READING ABBEY CARTULARIES I

In piam memoriam
F. M. STENTON

READING ABBEY
CARTULARIES

British Library Manuscripts:
Egerton 3031, Harley 1708 and Cotton
Vespasian E xxv

edited by

B. R. KEMP

I

General Documents and those relating to English Counties other than Berkshire

CAMDEN FOURTH SERIES
VOLUME 31

LONDON
OFFICES OF THE ROYAL HISTORICAL SOCIETY
UNIVERSITY COLLEGE LONDON
GOWER STREET WC1E 6BT
1986

© Royal Historical Society

British Library Cataloguing in Publication Data

Reading Abbey cartularies: British Library
   manuscripts: Egerton 3031, Harley 1708 and Cotton
   Vespasian E XXV.—(Camden fourth series; v.31)
   1, General documents and those relating to English
   counties other than Berkshire
   1. Reading Abbey   2. Church lands—England—
   Reading (Berkshire)   3. Cartularies
   I. Kemp, B. R.   II. Royal Historical Society
   III. British Library. Manuscript. Egerton 3031
   IV. British Library. Manuscript. Harley 1708
   V. British Library. Manuscript. Cotton
   Vespasian E XXV   VI.   Series
   333.3'22'0942293   BX2596.R/

ISBN 0-86193-108-4

Printed and bound in Great Britain by
Butler & Tanner Ltd, Frome and London

CONTENTS

ACKNOWLEDGEMENTS

I am grateful to the Trustees of the British Library for permission to print or calendar the contents of Egerton 3031, Harley 1708 and Cotton Vespasian E xxv and a number of original charters, and to cite items in Cotton Domitian A iii, Cotton Vespasian E v and Additional Roll 19617. Transcripts/translations of Crown-copyright records in the Public Record Office appear by permission of the Controller of H.M. Stationery Office. I am also grateful for similar permission from the owners of other manuscripts used in this edition, namely, T. M. Eyston, Esq., I. C. Malcolmson, Esq., R. M. Abel Smith, Esq., and the Dean and Chapter of Salisbury. Of these, Mr Eyston and Mr Malcolmson, who retain custody of their manuscripts, most generously made provision for me to inspect relevant charters in their own homes.

I should also like to express my appreciation of the unstinting help and co-operation which I have received from the staff of the Students' Room of the British Library; the staff of the Public Record Office, especially Dr David Crook; Miss S. M. Eward, Librarian of Salisbury Cathedral, and Canon J. R. Fenwick, Librarian of Worcester Cathedral; Mr Peter Walne, County Archivist, and the staff of the Hertfordshire Record Office; and the staff of the Wiltshire Record Office at Trowbridge. I must also thank Dr Christopher Kitching, Assistant Secretary of the Royal Commission on Historical Manuscripts, who kindly helped me to trace documents in private hands. The constant assistance received from the staff of Reading University Library is also gratefully acknowledged.

In preparing this edition I have benefited greatly from the helpful advice of numerous scholars, whom I have consulted on individual points and to whose kindness I owe a sincere debt of thanks, while reserving to myself entire responsibility for such deficiencies as remain. I should like especially to mention Dr B. C. B. Arnold, Dr M. C. Barber, Professor G. W. S. Barrow, Mr A. K. Bate, Mr N. P. Berry, Miss J. M. Boorman, Professor C. N. L. Brooke, Professor C. R. Cheney, Dr M. T. Clanchy, Dr D. Crook, Dr D. B. Crouch, Dr A. E. Curry, Miss B. Dodwell, Mr D. H. Farmer, Dr E. M. Hallam Smith, Dr N. M. Herbert, Professor J. C. Holt, Professor D. J. A. Matthew, Dr C. F. Slade, Dr D. Waley and the late Mr Denis Bethell.

The friendly encouragement and assistance of three successive Literary Directors of the Royal Historical Society, Professor G. W. S.

Barrow, Dr C. T. Allmand, and Dr D. E. Greenway, are warmly acknowledged. Dr Greenway in particular has shown me great kindness and patient understanding in the final stages of preparing the work for the press.

Finally I wish to thank the Research Board of the University of Reading for a generous grant of travel expenses towards the completion of this edition.

University of Reading   BRIAN KEMP

ABBREVIATED REFERENCES

Place of publication London unless otherwise stated

Abbreviatio Placitorum: *Placitorum in Domo Capitulari Westmonasteriensi asservatorium Abbreviatio* (Richard I – Edward II), ed. W. Illingworth, Record Commission, 1811

Aids: *Inquisitions and Assessments relating to Feudal Aids … preserved in the Public Record Office, 1284-1431*, 6 vols., 1899-1920

Ancient Charters: *Ancient Charters, royal and private, prior to A.D. 1200*, ed. J. H. Round, Pipe Roll Society, x, 1888

'Annales Radingenses', in *Ungedruckte anglo-normannische Geschichtsquellen*, ed. F. Liebermann, Strassburg, 1879

'Ann. Rad. Post.': 'Annales Radingenses posteriores, 1135-1264', ed. C. W. Previté-Orton, *EHR*, xxxvii (1922), 400-3

Ann. Mon.: *Annales Monastici*, ed. H. R. Luard, 5 vols., Rolls Series, 1864-9

Antiquaries Journ., xiv: H. C. Andrews, 'Two twelfth-century charters of Reading Abbey', *Antiquaries Journal*, xiv (1934), 7-12

Arch. Journ., xx; xxii: A. Way, 'Being contributions towards the history of Reading Abbey', *Archaeological Journal*, xx (1863), 281-96; xxii (1865), 151-61

Barfield, *Thatcham*: S. Barfield, *Thatcham, Berks., and its Manors*, 2 vols., London and Oxford, 1901

Berks. Place-Names: M. Gelling, *The Place-Names of Berkshire*, 3 vols., English Place-Name Society, xlix-li, 1973-6

BIHR: *Bulletin of the Institute of Historical Research*

BL: British Library

B.M. Cat. Seals: W. de G. Birch, *Catalogue of Seals in the Department of Manuscripts in the British Museum*, 6 vols., 1887-1900

Bracton's Note Book, ed. F. W. Maitland, 3 vols., 1887

Bucks. Feet of Fines: *A Calender of the Feet of Fines for the county of Buckingham, 7 Richard I – 44 Henry III*, ed. M. W. Hughes, Buckinghamshire Record Society, iv, 1942 (for 1940)

Cal. Chart. R.: *Calendar of the Charter Rolls preserved in the Public Record Office* (1226-1516), 6 vols., 1903-27

Cal. Close R.: *Calendar of the Close Rolls preserved in the Public Record Office* (Edward I – Henry VII), 47 vols., 1892-1963

Cal. Fine R.: *Calendar of the Fine Rolls preserved in the Public Record Office* (Edward I – Henry VII), 22 vols., 1911-62

Cal. Inq. P.M.: *Calendar of Inquisitions Post Mortem and other analogous documents preserved in the Public Record Office* (Henry III–   ), in progress, 1904– ; (Henry VII), 3 vols., 1898–1955

Cal. Liberate R.: *Calendar of the Liberate Rolls preserved in the Public Record Office* (Henry III), 6 vols., 1916–64

Cal. Misc. Inq.: *Calendar of Inquisitions Miscellaneous (Chancery) preserved in the Public Record Office* (Henry III–   ), in progress, 1916–

Cal. Papal L.: *Calendar of entries in the papal registers relating to Great Britain and Ireland* (1198–1492), 14 vols. in 15, 1893–1960

Cal. Pat. R.: *Calendar of the Patent Rolls preserved in the Public Record Office* (1232–1509), 52 vols., 1891–1916

'Cartl. Brecon': 'Cartularium Prioratus S. Johannis Evang. de Brecon', ed. R. W. Banks, *Archaeologia Cambrensis*, 4th series, xiii (1882), 275–308; xiv (1883), 18–311

Cartl. Lewes, iii: *The Chartulary of Lewes Priory. The portions relating to counties other than Sussex*, ed. W. Budgen and L. F. Salzman, Sussex Record Society, Additional vol., 1943

Cartl. Missenden: *The Cartulary of Missenden Abbey*, ed. J. G. Jenkins, 3 vols., Buckinghamshire Record Society, ii, x, xii, 1938–62

Cartl. Oseney: *Cartulary of Oseney Abbey*, ed. H. E. Salter, 6 vols., Oxford Historical Society, lxxxix–xci, xcvii–xcviii, ci, 1929–36

Cartl. Tutbury: *The Cartulary of Tutbury Priory*, ed. A. Saltman, Staffordshire Historical Collections, 4th series, iv, 1962

Cartl. Worc.: *The Cartulary of Worcester Cathedral Priory*, ed. R. R. Darlington, Pipe Roll Society, new series, xxxviii, 1968 for 1962–3

Cat. Anc. Deeds: *A Descriptive Catalogue of Ancient Deeds in the Public Record Office*, 6 vols., 1890–1915

Cheney, *Letters of Innocent III*: *The Letters of Pope Innocent III (1198–1216) concerning England and Wales*, ed. C. R. and M. G. Cheney, Oxford, 1967

Cheney, *BIHR*, xliv: C. R. and M. G. Cheney, 'The letters of Pope Innocent III …: additions and corrections', *BIHR*, xliv (1971), 98–115

Clanchy, *Berks. Eyre of 1248*: *The Roll and Writ File of the Berkshire Eyre of 1248*, ed. M. T. Clanchy, Selden Society, xc, 1973

Close Rolls: *Close Rolls of the Reign of Henry III preserved in the Public Record Office*, 14 vols., 1902–38

Coates, *Hist. of Reading*: C. Coates, *The History and Antiquities of Reading*, 1802; with supplement of 'Appendix' and 'Corrections and Additions', Reading, 1809

Complete Peerage: G.E.C(ockayne), *The Complete Peerage*, new edn, ed. V. Gibbs, H. A. Doubleday, Lord Howard de Walden, and G. H. White, 13 vols. in 14, 1910–59

Crook, *General Eyre*: D. Crook, *Records of the General Eyre*, PRO Hand-books, 20, 1982

Cur. Reg. R.: *Curia Regis Rolls ... preserved in the Public Record Office* (Richard I–Henry III), in progress, 1922–

Delisle and Berger: *Recueil des actes de Henri II, roi d'Angleterre et duc de Normandie, concernant les provinces françaises et les affaires de France*, ed. L. Delisle and E. Berger, Introduction and 3 vols., Académie des Inscriptions et Belles Lettres, Chartes et Diplômes, Paris, 1909–27

DNB: *Dictionary of National Biography*, ed. L. Stephen and S. Lee, 66 vols., 1885–1901

Duncan, 'Documents of May': A. A. M. Duncan, 'Documents relating to the Priory of the Isle of May, *c.* 1140–1313', *Proceedings of the Society of Antiquaries of Scotland*, xc, 1959, 52–80

EHR: *English Historical Review*

Excerpta e rot. fin.: *Excerpta e rotulis finium in Turri Londinensi asservatis, Henrico Tertio Rege*, ed. C. Roberts, 2 vols., Record Commission, 1835–6

EYC: *Early Yorkshire Charters*, i–iii, ed. W. Farrer, Edinburgh, 1914–16; iv–xii, ed. Sir C. T. Clay, Yorkshire Archaeological Society, Records Series, Extra Series, i–iii, v–x, 1935–65

Eyton: R. W. Eyton, *Court, Household, and Itinerary of King Henry II*, 1878

Farrer, *Honors and Knights' Fees*: W. Farrer, *Honors and Knights' Fees*, 3 vols., 1923–5

Farrer, *Itin.*: W. Farrer, *An Outline Itinerary of King Henry I*, Oxford, 1919

Fasti 1066–1300, ii: J. Le Neve *Fasti Ecclesiae Anglicanae 1066–1300*, ed. D. E. Greenway, vol. ii, *Monastic Cathedrals*, 1971

Fees: *Liber Feodorum. The Book of Fees commonly called Testa de Nevill*, 2 vols. in 3, 1920–31

Feet of Fines, 9 Richard I: *Feet of Fines of the ninth year of King Richard I, A. D. 1197 to A.D. 1198*, Pipe Roll Society, xxiii, 1898

Fines sive Pedes Finium: *Fines sive Pedes Finium ... A.D. 1195–A.D. 1214*, ed. J. Hunter, 2 vols., Record Commission, 1835–44

Flor. Hist.: *Flores Historiarum*, ed. H. R. Luard, 3 vols., Rolls Series, 1890

Foliot Letters and Charters: *The Letters and Charters of Gilbert Foliot*, ed. A. Morey and C. N. L. Brooke, Cambridge, 1967

Gallia Christiana, 16 vols., Paris, 1715–1865

Handbook of Brit. Chron.: *Handbook of British Chronology*, 3rd edn, ed. E. B. Fryde, D. E. Greenway, S. Porter and I. Roy, Royal Historical Society, Guides and Handbooks, 2, 1986

Hasted, *History of Kent*: E. Hasted, *The History and Topographical Survey of the County of Kent*, 2nd edn, 12 vols., Canterbury, 1797–1801

Heads of Relig. Houses: *The Heads of Religious Houses, England and Wales, 940–1216*, ed. D. Knowles, C. N. L. Brooke and V. C. M. London, Cambridge, 1972

Herefs. Domesday: *Herefordshire Domesday, circa 1160–1170*, ed. V. H. Galbraith and J. Tait, Pipe Roll Society, new series, xxv, 1950 (for 1947–8)

Holtzmann, *Papsturkunden*: *Papsturkunden in England*, ed. W. Holtzmann, 3 vols., Abhandlungen der Gesellschaft (Akademie) der Wissenschaften in Göttingen, phil.-hist. Klasse, new series, xxv; 3rd series, xiv-xv, xxxiii, Berlin, 1930, 1935–6, Göttingen, 1952

Humphreys, *Bucklebury*: A. Humphreys, *Bucklebury: a Berkshire parish*, Reading, 1932

Hurry, *Reading Abbey*: J. B. Hurry, *Reading Abbey*, 1901

JEH: *Journal of Ecclesiastical History*

Johnson, *Essays in Honour of Tait*: C. Johnson, 'Some Charters of Henry I' in *Historical Essays in Honour of James Tait*, ed. J. G. Edwards, V. H. Galbraith and E. F. Jacob (Manchester, 1933), 137–42

Journ. B. A. A., xxxi: W. de G. Birch, 'A fasciculus of the charters of Mathildis, Empress of the Romans, and an account of her Great Seal', *Journal of the British Archaeological Association*, xxxi (1875), 376–98

Kealey, *Roger of Salisbury*: E. J. Kealey, *Roger of Salisbury, viceroy of England*, University of California Press, Berkeley, Los Angeles and London, 1972*

Kennett, *Parochial Antiquities*: W. Kennett, *Parochial Antiquities attempted in the history of Ambrosden, Burcester, and other adjacent parts in the Counties of Oxford and Bucks.*, new edn, 2 vols., Oxford, 1818

Kent Feet of Fines: *Calendar of Kent Feet of Fines to the end of Henry III's reign*, prepared by I. J. Churchill, R. Griffin and F. W. Hardman, introduction by F. W. Jessup, Kent Archaeological Society, xv, 1956

Knowles and Hadcock: D. Knowles and R. N. Hadcock, *Medieval Religious Houses: England and Wales*, 2nd edn, 1971

Landon, *Itin.*: L. Landon, *The Itinerary of King Richard I*, Pipe Roll Society, new series, xiii, 1935

Lawrie, *Early Scottish Charters*: *Early Scottish Charters prior to A.D. 1153*, ed. Sir A. C. Lawrie, Glasgow, 1905

L. and P. For. and Dom., Hen. VIII: *Letters and Papers Foreign and Domestic of the reign of Henry VIII preserved in the Public Record Office, the British Museum, and elsewhere*, 21 vols., 1862–1910

List of Sheriffs: *List of Sheriffs from the earliest times to A.D. 1831*, PRO Lists and Indexes, ix, 1898

Matthew Paris, *Chronica Majora*: *Matthaei Parisiensis monachi Sancti Albani Chronica Majora*, ed. H. R. Luard, 7 vols., Rolls Series, 1872–83

Mayr-Harting, *Acta of Chichester*: *The Acta of the Bishops of Chichester, 1075–1207*, ed. H. Mayr-Harting, Canterbury and York Society, lvi, 1964

Med. Misc. for D. M. Stenton: *A Medieval Miscellany for Doris Mary Stenton*, ed. P. M. Barnes and C. F. Slade, Pipe Roll Society, new series, xxxvi, 1962 (for 1960)

Memoranda Roll I John: *The Memoranda Roll for the Michaelmas term of the first year of the Reign of King John*, ed. H. G. Richardson, Pipe Roll Society, new series, xxi, 1943

Migne: *Patrologiae cursus completus, series Latina*, ed. J. P. Migne, 221 vols., Paris, 1844–64

Mon. Ang.: W. Dugdale, *Monasticon Anglicanum*, rev. edn, J. Caley, H. Ellis and B. Bandinel, 6 vols. in 8, 1817–30

Morey, *Bartholomew of Exeter*: A. Morey, *Bartholomew of Exeter, Bishop and Canonist*, Cambridge, 1937

New Pal. Soc. Facs.: *The New Palaeographical Society. Facsimiles of Ancient Manuscripts*, ed. E. M. Thompson and others, 2 series, Oxford, 1903–30

Nichols, *History Leics.*: J. Nichols, *The History and Antiquities of the County of Leicester*, 4 vols. in 9, 1795–1815

Orderic Vitalis: *The Ecclesiastical History of Orderic Vitalis*, ed. M. Chibnall, 6 vols., Oxford, 1969–80

Oxon. Feet of Fines: *The Feet of Fines for Oxfordshire, 1195–1291*, calendared H. E. Salter, Oxfordshire Record Society, xii, 1930

Pal. Soc. Facs.: *The Palaeographical Society. Facsimiles of Manuscripts and Inscriptions*, ed. E. A. Bond and others, 2 series, 1873–94

Pat. Rolls: *Patent Rolls of the Reign of Henry III preserved in the Public Record Office* (1216–32), 2 vols., 1901–3

Patterson, *Gloucester Charters*: *Earldom of Gloucester Charters . . . to A.D. 1217*, ed. R. B. Patterson, Oxford, 1973

PR: *Pipe Rolls, 31 Henry I*, ed. J. Hunter, Record Commission, 1833, facsimile repr. Pipe Roll Society, 1929; *2–4 Henry II*, ed. idem, Record Commission, 1844; *5–34 Henry II*, Pipe Roll Society, various vols. between i and xxxviii, 1884–1925; *1 Richard I*, ed. J. Hunter, Record Commission, 1844; *2–10 Richard I* (Chancellor's Roll for 8 Richard I), Pipe Roll Society, new series, i-ix, 1925–32; *1–14, 16–17 John*, Pipe Roll Society, new series, various vols. between x and xxxvii, 1933–64

Placita de Quo Warranto temporibus Edw. I. II. and III in Curia Receptae Scaccarii Westm. asservata, ed. W. Illingworth, Record Commission, 1818

Potthast: *Regesta Pontificum Romanorum, inde ab a. post Christum natum MCXCVIII ad a. MCCCIV*, ed. A. Potthast, 2 vols., Berlin, 1874–5

PRO: Public Record Office, London

PRS: Pipe Roll Society

Rec. Comm.: Record Commission

Recueil des historiens des Gaules et de la France, ed. M. Bouquet and others, 24 vols. in 25, Paris, 1738–1904

Red Bk. Exch.: *The Red Book of the Exchequer*, ed. H. Hall, 3 vols., Rolls Series, 1896

Regesta: *Regesta Regum Anglo-Normannorum 1066–1154*: ii, *Regesta Henrici Primi*, ed. C. Johnson and H. A. Cronne, Oxford, 1956; iii, iv, *Regesta Regis Stephani ac Mathildis Imperatricis ...*, and *Facsimiles*, ed. H. A. Cronne and R. H. C. Davis, Oxford, 1968–9

Regesta Regum Scottorum 1153–1424: i, *The Acts of Malcolm IV;* ii, *The Acts of William I*, both ed. G. W. S. Barrow, Edinburgh, 1960–71

Reg. St Osmund: *Vetus Registrum Sarisberiense alias dictum Registrum S. Osmundi Episcopi*, ed. W. H. R. Jones, 2 vols., Rolls Series, 1883–4

Reg. Swinfield: *Registrum Ricardi de Swinfield Episcopi Herefordensis*, ed. W. W. Capes, Canterbury and York Society, vi, 1909

Richardson and Sayles, *Governance of Med. Eng.*: H. G. Richardson and G. O. Sayles, *The Governance of Medieval England from the Conquest to Magna Carta*, Edinburgh, 1963

Robert of Torigny: *The Chronicle of Robert of Torigny* in *Chronicles of the Reigns of Stephen, Henry II, and Richard I*, ed. R. Howlett, iv, Rolls Series, 1889

Rot. Chart.: *Rotuli Chartarum in Turri Londinensi asservati* (1199–1216), ed. T. D. Hardy, Record Commission, 1837

Rot. Cur. Reg.: *Rotuli Curiae Regis ... 6 Richard I – 1 John*, ed. F. Palgrave, 2 vols., Record Commission, 1835

Rot. de Ob. et Fin.: *Rotuli de Oblatis et Finibus in Turri Londinensi asservati temp. Regis Johannis*, ed. T. D. Hardy, Record Commission, 1835

Rot. Hug. de Welles: *Rotuli Hugonis de Welles Episcopi Lincolniensis*, ed. W. P. W. Phillimore and F. N. Davis, 3 vols., Canterbury and York Society, i, iii, iv, 1907–9

Rot. Hund.: *Rotuli Hundredorum temp. Hen. III and Edw. I in Turr. Lond' et in Curia Receptae Scaccarii Westm. asservati*, ed. W. Illingworth, 2 vols., Record Commission, 1812–8

Rot. Lit. Claus.: *Rotuli Litterarum Clausarum in Turri Londinensi asservati* (1204–27), ed. T. D. Hardy, 2 vols., Record Commission, 1833–44

Rot. Lit. Pat.: *Rotuli Litterarum Patentium in Turri Londinensi asservati* (1201–16), ed. T. D. Hardy, Record Commission, 1835

Round, *Cal. Docs. France*: *Calendar of Documents preserved in France, illustrative of the History of Great Britain and Ireland, I, A.D. 918–1206,* ed. J. H. Round, 1899

RS: Rolls Series (The Chronicles and Memorials of Great Britain and Ireland during the Middle Ages), 99 vols., 1858–96

Saltman, *Theobald*: A. Saltman, *Theobald, Archbishop of Canterbury,* 1956

Sanders, *English Baronies*: I. J. Sanders, *English Baronies: a study of their origin and descent, 1086–1327,* Oxford, 1960

Sarum Charters and Documents: *Charters and Documents illustrating the history of the cathedral, city, and diocese of Salisbury in the twelfth and thirteenth centuries,* ed. W. H. R. Jones and W. D. Macray, Rolls Series, 1891

Sir Christopher Hatton's Book of Seals, ed. L. C. Loyd and D. M. Stenton, Oxford, 1950

Slade, 'Reading': C. F. Slade, 'Reading' in *Historic Towns,* i, ed. M. D. Lobel, Oxford and London, 1969

Slade, 'Whitley Deeds': 'Whitley deeds of the twelfth century', ed. C. F. Slade in *Med. Misc. for D. M. Stenton,* 235–46

Smith, *Lincoln I*: *English Episcopal Acta, I, Lincoln 1067–1185,* ed. D. M. Smith, British Academy, 1980.

Stenton, *English Justice*: D. M. Stenton, *English Justice between the Norman Conquest and the Great Charter, 1066–1215,* 1965

Stuart, *Records of May*: *Records of the Priory of the Isle of May,* ed. J. Stuart, Society of Antiquaries of Scotland, 1868

Taxatio: *Taxatio Ecclesiastica Angliae et Walliae auctoritate P. Nicholai IV,* ed. J. Caley, Record Commission, 1802

Tout, *Chapters*: T. F. Tout, *Chapters in the Administrative History of Medieval England,* 6 vols., Manchester, 1923–35

Trans. East Herts. Arch. Soc., i: W. Brigg, 'Grant of the manor of Aston to Reading Abbey', *Transactions of the East Hertfordshire Archaeological Society,* i (1900), 129–35

Trans. Royal Soc. Lit., 2nd ser., xi: W. de G. Birch, 'On the Great Seals of King Stephen' and 'On the Seals of King Henry the Second, and of his son the so-called Henry the Third', *Transactions of the Royal Society of Literature of the United Kingdom,* 2nd series, xi, 1878

TRHS: *Transactions of the Royal Historical Society*

Van Caenegem, *Royal Writs*: R. C. van Caenegem, *Royal Writs in England from the Conquest to Glanvill,* Selden Society, lxxvii, 1959

VCH: *Victoria History of the Counties of England*

Walker, 'Hereford Charters': 'Charters of the earldom of Hereford, 1095–1201', ed. D. Walker, *Camden Miscellany, XXII,* Camden 4th Series, i (1964), 1–75

Warks. Eyre 1221–2: *Rolls of the Justices in Eyre for Gloucestershire, War-*

wickshire and Staffordshire (*recte Shropshire*), *1221*, *1222*, ed. D. M. Stenton, Selden Society, lix, 1940

Warks. Feet of Fines: *Warwickshire Feet of Fines, 7 Richard I, 1195–12 Edward I, 1284*, ed. E. Stokes and F. C. Wellstood, introduction by F. T. S. Houghton, Dugdale Society, xi, 1932

Warks. Place-Names: J. E. B. Gover, A. Mawer and F. M. Stenton, in collab. with F. T. S. Houghton, *The Place-Names of Warwickshire*, English Place-Name Society, xiii, 1936

Warner and Ellis: *Facsimiles of Royal and Other Charters in the British Museum*, ed. G. F. Warner and H. J. Ellis, i, 1903

MANUSCRIPTS

A   BL, Egerton 3031
B   BL, Harley 1708
C   BL, Cotton Vespasian E xxv
D   BL, Cotton Vespasian E v
E   BL, Cotton Domitian A iii
F   Cambridge University Library, Dd. ix. 38
G   Trowbridge, Wiltshire Record Office, D1/19

INTRODUCTION

I The manuscripts

This edition comprises the contents of Reading Abbey's three surviving general cartularies, all of which are now in the British Library
in London. In order of composition they are:

BL, Egerton 3031—cited in this edition as A;
BL, Harley 1708—cited as B;
BL, Cotton Vespasian E xxv—cited as C.

They were begun, respectively, in the 1190s, the 1250s and the 1340s
and, since the majority of Reading's original charters are lost, they
constitute the most important extant record of the development of
the abbey's muniments from its foundation in the early 1120s to the
late fourteenth century. They do not, however, contain all the surviving charter material from Reading in this period, since, apart
from a few extant originals which were not copied, the texts of many
additional charters are preserved in other more specialized cartularies and registers of the abbey or of its dependent priory at Leominster. Conversely, although Egerton 3031 and Harley 1708 were
originally confined to title-deeds, including in the latter case final
concords, all three general cartularies came ultimately to incorpor-
ate various other types of legal document which do not fall strictly
into that category. Each of the cartularies is described briefly in the
following notes.

BL, Egerton 3031

This fine early cartulary (A), which happily preserves its medieval
binding of white leather over oak boards,[1] contains 114 folios measuring approximately 28.5 × 21 cm. In addition to the modern foliation dating from 1922, there is a medieval foliation in thirteenth-
century Roman numerals, which runs from the present f 13, where
the transcript of charters begins, to the present f 112 (two folios
being inadvertently given the same number, xxi), and also a frag-
mentary pagination of the late sixteenth or early seventeenth century
occupying the present ff 3–14. The discovery of the cartulary some
time before June 1792 in a hidden chamber in the earl of Fingall's
house at Shinfield, near Reading, is recorded on a small paper

[1] For a colour illustration, see M. R. James, *Abbeys* (1925), facing p. 148.

insertion at the beginning in the hand of C. A. Buckler.[1] As Buckler noted elsewhere,[2] two folios had been cut out following the present f 12, an excision which must have been made after the abbey's dissolution, since the post-medieval pagination at the beginning of the cartulary originally included these missing folios. Another folio has been removed after f 8, but that had been done before the date of the post-medieval pagination, which ignores it, and was presumably for this reason not noticed by Buckler.

Of the 114 folios which now make up the cartulary, the first two are devoid of medieval writing, save for a fifteenth-century note of Reading's ownership on f 2v, and the last two are blank. The entry of charters in the original hand commences at f 13r, but this is preceded by a table of contents (ff 3r–6v), lists of relics and books at Reading (ff 6v–10v) and a list of books at Leominster (f 12v), all largely in the original hand, with additions of the early thirteenth century, including a list of vestments and liturgical objects (f 11r–v), and of the fourteenth century concerning the leper house (ff 11v–12r).[3] Charters in the original hand occupy the following folios: 13r–28v (English royal charters down to early Richard I, after which a gap was was left for subsequent additions); 36r–46r (charters from the laity, beginning with one from King David I of Scotland, arranged not according to the rank of the donors but apparently by place, though without strict classification); 47r–49v (abbatial acts mostly by heads of other houses but including one by Abbot Roger of Reading); 49v–60r (archiepiscopal and episcopal acts); 60v–63r (Scottish charters, mostly royal and comital); 63r (two acts by

---

[1] The paper is numbered i. The account reads:

'This book of the charters of Reading Abbey was found secreted in a very concealed & unknown corner in my Lord Fingall's house at Shinefield near Reading, it was brought to Woolhampton great house, now Mrs [*sic*] Crew's, by Gul. Corderoy the steward with several other books, found by a bricklayer necessitated to pull some part of the house or rather part of a wall down in order to repair thoroughly a chimney in Shinefield House. This account I had from the forementioned Mr Corderoy on Wednesday the twentieth of June 1792 who likewise supposes the bricklayer who is now living at Reading found no small sum of money, or something valuable as shortly after that time, he advanced much in the world, by means of money [*f i (v)*] which no one knows how he could be worth. Wrote this account—on June 23d. 1792. N.B. Mr Corderoy told me that in this concealed place there was convenient room for three persons there being three seats.'

A slightly shorter version of this account is in BL Additional Ms 37130 f 37v, where Woolhampton great house is said to be 'now Mr Crew's.'

[2] BL Add. Ms 37130 f 37r.

[3] For these items, apart from the table of contents, see below, nos. 225–8, 221–2. For a colour reproduction of the opening of the list of books at Reading (f 8v), see James, *Abbeys*, facing p. 82.

Henry II and the Empress Matilda concerning Herefordshire, for some reason omitted from the royal section but both included among the royal charters in the contemporary table of contents); and 63r–71r (papal acts down to Clement III). The folios in these original sections are ruled for 40 lines of writing, the prick-marks surviving at the outer edges of the folios, and have vertical lines defining the left and right margins but no rulings for headlines. The entries are provided with rubrics in red ink and have alternately red and blue initials decorated with a rather rudimentary form of ornament, the red initials being decorated in blue ink and vice versa. Very soon after the original composition, however, entries were made on f 46r–v (including two acts of John count of Mortain) and on f 71r–v (two acts of Hubert Walter as bishop of Salisbury and one as archbishop of Canterbury), all of which were included without differentiation in the table of contents, which ends with the last of them. These additions were made in the same hand as that of the original compilation, or one very similar, but their initials lack the decoration of those in the original parts.

The date of the original composition can be established with some certainty. It was most probably begun not earlier than 1191, since it contains three documents of, respectively, January, February and July 1191,[1] and was apparently finished by April × May 1193, since two important acts by Hubert Walter, bishop of Salisbury, dating from those months[2] were not included with his earlier act of 1189 × 90 in the original compilation, but were among the additions made very soon afterwards. With them was entered the act of Hubert Walter as archbishop, dating probably from February 1194,[3] while among further additions, perhaps made near the end of the century, were a general confirmation to Reading by Richard I granted after his release from captivity and possibly dating March × May 1194, and a gift by William d'Aubigny, second earl of Arundel, who died in December 1193.[4]

The cartulary was continued as far as f 112v in a succession of hands of the late twelfth century and the thirteenth century down to the 1250s, and the gap originally left between f 28v and f 35v was similarly filled over the same period with later royal charters and associated documents. Finally, four entries were made in the fourteenth century. In these additions no particular sequence of entries is apparent other than that of rough chronology, but close study of the texts, especially in the continuations after f 71, reveals that some dated from before the original compilation of the cartulary and were for some reason omitted at that time. The latest datable entries

---

[1] Nos. 155, 673, 1198.
[3] No. 206.
[2] Nos. 204–5.
[4] Nos. 38, 483.

made in the thirteenth century include three of February or July 1254[1] and, latest of all, the record of a dispute between the abbey and John de Turberville in East Hendred, which can be dated between November 1255 and May 1259, and probably earlier rather than later in this range.[2] By this time most of the folios were filled and it was decided to begin a new general cartulary, the present Harley 1708. The fourteenth-century additions were made long after Egerton 3031 had ceased to be a current register, one of them being entered in the second main hand of the fourteenth-century cartulary (Cotton Vespasian E xxv), but all were documents which dated from, or which concerned, the period of the cartulary's currency.[3] In all later sections the provision of rubrics and the treatment of initials are far less systematic than in the original sections. Some entries are given rubrics in red ink, but a number have black rubrics or none at all, while initials are either in red, blue or black ink, very occasionally in green ink, mostly without decoration.

The special virtue of Egerton 3031 is that in the original sections it by and large preserves full witness-lists of charters, which later cartularies as a rule omit, although the policy of copying out the witness-lists was abandoned for most of the later additions. The cartulary is of particular value for the history of Reading Abbey in the twelfth century in that, apart from the lists of relics and books which it alone contains, it preserves the texts of twenty-seven papal acts, very few of which survive in other copies, twenty-seven Scottish charters, of which only one appears in another Reading cartulary and no fewer than thirteen are not otherwise known, and a series of episcopal indulgences relating mostly to the Hand of St James, to say nothing of several other charters which became void or were of little interest by the time Harley 1708 was being written. On the other hand, the cartulary omits certain classes of deeds which the abbey is known from later cartularies to have possessed. For example, the original sections contain very few antecedent title-deeds received with new acquisitions of land, etc., although more were entered among the later additions, and most strikingly, and perhaps significantly, no final concords, although again a few were added subsequently.

[1] Nos. 69, 790, 859.

[2] No. 791. The date cannot be established with certainty, since the plea roll containing this case does not survive.

[3] They are: (1) a memorandum concerning Abbot Anscher's foundation of the leper house (no. 221); (2) an ordinance defining punishments for offending lepers (no. 222); (3) Henry III's charter of disafforestation in Berkshire in 1227 (no. 1306); and (4) a notification of the induction of Reading Abbey into the church of Bucklebury in 1239 (no. 700). Henry III's charter is the one which is entered in the second main hand of Cotton Vesp. E xxv.

BL, *Harley 1708*

This cartulary (B) was planned on a more ambitious scale and organized on a more rigorous topographical basis. It contains 247 numbered folios[1] of approximately 25.5 × 17.5 cm, except for the last two folios, which are somewhat smaller in size. The contemporary Roman foliation begins at the present f 16, where the original entries start, and runs with one break[2] to f 210, after which the sequence is continued in a later hand to f 230, where it ends. The folios preceding f 16 are a subsequent addition to the cartulary containing nothing in the original hand and bearing no medieval foliation. There is no table of contents, although BL, Additional Roll 19617, which appears to be part of a near-contemporary inventory of charters, contains folio references in Roman numerals to the relevant section of the cartulary.

The original sections of the cartulary are as follows: ff 16r-38v (royal charters down to 1253); ff 47r-133v (lay charters mostly relating to temporalities); ff 142r-161v (charters of the almoner's department, headed in a different hand *Carte Elemosinarie*); ff 166r-182v (final concords); ff 186v-187v (list of indulgences); and ff 188r-204v (archiepiscopal, episcopal, abbatial and other ecclesiastical acts concerning in the main the abbey's churches and other spiritualities and including a few lay charters regarding the same). Part of the last section has been lost, however, for five folios have been cut out between f 200 and f 201 with the result that the contemporary foliation now goes straight from clxxxvii to cxciii and the latter (the present f 201) begins some way into an act concerning Rowington vicarage.[3] Nevertheless, the contents of these folios, excluding possibly any mere notes of documents, are preserved on ff 119r-122v of a later cartulary, Cotton Vespasian E xxv, the main part of which consists of a fourteenth-century copy of Harley 1708. The missing folios were clearly still present at that time, but when and why they were subsequently removed is unknown.

The folios of the original sections are ruled for 34 lines of writing, with left and right margins but no rulings for headlines. The composition is very handsome and the writing clear and firm,[4] either in one hand or a few very similar hands. The rubrics are in red ink, as

---

[1] The modern foliation in pencil dates from April 1872, but it omits from the sequence two entirely blank folios which occur, respectively, after f 187 and after f 226.

[2] The break is caused by the subsequent loss of five folios after the present f 200 (see below).

[3] No. 635.

[4] For a specimen, see *New Pal. Soc. Facs.*, 1st ser., pl. 87, which reproduces f 47r.

are most of the mere notes of charters, unless several of the latter appear together, in which case they are alternately in red and black ink. The initials are striking and beautiful. The majority are alternately red and blue and have delicate decoration consisting mainly of coiled patterns within the letters and long ascenders and descenders occupying much of the left border of the text and enriched with tendril-work; very occasionally small birds or animals in outline are included. In each case the red initials are decorated in blue ink and vice versa. Some initials, however, are richer and more elaborate, chiefly on account of the importance of the documents concerned. Richest of all is the initial of the foundation charter on f 16r, which is blue and gold with the same type of decoration in blue and red ink, while four other initials are each partly blue and partly red, the blue parts having decoration in red ink and the red parts in blue ink.[1]

In all the original sections, apart from the list of indulgences, documents were grouped as far as possible by county, and by place within each county, the name of the relevant county being written in large capital letters at the head of each folio, except in the royal section, where the name of the appropriate king or member of the royal family appears instead. Both between and within the sections generous gaps were left for later additions, amounting to as many as eight folios originally left blank between the royal and lay sections and between the latter and the almoner's charters. In most cases these gaps were wholly or partially filled by subsequent entries, although some folios remain entirely blank.

The original composition of Harley 1708 was begun not earlier than 1257, since it includes at f 170v a final concord of late October or early November 1257.[2] It was probably largely complete by May 1258, since it does not include the agreement with Worcester cathedral priory concerning Tiddington, dated 15 May 1258,[3] which was added shortly after the original composition in the same hand but without the standard rubric and decorated initial, for which spaces were left; moreover, this agreement was entered in a gap left in the original composition after an earlier agreement with Worcester concerning the same place in 1222 × 42,[4] with which it would

---

[1] The four initials occur at the beginning of the following groups of charters: Henry II's (f 21r), John's (f 33r), Henry III's (f 36r), and Berkshire charters (f 47r), for the last of which see the preceding note. It may be significant that the cartulary chose in this way to distinguish the charters of Henry II, whose long reign brought the abbey several royal acts, of John, who maintained exceptionally good relations with the monks, and of Henry III, in whose reign the cartulary was written.

[2] No. 1128.   [3] No. 648.

[4] No. 640.

certainly have been entered at that stage if it was already then in the abbey's possession.

The cartulary appears to have remained in current use for about a century, since numerous additions were made in various hands down to the mid-fourteenth century, a deliberate effort being undertaken to maintain the basic plan and topographical arrangement by inserting the new entries as far as possible in appropriate spaces left in the original composition. By that time, however, a new general cartulary had been started (Cotton Vespasian E xxv) and Harley 1708 seems generally to have been left alone thereafter. Even so, a few subsequent entries were made, the latest being three acts of Richard II[1] and, exceptionally late, one of Henry VI,[2] but these had to be copied in wherever space was still available without particular regard to their relationship to surrounding material. At some point, too, the extra folios bound in at the beginning of the cartulary were incorporated. They contain a range of thirteenth-century royal and judicial documents touching the abbey's liberties, entered in a variety of later thirteenth-century hands, but when they became part of Harley 1708 is uncertain.

The main strengths of Harley 1708 lie both in its original compilation and in the additions. The former provides on the whole a very complete picture of the abbey's muniments as they stood in the 1250s, even extending to the careful noting of charters which are not copied out in full. Compared with Egerton 3031, however, there is much less Herefordshire material and all but one of the Scottish charters are omitted, possibly because these were increasingly the concern primarily of the abbey's priories at Leominster and May. Among other omissions the most striking is the almost total absence of papal acts. There are also some regrettable drawbacks in the recording of texts in the original sections, particularly the general omission of witness-lists and the tendency in royal acts to abbreviate royal styles and clauses of address. The later additions to the manuscript are in general an improvement in this respect, and it is arguably among these that some of the most valuable and interesting material is to be found, especially that entered on the folios bound in at the front of the cartulary before the original text begins. This includes, for example, two writs to the justices itinerant in Berkshire in 1210,[3] the recognition in 1219 regarding the abbey's right to the foreign hundred of Reading,[4] and the estreats of amercements due to the abbey from the Berkshire eyres of 1235 and 1241.[5] Among other additions of singular interest elsewhere in the cartulary are the

---

[1] Nos. 114-16. [2] No. 117.
[3] Nos. 51-2. See Stenton, *English Justice*, 105.
[4] No. 53. [5] Nos. 123-4.

texts of Pope Gregory X's constitutions *Pro zelo fidei* of 1274 and their associated bulls,[1] copies of which are extremely rare, and the extraordinary case of the forged Jewish bonds, which came to court in 1290.[2]

BL, Additional Roll 19617

Before moving on to Reading's third general cartulary, a little must be said about this roll. It is not, as has been supposed,[3] a surviving part of a contemporary table of contents for Harley 1708 covering the present ff 101v–134r, even though it undoubtedly has a close relationship with that section of the cartulary. It is in fact a fragment of an inventory of charters listed under the county headings, Kent, Sussex, Middlesex, Hampshire, Wiltshire, Gloucestershire, Herefordshire, Leicestershire and Warwickshire, an order which reflects the sequence on ff 101v–134r of Harley 1708, or, according to the original foliation, lxxxvi(v)–cxix(r). References to this contemporary foliation are given on the roll to indicate where copies of the charters may be found in the cartulary. It is clear, however, that the roll was not compiled by simply leafing through the folios of Harley 1708, for the following reasons: (a) although the items are very largely listed in the same order as they occur in the cartulary, there are three instances where this is not so;[4] (b) two deeds are listed which are neither copied nor noted in the cartulary;[5] and (c) whereas five charters are noted in the cartulary in a brief single reference in the margin, the roll lists them individually and in a fuller form.[6]

The roll is written throughout in one hand, which is very similar but not identical to the main original hand of Harley 1708, and may have been part of the same project of recording and cataloguing the abbey's muniments. It must date from after the initial composition of the cartulary, and probably very soon afterwards, since it includes the agreement with Worcester cathedral priory, dated May

---

[1] Nos. 1312–14.

[2] No. 234.

[3] See, e.g., G. R. C. Davis, *Medieval Cartularies of Great Britain* (1958), 91.

[4] These are as follows: (i) four Sussex charters, which appear on Harley 1708 ff 109r–110r in the order 1,2,3,4 (below, nos. 556, 553, 555, 557), are listed on the roll in the order 1,4,2,3; (ii) two charters on f 111v relating to the Turville gift in London (below, nos. 460–1) are listed in reverse order; and (iii) two writs of Eleanor of Aquitaine on f 113v concerning London properties (below, nos. 466–7) are listed in reverse order.

[5] Both are listed under Rowington (Warks.): (i) *Carta Hugonis de Boddebroc facta Waltero de Ruzerwik de una assarta in Screvele* [Shrewley]; (ii) *Cyr(ographum) de terra quam Symon clericus de Rokinton' tenuit. Vacat.* For neither of these items does the roll attempt to provide a folio reference in the cartulary.

[6] See below, no. 618a.

1258, which, as was mentioned above, was a subsequent addition to Harley 1708,[1] but no later documents. Moreover, the hand which wrote the roll also made minor additions to the cartulary, namely, the heading *Carte Elemosinarie* added in the margin at the top of f 142r where the almoner's charters begin, the specifications *junioris* and *senioris* added above two occurrences of the name *Henrici le Notte* on f 129r[2] (these specifications being also written in the same hand over these names in the roll), and *eodem* inserted in a note of a royal act in favour of John of Kington on f 129v[3] (*eodem* being present on the roll not as an insertion). The conclusion to which these observations lead is that Additional Roll 19617 was made by some one going through the abbey's muniments and listing them in the order in which they were kept, at the same time having in front of him Harley 1708, from which he took the folio references and in which he made minor amendments as he went along. The fact that in general the items in his list are in terms very similar or identical to the rubrics or notes of charters in the cartulary suggests further that he used these as a guide rather than the endorsements on the originals, especially since, in the one case where an original charter has survived of all those listed on the roll, the endorsement is in quite different terms.[4] Moreover, since the sequence of charters is virtually the same on the roll as in the cartulary, and assuming that the roll lists charters in the order in which they were kept, it may be inferred that the arrangement of entries in the original parts of Harley 1708 reflected the organization of the abbey's muniment room.[5]

BL, Cotton Vespasian E xxv

The reign of Edward III saw the compilation of this third general cartulary (C), which, though workmanlike, is altogether more hastily written and less prepossessing than either Egerton 3031 or Harley 1708. It seems likely that the present manuscript is not as it was first planned, however, but results from the combination of at least two originally separate parts, both of which suffered some trimming when put together. It contains 231 numbered folios, but the current

---

[1] See above and no. 648.

[2] See below, nos. 589, 586.

[3] No. 578a.

[4] The charter concerned is Hugh of Kilpeck's quitclaim of Broadward (Herefs.). The rubric in Harley 1708 and the item in Add. Roll 19617 read: *Carta Hugonis de Kilpeec* [*Kilpec* in the roll] *de quietaclamantia de Bradeford'*; the endorsement which the charter bore in the 13th century reads: *Hugo de Clipeet de Brad'* (see below, no. 327).

[5] On this point in general, see D. Walker, 'The organization of material in medieval cartularies' in *The Study of Medieval Records*, ed. D. A. Bullough and R. L. Storey (Oxford, 1971), 139-43.

foliation, which appears to be of the late seventeenth or the eighteenth century, omits several blank folios.[1] The folios measure approximately 24.5 × 17.5 cm, apart from ff 1–5 and 224–31, which are slightly shorter.

The main and probably earlier part occupies ff 6r–138v and consists of a copy in a single hand of the contents of Harley 1708 as they then were, excepting many of the mere notes of charters included in the latter and the list of indulgences.[2] The entries were copied in a continuous sequence almost entirely without gaps[3] and without any attempt to re-arrange the additions in the earlier cartulary into a more coherent order. There is no doubt, however, that this part of Vespasian E xxv is incomplete, since f 6r begins with a charter of King Stephen whose rubric reads *Carta eiusdem de Eston' et de Stauntone*,[4] indicating that at least one other act of the same king preceded it on the now lost previous folio, while at the end of f 138v the record of the abbey's dispute with the men of Blewbury in 1284[5] breaks off abruptly in the middle of a sentence and is not continued on the present f 139r, where indeed a new gathering begins. Since what survives is a copy of Harley 1708, it may be presumed that this part of Vespasian E xxv originally began with all the royal charters, including those of the founder, which in the earlier cartulary precede that of King Stephen mentioned above[6] and that it continued, or was planned to continue, with the remainder of the Blewbury dispute and, possibly, a good deal of the later thirteenth- and early fourteenth-century material following the account of that dispute in Harley 1708.[7] To compensate for these losses, however, the contents of the folios now missing from Harley 1708 (see above) were fortunately preserved by their being copied into Vespasian E xxv.

Throughout this section of the cartulary the folios are ruled only with two horizontal lines and two vertical lines defining the upper

[1] These are: one after the present f 1, one after f 152 (omitted also in the Arabic sequence, for which see below), two after f 219 (originally included in the Arabic sequence, although the former top corners of the folios bearing the numerals are lost), three after f 223 (where the Arabic foliation ends) and one after f 230. On the other hand, a number of folios had been lost from the cartulary before the current foliation was supplied (see below, p. 13 n. 1).

[2] No. 217.

[3] The only exception is a gap left before the beginning of Richard I's charters in the royal section.

[4] No. 13.

[5] No. 686.

[6] Apart from the founder's charters, these include charters of the Empress Matilda, Queen Adeliza and Henry II (both as duke and as king) as well as many of Stephen's.

[7] It presumably would not have included the royal and judicial material entered on the present ff 4r–15v of Harley 1708 (see above).

and lower limits of the text and the left and right margins. Inevitably, therefore, the number of lines of writing varies from folio to folio, but is generally in the region of 40. The entries are written in cursive script in black ink with simple large initials in red ink. There are two copies of the rubric for each item. The first was written in the margin in black ink by the scribe of the main text and has in many cases been partially lost through subsequent trimming of the folios. The second was written in red ink and, though wherever possible encompassed within the area of the text, was frequently entered wholly or partially in the margin. These facts suggest either that it was not originally intended to have red rubrics or that the rubrics in black ink were meant as a guide for the red rubricator, although, if the latter was the case, the first scribe usually did not leave enough room for the red rubrics to be inserted neatly.

Since this part of the cartulary is a copy of Harley 1708, it must have been written after the date of the latest addition made in Harley 1708 prior to the copying and, perhaps less securely, before the date of the earliest addition made afterwards and therefore not copied. This yields a date-range of 1339 × 48. The earlier *terminus* depends upon a royal writ concerning dies for the abbey's mint, dated 17 November 1338, which was copied from Harley 1708 into the new cartulary,[1] while the later date is derived from two documents, dated 24 September 1348 and 9 November 1348 respectively,[2] neither of which was copied into Vespasian E xxv, although both appear in sections of Harley 1708 which the scribe otherwise copied in full. Moreover, two documents of a little over three years later, namely, the writ and record of a legal action in Whitley dated February 1352, were similarly not copied from Harley 1708.[3]

The second part of Vespasian E xxv runs from the present f 139 to at least f 223, and probably by extension to the end of the manuscript (although its main hand ends on f 215v), and appears to consist of an originally separate work which was only later bound in with the main text. The recto face of f 139 is blank and has the rather grubby appearance of a leaf that was once exposed on the outside, while evidence of trimming exists at the tops of many subsequent folios. The original entries in this part were apparently made directly from the deeds themselves and are largely unique to this cartulary, although some of the texts were also among those copied from Harley 1708 in the first section. They comprise a large number of deeds relating to the town of Reading and other places in the immediate neighbourhood of which the abbey was lord. These occur

---

[1] No. 112. [2] Nos. 637, 1196.
[3] Nos. 1265–6.

on the following folios: 139v-148v and 151r-153v (Whitley), 155r-156r and 158v-167v (Tilehurst and Theale), and 168r-191v and 193v-215v (Reading). The folios are ruled with varying numbers of lines, ranging between 30 and 36, and the entries are in a distinct and rapid fourteenth-century cursive hand without separate initials, save that the first letter of each deed is rather larger than the rest, and without rubrics, although some later headings were added in the margin. The compilation was made after 9 July 1340, the date of the latest deed entered in this hand,[1] and was probably complete before May 1343, since deeds of May and October 1343 and others of 1345 and 1348 were added subsequently in different hands.[2] Despite its late composition, however, the work preserves the texts of some hundreds of deeds, mostly not otherwise known, ranging in date back to the time of the first abbot, Hugh of Amiens (1123-30), and including several abbatial deeds of the twelfth and early thirteenth centuries. As a whole the collection is of the utmost importance for the early tenurial history of the Reading area. Moreover, in many cases and especially with regard to the deeds of early abbots the scribe copied in full the witness-lists, which enable light to be shed on the personnel of the early abbatial households and on the people most prominent in Reading and its environs at that time. This part of the cartulary received additions in various other fourteenth-century hands, although none of the documents entered is dated later than Edward III's reign and some are much earlier. The most significant comprise further deeds concerning Reading (ff 216r-218v and ff 228r-230v), papal acts from the late twelfth to the early fourteenth centuries (ff 220r-223v) and mortmain licences granted by Edward II and Edward III (ff 224r-227v). Here, too, material not recorded elsewhere is included, more especially Pope Clement III's grant of pontificals to the abbot of Reading in 1191.[3] It seems likely, however, that the last folios in the manuscript, from f 224 to the end, constitute an addition to this part of the cartulary, since they are of a slightly smaller size than the rest and are not included in the medieval Arabic foliation, which ends at f 223 (see below). Even so, since the hand of the mortmain licences on ff 224-7 is the same as that of most of the papal acts, namely, those on ff 222-3, the extra folios were presumably bound in not long afterwards.

The key to when the two major parts of the cartulary were bound together, assuming that they were originally separate, is provided by the medieval foliation in Arabic numerals. This runs, or ori-

---

[1] No. 943.
[2] Nos. 1026-7, 1034-8.
[3] No. 154.

ginally ran,[1] continuously from 1 on the present f6 to 231 on f223 and thus covers the whole of the two parts, excluding the probable extension of the second part. As far as number 71, however, it is written over an erased but exactly equivalent foliation in Roman numerals. Though difficult to date precisely, the Arabic foliation appears to belong to the late fourteenth century, suggesting that the two parts were put together not many decades after each was written. It also suggests that the missing sections of the main part had been removed for some reason by the end of the fourteenth century. The same Arabic numerals are used in the incomplete table of contents, mostly in index-form, which appears on ff2v–5v, that is, on the folios subsequently bound in at the front of the cartulary preceding the commencement of the Arabic foliation.

II The abbey's foundation and initial endowment

This necessarily brief introduction is not the place in which to attempt either a general history of the abbey or a detailed account of the growth of its endowment. Nevertheless, some preliminary remarks on the circumstances of its foundation are called for, since they provide both the context for its early charters in general and, more particularly, the background against which discussions of possible forgery must be set. No valid interpretation or criticism of its charters can be complete without an appreciation of the founder's overall scheme for the house, from the type of monasticism he selected to the scale of privilege he granted.

Reading Abbey was founded by King Henry I in 1121, although for nearly two years it existed as a priory. It was among the last Black Monk houses of first rank to appear in England in the Middle Ages and owed its origins to the king's desire to establish a rich, respected and highly privileged monastic community befitting the royal dignity and charged with special obligations in relief of the poor and reception of pilgrims and guests.[2] More than this on his

---

[1] Parts of the medieval Arabic sequence are missing, indicating losses of folios since it was provided, namely, the numerals 145 (after the present f150), either 149 or 150 (after f153), 153–156 (after f156), and 158–163 (after f157). In the last case physical evidence remains of the removal of some folios after the present f157, which bears also the medieval Arabic numeral 157.

[2] A passage in the foundation charter (below, no. 1) specifically requires the abbot to devote the resources of the monastery to this end: '... non cum suis secularibus consanguineis seu quibuslibet aliis elemosinas monasterii male utendo disperdat, sed pauperibus et peregrinis et hospitibus suscipiendis curam gerat.' Moreover, in establishing a hospital at the abbey gate 'ad relevandam pauperum inopiam et subsidium peregrinorum' in the late 12th century, Abbot Hugh II cited 'susceptionem hospitum transeuntium, precipue tamen pauperum Christi ac peregrinorum' as one of Henry

aims one cannot say with certainty, but since the king's body was eventually to be brought from Normandy in very difficult winter conditions for burial in the abbey,[1] and since both his father, William I, and his nephew and successor, Stephen, were each laid to rest in their favourite foundations,[2] it is highly probable that Henry intended from the first to be buried at Reading. If such was the case, then the monastery was to be not simply a new royal abbey but more particularly a royal mausoleum.[3] The loss of Henry's only legitimate son in the wreck of the White Ship in November, 1120, which affected him deeply, may well have given a spur to his plans, but is unlikely by itself to have been the cause of so ambitious a project as the king undertook at Reading.[4]

For his new foundation Henry chose monks of the Cluniac observance. Given his links with Cluny and the high reputation which Cluniac monasticism then enjoyed in the Anglo-Norman world,[5] the choice was a natural one, but it was also one singularly well suited

---

I's main purposes in founding the abbey (below, no. 224). See also William of Malmesbury's elaborate tribute to the hospitality of Reading in its early years (*Gesta Regum*, ed. W. Stubbs. (RS, 1887-9), i. 489) and, for further discussion, see K. Leyser, 'Frederick Barbarossa, Henry II and the hand of St James', *EHR* xc (1975), 494-5.

[1] Henry died at Lyons-la-Forêt, in eastern Normandy, on 1 December 1135, having given instructions on his death-bed that his body was to be buried at Reading. It was taken first to Rouen for disembowelling and embalming, and thence to Caen where, the winds being contrary, it was lodged in St Stephen's abbey until after Christmas, when a crossing to England became possible (Orderic Vitalis, vi. 448-50; William of Malmesbury, *Historia Novella*, ed. K. R. Potter (1955), 12-14, 16; Henry of Huntingdon, *Historia Anglorum*, ed. T. Arnold (RS, 1879), 256-8; *The Letters of Peter the Venerable*, ed. G. Constable (Harvard, 1967), i. 22). The king was buried at Reading on 5 January 1136 ('Annales Radingenses', 11; continuator of Florence of Worcester, in *Florentii Wigorniensis ... Chronicon ex Chronicis*, ed. B. Thorpe (Eng. Hist. Soc., 1848-9), ii. 95; 'Winchcombe Annals', ed. R. R. Darlington, *Med. Misc. for D. M. Stenton*, 127). The date usually given for his burial is 4 January, which is derived from Gervase of Canterbury (*Historical Works*, ed. W. Stubbs (RS, 1879-80), i. 95), but this is strictly the date which Gervase gives for the bringing of the body from Normandy to England.

[2] For William I's burial at St Stephen's, Caen, see Orderic Vitalis, iv, 102-6. Stephen was buried at Faversham, where the original plan of the abbey church included what appears to have been a large royal funerary chapel occupying much of its eastern arm (E. M. Hallam, 'The burial places of English kings', *History Today* (July 1981), 46; B. Philp, *Excavations at Faversham, 1965* (Kent Archaeol. Research Group's Council, 1968), 15-17, 37).

[3] For evidence of Henry's concern that royal burials should only take place in suitably noble churches, see E. M. Hallam, 'Royal burial and the cult of kingship in France and England, 1060-1330', *Journ. of Medieval History*, viii (1982), 360.

[4] For a detailed account of the wreck of the White Ship and the king's grief at his son's death, see Orderic Vitalis, vi. 294-306. It is interesting in this respect that, according to the foundation charter, among the souls for whose welfare Reading Abbey was founded was that of Henry's son, William (below, no.1).

[5] D. Knowles, *The Monastic Order in England*. (2nd edn, Cambridge, 1963), 174.

to his purpose. Although Henry was later to patronize both the Cistercians and the Austin canons,[1] it was the typically Cluniac combination of reform and splendour which evidently appealed to him for his most important foundation. The first monks arrived in Reading on 18 June 1121. Of the initial community seven monks with a prior, Peter, had been sent from Cluny in response to Henry's request to Abbot Pons, and had been joined on their arrival in England by several others from the Cluniac priory of St Pancras at Lewes.[2] The community lived under the rule of Prior Peter until 15 April 1123, when Hugh of Amiens, formerly prior of Lewes, was appointed first abbot and Peter returned to Cluny.[3] It is clear that, whatever had been the case in the first two years, the appointment of an abbot entailed the liberation of the house from juridical dependence on Cluny.[4] Reading was the first Cluniac house in England to achieve independent abbatial status and the change was undoubtedly made at the king's insistence. He seems to have desired the best of two worlds, namely, all the benefits of the Cluniac observance but without the juridical ties to Cluny. That the final solution took nearly two years to achieve may indicate either a gradual development of the king's ideas in this respect or an element of resistance from Cluny, but the result was later to serve as a convenient model for King Stephen's foundation at Faversham, which was similarly colonized by Cluniac monks but was designated an abbey *ab initio*.[5] Shortly after the appointment of its first abbot, Reading received a papal confirmation from Calixtus II, dated 19

[1] For the Cistercians, see Knowles, *ibid.*, 175; *Gallia Christiana*, xi, 307-8 (for Mortemer in Normandy, although this did not become a full member of the Order until after Henry's death). For the Austin canons, see Knowles and Hadcock, 2nd edn, 156 (for Dunstable); *The Cartulary of Cirencester Abbey*, ed. C. D. Ross (1964), i. 21; *The Cartulary of the Priory of St Denys near Southampton*, ed. E. O. Blake (Southampton Records Ser., 1981), i, p. xxxv; ii. 211.

[2] 'Annales Radingenses', 10.

[3] *Ibid.* The precise date is given in *Flor. Hist.*, ii. 49; this work is now known certainly to be by Matthew Paris, who is presumed to have taken material from a lost chronicle of Reading (R. Vaughan, *Matthew Paris* (Cambridge, 1958), 37-41, 104), presumably that listed in the late 12th-century list of books at Reading as *Gesta regis Henrici et ystoria Rading' in uno volumine* (Egerton 3031, f 9r; see below, no. 225).

[4] This is clear from the tone of Peter the Venerable's *carta societatis* to Abbot Hugh and the convent of Reading (no. 218) and, more precisely, from the charter of La Charité cited in note 5.

[5] Faversham was founded in 1148 (*Heads of Relig. Houses*, 49 n.3) and was settled by Cluniac monks from Bermondsey, a dependency of La Charité-sur-Loire. Both the abbot of Cluny and the prior and convent of La Charité granted the new abbey complete freedom from all obedience and subjection to Cluny and La Charité, the latter adding that it was to enjoy the same freedom as Reading Abbey, also settled by Cluniac monks (Saltman, *Theobald*, 82-3; *Mon. Ang.*, iv. 575).

June 1123, and two years later the formal 'foundation charter' from the king.[1]

The endowment which Henry conveyed to his new abbey was generous by any standards. It comprised initially the manors and churches of Reading, Cholsey and Leominster, the manor of Thatcham and the church of Wargrave, to which were added later the church of Hanborough and, probably, the manor of Bucklebury and the manor and church of Pangbourne.[2] What made the initial endowment so significant, however, given the king's pious intentions, was its inclusion of the sites and properties of three old abbeys, Reading, Cholsey and Leominster, which had been destroyed on account of their sins, as the foundation charter has it, and whose lands had for long been in lay possession—in fact, in royal possession.[3] By giving the lands of these former abbeys to his new house Henry was at the same time satisfying the demands of the Gregorian Reform movement for the restitution of alienated Church property. This is the first of many indications in the foundation charter that Henry was prepared and willing to implement much of the monastic reformers' programme. Moreover, the king went to some lengths to provide his monks with neatly rounded endowments by removing the claims of other religious houses in the manors he intended to give. He recovered the church of Reading and its land from Battle

[1] See below, nos. 139, 1.

[2] Hanborough church (Oxon.) was given in c.1130 × 33 (see no. 494). No charter evidence survives for Bucklebury and Pangbourne (Berks.). Both were treated separately in Domesday Book and cannot, therefore, have come to the abbey as appurtenances of Reading: Bucklebury and one Pangbourne estate were held by the Crown, the other Pangbourne estate by Miles Crispin (*VCH Berks.*, i. 330, 334, 355). In 1212 both Bucklebury and Pangbourne were said to have been given to Reading Abbey by Henry I (*Fees*, i. 107-8), but this record is not uniformly accurate regarding other royal gifts to Reading. The monks' possession of Bucklebury can certainly be traced back to 1169 (*PR 15 Henry II*, 80) and probably to 1151 × 54, when they obtained the church by exchange from St Albans Abbey (see no. 688). They had demesne in Pangbourne by 1158 × 65 (BL Cotton Vesp. E v, f 19) and, according to a diocesan confirmation of 1193, had held the church since the time of Roger bishop of Salisbury (see no. 204). Great uncertainty surrounds the history of the two Domesday estates in Pangbourne in the twelfth century, but since no lord of Pangbourne other than Reading Abbey is mentioned after that time, they must both have come to the monks. The Crown's holding could well have been given by Henry I, while Miles Crispin's holding may have been detached from his other estates, which became the Honour of Wallingford, when they were in the control of his widow's second husband, Brian fitz Count, a protégé of Henry I (Sanders, *English Baronies*, 93); against this, however, a Richer of Pangbourne was listed among the knights of the Honour of Wallingford in 1166 (*Red Bk. Exch.*, i. 310).

[3] All were Anglo-Saxon houses, Reading and Leominster being nunneries, whose lands were held by the Crown in 1086. See Knowles and Hadcock, 2nd edn, 62, 69, 74. For Leominster, see also B. R. Kemp, 'The monastic dean of Leominster', *EHR*, lxxxiii (1968), 505-6.

Abbey, another estate in Reading from Tutbury Priory, and the church of Cholsey from the abbey of Mont St Michel, all by exchange for lands elsewhere.[1] In one case, however, he either failed or did not attempt to pursue this policy, for, although he gave the monks the manor of Thatcham, he did not include the church, which was held by his right-hand man, Roger bishop of Salisbury,[2] whom he may not have wished to disturb, and apparently substituted the church of Wargrave, which he had also recovered from Mont St Michel.[3]

The king's gifts were vastly more important than the bald recital of their names might suggest. In particular, the manor of Reading included not only the small town and central estate but also the later manors of Tilehurst, Beenham and Sulhamstead Abbots, while the church of Reading was the ancient mother church of a *parochia* formerly extending to the south and west of Reading, over much of which it still retained at least residual rights.[4] Leominster was even more complex, for the manor consisted of a *caput* with several members and the church was, like Reading, an ancient mother church whose extensive *parochia*, unlike Reading's, was still remarkably intact in the 1120s.[5] In fact, the temporal and ecclesiastical endowment at Leominster was rich enough to support a dependent priory, which was established in fully conventual form in 1139.[6]

[1] Battle was first given Funtington, which was very soon exchanged for Appledram, both in Sussex (*The Chronicle of Battle Abbey*, ed. E. Searle (Oxford, 1980), 122); Tutbury received the unidentified *Brincheale* (see below, no. 18 n.1); and Mont St Michel was given £12 worth of land at Budleigh (Devon) in exchange for the churches of Cholsey and Wargrave (see nos. 3, 771).

[2] See no. 1108.

[3] See above, n. 1.

[4] The later manors of Tilehurst, etc., are not mentioned in Domesday Book, but all appear in the abbey's possession in the twelfth century—Tilehurst by 1130 × 35 (see nos. 1132-9, etc.), Beenham by 1158 × 65 (BL Cotton Vesp. E v, f 19), and Sulhamstead Abbots by 1173 (see no. 1075)—and presumably formed parts of the 43 'hides which made up Reading in 1086 (*VCH Berks.*, i. 334). By virtue of its possession of the ancient minster church of St Mary in Reading, from which Minster Street in the town was named, the abbey acquired not only the younger churches in the lands of Reading but also the right to receive pensions from other churches formerly payable to St Mary's (see nos. 179, 797-9).

[5] For the manor and members of Leominster in Domesday Book, see *VCH Herefs.*, i. 314; an analysis of the charters in the Leominster cartulary (BL Cotton Domit. A iii) reveals that at least ten of the sixteen members which had belonged to Leominster in 1066 came with the *caput* into Reading's possession. For the church of Leominster and its *parochia*, see below, no. 354.

[6] See Kemp, 'The monastic dean of Leominster', 512-13, citing 'Annales Radingenses', 11. Henry's brother-in-law, King David I of Scotland, endowed Reading Abbey with possessions in Scotland which enabled a second dependent priory to be founded on the Isle of May (see below, no. 1276 n., and I. B. Cowan and D. E. Easson, *Medieval Religious Houses, Scotland* (2nd edn, 1976), 59-60).

Henry accompanied his gifts of manors and churches with an elaborate grant of immunities for the abbey and its possessions and of high liberties to be exercised by the monks over their lands and men. Although the king probably did not explicitly grant 'all immunity, power, quittance and liberty that the royal power can confer upon an abbey', as one of Reading's fabricated charters claims,[1] nevertheless, an exalted grant of individual liberties which together approximated to the same thing would have been wholly appropriate to his other plans for the abbey. Considered in this light, even the inclusion of *utfangenetheof*, which historians have thought fatal to the foundation charter's authenticity, becomes credible. The concept was certainly known in the late 1130s[2] and no compelling proof of its anachronism in the 1120s has been adduced. Indeed, one cannot exclude the possibility that its first known occurrence is in the early Reading charters, since, if it was being formulated in the 1120s, as is possible, it would have been entirely fitting for the king to grant it to the new house which he favoured so highly in other ways.

The detailed instructions in the foundation charter regarding the abbey's constitution reflect equally the king's desire to establish a house in impeccable conformity with reforming sentiments, an aim in which he was no doubt advised and encouraged by the first abbot, Hugh of Amiens. Much of the charter reads like a programme of contemporary monastic reform in a Black Monk context, containing as it does several provisions which distinguish Reading from older houses of similar type. Reading held its lands in free alms and not by feudal tenure, nor was it to create knights' fees within them. There was to be no division in the possessions of the house between the abbot and the convent; all were to be held in common, and during abbatial vacancies the prior and convent were to have custody. The appointment of abbots was to be by canonical election. The abbot was not to reward his lay relatives out of the abbey's lands, but to devote its resources to relief of the poor and reception of pilgrims and guests. There were to be no hereditary offices in the abbey or its possessions, but the appointment and dismissal of officials were to be in the sole control of the abbot and convent. The abbot was to take care not to accept boys into the community, but only adults of sound mind, whether clerks or laymen.[3] It is from such reforming provisions as these that the foundation of Reading derives at least part of its importance and significance in English monastic history.

The king's concern to establish his house on a proper footing

---

[1] No. 2.

[2] See no. 1 n.3.

[3] For these provisions, see the foundation charter (no. 1).

would equally have extended to the provision of relics. In the course
of the twelfth century Reading built up an impressive collection of
relics drawn from a variety of sources and, although Henry I's involvement can be demonstrated only in the case of a few, many
others are likely to have been given at the king's request in the early
years of the abbey's life.[1] Certainly it would have been very odd if
he had not taken an interest in this aspect of the abbey's endowment.
From this point of view the arrival of the monks' most important
relic, the Hand of St James, falls into place, despite the doubts which
have been cast on Reading's claim to have received it from Henry
I. If, as has been suggested, the king was keen to favour the abbey
in other respects, nothing would be more natural than his deciding
to send the relic to Reading after it had been brought to England
by his daughter, the Empress Matilda. He may not have given it
outright to the monks, as their fabricated charter alleges, but that
he lodged it with them on some kind of semi-permanent basis is
entirely possible and consistent with his general aims for the house.[2]

III A note on forgery

The vexed question of forgery can hardly be avoided in any collection of charters dating back to the first half of the twelfth century.
In Reading's case, however, although some of its twelfth-century
original charters and cartulary texts are certainly spurious, forgery
does not appear to have been rife among its muniments. In particular, very little is evident among its title-deeds to lands and
churches, and this is not surprising since the abbey was founded at
a time when gifts of real property to the religious were increasingly
accompanied by written acts, often no doubt at the request of the
recipients.[3] It is a fair assumption that the bulk of Reading's acquisitions of this kind were recorded in charters given at the same time
or very soon afterwards, and further that, even when the texts survive only as cartulary copies, they are for the most part authentic,
since where it is possible to compare cartulary texts with extant
originals there is very little or no evidence of alteration apart from
spelling and the like. Moreover, since the monks did not apparently
attempt to fabricate charters for the few gifts where they were

---

[1] The late 12th-century list of relics is preserved in Egerton 3031, ff 6v-8r (see
below, no. 227). For a valuable discussion, see D. Bethell, 'The making of a twelfth-
century relic collection', *Studies in Church History*, viii (1971), 61-72. Bethell discerned
several different elements in the collection, including Anglo-Saxon, Cluniac, Byzan-
tine and Holy Land groups. For Henry I's certain or probable involvement in the
acquisition of particular relics, see *ibid.*, 69.

[2] See no. 5 and n.

[3] M. T. Clanchy, *From Memory to Written Record* (1979), 38.

lacking,[1] it is reasonable to suppose that forgery was not employed on a large scale at Reading. Where forgery is detectable, it is mainly with regard to the abbey's privileges and liberties, and here the reason seems to lie in the monks' need to safeguard their liberties as new circumstances arose. Almost all the identifiable instances of fabrication date from before the end of the twelfth century, and most appear to belong to its last quarter, at which time the evolving nature of royal justice and administration may well have led the monks to adapt the terms of earlier grants to the different conditions in which their liberties had now to operate.

In dealing with prima-facie suspicious features in Reading's charters, certain considerations ought to be borne in mind before a definite conclusion of forgery is reached. In the first place, Reading's comparatively late foundation makes forgery a priori less likely there than in many of the older Black Monk houses, which felt the need to manufacture charters for lands, churches and rights which they had long held but for which they lacked the documentary title now increasingly regarded as necessary.[2] Secondly, the possibility cannot be excluded that some of Reading's early charters were composed and written by the monks as beneficiaries and merely sealed or otherwise authenticated by the donors. Such a procedure was not unusual in England in the twelfth century, when, apart from the king and some bishops, very few lords had organized writing offices, and it was even employed for royal acts, especially in the first half of the century.[3] With regard to the acts of kings and bishops in particular, however, it could give rise to charters containing features not normally found in the products of their own writing offices and therefore apparently suspect, despite their genuineness. Of a number of possible cases among the Reading charters, it seems likely, for example, that as late as the 1190s some of the abbey's episcopal acts were produced in this way and must be accepted as genuine, even though their somewhat archaic character might otherwise lead one

---

[1] Notably the Berkshire manors of Bucklebury and Pangbourne (see above, p. 16 n. 2) and property in Cambridge (see no. 8 and BL Add. Ch. 19579).

[2] Clanchy, *ibid.*, 253-4.

[3] *Ibid.*, 40-2 and pl. III. However, Dr Clanchy's statement that 'even bishops in England did not develop organized writing offices until *c.*1200' (*ibid.*, 40-1) must be doubtful, since Professor C. R. Cheney, whom he cites, expressly states that 'at the beginning of the thirteenth century we cannot fail to be impressed by the regularity and distinctiveness of the documents issued by the various bishops' (*English Bishops' Chanceries 1100-1250* (Manchester, 1950), 55), while the editors of Gilbert Foliot's *acta* observe that by the time of his death in 1187 a considerable degree of uniformity of practice and direction existed among the clerks of his writing office (*Foliot Letters and Charters*, 23-9). Even so, such developments did not exclude the writing of charters by beneficiaries down to the end of the century (see below).

to reject them as forgeries.[1] Thirdly, it is important not to consider individual charters in isolation but in relation to the abbey's muniments as a whole. This is especially true of the series of royal charters, beginning with the foundation charter of 1125, most of which exist today only in cartulary copies. The charters of Henry I have been particularly challenged as forgeries, but while some are undoubtedly very problematical in the forms in which they have survived, they need not in general be rejected as evidence of what the king actually gave to the abbey or stipulated for its constitution and privileges. For instance, the sweeping grant of liberties in the foundation charter, though seemingly unlikely when viewed in isolation from other texts, gains credibility from its inclusion in all subsequent general royal and papal confirmations down to the early thirteenth century, while being absent from the one earlier papal confirmation, that of Calixtus II in 1123. This last fact is of crucial importance in establishing the basic reliability of the abbey's royal and papal acts of the twelfth century, for, if it is argued that the text of the foundation charter was drastically altered and expanded in the later twelfth century, it would be necessary to argue also that precisely the same tampering was carried out on the texts of all general royal confirmations back to Stephen's and of all papal confirmations back to Honorius II's but not earlier. Equally, since by such an argument Calixtus II's bull would have been left untouched, one would have to credit the 'forgers' with a degree of precise calculation as to chronology which would have been, to say the least, exceptional in undertakings of this kind. In fact, however, where fabrication is evident beyond question, as in the text of Henry I's supposed gift of the hand of St James,[2] the result is so inept as to suggest that the abbey's forgers were not capable of such consistently sustained deception.

Nevertheless, fabrication there undoubtedly was, notably of some royal acts in the troubled reign of Stephen[3] and of certain general royal charters described as *gestatoria*, or 'portable', which contain statements of the abbey's privileges, particularly that purporting to have been granted by Henry I and one allegedly granted by Henry II.[4] These both assert that Henry I 'gave to the abbey all immunity, power, quittance and liberty that the royal power can confer upon an abbey', a statement which, though not impossible as an epitome of the king's intentions, is not found in the same all-embracing and unequivocal terms either in the foundation charter or in the fuller and on the whole more acceptable general confirmations of the

---

[1] See nos. 203, 205.　　　　[2] No. 5.
[3] See nos. 13, 17, 667.　　　　[4] Respectively, nos. 2 and 21.

twelfth century. Although the testimony of Pope Eugenius III that Reading was endowed with *regia libertas*[1] might be held to substantiate the assertion, and although it may have been broadly true in practice, the anomalies surrounding it must tell against the authenticity of the 'portable' charters in which it occurs. Even so, the statement was included in an apparently genuine charter of John and in an undoubtedly genuine charter of Henry III, both of which follow closely the text of Henry II's spurious 'portable' charter with its very extensive list of specific privileges.[2] Moreover, the same statement and liberties were confirmed by later kings who inspected the charter of Henry III which enshrined them.[3] Other instances of forgery or doubtful authenticity among the abbey's charters are discussed in this edition under the texts concerned.

IV The arrangement of the edition and the method of editing

For this edition the contents of the three general cartularies have been brought together and re-arranged into a new sequence. First come documents which are either of a general nature or are concerned with two or more different places; these are grouped as follows: (i) royal acts, (ii) documents relating to the abbey's liberties, (iii) papal acts, (iv) archiepiscopal and episcopal acts, and (v) abbatial acts and documents concerning the abbey as a community. These sections are followed by documents referring to individual places, arranged by county according to the boundaries which obtained before the local government re-organization of 1974, and by alphabetical order of place within each county. In the main the documents concerning each place have been dealt with chronologically, but in some cases it has been thought desirable to pursue, for example, the history of the church separately from the history of temporalities in the same place, while in other cases, especially where many deeds are not datable within sufficiently narrow limits, the sequence of entries in one or other of the cartularies has been followed. Any royal, papal or episcopal act referring to one place only has been put under that place, in order to render its history more readily apparent, rather than in the appropriate general section as is normally the practice of the cartularies. On the other hand, the small number of abbatial, comital and other acts relating to two places (none relate to more than two) appear under one of the places involved, with cross-referencing to the other. The edition concludes with the Scottish charters and finally a short section of

[1] See no. 144.
[2] Respectively, nos. 45, 56.
[3] E.g. Edward II and Edward III (nos. 102, 109).

such miscellaneous documents as the statutes of Marlborough and Gloucester which, though of interest to the abbey, did not concern it specifically.

The division of this material between the two volumes of the present edition is as follows:

Volume I: general documents and those relating to English counties other than Berkshire;

Volume II: Berkshire documents, Scottish charters and miscellaneous documents.

A consolidated index to both volumes is provided in volume II.

All items dating down to and including 1216 have been printed in full, except those already adequately and accessibly printed elsewhere, which have in the main been merely calendared. Items which date from after 1216 have also as a rule been calendared, whether or not printed elsewhere, unless they have seemed of sufficient interest or importance to warrant printing in full. In the case of all calendared items, however, witness-lists and most dating clauses have been given in full as in the manuscripts. Rubrics and other headings have in general been omitted, except where they contain information additional to that in the texts concerned. Where an original of an entry in the cartularies survives, this has been printed or calendared as the primary text, with notes of significant variants in the cartularies. A substantial number of documents appear in two or in all three of the general cartularies and, where this is so, the text printed or calendared is that of the first source cited (usually the earliest) with similar notes of variants in the other text or texts. The edition also takes account, however, of such additional copies of items in the general cartularies as occur in other Reading cartularies or occasionally elsewhere, although no notice has been taken of post-medieval transcripts. For these additional copies the noting of variant readings has been more selective. The other Reading cartularies concerned are these:[2]

BL Cotton Vespasian E v (13th-century Almoner's cartulary)— cited in this edition as D;

BL Cotton Domitian A iii (13th-century Leominster cartulary)— cited as E;

Cambridge University Library Dd.ix.38 (14th-century Reading register)—cited as F;

---

[2] For brief descriptions of the following, see G. R. C. Davis, *Medieval Cartularies of Great Britain* (1958), 91. The 14th-century register at Cambridge is described in detail by W. A. Pantin in *Chapters of the English Black Monks*, ii (Camden 3rd ser. xlvii, 1933), pp. v–viii.

Trowbridge, Wiltshire Record Office D1/19 [formerly Salisbury
Diocesan Registry] (15th-century Reading register)—cited as
G.

In the printing of texts dating from the twelfth and early thirteenth centuries, 'i' and 'j' have been standardized as 'i', the con-
sonantal 'u' and 'v' as 'v', 'c' and 't' as 't' when appropriate (i.e., in
such words as *ratio*) and, very occasionally and as appropriate, two
'u's as 'w' (as in *Niwetuna* in no. 354). For later texts, however, the
spellings printed or calendared are generally those of the first source
cited for each item unaltered. Modern conventions in punctuation
and use of capital letters have been adopted throughout, even for
originals. Expansions of abbreviations are not indicated unless the
exact form of the expansion is in doubt, in which case it is shown in
round brackets—e.g., *Rog(erus)*, *Linc(olniensis)*, *iustic(iarii)*, etc.

In the calendaring of charters the following practices have been
followed. Deeds conveying real property by use of the verb *donare*
are described as 'gifts', but those involving privileges, exemptions
and the like, and employing either *donare* or *concedere*, have been
rendered as 'grants'. In gifts in fee to an individual and his or her
heirs, reference to heirs has been omitted unless the relevant clauses
of the full text contain unusual features. The form 'in free alms' has
been employed to cover considerable variety in the diplomatic of
the deeds, ranging from the simple *in elemosinam* to the elaborate *in
liberam et puram et perpetuam elemosinam*. In *habendum* clauses, the persons of whom the donees are to hold are named only when different
from the donors or when unusual arrangements are specified. Warranty clauses, including the fully developed *warantizare acquietare et
defendere*, and sealing clauses appear, respectively, as 'warranty' and
'sealing' unless peculiarities in the complete text require a fuller
rendering. Conveyances of real property by means of *concedere* and
involving a rent-charge are described as 'leases'. Surnames and
place-names have been given in their modern equivalents, if known,
followed by the original form italicized in round brackets, although
original forms are not given for some obvious occupational surnames
nor for the place-name, Reading, all the various spellings of which
are otherwise represented in the edition. If a name is unidentifiable
or no satisfactory modern equivalent is known, it has been simply
incorporated in the calendar in its original form in italics.

Throughout the edition the use of square brackets indicates an
addition supplied by the editor, often the date of a saint's feast or
the location of a place mentioned in the text. In the printing of full
texts it indicates in addition the supply of words or passages either
lost from an original by damage and known from copies, or omitted

in the cartulary text being printed and available from other copies, or necessary to complete the sense. In the printing of cartulary texts in full (but not in calendars), transitions from one face of a folio to the other, or from one folio to the next, are similarly noticed in square brackets, this referring, in the case of multiple copies, only to the first source cited. Angle brackets are used to indicate words or phrases in the margins of manuscripts. In the textual notes, the abbreviation 'om.' is used for 'omitted.'

All items have been given a date. In the case of charters and documents which are themselves dated, the date is given without brackets, but dates which have been supplied by the editor appear in square brackets. For final concords and other legal documents dated only by 'return days', consisting of a number of calendar days and normally occurring at intervals of a week,[1] the date given is that of the beginning of the 'return day'.

The documents are numbered consecutively throughout the edition. However, where the cartularies merely note the existence of a deed and do not enter the text, this is indicated not by separate numbers but by the addition of lower-case letters to the relevant numbers in the sequence—e.g., below, nos. 11a, 49a, 366a-c, etc.

All references to previous printing are given immediately after the manuscript sources for each item ('pd.'). If unspecified the references are to the printing of the text in full, but references after the word 'cal.' (calendar) or 'transl.' (translation) or 'abstract', in round brackets, are to printings in that category. The precise source of the printing has not been given unless other than a Reading manuscript, in which case it is shown in round brackets after the reference concerned.

V List of abbots

For other lists published in this century see Hurry, *Reading Abbey*, 149-50; *VCH Berks.*, ii. 72-3; and, for the 12th and early 13th centuries, *Heads of Relig. Houses*, 63. The present list begins with the prior who ruled the house in its first two years before its elevation to abbatial status (see above, p. 15).

[**Peter**, initial prior, 18 June 1121 — 15 Apr. 1123
He was among the original monks from Cluny who, with others from Lewes, arrived in Reading on 18 June 1121; he returned to Cluny when the first abbot was appointed ('Annales Radingenses', 10).]

---

[1] See *Handbook of Dates*, ed. C. R. Cheney (Royal Hist. Soc., Guides and Handbooks, 4, revised 1982), 67.

1. **Hugh I**, of Amiens, 15 Apr. 1123—Sept. 1130
Formerly prior of Lewes. For his appointment as first abbot, see
ibid.; *Flor. Hist.*, ii. 49; above, p. 15. He was elected archbishop of
Rouen before 29 Mar. 1130 (*Papsturkunden in Frankreich*, v, ed. J.
Ramackers (Göttingen, 1956), 111–12), apparently left England with
Henry I on 8 Sept. (T. G. Waldman, 'Hugh "of Amiens"', Arch-
bishop of Rouen (1130–64)' (Oxford University D.Phil. thesis
(1970), 21) and was consecrated archbishop on 14 Sept. (Robert of
Torigny, 117).

2. **Anscher**, 1130 (? Sept.)—27 Jan. 1135
Formerly prior of Lewes. For his appointment as abbot and his
death, see 'Annales Radingenses', 11; also D f 11v (obit).

3. **Edward**, 1136—*c.*1154
For his appointment, see 'Annales Radingenses', 11; *Flor. Hist.*, ii.
58. No notice of his death or resignation has been found. His latest
recorded occurrence is in 1151 × 54 (see below, no. 688). His successor was appointed in 1154 before 7 Dec. (see under Reginald).

4. **Reginald**, 1154—1158
Formerly prior. For the year of his appointment as abbot, see *Flor.
Hist.*, ii. 72; he was in office before 7 Dec. (see below, no. 276). He
resigned at the king's insistence in 1158 ('Ann. Rad. Post.', 400;
Flor. Hist., ii. 75) and was later prior and first abbot of Walden
(*Heads of Relig. Houses*, 75–6). The only notice that he had been
prior of Reading is contained in the Walden Chronicle (see *The
Essex Review*, xlv (1936), 150). The evidence of the Reading charters
yields a prior Robert in 1136 × 54 (E f 117r) and a Hugh in 1151 ×
54 (below, no. 688), suggesting that, if Reginald held the priorate,
it was probably only for a short period before becoming abbot.

5. **Roger**, 1158—20 Jan. 1165
For his appointment, see 'Ann. Rad. Post.', 400; *Flor. Hist.*, ii. 75.
For his death, see 'Ann. Rad. Post.', 401; D f 11v (obit), but see
Reading Ms, BL Harley 978, f 15v (19 Jan.). The Winchester An-
nals have 1164 (*Ann. Mon.*, ii. 58), perhaps beginning the year on
25 March.

6. **William I,** the Templar, 1165—Feb. 1173
For his appointment, see 'Ann. Rad. Post.', 401. He was elected
archbishop of Bordeaux early in 1173 and consecrated on 25 Feb.
(*ibid.*; *Flor. Hist.*, ii. 84; Robert of Torigny, 255; *Recueil des historiens*

des Gaules et de la France, xii (Paris, 1877), 443; Delisle and Berger, Introduction, 474).

7. Joseph, 1173—1186

Formerly prior (see *Materials for the History of Thomas Becket, Archbishop of Canterbury*, ed. J. C. Robertson and J. B. Sheppard (RS, 1875–85), i. 418). For his appointment as abbot, see 'Ann. Rad. Post.', 401; *Flor. Hist.*, ii. 84. He resigned in 1186 and died 8 Feb. 1191 ('Ann. Rad. Post.', 401; D f 12r (obit)).

8. Hugh II, 1186—1199 (after 6 Apr.)

Formerly prior of Lewes. For his appointment as abbot of Reading, see 'Ann. Rad. Post.', 401; Waverley Annals, *Ann. Mon.*, ii. 244. He became Abbot Hugh V of Cluny in succession to Hugh IV, who died on 6 Apr. 1199 (*Gallia Christiana*, iv. 1144; Waverley, Winchester and Worcester Annals, *Ann. Mon.*, ii. 73, 251-2; iv. 390).

9. Elias, 1200—21 July 1213

Formerly chamberlain. For his appointment as abbot in 1200, see 'Ann. Rad. Post.', 401; the Worcester Annals note his 'succession' to Abbot Hugh II under 1199, but give his blessing under 1200 (*Ann. Mon.*, iv. 390 bis). The day of his death is given in D f 14v (obit). The year must be 1213, as is given in the Tewkesbury and Waverley Annals (*Ann. Mon.*, i. 61; ii. 273), although the Dunstable Annals give 1212, stating expressly that a successor was appointed at once, without royal custody (*ibid.*, iii. 38-9). It has been shown, however, that, while very important for the 'copious and excellent' information they contain, the Dunstable Annals for the years 1210-19 are chaotically unreliable in the dates they assign to events, many of those of 1213 for example being placed under 1212 (C. R. Cheney, 'Notes on the making of the Dunstable Annals', *Essays in Medieval History presented to Bertie Wilkinson*, ed. T. A. Sandquist and M. R. Powicke (Toronto, 1969), 93-6). Moreover, the Barnwell chronicler listed the abbey as vacant in 1213 (*Memoriale fratris Walteri de Coventria*, ed. W. Stubbs (RS, 1872-3), ii. 213).

10. Simon, 1213 (after 21 July)—13 Feb. 1226

Formerly chamberlain. For his appointment as abbot, see Dunstable Annals (see under Elias), *Ann. Mon.*, iii. 38 (s.a. 1212), 40 (election and blessing s.a. 1213). For his death, see 'Ann. Rad. Post.', 402; Dunstable, Tewkesbury, Waverley and Worcester Annals, *Ann. Mon.*, i. 69; ii. 302; iii. 100; iv. 419; *Pat. Rolls 1225-32*, 18 (below, no. 54); D f 12r (obit).

11. **Adam**, of Lathbury, Mar. 1226—6 Apr. 1238
Formerly prior of Leominster. His election as abbot received royal
assent at London on 7 Mar. 1226 (*Pat. Rolls 1225-32*, 21). He was
blessed by the diocesan on 15 Mar. (*Reg. St Osmund*, ii. 48). See also
'Ann. Rad. Post.', 402. For his death, see *ibid.*; D f13r (obit).
The Tewkesbury Annals give 8 Apr. (*Ann. Mon.*, i. 108), which is,
perhaps significantly, the date of the royal licence for a new election issued at Tewkesbury (*Cal. Pat. R. 1232-47*, 215—below, no.
60). The abbey was certainly vacant on 7 Apr. (*Close Rolls 1237-42*,
40).

12. **Richard I**, of Chichester, Apr. 1238—22 Mar. 1262
Formerly sub-prior. According to the Tewkesbury Annals, he was
elected on 12 Apr. 1238 (*Ann. Mon.*, i. 106-7). Royal assent to his
election was given at Eynsham on 18 Apr. (*Cal. Pat. R. 1232-47*,
216). For the date of his death, see 'Ann. Rad. Post.', 403. Royal
licence to elect a successor was given on the same day at Windsor
(*Cal. Pat. R. 1258-66*, 207).

13. **Richard II**, of Reading *alias* Bannister, Mar. 1262—11 July
1269
Formerly sub-prior. For his 'succession', see 'Ann. Rad. Post.', 403.
His election received royal assent at Windsor on 26 Mar. 1262 and
had been confirmed by the diocesan by 1 Apr. (*Cal. Pat. R. 1258-66*
207, 208). He resigned on grounds of ill health on 11 July 1269
(PRO C84/3/48).

14. **Robert**, of Burgate, July 1269—26 Oct. 1290.
Monk of Reading. His election received royal assent at Westminster
on 15 July and was confirmed by the diocesan on 19 July (*Cal. Pat.
R. 1266-72*, 354; PRO C84/3/50). The writ de intendendo to the
tenants of the abbey was issued on 20 July (*Cal. Pat. R. 1266-72*,
357). He resigned, at his monks' insistence, on 26 Oct. 1290 (PRO
C84/10/3; Stuart, *Records of May*, lxxxvii).

15. **William II**, of Sutton, Nov./Dec. 1290—June 1305
Formerly chamberlain. He was elected on 20 Nov. 1290, royal assent
was given on 27 Nov. and diocesan confirmation on 9 Dec. (PRO
C84/10/5-6; *Cal. Pat. R. 1281-92*, 409; cf. *Cal. Close R. 1288-96*, 154-
5). He was blessed by the diocesan on 14 Jan. 1291 (Salisbury
Chapter Muniments, Press II, Box 1/7; cf. *ibid.* 1/6). He was dead
by 24 June 1305 (*Cal. Close R. 1302-7*, 274); royal licence to elect his
successor was given on 27 June (*Cal. Pat. R. 1301-7*, 367).

16. **Nicholas**, of Whaplode, July/Sept. 1305—11 Jan. 1328

Formerly precentor. The abbacy was technically vacant for about two and a half months after William of Sutton's death, chiefly owing to irregularities in Nicholas's election. He was elected on 23 July 1305 (PRO C84/15/32; cf. *Cal. of Chancery Warrants*, i. 251) and presented as elect to the diocesan on 4 Aug., but the election was eventually quashed on 10 Sept. and Nicholas was 'provided' by episcopal authority (*Registrum Simonis de Gandavo Diocesis Saresbiriensis*, ed. C. T. Flower and M. C. B. Dawes (Canterbury and York Soc., xl-xli, 1934), ii. 655-9; PRO C84/15/33). Despite this, he was described in royal writs of 12 Sept. as having been elected (*Cal. Pat. R. 1301-7*, 377). He died on 11 Jan. 1328 (PRO C84/22/2).

17. **John I**, of Appleford, Feb./Mar. 1328—22 Jan. 1342

Monk of Reading. Royal assent to his election was given at York on 12 Feb. 1328 and restitution of temporalities ordered on 8 Mar. (*Cal. Pat. R. 1327-30*, 233, 250). He died on 22 Jan. 1342 (PRO C84/24/21); royal licence to elect his successor was given on 30 Jan. (*Cal. Pat. R. 1340-43*, 368).

18. **Henry**, of Appleford, Feb./Mar. 1342—July 1361

Monk of Reading. Royal assent to his election was given at Dunstable on 10 Feb. 1342 and restitution of temporalities ordered on 21 Mar. (*ibid.*, 372, 393). He probably died shortly before 29 July 1361, when the king at Swallowfield, south of Reading, allowed custody of the temporalities to the prior and convent (*Cal. Close R. 1360-4*, 197—below, no. 496).

19. **William III**, of Dumbleton, Aug./Sept. 1361—29 June 1369

Formerly prior of Leominster. His election as abbot received royal assent at Beaulieu on 15 Aug. 1361 and restitution of temporalities was ordered on 7 Sept. (*Cal. Pat. R. 1361-4*, 52, 58). In these letters he is described simply as a monk of Reading, but he was dean (i.e. prior) of Leominster in Oct. 1359 (G f15v) and significantly obtained royal licence to spend a year at Leominster in 1364 (*Cal. Pat. R. 1361-4*, 504). He died on 29 June 1369 (PRO C84/29/50).

20. **John II**, of Sutton, July/Aug. 1369—6 Apr. 1378

Formerly prior. He was elected on 11 July 1369, royal assent was given on 12 July and diocesan confirmation on 12 Aug., and restitution of temporalities was ordered on 15 Aug. (PRO C84/30/1, 11; *Cal. Pat. R. 1367-70*, 276, 295). He died on 6 Apr. 1378 (PRO C84/32/8).

21. **Richard III**, Yately, Apr. 1378—May × July 1409
Monk of Reading. His election was confirmed by the diocesan on 25 Apr. 1378 and restitution of temporalities was ordered on 29 Apr. (PRO C84/32/9; *Cal. Pat. R. 1377-81*, 193). No notice of his death or resignation has been found; he was still in office on 6 May 1409 (*ibid. 1408-13*, 72), but his successor's election received royal assent at Westminster on 6 Aug. (*ibid.*, 100).

22. **Thomas I**, Earley, Aug. 1409—Dec. 1430
Monk of Reading. Royal assent to his election was given at Westminster on 6 Aug. 1409 and restitution of temporalities ordered on 24 Aug. (*ibid.*, 100, 103). He was dead by 5 Dec. 1430, when royal licence to elect his successor was given at Westminster (*ibid. 1429-36*, 102).

23. **Thomas II**, Henley, Jan. 1431—11 Nov. 1445
Monk of Reading. He was elected on 9 Jan. 1431 (PRO C84/44/8); royal assent and diocesan confirmation had been given by 19 Jan., when restitution of temporalities was ordered (*Cal. Pat. R. 1429-36*, 103). He died on 11 Nov. 1445 (PRO C84/48/25; *VCH Berks.*, ii. 67); royal licence to elect his successor was given on 14 Nov. (*Cal. Pat. R. 1441-6*, 394).

24. **John III**, Thorne I, Jan. 1446—July 1486
Monk of Reading. His election had received royal assent and diocesan confirmation by 18 Jan. 1446, when restitution of temporalities was ordered at Westminster (*ibid.*, 396). He was dead by 10 July 1486, when warrant for royal licence to elect his successor was issued at Westminster (PRO C82/12).

25. **John IV**, Thorne II, July 1486—Jan. 1519
Formerly prior. He was elected on 22 July 1486 (*ibid.*), royal assent being given on 24 July (*Cal. Pat. R. 1485-94*, 119). He was dead by 17 Jan. 1519, when warrant for royal licence to elect his successor was issued at Greenwich (*L. and P. For. and Dom., Hen. VIII*, iii (1), 7).

26. **Thomas III**, Worcester, Feb. 1519—July 1520
Monk of Reading. On 27 Feb. 1519 the diocesan requested restitution of temporalities to him, which was ordered at Westminster on 15 Mar. (*ibid.*, 39; fuller details on Pat. R. 10 Hen. VIII (PRO C66/631), m.20). He was dead by 28 July 1520, when royal licence to elect his successor was given at Westminster (*L. and P.*, iii (1), 342).

27. **Hugh III**, Cooke *alias* Faringdon, Sept./Nov. 1520—15 Aug. ×
19 Sept. 1539

Formerly sub-chamberlain. His election was confirmed (by the diocesan) on 26 Sept. 1520 and restitution of temporalities ordered on
8 Nov. at Westminster (*ibid.*, 370, 388). The dates of the end of his
abbacy and of the suppression of the abbey are uncertain (see D.
Knowles, *The Religious Orders in England*, iii (Cambridge, 1959), 378–
9, 483-91). He was still in office on 15 Aug. 1539 (*L. and P.*, xiv (2),
15), but by 19 Sept. the town of Reading regarded him as having
been deprived and the abbey suppressed (*Reading Records. Diary of
the Corporation*, ed. J. M. Guilding (1892), i. 172). He was tried and
convicted of treason on 13 Nov. and drawn and hanged on the
following day (J. E. Paul, 'The last abbots of Reading and Colchester', *BIHR*, xxxiii (1960), 119-20, 116).

GENERAL DOCUMENTS

I ROYAL ACTS

1 *Notification by King Henry I of his foundation of Reading Abbey and gift of Reading, Cholsey and Leominster with their churches and with a mint and moneyer at Reading, Thatcham and the church of Wargrave; and grant of specified liberties and immunities* [? March] 1125

A f13r–v; B f16r–v; D ff17r–18r; E ff48r–49r; F f75r–v (not fully collated); PRO Cartae Antiq. Roll, C52/22(X), no. 9 (not fully collated)

Pd. *Mon. Ang.*, iv. 40–1 (no. ii); Barfield, *Thatcham*, ii. 5–6; (cal.) *Regesta*, ii. 192–3 (no. 1427); Farrer, *Itin.*, 111 (no. 512), reprinted from *EHR*, xxxiv (1919), 535; (transl.) Hurry, *Reading Abbey*, 151–5

Henricus dei gratia rex Anglorum et dux Normannorum archiepiscopis, episcopis, abbatibus, comitibus baronibusque suis et omnibus christianis tam presentibus quam futuris, salutem perpetuam. Sciatis quia tres abbatie in regno Anglie peccatis*ᵃ* exigentibus olim destructe sunt, Radingia scilicet atque Chealseia*ᵇ* et Leoministria, quas manus laica diu possedit earumque terras et possessiones alienando distraxit. Ego autem consilio pontificum et aliorum fidelium meorum*ᶜ* pro salute anime mee et Willelmi regis patris mei et Willelmi regis fratris mei et Willelmi filii mei et Mathildis*ᵈ* regine matris mee et Mathildis*ᵈ* regine uxoris mee et omnium antecessorum et successorum meorum edificavi novum apud Radingiam monasterium in honore et nomine dei genitricis semperque virginis Marie et beati Iohannis ewangeliste.*ᵉ* Et donavi eidem monasterio ipsam Radingiam, Chelseiam*ᶠ* quoque et Leoministriam cum appendiciis suis cum silvis et agris et pasturis, cum pratis et aquis, cum molendinis et piscariis, cum ecclesiis quoque et capellis et cimiteriis et oblationibus et decimis, cum moneta et uno monetario apud Radingiam. Dedi etiam prefato monasterio Thacheham*ᵍ* et ecclesiam de Waregrava.*ʰ* Ita ut quomodo ea in manu mea fuere sic libera sint et absoluta et plena in manu abbatis et monachorum Radingie. Nulla autem persona parva vel magna per debitum seu per consuetudinem aut per violentiam aliquid ab hominibus et terris et possessione Radingensis monasterii exigat, non equitationem sive expeditionem, non pontium vel castrorum edificationem, non vehicula, non summagia, non vectigalia, non navigia, non opera, non tributa, non xenia, sed sint monachi Radingenses et familia eorum et res ipsorum absoluti ab omni geldo et theoloneo*ⁱ* et alia qualibet consuetudine in terris et aquis, in transitibus pontium et maris portuum per totam Angliam.

Sintque abbatis et monachorum eius de hominibus suis et de tota possessione sua et de alienis in ea forisfacientibus vel ibi cum forisfacto interceptis hundreda et placita omnia cum socca et sacca et toll[j] et theam et infangentheof[k] et hutfangentheof[l] et hamsochna[m] infra burgum et extra burgum in viis et semitis et in omnibus locis, cum omnibus causis que sunt vel esse possunt. Habeantque abbas et monachi Radingenses in tota possessione sua omnem iustitiam de assaltu et furtis et murdris, de sanguinis effusione et pacis infractione quantum ad regiam pertinet potestatem et de omnibus forisfactis. Quod si abbas et monachi de his[n] iustitiam facere neglexerint, rex fieri compellat ita ut in nullo libertatem Radingensis ecclesie minuat. Veniantque ad hundreda [o]de Radingia et[o] de Leoministria homines circumiacentium maneriorum secundum consuetudinem temporum precedentium, qui si quando vocati fuerint ad iustitiam venire contempserint, rex inde forisfactum accipiat et venire et satisfacere compellat. Statuimus autem tam ecclesiastice quam et[p] regie prospectu potestatis ut decedente abbate Radingensi omnis possessio monasterii ubicumque fuerit remaneat integra et libera cum omni iure et consuetudine sua in manu et dispositione prioris et monachorum capituli Radingensis. Hoc autem ideo statuimus statutumque perpetuo servandum firmavimus, quia abbas [f 13v] Radingensis non habet proprios redditus sed communes cum fratribus. Qui autem deo annuente canonica electione abbas substitutus fuerit non cum suis secularibus consanguineis seu quibuslibet aliis elemosinas monasterii male utendo disperdat, sed pauperibus et peregrinis et hospitibus suscipiendis curam gerat. Terras censuales non ad foedum[q] donet nec faciat milites nisi in sacra veste Christi, in qua parvulos suscipere modeste caveat, maturos autem seu discretos tam clericos quam laicos provide[r] suscipiat. Nemo de possessione Radingensis monasterii aliquid teneat feodaliter absolutum, sed ad censum annuum et servitium abbati et monachis debitum. In abbatis et monachorum domo Radingensium et possessione nullus per hereditatem officium teneat, sed in arbitrio abbatis et monachorum de transmutandis prepositis seu aliis quibuslibet officiariis causa consistat. Hanc monasterio Radingensi et omnibus ad ipsum pertinentibus in perpetuum dono et confirmo liberam immunitatem et immunem libertatem quam regibus post me in Anglia regnaturis causa dei commendo servandam, ut eis conservet deus eternam. Siquis autem hoc nostre donationis decretum infringere seu minuere vel transmutare scienter presumpserit, summus iudex omnium contrahat eum et eradicet[s] cum sua posteritate ut permaneat sine aliqua hereditate in clade et fame. Quisquis vero Radingense monasterium cum prefata libertate et possessione servaverit altissimus qui dominatur in regno hominum bonis omnibus stabiliat eum et servet in evum.[t] Ego

Henricus dei gratia rex Anglorum et dux Normannorum dono et
subscribo. [a]Signum Adeleidis regine. Signum Iohannis presbiteri
cardinalis sedis apostolice legati. Signum Willelmi archiepiscopi
Cantuariensis. Signum Turstani archiepiscopi Eboracensis. Signum
Gaufredi[v] archiepiscopi Rothomagensis.[w] Signum Willelmi episcopi
Wintonie. [x]Signum Bernardi episcopi Sancti David. Signum Willelmi episcopi Exonie.[x] Signum Siefredi episcopi Cicestrensis. Sig-
num Simonis episcopi Wigornensis. Signum Iohannis episcopi Lux-
oviensis. Signum Odini[y] episcopi Ebroicensis. Signum Turgisi
episcopi Abricatensis. Signum Anselmi abbatis Sancti Eadmundi.
Signum Warnerii abbatis Sancti Martini de Bello. Signum Bosonis
abbatis Beccensis. Signum Gileberti abbatis Sagiensis. Signum Ricardi abbatis Sancti Michaelis de Monte. Signum Roberti comitis
Gloecestrie. Signum Willelmi comitis Surreie. Signum Rogerii[z] comitis Warwicensis.[aa] Signum Stephani comitis Albemarle. Signum
Willelmi camerarii de Tancarvilla. Signum Brientii filii Comitis de
Warengeforda. Signum Hunfredi[bb] de Buhun. [Signum Roberti de
Haia.][cc] Signum Willelmi filii Oddonis. Signum Hugonis Bigoti.
[dd]Actum anno verbi incarnati MCXXV, papa Romano Honorio[ee]
secundo, Romanorum imperatore augusto Henrico quarto.[ff]

[a] *Insert* suis *D*
[b] Chelseya *D*, Cealseia *E*
[c] *Om. in B, D, E*
[d] Matildis *B, D, E*
[e] evangeliste *B, D*
[f] Cheals' *B*, Cealseiam *E*
[g] Tacheam *D*
[h] Weregrava *B, E*, Weregrave *D*
[i] theloneo *B, D, E*
[j] toll' *B*, tol *D, E*
[k] infangenthef *D*
[l] hutfangenthef *D*
[m] hamsocna *B*
[n] hiis *B, D, E*
[o-o] *Om. in E*
[p] *Interlined in A, om. in D*
[q] feodum, *B, E*, feudum *D*
[r] *Om. in D*
[s] *Insert* eum *B, D, E*
[t] *B ends with* T', *E omits the following list and resumes at dd, F and PRO text end*
[u] *D divides the following names into two columns, beginning the second column with Anselm abbot of St Edmunds*
[v] Galf' *D*
[w] Rotomag' *D*
[x-x] *D reverses these signs*
[y] Odonis *D*
[z] Rogeri *D*
[aa] Warwichen' *D*
[bb] Hunfridi *D*
[cc] *Om. in A, supplied from D*
[dd] *E resumes*
[ee] Henr' *D*
[ff] *rectius* quinto

The text is certainly spurious as it stands, but may well represent an 'improved' and
interpolated version of an original charter given in 1125, as suggested by Johnson,
Essays in Honour of Tait, 139. Among its suspicious features are: the inclusion of *dei
gratia* and, perhaps, *dux Normannorum* in the king's style; the use of first person plural
for two of the king's acts; the inclusion of *hutfangentheof* among the liberties granted;
and difficulties in the list of signatories and the dating clause. However, these 'anomalies' do not require the rejection of the entire text, since all can be accounted for

by making two reasonable assumptions: firstly, that the king was prepared to grant to his new abbey, where he probably planned to be buried,[1] liberties so exalted[2] as to include the exceptional *hutfangentheof*, which, though not otherwise known at this early date, was certainly current by 1135 × 40;[3] and, secondly, that the 'improved' version of the text was made in the later twelfth century, perhaps between 1189 and 1193. The addition of *dei gratia* would be normal by that date; equally an 'improver' might then understandably slip into first person plural when adding short passages to the text. It is significant that the only occurrences of first person plural are in the following passages: 'Statuimus autem tam ecclesiastice quam et regie prospectu potestatis ut ...', and 'Hoc autem ideo statuimus statutumque perpetuo servandum firmavimus ...'. These are absent from King Stephen's general confirmation to Reading, given probably in Jan. 1136 (no. 8; pd. *Regesta*, iii. 249-50), which is largely a re-issue of Henry I's charter and arguably reproduces more accurately what that charter originally said. Moreover, the general confirmation by Pope Honorius II, dated 13 Apr. 1125, is closely similar to the text of Henry's charter as it survives, especially concerning the abbey's liberties and even including *utfangenethef* (no. 140; pd. Holtzmann, *Papsturkunden*, iii. 136-7, where the passages common to both are indicated), and could only have been given after an original grant by the king. The same similarity occurs in later papal confirmations but significantly not in the earlier bull of Calixtus II, dated 1123 (no. 139; pd. Holtzmann, *ibid.*, 133-4).[4] This being the case, Henry's original charter was probably given in March 1125, and not October (as suggested by Farrer, *Itin.*, and *Regesta*, ii), particularly since the dating clause shows the Emperor Henry V, who died 23 May, to be still alive, although it erroneously calls him Henry IV. The difficulties which a date in March appears to raise are not insuperable. Although John of Crema, here called papal legate, did not strictly hold that position between the death of Calixtus II in Dec. 1124 and the renewal of his commission by Honorius II on 12/13 Apr. 1125, he may nevertheless have continued to act as such (see M. Brett, *The English Church under Henry I* (Oxford, 1975), 42 n. 4). More awkwardly, Seffrid and Simon, though here styled bishops of Chichester and Worcester, and though elected to these sees before Easter (29 Mar.) while they were with the king in Normandy (*The Chronicle of John of Worcester*, ed. J. R. H. Weaver (Oxford, 1908), 18; Robert of Torigny, 110), were not consecrated until 12 Apr. and 24 May, respectively. It is probably significant, however, that they come at the end of the list of English bishops signing, suggesting that the text of an original charter may have read 'elect' for each and that this was changed to 'bishop' when, as is here suggested, the text was later tampered with. The presence of so many Norman prelates is consistent with an original charter having been given in Normandy, perhaps at Rouen.

---

[1] See above, p. 14.

[2] See above, p. 18, and cf. Pope Eugenius III's reference to Reading's *regia libertas* (below, no. 144).

[3] It appears in the forged charter of Edgar for Glastonbury quoted by William of Malmesbury in the third recension of his *Gesta Regum* (ed. W. Stubbs (RS, 1887-9), i. 170).

[4] The clauses concerning the abbey's liberties seem also to have provided the basis for a spurious charter of William I for Battle (*Mon. Ang.*, iii. 245; *Regesta*, i. 29, no. 113), forged in 1211 × 15 (E. Searle, 'Battle abbey and exemption: the forged charters', *EHR* lxxxiii (1968), 464).

2 *Notification by King Henry I of his foundation of Reading Abbey and grant of all immunity, power, quittance and liberty that the royal power can confer upon an abbey, with specified privileges* [? *c.* Jan. 1127]

Fabricated original charter: BL Add. Ch. 19571
A ff 13v–14r; B ff 16v–17r; F f 75v (not fully collated); PRO Cartae Antiq. Roll, C52/22(X), no. 9 (not fully collated)
Pd. Johnson, *Essays in Honour of Tait*, 138 (with facsimile); *Arch. Journ.*, xx. 286–7; Coates, *Hist. of Reading*, App. 1; Barfield, *Thatcham*, ii. 6–7; (cal.) Hurry, *Reading Abbey*, 157–8; Farrer, *Itin.*, 116 (no. 535), reprinted from *EHR* xxxiv (1919), 540; *Regesta*, ii. 203 (no. 1474)

H(enricus) dei gratia rex Anglorum *a*et dux Normannorum archiepiscopis, episcopis, abbatibus, comitibus baronibusque suis et omnibus Christianis tam presentibus quam futuris,*a* salutem perpetuam. Sciatis me pro salute anime mee et omnium antecessorum et successorum meorum novam apud Radingiam abbatiam construxisse eidemque abbatie omnem immunitatem et potestatem, quietantiam et libertatem dedisse quam regia potestas alicui abbatie conferre potest. Quare volo et firmiter precipio quod abbas et monachi de Rading(ia) omnia tenementa sua tam laica quam ecclesiastica quecumque in presenti habent vel in posterum donatione fidelium habituri sunt bene et in pace, libere et quiete, plenarie et honorifice teneant in omnibus locis et in omnibus rebus ubicumque fuerint quieta de Denegeldis et omnibus geldis, *b*et auxiliis,*b* et sciris et hundredis, et omnibus placitis et querelis, de scutagiis et hidagiis et stallagiis, de summagiis et careagiis, de navigiis et clausuris, de pontium et castrorum edificatione, de conductu thesauri et omni operatione, de tributis et lestagiis, de thedinpeni*c* et tinpeni,*d* de summonitionibus, de assisis et superassisis,*e* de merciis quacumque occasione exigendis et de omnibus forisfacturis undecumque fuerint, de essartis et nemorum wastis. Nullus vero de forestariis regis quicquam se intromittat de boscis abbatis et monachorum qui sunt intra forestam, sed omnem potestatem et libertatem quam habet rex in boscis suis habeant abbas et monachi et ministri eorum in omnibus boscis qui ad abbatiam pertinent ubicumque fuerint. Sintque abbas et monachi Rading(enses) et omnes homines eorum et res ipsorum quieti de hedagiis*f* et theloneis et omnibus exactionibus et consuetudinibus in nundinis et foris quorumcumque sunt, in terris et aquis, in viis et transitibus pontium et portibus maris per totam Angliam et Normann(iam). Habeatque*g* abbas et monachi omnem iustitiam de assaltu et murdris et sanguinis effusione et pacis infractione et thesauri inventione quicquid ad regiam pertinet potestatem. Mercie nulle de abbate Rading(ensi) vel monachis nec de tenementis vel boscis eorum exigantur, nec exacte solvantur, sed sint omnes homines eorum et eorum dominia ita quieta et libera sicut mea propria et

soli abbati et monachis de omnibus respondentia. Et habeant abbas
et monachi de hominibus suis et de tota possessione sua et de alienis
in ea forisfacientibus vel ibi cum forisfacto interceptis hundreda et
placita omnia cum sacha[h] et socca et toll et theam et infangenetheof[i]
et hutfangenth(eof)[j] in omnibus locis cum omnibus [causis][k] que
sunt vel esse possunt. Hanc monasterio Rading(ensi) quantamcumque rex donare potest dono et confirmo libertatem et immunitatem quam regibus post me in Anglia regnaturis pro deo servandam
commendo. Quam qui infringere vel minuere presumpserit, contrahat eum dominus et conterat de terra viventium cum omni posteritate sua.[l] Huius nostre donationis hos testes adhibemus: Willelmum
archiepiscopum Cant(uariensem), T(urstanum) et G(aufredum)
Eborac(ensem) et Rothomag(ensem) archiepiscopos, Willelmum et
S(iefredum)   Wint(oniensem)   et   Cicestr(ensem)   episcopos,
R(obertum) et W(illelmum) comites Gloec(estrie) et Surreie. Apud
Westim(onasterium).

Endorsed: Carta regis Henrici primi gestatoria de libertatibus
    [*12th cent.*]
Size: 361 × 150 mm
Seal: missing, deerskin tag through slit in fold at bottom

[a-a] et cetera ut supra B, *referring to no. 1*
[b-b] *Om. in B*   [c] tedinpeni B
[d] timpeni B   [e] *Original has* superassis
[f] *Original has* hed'agiis; hidagiis A, B
[g] *Sic in original and all copies except F, which has* habeantque
[h] sacca B   [i] *Original has* infagenetheof
[j] hutfangenetheof A
[k] *Om. in original, supplied from A, B, F*
[l] *B ends with* T', *F and PRO text end*

The charter has long been regarded as a forgery (Johnson, *Essays in Honour of Tait*,
138-9). Although the inclusion of *hutfangentheof* need not be impossible (see no. 1, n.),
the royal style and the switch to first person plural in the attestation clause are highly
suspect features. Most problematical, however, is the king's alleged grant of 'all
immunity (etc.) that the royal power can confer upon an abbey', a formula which is
not present in the foundation charter and whose all-embracing terms must undermine
this charter's credibility (see above, pp. 21-2; and cf. below, no. 21). It is written in
a standard 12th-century book hand and was probably fabricated in the later 12th
century. If genuine it would date between Apr. 1125 (consecration of Seffrid bishop
of Chichester) and Jan. 1129 (death of William Giffard bishop of Winchester). During
these years the king was in England only between 11 Sept. 1126 and 26 Aug. 1127
(*Regesta*, ii. 203) and was in London with Thurstan archbishop of York at the turn
of the year (Farrer, *Itin.*, 115). Both the endorsement of the 'original' and the cartulary rubrics describe the charter as *gestatoria*, i.e. 'portable', indicating presumably
that it, rather than the foundation charter (no. 1), was the one to be taken before
courts and other authorities whenever the abbey's liberties were in question. Both A
and B note that another copy was at Leominster.

3 Notification by King Henry I, addressed generally for England, that he has acquired from the abbot and monks of Mont St Michel the churches of Wargrave and Cholsey in Berkshire in exchange for £12 worth of land which he has given them in the manor of Budleigh in Devon; and that he has given the two churches in free alms to Reading Abbey   [latter half of 1123]

A f 14v; B f 17v
Pd. *Regesta*, ii. 350–1 (no. clxxiii); (cal.) *ibid.*, 190 (no. 1418)

Testibus:[a] Iohanne episcopo Luxov(iensi), et G(aufredo) cancellario, et Willelmo comite de Warenna, et Willelmo de Tancardivilla, et Willelmo de Albini, et Gaufr(edo) de Glint(ona), et Thoma de Sancto Iohanne, et Drogone de Monceio. Apud Pirarios super Andelam.

[a] *B ends*

After 11 June, when Henry sailed from Portsmouth to Normandy (Farrer, *Itin.*, 107), and before the end of 1123, since the letter from Mont St Michel requesting the bishop of Salisbury to execute the exchange (no. 771) is in the name of Abbot Roger, who resigned in 1123 (*Regesta*, ii. 190). The editors of *Regesta*, ii, believed that this charter was the same as that entered in the cartulary of Mont St Michel relating to the same exchange, calendared by Round, *Cal. Docs. France*, 259; also Farrer, *Itin.*, 108 (no. 502). However, the latter is a different, complementary charter which gives the land in Budleigh for the two churches which the king has given to Reading, and has a slightly different witness list (see PRO Transcripts, PRO 31/8/140B, part II, p. 247). The charter to Mont St Michel has therefore never been printed.

4 Precept by King Henry I to all who have lands in the hundred of Leominster to come to the hundred-courts at the summons of the abbot of Reading and his ministers as fully as they used to come when the hundred was in the king's demesne. If not the abbot may distrain them by judgement of the hundred-court   [1123 × 33]

A f 14r-v; B f 18v
Pd. *Regesta*, ii. 384 (no. ccxcviii); (cal.) *ibid.*, 282 (no. 1865)

T(estibus):[a] episcopo Sar(esburiensi), et Cancellario. Apud Radingiam.

[a] *B ends*

Given at Reading, this could date from any year when the king was in England between the appointment of the first abbot in 1123 and Henry's final departure in 1133.

5 *Gift by King Henry I to Reading Abbey of the Hand of St James at the request of his daughter, the Empress Matilda, who gave it to him on her return from Germany; and mandate to receive and treat it with all due reverence*
[? *c.* 11 Sept. 1126]

A f 14r; B f 17v
Pd. *Mon. Ang.*, iv. 41 (no. iii); (cal.) *Regesta*, ii. 198 (no. 1448); (noted) Farrer, *Itin.*,
113, reprinted from *EHR* xxxiv. 537

Henricus rex Anglie et dux Normannie abbati et conventui de Rad-
ing(ia), salutem. Sciatis quod gloriosam manum sancti Iacobi apostoli quam Matillis *ᵃ*imperatrix filia mea*ᵃ* de Alemannia rediens mihi
dedit ipsius petitione vobis transmitto et in perpetuum ecclesie de
Rading(ia) dono. Quare vobis mando quod eam cum omni vener-
atione suscipiatis, et tam vos quam posteri vestri quantum honoris
et reverentie potestis sicut dignum est tantis tanti apostoli reliquiis
iugiter in ecclesia de Rading(ia) exhibere curetis. Testibus:*ᵇ* Willelmo Cant(uariensi) archiepiscopo, Matill(e) imperatrice filia mea,
Simone Wigorn(ensi) episcopo, Rannulfo cancellario, Roberto de
Sigillo, Brientio filio Comitis, Rogero Bigot dapifero meo, Willelmo
de Crevequer. Apud Port(esmudam).

ᵃ⁻ᵃ A has filia mea imperatrix filia mea
ᵇ B ends

The text is either forged or corrupt in its present form, for the witnesses include
Roger Bigod the steward, who died in 1107, and Rannulf the chancellor, who died
in 1123 before the death of Matilda's first husband and the consecration of Simon as
bishop of Worcester in 1125. These anomalies, with the form of the royal style, have
led scholars to question its genuineness (Johnson, *Essays in Honour of Tait*, 142 n. 3;
Regesta, ii. 198) and even to doubt whether the gift itself was ever made by Henry I,
since no cult of St James developed at Reading in his time (H. E. Mayer, in *Festschrift
Karl Pivec*, ed. A. Haidacher and H. E. Mayer (Innsbruck, 1966), 273-4). If based on
a genuine original given at Portsmouth, the deed would date from about the time
when Henry, accompanied by Matilda, landed in England from Normandy (Farrer,
Itin., 114), but according to Matthew Paris, who may have been relying on a Reading
source, the hand was sent to Reading by Henry I on his last crossing to Normandy
in 1133 (Matthew Paris, *Chronica Majora*, ii. 159). For further discussion, and support
for the assertion that the king gave the Hand to Reading, whether or not with a
charter, see Kemp, 'Miracles of the Hand of St James', *Berks. Arch. Journ.*, lxv (1970),
1-2; Leyser, 'Frederick Barbarossa, Henry II and the Hand of St James', *EHR*, xc
(1975), 491-4, the latter believing that the gift was made in 1133. See also above, p.
19.

6 *Notification by King Henry I, addressed generally for England, that he
has granted to Reading Abbey a fair at Reading on the feast of St Laurence
and three days following. No one shall disturb those attending it on pain of a
forfeiture of £10*   [*c.* 1129 × 33]

A f 14v; B f 17v
Pd. *Mon. Ang.*, iv. 41 (no. iv); (cal.) *Regesta*, ii. 282 (no. 1864)

Henricus rex Anglie archiepiscopis, episcopis, abbatibus, comitibus
et omnibus baronibus suis et vicecomitibus totius Anglie, salutem.
Sciatis me concessisse ecclesie [sancte]*ᵃ* Marie de Rading(ia) et ab-

bati et monachis ibidem servientibus deo quod habeant feriam unam Rading(ie) ad festum sancti Laurentii, scilicet die festi et per tres subsequentes dies. Et prohibeo ut nullus super hoc iniuste disturbet aliquem illuc euntem*b* vel inde redeuntem super .x. libras forisfacture, sed pacem meam habeant. Et feriam illam ita quietam in omnibus habeant sicut terras et reliquas ecclesie possessiones quietas concessi et per cartam meam confirmavi. Testibus:*c* G(aufredo) cancellario, et R(oberto) de Sig(illo), et Unfr(edo) de Buhun, et Iohanne marisc(allo). Apud Wind(resores).

ª *Om. in A, supplied from B*
b *A has* eundi   *c* *B ends*

After John succeeded his father as marshal (*PR 31 Henry I*, 18; *Regesta*, ii, p. xvii) and before Henry's final departure from England.

7 *Precept by King Henry I to the justices, sheriffs and ministers of England that the men of Reading Abbey shall be quit of shires, hundreds, tolls, passage-money and all customs, and of gelds, aids, pleas and plaints*

[*c.* 1129 × 35]

A f 25r

Henricus rex Anglie et dux Normannie iustic(iariis) et omnibus vicecomitibus et ministris totius Anglie, salutem. Precipio quod homines monachorum meorum de elemosina mea de Rading(ia) sint omnino quieti de schiris et hundredis et theloneis et passagiis et omnibus aliis consuetudinibus. Et emant et vendant sine thelon(eis) et passag(iis) ubicumque venerint. Et nominatim sint omnimodo quieti de geldis et auxiliis et omnibus placitis et querelis. Et prohibeo ne aliquis eos super hoc breve meum nec res suas iniuste disturbet super .x. libras forisfacture. Testibus: Gaufredo filio Pagani, et Roberto de Curci dapifero, et Iohanne maresc(allo). Apud Winars.

Although this writ is entered in the cartulary among the acts of Henry II, it clearly belongs to Henry I. Robert de Courcy occurs as steward (of Normandy) under Henry I in *c.* 1129 and 1132 (*Regesta*, ii. 226, 258); John succeeded to the office of marshal in or shortly before 1130 (*ibid.*, p. xvii). *Winars* has proved unidentifiable.

8 Confirmation by King Stephen of the foundation of Reading Abbey by Henry I and of its possessions, viz., Reading, Cholsey and Leominster with their churches, Thatcham, the churches of Wargrave and Hanborough, and a mint and moneyer in London, all given by Henry I, and Whitsbury, Rowington, Houghton [Conquest] and houses and lands in Cambridge and Southampton, which the abbey held in that king's time; and confirmation of the abbey's liberties [specified as in no. 1]. Also gift of [East] Hendred, for which

the abbot shall pay annually 100s for as long as the king
pleases.   [prob. Jan. 1136]

A f 17r–v; B f 28r–v
Pd. *Regesta*, iii. 249–50 (no. 675)

Probably at the funeral of Henry I in Reading Abbey (5 Jan. 1136—see above, p.
14, n. 1), as suggested by *Regesta*, and by the omission of any possession of the abbey
certainly acquired after that date. The text follows closely that of the foundation
charter, of which it is largely a re-issue (see no. 1, n.), and the original may have
been prepared by the monks for the king's sealing. There are no witnesses, but there
is no compelling reason to doubt its fundamental authenticity, although the inclusion
of *dei gratia* and *dux Normannorum* in the royal style and an odd lapse into first person
plural probably indicate 'improvement' in the later twelfth century.

9 Precept by King Stephen, addressed generally for England, that
Reading Abbey shall hold its lands and churches [etc.], and its
liberties as freely as in the time of Henry I, and especially the
meadow which Thurstan was claiming   [1136 × 37]

A f 19r–v; B f 29v
Pd. *Regesta*, iii. 251 (no. 678)

Testibus:[a] Regina, et R(ogero) de Fisc(anno), et W(illelmo) Martel,
et Hugone Bigoto. Apud Rading(iam).

[a] *B ends*

Roger de Fécamp had become an archdeacon by Nov. 1137 (*Regesta*, iii, p. xii). Since
this precept was issued at Reading, it dates possibly from the occasion of Henry I's
funeral there, 5 Jan. 1136. The identity of Thurstan and the meadow is uncertain,
but the possibility that he may be the Thurstan of Whitley who occurs possibly before
Oct. 1154 (see no. 1197), ? alias Thurstan of Cosham (cf. nos. 1214, 1218–1220),
suggests that the meadow was in Whitley or Reading.

10 Confirmation by King Stephen, addressed generally for England, to Reading Abbey of the manor of Rowington in Warks.,
given by Adeliza d'Ivry, 1½ hides of land in Houghton [Conquest]
by gift of Robert earl of Leicester, and the land of Whitsbury formerly belonging to the monk Ingelram Apostolicus. All are to be
held as freely as the abbey holds its other lands and as the charters
of Henry I testify   [1136 × 39]

A f 18r–v; B f 29r
Pd. *Regesta*, iii. 253–4 (no. 686)

Testibus:[a] H(enrico) episcopo Wint(oniensi), et R(ogero) episcopo
Sar(esburiensi), et A(lexandro) episcopo Linc(olniensi), et
R(oberto) de Ver, et A(lberico) de Ver, et Willelmo Martel. Apud
Oxon(iam)

[a] *B ends*

Given at Oxford before the arrest of the bishops in June 1139.

11 Gift in free alms by King Stephen to Reading Abbey of all the land at Windsor and Catshill which belonged to Geoffrey Purcell, in such manner that Ralph Purcell shall hold of the abbey 20s worth of land at Windsor as he fined with the monks before the king

[1139 × 40]

Original charter: BL Add. Ch. 19584
A ff 18v–19r; B f 28v
Pd. *Arch. Journ.*, xx. 291; *Regesta*, iii. 254–5 (no. 690); (cal.) Hurry, *Reading Abbey*, 159–60

Testibus:*a* G(aufredo) de Magnavilla, et Ricardo de Luci, et Turgis(io) de Abrincis, *b*et Elya de Amundevilla, et Iohanne vicecomite, et Roberto Burnell(o), et Rad(ulfo) Purcell(o).*b* Apud Norwicum.

Endorsed: de terra Gaufredi Purcelli. Stephani regis [*both 12th cent., but in different hands*]
Size: 182 × 145 mm
Seal: missing, slit for tag in fold at bottom

a B ends   *b-b* et multis aliis A

Date as given by *Regesta*. After Richard de Lucy's return to England at the end of 1138, and before Geoffrey de Mandeville became an earl in 1140. The Windsor estate was 1 hide in Windsor Underoure (see nos. 19, 34, 1268).

11a Note of charter by King Stephen to the Earl de Warenne concerning the same

[1140 × 47]

A f 19r; (prob.) B f 28v[1]

This note refers almost certainly to the original charter which survives as BL Add. Ch. 19583, pd. *Regesta*, iii, 255 (no. 692), q.v. for other printings; but, contrary to the latter's assertion, the text is not entered on B f 28v nor does it appear in any other Reading cartulary. Moreover, whereas the cartulary notes imply references to Windsor and Catshill, the charter in fact concerns only the latter—it orders the earl to permit Reading Abbey to hold in peace its land of Catshill which Geoffrey Purcell gave to it, and to restore anything he has taken. The date is after Robert, the first witness, became chancellor and before Earl William de Warenne II set out on crusade in 1147 (*Complete Peerage*, xii(1), 497); the tone of the order rules out the possibility that the earl might be Stephen's second son, William, who acquired the title by marriage to Isabel de Warenne in 1148–9.

[1] B has *Item alia de eodem*, following no. 11.

12 Notification by King Stephen to William Martel and his ministers that he has given in free alms to Reading Abbey the land which belonged to Geoffrey Purcell at Windsor and Catshill; and precept that the abbey shall hold it as freely as its other lands, and that, if anything of the chattels of its men has been seized, it is to be returned. Witnesses [omitted]

[1135 × 54; ? 1139 × 54]

B f29r; (noted) A f19r
Pd. *Regesta*, iii. 255 (no. 691)

If this is after no. 11, it cannot be earlier than 1139, but there is no certain proof. William Martel was sheriff of Surrey for part of Stephen's reign (*Regesta*, iii, loc. cit. and p. xxv), but it may also be significant that he occupied the Windsor estate against the abbey's will (see no. 1268).

13 Confirmation by King Stephen to Reading Abbey of the gifts by Queen Adeliza of the manor and church of Aston, equivalent to £20 (*pro .xx. libris*), and of 100s worth [of land] in Stanton [Harcourt]; to be held as freely as its other alms and as the queen's charter conceded them   [? Mar. × June 1139]

Original charter: Hertford County Record Office, D/E AS 1
A f18v; B ff29v–30r; C f6r
Pd. *Antiquaries Journ.*, xiv (1934), 10 (with facsimile); *Trans. East Herts. Arch. Soc.*, i (1900), 135; *Regesta*, iii. 251 (no. 679); (facsimile) *ibid.*, iv, pl. x.

Testibus:[a] H(enrico) episcopo Wint(oniensi), et S(effrido) episcopo Cicestr(ensi), et G(ualerano) comite Metll(enti), et R(annulfo) comite Cestr(ie), et comite Gisl(eberto), [b]et R(oberto) de Ferr(ariis) comite de Noting(eham), et Willelmo de Ip(ra), et W(illelmo) Mart(el), et R(oberto) de Ver, et W(illelmo) de Albini pincerna, et Eud(one) Mart(el).[b] Apud Arundell'.

Endorsed: Stephani regis de Hestona et de Stantona [*12th cent.*]; *also 17th-cent. endorsement*
Size: 243 × 120 mm
Seal: fragment of forgery of Stephen's first seal, white wax, on tongue partially torn off and sewn back on to the root

  [a] *B and C end*   [b-b] et multis aliis *A*

For discussion of the date, if genuine, see *Regesta*, iii. 251, and iv, pl. x. The charter is highly suspect, however, since, though in the hand of a known royal scribe, the seal is forged and Waleran count of Meulan was in Normandy from May 1138 to Dec. 1139 (*ibid.*). I am grateful to Mr R. M. Abel Smith for permission to print from the original charter.

14 Precept by King Stephen to the sheriff [a]and reeve[a] of Southampton, and to all sheriffs, barons and ministers of England, that the provisions and goods of Reading Abbey shall be quit of toll, passage-money and all custom. No one shall disturb it on this account on pain of a forfeiture of £10   [1136 × 54; prob. 1140 × 54]

A ff19v–20r; B f29v
Pd. *Regesta*, iii. 250 (no. 676)

Testibus:[b] R. cancellario, et Willelmo Martel. Apud Oxon(iam).

a-a Om. in B
b B ends

Comparison of the witness lists of this and the following precept suggest that R. the chancellor is Robert de Gant, who held office from 1140 (*Regesta*, iii, p. x).

15 Precept by King Stephen to the justices, sheriffs, barons, ministers and all his faithful of England, that Reading Abbey's men shall be quit of pleas, plaints, shires, hundreds, tolls, gelds and aids, as a writ of Henry I testifies [1140 × 54]

A f 19v (twice); B f 29v
Pd. *Regesta*, iii. 250-1 (no. 677)

Testibus:[a] Roberto cancellario, et W(illelmo) Martel. Apud Oxon(iam).[b]

a B ends
b Oxen' second copy on A f 19v

Probably contemporary with no. 14. After Robert de Gant became chancellor. The abbey had at least three copies of this act: B says, *Hec triplex est*, while A, after giving the text once, says that there were two more deeds concerning the same, and a little further down the folio gives the text again.

16 Confirmation by King Stephen to Reading Abbey of all its possessions [unspecified], given by Henry I, himself and others, and confirmed by Henry I and himself, up to the first Easter after the agreement made between him and Henry duke of Normandy [4 Apr. × 25 Oct. 1154]

A ff 17v-18r; B f 28v
Pd. *Regesta*, iii. 257 (no. 696)

Testibus:[a] Comite Hugone, et Henrico de Essexa, et Ricardo de Luci, et Warino de Lusor(iis). Apud Lundon(iam).

a B ends

Between Easter 1154 (the first after Stephen's agreement with Duke Henry in the summer of 1153) and the king's death.

17 Gift in free alms by Empress Matilda, daughter of King Henry and queen of the English, to Reading Abbey of the land of Windsor and Catshill which belonged to Geoffrey Purcell and which he gave to the abbey when he became a monk there [2 Feb. × 25 July 1141]

Original charter: BL Add. Ch. 19576
A f16r; B f19v
Pd. *Arch. Journ.*, xx. 289; *Journ. B. A. A.*, xxxi. 389; *Regesta*, iii. 258 (no. 699); *Pal. Soc. Facs.*, 1st ser., pl. 193 (with facsimile); (cal.) Hurry, *Reading Abbey*, 160-1

Testibus:[a] Henrico episcopo Wint(oniensi), Alexandro Linchoniensi[b] episcopo, Nigello episcopo Heliensi, Bernardo episcopo de Sancto David, Rodberto[c] episcopo Herefordensi,[d] et testibus Roberto comite de Gloecestria, et Reginaldo comite filio regis, et Rodberto fratre eius, et Brien(tio) filio Comitis, Milone constabulo, Iohanne maresc(allo). Apud Rading(iam).

Endorsed: Matild(is) imperatricis de terra Gaufr(edi) Purcell(i) de Windesor(es) et Cateshella [*12th cent.*]
Size: 214 × 116 mm (measuring from the fold at the bottom, which is now opened out)[1]
Seal: missing, slit for tag in fold at bottom, now opened out

[a] *B ends*	[b] *Sic in charter;* Lincoln' *A*
[c] Roberto *A*	[d] Herefordense *in charter*

Probably a forgery (see *Regesta*). If genuine, it would date after Stephen's capture at the Battle of Lincoln (2 Feb.) and before Miles the constable was created earl of Hereford (25 July) in 1141; possibly, since given at Reading, May, 1141.

[1] The size including the opened-out fold is 214 × 121 mm.

18 *Confirmation by King Henry II to Reading Abbey of its possessions given by either Henry I or the Empress—viz., Reading, Cholsey and Leominster with their churches and a mint and moneyer at Reading, Thatcham, the churches of Wargrave and Hanborough, Rowington and its church, land in Wigston [Parva], Whitsbury and its church, land in Houghton [Conquest], land in Southampton, the land which Robert de Ferrers had in Reading,[1] Blewbury, [East] Hendred, the church of Berkeley with its churches and chapels, the church of Stanton [Harcourt], the church of Thatcham—and of its liberties* [Jan. 1156 × Apr. 1157]

A ff20r-21r; B ff21r-22r; PRO Cartae Antiq. Roll, C52/22(X), no. 11 (not fully collated)

Henricus rex Anglie et dux Normannie et Aquitanie et comes Andegavie omnibus archiepiscopis, episcopis, abbatibus, comitibus, baronibus, iustic(iariis), vicecomitibus, ministris et omnibus fidelibus suis [*f 20v*] totius Anglie, salutem. Sciatis me concessisse et in perpetuam elemosinam presenti carta confirmasse deo et sancte Marie et monachis de Rading(ia) omnes terras et tenuras et elemosinas quas rex Henricus avus meus eis in elemosinam dedit et concessit. Videlicet, ipsam Radingiam et Chealseiam et Leoministriam[a] cum omnibus appendiciis[b] suis cum silvis et agris et pasturis, cum pratis et aquis, cum molendinis et piscariis, cum ecclesiis et capellis et cimiteriis et oblationibus et decimis, cum moneta et uno monetario apud Rading(iam); et Tacheam[c] et ecclesiam de Weregrava,[d] et ecclesiam de Haneberga, et Rokintonam in Warwicschir(a)[e] cum ecclesia eiusdem ville, et Wigestanam que fuit terra Willelmi elemosinarii, et in Wiltescir(a)[f] Wicheberiam cum ecclesia eiusdem ville, et in Bedefordscir(a)[g] terram Abbodi[h] de Hoctona, et terram Roberti sacerdotis de Hamtona, et terram quam Robertus de Ferrariis habuit in villa Rading(ie). Preterea concedimus[i] eis et confirmamus[j] quicquid domina nostra[k] imperatrix eis in elemosinam dedit et concessit, videlicet, Bleoberiam cum omnibus appendiciis suis, et Heandredam,[l] et ecclesiam de Berkel(eia) cum ecclesiis et capellis et decimis et ceteris suis appendiciis, et ecclesiam de Stantona cum suis appendiciis, et ecclesiam de Tacheham cum omnibus suis pertinentiis. Nulla autem persona parva vel magna per debitum seu per consuetudinem aut per violentiam aliquid ab hominibus et terris et possessione Radingensis monasterii exigat, non equitationem sive expeditionem, non pontium vel castrorum edificationem, non vehicula, non summagia, non vectigalia, non navigia, non opera, non tributa, non xenia, sed sint monachi Rading(enses) et familia eorum et res ipsorum absoluti ab omni geldo et theloneo et alia qualibet consuetudine, in terris et aquis, in transitibus pontium et maris portuum per totam Angliam et Norm(anniam). Sintque abbatis et monachorum eius de hominibus suis et de tota possessione sua et de alienis in ea forisfacientibus vel ibi cum forisfacto interceptis hundreda et placita omnia, cum socca et sacca et toll et theam[m] et infangenetheof et utfangenetheof et hamsochna[n] infra burgum et extra burgum, in viis et semitis et in omnibus locis cum omnibus causis que sunt vel esse possunt. Habeantque abbas et monachi Rading(enses) in tota possessione sua omnem iustitiam de assaltu et furtis et murdris et sanguinis effusione et pacis infractione quantum ad regiam pertinet potestatem, et de omnibus forisfactis. Quod si abbas et monachi de his[o] iustitiam facere neglexerint, rex fieri compellat ita ut in nullo libertatem Radingensis ecclesie minuat. Veniantque ad hundreda de Rading(ia) et de Leoministria[p] homines circumiacentium maneriorum secundum consuetudinem temporum precedentium, qui si quando vocati fuerint ad iustitiam venire contempserint, rex inde forisfactum accipiat et venire et satisfacere compellat. Statuimus autem tam ecclesiastice quam et regie prospectu potestatis ut decedente abbate Radingensi omnis possessio monasterii ubicumque fuerit remaneat integra et libera cum omni iure et consuetudine sua in manu et dispositione prioris et monachorum capituli Rading(ensis). Hoc autem ideo statuit rex H(enricus) avus meus^q et ego^r statutum illud 'concedo et confirmo^s [f21r] et ut in perpetuum servetur precipio,^{t} quia abbas Rading(ensis) non habet proprios redditus sed communes cum fratribus. Qui autem deo annuente canonica electione abbas substitutus fuerit non cum suis secularibus consanguineis seu quibuslibet aliis elemosinas monasterii male utendo disperdat, sed pauperibus et peregrinis et hospitibus suscipiendis curam gerat. Terras censuales non ad feodum donet nec faciat milites nisi in sacra veste Christi, in qua parvulos suscipere modeste caveat, maturos autem seu discretos tam clericos quam laicos provide suscipiat. Nemo de possessione Radingensis monasterii feodaliter absolutum aliquid teneat, sed ad censum annuum et servitium abbati et monachis debitum. In abbatis et monachorum domo Rading(ensium) et possessione nullus per hereditatem officium teneat, sed in arbitrio abbatis et monachorum de transmutandis prepositis seu aliis quibuslibet^u officiariis causa consistat. Hanc monasterio Rading(ensi) et omnibus ad ipsum pertinentibus in perpetuum ^{v}concedo et confirmo^v liberam immunitatem et immunem libertatem quam regibus post me in Anglia regnaturis causa dei commendo servandam, ut eis conservet deus eternam. Siquis autem hoc^w nostre donationis decretum infringere seu minuere vel transmutare scienter presumpserit, summus iudex omnium contrahat eum et eradicet cum sua posteritate, ut permaneat sine aliqua hereditate in clade et fame. Quisquis vero Radingense monasterium cum prefata libertate servaverit altissimus qui dominatur in regno hominum bonis omnibus stabiliat eum et servet in evum. ^{x}Et volo et firmiter precipio^x quod predicti monachi de Rading(ia) hec omnia predicta cum omnibus libertatibus et liberis consuetudinibus et quietantiis predictis in perpetuam elemosinam habeant et teneant, ita bene et in pace et libere et quiete et integre sicut carta predicti regis H(enrici) avi mei testatur et sicut carta domine mee imperatricis eis testatur.^{y} Testibus: Domina Imperatrice,^{z} et Hugone Rothomag-(ensi) archiepiscopo, et Nigello Eliensi episcopo, et Hilario Cicestr-(ensi) episcopo, et Philippo Baioc(ensi) episcopo, et Arn(ulfo) Lexov(iensi) episcopo, et Rotroco Ebroic(ensi) episcopo, et Ricardo Constanc(iensi) episcopo, et Herberto Abrinc(ensi) episcopo, et abbate Becc(i), et abbate Fiscann(i), et abbate Sancti Wandrag(esili), et abbate Gimetic(i), et abbate de Pratell(is), et abbate de Monte Sancte Katerine Rothom(agensis), et abbate Sancti Victoris, et Gaufredo et Willelmo fratribus domini regis, et Rag(inaldo) comite Cornubie, et Gualer(anno) comite de Mellent(o), et Simone comite Ebroic(ensi), et comite Giffardo, et comite de Augo, et Roberto de Novo Burgo tunc temporis dapifero Norm(annie), et Ragin(aldo) de Sancto Walerico, et Hugone de Mortuomari, et Mann(assero) Biset dapifero, et Huberto de Vallibus. Apud Rothomagum.

[a] Liministr' *B*
[c] Tacheham *B*
[e] Warwicsir' *B*
[g] Bedefordsir' *B*
[i] concedo *B and PRO text*
[k] mea *B*
[m] team *B*
[o] hiis *B*
[b] *A has* appentiis
[d] Weregrave *B*
[f] Wiltesir' *B*
[h] Albodi *B*
[j] confirmo *B and PRO text*
[l] Henredam *B*
[n] hamsocna *B*
[p] Lim' *B*
[q] *A has* patris nostri *written in a later hand under* meus
[r] *A has* nos *written under* ego (*as q*)
[s-s] *A has* concedimus et confirmamus *written under these words* (*as q*)
[t] *A has* precipimus *written over this word* (*as q*)
[u] *A repeats* aliis *here*
[v-v] *Underlined in A with* concedimus et confirmamus *written in margin* (*as q*)
[w] *Interlined in A*
[x-x] *Underlined in A with* Et volumus et firmiter precipimus *written in margin* (*as q*)
[y] *PRO text ends*
[z] *B ends with* et cetera

No original exists and the text in all copies seems suspect in its mixing of first person singular and plural. However, the royal style and witness list are in order, and the text may be accepted as a slightly 'improved' version of a genuine original. It must be earlier than July 1158, when the king's brother, Geoffrey, died (Robert of Torigny, 196). Between Dec. 1154 and Aug. 1158 the king was on the Continent only from Jan. 1156 to Apr. 1157 (Eyton, 16, 25). The projected amendments in notes *q, r, s-s, t, v-v, x-x*, would suit a confirmation by Richard I or John, presumably in this case the latter, since they are made in a hand later than that of the original part of the cartulary which includes Richard's confirmation.

[1] This land may be identified with the Domesday holding of Henry de Ferrers in Reading (*VCH Berks*, i. 334), which appears to have been given to Tutbury Priory, probably before the foundation of Reading, and subsequently, according to Pope Alexander III's confirmation to Tutbury (dated 1162-3), exchanged for *Brincheale* (unidentified) by 'King Henry' (*Cartl. Tutbury*, 24). Since this probably refers to Henry I, the Robert de Ferrers named in Henry II's confirmation to Reading is probably Henry de Ferrers' son, who succeeded him by 1130 and died in 1139.

19 Confirmation by King Henry II to Reading Abbey of its possessions given by either Henry I or the Empress—viz., Reading with churches and the land which Robert de Ferrers had, Leominster with churches, Thatcham, Cholsey with the farm of 100s which William son of Gerold used to pay to Henry I, Whitsbury and Rowington with their churches, land in Wigston [Parva], in Southampton and in Houghton [Conquest], 1 hide in Underoure [Windsor], Blewbury, [East] Hendred, land in Marlborough, the churches of Berkeley, Thatcham and Stanton [Harcourt], a fair of St Laurence, and a mint and moneyer at London or Reading—and of its liberties   [Jan. 1156 × Apr. 1157]

Original charter: BL Add. Ch. 19591
A f21r-v; B ff22v-23r
Pd. *Arch. Journ.*, xx. 293-4; Delisle and Berger, i. 133-4 (no. xxxiii); *Trans. Royal Soc. Lit.*, 2nd ser., xi. 316-17; Warner and Ellis, i. no. 40 (with facsimile); Barfield, *Thatcham*, ii. 7-8 (with facsimile); (cal.) Hurry, *Reading Abbey*, 165

Testibus:[a] Domina Imperatrice, et Phil(ippo) Baioc(ensi) episcopo, et comite Reginaldo, et Roberto de Novo Burgo, et Man(assero) Biset dapifero, et Stephano de Bello Campo. Apud Rothomagum.[b]

Endorsed: Carta regis H(enrici) .ii.[c] gestatoria de libertatibus [*12th cent.*]

Size: 258 × 225 mm

Seal: substantial portion of great seal (approximately half) in yellow-green wax on plaited cords; seal contained in bag of fine tissue

a B ends
b Rotom(agum) A
c Above the line in the same hand

Probably contemporary with no. 18. The endorsement of the original calls it a 'portable' charter (see no. 2 n.). There is no reason to doubt its authenticity.

20   *Confirmation by King Henry II to Reading Abbey of the gifts of lands, etc. [unspecified], made by Henry I and the Empress, and of specified liberties and immunities*   [Jan. 1156 × Apr. 1157]

A ff 21v–22v; B f 23r–v

Henricus rex Angl(ie)[a] et dux Norm(annie) et Aquitanie et comes Andegavie archiepiscopis, episcopis, abbatibus, comitibus, baronibus, iustic(iariis), vicecomitibus, ministris et omnibus fidelibus suis Francis et Anglis totius Anglie,[a] salutem. Sciatis me concessisse et in perpetuam elemosinam confirmasse deo et sancte Marie de Rading(ia) et monachis ibidam [b]deo servientibus[b] omnes terras et tenuras [c]et elemosinas[c] quas rex H(enricus) avus meus eis in elemosinam dedit et concessit, et preterea quicquid domina imperatrix mater mea eis in elemosinam dedit et concessit. Nulla autem persona parva vel magna [*f 22r*] per debitum seu per consuetudinem aut per violentiam aliquid ab hominibus et terris et possessione Rading(ensis) monasterii exigat, non equitationem sive expeditionem, non pontium vel castrorum edificationem, non vehicula, non summagia, non vectigalia, non navigia, non opera, non tributa, non xenia, sed sint monachi Rading(enses) et familia eorum et res ipsorum absoluti ab omni geldo et theloneo et alia qualibet consuetudine in terris et aquis, in transitibus pontium et [b]maris portuum[b] per totam Angliam et Norm(anniam). Sintque abbatis et monachorum eius de hominibus suis et de tota possessione sua et de alienis in ea forisfacientibus vel ibi cum forisfacto interceptis hundreda et placita omnia, cum socca et sacca et toll et theam[d] et infangenetheof et utfangenetheof et hamsocna infra burgum et extra burgum,[e] in viis et in semitis et in omnibus locis cum omnibus causis que sunt vel esse possunt.

Habeantque abbas et monachi Rading(enses)^e in tota possessione
sua omnem iustitiam de assaltu et furtis et murdris et sanguinis
effusione et pacis infractione quantum ad regiam pertinet^e potestatem, et de omnibus forisfactis. Quod si abbas et monachi de his^f
iustitiam facere neglexerint, rex fieri compellat ita ut in nullo libertatem Rading(ensis) ecclesie minuat. Veniantque ad hundreda de
Rading(ia) et de Leoministria^g homines circumiacentium maneriorum secundum consuetudinem temporum precedentium, qui si
quando vocati fuerint ad iustitiam venire contempserint, rex inde
forisfactum accipiat et venire et satisfacere compellat. Statuimus
autem tam ecclesiastice quam et^h regie ^{b}prospectu potestatis^b ut decedente abbate Rading(ensi) omnis possessio monasterii ubicumque
fuerit remaneat libera et integra cum omni iure et consuetudine sua
in manu et dispositione prioris et monachorum capituli Rad-
ing(ensis). Hoc autem ideo statuit rex H(enricus) avus meus et ego
statutum illud concedo et confirmo et ut in perpetuum servetur
precipio, quia abbas Rading(ensis) non habet proprios redditus sed
communes cum fratribus. Qui autem deo annuente canonica electione abbas substitutus fuerit non cum suis secularibus consanguineis
seu quibuslibet aliis elemosinas monasterii male utendo disperdat,
sed pauperibus et peregrinis et hospitibus suscipiendis curam gerat.
Terras censuales non ad feodum donet nec faciat milites nisi in sacra
veste Christi, in qua parvulos suscipere modeste caveat, maturos
autem seu discretos tam clericos quam laicos^i provide suscipiat.
Nemo de possessione Rading(ensis) monasterii feodaliter absolutum
aliquid teneat sed ad censum annuum et servitium abbati et monachis debitum. In abbatis et monachorum domo Rading(ensium) et
possessione nullus per hereditatem officium teneat, sed in arbitrio
abbatis et monachorum de transmutandis prepositis seu aliis quibuslibet officiariis causa consistat. Hanc monasterio Rading(ensi) et
omnibus ad ipsum pertinentibus in perpetuum dono et concedo
liberam immunitatem et immunem libertatem quam regibus post
me in Anglia regnaturis causa dei commendo servandam, ut eis
conservet deus eternam. Siquis autem hoc nostre donationis decretum infringere seu minuere vel transmutare scienter presumpserit,
summus iudex omnium contrahat eum et eradicet cum sua posteritate, ut permaneat sine alique hereditate in clade et fame. Quisquis
vero Rading(ense) monasterium cum prefata libertate servaverit altissimus [f 22v] qui dominatur in regno hominum bonis omnibus
stabiliat eum et servet in evum. Et volo et firmiter precipio quod
predicti monachi Rading(enses) omnes possessiones suas cum omnibus libertatibus et liberis consuetudinibus et quietantiis predictis in
perpetuam elemosinam habeant et teneant ita bene et in pace et
libere et quiete et integre sicut carta predicti regis H(enrici) avi mei

testatur et sicut carta domine*ʲ* imperatricis matris mee testatur. Testibus:*ᵏ* M(athilde) Imperatrice, Hugone archiepiscopo Roth(omagensi), Nigello episcopo Eliensi, Ph(ilippo) episcopo Baioc(ensi), R(otroco) episcopo Ebr(oicensi), Th(oma) cancellario, Galfr(edo) et Willelmo fratribus regis, Roberto de Novo Burgo. Apud Rothomagum.

ᵃ⁻ᵃ et cetera *B*
ᵇ⁻ᵇ In reverse order in *A*, marked for transposition
ᶜ⁻ᶜ Om. in *B*   *ᵈ* team *B*
ᵉ Om. in *B*   *ᶠ* hiis *B*
ᵍ Lemin' *B*   *ʰ* Interlined in *A*
ⁱ quam laicos repeated in *A* and marked for deletion
ʲ Insert mee *B*   *ᵏ* B ends

Probably contemporary with no. 18. There is one lapse into first person plural, but otherwise the charter seems in order. The rubric of A has *gestatoria* added in a slightly later hand, and A notes in the margin that another copy was at Leominster.

21 *Notification by King Henry II, addressed generally, that Henry I founded Reading Abbey with all the immunity [etc.] that the royal power can confer upon an abbey, and precept that the abbey shall hold its possessions with specified liberties and immunities* [1154 × 89]

A f92r-v; B f22r-v

Henricus dei gratia rex Angl(ie) et dux Norm(annie) et Aquit(anie) et comes Andeg(avie) archiepiscopis, episcopis, comitibus, baronibus et omnibus bailliis*ᵃ* et fidelibus suis, salutem. Sciatis H(enricum) regem avum meum pro salute anime sue et omnium antecessorum et successorum suorum abbatiam de Rading(ia) construxisse, eidemque abbatie omnem immunitatem et potestatem, quietantiam et libertatem dedisse quam regia potestas alicui abbatie conferre potest. Quare volo et firmiter precipio quod abbas et monachi de Rading(ia) omnia tenementa sua tam laica quam ecclesiastica quecumque in presenti habent vel in posterum emptione vel donatione fidelium habituri sunt bene et in pace, libere et quiete teneant in omnibus locis et in omnibus rebus ubicumque fuerint, *ᵇ*quieta de Danegeldis*ᵇ* et de omnibus geldis et siris et hundredis et omnibus placitis et querelis et auxiliis et scutagiis, de hidagiis et summagiis et careagiis*ᶜ* et navigiis et clausuris, de pontium et castrorum edificatione, de conductu thesauri et omni operatione, de tributis et lestagiis et stalagiis,*ᵈ* de teoþincpeni*ᵉ* et tinpeni, de summonitionibus, de assisis et superassisis et*ᶠ* omnibus forisfactis quacumque occasione emerserint, de assartis*ᵍ* et nemorum wastis. Nullus vero de forestariis regis quicquam se intromittat de boscis abbatis et monachorum qui sunt intra forestam, sed omnem potestatem et libertatem quam

habet rex in boscis suis habeant abbas et monachi in omnibus boscis
qui ad abbatiam pertinent ubicumque fuerint. Habeantque abbas et
monachi warennas suas ubicumque eis placuerit in terra sua liberas
et quietas ad capiend(um) capream, leporem et vulpem. Nullus
dominicos canes abbatis [et]^h monachorum espealtare^i cogat, verum
canes hominum suorum intra forestam manentium abbas et monachi
espealtare^j faciant, et si que mercie hinc inde provenerint, abbas et
monachi eas soli habeant. Sintque abbas et monachi Rading(enses)
et homines eorum et res ipsorum quieti de hidagiis^k et theloneis et
omnibus exactionibus [$f92v$] et consuetudinibus in nundinis et foris
quorumcumque sint in omnibus locis et in omnibus rebus per totam
Angliam et Norm(anniam). Habeant autem abbas et monachi
omnem iustitiam de assaltu et murdris et sanguinis effusione et pacis
infractione et thesauri inventione quicquid ad regiam pertinet potestatem. Mercie nulle quacumque occasione de abbate vel monachis vel de tenementis vel de^l hominibus eorum exigantur nec exacte solvantur, sed omnia que eorum sunt ita quieta sint et libera
sicut mea propria et soli abbati et monachis de omnibus respondent-
tia. De assisis etiam et recognitionibus que per preceptum regis vel
iusticiar' eius fieri mandantur de terris et hominibus qui sunt in
baillia^m abbatis et monachorum habeant abbas et monachi curiam
suam, quod si de hiis iustitiam facere negglexerint^n rex fieri compellat in curia abbatis et monachorum de Rading(ia), ita ut in nullo
libertatem Rading(ensis) ecclesie minuat. Nemo homines abbatis et
monachorum absque eorum licentia ad aliam quam ad abbatis curiam propter aliquam recognitionem venire faciat. Habeant autem
abbas et monachi de hominibus suis et de tota possessione sua et de
alienis in ea forisfacientibus vel ibi cum forisfacto interceptis hundreda et placita omnia ^{o}cum socha, sacha, et tol et theam, et infan-
geneþeof et hutfangeneþeof^o in omnibus locis cum omnibus causis
que sunt vel esse possunt. Hanc monasterio Rading(ensi) et quantamcumque rex donare potest dono et confirmo liberam immunitatem et immunem libertatem quam regibus in Anglia regnaturis post
me servandam commendo. T(estibus).

^{a} ball'is B	$^{b-b}$ quieta de negeldis A
^{c} cariag' B	^{d} stallagiis B
^{e} teþinpeni B	^{f} *Insert* de B
^{g} essartis B	^{h} *Om. in A, supplied from B*
^{i} *Sic in A and B, ? rectius* espealtari	^{j} *Sic in A; B has* espealtari
^{k} hedagiis B	^{l} *Om. in B*
^{m} ballia B	^{n} neglexerint B

$^{o-o}$ cum socca et sacca et toll' et team et infangentheof et utfangentheof B

The text is suspect in several respects. It is largely an expanded version of no. 2,
which in its present form is itself a forgery; no original exists and neither of the

cartulary copies gives witnesses. Moreover, in the late 12th-century cartulary A it appears rather suspiciously in a section added after the main text was written, far away from the other acts of Henry II assembled among the royal charters. The royal style would not be impossible especially after 1172, but the extent of the privileges granted and confirmed is so sweeping as to cast doubts on the charter's authenticity. Nonetheless, these liberties were confirmed by King John and later kings (see nos. 45, 56, 102, 109). The rubric of A describes the charter as 'portable'.

22   *Precept by King Henry II to the justice and sheriff of Herefordshire that Reading Abbey shall hold its lands in Herefordshire freely and quietly as his grandfather gave them* [1154 × 73]

A f63r

Henricus rex Angl(ie) et dux Norm(annie) et Aquit(anie) et comes Andeg(avie)*ᵃ* iustic(iario) et vicecomiti de Heref(ordscira), salutem. Precipio quod monachi de Rading(ia) teneant terras suas de Herefordsc(ira) bene et in pace et libere et quiete, sicut rex avus meus eas illis dedit. Nec inde in placitum ponantur nisi coram me. T(este) Ricardo de Hum(eto) constabulario. Apud Windr(esores).

a Endeg' *in Ms*

This is entered in the original hand of A, though not with the other acts of Henry II, and is listed in the contemporary table of contents. Richard de Humez was constable of Normandy 1154–80. The omission of *dei gratia* in the royal style, on which point A is generally scrupulous, dates the act not later than 1173; Henry was abroad from May 1172 to July 1174, except probably for a few days in July 1173 (Eyton, 167, 173, 179).

23   *Precept by King Henry II to the constables of Windsor and Guildford and his foresters and ministers to allow the abbot of Reading's men to bring timber through the king's forest for the work of the abbey without disturbance* [1154 × 73; ? 1164]

A f26v; B f27v

Henricus rex Angl(ie) *ᵃ*et dux Norm(annie) et Aquit(anie) et comes Andeg(avie)*ᵃ* conest(abulariis) de Windr(esores)*ᵇ* et de Gerdeford(a)*ᶜ* et forestariis et ministris suis, salutem. Precipio quod permittatis homines abbatis de Rading(ia) in pace ducere per forestam meam mairemium ad opus ecclesie de Rading(ia) et eos non disturbetis. T(este)*ᵈ* magistro Iohanne Cumin'. Apud Radingiam.

ᵃ⁻ᵃ et cetera *B*   *ᵇ* Windlesor' *B*
ᶜ Guldef' *B*   *ᵈ* B ends

The date depends upon the omission of *dei gratia* in the royal style. Since it was given at Reading and concerned the abbey's works, it may perhaps date from the time of the consecration of the abbey church in Apr. 1164. John Cumin was elected archbishop of Dublin in 1181.

24 *Precept by King Henry II to the men who ought to hold of Reading Abbey to do their service as in the time of Henry I*   [Jan. 1155]

A f 25v; B f 26v

Henricus rex Anglie *et dux Norm(annie) et Aquit(anie) et comes Andeg(avie)*ᵃ omnibus hominibus qui de ecclesia Rading(ensi) tenere debent, salutem. Precipio quod faciatis idem servitium abbati de Rading(ia) quod vos et antecessores vestri soletisᵇ facere abbati eiusdem ecclesie tempore regis H(enrici). Et nisi feceritis, ipse abbas vos iustitiet per terras et catalla vestra. Test(e)ᶜ Philippo episcopo Baioc(ensi). Apud Niwerc(am).

   ᵃ⁻ᵃ et cetera *B*
   ᵇ solebatis *B*   ᶜ *B ends*

1155 was the only year in which Philip bishop of Bayeux was with the king in England, accompanying him from London to Northampton and Nottingham in Jan. and to York in Feb. (Eyton, 2–5). This writ was no doubt issued at Newark when the king was in Notts. in Jan.

25 *Precept by King Henry II to his justices, sheriffs and ministers that the land and men of Reading Abbey be quit of assizes and plaints as in the time of Henry I*   [? summer 1155]

A f 26v

Henricus rex Anglie et dux Normann(ie) et Aquitan(ie) et comes Andeg(avie) iustic(iariis) et vicecom(itibus) et ministris suis, salutem. Precipio quod terra monachorum de Rading(ia) et homines sui sint quieti de assisis et omnibus querelis sicut fuerunt tempore regis H(enrici) avi mei et sicut carta eius testatur. T(este) Ricardo de Hulm(eto) const(abulario). Apud Brug(iam).

Probably during the time between May and July 1155 when the king was occupied with the revolt of Hugh de Mortimer and the siege of Bridgnorth (Eyton, 10).

26 *Precept by King Henry II to his justices, sheriffs, ministers and reeves of England and Normandy and of sea ports that all goods of Reading Abbey be quit of toll, passage-money and all custom*   [1156 × 59]

A ff 24v–25r; B f 27r

Henricus rex Anglie *et dux Norm(annie) et Aquit(anie) et comes Andeg(avie)*ᵃ omnibus iustic(iariis) et vic(ecomitibus) et ᵇprepositis et ministrisᵇ suis Anglie et Norm(annie) et portuum maris, [*f 25r*] salutem. Precipio quod omnes res monachorum meorum de Rading(ia) quas homines sui poterunt affidare suas esse proprias sint quiete de thelon(eis) et passag(iis) et omni consuetudine per totam terram meam et per portus maris. Et prohibeo ne quis eos inde super hoc disturbet, super .x. libras forisfacti. Testibus:^{c} Imperatrice, et Philippo Baioc(ensi) episcopo, et Roberto de Novo Burgo. Apud Rothomagum.

$^{a-a}$ et cetera B
$^{b-b}$ A has ministris et prepositis, *marked for transposition*
^{c} B ends

Robert de Newburgh is no doubt the seneschal of Normandy who entered Bec Abbey in July 1159 shortly before his death. The writ dates before this and after Henry's return from England to Normandy in Jan. 1156 (Eyton, 16).

27   *Precept by King Henry II to the abbot and convent of Reading to hold their lands in demesne and to recall into demesne any that may have been given in fee since the death of Henry I*   [1156 × 59]

A f25v; B f27v

Henricus rex Anglie ^{a}et dux Norm(annie) et Aquit(anie) et comes Andeg(avie)^a abbati Rading(ensi) et toti conventui ecclesie Rading(ensis),^{b} salutem. Volo et firmiter precipio quod omnes terras et tenuras vestras teneatis in dominio vestro liberas et absolutas, ita quod nemini detur in feudum^c sicut rex H(enricus) avus meus precepit per cartam suam. Et siquid inde alicui datum est in feudum^c post mortem predicti regis H(enrici) avi mei, totum resaisiatis sine dilatione in dominium vestrum et in pace teneatis. Et siquis aliquod tenementum calumpniaverit de vobis in feudum^c et hereditatem, non respondeatur ei contra cartam H(enrici) regis avi mei et meam. Et siquis inde vobis vim et iniuriam fecerit, iustic(iarii) et vicecom(ites) et ministri mei vobis inde iustitiam et pacem sine dilatione faciant. Testibus:^{d} Imperatrice, et episcopo Baiocensi, et Roberto de Novo Burgo. Apud Rothomagum.

$^{a-a}$ et cetera B ^{b} Om. in B
^{c} feodum B ^{d} B ends

Probably contemporary with no. 26.

28   *Grant by King Henry II to Reading Abbey of a fair at Reading on the feast of St James and three days following. All attending shall have the king's firm peace*   [1163 × 65; ? 1164]

A f23r-v; B ff23v-24r
Pd. *Mon. Ang.*, iv. 42 (no. x)

Henricus rex Anglie ^{a}et dux Norm(annie) et Aquit(anie) et comes Andeg(avie) archiepiscopis, episcopis, abbatibus, comitibus, baronibus, iustic(iariis), vicecomitibus, ministris et omnibus hominibus suis Francis et Anglis totius Anglie,*a* salutem. Sciatis me dedisse et carta mea confirmasse ecclesie beate Marie de Rading(ia) et monachis meis in ea deo servientibus feriam unam apud Rading(iam) durantem per totum diem festivitatis sancti Iacobi apostoli mense Iulio et per tres continuos dies sequentes annua[*f23v*]tim. Quare volo et firmiter precipio quod predicta ecclesia et monachi feriam illam habeant et teneant bene et in pace et integre et quiete, et quicumque ad eandem feriam annuam venerint, in eundo et manendo et redeundo, meam firmam pacem habeant. Testibus:*b* Rotr(oco) Ebr(oicensi), Arn(ulfo) Lex(oviensi) episcopis, Roberto comite Leg(recestrie), Gaufredo Cant(uariensi), Ricardo Pictav(ensi) archidiaconis, Iohanne de Oxoneford(ia), Ricardo de Hum(eto) constabulo. Apud Clarendonam.

a-a et cetera B   *b* B ends

Geoffrey Ridel became archdeacon of Canterbury in 1163 (*Fasti 1066–1300*, ii. 13); in 1165 Rotrou bishop of Evreux became archbishop of Rouen, and John of Oxford became dean of Salisbury. The charter may date from the early part of 1164, when Rotrou bishop of Evreux was in England (Eyton, 70).

29 Precept by King Henry II to his justices, sheriffs and ministers of England to cause to be returned to Reading Abbey its villeins and fugitives who have absconded since the death of Henry I. No one shall detain them on pain of £10 forfeiture

[Jan. 1163 × Mar. 1166; ? not before Jan. 1164]

A f 23v; B f 26v
Pd. van Caenegem, *Royal Writs*, 474

T(este)*a* Ricardo archidiacono Pictav(ensi). Apud Clarend(onam).

a B ends

Richard of Ilchester was archdeacon of Poitiers 1162/3–74. The king returned to England Jan. 1163 and remained until Mar. 1166 (Eyton, 58,92). He appears not to have been at Clarendon before Jan. 1164, returning there several times before his departure from England in 1166. In later years he is not known to have visited Clarendon until after Richard of Ilchester became bishop of Winchester in 1174. In A the writ was entered at the foot of the folio after the original composition, but in a smaller version of the same hand, and was added to the table of contents (cf. no. 609).

30 *Precept by King Henry II, addressed generally, that the men of Reading Abbey be quit of shires, hundreds, pleas, plaints, tolls, passage-money and carriage-money, and may sell and buy throughout England without toll. No-one shall disturb them on pain of £10 forfeiture*   [prob. May 1175]

A f 25r; B f 27v

Henricus dei gratia rex Angl(ie) *a*et dux Norm(annie) et Aquit(anie) et comes Andeg(avie) archiepiscopis, episcopis, abbatibus, comitibus, baronibus, vicecomitibus et omnibus baillivis et fidelibus suis,*a* salutem. Precipio quod omnes homines monachorum de Rading(ia) sint quieti de schir(is)*b* et hundr(edis) et omnibus placitis et querelis et theloneis et passagiis et carreagiis.*c* Et vendant et emant ubicumque voluerint per totam Angliam sine theloneo. Et nullus eos disturbet super forisfactum .x. librarum. Testibus:*d* Ricardo de Luci, magistro Waltero de Insul(a), Iohanne filio Luce. Apud Westm(onasterium).

a–a et cetera B	*b* syr' B
c cariag' B	*d* B ends

John fitz Luce, canon of Rouen, was in England in 1175 (Eyton, 192) and may have attended the archbishop of Canterbury's council at Westminster in May, at which the king was present. Master Walter de Insula acted as keeper of the seal while Geoffrey Ridel was chancellor, 1162–73.

31 Precept by King Henry II to his justices, sheriffs and bailiffs in whose bailiwicks Reading Abbey has lands to protect the abbey's men and possessions as the king's own. The abbey shall not be impleaded for its demesne tenements except before the king or his chief justiciar   [May 1175 × July 1188]

Original charter: BL Add. Ch. 19592
A f 25r–v

Pd. *Arch. Journ.*, xx. 294; *Trans. Royal Soc. Lit.*, 2nd ser., xi. 327–8; Delisle and Berger, ii. 13; (facsimile) L. Delisle, *Recueil des actes de Henri II: Atlas* (Paris, 1909), pl. V 7 *bis*; *Bulletin de l'Ecole des Chartes*, lxviii (1907), pl. II. 6; (cal.) Hurry, *Reading Abbey*, 169

T(este) G(aufredo) El(iensi) episcopo. Apud Windesor(es).*a*

Endorsed: Carta regis H(enrici) secundi de protectione [*late 12th or early 13th cent.*]

Size: 156 × 92 mm

Seal: large fragment of great seal in red wax on tongue

a Windresores *A*

Geoffrey Ridel was consecrated bishop of Ely on 6 Oct. 1174, the king being on the Continent and not returning to England until May 1175 (Eyton, 190). Henry left England for the last time in July 1188 (*ibid.*, 288). Geoffrey Ridel died in Aug. 1189.

32 *Notification by King Henry II, addressed generally, that Reading Abbey and its possessions are in the royal protection, and precept to protect them as the king's own. The abbey shall not be impleaded for any demesne tenement except before the king or his chief justiciar*   [1181/2 × July 1188]

A f 25r; B f 26v

Henricus dei gratia rex Anglie *et dux Norm(annie) et Aquit(anie)
et comes Andeg(avie) archiepiscopis, episcopis, abbatibus, archidiaconis, decanis, comitibus, baronibus, vicecomitibus, iustic(iariis) et
omnibus bailivis et fidelibus suis, salutem.* Sciatis quod abbatia de
Rading(ia) et monachi in ea deo servientes et omnia tenementa sua
et res et possessiones sue tam ecclesiastice quam laice sunt in manu
et *protectione et custodia* mea. Et ideo precipio quod eandem
abbatiam et abbatem et monachos ipsius abbatie in ea deo servientes
et omnes terras et tenementa et redditus et homines et res et possessiones suas custodiatis et manuteneatis et protegatis sicut meas
proprias, ita ut nullam violentiam vel iniuriam aut gravamen eis
faciatis nec fieri permittatis. Et siquis eis super hoc in aliquo forisfacere presumpserit, plenariam eis inde sine dilatione iustitiam fieri
faciatis. Et prohibeo ne de ullo dominico tenemento suo ponantur
in placitum nisi coram me vel coram capitali iusticia mea. Testibus:*
G(aufredo) cancellario filio meo, et Rann(ulfo) de Glanv(illa). Apud
Stokes.

a-a et cetera B
b-b custodia et protectione B   *c* B ends

Geoffrey, the king's illegitimate son, became chancellor in 1181/2; Henry left England
for the last time in July, 1188. *Stokes* is a common place-name and not precisely
identifiable.

33 *Confirmation by King Henry II to Reading Abbey of the gifts of land in
Carswell and Burghfield made by Aumary son of Ralph*   [1185 × 87]

A f 23v; B f 27r

Henricus dei gratia rex Anglie *et dux Norm(annie) et Aquitan(ie)
et comes Andegav(ie) archiepiscopis, episcopis, abbatibus, comitibus, baronibus, iustic(iariis), vicecomitibus et omnibus baillivis et
fidelibus suis, salutem.* Sciatis me concessisse et presenti carta mea
confirmasse deo et abbatie sancte Marie de Rading(ia) et monachis
ibidem deo servientibus subscriptas rationabiles donationes quas Almaricus filius Rad(ulfi) eis fecit et cartis suis confirmavit, scilicet
totam terram quam de predicto Almarico tenuerunt in Kersewella
Rog(erus) prepositus, Ricardus vallet, Rod(bertus) de Buleflet, Edwardus de Effedford',* Alanus piscator, Sewaldus, Edwinus, Fre-
winus, Godricus cum omnibus pertinentiis suis, et terram Iacobi de
Berchefeld' cum pertinentiis suis. Quare volo et firmiter precipio
quod predicta abbatia de Radingia et monachi in ea deo servientes
prenominatas terras teneant et habeant in libera et perpetua elemosina bene et in pace, libere et quiete, integre et plenarie et honorifice, cum omnibus pertinentiis et libertatibus et liberis consuetu-

dinibus suis, sicut prefatus Almaricus eas ipsis dedit et sicut carte
eius testantur. Testibus:[c] H(ugone) Dunel(mensi) et Iohanne
Ebroic(ensi) episcopis, Willelmo filio Rad(ulfi) senescallo
Norm(annie), Seero de Quint(i), Hugone de Creissi, Thoma
Bard(ulfo), Alvredo de Sancto Martino. Apud Rothomagum.

a-a et cetera B
b Heffedford B   c B ends

The presence of John bishop of Evreux among the witnesses limits the date to 1181 ×
89. During this period Hugh of Durham accompanied Henry II to Normandy with
Heraclius, patriarch of Jerusalem, in Apr. 1185, remaining with the king until sent
home in Mar. 1186 (Eyton, 263–7). The bishop was again with the king in Normandy
in 1187, at a time when the bishop of Evreux is found witnessing royal charters (ibid.,
282). For Aumary's charters, see nos. 705, 769.

34 Confirmation by King Richard I to Reading Abbey of its possessions—
viz., Reading, Cholsey and Leominster with their churches, a mint and moneyer
at Reading or London, Thatcham, the churches of Wargrave and Hanborough,
Rowington and its church, land in Wigston [Parva], Whitsbury and its
church, lands in Houghton [Conquest] and Southampton, the land which Robert
de Ferrers had in Reading, lands in Carswell, in Burghfield, in Kiddington
and in Whitley, Aston and its church, lands in Quidenham, in Stanford[-in-
the-Vale], in Sawbridgeworth, in Lashbrook, in Cambridge and in Ufton
[Robert], the church of Englefield, land in Warwick, Blewbury, [East]
Hendred, the church of Berkeley with its churches and chapels, the churches of
Stanton [Harcourt] and Thatcham, and 1 hide in Underoure [Windsor]—and
of its liberties   12 Sept. 1189

A ff26v–28r; B ff31r–32r; C f7r–v; PRO Cartae Antiq. Roll, C52/22(X), no. 12
(not fully collated)
Pd. (incomplete) Mon. Ang., iv. 42 (no. xi)

Ricardus dei gratia rex Anglie dux Norm(annie)[a] Aquit(anie) comes
Andeg(avie) archiepiscopis, episcopis, [b]abbatibus, comitibus, baronibus, iustic(iariis), vicecomitibus et omnibus ministris et fidelibus suis
totius Anglie, salutem.[b] Sciatis nos concessisse et presenti carta nostra
confirmasse deo et sancte Marie et monachis de Rading(ia) in perpetuam elemosinam omnes terras et tenuras et elemosinas quas rex
H(enricus)[c] avus domini regis H(enrici) patris nostri et omnes alii
donatores eis[d] concesserunt et dederunt. Videlicet ipsam Rad-
ing(iam) et Chealseiam et Liminiistriam[e] cum omnibus appendiciis
suis, cum silvis et agris et pasturis, cum pratis et aquis, cum molendinis et piscariis, cum ecclesiis et capellis et cimiteriis et oblationibus
et decimis, cum moneta et uno monetario apud [f27r] Rading(iam)
vel apud Londoniam. Et Thacheham,[f] et ecclesiam de Waregrava,[g]
et ecclesiam de Haneberga, et Rokintonam in Warewicsc(ira)[h] cum

ecclesia eiusdem ville, et Wigestanam que fuit terra Willelmi elemosinarii, et in Wilthesc(ira)[i] Wicheberiam[j] cum ecclesia eiusdem
ville, et in Bedefordsc(ira)[k] terram Albodi de Hoctuna, et terram
Roberti sacerdotis de Hamtona, et terram quam Robertus de Ferrariis habuit in villa Rading(ie), et terram quam Amalricus eis dedit
in Kersewella[l] et in Burgefeld',[m] et terram quam Willelmus comes
de Mandevill' eis dedit in Katedena,[n] et terram de Witheleia[o] quam
Petrus de Cosham eis concessit et carta sua confirmavit, et Hes-
tonam[p] in Hertfordsc(ira)[q] cum ecclesia eiusdem ville et omnibus
appendiciis suis, et parcum quem dominus rex pater noster eis dedit
et confirmavit, et unam feriam apud Rading(iam) die sancti Iacobi
et per tres dies sequentes, [r]et unam feriam apud Leomimistriam in
die sanctorum Petri et Pauli et per tres dies sequentes,[r] et terram
quam Willelmus comes de Sussex' eis dedit in Quidenham, et terram
quam Willelmus comes de Ferrariis eis dedit in Stanford, et terram
quam Henricus filius Geroldi eis dedit in Sebrihteswrd',[s] et terram
quam Michael de Basevill' eis dedit in Lechebroch,[t] et terram quam
Laurentius hostiarius[u] de eis tenet in Cantebrig(ia),[v] et terram quam
Rad(ulfus) de Offentuna[w] eis dedit, et ecclesiam de Englefeld cum
pertinentiis suis, et terram quam Stephanus de Mortona eis dedit in
suburbio de Warewic.[x] Et quecumque Matill(is) imperatrix avia
nostra eis dedit et concessit, scilicet Bleoberiam[y] cum omnibus pertinentiis suis, et Hendredam,[z] et ecclesiam de Berkelai cum ecclesiis
et capellis et omnibus appendiciis suis, et ecclesiam de Stant(ona)
cum omnibus appendiciis suis, et ecclesiam de Tacheham cum omnibus pertinentiis suis, et forum in eadem villa dominicis diebus,[aa]et
hidam de Underore cum omnibus pertinentiis suis.[aa] Nulla autem
persona parva vel magna per debitum seu per consuetudinem aut
per violentiam aliquid ab hominibus et terris et possessione Rad-
ing(ensis) monasterii exigat, non equitationem sive expeditionem,
non pontium vel castrorum edificationem, non vehicula, non summagia, non vectigalia, non navigia, non opera, non tributa, non
xenia, non lestagia, non tethinpani,[bb] non timpani,[cc] et habeant quietantiam de wastis nemorum et de essartis. [dd]Nullus vero de forestariis
regis quicquam se intromittat de boscis abbatis et monachorum qui
sunt in foresta, sed omnem libertatem et potestatem quam habet rex
in boscis suis habeant abbas et monachi in omnibus boscis suis ubicumque fuerint.[dd] Et sint monachi Rading(enses) et omnes homines
eorum et res ipsorum absoluti a Danegeldo[ee] et omni geldo et hidagio
et pontagio et theloneo et omni alia exactione et consuetudine, in
nundinis et foris quorumcumque sint, in terris et aquis, in transitibus
pontium et maris portuum per totam Angliam et Norm(anniam) et
per totam terram nostram, in omnibus locis et in omnibus rebus.
Sintque abbatis et monachorum de hominibus suis et de tota poss-

essione sua et de alienis in ea forisfacientibus vel ibi cum forisfacto interceptis hundreda et placita omnia, cum socha et sacha et toll et theam et infangenetheof*ff* et utfangenetheof*gg* et hamsocna infra burgum et extra burgum, in viis et semitis et in omnibus locis, cum omnibus [*f 27v*] causis que sunt vel esse possunt. Habeantque abbas et monachi Rading(enses) in tota possessione sua omnem iustitiam de assaltu et furtis et murdris et sanguinis effusione et pacis infractione et thesauri inventione quantum ad regiam pertinet potestatem et de omnibus forisfactis. De assisis etiam et recognitionibus que per preceptum regis vel iusticiar' eius fieri mandantur de terris et de hominibus qui sunt in ballia*hh* abbatis et monachorum habeant abbas et monachi curiam suam. Quod si abbas et monachi de his iustitiam facere*ii* neglexerint, rex fieri compellat *jj*in curia abbatis et monachorum*jj* ita ut in nullo libertatem Rading(ensis) ecclesie minuat. Veniantque ad hundreda de Rading(ia) et de Leoministria*kk* homines circumiacentium maneriorum secundum consuetudinem temporum precedentium, qui si quando vocati fuerint ad iustitiam venire contempserint, rex inde forisfactum accipiat et venire et satisfacere compellat. Statuimus autem tam ecclesiastice quam et regie*ll* prospectu potestatis ut decedente abbate Rading(ensi) omnis possessio monasterii ubicumque fuerit remaneat integra et libera cum omni iure et consuetudine sua in manu et dispositione prioris et monachorum capituli Rading(ensis). Hoc autem ideo statuit H(enricus) rex avus patris nostri et H(enricus) rex pater noster confirmavit. Et nos illud statutum concedimus et confirmamus et ut in perpetuum servetur precipimus, quia abbas Radingie non habet proprios redditus sed communes cum fratribus. Qui autem deo annuente canonica electione abbas substitutus fuerit non cum suis secularibus consanguineis seu quibuslibet aliis elemosinas monasterii male utendo disperdat, sed pauperibus et peregrinis et hospitibus suscipiendis curam gerat. Terras censuales non ad feodum donet nec faciat milites nisi in sacra veste Christi, in qua parvulos suscipere modeste caveat, maturos autem seu discretos tam clericos quam laicos provide suscipiat. Nemo de possessione monasterii Rading(ensis) feodaliter absolutum aliquid teneat, sed ad censum annuum et servitium abbati et monachis debitum. In abbatis et monachorum domo Rading(ensium) et possessione nullus per hereditatem officium teneat, sed in arbitrio abbatis et monachorum de transmutandis prepositis seu aliis quibuslibet officiariis causa consistat. Hanc monasterio Rading(ensi) et omnibus ad ipsum pertinentibus in perpetuum concedimus et confirmamus liberam immunitatem et immunem libertatem, quam regibus post nos in Anglia regnaturis causa dei commendamus servandam, ut eis conservet deus eternam. Siquis autem hoc nostre donationis decretum infringere seu

minuere vel transmutare scienter presumpserit, summus iudex omnium contrahat eum et eradicet cum sua posteritate, ut permaneat
sine aliqua hereditate in clade et fame. Quisquis vero Rading(ense)
monasterium cum prefata libertate servaverit, altissimus qui dominatur in regno hominum bonis omnibus stabiliat eum et servet in
evum. Volumus igitur et firmiter precipimus quod predicti monachi
de Rading(ia) hec omnia predicta cum omnibus libertatibus et liberis consuetudinibus et quietantiis predictis in perpetuam elemosinam bene et in pace, libere et quiete et integre habeant et teneant
in perpetuum.*mm* [*f28r*] Testibus: B(aldewino) Cant(uariensi) archiepiscopo,*nn* H(ugone) Linc(olniensi) et H(ugone) Covintr(ensi) et
G(ilberto) Roff(ensi) episcopis, comite Willelmo de Mandevill',
Rann(ulfo) de Glanvill', Willelmo Maresc(allo), Roberto de Witefeld. Apud Gaitint(onam). Datum per manum Willelmi canc(ellarii)
nostri die xii. Septembris anno primo regni nostri.

a *Insert* et *B*
c *Interlined in A*
e Leministr' *B,C*
g Weregrave *B,C*
i Wiltesir' *B,C*
k Bedefordsir' *B,C*
m Burgf' *C*
o Witeleya *B,C*
q *A has* Herefordsc' (*in error*); Hertfordsir' *B,C*
s Sebrichteswrþe *B,C*
u ostiarius *B,C*
w Offinton' *B,C*
y Bleobir' *B,C*
aa-aa *Om. in B,C*
cc tinpeni *B*; *om. in C*
ee Denegeldo *B,C*
gg utfong' *B,C*
ii *A has* fieri (*in error*)
kk Lem' *B,C*
mm *PRO text ends*

b-b et cetera *B,C*
d *Insert* rationabiliter *B,C*
f Tacheham *B*, Tacheam *C*
h Warwicsyr' *B,C*
j Wichebir' *B,C*
l Kereswell' *C*
n Ketenden' *B,C*
p Eston' *B,C*
r-r *Om. in B,C*
t Lechebroc *B,C*
v Kantebrig' *B,C*
x Warwic *B,C*
z Henredam *B,C*
bb tethinpeni *B,C*
dd-dd *Om. in B,C*
ff infongenetheof *B,C*
hh baillia *B*, balliva *C*
jj-jj *Om. in B,C*
ll *B,C repeat* ecclesiastice (*in error*)
nn *B,C end with* et cetera

The text is closely modelled on nos. 1 and 18. Cartulary A notes that there was
another charter by the same concerning the same at Leominster. The passages included in A, but omitted in B and C, especially that marked *jj-jj*, may indicate
'improvements' to the text in A.

35 *Notification by King Richard I that he has taken the lands and possessions
of Reading Abbey into his protection, and confirmation of specified liberties and
immunities*   12 Sept. 1189

A f28r; B f32r–v; C ff7v–8r; PRO Cartae Antiq. Roll, C52/22(X), no. 13 (not
fully collated)

Ricardus dei gratia rex Angl(ie) *a*dux Norm(annie) Aquit(anie) comes Andeg(avie) archiepiscopis, episcopis, abbatibus, comitibus, baronibus, iustic(iariis), vicecomitibus et omnibus ministris et fidelibus suis totius Anglie, salutem.*a* Sciatis nos recepisse in nostra propria manu et custodia et protectione sicut liberam et specialem elemosinam nostram omnes terras et possessiones monachorum de Radingia tam ecclesiasticas quam laicas. Quare volumus et firmiter precipimus quod monachi predicti*b* omnia tenementa sua teneant bene et in pace, libere et quiete, integre, plenarie et honorifice in omnibus locis et in omnibus rebus, tam in burgo quam extra burgum, quieta de Denegeldis et omnibus geldis et auxiliis, de sciris et hundredis, de placitis et querelis, de scutagiis et hidagiis et stalagiis,*c* de assisis et summonitionibus, de wardis et merciis*d* et*e* forisfacturis, de essartis et nemorum wastis, de summagiis et careagiis,*f* de navigiis et omnibus operibus, de tributis et lestagiis, de tedinpani*g* et timpani,*h* de theloneis et omnibus aliis exactionibus et consuetudinibus. Sintque abbatis et monachorum de hominibus suis et de tota possessione sua et de alienis in ea forisfacientibus vel ibi cum forisfacto interceptis hundr(eda) et placita omnia, cum socca*i* et sacca*j* et toll et theam et infangeneth(eof) et utfangeneth(eof) et hamsocna infra burgum et extra burgum et in omnibus locis cum omnibus causis que sunt vel esse possunt. Habeantque omnem iustitiam de assaltu et furtis et murdris et sanguinis effusione et pacis infractione et thesauri inventione, quantum ad regiam pertinet potestatem et de omnibus forisfactis. De assisis etiam et recognitionibus que per preceptum regis fieri mandantur de terris et hominibus qui sunt in ballia*k* abbatis et monachorum habeant abbas et monachi curiam suam. Quod si abbas et monachi de his iustitiam facere neglexerint, rex fieri compellat in curia abbatis et monachorum ita ut in nullo libertatem Rading(ensis) ecclesie minuat. Siquis versus prefatum abbatem et monachos aliquid de possessionibus quas habent clamaverit sive eos vexare vel in placitum ponere voluerit, prohibemus ne pro aliquo respondeant neque in placitum intrent nisi coram nobis, neque aliquis eos placitare faciat nisi coram nobis.*l* Testibus:*m* B(aldewino) Cant(uariensi) archiepiscopo, H(ugone) Linc(olniensi) et H(ugone) Covintr(ensi) et G(ilberto) Roff(ensi) episcopis, comite Willelmo de Mandevill', Rann(ulfo) de Glanvill', Willelmo Maresc(allo), Roberto de Witefeld. Apud Gai(ti)nt(onam), xii. die Septembris. Datum per manum Willelmi de Longo Campo cancellarii nostri, anno primo regni nostri.

a-a et cetera *B,C*
c stallag' *B,C*
e de *B, insert* de *C*
g teþinpeni *B,C*

b prefati *B,C*
d A *has* mercis
f cariag' *B,C*
h tinpeni *B,C*

ⁱ socha B,C   ^j sacha B,C
^k balliva C   ^l PRO text ends
^m B,C end

The cartulary rubrics describe this as a 'portable' charter.

36   *Precept by King Richard I, addressed generally, that the men of Reading Abbey be quit of shires, hundreds, pleas, plaints, tolls, passage-money and carriage-money, and may sell and buy without toll. No-one shall disturb them on pain of £10 forfeiture*   12 Sept. [1189]

A f 28v; B f 32v; C f 8r

Ricardus dei gratia rex Anglie ^adux Norm(annie) Aquit(anie) comes Andeg(avie) archiepiscopis, episcopis, abbatibus, comitibus, baronibus, iustic(iariis), vicecomitibus et omnibus baillivis et fidelibus suis, salutem.^a Precipimus vobis quod omnes homines monachorum de Rading(ia) sint quieti de scir(is) et hundr(edis) et omnibus placitis et querelis et theloneis et passagiis et careagiis.^b Et vendant et emant ubicumque voluerint per totam Angliam sine theloneo. Et nullus eos disturbet super forisfactum .x. librarum. T(este)^c comite Willelmo de Mandevilla. Apud Gaitintonam, xii. die Septembris.

^{a-a} et cetera B,C
^b cariag' B,C   ^c B,C end

Contemporary with nos. 34–5. The text follows almost exactly that of no. 30.

37   Precept by King Richard I to the abbot and convent of Reading to hold their lands in demesne and to recall into demesne any that may have been given in fee since the death of Henry I
                                                12 Sept. [1189]

Original charter: BL Add. Ch. 19609
A f 28v; B ff 32v–33r; C f 8v
Pd. *Arch. Journ.*, xx. 296; *New Pal. Soc. Facs.*, 2nd ser., pl. 134 a & b (with facsimile
   of original charter and of text in A); (cal.) Hurry, *Reading Abbey*, 171–2

T(este)^a comite Willelmo de Mand(evilla). Apud Gaitinton(am), xii. die Septembris.

Endorsed: Ricardi regis de dominicis terris ne dentur in feudum [*early 13th cent.*]
Size: 160 × 116 mm
Seal: fragment of Richard's first seal in discoloured white wax on
   tag

^a B,C end

Contemporary with nos. 34–5. The text follows closely that of no. 27.

38 *Confirmation by King Richard I to Reading Abbey of its lands and liberties [unspecified] to be held as freely as they have been hitherto and as the abbey's charters testify*   [prob. 13 Mar. × 12 May, 1194]

A f95r–v; B f32v; C f8r

Ricardus dei gratia rex Angl(ie) ^adux Norm(annie) Aquit(anie) comes And(egavie) archiepiscopis, episcopis, abbatibus, comitibus, baronibus, iustic(iariis), vicecomitibus, baill(ivis) et omnibus [*f95v*] ministris et fidelibus suis totius terre sue, salutem.^a Noveritis nos pro salute anime nostre et animarum^b omnium antecessorum^c et successorum nostrorum concessisse et presenti carta nostra confirmasse deo et ecclesie sancte Marie de Rading(ia), abbati etiam et monachis ibidem deo servientibus, omnes donationes terrarum, tenementorum, libertatum et liberarum consuetudinum, quietantiarum et omnium aliarum rerum et possessionum que ex donatione nostra vel antecessorum nostrorum vel ex donatione quarumlibet aliarum personarum ecclesiasticarum vel secularium adepti sunt, statuentes et firmiter precipientes ne quis eis contra prefatas donationes aliquam iniuriam, vexationem vel molestiam inferat aut in aliquo contra libertatem prefatarum donationum venire presumat. Volumus enim et firmiter precipimus quod predicti abbas et monachi de^b Rading(ia) omnia predicta habeant in omnibus et possideant adeo bene et in pace et quiete,^d libere et integre, in perpetuum sicut debent et solent et sicut hucusque habuisse et possedisse dinoscuntur et sicut carte quas inde habent rationabiliter testantur.^e Hiis testibus: H(uberto) Cant(uariensi) archiepiscopo, Adam abbate Colec(estrensi), magistro R(ogero) de Sancto Edmundo archidiacono de Richem(un)d', Willelmo de Stagno, Roberto de Harecort'.

^{a–a} et cetera *B,C*
^b *Om. in B,C*   ^c *A has* meorum *deleted here*
^d *Insert* et *B,C*   ^e *B,C end with* T'

Hubert Walter was translated to Canterbury in 1193; Adam became abbot of Colchester in *c.* 1194/5 (*Heads of Relig. Houses*, 40). This confirmation must therefore date after Richard's release from captivity in Feb. 1194. It seems likely that it was given in England and accordingly belongs to the period spent by the king in England in 1194 (Landon, *Itin.*, 85–93), although Robert de Harcourt is not otherwise recorded as having accompanied him to England.

39 *Notification by King Richard I, addressed generally, that Reading Abbey and its possessions are in the royal protection, and precept to protect them as the king's own. The abbey shall not be impleaded for any demesne tenement except before the king or his chief justiciar*   [1189 × 99]

A f28v; A f93v; B f33r; C f8v

Ricardus dei gratia *a*rex Anglie dux Norm(annie) Aquit(anie) comes And(egavie) archiepiscopis,*b* episcopis, abbatibus, archidiaconis, decanis, comitibus, baronibus, iustic(iariis), vicecomitibus et omnibus baill(ivis)*c* et fidelibus suis, salutem.*a* Sciatis quod abbatia de Rading(ia) et monachi in ea deo servientes et omnia tenementa sua et res et possessiones sue tam ecclesiastice quam laice sunt in manu et custodia et protectione nostra. Et ideo precipimus quod eandem abbatiam et abbatem et monachos ipsius abbatie in ea deo servientes et omnes terras et tenementa et redditus et homines et res et possessiones suas custodiatis, manuteneatis et protegatis sicut meas proprias, ita quod nullam violentiam vel iniuriam aut gravamen eis faciatis nec fieri permittatis. Et si quis eis super hoc in aliquo forisfacere presumpserit, plenariam eis inde sine dilatione iustitiam fieri faciatis. Et prohibemus*d* ne de ullo dominico tenemento suo ponantur in placitum nisi coram nobis vel coram capitali iusticia nostra. Test(ibus).*e*

a-a et cetera *B,C*
c ball' *A f93v*
e Perhaps Test(e) (*see note*); om. in *A f93v*
b Om. in A f93v
d precipimus *A f93v*

The text follows closely that of no. 32. This suggests that, since Richard I's writs, nos. 36–7, dating 12 Sept. 1189, were also virtual re-issues of Henry II's, the present writ may also date from the same time; in that case, the final word should perhaps be expanded as *Teste*, since only Earl William de Mandeville witnessed nos. 36–7. On the other hand, the entry was not made in the original composition of A and does not appear in the original table of contents.

40   *Precept by John count of Mortain to his justices, sheriffs, bailiffs, ministers and faithful that the men of Reading Abbey be quit of shires, hundreds, pleas, plaints, tolls, passage-money and carriage-money, and may sell and buy without toll throughout his land and ports. No-one shall disturb them on pain of £10 forfeiture*   [1189 × 94]

A f46r-v; (noted) B f35r

Iohannes comes Moret(onii) iusticiis,*a* vicecomitibus, baillivis, ministris et omnibus fidelibus suis, salutem. Precipio quod omnes homines monachorum de Rading(ia) sint quieti de sciris et hundredis et omnibus placitis et querelis et theloneis et passagiis et carreagiis, et vendant et emant ubicumque voluerint per totam terram meam et per omnes portus meos sine theloneo. Et nullus eos *b*distur [*f46v*] disturbet*b* super forisfactum decem librarum. Testibus: Stephano Ridell(o) cancellario meo, Waltero de Dunestanvill(a), Willelmo de Kahaingn(es), Ingelram de Pratell(is), Gileberto Basset, et multis aliis.

a Sic   *b-b Sic*

The text follows closely those of nos. 30, 36. John was created count of Mortain in 1189; Walter de Dunstanville II died in 1194, leaving a son and heir Walter, who came of age in 1213 (Sanders, *English Baronies*, 28). The precept was added immediately after the original composition of A and may date from 1192—cf. witness list and note to no. 42.

41 *Precept by John count of Mortain to justices, sheriffs, bailiffs, etc., that the men of Reading Abbey be quit of suits of shire and hundred, of pleas, plaints, tolls, pontage, stallage, passage-money and carriage-money, and may buy without toll throughout his land and ports. No one shall disturb them on pain of £10 forfeiture*   [1189 × 99]

B f 35r; C f 10v

Iohannes comes Moret(onii) iust(iciariis), vic(ecomitibus), baill(ivis),[a] et cetera. Precipio vobis quod homines monachorum de Rading(ia) quieti sint de sectis syr(arum) et hundr(edorum) et de omnibus placitis et querelis et thelon(eis) et pontag(iis) et stall(agiis) et passag(iis) et cariag(iis), et emant ubicumque voluerint per totam terram meam et per omnes portus meos sine thelon(eo). Et prohibeo ne quis illos inde disturbet super forisfactum .x. librarum. T(estibus).

[a] ball' C

Similar to no. 40, and perhaps of the same date.

42 *Gift in free alms by John count of Mortain to Reading Abbey, inspired by the Hand of St James there, of 1 mark of gold annually at his exchequer*   [1192]

A f 46r; B ff 34v–35r; C f 10r
Pd. *Mon. Ang.*, iv. 44 (no. xix)

Iohannes comes Moret(onii) omnibus hominibus et amicis suis [a]Francis et Anglicis presentibus et futuris, salutem.[a] Sciatis me, pro salute anime mee et pro anima regis Henrici patris mei et pro animabus antecessorum necnon[b] successorum meorum et intuitu manus beati Iacobi apostoli que in conventuali ecclesia sancte Marie de Rading(ia) reposita est, dedisse et concessisse et hac carta mea confirmasse deo et eidem ecclesie et monachis ibidem deo servientibus unam marcam auri de redditu singulis annis recipiendi de me et de heredibus meis ad festum sancti Michaelis ad scaccarium meum in puram [c]et liberam[c] et perpetuam elemosinam. Quare volo et firmiter precipio quod prenominati monachi unam marcam auri habeant de me et de heredibus meis singulis annis sicut prescriptum est absque omni molestia et difficultate que eis inde fieri possit. Testibus:[d] Stephano Ridell(o) cancellario meo, Waltero de Dunestanvilla, Willelmo de Cahaign(es), et multis aliis.

a-a et cetera *B,C*　　　　　　　　　　*b* et *B,C*
c-c Interlined in *A*　　　　　　　　　*d B,C* end

For the date of this gift, see 'Annales Radingenses Posteriores', 401. For John's confirmation of the gift as king, see no. 46. For the gift of the Hand of St James to Reading, see no. 5.

43　Precept by John count of Mortain to his steward of the honour of Gloucester to cause Reading Abbey to have 1 mark of gold annually from his revenues of Tewkesbury, in order to make a cover for the Hand of St James. Witnesses [omitted]　　　　[*c.* 1192]

B f 35r; C f 1or
Pd. *Mon. Ang.*, iv. 44 (no. xx); Patterson, *Gloucester Charters*, 151 (no. 165)

Probably of the same date as no. 42. The Hand of St James was deprived of its reliquary by Richard I in 1189 (see no. 46).

44　*Precept by John count of Mortain to Robert de Fern' and master Swein to assign to the abbot of Reading annually in the manor of Faringdon 1 mark of gold which he owes annually to the abbey*　　　　[1192 × 99]

B f 35r; C f 1or
Pd. *Mon. Ang.*, iv. 44 (no. xxi)

Iohannes comes Moret(onii) dilectis et fidelibus suis Roberto de Fern' et magistro Suano, salutem. Precipio vobis quod assignetis abbati de Rading(ia) ad recipiend(am) singulis annis in manerio de Ferendon(a) unam marcam auri quam ecclesie sancte Marie Rading(ensi) singulis annis debeo et computabitur vobis. T(estibus).

This must be subsequent to no. 43, since the obligation continued to rest upon Faringdon after John became king—see *PR 2 John*, 128, which includes, among the disbursements from Faringdon in the Honour of Gloucester for 1200, 10 marks for Reading *ad operationem capsule manus sancti Iacobi*.

45　*Notification by King John, addressed generally, that Henry I founded Reading Abbey with all immunity [etc.] that the royal power can confer upon an abbey, and precept that the abbey shall hold its possessions with specified liberties and immunities*　　　　20 June 1199

A f 30r-v; B f 33r-v; C ff 8v-9r

Iohannes dei gratia rex*a* Angl(ie) dominus Hib(ernie) dux Norm(annie) Aquit(anie) comes Andeg(avie) archiepiscopis,

episcopis, abbatibus, comitibus, baronibus, iustic(iariis), vicecomitibus, prepositis, ministris et omnibus baill(ivis) et fidelibus suis, salutem.[b] Sciatis H(enricum) regem avum H(enrici) patris nostri pro salute anime sue et omnium antecessorum et successorum suorum abbatiam de Rading(ia) construxisse eidemque abbatie omnem immunitatem et potestatem, quietantiam et libertatem dedisse quam regia potestas alicui abbatie conferre potest. Quare volumus et firmiter precipimus quod abbas et monachi de Rading(ia) omnia tenementa sua tam laica quam ecclesiastica quecumque in presenti habent vel in posterum emptione vel donatione fidelium habituri sunt bene et in pace, libere et quiete teneant in omnibus locis et in omnibus rebus ubicumque fuerint quieta de Danegeldis et de omnibus geldis et sciris[c] et hundredis et omnibus placitis et querelis et auxiliis et scutagiis et de hydagiis et summagiis et cariagiis et navigiis et clausuris, de pontium et castrorum edificatione, de conductu thesauri et omni operatione, de tributis et lastagiis et stallagiis, de thethinpeni,[d] tinpeni, de summonitionibus, de assisis et superassisis et de omnibus forisfactis quacumque occasione emerserint, de assartis et nemorum wastis. Nullus vero de forestariis regis quicquam se intromittat de boscis abbatis et monachorum qui sunt intra forestam, sed omnem potestatem et libertatem quam habet rex in boscis suis habeant abbas et monachi in omnibus boscis qui ad abbatiam pertinent ubicumque fuerint. Habeantque abbas et monachi warennas suas ubicumque eis placuerit in terra sua liberas et quietas ad capiend(um) capream, leporem et vulpem. Nullus dominicos canes abbatis et monachorum espaaltare[e] cogat, verum canes hominum suorum intra forestam manentium abbas et monachi espaaltari faciant. Et si que mercie hinc inde provenerint, abbas et monachi eas soli habeant. Sintque abbas et monachi de Rading(ia) et homines eorum et res ipsorum quieti de hidagiis et theloneis et omnibus exactionibus et consuetudinibus in nundinis et foris quorumcumque sint in omnibus locis et in omnibus rebus per totam Angl(iam) et Norm(anniam). Habeant autem abbas et monachi omnem iustitiam de assaltu[f] et murdris et sanguinis effusione et pacis infractione et thesauri inventione, quicquid ad regiam pertinet potestatem. Mercie nulle quacumque occasione de abbate [g][et monachis][g] vel de tenementis vel de[h] hominibus eorum exigantur nec exacte solvantur, sed omnia que eorum sunt ita quieta sint et libera sicut nostra propria et soli abbati et monachis de omnibus respondentia. De assisis etiam et recognitionibus que per preceptum regis vel iustic' eius fieri mandantur de terris et hominibus que sunt in baill(iv)a[i] abbatis et monachorum habeant abbas et monachi curiam suam, quod si de his iustitiam facere neglexerint, rex fieri compellat in curia abbatis et monachorum de Rading(ia), ita ut in nullo libertatem Radingensis ecclesie minuat. Nemo homines abbatis et monachorum [*f30v*] absque eorum licentia ad aliam quam abbatis curiam propter aliquam recognitionem venire faciat. Habeant autem abbas et monachi de hominibus suis et de tota possessione sua et de alienis in ea forisfacientibus vel ibi cum forisfacto interceptis hundreda et placita omnia cum socch(a)*ʲ* et sacch(a)*ᵏ* et toll' et theam et infangenthef*ˡ* et utfangenthef*ᵐ* in omnibus locis cum omnibus causis que sunt vel esse possunt. Hanc monasterio de Rading(ia) et quantamcumque rex donare potest concedimus et confirmamus liberam immunitatem et immunem libertatem quam regibus in Anglia regnaturis post nos servandam commendamus. Que omnia pater noster rex H(enricus) eis donavit et carta sua confirmavit. Testibus:*ⁿ* W(illelmo) Lond(oniensi), E(ustachio) Eliensi et G(odefrido) Wint(oniensi) episcopis, Willelmo Marescallo comite de Penbroc, W(illelmo) comite Sarr(esburie), W(illelmo) Briwer', Hugone Bard(ulf). Dat' per manum H(uberti) Cant(uariensis) archiepiscopi cancellarii nostri, apud Soram xx. die Iunii, anno regni nostri primo.

ᵃ Om. in B	*ᵇ⁻ᵇ* et cetera *B,C*
ᶜ schyr' *B,C*	*ᵈ* teþingpeni *B,C*
ᵉ Sic in Ms, ? rectius espaaltari	*ᶠ Insert* et furtis *B,C*
ᵍ⁻ᵍ Om. in A; vel monachis *B,C*	*ʰ Om. in B,C*
ⁱ balliva *C*	*ʲ* socca *B,C*
ᵏ sacca *B,C*	*ˡ* infangenetheof *B,C*
ᵐ utfong' *B,C*	*ⁿ B,C end*

The text follows very closely that of no. 21. The rubric of B calls it a 'portable' charter, and the rubrics of A and B note that there were two copies—*Hec duplex est.* In the margin of A there is written in a much later hand the note: *Iste dedit nobis capud Phylippi Apostoli.* The earliest surviving Charter Roll of John's reign begins with charters given on 14 July 1199; the present charter may have been enrolled, however, on the missing roll, of which one membrane only survives containing charters issued at Shoreham on 17 and 18 June 1199 (see *Rot. Chart.*, xxxix-xl).

46 *Gift in free alms by King John to Reading Abbey, inspired by the Hand of St James there, of 1 mark of gold annually at the Exchequer at Westminster* 11 Mar. 1200

A f31r-v; B f35r; C f10r
Pd. *Mon. Ang.*, iv. 44 (no. xxii); *Rot. Chart.*, 37 (from Charter Roll)

Iohannes dei gratia rex Angl(ie) *ᵃ*dominus Hibern(ie) dux Norm(annie) Aquit(anie) comes Andeg(avie) archiepiscopis, episcopis, abbatibus, comitibus, baronibus, iustic(iariis), vicecomitibus et omnibus baill(ivis) et fidelibus suis, salutem.*ᵃ* Sciatis nos, pro salute anime nostre et pro [anima]*ᵇ* regis Henrici patris nostri et pro animabus antecessorum et successorum nostrorum et intuitu manus [beati]*ᵇ* Iacobi apostoli quam Ricardus rex frater noster in itinere

peregrinationis*c* sue denudavit, que in conventuali ecclesia sancte
Marie de Rading(ia) posita est, dedisse et concessisse et presenti
carta confirmasse deo et eidem ecclesie et monachis ibidem deo
servientibus unam marcam auri de reditu singulis annis recipiendi
de nobis et heredibus nostris ad festum sancti Michaelis ad scaccarium de Westmon(asterio) in puram et liberam et perpetuam elemosinam. Quare volumus et firmiter precipimus quod prenominati
monachi unam marcam auri habeant de nobis et heredibus nostris
singulis annis sicut predictum est absque omni molestia et difficultate
que eis inde fieri possit. Testibus:*d* Willelmo Maresc(allo) comite
[*f31v*] Penbroc, Willelmo comite Sar(esburie), Roberto filio
Rog(eri), Hugone Bardulf'. Dat' per manus S(imonis) Well(ensis)
archidiaconi et Iohannis de Gray archidiaconi de Cliveland', apud
Wudestok' xi. die Marcii, anno regni nostri primo.

a-a et cetera *B,C*
c A has peregnationis

b Hole in Ms in A, supplied from B,C
d BC end

This is John's confirmation as king of his earlier gift as count of Mortain (no. 42).

47 *Confirmation by King John to Reading Abbey of the churches of Wargrave and Cholsey given by Henry I*   27 June 1202

A f31r; B f35v; C f10v

Iohannes dei gratia *a*rex Angl(ie) dominus Hibern(ie) dux
Norm(annie) Aquit(anie) comes Andeg(avie) archiepiscopis, episcopis, abbatibus, comitibus, baronibus, iustic(iariis), vicecomitibus
et omnibus baill(ivis) et fidelibus suis, salutem.*a* Sciatis nos concessisse et presenti carta confirmasse abbatie de Rading(ia) et abbati et
monachis ibidem deo servientibus rationabilem donationem quam
H(enricus) rex avus patris nostri eis fecit de duabus ecclesiis de
Weregrave et de Chelsea.*b* Quare volumus et firmiter precipimus
quod predicti abbas et monachi habeant eas et teneant bene et in
pace cum terris et decimis et omnibus rebus eisdem ecclesiis pertinentibus, sicut carta H(enrici) regis avi patris nostri rationabiliter
testatur.*c* Testibus:*d* W(illelmo) Marescallo comite Penbroc, Willelmo comite Sar(esburie), Roberto de Haracurt, Petro de Pra-
tell(is). Dat' per manum Simonis archidiaconi Well(ensis), apud
Rothomagum xxvii. die Iunii, regni nostri anno .iiii.

a-a et cetera *B,C*
c C ends

b Cheals' *B,C*
d B ends

Given two days before the general confirmation (no. 48), which includes these
churches. The Charter Roll for 4 John has not survived.

48 *Confirmation by King John to Reading Abbey of its possessions given by Henry I or the Empress—viz.*, *Reading, Cholsey and Leominster with their churches, a mint and moneyer at Reading, Thatcham, the churches of Wargrave and Hanborough, Rowington and its church, land at Wigston [Parva], Whitsbury and its church, land in Houghton [Conquest], land in Southampton, the land which Robert de Ferrers had in Reading, Blewbury, [East] Hendred, the church of Berkeley with its churches and chapels, the church of Stanton [Harcourt] amd the church of Thatcham—and of its liberties*   29 June 1202

A ff 29r–30r; B ff 33v–34v; C f 9r–v
Pd. *Cal. Chart. R.*, i. 15–16 (in inspeximus by Henry III, see below, no. 55)

Iohannes dei gratia *a*rex Angl(ie) dominus Hib(ernie) dux Norm(annie) Aquit(anie) comes Andeg(avie) omnibus archiepiscopis, episcopis, abbatibus, comitibus, baronibus, iustic(iariis), vicecomitibus, ministris et omnibus fidelibus suis totius Angl(ie), salutem.*a* Sciatis nos concessisse et in perpetuam elemosinam presenti carta confirmasse deo et sancte Marie et monachis de Rading(ia) omnes terras et tenuras et elemosinas quas rex Henricus avus patris nostri eis in elemosinam dedit et concessit. Videlicet ipsam Rading(iam) et Chealseiam et Leominist(riam)*b* cum omnibus appendiciis suis cum silvis et agris et pasturis, cum pratis et aquis, cum molendinis et piscariis, cum ecclesiis et capellis et cimiteriis et oblationibus et decimis, cum moneta et uno monetario apud Rading(iam). Et Thacheam*c* et ecclesiam de Weregrava,*d* et ecclesiam de Haneberga, et Rokinton(am)*e* cum ecclesia eiusdem ville, et Wigestanam que fuit terra Willelmi elemosinarii, et in Wiltescir(a)*f* Wichebyr(iam) cum ecclesia eiusdem ville, et in Bedefordescir(a)*g* terram Albodi de Hocton(a), et terram Roberti sacerdotis de Hamton(a), et terram quam Robertus de Ferrariis habuit in villa de Rading(ia). [*f 29v*] Preterea concedimus eis et confirmamus quicquid domina nostra Imperatrix eis in elemosinam dedit et concessit, videlicet Bleobir(iam)*h* cum omnibus appendiciis suis, et Henredam,*i* et ecclesiam de Berkel(eia) cum ecclesiis et capellis et decimis et ceteris suis appendiciis, et ecclesiam de Stanton(a)*j* cum suis appendiciis, et ecclesiam de Thacheam*c* cum omnibus suis pertinentiis. Nulla autem persona parva vel magna per debitum seu per consuetudinem aut per violentiam aliquid ab hominibus et terris et possessione Rading(ensis) monasterii exigat, non equitationem sive expeditionem, non pontium vel castrorum edificationem, non veicula,*k* non summagia, non vectigalia, non navigia, non opera, non tributa, non xenia, sed sint monachi Rading(enses) et familia eorum et res ipsorum absoluti ab omni geldo et theloneo et alia qualibet consuetudine in terris et aquis, in transitibus pontium et maris portuum per totam Angl(iam) et Norm(anniam). Sintque abbatis et monachorum eius de hominibus suis et de tota possessione[l] et de alienis in ea forisfacientibus vel ibi cum forisfacto interceptis hundreda et placita omnia cum socc(a) et sacc(a) et toll' et theam et infangenthef[m] et utfangenthef[n] et hamsocna infra burgum et extra burgum, in viis et semitis et in omnibus locis cum omnibus causis que sunt vel esse possunt. Habeantque abbas et monachi Rading(enses) in tota possessione sua omnem iustitiam de assaltu et furtis et murdris et sanguinis effusione et pacis infractione quantum ad regiam pertinet potestatem et de omnibus forisfactis. Quod si abbas et monachi de hiis iustitiam facere neglexerint, rex fieri compellat ita ut in nullo libertatem Radingensis ecclesie minuat. Veniantque ad hundreda de Radingia et de Leomenist(ria)[o] homines circumiacentium maneriorum secundum consuetudinem temporum precedentium, qui si quando vocati fuerint ad iustitiam venire contempserint, rex inde forisfactum accipiat et venire et satisfacere compellat. Statuimus autem tam ecclesiastice quam et regie prospectu potestatis ut decedente abbate Radingensi omnis possessio monasterii ubicumque fuerit remaneat integra et libera cum omni iure et consuetudine sua in manu et dispositione prioris et[p] capituli Radingensis. Hoc autem ideo statuit rex Henricus avus patris nostri et nos statutum illud concedimus et confirmamus et ut in perpetuum servetur precipimus, quia abbas Radingensis non habet proprios redditus sed communes cum fratribus. Qui autem deo annuente canonica electione abbas substitutus fuerit non cum suis secularibus consanguineis seu quibuslibet aliis elemosinas monasterii male utendo disperdat, sed pauperibus et peregrinis et hospitibus suscipiendis curam gerat. Terras censuales non [ad][q] feodum donet nec faciat milites nisi in sacra veste Christi, in qua parvulos suscipere modeste caveat, maturos autem seu discretos tam laicos quam clericos provide suscipiat. Nemo de possessione Rading(ensis) monasterii feodaliter absolutum aliquid teneat, sed ad censum annuum et servitium abbati et monachis debitum. In abbatis et monachorum domo Rading(ensium) et possessione nullus per hereditatem officium teneat, sed in arbitrio abbatis et monachorum de transmutandis prepositis seu aliis quibuslibet officiariis causa consistat. Hanc monasterio Rading(ensi) et omnibus ad ipsum pertinentibus in perpetuum concedimus et confirmamus liberam immunitatem et immunem libertatem quam regibus post nos in Anglia regnaturis causa dei commendamus[r] servandam, ut eis conservet deus eternam. Siquis autem hoc nostre donationis decretum infringere seu minuere vel transmutare scienter presumpserit, summus iudex omnium contrahat eum et eradicet cum sua posteritate ut permaneat sine aliqua hereditate in clade et fame. Quisquis vero Radingense monasterium cum pre[*for*]fata libertate servaverit, altissimus qui dominatur in regno hominum bonis om-

nibus stabiliat eum et servet in evum. Et volumus et firmiter precipimus quod predicti monachi de Rading(ia) hec omnia predicta
cum omnibus libertatibus et liberis consuetudinibus et quietantiis
predictis in perpetuam elemosinam habeant et teneant ita bene et
in pace et libere et quiete et integre sicut carta predicti regis Henrici
avi patris nostri testatur et sicut carta domine nostre Imperatricis eis
testatur et sicut carta H(enrici) regis patris nostri rationabiliter testatur.[s] Hiis testibus: Waltero Rotomag(ensi) archiepiscopo,
W(illelmo) Marescallo comite de Pembroc, W(illelmo) comite
Sarr(esburie), Roberto de Haracurt, Petro de Pratell(is), Fulcone de
Cantilup(o). Dat' per manum S(imonis) Well(ensis) archidiaconi,
apud Rothomag(um) xxix. die Iunii, anno regni nostri .iiii.

[a-a] et cetera B,C
[c] Tacheham B,C
[e] Insert in Warwiksir' B, in Warwicsyre C
[g] Bedefordsir' B,C
[i] Hanredam B, Handredam C
[k] vehicula B,C
[m] infangenetheof B,C
[o] Limin' B,C
[q] Om. in A, supplied from B,C
[s] B ends with T', C ends

[b] Liministr' B,C
[d] Weregrave B,C
[f] Wiltesir' B,C
[h] Bleobur' C
[j] Staunton' C
[l] Insert sua B,C
[n] utfang' B,C
[p] Insert monachorum B,C
[r] A has comendamus

The Charter Roll for 4 John has not survived. The text printed in *Cal. Chart. R.*, i,
is dated 19 June. This charter follows almost exactly the text of Henry II's confirmation (no. 18). It formed the basis of all later royal confirmations by Inspeximus (see
nos. 55, 102, 109, 116 n. 1).

49 *Grant by King John to Abbot Elias and his successors and the monks of
Reading of an annual fair at Reading on the vigil and feast of St Philip and
St James [1 May] and the two days following, provided that it be not to the
damage of neighbouring fairs*   1 May 1205

A f 30v; B f 35v; C f 10v
Pd. *Rot. Chart.*, 148 (from Charter Roll)

Iohannes dei gratia [a]rex Angl(ie) dominus Hibern(ie) dux
Norm(annie) Aquit(anie) comes Andeg(avie) archiepiscopis, episcopis, abbatibus, comitibus, baronibus, iustic(iariis), vicecomitibus,
prepositis, ministris et omnibus baillivis et fidelibus suis, salutem.[a]
Sciatis nos concessisse et hac carta nostra confirmasse deo et ecclesie
beate Marie de Rading(ia) et Elye[b]abbati et successoribus suis et
monachis ibidem deo servientibus quod habeant in perpetuum unam
feriam singulis annis apud Rading(iam) per quatuor dies duraturam, scilicet vigilia beatorum apostolorum Philippi et Iacobi et[c]
die et duobus diebus sequentibus, ita tamen quod non sit ad nocu-
mentum vicinarum feriarum. Quare volumus et firmiter precipimus

quod predictus abbas de Rading(ia) et successores sui et monachi ibidem [deo]^d servientes habeant et teneant predictam feriam in perpetuum bene et in pace et integre cum omnibus libertatibus et liberis consuetudinibus ad huiusmodi feriam pertinentibus sicut predictum est.^{e} Testibus:^{f} R(anulfo) comite Cestr(ie), War(ino) filio Geroldi, Henrico Biset, Hugone de Lascy, Petro de Stok'. Dat' per manum Ioscelini de Well(es), apud Rading(iam) prima die Maii, anno regni nostri vi.

$^{a-a}$ et cetera *B,C*	^{b} Hel' *B,C*
^{c} *Om. in B,C*	^{d} *Om. in A, supplied from B,C and* Rot. Chart.
^{e} *C ends*	^{f} *B ends*

This grant was associated with the same king's gift to Reading of the Head of St Philip; see A f 7r: *Iohannes rex Anglie dedit nobis caput Philippi apostoli venerandum. Et nobis nundinas ipso die concessit habere.* See also no. 230 n. In fact, the king probably gave only part of the Head of St Philip, whose relics with others were brought to the West after the sacking of Constantinople in 1204 (D. Bethell, 'The making of a twelfth-century relic collection', *Studies in Church History*, viii (1971), 64 and n. 1).

49a Notes of the following:
  (i) charter testimonial by King John for the receipt of certain charters;
  (ii) another for the receipt of three letters patent formerly deposited in the abbey (*in deposito nostro*).

B f 35v

These are possibly the letters patent issued, respectively, on 19 June 1213 and 17 June 1207 (*Rot. Lit. Pat.*, i. 100, 73).

50 *Restoration in free alms by King John to the abbot and monks of Reading of what was lacking to them of the hundred of Reading, viz., the foreign hundred, which was in the King's hand and which Henry I gave to them*

24 Feb. 1208

A f 30v; A f 31v (deleted); B f 34v; C f 10r
Pd. *Mon. Ang.*, iv. 44 (no. xviii); *Rot. Chart.*, 175 (from Charter Roll)

Iohannes dei gratia ^{a}rex Angl(ie) dominus Hibern(ie) dux Norm(annie) Aquit(anie) comes Andeg(avie) archiepiscopis, episcopis, abbatibus, comitibus, baronibus, iustic(iariis), vicecomitibus,^{b} ministris et omnibus baill(ivis) et fidelibus suis, salutem.^{a} Sciatis nos reddidisse, dedisse, concessisse et hac^c carta nostra confirmasse deo et ecclesie sancte^d Marie de Rading(ia) et abbati et monachis ibidem deo servientibus id quod eis defuit de hundredo suo de Rading(ia), scilicet totum forinsecum hundredum quod fuit in manu

nostra, sicut ius suum cum omnibus pertinentiis, sectis, consuetudinibus et libertatibus suis, quod H(enricus) rex avus regis H(enrici)
patris nostri eis dedit et carta sua confirmavit, habendum et tenendum in liberam puram et perpetuam elemosinam in perpetuum.
Quare volumus et firmiter precipimus quod predicti abbas et monachi habeant et teneant totum predictum hundredum libere et^e
quiete, integre, plenarie et honorifice cum omnibus pertinentiis, sectis, consuetudinibus et libertatibus ad predictum hundredum pertinentibus in perpetuum, sicut predictum est.^f His testibus: P(etro)
Wint(oniensi), I(ocelino) Bath(oniensi) episcopis, Willelmo Briwer',
Roberto de Veteri Ponte, Simone de Pateshull', Willelmo de Can-
tilup(o), Iacobo de Pot(erna), Ricardo de Riveriis, Petro de Maulay,
Gaufr(edo) Luterell'. Dat' per manum H(ugonis) de Well(es) archidiaconi, apud Wint(oniam) xxiiii. die Februarii, anno regni nostri ix.

^a-a et cetera B,C	^b Insert prepositis A f31v
^c Insert presenti B,C, A f31v	^d beate B,C, A f31v
^e Om. in B,C, A f31v	^f B,C end with T', A f31v ends with Testibus dominis

The rubrics of A f30v, B, C state that there were two copies of this charter (Hec duplex
est). In view of the slight variations in reading, the deleted text on A f31v and the
text in B and C may be of the second copy. The Charter Roll entry is dated 23 Feb.

51 Notification by Geoffrey fitz Peter, earl of Essex, to the sheriff
of Berkshire and his fellow justices itinerant in Berkshire that, the
charters of Reading Abbey having been read before him and Peter
[des Roches], bishop of Winchester, and others, both magnates and
barons of the Exchequer, it was judged that the abbey ought to
have its court of the foreign hundred of Reading which the king has
returned to it, for all assizes, recognitions, pleas of the Crown and
all manner of liberties and customs; and mandate to permit the
abbey to have the same and not to impede it regarding these
liberties.   3 Aug. 1210

A f29r; B f4r
Pd. Stenton, *English Justice*, 212 (with transl., 213); *Memoranda Roll 1 John*, lxxv;
   Coates, *Hist. of Reading*, App. VI

T(este) domino P(etro) Winton(iensi) episcopo, apud Westm-
(onasterium) iii. die Augusti, anno regni regis Iohannis xii.

This was issued by Geoffrey fitz Peter as justiciar. It does not relate to a general eyre
in the county. For discussion, see Stenton, 105; *Memoranda Roll 1 John*, lvi n. 1, lxxv.

52 Notification by William the king's treasurer, William archdeacon of Taunton, William archdeacon of Huntingdon and the

other barons of the Exchequer to the justices itinerant in Berkshire that, having inspected the charters of Reading Abbey, they are in no doubt that the abbey ought to have its court for assizes and recognitions made by order of the king or his justiciar (*iusticiar'*) in the foreign hundred of Reading which the king has restored to the abbey, upon which matter the justices were in doubt because there has been no eyre in those parts since the hundred was restored. The justices are advised to allow the same liberties in the foreign hundred as in the abbey's other lands and bailiwicks. *Valete*

[*c.* 3 Aug. 1210]

A f 29r
Pd. Stenton, *English Justice*, 212, 214 (with transl., 213, 215)

Certainly of about the same date as no. 51 (Stenton, 105). Unlike no. 51, this was not entered in B, despite Lady Stenton's reference.

53   *Recognition before Richard [Poore], bishop of Salisbury, and his fellow justices-in-eyre in Berkshire that Reading Abbey is in full seisin of the foreign hundred of Reading and has all assizes, recognitions, pleas of the Crown and all manner of liberties as in its demesne lands. The hundred was given to the abbey by Henry I, given up by one of the abbots during the Anarchy and restored to the abbey by King John, after which, a dispute arising in the next eyre to take place [in the county], judgement was given at the Exchequer in favour of the abbey that it should have its court of the foreign hundred for all assizes, recognitions, pleas of the Crown and liberties, as the king so ordered by his letters*   [Jan. × Feb. 1219]

B f 4r
Pd. (transl. of greater part) H. M. Cam, *Liberties and Communities in Medieval England* (Cambridge, 1944), 72

Recognitum fuit coram venerabili patre Ricardo episcopo Sar(esburiensi) et sociis suis iustic(iariis) itinerantibus in comitatu Berk' quod abbas et monachi Rading(enses) sunt in plenaria seisina de forinseco hundredo de Rading(ia), de quo habent et habere debent omnes assisas et recognitiones et omnia placita corone et omnimodas libertates sicut in omnibus dominicis terris suis. Istud enim hundredum cum omnibus predictis libertatibus eis datum fuit a fundatore suo in prima fundatione ecclesie sue, sicut carta eiusdem fundatoris sui et carte regum aliorum Anglie que ibi vise et lecte fuerunt testantur, et illud semper pacifice habuerunt usque ad guerram inter regem S(tephanum) et regem H(enricum). Et tunc quidam abbas eiusdem domus sponte dimisit illud. Postmodum vero dominus rex Johannes reddidit eis dictum hundredum cum dictis libertatibus sicut ius suum per cartam que ibi visa et lecta fuit et plenariam seisinam eis inde fecit. Unde, cum aliquando quedam contentio mota fuisset coram iustic(iariis) cito post itinerantibus propter novam disseisinam super quibusdam libertatibus ad predictum hundredum pertinentibus, iudicium predictis abbati et conventui datum fuit ad scaccarium coram P(etro) Wint(oniensi) episcopo tunc iustic(iario) et multis aliis comitibus [et]*a* baronibus cum baronibus de scaccario quod abbas et monachi de Rading(ia) habere debent curiam suam de forinseco hundredo et de omnibus assisis et recognitionibus et omnibus placitis corone et de omnibus libertatibus ad dominum regem pertinentibus. Et ita precepit dominus rex per litteras suas quod predicti abbas et monachi de Rading(ia) habeant predictum hundredum cum omnibus predictis libertatibus bene et in pace. Et eo modo per preceptum suum et per cartas dictorum abbatis et monachorum novas et veteras et per iudicium scaccarii usi semper fuerunt libertatibus illis, ita quod nullus vicecomes quicquam se de predictis intromisit postquam predicta libertas eis reddita fuit, ut predictum est. Hoc etiam recognovit comitatus de Berk' coram predictis iust(iciariis) quod in tali seisina fuerunt et talibus libertatibus usi sunt. Et propter hoc dicti iustic(iarii) seisinam suam de predictis libertatibus dicte ecclesie de Rading(ia) bene et in pace dimiserunt.

Rubric: De forinseco hundredo in manu regis aliquando dimisso et iterum reddito et in rotul' scaccarii notato

a Supplied

The justices were appointed in 1218 (*Pat. R. 1216-25*, 207) and held the main session of their eyre at Reading in Jan. and Feb. 1219 (Clanchy, *Berks. Eyre of 1248*, xciii). On 10 July 1218, possibly in anticipation of the forthcoming eyre, the sheriff of Berkshire was instructed to enquire with John of Wickenholt (a former sheriff and one of the eyre justices in 1219) and others of the county what liberties the abbey ought to have in the county, and to allow the same (*Rot. Lit. Claus.*, i. 365). The present recognition refers to judgement at the Exchequer before Peter des Roches as justiciar, but no such judgement is known and the reference is probably to that before Geoffrey fitz Peter and the bishop (no. 51), especially since that follows immediately in the cartulary. For further discussion, see Cam, *Liberties and Communities*, 71-3; Clanchy, *Berks. Eyre of 1248*, xxx.

54 Licence by King Henry III to the prior and convent of Reading to elect an abbot in place of Abbot Simon, whose death has been reported to the king by Ralph the sacrist and Thomas of Osney, monks of Reading   16 Feb. 1226

B f 37r; C ff 11v-12r
Pd. *Pat. Rolls 1225-32*, 18 (from Patent Roll)

Teste me ipso apud Westm(onasterium) xvi. die Februarii, anno regni nostri x.[a]

[a] *The Patent Roll entry adds:* coram iusticiario et Bathoniensi et Sarresburiensi episcopis

Abbot Simon died 13 Feb. 1226 (D f 12r; *Rot. Lit. Claus.*, ii. 99).

55 Inspeximus and confirmation by King Henry III of King John's general confirmation [no. 48]   19 Feb. 1227

A ff 31v–32v; B f 36r; C ff 10v–11r
Pd. (cal. quoting John's charter in full) *Cal. Chart. R.*, i. 15–16 (from Charter Roll)

Hiis testibus:[a] [[b]Eustachio London(iensi), Petro Wynt(oniensi), Jocel(ino) Bathon(iensi), Ricardo Sar(esburiensi) episcopis, Huberto de Burgo comite Kant(ie) justiciario nostro, Willelmo de Forz comite Albemarl', Humfredo de Buun comite Herford', Willelmo de Eineford', Ricardo de Arg(enteom), Henrico de Capella, et aliis.[b] 'Dat' per manum venerabilis patris Radulfi Cicestr(ensis) episcopi et cancellarii nostri apud Westm(onasterium) xix. die Februarii, anno regni nostri xi.[c]]

[a] *A ends; B,C have* T' *et cetera, resuming at first* c
[b–b] *Supplied from Edward II's inspeximus* (no. 102)
[c–c] *B and C only*

The cartulary rubrics state that there were 3 copies of this charter (*Hec triplex est* A; *Hec triplicata est* B,C).

56 Notification by King Henry III, addressed generally, that Henry I founded Reading Abbey with all immunity [etc.] that the royal power can confer upon an abbey, and precept that the abbey shall hold its possessions with specified liberties and immunities
19 Feb. 1227

A ff 32v–33v; B f 36r–v; C f 11r–v; D ff 18r–19r; E ff 49r–50r
Pd. (cal.) *Cal. Chart. R.*, i. 20 (from Charter Roll)

[a]Hiis testibus:[b] '[E(ustachio) London(iensi), J(ocelino) Bathon(iensi), R(icardo) Sar(esburiensi) episcopis, H(uberto) de Burgo comite Kant(ie) justiciario nostro, W(illelmo) de Forz comite Albemarl', H(umfredo) de Buhun comite Herford', W(illelmo) de Eyneford, Ricardo de Argenteom, Henrico de Capella, et aliis. Dat' per manum venerabilis patris Rad(ulfi) Cicestr(ensis) episcopi et cancellarii nostri apud Westmonasterium decimo et nono die Februarii, anno regni nostri undecimo.][c]

[a] *B,C end with* T'
[b] *A ends, E ends with* et cetera
[c–c] *Supplied from D*

This is in effect a re-issue of John's charter (no. 45), which itself closely follows Henry II's (no. 21). The rubrics of B and C describe it as a 'portable' charter, and state that there were 2 copies.

57 Precept by King Henry III, addressed generally, that the men of Reading Abbey be quit of shires, hundreds, pleas, plaints, tolls, passage-money and carriage-money, and may sell and buy throughout England without toll. No one shall disturb them on pain of £10 forfeiture   19 Feb. 1227

A f 33v; B f 37r; C f 11v; E f 50v
Pd. (cal.) *Cal. Chart. R.*, i. 13, 14 (twice, from Charter Roll)

*a*Hiis testibus: E(ustachio) London(iensi), J(ocelino) Bathon(iensi), R(icardo) Sar(esburiensi) episcopis, H(uberto) de Burgo comite Cant(ie) justiciario nostro, Willelmo de Forz comite Albemarl', H(umfredo) de Boun comite Hereford', Willelmo de Eyneford', Ricardo de Argent(eom), Henrico de Capella, et aliis. *b*Dat' per manum venerabilis patris Rad(ulf)i Cicestr(ensis) episcopi, cancellarii nostri, apud Westm(onasterium) xix. die Februarii, anno regni nostri undecimo.*b*

a B,C end with T', but B has the dating clause in the margin; E ends
b-b B has this in the margin

This is in effect a re-issue of nos. 30, 36 and 40. Neither of the two copies on the Charter Roll has the same date as the Reading text, one being dated 17 Feb., the other 20 Feb.

58 Grant in free alms by King Henry III to Reading Abbey of 10 marks [of silver] to be received annually at Michaelmas at the king's Exchequer, in place of the 1 mark of gold annually given by King John. Witnesses [omitted]   [9 Apr. 1230]

B f 36v; C f 11v
Pd. *Mon. Ang.*, iv. 44 (no. xxiii); (cal.) *Cal. Chart. R.*, i. 116 (from Charter Roll)

The date is taken from the Charter Roll, the king being then at Reading. For King John's charter, see no. 46. 1 mark of gold was confirmed by Henry III in 1218 (*Rot. Lit. Claus.*, i. 381), but converted in the following year to 10 marks of silver (*ibid.*, 390). In 1226, 1228 and 1229 the writs to the treasurer and chamberlains of the Exchequer were for 9 marks (*ibid.*, ii. 143; *Cal. Liberate R. 1226–40*, 109, 149), but in 1230 and 1250 for 10 marks (nos. 59, 74 n.).

59 Writ *Liberate* by King Henry III to the treasurer and chamberlains [of the Exchequer] for the annual payment to Reading Abbey of 10 marks [of silver] in place of 1 mark of gold annually given by King John   9 Apr. 1230

B f 37r; C f 11v

Teste me ipso apud Rading(iam) ix. die Aprilis, anno regni nostri xiiii.

The rubrics say: *Hec duplex est.*

60 Licence by King Henry III [to the prior and convent of Reading] to elect an abbot in place of Abbot Adam [of Lathbury], whose death has been reported to the king by N., N. and N., monks of Reading.   8 Apr. 1238

B f 37r; C f 12r
Pd. (cal.) *Cal. Pat. R. 1232–47*, 215 (from Patent Roll)

Teste me ipso apud Theok(es)bir(iam) viii. die Aprilis, anno regni nostri xxii.

Adam of Lathbury died 6 Apr. 1238 (D f 13r)

61 Mandate by King Henry III to the treasurer and barons of the Exchequer to cause to be allowed to the abbot of Reading the liberty of amercements of his men as they were allowed in the king's and his predecessors' times by record of the rolls of the Exchequer

30 May 1241

A f 34r
Pd. *Close Rolls 1237–42*, 304 (from Close Roll)

Teste me ipso apud Westmonast(erium) iii. kl' Junii, anno regni nostri xxv.

62 *Request by King Henry III to the knights, free men and other tenants of Reading Abbey to assist the abbey in relieving its debts by giving a subsidy*   [c. 1242 × Mar. 1245]

B f 38r; C f 12v

Henricus dei gratia, et cetera, omnibus militibus, liberis hominibus et aliis tenentibus de abbatia de Rading(ia), salutem. In necessitate probatur amicus qui necessitatis temporibus libenter impartitur subsidium. Cum igitur, sicut pro certo intelleximus, abbatia Rading(ensis), quam inter ceteras abbatias regni nostri affectione diligimus speciali, tam ob hospitalitatis gratiam liberaliter petentibus impartitam quam ob alia multiplicia eiusdem domus negotia sit ere alieno non modicum onerata, nos egestati sue pio compatientes affectu universitati vestre duximus concedend' et dilectionem vestram de qua plenam reportamus fiduciam affectuose rogandam quatinus, intuitu precum nostrarum et ob favorem dilecti nobis in Christo abbatis predicte domus domini vestri, ad domum suam debitis exonerandam eidem liberaliter et competenter subvenire velitis, tale ei subsidium impendentes quod tam nos quam ipse liberalitatem vestram gaudere possimus prefate domui*a* profuisse, et ut tam nos quam prefatum dominum vestrum in negotiis vestris oportunis temporibus favorabiliores invenire merito debeatis. Cum specialibus actionibus gratiarum. T'.

a domini *C (in error)*

The date depends upon this being earlier than no. 63, which it immediately precedes in the cartularies.

63 *Letter by King Henry III to the same*a *regretting that they have not complied with his earlier request and repeating the same*

17 Mar. [1242 or 1245]

B f 38r; C f 12v

Henricus dei gratia, et cetera. Plenam de vobis optinuimus fiduciam quod preces regias vobis pro honore vestro et pro commodo dilecti nobis in Christo abbatis de Rading(ia) domini vestri nuper factas libenter exaudiretis, sed, sicut audivimus, in contrarium res est versa. Preces ipsas obaudistis et in nullo in hac parte nostre curastis annuere voluntati. Verum, ne adhuc super hoc noster animus moveatur, sperantes de vobis quod tam nobis quam prefato domino vestro adhuc optemperare velitis, iterato vos monendos et rogandos duximus cum affectu quatinus intuitu precum nostrarum prefato domino vestro ad domum suam exonerandam tale subsidium impendatis quod ob favorem quem gerimus erga ecclesiam Rading(ensem) nos in negotiis vestris favorabiles invenire merito debeatis, et ne, si secus egeritis, nos ad motum animi nostri vos provocare contingat, quod quidem nollemus. Immo potius pro gratia vestra vobis mallemus impendere gratias speciales. Teste me ipso apud Sanctum Edmundum xvii. die Marcii.

a As indicated by the rubrics

The king was at Bury St Edmunds on 17 Mar. only in the years 1242 and 1245 (*Cal. Pat. R. 1232-47*, 277, 449).

64 Notification by King Henry III that he has received from Abbot Richard [I] of Reading 100 marks which the abbot had promised him in aid for his crossing to Gascony. Letters patent

25 Apr. 1242

B f 37v; C f 12r

Teste me ipso apud Rading(iam) xxv. die Aprilis, anno regni nostri xxvi.

Cf. *Close Rolls 1237-42*, 420-1. The abbot was Richard of Chichester, 1238-62.

65 *Judgement by the archbishop of York [Walter de Gray, acting as Regent] and the king's council that the abbot of Reading be allowed his liberties as well for fines before judgement as for other amercements, since the abbot has his court in such manner that the justices-in-eyre at Reading enter his court and hold it with his steward* [prob. Nov. 1242]

B f6r

Consideratum est per dominum Eborac(ensem) et alios de consilio domini regis, anno xxvii, quod libertates abbatis de Rading(ia) ei allocentur tam de finibus ante iudicium quam de aliis amerciamentis, eo quod idem abbas habet curiam suam ita quod iusticiarii itinerantes apud Rading(iam) intrant curiam ipsius abbatis et tenent curiam illam cum senescall(o) ipsius abbatis ad videndum quod iustitia omnibus exhibeatur.

Rubric: In memorand' anno xxvii. In termino sancti Michaelis. In quarto rotulo

This decision is entered on L.T.R. Memoranda Roll, PRO E368/14, m. 4. It is undated but preceded on the roll by an entry dated 18 Nov. 1242. The judgement was no doubt called forth by difficulties or objections experienced in the Berks. eyre of Oct.-Nov. 1241. For further discussion, see Clanchy, *Berks. Eyre of 1248*, xxxi, xxxviii.

66 Restoration by King Henry III to the abbot of Reading of all his liberties which were seized into the king's hand on account of homicides and other serious transgressions committed by his men in 28 Henry III. Letters patent. Witness [omitted]   [1244]

B f38r; C f12r-v

The abbot's liberty was taken into the king's hand 4 May, 1244—writ to the sheriff of Berks. (*Close Rolls 1242-47*, 181)—but recovered by the abbot before 27 Oct. 1244 by making a fine of £100 for the homicides and other transgressions of his men in Berks. (*Rotulorum Originalium ... Abbreviatio* (Record Comm., 1805), i. 5). See also Clanchy, *Berks. Eyre of 1248*, xxxviii n. 10.

67 Mandate by King Henry III to Roger of Thirkleby (*Turkeby*) and his fellow justices-in-eyre at Reading to cause to be made and delivered to the abbot and convent of Reading an estreat of amercements touching their liberty; no estreat is to be sent to the Exchequer   18 July 1248

A f34r; B f7r
Pd. cf. *Close Rolls 1247–51*, 65

Teste me ipso apud Westm(onasterium) xviii. die Julii, anno regni nostri xxxii.

The Close Roll entry, which is not a full copy, is dated 17 July and contains a few details which do not exactly coincide with the text in the Reading cartularies. Reference to the writ was made on the roll of the 1248 eyre in Berks. (Clanchy, *Berks. Eyre of 1248*, 175). Cf. *Close Rolls 1259–61*, 358; and below, no. 90.

68 *Precept by King Henry III to the sheriff of Berkshire that, whereas the men of Reading were summoned before the king to show warrant for the liberties which they say they have by grant of King Edward [the Confessor] and which are contrary to the liberties of the abbot of Reading, and why they have used violence against the abbot's officers in the town of Reading; and whereas the said men came and were unable to show, except by their own voice, that they have any liberty unless through the abbot; the sheriff is not to permit the said men of Reading to assume any liberty over the abbot, but to maintain the abbot and his men and bailiffs in their liberties*   4 Feb. 1253

A f34v; B f165v
Pd. Coates, *Hist. of Reading*, App. VII

H(enricus) dei gratia,[a] et cetera, vicecomiti Berkesir(e),[b] salutem. Scias quod, cum homines de Rading(ia) submoniti fuissent coram nobis ad ostendendum warentum libertatum suarum quas dicebant se habere per regem Edwardum, que quidem libertates ut dicebant contrarie fuerunt libertatibus quas abbas Rading(ensis)[c] habet per cartas H(enrici) regis avi [patris][d] domini J(ohannis) regis patris nostri, et quare venerunt armati in villa de Rading(ia)[e] et baillivos eiusdem abbatis vi repulerunt contra libertates[f] eiusdem abbatis quas[g] habet per cartas predecessorum nostrorum regum Anglie et per cartam nostram; et similiter quare de die et nocte in villa predicta posuerunt insidias baillivis et servientibus eiusdem abbatis et ipsos impedierunt quo minus [h]poterunt exercere[h] officium suum ex parte dicti abbatis eis iniunctum; dicti homines venerunt et nullam libertatem ostenderunt, neque per cartam neque alio modo nisi per simplicem vocem suam, per que aliquam libertatem habere debent nisi per ipsum abbatem dominum suum et per cartas quas dictus abbas habet de predecessoribus nostris; tibi precipimus quod non permittas dictos homines Rading(ie) occupare aliquam libertatem super dictum abbatem contra cartas suas, sed ipsum abbatem et homines suos et baillivos suos in libertatibus suis manuteneas et protegas, non permittens eis inde aliquam molestiam fieri. Et ita in negotio isto te geras quod pro defectu tui ad nos non perveniat

querimonia.   T(este)   Gileberto   de   Segrava,[i]   apud
Westm(onasterium) quarto die Februarii, anno regni nostri xxxvii.

[a] *Insert* rex Anglie *B*
[c] Radingie *B*
[e] Reding' *B*
[g] quam *B*
[i] Segrave *B*

[b] Bark' *B*
[d] *Supplied; B has here* nostri
[f] libertatem *B*
[h-h] exercere potuerunt *B*

For discussion of this episode, see Coates, *Hist. of Reading*, 49–50; *VCH Berks.*, iii. 344.
The text in B is a 15th-century copy.

69 *Final concord in the king's court at Westminster between Henry Wille
and Daniel Wolvesey, stewards of the gild of Reading, and the burgesses of
the same, seeking, and Abbot Richard [I] of Reading, defending, concerning
the customs and services which the abbot was demanding from the said burgesses
and which they do not recognize*   3 Feb. 1254

A ff 34v–35r; B f 166r–v; C ff 96v–97v; cf. F f 123r[1]
Pd. *Reading Records. Diary of the Corporation*, ed. J. M. Guilding (1892), i. 280–2
    (from the Corporation Diary); cf. English transl., prob. of 15th cent., Coates,
    Hist. of Reading, App. V

Hec est finalis concordia facta in curia domini regis apud
Westm(onasterium) in crastino Purificationis beate Marie, anno
regni regis Henrici filii regis Johannis tricesimo octavo, coram Henrico de Bathon(ia), Henrico de la Mare, Henrico de Bratton'[a] et
Nicholao de Turry,[b] justiciariis, Radulfo filio Nicholai et Bertranno
de Curiel tunc senesc(allis) et aliis domini regis fidelibus tunc ibi
presentibus, inter Henricum Wille et Danielem Wlveseie[c] tunc se-
nesc(allos) gilde de Rading(ia) et burgenses eiusdem ville, querentes,
et Ricardum abbatem de Rading(ia), deforc(iantem), de consuetudinibus et serviciis que idem abbas exigebat de predictis
burgensibus; unde iidem burgenses questi fuerunt quod predictus
abbas distrinxit eos ad placitandum alibi quam in gilda sua communi, et quod abstulit ab eis gildam suam mercandam cum pertinenciis, et preterea quod predictus abbas amovit mercatum ville de
Rading(ia) a loco quo antiquitus teneri solet, et preterea quod exigebat ab eisdem burgensibus alias consuetudines et alia servicia
quam facere debuerunt et facere consueverunt temporibus predecessorum predicti domini regis regum Anglie, quas consuetudines et
que servicia dicti [*f 35r*] burgenses eidem abbati non cognoverunt,
et unde placitum fuit inter eos in eadem curia. Scilicet quod predictus abbas concessit pro se et successoribus suis et ecclesia sua de
Rading(ia) predictis burgensibus et eorum heredibus quod mercatum bladi in villa de Rading(ia) sit in loco illo in perpetuum ubi
prius esse solebat, et quod omnia alia vendantur in locis illis in
quibus prius vendi consueverunt; et quod predicti burgenses habeant

gildhallam suam mercandam in villa de Rading(ia) cum duodecim
mesuagiis que ad gildhallam illam pertinent, simul cum prato quod
vocatur Portmanebrok,[d] reddendo inde annuatim dicto abbati et
successoribus suis et ecclesie sue predicte dimidiam marcam ad festum sancti Michaelis ubi prius non solebant reddere nisi unum denarium tantum; et quod habeant gildam suam mercandam cum omnibus pertinentiis suis in perpetuum. Et pro hac concessione, fine et
concordia, predicti burgenses concesserunt pro se et heredibus eorum
quod predictus abbas et successores sui de cetero assumant unum
burgensem de predictis burgensibus qui sit in gilda mercanda et de
quo predicti burgenses sint contenti, qui sit custos gilde mercande et
qui faciat sacramentum tam dictis abbati quam burgensibus ad
omnia que ad gyldam mercandam pertinent fideliter observanda, et
qui de anno in annum amovebitur et tunc loco 'ipsius alius' substi-
tuetur, secundum quod predictum est. Concesserunt etiam dicti burgenses pro se et heredibus ipsorum quod predictus abbas et successores sui habeant de cetero de filio cuiuslibet burgensis legittime
nato quatuor solidos ad introitum gilde mercande, et de quolibet
homine forinseco med(ietatem) finis quem facere poterit cum predicto custode per visum unius monachi dicti abbatis et successorum
suorum ad hoc testificandum assignati, ita quod si finis ille testifi-
cetur per sex legales homines dicte gilde quod finis ille sit rationabilis
dictus monachus non poterit finem illum refutare. Et preterea dicti
burgenses concesserunt pro se et heredibus eorum quod predictus
abbas et successores sui de cetero habeant singulis annis ad festum
sancti Petri ad Vincula quinque denarios de quolibet burgense in
gilda mercanda nomine Chepinggavel. Et preterea concesserunt pro
se et heredibus ipsorum quod bene licebit dicto abbati et successoribus suis talliare dictam villam de Rading(ia) quando dominus rex
talliat dominica sua. Concesserunt etiam predicti burgenses pro se
et heredibus eorum quod bene licebit dicto abbati et successoribus
suis vel eorum ball(ivis) placitare in predicta gildhalla omnia placita
que ad predictam villam de Rading(ia) pertinent placitanda, et
quod habeant omnes emendas tam de gyldanis quam de aliis, et
quod clavis gildhalle remaneat custodi gyldhalle qui ipsam tradet
dicto abbati vel ballivis suis sine contradictione quando ibi placitare
voluerint. Et si contingat quod aliquis predictorum burgensium de
gylda mercanda pro aliquo delicto in misericordiam inciderit, secundum quantitatem delicti et eius facultatem amercietur. Preterea dicti
burgenses recognoverunt pratum quod iacet ad capud[f] prati quod
vocatur Portmanebrok[d] esse ius ipsius abbatis et ecclesie sue de Rad-
ing(ia) et illud ei reddiderunt in eadem curia et remiserunt et quietum clamaverunt de se et heredibus ipsorum[g] dicto abbati et successoribus suis et ecclesie sue de Rading(ia) in perpetuum.

^a Bracton' C   ^b Turri B,C
^c Wolves' C; PRO foot has de Wolveseye   ^d Portmanebroc B,C
^{e-e} illius C   ^f caput B,C
^g eorum C

This is interestingly a *coram rege* fine. The foot is PRO CP 25(1)/284/19/112. Though not a royal act, it has been included at this point on account of its close relationship to the preceding writ.
[1] This is an abstract of the terms of the final concord, written in a 14th-century hand.

70   Request by King Henry III to the free men and free tenants of Reading Abbey for a reasonable aid for the abbey to pay off its manifold debts. Letters patent   7 June 1253

B f 38v; C f 12v
Pd. (cal.) *Cal. Pat. R. 1247–58*, 233 (from Patent Roll)

Teste me ipso apud Westm(onasterium) vii. die Junii, anno regni nostri xxxvii.

71   Notification by King Henry III to all his bailiffs and faithful that he has taken into his protection the men, lands, goods, revenues and all possessions of Reading Abbey, and mandate to protect the same   6 July 1253

A f 34v; B f 37r; C f 11v
Pd. (cal.) *Cal. Pat. R. 1247–58*, 208 (from Patent Roll)

Teste me ipso apud Portesmuth(am) sexto die Julii, anno regni nostri xxxvii.

72   Grant by King Henry III to the prior of Leominster of an annual fair at Leominster of 6 days duration, viz., on the vigil and feast of St Michael and the 4 days following, unless the fair be to the damage of neighbouring fairs.   1 Nov. 1265

B f 120r; B ff 212v–213r; C f 65v; C f 128v
Pd. *Mon. Ang.*, iv. 57 (no. xii)

Hiis testibus:^a venerabili patre W(altero) Bath(oniensi) et Well(ensi) episcopo, Hugone le Bigod, Rogero de Mort(uomari), Rogero de Cliff(ord), Rogero de Lay(burn), Roberto Waler(and), Willelmo Belet, Petro de Chauvent, et aliis. Dat' per manum nostram apud Cantuar(iam) primo die Novembris, anno regni nostri quinquagesimo.

^a *B ff 212v–213r ends, C f 128v ends with* et cetera

The rubric of B f 120r states that the charter was at Leominster. The Charter Roll for 50 Henry III does not survive. This fair was moved in 1281 to the feast of St Cosmas and St Damian (*Cal. Chart. R.*, ii. 261) and in 1290 to the feast of St Edfrid

(*ibid.*, 356). Another fair of 6 days duration was granted in 1281 for the feast of St
Philip and St James (*ibid.*, 253).

73 Precept by King Henry III to the justices of the Jews [Sir
Robert of Fulham (*Foleham*) and Sir William of Orlestone (*Orleweston'*)]ᵃ that, whereas the king by his charter has granted to the abbot
of Reading that no amercements shall be taken from him or his men
by any royal bailiff, they are to desist from their demands for
amercements by summons of the Exchequer of the Jews, which con-
travene the abbot's liberties   12 Oct. 1266

B f6r

Teste Willelmo de Orleweston' apud Westm(onasterium) xii. die
Octobris, anno regni nostri l. Per breve de magno sigillo.
Et istud breve sub eisdem verbis directum fuit vicecomiti Berk' sub
sigillo de scaccario.

  ᵃ *Names om. in text, supplied from rubric*

74 *Certification by John Chishull, the treasurer, and the barons of the Exchequer to King Henry III that, having at the king's mandate searched the
rolls of the Exchequer of Receipt, they find that by the king's writ the abbot
of Reading received at the Exchequer 40 marks for 4 marks of gold for 33–36
Henry III [1249–52] and thereafter nothing up to the feast of St Lucy, 55
Henry III [13 Dec. 1270], except for 54s 10d which he received in part
payment in Michaelmas term at the beginning of 42 Henry III [1257]. The
abbot is thus owed 78s 6d for 42 Henry III and 170 marks for 17 full
years   [c. 13 Dec. 1270]*

  B f6v

Excellentissimo domino suo Henrico dei gratia illustri regi Anglie,
et cetera, devoti sui J(ohannes) de Chishull' thesaurarius suus et
ceteri barones de scaccario suo, salutem et fidele semper servitium.
Ad mandatum vestrum scrutatis rotulis scaccarii vestri de recepta,
invenimus quod abbas de Rading(ia) recepit ad idem scaccarium
triginta marcas de anno regni vestri tricesimo tertio, tricesimo
quarto et tricesimo quinto pro tribus marcis auri per breve vestrum
patens; et anno regni vestri tricesimo sexto per idem breve decem
marcas argenti pro predicta marca auri. Et ab illo tempore nichil
ibidem recepit dictus abbas de predictis denariis usque ad festum
sancte Lucie anno regni vestri quinquagesimo quinto, preter quam
.liiii. sol' .x. d' quos recepit in termino sancti Michaelis anno regni
vestri .xlii. incipiente in partem solutionis dictorum denariorum. Et
sic restant predicto abbati per predictum tempus, videlicet de pre-

dicto anno .xlii., sexaginta decem et octo sol' et .vi. d', et de .xvii. annis transactis integris C. lxx. marce.

The date is approximately that of the *terminus ad quem* mentioned in the text. The writ to the barons is on KR Memoranda Roll, PRO E159/45, m. 4d. John Chishull was treasurer 6 Feb. 1270–9 June 1271. This document concerns the annual payment of 10 marks due to the abbey at the Exchequer for the mark of gold given by King John (see nos. 46, 58). On 16 Dec. 1250 the king ordered payment of the arrears of this sum (*Close Rolls 1247–51*, 389). The treasurer and barons computed the arrears in 1270 with complete accuracy: the total of payment and arrears for 42 Henry III is exactly 10 marks, and the 17 full years accurately comprise the 5 years 37–41 Henry III and the 12 years 43–54 Henry III, the year 55 Henry III having begun only on 28 Oct. 1270.

75 Letters patent by King Henry III giving quittance to the abbot of Reading and his villeins of the twentieth contingent upon them, since the abbot has satisfied the king and Edward, his eldest son, of the same   7 Mar. 1271

B f 11r
Pd. (cal.) *Cal. Pat. R. 1266–72*, 520 (from Patent Roll)

Teste me ipso apud Westm(onasterium) vii. die Marcii, anno regni nostri lv.

The Patent Roll entry is dated 6 March.

76 Order by King Henry III to the sheriff of Sussex to respite until the quindene of Easter the demand which he is making by summons of the Exchequer upon the abbot of Reading and his men concerning certain amercements, chattels, murder and fines from which the abbot claims quittance by his royal charters, and to return in the meantime any cattle (*averia*) he may have taken on this account   24 Oct. 1271

B f6r

Teste Matheo Heym apud Westm(onasterium) xxiiii. die Octobris, anno regni nostri quinquagesimo quinto.

77 Mandate by King Henry III to the treasurer and barons of the Exchequer to inform him, after searching the rolls of the Exchequer, of the time when amercements of the abbot of Reading and his men, fines, murders and his felons' and fugitives' chattels were allowed to the abbot at the Exchequer, and from what time, how and why the allowance was withdrawn or respited, in order that the king may cause to be done for the abbot, as of his right or of the king's grace, what shall appear necessary in this matter with the advice of the king's council   24 June 1272

B f6v

Teste me ipso apud Rading(iam) xxiiii. die Junii, anno lvi.

This is a writ *Certiorari*, to which no. 78 is the reply. The writ is noted on KR Memoranda Roll, PRO E159/46, m. 8. In the autumn of 1270 the king had sent a similar but less extensive writ, omitting reference to the withdrawal of the allowance (E159/45, m. 4), but neither this nor any reply it elicited was entered in the Reading cartularies.

78 *Reply [by the treasurer and barons of the Exchequer] to King Henry III concerning the same* [5 July 1272]

B f6v

Excellentissimo domino suo, et cetera. Ad mandatum vestrum scrutatis rotulis de scaccario vestro invenimus quod in primo anno regis Ricardi in comitatu Berksyr'[a] allocantur abbati Rading' et monachis per libertates cartarum predecessorum vestrorum regum Anglie de amerciamentis quorumdam hominum suorum .lx. sol' quia non habuerunt quem plegiaverunt.[1] Et in secundo rotulo eiusdem regis allocantur eisdem .iii. sol' .vi. d' pro assartis factis in foresta vestra in comitatu Berk', et hominibus eiusdem abbatis in eodem comitatu in villa de Crokham .iii. sol' .v. d' pro purprestur' et dimidiam marcam pro vasto.[2] Et sextodecimo anno regni vestri in comitatu Bukingeham .xx. sol' de fine quem fecit Robertus Boistard pro Reginaldo de Kenebelle et plegiis suis, quia retraxit se, et .xl. d' pro concelamento et receptamento. Et in eodem anno in comitatu Warwiksir' de villata de Rokenton' pro murdro .xl. sol' et .xx. d' pro fuga Ricardi filii Henrici. Et anno regni vestri .xxv. de catallis Symonis Morewyne .xxix. sol' .viii. d' in itinere W(illelmi) de Eboraco, et de villata de Aldermaneston' .xx. sol' quia non fecit sectam, et dimidiam marcam de Roberto de la More de fine pro falso appello, et dimidiam marcam de Willelmo Reyner quia retraxit se, et dimidiam marcam de Phil(ippo) de Kovel(e) quia non est prosecutus, et .iiii. marcas de Johanne de la Huse et sociis suis iuratoribus de fine pro transgressione, et .xl. sol' de Roberto Wille pro panno vendito contra assisam, et dimidiam marcam de Ricardo de Dunmere pro dissaisina, et de Willelmo filio Wygayn dimidiam marcam pro falso clamore, et de Galfrido filio Johannis dimidiam marcam[b] pro iniusta detentione, et .xx. sol' de eodem pro licentia concordandi, et de magistro Ricardo de Benham dimidiam marcam pro habenda inquisitione.[3] Et anno regni vestri .xxvii.[c] de villata de Rading(ia) .xv. marcas de fine ante iudicium,[4] et de Radulfo de Wodehacche dimidiam marcam pro vinis venditis contra assisam, et .vii. sol' pro viridi, et dimidiam marcam[d] pro iniusta detentione, et dimidiam marcam pro plegiagio. Et cessavit[e] ista allocatio per vos et consilium vestrum anno regni vestri .xviii. ita quod ab eo tempore usque nunc nulla facta fuit allocatio eidem abbati vel aliquibus viris religiosis nisi per brevia vestra specialia.[5] Valeat[f] excellentia vestra diu.

Rubric: Quinto die Julii anno lvi. rescriptum fuit domino regi sub hac forma.

[a] *Sic in Ms, rectius* Hertfordsyr' (*see Note 1*)
[b] *Inserted in margin*
[c] *Sic in Ms, rectius* xxvi (*see note 4*)
[d] *Interlined*
[e] *From here the text continues in the margin alongside no. 77, repeating* Et cessavit.
[f] *Ms has* Valea

The date is taken from the rubric. For discussion of this reply, see Clanchy, *Berks. Eyre of 1248*, xxxvii.

[1] *PR 1 Richard I* (Rec. Comm., 1844), 26. A total of 60s was allowed to the abbot as amercements imposed on 4 of his men at Aston in Herts.
[2] *PR 2 Richard I*, 34, 33.
[3] All the allowances under 25 Henry III appear in the estreat of amercements from the Berks. eyre of 1241 (see no. 124).
[4] *PR 26 Henry III*, 66; see also Clanchy, *ibid.*, xxxviii. The following amercements do not appear on the Pipe Roll for 26 Henry III and probably belong to 27 Henry III.
[5] For this ruling in 1233-4, see Clanchy, *ibid.*, xxxvii. The present reply confusingly cites what appear to be automatic allowances to the abbey after this date, but these were in fact made by special writ (Clanchy, xxxviii).

79 Mandate by King Henry III to P(hilip) [of Eye], the treasurer, and the barons of the Exchequer to cause Reading Abbey to have 10 marks for Michaelmas of the previous year, being the annual 10 marks which it receives by the king's charter at the Exchequer, according to the tenor of the writ *Liberate* which is at the Exchequer   21 Oct. 1272

B f6r

Teste me ipso apud Westm(onasterium) xxi. die Octobris, anno regni nostri lvi.

80 Precept by King Edward I to the sheriff of Herefordshire that, since the abbot of Reading has satisfied the king of the twentieth contingent upon him and his villeins, as the king has learnt from the letters patent of Henry III which the abbot has, he is to desist from exaction of the same from the abbot's villeins of his tenure of Leominster and restore anything he has taken   20 Jan. 1273

B f11r; B f11v

Dat' per manum W(alterum) de Merton' cancellarii nostri apud Westm(onasterium) xx. die Januarii, anno regni nostri primo.

The letters patent of Henry III are presumably those of 7 Mar. 1271 (no. 75).

81 Request by King Edward I to the knights, free men and other tenants of Reading Abbey to assist the abbey in relieving its debts by giving a subsidy   5 Feb. 1275

B f 39r; C f 13r
Pd. (cal.) *Cal. Pat. R. 1272-81*, 78 (from Patent Roll)

Teste me ipso apud Kaversham v. die Februarii, anno regni nostri iii.

This is in effect a re-issue of Henry III's request (no. 62). However, by 1275 the abbey's debts were far more serious and it was probably at this time that Archbishop Kilwardby attempted to restore financial order (*Registrum Epistolarum Johannis Peckham*, ed. C. T. Martin (RS, 1882-5), I. 223). Further efforts were made by Archbishop Pecham in 1281 (*ibid.*, 223-6) and by Walter Scammel, bishop of Salisbury, in 1284, the latter confirmed by Pecham in 1285 (*Reg. Swinfield*, 165-9), but these were unsuccessful and eventually, in 1286, the Crown took over the administration of the abbey, and by 1289 had restored it to solvency (see nos. 92-3, 98-9). See also D. Knowles, *The Religious Orders in England*, i (Cambridge, 1948), 107, 109.

82 Request by King Edward I to Hugelinus Bonaventure and Bonaventurus Johannis and their fellow merchants of Siena that, since Reading Abbey is greatly in debt to various creditors, they should allow the abbey two years in which to repay its debts to them   5 Feb. 1275

B f 11v

Teste me ipso apud Kaversham' v. die Februarii, anno regni nostri iii.

83 Mandate by King Edward I to the abbot of Reading that, since the abbey is heavily in debt, he shall cause to be removed from the abbey and from Leominster Priory all servants and horses with their keepers lodged there by the king or by others, and to receive no more until the abbey and priory are relieved of their indebtedness   23 Feb. 1275

B f 11v
Pd. (cal.) *Cal. Pat. R. 1272-81*, 81 (from Patent Roll)

Teste me ipso apud Windes(ores) xxiii. die Februarii, anno regni nostri tercio.

The Patent Roll entry is dated 24 Feb.

84 Precept by King Edward I to the sheriff of Cambridgeshire (*Cantebir'*) to allow the abbot of Reading the liberties in that county which he claims to have by royal charters and has enjoyed hitherto, according to the statute of the king's council on this matter or until the king shall order otherwise   6 Jan. 1280

B f 11r

Teste me ipso apud Wynton(iam) vi. die Januarii, anno regni nostri octavo.

This writ was probably issued to cover the abbey's first major acquisition in Cambs., the manor of Southwood (in Doddington), recently given by Ela, dowager countess of Warwick (BL Harl. Ch. 54 D 15, pd. *Mon. Ang.*, iv. 45 (no. xxvi); *VCH Cambs.*, iv. 112).

85 Precept by King Edward I to the bailiffs of the abbot of Reading to deliver to the sheriff of Berkshire, to be taken where the king has ordered him, Albert Morin, Guy his brother and Adam of Cremona (*de Cremone*) lately taken for the death of Leonard of Cremona at Reading   19 Jan. 1280

B f 39r; C f 13r

Teste me ipso apud Lindhurst nonodecimo die Januarii, anno regni nostri octavo.

86 Mandate by King Edward I to the abbot of Reading, as he previously ordered, to deliver to the sheriff of Berkshire Albert Morin, Guy his brother and Adam of Cremona[a] lately taken at Reading and detained in prison there for the death of Leonard[b] of Cremona lately killed there, and this shall not be to the prejudice of the abbot's liberty of Reading. Letters patent   28 Feb. 1280

B f 39r; C f 13r
Pd. (cal.) *Cal. Pat. R. 1272–81*, 364 (from Patent Roll)

Teste me ipso apud Dunameneye xxviii. die Februarii, anno regno nostri octavo.

[a] de Pavye *on Patent Roll*
[b] Gerard *on Patent Roll*

These letters patent were clearly sought by the abbey to protect its liberty, which obedience to the earlier writ might have jeopardised.

87 Memorandum that in 9 Edward I John *Fachel* and Richard *le Sumenur* were indicated by the men of Surrey and Berkshire of breaking the park of Windsor and were taken and imprisoned at Reading, where they were detained for a fortnight. Then, against the king's coming from Norfolk to Windsor, the abbot, at the mandate of Sir Geoffrey of Pitchford (*Picheford'*) constable of Windsor Castle, sent them to Windsor by William of Ufton (*Uffinton'*) his bailiff of Reading. Then, on Thursday before St Peter in Cathedra [22 Feb.], before the king's justices at Windsor the abbot sought them for his prison by J(ohn) Gerard and William of Blewbury (*Blebir'*), and they were adjourned at Reading *coram rege*   20 Feb. 1281

The king conceded them to the abbot and ordered the sheriff of Hampshire, to whom he had sent them for custody, to deliver them to him, as follows:

Precept by King Edward I to the sheriff of Hampshire or the constable of Winchester Castle to deliver to the abbot of Reading John *Fachel* and Richard *le Sumenur*, whom he sent to him for custody for breach of the park of Windsor, to be kept in prison at Reading within the abbot's liberty and for the abbot to have them before the king at the king's will to answer the charge

Teste me ipso apud Chaversham xxv. die Februarii, anno regni nostri nono.   25 Feb. 1281

B f 245v

John Gerard was a monk of Reading (*Cal. Chart. R.*, ii. 261); William of Blewbury was steward of the abbey (BL Add. Ch. 19627; below, nos. 1045, 1240).

88   Mandate by King Edward I to Geoffrey of Pitchford (*Picheford'*), constable of Windsor Castle that, since the abbot of Reading has by his royal charters attachments of his men and of others within his fee for custody in the king's gaol at Reading until delivered by the law of the land, he is to surcease in his demand upon the abbot for the person of William Brown (*Brun*), whom the royal foresters of Windsor pursued for a hunting offence into the vill of Reading, and to release to the abbot any distress he may have taken in this regard   18 July 1283

B f 11r

Teste me ipso apud Kaernarvan xviii. die Julii, anno regni nostri undecimo.

89   Mandate by King Edward I to Solomon of Rochester and his fellow justices-in-eyre in Berkshire to allow to the abbot of Reading in this present eyre the liberties which he has by his royal charters and which he and his predecessors have enjoyed hitherto

30 Sept. 1284

B f 40v; C ff 13v–14r

Teste me ipso apud Overton' xxx. die Septembris, anno regni nostri xii.

Rubric: Breve domini regis de libertatibus placitandis apud Rading(iam) in itinere de Berkesyr'[a] et non alibi.
Marginal note (B only): Ista duo brevia [*nos. 89–90*] invenientur in rotul' domini regis Edwardi anno eiusdem xii.

[a] Barkesyr' *C*

The rubric suggests that, from the abbey's point of view, the most valuable part of the liberties was the special session of the eyre for the abbey's jurisdiction at Reading.

90 Mandate by King Edward I to Solomon of Rochester and his fellow justices-in-eyre in Berkshire to deliver to the abbot of Reading an estreat of fines and amercements touching him and his men in the present eyre

30 Sept. 1284

B f 40v; C f 14r

Teste me ipso apud Overton' xxx. die Septembris, anno regni nostri xii.

Marginal note (B only): see no. 89.

91 Mandate by King Edward I to the treasurer and barons of the Exchequer to cause the abbot of Reading to be acquitted of the 20s at which he was amerced before the justices-in-eyre last in Hertfordshire for the common summons, as the king has pardoned him the amercement

23 Jan. 1286

B f 40v; C f 14r
Pd. (cal.) *Cal. Close R. 1279–88*, 381 (from Close Roll)

Teste me ipso apud Merleberg(am) xxiii. die Januarii, anno regni nostri quartodecimo.

92 Letters patent by King Edward I declaring that, although he has committed custody of Reading Abbey, with all goods and revenues pertaining to it and to the manor of Leominster and its other places, to his clerk Ralph of Broughton (*Broghton'*) to relieve the abbey of its indebtedness, this shall not be to the prejudice of the

abbey's immunity from royal custody in future abbatial
vacancies   15 Mar. 1286

B f 232v

Teste me ipso apud Wodestok' xv. die Marcii, anno regni nostri
quartodecimo.

See no. 81 n.

93 Mandate by King Edward I to the abbot of Reading that,
whereas he has committed custody of the same to his clerk Ralph of
Broughton (*Broghton'*) to relieve the abbey of its debts in accordance
with the abbot and convent's arrangement (*ordinatio*), taking for
himself or for the king only reasonable expenses, and this custody
shall not be to the prejudice of the abbey in future vacancies, the
abbot shall admit the said Ralph to the custody as set out in the
letters patent which the king sends to the abbot   16 Mar. 1286

B f 232v

Teste me ipso apud Wodestok' xvi. die Marcii, anno regni nostri
quartodecimo.

94 Mandate by King Edward I to the treasurer and barons of the
Exchequer that, after inspecting the charter of Henry III and his
letters patent to the then treasurer and barons regarding 10 marks
to be paid annually to Reading Abbey for the 1 mark of gold
annually given by King John, which charter and letters patent the
king has seen, they are to pay the 10 marks and arrears of the same
in accordance with the charter and letters patent and as they shall
consider the king is bound in this   28 Apr. 1286

B f 14r

Teste me ipso xxviii. die Aprilis, anno regni nostri quartodecimo.

This relates to the 10 marks due to the abbey annually for the mark of gold given by
King John (see nos. 46, 58-9, 74). In 1292 the abbey released the Crown from this
obligation and all arrears thereof, and surrendered the charters of John and Henry
III (nos. 46, 58) in return for £100 (*Extracts from the Issue Rolls of the Exchequer, Henry
III to Henry VI* (Rec. Comm., 1837), 104; *Kalendars and Inventories of His Majesty's
Exchequer* (Rec. Comm., 1836), i. 49).

95 Mandate by King Edward I to the sheriff and all bailiffs and
faithful of Berkshire to aid the king's clerk, Ralph of Broughton
(*Broghton'*), to whom custody of Reading Abbey and its manor of

Leominster and other manors has been committed to relieve the
abbey of its debts. Letters patent   4 May 1286

B f 233r
Pd. (cal.) *Cal. Pat. R. 1281–92*, 242 (from Patent Roll)

Teste me ipso apud Ledes quarto die Maii, anno regni nostri quartodecimo.

96   Precept by King Edward I to the sheriff of Kent that, whereas,
as the abbot of Reading has shown the king, he ought to have by
his royal charters amercements of his men, fugitives' and felons'
chattels, gallows, tumbrel, pillory and quittance of *murdrum*, and the
sheriff of his own will is impeding the abbot in the enjoyment of the
same, he is to permit him to enjoy these liberties and entirely to
desist from disturbing him   10 June 1286

B f 13v

Teste Edmundo comite Cornubie consanguineo nostro apud
Westm(onasterium) x. die Junii, anno regni nostri xiiii.

Edmund earl of Cornwall, who witnesses, served as regent while the king was in
France, 13 May 1286 – 12 Aug. 1289.

97   Order by King Edward I to the sheriff of Herefordshire to
respite until his next account the demand which he is making on the
abbot of Reading and his men by summons of the Exchequer of the
Jews and in the meantime to deliver to him any cattle (*averia*) he
may have taken on that account, since the abbot has by his royal
charters quittance of all manner of amercements touching him and
his men, as he says   18 Apr. 1287

B f 14r

Teste W(illelmo) de Carlton' apud Westmonasterium xviii. die
Aprilis, anno regni nostri xv.

William de Carlton was a baron of the Exchequer (*Cal. Close R. 1279–88*, 480).

98   Mandate by King Edward I to his clerk, Ralph of Broughton
(*Broghton'*), that, since the king has learnt that Reading Abbey, to
which the king assigned Ralph at the abbot and convent's request
to relieve its debts, has been restored to solvency, he is to relinquish
control of the house to the abbot and convent   10 Jan. 1289

B f 233r

Teste me ipso apud Bonam Wardam in Vascon(ia) x. die Januarii, anno regni nostri decimo septimo.

99 *Letter [by Robert Burnell, the chancellor,ᵃ to Ralph of Broughtonᵇ] rejoicing that he has restored Reading Abbey to solvency and urging him to free himself from his responsibility as honourably and quickly as possible, since the king does not wish him to tarry there longer* 10 Jan. 1289

B f 233r

Salutem, et cetera. Cum dominus abbas Rading(ensis) significaverit domino nostro regi et nobis quod de cura vestra de cetero non indigent desicut domus sua ad statum prosperum reducitur, de quo quamplurimum congaudemus, per quod idem dominus noster rex per suas litteras vobis mandat ut de cura domus eiusdem vos non intromittatis de cetero quoquo modo, vobis consulendo mandamus ut honestiori modo quo poteritis vos exoneretis ex ea et hoc quamcitius poteritis facere non tardetis, maxime cum domino nostro regi non placeat quod occasione predicta amplius perhendinetis ibidem. Dat' ut supra.ᶜ

Marginal note (in different hand): Littere R. Burn' cancellarii

ᵃ *See marginal note*
ᵇ *Supplied from the context*
ᶜ *Referring to no. 98*

100 Mandate by King Edward I to the abbot of Reading that, since it is part of the royal dignity to require the service of any inhabitant of the realm the king needs, notwithstanding service to anyone else, and since the king wishes to obtain the service of Roger of Burghfield (*Burghfeld*), coroner of the abbot's liberty of Reading, he is to cause to be elected by the oath of good and lawful men of the said liberty a knight or other to the office of coroner in Roger's place 15 Aug. 1297

B f 15r

Teste P(hilippo) de Wylugby tenente locum thes(aurarii) nostri, apud Westm(onasterium) xv. die Augusti, anno regni nostri xxv.

Note that Robert Adelard was duly elected coroner by oath of good and lawful men of the liberty of Reading.

Philip of Willoughby was appointed chancellor of the Exchequer in 1283 (*Cal. Pat. R. 1281-92*, 60) and retained the office until his death in 1305 (Tout, *Chapters*, ii. 7 n.4). He often served as locum tenens for the treasurer, Walter Langton (*ibid.*).

101 Licence by King Edward II, at the instance of Queen Isabella and by a fine made by the abbot of Reading, to William *Pouche* and Alice his wife to alienate in mortmain to Reading Abbey 2 messuages, 154 acres of land, 10 acres of meadow, 8 acres of wood and 1d rent in *Purtleton'* and *la Hyde;* and to John *de Danhurst*[a] to alienate in mortmain to the same £6 rent in Leominster, Ivington (*Ivynton'*), Luston (*Luston'*) and Eyton (*Eiton'*) [all Herefordshire]. Licence also to the abbot and convent to receive and hold the same

13 Sept. 1308

C f 227r; E f 183r; (noted) C f 225v
Pd. (cal.) *Cal. Pat. R. 1307-13*, 138 (from Patent Roll)

Teste me ipso apud Guldeford xiii. die Septembris, anno regni nostri[b] secundo.[c]

[a] Danehurst *E*
[b] *E ends with* et cetera
[c] *C adds:* scilicet Edwardi filii regis Edwardi

102 Inspeximus and confirmation by King Edward II of the following three charters for Reading Abbey: 1. Henry III's inspeximus and confirmation of John's general confirmation [no. 55], excluding the clause relating to a mint and moneyer; 2. Henry III's general notification and precept regarding the abbey's liberties [no. 56]; 3. Henry II's confirmation of the manor of Aston [no. 372]. The king further grants that, although the abbey may not have enjoyed all its liberties to the full in the past, it shall do so henceforth, except for a mint and moneyer, and shall moreover be quit of prises and cheminages (*chiminagium*) and shall have the assize of bread and ale and other things pertaining to the office of the marshalsea, in such manner that no royal steward or marshal or clerk of the market shall enter the abbey's liberty in pursuit of his office except by default of the abbot and monks, and if they do enter the liberty for any reason the abbey shall have the fines, amercements and other profits and, after their withdrawal, have the liberty as before, unless the default has been such that the liberty ought to remain forfeit to the king and his heirs. Grant also that royal justices dealing with lands, tenements and other matters which are outside the liberty shall not enter the liberty or sit on these cases in the liberty, but elsewhere in the county   3 July 1315

B ff 41v-44r; C ff 14r-16v; F ff 75v-77r (not fully collated)
Pd. (cal) *Cal. Chart. R.*, iii. 279-80 (from Charter Roll)

Hiis testibus: venerabili patre W(altero) Cantuar(iensi) archiepiscopo tocius Anglie primate, Johanne de Britannia comite Riche-

mund', Adomar(o) de Valenc' comite Penbrok', Humfr(edo) de
Bohoun comite Herford' et Essex', Edmundo comite Arundell', Bartholomeo de Badelesmer', Johanne de*a* Crumbewell' senescallo
hospicii nostri, et aliis. Dat' per manum nostram apud
Westm(onasterium) tercio die Julii, anno regni nostri octavo.

a Om. in C

103 Mandate by King Edward II to the clerk of the market to
permit Reading Abbey to enjoy the assize of bread and ale and
other appurtenances of the marshalsea within its liberty in accordance with the terms of the king's charter   27 Feb. 1317

B f 242v

Teste me ipso apud Claryndon' xxvii. die Februarii, anno regni
nostri decimo.

Marginal note (in later hand), slightly clipped by trimming of the folio: Nota
peroptime ista duo brevia[1] pro carta (a)llocand' et specialiter pro
(j)usticiar' ad ass' et pro exoneracione clerici mercati. [?] aliud
seq(uitur) pro exoneracione custodie maris.[2]

The cartulary text omits the opening words of this writ, beginning: *Clerico mercati sui
salutem.* However, that it is by Edward II is certain, since he made the grant of the
assize of bread and ale (no. 102) and was, moreover, at Clarendon on this date. The
terms of the privilege are detailed and follow those set out in no. 102. In 1339, during
Edward III's absence abroad, a similar mandate was directed to Robert Jovel, clerk
of the market and coroner of the household of Edward, duke of Cornwall, acting as
regent (F f 83v).

[1] Referring to nos. 103 and 104
[2] Referring to no. 108, which follows on the next folio

104 Mandate by King Edward II to R(obert) of Sindlesham (*Syn-
dlesham*) and H(enry) of Pentlow (*Pentelawe*), keepers of the Peace
and of the Statute of Winchester in Berkshire, that, since the king
has confirmed to Reading Abbey all justice of assault, theft, murder,
bloodshed and breach of the peace throughout its possessions, and
since the king has granted that, although the abbey may not have
enjoyed these liberties fully hitherto, it shall do so, and that royal
justices dealing with lands, tenements and other matters which are
outside the liberty shall not enter the liberty or sit on these cases
within the liberty but elsewhere in the county, they are to allow the
same to the abbey. Witness [omitted]
                    [June 1316 × Nov. 1326; ? Feb. 1317]

B ff 242v-243r

The cartulary text begins simply with: 'Rex dilectis et fidelibus suis', but the king is clearly Edward II. In June 1316 Robert of Sindlesham and Henry of Pentlow were appointed conservators of the peace in Berks. (*Cal. Pat. R. 1313-17*, 482) and again in June 1320 (*ibid. 1317-21*, 460); the king lost all authority in Nov. 1326 (N. Fryde, *Tyranny and Fall of Edward II* (Cambridge, 1979) 192). However, the mandate may well be of the same date as no. 103.

105   Licence by King Edward III, by a fine made by the abbot of Reading, to Hugh of Reading to alienate in mortmain to Reading Abbey 3 messuages, 240 acres of land, 10 acres of meadow, 3 acres of pasture, 40 acres of wood and 16s rent in *Mileshop,*[a] Leominster, Luston (*Luston'*), *Purtleton'*, Stockton (*Stokton'*),[b] Stoke [Prior] (*Stok'*), Ivington (*Ivynton'*) and *la Hulle*[c] [all Herefordshire], to find 2 chaplains to celebrate in the conventual church of Reading for ever in accordance with Hugh's appointment. Licence also to the abbot and convent to receive and hold the same on these terms   28 Nov. 1331

C f 227v; E ff 183v-184r; (noted) C f 225v
Pd. (cal.) *Cal. Pat. R. 1330-34*, 221 (from Patent Roll)

Teste me ipso apud Wynton(iam) xxviii. die Novembris, anno regni nostri quinto.[d]

[a] Milleshop *E*   [b] Stoctu(n) *E*
[c] la Hull *E*   [d] *Om. in E*

106   Licence by King Edward III to master Hubert Constable (*le Constable*) to alienate in mortmain to Reading Abbey 1 messuage in Reading;[1] to William of Whitley (*Whytele*), chaplain, to alienate similarly 7 acres of land in Whitley; and to John *atte Broke* to alienate similarly 8 acres of land in Burghfield (*Burghfeld*) and Sulhamstead (*Sylhamsted'*) [all Berks.], all of which are not held of the king and are worth annually 9s 2d, as appears by the inquest held by William *de Northo*, lately escheator in Hants., Wilts., Oxon., Berks., Beds. and Bucks.; to be held by the abbey at the value of 15s annually in part satisfaction of the £10 worth of land and rent which the abbey has the king's licence to acquire. Licence also to the abbot and convent to receive and hold the same   10 Dec. 1335

C f 224r (abridged)
Pd. (cal.) *Cal. Pat. R. 1334-38*, 189 (from Patent Roll)

Teste me ipso apud Aukland' x. die Decembris, anno regni nostri nono.

The Patent Roll entry lacks the day date. The mortmain licence for £10 worth of land and rent is *Cal. Pat. R. 1327-30*, 61.

[1] See no. 976.

107 Licence by King Edward III to Hugh of Reading, chaplain, to alienate in mortmain to Reading Abbey 110 acres of land, 10 acres of meadow, 20 acres of pasture, 80 acres of wood and 16s rent in Leominster, Ivington (*Ivynton'*), Luston (*Luston'*), Stockton (*Stokton'*)[a] and *Hopemile* [all Herefordshire]; and to Adam *de Kynton'*, chaplain, to alienate similarly 10 acres of land in Whitley (*Whytelegh'*)[b] [Berks.], which are held of the abbot; which land, meadow, pasture and wood are worth annually 46s 4d, as appears by the inquests held by William Trussel, escheator this side of the Trent; to be held by the abbey at the value of £4 in part satisfaction of the £10 worth of land and rent which the abbey has the king's licence to acquire. Licence also to the abbot and convent to receive and hold the same   2 May 1336

C f 224r (abridged); E f 184r–v
Pd. (cal.) *Cal. Pat. R. 1334–38*, 257 (from Patent Roll)

Teste me ipso apud Westm(onasterium)[c] secundo die Maii, anno regni nostri decimo.

   [a] Stoktone *E*   [b] Wythele *E*   [c] *E ends*

For the mortmain licence for £10, see no. 106 n.

108 Mandate by King Edward III to Bartholomew *de Insula*, John *de Scures* and Thomas Cowdray (*Coudrey*), keepers of ports, sea-shores and maritime land in Hampshire, Wiltshire and Berkshire and commissioners of array in the same, not to intermeddle in an array on the abbot of Reading's demesne temporalities, as the abbot says they are attempting to do, and to release any distress they may have taken in this regard, since it is not the king's intention that religious and other ecclesiastics should be liable to such array on their demesne temporalities   25 Jan. 1336 x 24 Jan. 1337

B f 243r

Teste me ipso, et cetera, anno regni nostri decimo.

Note of similar writs in favour of the abbot of Reading sent to the arrayers in Kent, viz., William of Ellington (*Elynton'*), John of Cobham, Roger of Heigham (*Hegham*) and Thomas of Aldon (*Aldone*), and to the arrayers in Sussex, viz., Henry *de Huse*, Thomas of Poling (*Polyngges*) and Edward of St Albans.

109 Inspeximus and confirmation by King Edward III, in favour of Abbot John of Appleford and the monks of Reading, of Edward

II's inspeximus and confirmation of charters by Henry III and Henry II [no. 102]. The king further grants that, although the abbey may not have enjoyed all its liberties fully in the past, considering the subvention of great and precious jewels which the abbey has made to him for his passage overseas in defence of the realm and the rights of the Crown, it shall do so henceforth without hindrance from the king, his heirs or royal justices, escheators, sheriffs, bailiffs and ministers. Also restoration of a mint and moneyer at Reading, withdrawn by Edward II, for the coining of pennies, halfpennies and farthings. Moreover, whereas the charters by King John and Henry III referred to the abbey's having all justice of assault [etc.], as pertained to the royal power and all immunity, power, quittance and liberty that the royal power can confer upon an abbey, and by virtue of these general words the abbey has had return of writs and of summonses of the Exchequer, attachments, animals called 'waifs', felons' and fugitives' chattels, deodands, year day and waste, and escapes of felons within its liberty of Reading, as also fines and amercements of its men and tenants in the same and quittance of tallages and escapes of felons, but, because these liberties are not specified expressly in the above charters, the abbey has been frequently challenged and hindered in the royal courts over their allocation, the king grants and confirms these liberties to the abbey specifying that the abbey may, without the interference of any royal officer, levy amercements, fines, deodands and all that pertains to the king from year day and waste and escapes of felons within the said liberty, and the abbey is to be quit of tallages and escapes of felons within the same   19 June 1338

B ff 44v–45v; C ff 17r–18r; F ff 78v–79r (not fully collated)
Pd. (cal.) *Cal. Chart. R.*, iv. 448 (from Charter Roll)

Hiis testibus: venerabilibus patribus J(ohanne) archiepiscopo Cantuar(iensi) tocius Anglie primate, R(icardo) episcopo Dunolm(ensi), R(oberto) Cicestr(ensi) episcopo cancellario nostro, Th(oma) de Bello Campo comite Warr', Willelmo de Monte Acuto comite Sar', Henrico de Ferrariis, Johanne Darcy senescallo hospicii nostri, et aliis. Dat' per manum nostram apud Walton' decimo nono die Junii, anno regni nostri duodecimo.
Per ipsum regem et per breve de privato sigillo.

110   Licence by King Edward III to Hugh of Reading, chaplain, to alienate in mortmain to Reading Abbey 1 messuage, 1 carucate of land and 14 acres of meadow in Stockton (*Stocton'*),[a] Middleton (*Mittelton'*),[b] Luston (*Luston'*), Ivington (*Ivynton'*) and Leominster [all Herefordshire], which are held of the abbey by the annual service of 24s 11d and, apart from the said rent, are worth annually 27s, as appears by the inquest held by William Trussel, escheator this side of the Trent; to be held by the abbey at the value of 40s annually in part satisfaction of the £10 worth of land and rent which the abbey has the king's licence to acquire. Licence also to the abbot and convent to receive and hold the same   26 Oct. [1338]

> C f 224v (abridged); E f 187r–v
> Pd. (cal.) *Cal. Pat. R. 1338–40*, 156 (from Patent Roll)

Teste E(dwardo) duce Cornubie et comite Cestrie filio nostro carissimo, custode Anglie, apud Kenyngton' ᶜxxvi. die Octobris.ᶜ

> ᵃ Stoctu(n) *E*   ᵇ Mittilton' *E*   ᶜ⁻ᶜ et cetera *E*

The year date is supplied from the Patent Roll.

111 Mandate by King Edward III to the treasurer and barons of the Exchequer to have made and delivered to the abbot and monks of Reading, or their representatives, three dies for pennies, halfpennies and farthings, if one die is insufficient for this purpose, for use in their mint at Reading, which the king by his charter has granted to them   8 Nov. 1338

> B ff 45v–46r; C f 18r; F f 84r
> Pd. *Mon. Ang.*, iv. 46 (no. xxix)

Teste Edwardo duce Cornubie et comite Cestrie filio nostro carissimo, custode Anglie, apud Kenyngton' viii. die Novembris, anno regni nostri duodecimo.

On 26 Aug. 1338 the treasurer and barons were ordered to provide the abbey with one die for the three coins (*Cal. Close R. 1337–9*, 450), but that seems to have raised problems which this writ was designed to meet. This writ is enrolled as part of a longer entry concerning the dies for Reading on K. R. Memoranda Roll, PRO E159/115, m. 216d, which in turn is entered in F f 84r.

112 Mandate by King Edward III to John of Fleet (*Flete*), keeper of the king's exchange of London, to cause to be made at the abbot of Reading's expense, and with the impression and circumscription which the abbot shall determine, three dies for pennies, halfpennies and farthings for use in the abbey's mint at Reading, which the king by his charter has granted, and to send them to the Exchequer at Westminster as soon as possible and not later than the quindene of St Martin next [11 Nov.], for delivery to the abbot   17 Nov. 1338

> B f 46r; C f 18r

Teste J(ohanne) de Shordich' apud Westm(onasterium) xvii. die Novembris, anno regni nostri duodecimo.

Per rotulum memor' de anno xiii. Mich' record'.

John of Shoreditch was appointed second baron of the Exchequer in 1336 (*Cal. Pat. R. 1334-38*, 341). This writ was abstracted as part of the entry on K.R. Memoranda Roll for 12 Edward III, copied in F f 84r (see no. 111 n.). This account continues that the dies were duly delivered into the Exchequer on the quidene of St Martin and that, on 6 Dec., a royal writ ordered their delivery into the Chancery, to which they were sent on 10 Dec. The Close Roll, however, records the sending of a die for pennies to Reading Abbey on 4 Dec. (*Cal. Close R. 1337-9*, 577). The Memoranda Roll continues that, after the delivery of the three dies into Chancery, those for halfpennies and farthings were returned to the Exchequer and not finally delivered to Reading Abbey until 27 Feb. 1339. By July, 1340, however, the three dies were worn out, and the king had to order new ones to be made (F ff 83v-84r).

113 Licence by King Edward III for Reading Abbey to acquire in mortmain lands and tenements, not held of the king in chief, to the annual value of £10   25 Aug. 1345

C f 225v
Pd. (cal.) *Cal. Pat. R. 1343-45*, 539 (from Patent Roll)

Teste me ipso apud Westm(onasterium) xxv. die Augusti, anno regni nostri Anglie xix, regni vero nostri Francie sexto.

113a Note of a charter concerning certain lands at Leominster, and a croft called *Utham* and 1 acre adjacent to the east in Whitley (*Whytele*), which belonged to Humphrey Carpenter (*le Carpenter*)
[? 14th cent.]

C f 225v

This appears among notes mostly of royal licences of mortmain, but, if it does relate to one such licence, I have been unable to trace the connection.

114 Memorandum that William Draper (*Drapere*) of Cambridge (*Cantebrygge*) was taken and held in the king's prison at Reading by order of Robert Bracy, the king's janitor, and afterwards sent *coram rege* by virtue of the following royal writ sent to the abbot of Reading's bailiffs

Writ of *venire facias* by King Richard II to the bailiffs of the abbot of Reading to cause William Draper of Cambridge, held in the king's prison under their custody, to come before the king in the quindene of Easter to answer the charges there to be put to him
20 Mar. 1382

B f 243r

Et cetera, xx. die Marcii, anno quinto.

Marginal note: Virtute istius brevis Willelmus Drapere missus fuit coram domino rege.

115 Writ of *venire facias* by King Richard II to the bailiffs of the abbot of Reading to cause Walter *Wolfeld'* of Thorpe (*Thorp'*), skinner, taken and held in the abbot's prison at Reading under their custody, to come before the king in one month from Easter, with the cause of his arrest, to answer the charges there to be put to him

5 Apr. 1382

B f 242r

Teste me ipso apud Westm(onasterium) quinto die Aprilis, anno regni nostri quinto.

116 *Mandate by King Richard II to the treasurer and barons of the Exchequer that, since the tomb and effigy of Henry I in Reading Abbey have been repaired within the year set by the king as the condition for the king's confirmation of the abbey's franchises, liberties and quittances, they are to permit the abbey to enjoy the same* 25 May 1398

B f 76v; F f 79v
Pd. *Mon. Ang.,* iv. 46–7 (no. xxx)

Rex thesaurario et baronibus suis de scaccario, salutem. Cum nos nuper per litteras nostras patentes sub magno sigillo nostro ratificaverimus et confirmaverimus dilectis nobis in Christo abbati et conventui abbatie de Redyng', que de fundacione progenitorum nostrorum quondam regum Anglie et nostro patronatu existit, diversas franchesias, libertates et quietancias sibi per progenitores nostros predictos cum clausula licet concessas, sic quod iidem abbas et conventus et successores sui tumbam et ymaginem Henrici quondam regis Anglie progenitoris nostri et fundatoris abbatie predicte in eadem humati infra annum post confirmacionem nostram predictam honeste facerent reparari, prout in litteris nostris predictis[a] plenius continetur; iamque iidem abbas et conventus nobis supplicaverint ut, cum vos pro eo quod de factura tumbe et ymaginis predictarum certificati non estis libertates, franchesias et quietancias predictas eisdem abbati et conventui allocare renuatis, velimus facturam tumbe et ymaginis predictarum vobis notum facere et testificari; et nos supplicacioni predicte annuentes premissa infra annum predictum bene et honeste facta modo quo inde contenti sumus testificati fuerimus, et hoc omnibus quorum interest innotesci fecerimus prout

in litteris nostris patentibus inde confectis plenius similiter continetur;[1] vobis mandamus quod ipsos abbatem et conventum libertatibus, franchesiis et quietanciis in cartis dictorum progenitorum nostrorum et confirmacione nostra predictis contentis coram vobis uti
et gaudere permittatis iuxta tenorem cartarum et confirmacionis
predictarum, ipsos contra tenorem earundem non molestantes in
aliquo seu gravantes. Teste me ipso apud Westm(onasterium) xxv.
die Maii, anno regni nostri vicesimo primo.

Irrotulatur inter brevia directa baronibus de termino Trinitatis
anno xxi. regis Ricardi secundi, rotulo videlicet secundo.

a Om. in F

The official enrolment is on K. R. Memoranda Roll 21 Richard II, PRO E159/174,
rot. 2d, which adds at the end: *Hoc breve alloc(atur) in magno rotulo de anno xx. in
Res(idua) Hereford'*.

[1] The letters referred to here are *Cal. Pat. R. 1396–99*, 346. The letters patent by
which the king confirmed the liberties with the above condition are neither in the
Reading cartularies nor on the Patent Roll. The king had confirmed the abbey's
liberties by inspeximus of Edward III's inspeximus (no. 109) in 1381 (*Cal. Chart. R.*,
v. 276).

117 *Order by King Henry VI to the warden of the Gild of Reading that,
although when the king was last in Reading he licensed him to bear a mace
before the king, but has since learnt that it is against the liberties of Reading
Abbey for anyone to bear any sign of office within the town and franchise of
Reading apart from 2 tipped staves borne by the abbot's bailiff(s), the warden
is not to use or bear a mace or other sign, nor to cause such to be borne by any
other within the said town and franchise apart from the said 2 tipped
staves* 30 July [*either* ?1443 *or* 1449 *or* 1451]

B f 164v
Pd. Coates, *Hist of Reading*, 60; *Mon. Ang.*, iv. 47 (no. xxxi)

Littere regis Henrici Sexti directe Custodi Gilde de Redyng'.
Welbeloved we grete you wel, and how be hit that we calle to oure
remembraunce how that at oure last beyng' at the towne of Redyng'
we licenced you to bere oonly the mase by fore us so that it be not
preiudiciall' unto oure church' and monasterie of Redyng', yet
nathelesse ye use it other wise than was or is accordyng' to oure
entent. In so much that as we sithens have clierly perceyved by
sheweng' of evidenc' and credible report made unto us of the antique
usage and custume had in the same towne that hit is contrarie to
the ffranchisse and libertees of oure said church' and monasterie by
oure noble aunciesteres graunted and by us confermed you to be
called or bere other in name or in signe other wise than as keper of

the Gilde of Reding' admitted by the abbot of owre said monasterie
and not by us, for to have any mase or eny other signe of officere or
office to be born' by you or any other man with in the said town'
and ffranchise of Redyng' savyng' oonly two tipped stafis to be born'
by the baylif' of thabbott' of oure said monasterie graunted and
yeven' to thabbot' and convent of the same oure monasterie at' the
first ffundacion ther of oute of Court of Marchalsie eldest' of recorde
with' al maner court' plees of dette of trespace and other, and also
execucion of the same to be doon by his baylif' and by noon' other
as in theire charters of graunte and confirmacion more evidently hit
appereth'. We therfor woll' and charge you straitly that ye ne use
nor bere any mase nor other signe nor do to be born' by non other
persoune with' in the said town' and ffranchise ther of wherby the
interesse and right of oure said monasterie might' in any wyse be
interrupted or hurted wich' we ne wolde nor never entended, savyng' oonly the two tipped staf(is) in maner and fourme as is above
rehersed, as ye desire to please us and wol eschew the contrary.
Yeven' under oure signet' at Eltham, the xxx. day of Juill'.

Henry VI used the signet for public business of this kind mainly from 1437 to 1453
(A.J. Otway-Ruthven, *The King's Secretary and the Signet Office in the XV Century* (Cambridge, 1939), 13-15, 47, 74). In the reign as a whole the only years in which the
king is known to have been at Eltham on 30 July were 1449 and 1451 (B. Wolffe,
Henry VI (1981), 368-9), but he was possibly there on that day in 1443, since his
whereabouts between Windsor on 29 July and Eltham on 3 Aug. are unknown (*ibid.*,
364). The king was in Reading in 1438, 1440, 1447, 1451 and 1453 (*ibid.*, 361-2,
366, 369-70). None of the Eltham dates can be reconciled with the earliest known
appearance of a mace at Reading. According to the town records, the mace was
introduced in late Oct. 1458 (*Reading Records. Diary of the Corporation*, ed. J.M. Guilding (1892), i. 48). Since the king was deposed 4 Mar. 1461 and was in the midlands
in July 1459 (Wolffe, 371), the only year after 1458 when the king might conceivably
have been at Eltham on 30 July was 1460 (*ibid.*), but, since he was then under Yorkist
control following the Battle of Northampton on 10 July, his use of the signet for an
order of this kind would have been out of the question.

II DOCUMENTS RELATING TO THE ABBEY'S LIBERTIES

118 *Certification by Robert of Bassingbourn to Abbot Simon of Reading containing evidence from Pipe Roll 1 Richard I of the allocation of the abbot's liberty*   [1213 × 26]

A f 34r

Robertus de Bassingeburn' misit literas istas Symoni abbati Rading(ensi) ad certificandum eum super articulis istis.

Robertus de Bassingebur' abbati Rading(ensi), et cetera. Quoniam perpendi vos nuper multum admirari et magnam ferentes angustiam eo quod libertas vestra non potuit inveniri in rotulis de scaccario, postea ad memoriam revocatus inveni libertatem vestram allocatam in primo rotulo regis Ricardi in hec verba. Idem vicecomes reddidit compotum suum de .xl. sol' de Johanne de Eston' quia non habuit quem pleg(iavit), et de dimidia marca de Johanne filio Galfr(edi) pro eodem, et de dimidia marca de Roberto filio Kane pro eodem, et de dimidia marca de Rad(ulfo) fabro pro eodem, et in perdonis per libertatem carte regis monachis de Rading(ia).[1]

The dating limits are those of Simon's abbacy. The document is concerned with the abbot's liberty of amercements of his men, but the text has clearly not been copied out in full. Robert of Bassingbourn was a royal clerk by Nov. 1204 (*Rot. Lit. Pat.*, 47) and by Oct. 1219 a clerk of the Exchequer (*Rot. Lit. Claus.*, i. 402), where in the early 1220s he was either the chancellor's or the treasurer's scribe (D. Crook, 'The early remembrancers of the Exchequer', *BIHR*, liii (1980), 17 n. 51; *Cal. Liberate R. 1267-71*, nos. 2157, 2163, 2167, 2182). I am grateful to Dr Crook for help on this point.

[1] *PR 1 Richard I* (Rec. Comm., 1844), 26.

119 *Extracts from Pipe Roll 2 Richard I showing allocation to Reading Abbey of amercements of it or its men*   [1190]

A f 34r; cf. B f 4v (see no. 120, n. 2)
Pd. see note

Homines abbatis de Rading(ia) in Crocham r(eddiderunt) compotum suum de tribus solidis et .v. denariis de purprestura. In perdonis per libertatem carte regis ipsi abbati .iii. sol', et quietus est.

Idem abbas r(eddidit) compotum de dimidia marca pro vasto. In perdonis per libertatem carte dimidia marca, et quietus est.

In eodem rotulo continetur: abbati de Rading(ia) de minutis particulis foreste .iii. sol' et .vi. d'.

Marginal note: Berchsire. In ii° rotulo regis Ricardi

These extracts are to be found, with slight differences, in *PR 2 Richard I*, 33, 34. The cartulary scribe has omitted the additional 5d allowed to the abbot in respect of the men of Crookham, but the Pipe Roll shows the whole amount to have been allowed. Since these extracts immediately follow no. 118 in A, though in a different hand, they may have been part of the same document.

120 *Extracts from Pipe Rolls between 1 Richard I and 26 Henry III showing allocation to Reading Abbey of amercements and fines before judgement*   [1189–1242]

B f 4v; (partial) A f 34r (passages marked *d–d* and *h–h* only)
Pd. see notes 1–3

Libertas abbatis et monachorum de Rading(ia) allocata est ad scaccarium anno regni regis Ricardi primo in hec verba. Idem vicecomes reddidit compotum suum de .xl. s' de Johanne*ᵃ* de Eston'*ᵇ* quia non habuit quem plegiavit, et de dimidia marca de Johanne filio Galfredi*ᶜ* pro eodem, et de dimidia marca de Roberto filio Kane pro eodem, et de dimidia marca de Rad(ulfo) fabro pro eodem, et in perdonis per libertatem carte regis monachis de Rading(ia) .lx. s', et quietus est.[1]
Marginal note: Hertford'

Anno secundo regis Ricardi reddidit vicecomes Berk' compotum suum de tribus s' et .v. d' de purprestur'. In perdonis per libertatem carte regis abbati .iii. s', et quietus est. Idem abbas reddidit compotum suum de dimidia marca pro vasto. In perdonis per libertatem carte dimidia marca, et quietus est.[2]
Marginal note: Itinere G. filii Petri. Berk'

*ᵈ*Liberati sunt abbati 'et monachis*ᵉ* de Rading(ia) .xx. s' de fine quem fecit Robertus Bostard'*ᶠ* pro Reginaldo de Kenebell' et plegiis suis, quia retraxit se, per libertatem carte domini regis et quietus est, anno regni regis H(enrici) filii regis J(ohannis) xvi.*ᵈᵍ*
Marginal note: Itinere W. de Ralege. Bukingh'

*ʰ*Villata de Alveston' reddidit compotum suum de .xl. s' pro receptamento et concelatione*ⁱ* Walteri de Oclive.*ʲ* In thesaur(o) domini*ᵏ* regis .xxxvi. s' .viii. d', et abbati et monachis de Rading(ia) .xl. d' per libertatem carte domini*ᵏ* regis, et quieta est, anno regni*ᵏ* regis Henrici filii regis Johannis xvi.*ʰ*
Marginal note: Warwik

Villata Rading(ie) exceptis vinetar(iis) et drap(eriis) reddidit compotum suum de .xv. marcis de fine ante iudicium. In thesaur(o) regis nichil, et abbati Rading(ensi) .xv. marc(e) per libertatem cart(arum) regum Anglie et quieta est, anno regni regis H(enrici) filii regis J(ohannis) xxvi.[l3]

Marginal note: Berk' finis

General rubric: De libertate allocata ad scaccarium

[a] Ph' *B (in error)*	[b] *Insert* dimid' m' *B (in error)*
[c] Godefr' *B (in error)*	[d-d] *A f 34r* (slightly different word order)
[e-e] *Om. in A*	[f] Boistard *A*
[g] *B adds in a later hand:* in itinere W. de Raley in fine magni rotuli	
[h-h] *A f 34r*	[i] concelamento *A*
[j] Clive *A*	[k] *Om. in A*
[l] *B has* xxvii, *but* xxvi *is correct (see Note 3)*	

See also no. 138.

[1] *PR 1 Richard I*, 26. The extract also appears in no. 118.
[2] *PR 2 Richard I*, 33. Another version of this is in no. 119.
[3] *PR 26 Henry III*, 66.

121   *Memorandum that in 8 Henry III ½ mark was paid to Reading Abbey [at the Exchequer] from Thomas le Prude by liberty of the king's charter*   1224

A f 33v

Anno octavo eiusdem regis[1] liberata fuit dimidia marca abbati et monachis de Rading(ia) de Thoma le Prude per libertatem carte regis, et quietus est.

Marginal note: in comitatu Sudsexie (*? corrected from* Msexie)

[1] This immediately follows a quite unconnected mandate by Henry III concerning quittance of scutage in Showell (no. 528).

122   *Agreement, reached before justices-in-eyre in Berkshire, between Abbot Adam [of Lathbury] and the convent of Reading, and Prior Robert de Diva and the Hospitallers of England, concerning the [hundred court] suit of the men of Woolhampton [Berks.] of the fee of Roger Pantulf*

[prob. Jan. 1228]

A f 81r; B f 63v; C f 30r–v

Hec est concordia facta inter[a] Adam abbatem de Rading(ia) et conventum eiusdem loci, ex una parte, et fratrem Robertum de Diva[b] priorem et fratres hospitalis Ierusalem in Anglia, ex altera, de secta hominum de Wullavint(ona)[c] de feodo Rogerii Pantulf, unde placitum fuit inter eos in curia domini regis Henrici filii regis Iohannis, anno regni ipsius duodecimo. Scilicet quod dicti prior et fratres concesserunt pro se et successoribus suis dictis abbati et monachis de Rading(ia) et successoribus suis quod medietas ville de Wullavint(ona)[d]que est de feodo Rogerii Pantulf, quod feodum Henricus de Scakario[e] in manu sua tunc tenuit, faciat omnimodam sectam ad

hundredum de Rading(ia). Et pro hac concessione idem abbas re-
misit et quietum clamavit pro se et successoribus suis in perpetuum
dictis priori et fratribus totum ius et clamium quod habuit in secta
residue medietatis eiusdem ville, que est de dominio dicti prioris, et
totum ius quod habuit in amerciamentis hominum suorum in eodem
feodo et catallis fugitivorum, salvis tamen eidem abbati et successoribus suis in perpetuum omnibus placitis corone, inquisicionibus et
attachiamentis ad placita corone pertinentibus. Et ut hec concordia
rata et stabilis in perpetuum perseveret, huic parti cirographi, que
penes abbatem et monachos de Rading(ia) remanet, dicti prior et
fratres hospitalis Ierusalem in Anglia sigilla sua apposuerunt. Hiis
testibus:*f* domino Roberto de Lexintun(a), Radulfo Musard, Mauricio de Gaunt, tunc justic(iariis) domini regis itinerantibus in comitatu Berkesire, coram quibus dicta concordia facta fuit et per quos
eadem concordia in rotulo domini regis fuit inrotulata, et multis
aliis.

a Interlined in A   *b* A has Avia (in error), Diva B, C
c Wlhavent' B, C   *d* Wlavint' B, C
e Scacc(ario) B, C   *f* B, C end

This agreement was made during the Berks. eyre of 12 Henry III, the main sessions
of which were held in Dec. 1227 (Clanchy, *Berks. Eyre of 1248*, xciv). However, since
in Hilary term, 12 Henry III, the prior of the Hospitallers appointed his attorney
against the abbot of Reading in a plea of suit (*Cur. Reg. R.*, xiii. 102), this agreement
probably dates from the subsidiary session of the eyre at Wallingford in Jan. 1228
(Clanchy, *ibid.*).

123 *List of amercements which the abbot of Reading ought to receive from
the eyre of Robert of Lexington by liberty of the king's charter* [1235–36]

B f 4v

Amerciamenta que debet abbas Rading(ensis) percipere per libertatem carte domini regis de itinere Roberti de Lexinton'.
< Berk. >

De Willelmo de Englefeld .v. marc(e) pro defalta.

De Nicholao le Butiler dim(idia) marc(a) pro eodem.

De Symone filio Nicholai et Roberto de Offinton' pro eodem
dim(idia) m(arca).

De Rad(ulfo) de Wodehache de Windesor(es) dim(idia) m(arca)
pro vinis venditis contra assisam.

De Godefr(ido) Underhor'	.ii. s'.	
De Petro Page	.ii. s'.	pro viridi
De Rogero de Haga	.xii. d'.	
De Johanne de la Dene	.ii. s'	

< Warwik >
De Rokinton' .xl.ª pro murdr'.
De Tidinton' .xix. d' pro fuga Ricardi filii Henrici.

< Hertford' >
De Roberto de Broke et Waltero filio Angerii de Eston' dim(idia)
m(arca) pro iniusta detencione.

ª *Sic*

The eyres in Berkshire and Hertfordshire took place in 1235, the eyre in Warwickshire
in 1236 (Crook, *General Eyre*, 93, 90, 95). For the Berkshire portion of this list, see
Clanchy, *Berks. Eyre of 1248*, xxxviii.

124 *Estreat of amercements which the abbot of Reading ought to receive by
liberty of the king's charter from the eyre of William of York in Berkshire, 25
Henry III*   [Nov. 1241]

B ff 4v–5v

Amerciamenta que debet abbas percipere per libertatem carte
domini regis de itinere Willelmi de Eboraco et sociorum suorum,
anno xxv.
< Berk' >
De decena Alani Morel in Silamsted' pro fuga Simonis la Pappe
.i. mª.
De Henrico Otvy pro plegio Alicie que fuit uxor Ricardi de Lam-
bur' dim' mª.ª
De decena Simonis Merwyne in Silamsted' Abbatis pro fuga Rob-
erti le Franceis .i. mª.
De abbate de Rading(ia) de catallis eiusdem Symonis .xxix. s'
.viii. d'.
De decena Ade Blakeman pro fuga Stephani de Benham .x. s'.
De villata de Aldermanston' quia non fecit sectam .xx. s'.
De decena Wydonis de Englefeld pro fuga Hugonis molend(inarii)
de la Thele .x. s'.
De catallis eiusdem Hugonis .vii. s'.
[*f 5r*]
De decena Galfr(edi) Blostine in Pangeburn' pro fuga Johannis le
Coliere .x. s'.
De abbate de Rading(ia) de catallis eiusdem Johannis .iiii. s'.
< finis > De Roberto de la More de fine pro falso appellatione dim'
mª per plegium Johannis Blancboli.
De Ricardo de Colley pro plegio eiusdem dim' mª.
De abbate de Rading(ia) de catallis Rad(ulfo) de Quercu sus-
penso .vii. mª.

De Willelmo Reyner quia retraxit se dim' m².

De Petro Jordan et Ricardo porcario de Aldermanston' pro plegio eiusdem Willelmi dim' m².

De Roberto de Fonte pro eodem dim' m². De Willelmo de Broka pro eodem dim' m².

De Johanne Jordan et Waltero de Frith' pro eodem dim' m².

De Johanne de la Pirie et Eudone Wardbudell' pro plegio Johannis Bassing' dim' m².

De Ph(ilippo) de Covel' quia non est prosecutus dim' m².

De Rogero preposito de Padewrth' et Martino de Shefeld dim' m² pro pleg' eiusdem.

De Johanne Lilie et Eudone Wardbudell' quia non habuerunt quem pleg(iaverunt) dim' m².

De Willelmo de la Bure pro eodem dim' m². De Rad(ulfo) fabro de Thedmerse pro eodem dim' m².

De Roberto de la More et Willelmo filio Warini pro eodem dim' m².

De Ada filio Hervei pro transgressione dim' m².

De Roberto le Taillur et Willelmo molend(inario) quia non habuerunt quem pleg(iaverunt) dim' m².

De Rogero Rufo et Roberto de la Bure pro eodem dim' m².

De Wygano de Stapel et Willelmo de Marruge pro eodem dim' m².

De Rad(ulfo) de Scaccario pro eodem dim' m². De Willelmo Revel pro eodem dim' m².

De Henrico de Wicumbe pro eodem dim' m². De Herveo Coco pro eodem dim' m².

De Johanne Coco et Roberto filio Elye pro eodem dim' m².

De Waltero Prest et Johanne de la Cumbe pro eodem dim' m².

< finis > De Johanne de la Hose et sociis suis iur(atoribus) de fine pro transgressione .iiii. m².

De villata de Tacham quia non fecit sectam .i. m².

De Willelmo le Marre et Johanne Coterel quia non habuerunt quem pleg(iaverunt) dim' m².

De decena Bartholomei Hollepuke in Burhildebur' pro eodem dim' m².

De decena Nicholai Dod in Blebur' pro fuga Walteri sutoris .i. m².

De Ricardo filio Petri in Chaus' pro transgressione .i. m².

De decena Henrici de Coleburn' in Wyndel' Abbatis pro fuga Johannis Swetrig .x. s'.

< finis > ᵇ De Willelmo de Benham et sociis suis de fine pro transgressione .xl. s'.

De villata de Rading(ia) de fine ante iudicium .xv. m².

De warda que vocatur Vicus Lond' pro fuga Ricardi de Wicumb' .xl. s'.

De abbate de Rading(ia) de catallis cuiusdam extranei fug(ati) .v. s'.

De warda de Alto Vico pro fuga Colini pistoris .xl. s'.

De warda Novi Vici pro fuga Roberti de Hollebroc et Reginaldi Rufi .i. mᵃ.

De Henrico Wille pro vinis venditis contra assisam dim' mᵃ.

De Alano vinetario pro eodem dim' mᵃ.

De Agatha que fuit uxor G(ileberti)ᶜ Rufi pro eodem dim' mᵃ.

De Alano le Porter pro transgressione dim' mᵃ.

De Th(oma) le Taillur pro eodem dim' mᵃ.

De Roberto Wille pro paneᵈ vend' contra assisam .xl. s'.

De Roberto del Parlur pro eodem dim' mᵃ. De Johanne filio Ph(ilippi) pro eodem dim' mᵃ.

De Gileberto de Ponte pro eodem dim' mᵃ.

[f 5v]

< finis > De Willelmo de Musseden' et sociis suis iur(atoribus) de fine pro transgressione .iiii. mᵃ.

< diss' >ᵉ De Ricardo de Dunmere pro dissens'ᶠ dim' mᵃ.

De Willelmo le gardiner pro falso clamore dim' mᵃ per plegium Henrici de Fonte.

De Roberto de la More pro eodem et pro transgressione dim' mᵃ per plegium Amis(ii) de Peletot et Symonis de molend(ino).

De Ricardo Blundo quia retraxit se dim' mᵃ per plegium W(illelmi) de Englefeld.

De Godefr(ido) de Colley et Ricardo de Colley per plegium eiusdem Ricardio dim' mᵃ.

De Amis(io) de Peletot dim' mᵃ.

< diss' > De Waltero Fachel .x. s' pro diss'.

De Roberto Wandri quia retraxit se dim' mᵃ per plegium Roberti Kibbe.

De Willelmo de la Haith' et Elena Ravening per plegium eiusdem Roberti dim' mᵃ.

De Willelmo de la Heche quia retraxit se et Laurentio Kipping et Roberto le Eir per plegium eiusdem W(illelmi) dim' mᵃ.

De Johanne Banastr' quia retraxit se dim' mᵃ per plegium Willelmi de Englefeld.

< diss' > De Roberto capellano de Offinton' pro diss' dim' mᵃ.

De Willelmo filio Wygani pro falso clamore dim' mᵃ. De Roberto de Offinton' pro eodem dim' mᵃ.

De Roberto de la More quia retraxit se dim' mᵃ.

De Galfr(edo) filio Johannis et Ada filio Hervey pro iniusta detentione dim' mᵃ.

<diss'> De Roberto de Auvers pro diss' dim' m^a.

<finis> De Galfr(edo) filio Johannis pro licentia concordandi .xx. s' per plegium Petri Auris et Petri de Mulleford'.

De Roberto de Auvers pro eodem dim' m^a.

De Gileberto de la More pro eodem .i. m^a per plegium Johannis Blanbulli.

De magistro Ricardo de Benham pro habenda inquisicione dim' m^a.

De Amisio de Peletot pro eodem .i. m^a per plegium Gileberti de la^g More et Roberti Kibbe.

De Rogero de la Hyde pro eodem .ii. m^a.

De Gervasio Cacoberd pro eodem dim' m^a per plegium Henrici de Braihof.

<finis>^e De Gileberto Lil pro habenda inquisitione dim' m^a per plegium Gregorii le Mazun.

De Willelmo de Englefeld pro licentia concordandi dim' m^a.

De Roberto Basseth pro eodem dim' m^a per plegium Rad(ulfi) Basseth.

De Gunnild(a) que fuit uxor Henrici Chanterel pro habenda inquisitione dim' m^a per plegium J(ohannis) Blancbulli.

De Henrico ostiario pro eodem dim' m^a.

De Henrico Snuker pro eodem dim' m^a per plegium Willelmi Russel et Gileberti le Hyreis.

<finis> De Ricardo de Russehal' pro licentia concordandi dim' m^a.

De Agatha de Sancto Laurentio quia retraxit se dim' m^a de itinere Henrici de Barthon' in Sutht'.

De Hugone de Porta dim' m^a pro fuga Willelmi filii Willelmi.

De Henrico tannur dim' m^a quia non habuit quem pl(egiavit).

De Nicholao le Tannur dim' m^a pro eodem. De Willelmo Neol et Willelmo Waker dim' m^a.

<finis> De Ada filio Hervi de fine pro licentia concordandi .xx. s'.

^a This and the following item appear in reverse order in Ms and marked for transposition
^b Bracketed in Ms with next item
^c For this expansion, see the Eyre Roll for 1241, PRO JUST 1/37, m. 35d
^d Sic, probably error for pannis (see Eyre Roll, m. 35d)
^e Bracketed in Ms with next two items
^f Sic, probably error for disseis'
^g Interlined

This list gives the profits of justice due to the abbot of Reading from the Berkshire eyre of William of York and his colleagues, who closed their main session on 3 Nov. 1241 (Clanchy, *Berks. Eyre of 1248*, xciv). For discussion of the list and of its significance in the abbey's defence of its liberties, see *ibid.*, xxxvii–xxxviii. The noting of fines, where appropriate, in the margin is connected with a dispute which the abbey was then engaged upon with the Crown over the allocation to it of fines as well as amercements, a dispute which was not settled until the judgement of the king's council in Nov. 1242 that the abbey should have fines before judgment and other amercements (see no. 65).

125   *Precept by Richard de Turri, steward of Richard earl of Cornwall, to Robert de Luches, bailiff of the honour of Wallingford, to cause the abbot of Reading to have the chattels of Ralph de Quercu in Burghfield and all amercements of the justices' eyre in his liberty*   28 Oct. 1241 × 27 Oct. 1242

    B f 4r

R(icardus) de Turri, senescallus Ricardi comitis Cornubie, Roberto de Luches, baillivo de honore de Walingf(ordia), salutem. Vehementer miramur super eo quod mandatum et preceptum nostrum nondum fecisti tibi iniunctum apud Rading(iam). Unde tibi iterato precipimus quod visis litteris istis habere facias domino abbati de Rading(ia) catalla que fuerunt Radulfi de Quercu in Burchefeld' prout extenta sunt, insuper et omnes denarios amerciamentorum itineris justic(iariorum) in libertate sua secundum tenorem libertatis sue optente per cartas quas habet a regibus Anglie. Anno regni regis H(enrici) filii regis Johannis xxvi.

The text appears to have been abridged towards the end. The eyre in question was that of William of York and his colleagues at Reading in Oct.–Nov. 1241. The estreat of amercements due to the abbot from this eyre includes an item of 7 marks for Ralph de Quercu's chattels (see no. 124).

126   *Memorandum concerning demands by the treasurer and barons of the Exchequer upon the abbot of Reading for fines and amercements*   [1256–60]

    B f 6r

Memorandum quod thesaurarius et barones de scaccario exigunt ab abbate Rading(ensi) debita subscripta. Scilicet in rotulo quadragesimo quarto pro licencia concordandi dimidiam marcam. Item de fine pro eodem .i. marcam. Item in rotulo quadragesimo secundo pro disseisina .xx. marcas. Et pro falso clamore .v. marcas. Item in rotulo quadragesimo pro attincta habenda .xx. solidos. Et pro licencia concordandi .v. marcas.

127   *Note that the abbot of Reading is allowed at the Exchequer 1 mark for licence to agree in the eyre of Richard of Middleton*   [1268]

    B f 5v

De abbate de Radingia pro licentia concordandi .i. marc(a), et allocatur in itinere dicti Ricardi de Midlentone ad scaccarium in rotulis suis, et in rotulis de scaccario.

Marginal note: De itinere Ricardi de Midlentone

This presumably relates to the eyre of Richard of Middleton and his fellow justices in Berks. in June, 1268 (Clanchy, *Berks. Eyre of 1248*, xcvii). It is written in a later hand at the end of the estreat of amercements from the 1241 eyre (no. 124).

128 Final concord in the king's court at Windsor in the quindene of the Purification, 3 Edward I, before the king himself, between Peter Achard, plaintiff, and Robert [of Burgate], abbot of Reading, on a plea that the abbot should permit Peter to have all kinds of waifs found in his fee and all swarms of bees and all fowls taken in his park or garden. Namely, Peter conceded for him and his heirs that the abbot and his successors and the abbey of Reading shall have all waifs in Peter's fee within the abbot's liberty, and that they shall be handed over to the abbot's bailiffs 8 days after their discovery, recompense being paid to Peter and his heirs for damages caused by the waifs. In return, the abbot granted for him and his successors to Peter and his heirs all manner of fowls and swarms of bees taken in his park and garden; also that, by reasonable summons of 8 days, Peter and his heirs shall come by one of their free men to the abbot's view of frankpledge at Theale (*la Thele*) once a year before Martinmas to demand the court of Peter and his heirs, so that a day be assigned to the latter by the abbot or his bailiffs for the holding of the view of frankpledge by the abbot's bailiffs at the bridge of Aldermaston (*Aldermaneston'*),[a] all profits of the view remaining to Peter and his heirs, as was previously the custom. The abbot granted also that Peter and his heirs may exercise *infongeneþef* in their court in respect of thieves taken with mainour, the chattels of such thieves remaining to Peter and his heirs unless the thief were the abbot's man or of the abbot's liberty outside Peter's fee; if a thief attached within that fee turns approver and someone accused in the fee is able to be attached, both the approver and the accused with their chattels shall be handed over to the abbot or his successors or their bailiffs; if any man of the abbot or his successors, resident in the fee of Peter or his heirs or outside in the liberty of the abbot or his successors, be taken or attached within that fee in mainour or for any reason, he shall be handed with his chattels to the abbot and his successors or their bailiffs. The abbot granted also that felons' and fugitives' chattels within Peter's fee, or a reasonable value instead, shall, by view and office of the coroners of the abbot and his successors, be handed to the tithing man (*theþing mannus*) of Peter and his heirs for safe-keeping until the arrival of the itinerant justices in Berkshire, when the chattels or their value shall be restored to the abbot and his successors or their bailiffs. The abbot granted also that Peter, his heirs and all his men shall be quit of tolls throughout the abbot's liberty for all trading for their own needs and uses, but that, if any of their men trade commercially in the abbot's market towns, they shall pay tolls like other outsiders; also that, when any attachment or summons needs to be made within the fee of Peter and his heirs, by a royal writ or without it, the abbot and his successors or their bailiffs will order the bailiffs of Peter and his heirs to make the same; if the latter refuse to do so, the bailiffs of the abbot and his successors shall make the attachment or summons without impediment from Peter or his heirs   16 Feb. 1275

B f 171r–v; C ff 101r–102r

a Aldermanstone C

The foot of this fine is PRO CP 25(1)/9/29/18; also 17, but this is an earlier version corrected to give the text of 18. The fine is highly exceptional in having been made before the king alone, without reference to other justices (cf. no. 456). The explanation lies partly in the close links between both parties and the Crown, Reading being a royal abbey and the Achards having a record of royal service in the 13th century (K. J. Stringer, 'Some documents concerning a Berkshire family and Monk Sherborne priory, Hampshire', *Berks. Arch. Journ.*, lxiii (1967-8), 25) and partly in the exalted nature of the liberties at issue. Peter Achard was lord of Aldermaston (*VCH Berks.*, iii. 308), which lay within the foreign hundred of Reading (also called the hundred of Theale), part of the abbot of Reading's Liberty. By a grant of Henry I to Robert Achard, his ancestor, Peter claimed high franchises, including *infangenetheof* and exemption from attendance at hundred courts (Stringer, loc. cit.; F. M. Stenton, *The First Century of English Feudalism* (2nd edn, Oxford, 1961), 101 n.1), which clearly conflicted with the abbey's liberties and had been the subject of earlier disputes (Stringer, 28 n. 41; Stenton, loc. cit.). By this complex agreement, reached with the personal intervention of the king, Peter secured a definition of his and his heirs' liberties in relation to those of Reading Abbey.

129 Quo warranto proceedings concerning the abbot of Reading's liberties in Hertfordshire   [Nov. 1278]

B ff 12r–11v (begun on f 12r and completed on f 11v)
Pd. *Placita de Quo Warranto*, 282-3 (from Eyre Roll)[1]

Rubric: Libertates abbatis Rading' allocate per veredictum militum in comitatu Hertford' in itinere dominorum Johannis de Reygat', Willelmi de Northburg', Galfr(edi) de Leukenor', Walteri de Hopton', Rogeri Loveday et Salomonis de Roff'

The justices sat at Hertford 3-27 November or later, 1278 (Crook, *General Eyre*, 158).

[1] The printed text is slightly less extensive than that in the cartulary, for the latter includes quittance of *tynpeni* and the claims that the abbot's men are quit of assizes and recognitions and that the dogs of the abbot's men are quit of hambling.

130 Quo warranto proceedings concerning the abbot of Reading's
liberties in Kent [Jan. x June 1279]

B f 12r
Pd. *Placita de Quo Warranto*, 347 (from Eyre Roll)[1]

Rubric (*in margin*):[2] Libertates abbatis Rading' allocate per veredictum militum in comitatu Kanc(ie) anno regni regis Edwardi septimo
in itinere dominorum J(ohannis) de Reygat', Willelmi de Northburg', Galfr(e)di de Leukenor', Walteri de Hopton', Ricardi de
Boyland' et Salomonis de Roff'

For the dates of the justices' main sessions in Kent in 1279, see Crook, *General Eyre*,
158.

[1] The printed text is slightly different from that in the cartulary, for the latter,
while omitting *furcas*, includes *pillori* and quittance of *tynpeni* and the abbot's claims
to have free warren in all his lands and that his men are quit of assizes and recognitions. It concludes: *Salvo iure domini regis cum inde loqui voluerit.* See also no. 447.
[2] The extreme right edge of the rubric was shaved when the folio was subsequently
trimmed.

131 Quo warranto proceedings concerning the abbot of Reading's
liberties in Sussex [June x Nov. 1279]

B f 12v; G f 3r–v
Pd. *Placita de Quo Warranto*, 754 (from Eyre Roll)[1]

Rubric (*in margin*):[2] Libertates domini abbatis de (R)ading(ia) in
comitatu (S)usex' allocate per vere(d)ictum militum in itinere
(dom)inorum Johannis de Regat', W(illelmi) de Northburg',
G(alfredi) de Leuk', Ricardi de (B)oylond', Salomonis de Rovec',
anno regni (r)egis E(dwardi) octavo

For the dates of the justices' main sessions at Chichester in Sussex in 1279, see Crook,
General Eyre, 159.

[1] This text is the same as that in G, but slightly different from that in B, which
may have been taken from another roll (see Crook, loc. cit.). The only significant
difference in B, however, is that it calls the abbot's attorney Adam Scot, while G and
the printed text have Andrew Scot. Cf. no. 558.
[2] The extreme left edge of the rubric was shaved when the folio was subsequently
trimmed.

132 Record of the action brought by [Roger Longespee] bishop of
Coventry and Lichfield, guardian of the land and heir of William of
Englefield (*Englefeud*), against the abbot of Reading concerning 13½
marks which John, monk and chamberlain of Reading Abbey, re-
ceived from the said William when John of St Valery was sheriff of
Berkshire by estreat of the summons of the Exchequer which he had

from the sheriff for the levying of the king's debts within the abbot's liberty, in respect of which sum the chamberlain should have acquitted William at the Exchequer and did not do so. In pleading the abbot's attorney acknowledged that the chamberlain had received from William 5 marks because he did not proceed and 5 marks for escape [of thieves],[a] which William owed to the king, as is contained in the Account Roll of 4 Edward I in Berkshire, and which 10 marks the abbot claimed to have by liberty of his royal charters. The remaining $3\frac{1}{2}$ marks the abbot paid into the king's treasury. The bishop thus withdrew quit of the said moneys.

[9 Feb. 1284]

B f 13v

Rubric: Memorand' et inrotulacio de scaccario pro evasione latronum et allocatio in oct' Purific(ationis) beate Marie, anno domini M.CC. octogesimo tercio

[a] *Supplied from rubric*

The date is taken from the rubric. William of Englefield was dead by 8 Aug. 1275 (see nos. 762–3).

133 Record of a recognition concerning the abbot of Reading's liberties in Hertfordshire [a][during the eyre of Solomon of Rochester and his colleagues].[a] The abbot claims view of frankpledge, assize of bread and ale, waif, *infongenethef*, *utfongenethef*, gallows, felons' and fugitives' chattels of his men, and fines and amercements of his men in his manor of Aston (*Eston'*) and that he and his men are to be quit of suits of shires and hundreds, sheriff's tourns and all toll, etc., in all his lands and manors in the county, and free warren in the same. The abbot, through his attorney, says that he and his predecessors have held the manor of Aston (*Aston'*) with these liberties by gift of Queen Adeliza (*Alic'*), confirmed by Richard I and by Henry III, all of whose charters he proffers. Both he and the king's attorney, William of Gislingham (*Giselingham*), agree to an inquiry. The jury find for the abbot, who is accordingly *sine die*, saving the king's right, etc. [Apr. x May 1287]

B f 14r

Rubric (in margin):[1] Libertates allocate [in] comitatu Hertford' i(n) itinere domini S. de [Roff'] et sociorum suorum

[a-a] *Supplied from rubric*

For Solomon of Rochester's eyre in Hertfordshire in 1287, see Crook, *General Eyre*, 168. This case does not appear in the printed edition of Quo warranto proceedings.

¹ Extreme right edge of rubric shaved by subsequent trimming of the folio.

134 *Memorandum of liberties not specified in the king's charter*
[? early 14th cent.]

B f 15v

Isti articuli non sunt specificati in carta regis. Videlicet returnum omnium brevium regis in omnibus terris nostris. Et quod respondere possimus per manus nostras ad scaccarium de omnibus debitis exactis in cunctis com(itatibus). Et quod placitum namii vetiti specificetur. Et quod fines omnimode specificentur.

This is written in an early 14th-century hand at the top of the folio, the remainder being blank. The tone of the entry suggests that the abbey claimed or exercised these liberties and that an attempt was to be made to have them specified in a future royal charter. They do not appear in the general charter of Edward II (no. 102), which may be the charter referred to, but most of them were included in that of Edward III (no. 109).

135 *Extract from the Warwickshire and Leicestershire section of Pipe Roll 10 Edward II concerning the allocation to Reading Abbey of a fine of 50 marks from 13 men of the abbey for transgression* [1317]

B f 44r-v; C ff 16v-17r; F f 82r-v (not collated)

Idem vicecomes redd' compotum de .L. marcis de Willelmo de Aboneton' in Wyngeston', Bate filio Henrici de eadem, Willelmo de Wolveye, Willelmo sur la grene, Willelmo Haliday,ᵃ Petro filio Rogeri, Radulfo filio Henrici, Gilberto de Wyngeston', Willelmo filio Henrici, Waltero de Wygeston', Symone Wodecok', Galfr(ed)o filio Petri et Roberto filio Henrici Drak' de fine suo pro trans(gressione) per plegium Johannis Jurdan de Stapelton', Rogeri de Keleby de Haston', Walteri filii Ran(ulfi) de Sharneford', Willelmi filii Ricardi de Stratton', Ade filii Mabil(ie) de Bulginton', Henrici de Frellesworth', Johannis filii Thome de Scharneford', Johannis le Joeveneᵇ de Wolveye, Roberti fratris eius et Roberti filii Ricardi de Stratton', sicut continetur ex alia parte rotuli. In thesauro nichil. Et abbati et monachis Rading', quorum tenentes predicti homines sunt, sicud idem vicecomes testatur, .L. mar' per libertatem cartarum reg(um) Anglie et perᶜ confirmacionem regis nunc et per breve regis inter Communia de anno xi.; in quo continetur quod, cum progenitores regis quondam reges Anglie per cartas suas concessissent abbati et monachis de Rading' diversas libertates et immunitates sub generalibus verbis in eisdem cartis contentis, virtute quorum verborum generalium abbas et monachi loci predicti a tempore confectionis

cartarum[d] illarum semper hactenus habuerunt fines et amerciamenta hominum et tenencium suorum ex quacumque causa emer-
gencia, catalla etiam dampnatorum et fugitivorum, annum et vastum et diem, finesque illi et amerciamenta ac etiam catalla illa,
annus et vastum et dies ad scaccarium predictorum progenitorum
regis allocata fuerunt [f 44v] sicud dicunt; ac rex cartas predictas
confirmaverit et de gratia sua speciali concesserit eisdem abbati et
monachis quod, licet ipsi vel predecessores sui predicti libertatibus
vel immunitatibus in eisdem cartis contentis vel earum aliqua usi
non fuerint, ipsi tamen abbas et monachi et successores sui libertatibus et immunitatibus predictis et earum qualibet plene de cetero
guadeant et utantur prout in carta regis eis inde confecta plenius[e]
continetur; rex per idem breve mandat thesaurario et baronibus suis
de scaccario quod, scrutatis rotulis et memor(andis) scaccarii predicti de temporibus progenitorum regis predictorum, si invenerint
predicta fines et amerciamenta hominum et tenencium predictorum
abbatis et monachorum, catalla, annum et vastum et diem predicta
eis ad scaccarium progenitorum regis predictorum allocata fuisse,
sicut predictum est, tunc eisdem abbati et monachis fines, amerciamenta, catalla, annum et vastum et diem huiusmodi faciant ad
dictum scaccarium tempore regis allocari et nichilominus cartam
regis predictam in singulis suis articulis coram eis in dicto scaccario
allocent, ac ipsos abbatem et monachos libertatibus et immunitatibus in eadem carta contentis coram eis in scaccario predicto uti et
gaudere permittant iuxta tenorem carte eiusdem, eo non obstante
quod ipsi vel eorum predecessores libertatibus vel immunitatibus
predictis vel earum aliqua hactenus usi vel gavisi non fuerint; et
sicut allocatum est eisdem abbati et monachis in rotulo xxv. regis
E(dwardi) patris regis huius in Berk', ubi allocatur pro diss(eisina),
pro falso clamore, pro licencia concordandi, pro fine de licencia
concordandi; et sicud allocatum est eisdem in rotulo xvi. regis
H(enrici) avi regis huius in Buk', Bed', ubi allocatur de fine, et in
eodem rotulo xvi. in Warr', Leic', ubi allocatur pro concelamento;
et in rotulo xii. eiusdem regis H(enrici) in Essex', ubi allocatur quia
non h(abuit); et in rotulo primo regis Ricardi, ubi allocatur quia
non h(abuit). Et quietus est.

Rubric: In magno rotulo de anno decimo regis Edwardi filii regis
E(dwardi) in Warr'. Leic'.

[a] Haleday C
[b] Jeovene C
[c] Om. in C
[d] B has here predictarum deleted
[e] Insert inde C (in error)

136 Grant and acknowledgment [in French] by Richard of Hampton (*Hompton'*), Thomas of Edvin (*Yeddefen*), John of Sarnesfield (*Sarnefeld*), James of Ford (*la Forda*), Walter of Sarnesfield (*Sarnesfeld*), Henry Bernard, John of Eaton (*Eton'*), John of Humber (*Humbr'*), Hugh *Hakelud*, John *Coykings*, William of Stanton (*Staunton'*), Roger of Brimfield (*Brumfeld*), John of Eyton (*Eyton'*), John of Wharton (*Waverton'*), Ralph of Stockton (*Stokeston'*), Richard *de Paccheshale*, Walter *de Mappenore*, John of Reading, Richard *Lyulf'*, John *Melide*, John of Monmouth (*Monemwe*)ᵃ William of Salisbury (*Salesbur'*), William *Pril*, Philip *Gody*, William Bernard, Philip *le Romayn*, Roger Porter (*le Porter*) and William son of Ralph. Whereas there has been a dispute between them and Abbot Nicholas [of Whaplode] and the convent of Reading over the franchise of bloodshed (*saunk' espaundu*), which with other franchises the abbot and convent have by grant of the king and his progenitors, which bloodshed and various other trespasses the above-named have refused to present, they and all others of the abbot's franchise of Leominster grant and acknowledge for themselves and their heirs that presentment of bloodshed should be made on all days in the abbot's court of Leominster or wherever the court is held in the said franchise. Because of their contrariness in this and other matters, they are obliged to pay the abbot £100 all together on the quindene of Easter, 17 Edward [II]. Sealing with their seals. Given at Leominster, Thursday the feast of the Purification of Our Lady in the said year

2 Feb. 1324

B f 233v; F f 212v (not fully collated)

Rubric (B only): Concordia facta est inter abbatem Rading' et tenentes suos in libertate Leomenistrie de effusione sanguinis

ᵃ Monemuwe F

The naming of Abbot Nicholas (1305–28) and the precision of the dating clause enable the king to be identified as Edward II.

137 Quo warranto proceedings concerning the abbot of Reading's liberties in Houghton [Conquest, Bedfordshire]. [June x Nov. 1330]

B ff 137v–139v; C ff 79v–81r
Pd. *Placita de Quo Warranto*, 27–8 (from Eyre Roll)¹

Rubric: Allocatio libertatum abbatis Radyng' in comitatu Bedeford' coram Roberto de Ardern' et Johanne de Cauntebrygge et sociis suis justic(iariis) itinerantibus anno regni regis E(dwardi) tercii a Conquestu quarto, rotulo octavo itineris predicti, et cetera

For the justices' sessions in Bedfordshire in 1330, see Crook, *General Eyre*, 184; the case was adjourned *coram rege* on 23 Nov. Although nos. 137–8 relate to one place only, they are included here since they raise fundamental questions touching the abbey's liberties in general.

¹ The only significant differences between the printed text and that in the cartularies are these:

For *Abbat' de Hoctona* (printed, para. 1, line 3) read *Albodi de Hoctona*

For *Rogerum Vagel* (para. 2, line 1) read *Rogerum Vachel*

After *weyf* (para. 2, line 7) add *tanquam pertinentes ad terram suam predictam et cetera*

The sentence *Et de exitibus ... Regi respondeat* (para. 7, lines 11–12) is omitted in the cartularies

The word *alias* (para. 9, line 16) is omitted in the cartularies.

138 Continuation of the same case *coram rege*, to which it was adjourned by the itinerant justices   Jan. 1331–Jan. 1332

B ff 139v–141r; C ff 81r–82r

In the quindene of St Hilary [4 Edward III] Adam of Fincham (*Fyncham*), for the king, and the abbot of Reading, by Walter of Walgrave (*Waldegrave*) his attorney, came and were given a day in the octave of Holy Trinity [26 May], on which day both Adam and the abbot's attorney came. The king sent from his Chancery to his justices *coram rege* evidence of the allocation of certain liberties to the abbot of Reading in the Exchequer, as follows.

Mandate by King Edward III to Geoffrey le Scrope and his fellow justices *coram rege* that, having inspected the certification which the treasurer and barons of the Exchequer sent into Chancery by the king's mandate concerning certain liberties allowed to the abbot in the Exchequer, which the king encloses with the writ, they are to cause to be done what is right for the abbot.

Teste me ipso apud Langele xii. die Februarii, anno regni nostri quinto.   12 Feb. 1331

The king's writ to the treasurer and barons is as follows.

Mandate by King Edward III to the treasurer and barons of the Exchequer that, whereas a case is pending *coram rege* between the king and the abbot of Reading concerning certain liberties claimed by the abbot in the eyre of the justices itinerant in Bedfordshire, and because it is expedient and necessary that the king be informed as to the allocation of liberties to the abbot at the Exchequer in the past, they are to search the rolls and memoranda of the Exchequer and inform the king of their findings concerning this matter without delay.

Teste me ipso apud Westm(onasterium) xxii. die Januarii, anno regni nostri quarto.   22 Jan. 1331

By virtue of this writ the treasurer and barons sent to Chancery the following certification, which the king forwarded *coram rege*.

[*f 140r*]

In rotulo primo regis Ricardi in Essex' vicecomes redd' compotum de .xl. solidis de Johanne de Eston' quia non habuit quem pl(egiavit), et de dimidia marca de Johanne filio Galfr(ed)i pro eodem, et de dimidia marca de Roberto filio Kane de misericordia pro eodem, et de dimidia marca de Radulfo fabro pro eodem. In perdonis per libertatem carte regis monachis de Redyng' .lx.ª s'. Et quietus est.

In secundo rotulo regis Ricardi in Berk' annotatur sic. Homines abbatis de Radyng' in Crokham redd' compotum de .iii. s' et .v. d' pro purprestur'. In perdonis per libertatem carte regis ipsi abbati .iii. s' .v. d'. Abbas de Redyng' redd' compotum de dimidia marca pro vasto. In perdonis per libertatem carte regis ipsi abbati dimid' marc', et quietus est.

In rotulo quinto regis Ricardi in Bed', Buk' annotatur sic. Vicecomes redd' compotum de .xx. s' de Redburnstok' hundredo pro murdro. In thesauro .xi. s', in perdonis per cartam regis fratribus Hospitalis .xviii. d' et milicie Templi .xii. d' et monachis de Redyng' .ix. d'.

In rotulo .xvi. regis Henrici in Bed', Buk' sub titulo de amerciamentis per Willelmum de Ralegh', R(obertum) de Lexinton' et socios suos vicecomes redd' compotum de .CC. li' .xvii. s' de amerciamentis hominum francorum [*f 140v*] plegiorum et villarum hundredorum quorum nominibus preponitur littera .T. in rotulo quem predicti W(illelmus) et R(obertus) liberaverunt in thesauro. In thesauro .C. .iiiiˣˣ. .vi. li' .x. s' .iiii. d'. Et Ade filio Willelmi et Ricardo Duket itinerantibus in comitatibus Buk' et Bed' ad expensas suas .xx. marc' per litteras regis. Et abbati de Redyng' .xx. s' de fine quem Robertus Bustard' fecit pro Reginaldo de Kynebelle et plegiis suis quia retraxit se per libertatem carte regis. Et quietus est.

In eodem rotulo in Warr' annotatur sic. Villa de Alveston' redd' compotum de .xl. s' pro concelamento et receptamento Walteri de Clyve. In thesauro .xxxvi. s' .viii. d', et abbati et monachis de Redyng' .xl. d' per libertatem cartarum reg(um). Et quietus est.

In rotulo .xxvi. regis Henrici in Berk' annotatur sic. Villata de Redyng' exceptis draperiis et vinetariis redd' compotum de .xv. marcis de fine ante iudicium. In thesauro nichil, et abbati et monachis de Redyng' .xv. mar' per libertatem carte reg' Angl'. Et quietus est.

In rotulo .xxv. regis E(dwardi) filii regis H(enrici) in Berk' annotatur sic. Abbas de Redyng' debet .xxi. li' de pluribus debitis, scilicet .xx. mar' pro disseisina et .v. mar' pro falso clamore et .v. mar' pro licencia concordandi et .xx. s' de fine pro licencia concordandi. In thesauro nichil, et abbati et monachis de Redyng' .xxi. li' per libertatem cart' reg'. Et quietus est.

In rotulo .xiii. regis E(dwardi) filii regis E(dwardi) in Berk' annotatur sic. Johannes de la Weye redd' compotum de .x. s' de fine pro transgressione per plegium Elye de Sancto Albano et Rogeri de Lynch'. Willelmus de Blebury redd' compotum de .xx. s' pro licencia concordandi de tenementis in Blebury, Ufton' et Bradefeld'. Summa .xxx. s'. In thesauro nichil. Et abbati et monachis de Redyngia, cuius tenentes dicti Johannes et Willelmus sunt sicut vicecomes testatur, .xxx. s' per libertatem cartarum reg(um). Et quieti sunt.

The case was adjourned from the said octave of Holy Trinity, 5 Edward III, to the octave of St Hilary, 6 Edward III, when both the said Adam, for the king, and the abbot, by Walter of Walgrave his attorney, came. On inspection of the said allocations, it was clear that amercements, which the abbot claimed were not exacted from him and his monks, amercements of his men and tenants, and moneys for *murdrum* were allowed to them before the treasurer and barons. Therefore, concerning these, the abbot *sine die, salvo iure regis cum alias inde loqui voluerit et cetera.* As to felons' and fugitives' chattels and treasure trove, the abbot sought a writ *certiorari* to the treasurer and barons of the Exchequer, and a day was given to him *coram rege* in the octave of Holy Trinity.

Rubric (in margin) B only:[1] (I)nter rotulos regis rotulo xiiii. de termino Hillar' anno sexto

---

[a] *Ms has .xl., but see no. 120 and PR 1 Richard I, 26*

[1] In the margin of f 139v, where this account begins, partially trimmed and possibly not complete.

III PAPAL ACTS

139 Grant by Pope Calixtus II to Abbot Hugh [I] of Reading and his successors of papal protection for Reading Abbey, newly founded by King Henry I, and confirmation of its possessions, viz., the manors of Reading, Leominster and Thatcham with their appurtenances   [19 June 1123]

A ff 64v-65r
Pd. Holtzmann, *Papsturkunden*, iii, 133-4 (no. 9)

Marginal note (in a later hand): Prima confirmatio possessionum monasterii Radyng(ensis) .xiii. kl' Iulii anno domini M.C. xxiii

The date of this bull, which is not itself dated, is given in the marginal note. Holtzmann has misread this as the 12th kalend of July, thereby dating the bull to 20 June.

140 Confirmation by Pope Honorius II to Abbot Hugh [I] of Reading and his successors of the foundation of Reading Abbey by King Henry I and of the king's gifts—viz., Reading, Cholsey and Leominster with their churches and other appurtenances, a mint and moneyer at Reading, Thatcham and the church of Wargrave—and of the abbey's liberties and immunities   13 Apr. 1125

A f 63r-v; F ff 77v-78r
Pd. Holtzmann, *Papsturkunden*, iii, 136-7 (no. 12)

[Dat' Lateran(i) per manum Aimerici sancte Romane ecclesie diaconi cardinalis et cancellarii, idus Aprilis, indictione iii. anno dominice incarnationis M.C.xxv, pontificatus autem domini Honorii secundi pape anno primo.]

a-a Om. in A, supplied from F

   The content of this bull has a direct bearing on the question of the authenticity of Henry I's foundation charter (no. 1), for, as indicated by Holtzmann, the bull contains a long passage relating to the liberties, privileges and constitution of the abbey which is almost identical with the equivalent sections of the king's charter. The same passage occurs in all subsequent general papal confirmations to Reading in the 12th century, but is significantly absent from the earlier bull of Calixtus II (no. 139). Honorius II's bull was clearly composed with knowledge of the text of the king's charter in the Curia. There is no reason to doubt its authenticity, even as regards its inclusion of *utfangeneth(ef)*, on which see no. 1 n.

141 Confirmation by Pope Innocent II to Abbot Anscher of Reading and his successors of the foundation of Reading Abbey by King

Henry I and of the gifts made by the king and others – viz., Reading, Cholsey and Leominster with their churches and other appurtenances, Thatcham, the churches of Wargrave and Hanborough, the land of Houghton [Conquest] in Bedfordshire given by Albold, Whitsbury in Wiltshire given by Ingelram Apostolicus, land in Warwickshire given by Adeliza d'Ivry, a moneyer in London with the same liberties as though he were in Reading, and houses and land given by Wulvard of Dover in London and other lands and houses in the same city, and tithes conceded by diocesan bishops from the abbey's churches – and of the abbey's liberties and immunities   [1130 × 35]

A ff 63v–64v
Pd. Holtzmann, *Papsturkunden*, iii. 148–50 (no. 28)

The dating limits are those of Anscher's abbacy. *Mutatis mutandis* and with a longer list of gifts, this follows closely the bull of Honorius II (no. 140).

142   Indult by Pope Innocent II to Abbot Anscher and the monks of Reading of freedom to receive as monks any clerk or secular priest, whether he be canon, archdeacon or dean, without interference from any archbishop or bishop.   [1130 × 35]

A f 64v
Pd. Holtzmann, *Papsturkunden*, iii. 150 (no. 29)

The dating limits are those of Anscher's abbacy.

143   Confirmation by Pope Eugenius III to Abbot Edward of Reading and his successors of the foundation of Reading Abbey by King Henry I and of the gifts made by the king and others—viz., Reading, Cholsey and Leominster with their churches and other appurtenances, Whitsbury and its church, the churches of Wargrave and Hanborough, land in Houghton [Conquest] in Bedfordshire given by Albold, Thatcham and its church, Rowington and its church in Warwickshire given by Adeliza d'Ivry, a moneyer in London with the same liberties as though in Reading, houses and land given by Wulvard of Dover in London and other lands and houses in the same city, tithes conceded by diocesan bishops from the abbey's churches, houses and lands in Cambridge and Southampton, [East] Hendred in Berkshire, Blewbury in the same, 4 hides in Stratton [St Margaret] in Wiltshire given by Richard *de Mersi* of the fee of William d'Aubigny, Aston with its church in Hertfordshire, 100s worth of land and the church in Stanton [Harcourt] in Oxfordshire with the chapel of [North]moor, 100s annually from a hithe in London which King Henry I gave to his wife Queen Adeliza, the land of William the king's almsman at Wigston [Parva] in Leicestershire, the land of Herbert son of Fulcher at Marlborough, the lands of Geoffrey Purcell when he became a monk at Reading, land of Alan son of Robert and 1 hide of Ralph de Langetot in Lenborough in Buckinghamshire, land of Payn at Moulsford in Berkshire, land by Wallingford given by Rannulf *Grossus*, and the church of Berkeley with appurtenances—and of the abbey's liberties and immunities [1145 × 53]

A ff 65r-66r

Pd. Holtzmann, *Papsturkunden*, iii. 216-18 (no. 85)

The dating limits are those of Eugenius III's pontificate. This follows closely the text of Innocent II's confirmation (no. 141) but with a longer list of gifts.

144 Mandate by Pope Eugenius III to Theobald, archibishop of Canterbury, and his suffragans in whose dioceses the possessions of Reading Abbey are situated that, since the abbey, endowed with royal liberty (*regia libertas*), is under papal protection and the pope prohibits the construction of any fortification or castle in the abbey's lands against its will, they are to prohibit the people of their dioceses from any such intrusion [1145 × 53]

A f 66r

Pd. Holtzmann, *Papsturkunden*, iii. 218 (no. 86)

Rubric: Item carta eiusdem de non faciendo castrum apud Radingiam

The dating limits are those of Eugenius III's pontificate. This bull may have been called forth by the abbey's annoyance at a castle constructed in its precinct at Reading by King Stephen—contrary to divine and human law, as Robert of Torigny has it—which was destroyed by an Angevin force from Wallingford in 1153 (Robert of Torigny, 174). The cartulary rubric significantly relates the bull to the prohibition of building a castle at Reading.

145 Grant by Pope Adrian IV to Abbot Reginald of Reading and his successors of papal protection and confirmation for Reading Abbey and its possessions [specified as in Eugenius III's bull (no. 143) with the following additions] the gift by Jocelin brother of Queen Adeliza in Diddlesfold, a 4-day fair of St Laurence in Reading by grant of Henry I, Broadward given by Roger earl of Hereford, Rhynd (*Rindalgros*) and the Isle of May by gift of David king of Scotland, and a house given by Gospatrick earl [of Dunbar]— and the abbey's liberties and immunities [1154 × 58]

A ff 66r-67r

Pd. Holtzmann, *Papsturkunden*, iii. 269-71 (no. 126)

After 5 Dec. 1154, when Adrian IV was consecrated and before the end of 1158, in which year Abbot Reginald was deposed. The text follows closely that of Eugenius III (no. 143).

146 Confirmation by Pope Adrian IV to Abbot Reginald of Reading of the abbey's *societas* and fraternity with the abbey of Cluny   [1154 × 58]

A f 67v
Pd. Holtzmann, *Papsturkunden*, iii. 271 (no. 127)

Date as for no. 145. The text refers to a sealed *scriptum* of the abbot of Cluny concerning the same, which probably means the letter sent by Peter the Venerable to Abbot Hugh I (no. 218).

147 Mandate by Pope Adrian IV to Theobald, archbishop of Canterbury and papal legate, and his suffragans to compel those of their dioceses who have caused loss or injury to Reading Abbey to make satisfaction, and to admonish debtors of the abbey to pay the money owed; also to forbid that the chapels erected within the abbey's parishes during the time of war should prejudice the rights of its parish churches, since what is done in an emergency ought to cease when the emergency is over. The pope further inhibits the people of the addressees' dioceses from despoiling the abbey of its possessions given in free alms   [1154 × 59]

A f 67r-v
Pd. Holtzmann, *Papsturkunden*, iii. 274 (no. 131)

Rubric: Item carta eiusdem de capellis tempore belli erectis diruendis

The dating limits are those of Adrian IV's pontificate. This bull was no doubt occasioned by difficulties experienced by the abbey during the reign of Stephen, but the rubric indicates that the most serious problem was the unlawful building of chapels within the parishes of the abbey's churches.

148 Confirmation by Pope Alexander III to the abbot and monks of Reading, of Leominster and other possessions on the March of Wales or in Wales, and the Isle of May and other possessions in Scotland, forbidding anyone to make the said cells into abbeys or to dispose of their possessions without Reading Abbey's consent

[1159 × 81]

A f 70v
Pd. Holtzmann, *Papsturkunden*, iii. 421-2 (no. 300); Duncan, 'Documents of May', 76 (no. 55)

The dating limits are those of Alexander III's pontificate.

149 Mandate by Pope Alexander III to the bishops in whose dioceses Reading Abbey has churches to compel the clerks in possession of such churches who have 'hearth-ladies' (*focarie*) to remove them   [1159 × 81]

A f 70v
Pd. Holtzmann, *Papsturkunden*, iii. 422 (no. 301)

The dating limits are those of Alexander III's pontificate.

150 Grant by Pope Alexander III to the abbot and monks of Reading of papal protection for the abbey and its possessions, and that they may increase the pensions from their churches for the reception of guests or poor or for certain uses of the abbey, and may appoint vicars in their churches and remove those who are found to be unsuitable   22 Apr. [1166 × 79]

A f 78r; D f 78v
Pd. Holtzmann, *Papsturkunden*, iii. 389–90 (no. 258)

Dat' Lateran(i) x. kl' Maii.

The date is that given by Holtzmann. He doubts the authenticity of this text. It is not with other acts Alexander III in the original section of A, but added in a 13th-century hand.

151 Grant by Pope Alexander III to Abbot Joseph and the monks of Reading of papal protection for Reading Abbey and its liberties, and confirmation of its possessions [specified as in Adrian IV's bull (no. 145)]—and of its liberties and immunities   [1173 × 81]

A ff 67v–68v
Pd. Holtzmann, *Papsturkunden*, iii. 405 (no. 278)

After Joseph became abbot and before the death of Alexander III. The text follows closely those of earlier papal general confirmations.

152 Exhortation and injunction by Pope Alexander III to the faithful of the province of Canterbury to visit Reading Abbey on the anniversary of its dedication and on the feast of St James, in order to avail themselves of the indulgence established by the glorious martyr, blessed Thomas, with the advice of his suffragans, when with them he dedicated the abbey   [1173 × 81]

A f 69v
Pd. Holtzmann, *Papsturkunden*, iii. 429 (no. 312)

After the canonization of Thomas Becket in Feb. 1173, and before the pope's death. Reading Abbey was dedicated 19 Apr. 1164 ('Ann. Rad. Post.', 400). For Archbishop Becket's indulgence, see no. 186.

153 Grant by Pope Alexander III to Abbot Joseph and the monks of Reading, following the example of his predecessors Popes Eugenius III and Adrian IV, of papal protection for Reading Abbey, and confirmation of its possessions [unspecified] and ecclesiastical privileges and ancient liberties   22 June 1175

A ff 68v–69v; F f 77r–v
Pd. Holtzmann, *Papsturkunden*, iii. 354–5 (no. 221)

[Dat' Ferentin(i) per manum Gratiani sancte Romane ecclesie subdiaconi et notarii, x. kl' Iulii, indictione viii, incarnationis dominice anno M.C.lxxv, pontificatus vero domini Alexandri pape tertii anno sextodecimo.]

a–a Om. in A, supplied from F

This is the earliest papal bull to set out in detail the abbey's ecclesiastical and spiritual privileges. It is significant, therefore, that of all the papal bulls to Reading in the 12th century only this and Honorius II's general confirmation (no. 140), which first detailed the abbey's temporal immunities, were copied into F, which is primarily concerned with the abbey's rights and privileges.

154 Indult by Pope Clement III to Abbot Hugh [II] and the monks of Reading that the abbot and his successors may use the mitre, ring, gloves, dalmatic, tunicle and sandals on feast days within the abbey and its obediences, in processions of the abbey, in papal and legatine councils and in episcopal synods   25 Jan. 1191

C f 222r
Pd. Holtzmann, *Papsturkunden*, iii. 525 (no. 433)

Dat' Lateran(i), viii. kl' Februarii, pontificatus nostri anno quarto.

155 Grant by Pope Clement III to Reading Abbey that it may assign its churches of Thatcham, Bucklebury, Aston, Reading St Mary's and Reading St Giles', when they fall vacant, to the maintenance of the monks and of guests and the poor, assignment having been made to the vicars that they may live properly and answer in spirituals and synodals to the bishops and their officials   25 Jan. 1191

A f 71r
Pd. Holtzmann, *Papsturkunden*, iii. 524–5 (no. 432); Barfield, *Thatcham*, ii. 52–3; (transl.) Humphreys, *Bucklebury*, 157

Dat' Lateran(i), viii. kl' Februarii, pontificatus nostri anno quarto.

Rubric: Carta Clementis pape iii.*b* de eo quod liceat nobis pensiones ecclesiarum nostrarum augere

a–a Interlined in a later hand   *b Superscribed in a later hand*

It is highly instructive to see from the rubric how the abbey interpreted the force of this grant.

156 Indult by Pope Celestine III to Reading Abbey to assign to the maintenance of the poor, the infirm and pilgrims the tithes of the abbey's demesne (*decimas laborum vestrorum*)   [1191 × 98]

A f 93r
Pd. Holtzmann, *Papsturkunden*, iii. 581 (no. 489)

The dating limits are those of Celestine III's pontificate.

157 Mandate by Pope Celestine III to the bishop of London, the abbot of Westminster and the prior of Merton, or two of them, to do justice to the abbot and convent of Reading, with papal authority in their complaint against Gilbert (*Gill'*)[1] Martel and others concerning injury and vexation   [1191 × 98; ? 1196]

A f 94r-v
Pd. Holtzmann, *Papsturkunden*, iii. 581-2 (no. 490)

The outside dating limits are those of Celestine III's pontificate, but it may be contemporary with no. 159.

[1] Holtzmann expands this as *Gill(elmus)*, but *Gill(ebertus)* is far more likely (see below, no. 211 n. 2, and cf. nos. 224, 694-6).

158 Confirmation by Pope Celestine III to Reading Abbey of the chapel of St Laurence, Reading, and the churches of Thatcham and Bucklebury, and indult that, when they become vacant, the abbey may retain them in its hands and divert the revenues to the support of the poor of the abbey   [prob. 12 Sept. 1196]

A f 94r
Pd. Holtzmann, *Papsturkunden*, iii. 575-6 (no. 481)

Probably of the same date as the following bull.

159 Mandate by Pope Celestine III to the bishop of London, the abbot of Westminster and the prior of Merton that, since the pope has, at the request of the archbishop of Canterbury, allowed Reading Abbey to appropriate to the use of the poor of the abbey the chapel of St Laurence, Reading, and the churches of Thatcham and Bucklebury, they are to permit nobody to molest the abbey in this regard   12 Sept. 1196

A f 94r; D f 78r
Pd. Holtzmann, *Papsturkunden*, iii. 576-7 (no. 482); (transl.) Humphreys, *Bucklebury*, 158-9

a Dat' Lateran(i), ii. idus*b* Septembris, pontificatus nostri anno sexto.*a*

a-a In the margin in a later hand in A
b Om. in D

For the involvement of the archbishop of Canterbury, Hubert Walter, see no. 208.

160 Confirmation by Pope Celestine III to the poor of the hospital before the gate of Reading [Abbey] of the churches of Thatcham and Bucklebury and the fruits and obventions of the chapel of St Laurence, Reading, conceded to them by Hubert [Walter], now archbishop of Canterbury but then bishop of Salisbury

[1193 × 98; ? 1196 × 98]

A ff 93v–94r
Pd. Holtzmann, *Papsturkunden*, iii. 585 (no. 493)

After Hubert Walter became archbishop in 1193, and possibly after the pope's bulls of Sept. 1196 (nos. 158–9). For Hubert Walter's grants, see nos. 203, 205, 208.

161 Mandate by Pope Innocent III to the abbots of Evesham, Gloucester and Wigmore to hear and decide the complaint by Reading Abbey against the bishop of Salisbury concerning unjust disturbance over the churches of Thatcham and Bucklebury, despite papal confirmation   19 June 1206

C f 222r
Pd. Cheney, *BIHR*, xliv (1971), 104 (no. 1192)

Dat' Ferentin(i) xiii. kl' Iulii, pontificatus nostri anno nono.

For the situation regarding these churches, see no. 211 n.

162 Grant by Pope Innocent III to Abbot Elias and the convent of Reading, of the Cluniac Order, of papal protection and confirmation of their possessions and liberties [unspecified], forbidding anyone to disturb them over privileges from previous popes

26 Feb. 1207

A f 102r
Pd. Migne, ccxv. 1115 (no. xvi); (cal.) Potthast, i. 257; *Cal. Papal. L.*, i. 28; Cheney, *Letters of Innocent III*, 122 (no. 739) (all except Cheney solely from Papal Register)

Dat' Rom(e) apud Sanctum Petrum, iiii. kl' Martii, pontificatus nostri anno decimo.

163 Grant by Pope Innocent III to Reading Abbey, of the Cluniac Order, that it may revoke alienations of property made to the prejudice of the abbey by the negligence of previous heads and not contradicted by their convents   26 Feb. 1207

A f 78r-v

Pd. Migne, ccxv. 1115 (no. xvii); (cal.) Potthast, i. 257; *Cal. Papal L.*, i. 28; Cheney, *Letters of Innocent III*, 122 (no. 740) (all except Cheney solely from Papal Register)

Dat' Rom(e) apud Sanctum Petrum, iiii. kl' Martii, pontificatus nostri anno x.

164 Grant by Pope Innocent III to the abbot of Reading that he may, with the advice of his chapter or the greater or wiser part, appoint suitable monks of the house to manage its external affairs and, if necessary, recall them, so that the goods and revenues of the abbey shall only be administered by those monks to whom they were committed by the abbot and chapter 10 Mar. 1207

A f 78v

Pd. Migne, ccxv. 1115 (no. xviii); (cal.) Potthast, i. 258; *Cal. Papal L.*, i. 28; Cheney, *Letters of Innocent III*, 123 (no. 742) (all except Cheney solely from Papal Register)

Dat' Lateran(i) vi. idus Martii, pontificatus nostri anno x.

165 Grant by Pope Innocent III to Abbot Elias and the monks of Reading, of the Cluniac Order, of papal protection, decreeing that the Rule of St Benedict shall be observed in the abbey for ever; and confirmation of their possessions—viz., Reading, Cholsey and Leominster with their churches, Thatcham, the church of Wargrave, Whitley, Whitsbury, Blewbury, land in [East] Hendred, Aston and its church, Rowington and its church, the churches of Stanton [Harcourt], Hanborough and Englefield, Diddlesfold, land in Houghton [Conquest], lands in Lenborough, Stratfield [Mortimer] and Sawbridgeworth, lands and rents in London and Berkhamstead, land in Hoo, and the priory of May and Rhynd in Scotland—and of their ecclesiastical privileges, their immunities granted by previous popes and their secular liberties granted by kings and others

23 Mar. 1207

A ff 101v-102r

Pd. Migne, ccxv. 1123-5 (no. xxviii); (cal.) Potthast, i. 259; *Cal. Papal L.*, i. 28; Cheney, *Letters of Innocent III*, 123 (no 744) (all except Cheney solely from Papal Register)

a[x. kl' Aprilis, indictione ix, incarnationis dominice anno 1207, pontificatus vero domini Innocentii pape iii. anno decimo.]*a*

a-a Om. in A, supplied from papal register as in Migne

166 Grant by Pope Innocent III to the brethren of the hospital before the gate of Reading [Abbey] of papal protection, and confirmation of the churches of Thatcham and Bucklebury and their right in the chapel of St Laurence, Reading, with their other possessions [unspecified]   20 May 1215

C f 222v
Pd. Cheney, *BIHR*, xliv (1971), 104–5 (no. 1202)

Dat' Lateran(i) xiii. kl' Iunii, pontificatus nostri anno octavodecimo.

167 Annulment by Pope Alexander IV in favour of the abbot and convent of Reading, of the Cluniac Order, of the sentences imposed by any ordinary on them or their subjects for refusing to pay procurations in excess of the maximum of 4 marks laid down by Pope Innocent [III], saving any adjustment by a general council; and prohibition of the exaction of more than the customary sum from their poor churches and places, which are to contribute to procurations with other churches and places according to their poverty and as has been observed hitherto   25 Feb. 1257

C f 222r–v

Dat' Lateran(i) v. kl' Marcii, pontificatus nostri anno tercio.

The pope is identified as Alexander IV by *Quartus* in the margin of C.

168 Indult by Pope Alexander IV to the abbot and convent of Reading, of the Cluniac Order, that they cannot be bound by papal or legatine letters of provision to pensions or ecclesiastical benefices without a special mandate of the apostolic see making express mention of this indult   27 Feb. 1257

C f 222r–v

Dat' Lateran(i) iii. kl' Marcii, pontificatus nostri anno tercio.

The identification of Pope Alexander is not clear from the cartulary entry, but the time and place dates show him to be Alexander IV (see *Cal. Papal L.*, i. 344).

169 Grant by Pope Alexander IV to the abbot and convent of Reading, *[of the Cluniac Order],* that, since they assert that the cold in winter is so severe in their region that they cannot attend divine office bare-headed without danger to health, they may wear appropriate felt caps in the monastery when necessary

8 Nov. 1257

C f 222r; F f 77r

Dat' Viterbii, vi. idus Novembris, pontificatus nostri anno tercio.

a–a Om. in C, supplied from F

Neither copy of this bull identifies the Pope Alexander concerned, but Alexander IV was in Viterbo at this time (see *Cal. Papal L.*, i. 345 ff).

170 Inhibition by Pope Nicholas III in favour of the abbot and convent of Reading, of the Cluniac Order, against those, both clerks and laymen, who, having a complaint against the abbey, presume by a bad custom to seize in pledge, take and detain animals and other goods of the abbey until they obtain satisfaction in such complaints according to their will, even though they have no jurisdiction, either ordinary or delegated, by which they can do this. No one by virtue of the said custom is to inflict such annoyances on the abbot and convent or presume to occupy, take in pledge or in any way detain the goods of the abbey without process of law (*absque iuris ordine*)   7 May 1278

C f 222v

Dat' Rome apud Sanctum Petrum, non' Maii, pontificatus nostri anno primo.

The pope is identified by *Tercius* in the margin. Nicholas III was at St Peter's on this day (*Cal. Papal L.*, i. 454). The bull appears to relate to the thorny question of distraint, which was the subject of legislation in England in the statutes of Marlborough (1267), Westminster I (1275) and Westminster II (1285).

171 *Grant by Pope Nicholas [III or IV] [to the abbot and monks of Reading]*[1] *of papal protection for the abbey, decreeing that the monastic order according to the Rule of St Benedict and the institution of the monks of Cluny be perpetually observed there; with confirmation of its possessions [specified] and of its ecclesiastical privileges*   [*either 1277 × 80 or 1288 × 92*]

C ff 220r–221v

Nicholaus episcopus servus servorum dei *ª[dilectis filiis]ª* [.....]*ᵇ* eiusque fratribus tam presentibus quam futuris, regularem vitam professis imperpetuum. Religiosam vitam eligentibus apostolicum convenit adesse presidium ne forte cuiuslibet temeritatis incursus aut eos a proposito revocet aut robur quod absit sacre religionis infringat. ᶜEapropter dilecti in domino filii vestris iustis postulacionibus clementer annuimus et monasterium de Raddinghes Saresburien(sis) diocesis, in quo divino estis obsequio mancipati, sub beati Petri et nostra protectione suscipimus et presentis scripti privilegio communimus, in primis siquidem statuentes ut ordo monasticus qui secundum deum et beati Benedicti regulam atque institucionem fratrum Cluniacen(sium) in eodem monasterio institutus esse dinoscitur perpetuis ibidem temporibus inviolabiliter observetur. Preterea quascumque possessiones quecumque bona idem monasterium impresen-

ciarum iuste ac canonice possidet aut in futurum concessione
pontificum largicione regum vel principum oblacione fidelium seu
aliis iustis modis prestante domino poterit adipisci firma vobis vestrisque successoribus et illibata permaneant. In quibus hec propriis
duximus exprimenda vocabulis:ᶜ locum ipsum in quo prefatum monasterium situm est cum omnibus pertinenciis suis; in predicta diocesi
Saresburien(si) Raddingiam, Chelseyam, Burghildebury et Benham
cum ecclesiis capellis decimis redditibus hundredis nundinis possessionibus silvis terris pratis aquis molendinis piscariis et omnibus aliis
pertinenciis et appendiciis suis, Whitele cum omnibus pertinenciis
suis, Wychebury cum omnibus pertinenciis suis, villam de Thacham
cum pertinenciis suis et ius patronatus, annuum redditum viginti
marcarum argenti quem percipitis in ecclesia de Thacham a rectore
qui est pro tempore in eadem et quicquid iuris habetis ibidem, in
Henrede terram cum pertinenciis suis, terram quam habetis in Stratfeld' cum omnibus pertinenciis suis, villam et ius patronatus de Pangeburn' necnon redd(itum) et quicquid iuris habetis ibidem, terras
et redditus quos habetis in loco qui dicitur Offintona, ius patronatus,
annuum redditum denariorum et quicquid iuris habetis in ecclesia
de Silhamsted' necnon terras et possessiones quas habetis ibidem,
terras redditus possessiones et quicquid iuris habetis in locis qui
Burgefeud', Sefeud, Wyndesore, Kendindon' et Walingeford' vulgariter nominantur, ecclesiam de Wergrave cum pertinenciis suis,
annuum redditum denariorum quem percipitis in ecclesia de Englefeld'; in diocesi Lyncoln(iensi) Estonam, ius patronatus et annuum
redditum denariorum et quicquid iuris habetis in ecclesia de Estona
cum iurisdictione temporali et omnibus pertinenciis suis, ius patronatus in ecclesia de Stantona et annuum redditum viginti marcarum
quem percipitis a rectore qui pro tempore fuerit in eadem ecclesia
et quicquid iuris habetis in ecclesia ipsa, ius patronatus et annuum
redditum denariorum et quicquid iuris habetis in ecclesia de Hane-
berghe, terras redditus possessiones et quicquid iuris habetis in locis
qui Hocton', Sewell', Linthingebergh', Audewell', Grendon', Ky-
nebell', Langetot', Nehnham_d_ et Caversham vulgariter nuncupan-
tur; in diocesi Wygorn(iensi) villam et ecclesiam de Rokenton' cum
pertinenciis suis, terras redditus possessiones et quicquid iuris habetis
[_f 220v_] in villis de 'Tidynton', Preston', Wiggeston',ᵉ Stratford',
Warewyk', Glovern(ia) et de Bristoll' ac omnibus pertinenciis earundem; in diocesi Herforden(si) Leoministriam cum omnibus villulis
maneriis casalibus nundinis undredis_f_ necnon iurisdictione temporali
redditibus possessionibus terris cultis et incultis molendinis aque-
ductibus pratis pascuis piscariis ac omnibus appendiciis et pertinenciis suis, ecclesias eciam apostolorum Petri et Pauli de Leoministria
et sancti Petri de Eya cum capellis dependentibus ab eisdem, scilicet

Stoke, Hope, Dochelowe, Forda, Eytone, Lucton', Yarpoll',[g] Halre-
tune, Brumfeld', Michyname,[h] Kynebaltune et Hopemile, decimas
quas percipitis in parochia ecclesie de Leom(inistria), decimas annuos redditus denariorum et quicquid iuris habetis et percipitis in
capellis de Humbur, de Monkenelane, de Hatfeud' Minori et de
Hatfeud Maiori, annuos redditus et quicquid iuris habetis in capellis
de Luctun', de Crofte, de Titeley necnon et in ecclesia Kenardesleye
et in parochiis et pertinenciis earundem; in diocesi Cicestren(si) terras et redditus de Dudelesfaude, locum qui dicitur Bove3ate cum
omnibus pertinenciis suis, in diocesi Roffen(si) terras et redditus sitos
infra tenementum de Hoo et quicquid iuris habetis ibidem; in Scotia
in diocesi Sancti Andree prioratum de May cum omnibus pertinenciis suis, duas carucatas terre in Rindelgros et ecclesiam loci eiusdem
cum capella de Pert et aliis capellis dependentibus ab eadem cum
omnibus pertinenciis earundem; domos possessiones et redditus quos
habetis in civitate et diocesi London(iensi); et domos et redditus
quos habetis in diocesi Wynton(iensi) in loco qui dicitur Guldeford',
cum terris pratis vineis nemoribus usuagiis et pascuis in bosco et
plano, in aquis et molendinis, in viis et semitis et omnibus aliis
libertatibus et immunitatibus suis. [i]Sane novalium vestrorum que
propriis manibus aut sumptibus colitis de quibus aliquis[j] hactenus
non percepit sive de vestrorum animalium nutrimentis nullus a vobis
decimas exigere vel extorquere presumat.[i] Liceat quoque vobis clericos vel laicos liberos et absolutos e seculo fugientes ad conversionem
recipere et eos absque contradictione aliqua retinere. Prohibemus
insuper ut nulli fratrum vestrorum post factam in monasterio vestro
professionem fas sit sine abbatis sui licencia de eodem loco nisi artioris religionis obtentu discedere; discedentem vero absque com-
munium litterarum caucione nullus audeat retinere. [k]Cum autem
generale interdictum terre fuerit, liceat vobis clausis ianuis, exclusis
excommunicatis et interdictis, non pulsatis campanis, suppressa voce
divina officia celebrare dummodo causam non dederitis interdicto.
Crisma vero, oleum sanctum, consecrationes altarum seu basilica-
rum, ordinaciones clericorum qui ad ordines fuerint promovendi, a
diocesano suscipietis episcopo siquidem catholicus fuerit et gratiam
et communionem sacrosancte Romane sedis habuerit et ea vobis
voluerit sine pravitate aliqua exhibere. Prohibemus insuper ut infra
fines parochie vestre, si eam habetis, nullus sine assensu diocesani
episcopi et vestro capellam [f 221r] seu oratorium de novo construere
audeat, salvis privilegiis pontificum Romanorum.[k] Ad hec novas et
indebitas exactiones ab archiepiscopis episcopis archidiaconis seu
decanis aliisque omnibus ecclesiasticis secularibusve personis a vobis
omnino fieri prohibemus. Sepulturam quoque ipsius loci liberam
esse decernimus ut eorum devocioni et extreme voluntati qui se illic

sepeliri deliberaverint, nisi forte excommunicati vel interdicti sint
aut eciam publice usurarii nullus obsistat, salva tamen iusticia illarum ecclesiarum a quibus mortuorum corpora assumuntur. Decimas preterea et possessiones ad ius ecclesiarum vestrarum spectantes
que a laicis detinentur redimendi et legitime liberandi de manibus
eorum et ad ecclesias ad quas pertinent revocandi libera sit vobis de
vestra auctoritate facultas. Obeunte vero te nunc eiusdem loci abbate vel tuorum quolibet successorum, nullus ibi qualibet surrep-
cionis astutia seu violencia preponatur nisi quantum fratres communi consensu vel fratrum maior pars consilii sanioris secundum
deum et beati Benedicti regulam providerint eligendum. Paci quoque et tranquillitati [*etc., as general confirmation by Innocent III* (*Migne,
ccxv, cols. 1123–5*),² *col. 1125, lines 1–22, with minor variants only, but
adding after* justitia *in line 22 the following:* et in predictis decimis
moderacione concilii generalis]. Si qua igitur [*etc., as ibid., lines 22–
32, but without the abridgements and ending:* Amen. Amen. *The transition
to f 221v occurs between* examine *and* districte].

ᵃ⁻ᵃ *Supplied conjecturally, only traces of the words surviving* (*see note 1*)
ᵇ *Four or five words totally lost by trimming of folio and fading* (*see note 1*)
ᶜ⁻ᶜ *Following closely Innocent III's general confirmation* (*Migne, ccxv. 1123–5*), *with addition*
ᵈ *Doubtful reading, corrected from Ms.?* Sehnham
ᵉ⁻ᵉ *Suspensions uncertain owing to trimming and fading* (*see note 1*)
ᶠ *Ms has* undrdedis   ᵍ *Ms has* Varpoll'
ʰ *Doubtful reading*   ⁱ⁻ⁱ *As c–c, with addition*
ʲ *Interlined*   ᵏ⁻ᵏ *As c–c, with additions*

The pope is either Nicholas III (1277–80) or Nicholas IV (1288–92). The greater
part of this bull is printed here in full, since it is the only detailed papal confirmation
to Reading known to survive after that of Innocent III (no. 165), of which it is a
much amplified version, and seems to have gone unnoticed by historians.

¹ The text is missing in places owing to the trimming of the tops of ff 220–221,
while at the top and bottom of f 220r the writing is so faded as to be illegible except
under ultra-violet light.
² See no. 165.

172   Confirmation by Pope Nicholas IV to the abbot and monks of
Reading of Pope Clement III's grant to the abbot and his successors
of the use of the mitre, ring, gloves, dalmatic, tunicle and sandals
on feast days within the abbey and its obediences, in processions of
the abbey and in episcopal synods   27 Aug. 1288

C f 222r; F f 77r
Pd. (cal.) *Cal. Papal L.*, i. 495 (from Papal Register)

Dat' Reate vi. kl' Septembris, pontificatus nostri anno primo.

The grant here is slightly less extensive than Clement III's (no. 154), omitting papal
and legatine councils from the occasions when pontificals may be worn.

173 Confirmation by Pope Clement V to the abbot and convent of Reading, of the Cluniac Order, of the privileges and indults granted by previous popes but not always enjoyed through simplicity and ignorance of their right, unless such privileges and indults have been lawfully withdrawn 14 July 1310

C f 223r

Dat' Avinion', ii. idus Julii, pontificatus nostri anno quinto.

IV ARCHIEPISCOPAL AND EPISCOPAL ACTS

174 Confirmation by William [of Corbeil], archbishop of Canterbury, to Abbot Hugh [I] and the monks of Reading of the gifts made to the abbey by King Henry I—viz., Reading with its churches and chapels, Leominster with its churches and chapels, Thatcham, Cholsey and its church, which church with that of Wargrave the king obtained by exchange with the abbey of Mont St Michel and gave to Reading Abbey. The archbishop makes this confirmation because Reading, Leominster and Cholsey were formerly abbeys and have now been restored to Reading Abbey   [1123 × 30]

A ff 49v-50r; B f 188r; C f 108v
Pd. Saltman, *Theobald*, 438-9

The dating limits are those of Abbot Hugh I's abbacy. The text of the act may have been tampered with, since, though mostly in first person singular, it moves to first person plural for the final sentence.

175 Confirmation by Roger, bishop of Salisbury, to Abbot Hugh [I] and the monks of Reading of the gifts in his diocese made by King Henry I—viz., Reading, St Mary's church in Reading with its appurtenant *parochia*, Thatcham, Cholsey, 100s worth of land in Cholsey held of the abbey by William son of Gerold for 100s annually, the churches of Cholsey and Wargrave for which the king exchanged 12 librates of land with the abbey of Mont St Michel   [1123 × 30;? late 1123]

A f 51r-v; B f 189r-v; C f 109v
Pd. Barfield, *Thatcham*, ii. 49; Kealey, *Roger of Salisbury*, 239-40 (no. 8)

The dating limits are those of Hugh I's abbacy, but, since the act refers to Henry I's exchange with Mont St Michel (no. 3) and to a request from Mont St Michel to the bishop regarding the same, which probably dates from the latter half of 1123 (no. 771), it may date from soon after these.

176 Notification by Roger, bishop of Salisbury and *procurator* of England, addressed generally, that King Henry I has granted to Reading Abbey certain liberties [specified] in its possessions—viz., Reading, Cholsey, Leominster and Thatcham—and a mint and moneyer at Reading; and precept that the abbey shall hold all its possessions in accordance with the king's charter. At Westminster. By the king's writ   [?1125]

Original charter: BL Add.Ch. 19575

A f 51v; B ff 189v-190r; C ff 109v-110r

Pd. Johnson, *Essays in Honour of Tait*, 141-2 (with facsimile); D.M. Stenton, 'Roger of Salisbury, *Regni Angliae Procurator*', *EHR*, xxxix (1924), 79-80; Kealey, *Roger of Salisbury*, 241-2 (no. 9); Barfield, *Thatcham*, ii. 49-50; (cal.) *Regesta*, ii. 203 (no. 1471); Hurry, *Reading Abbey*, 157

Endorsed: Rogerii episcopi Sar' de libertate Radingensis ecclesie [*12th cent.*]

Size: 173 × 377 mm

Seal: missing, slit for tag in fold at bottom

As indicated by Johnson (loc. cit.), a substantial portion of this act follows closely the relevant part of Henry I's foundation charter (no. 1), which in turn is also largely embodied in Honorius II's general confirmation (no. 140). If genuine, therefore, it would date from after ?Mar. 1125, when the contents of the king's charter were known both to the pope and to Bishop Roger by means of a writ from Normandy. The doubts which have been cast on its authenticity (Johnson, loc. cit.; N. D. Hurnard, 'The Anglo-Norman franchises', *EHR*, lxiv (1949), 442-3) seem insufficient to prove forgery beyond doubt, even concerning the inclusion of *hutfangentheof* (see no. 1 n.), particularly in view of the elements common both to it and to Henry I's charter and Honorius II's bull. Moreover, both the primitive and unsophisticated form of the bishop's title as justiciar and the fact that the original charter uses the 'cedilla' under the letter *e* to denote the classical *ae* probably indicate an early date and arguably support the case for the charter's authenticity.

177 Notification by Roger, bishop of Salisbury and *procurator* of England, to A(ubrey) [de Vere], the sheriff, and all present and future ministers of the king in London and all England that, on the order of King Henry I, he has given to Abbot Hugh [I] and the monks of Reading a moneyer in London, to have a mint and hold an exchange there, viz., Edgar, who shall be as free and in the possession (*in manu*) of the abbot and monks as if he dwelt at Reading, as shall be any successor appointed by the abbot and monks. Edgar and his successors shall pay to the abbey the same dues for the mint as the other London moneyers pay to the king, and shall change money (*cambiare*) in the abbot's land[a] as the abbot shall grant [1125 × 29]

B f 113r; C f 60r-v

Pd. *Mon. Ang.*, iv. 41 (no. vi); W.J. Andrew, *A Numismatic History of the Reign of Henry I* (Numismatic Chronicle, 1901), 373-4; Kealey, *Roger of Salisbury*, 243-4 (no. 10); (cal.) *Regesta*, ii. 203 (no. 1472)

[a] *C has 'in the land of the abbot and monks'*

Presumably after no. 176, since the mint and moneyer are now to be in London, and probably during one of the king's absences abroad while Aubrey de Vere was sheriff of London (S. Reynolds, 'The rulers of London in the twelfth century', *History*, lvii (1972), 354). Certain surviving late coins of Henry I (type xv), minted in London and bearing the name of the moneyer Edgar, were probably produced by the abbey's mint there (Andrew, *ibid.*, 375-7; G. C. Brooke, *A Catalogue of English Coins in the British Museum: the Norman Kings*, i (London, 1916), p. clxxix).

178 Order by Roger, bishop of Salisbury, to the archdeacon of Berkshire and all deans and clergy of Berkshire that no one shall have charge of a school at Reading without the consent of the abbot and convent   [*c.* 1133 × 39]

A f 51v; B f 190v

Pd. A. F. Leach, *Educational Charters and Documents 598-1909* (Cambridge, 1911), 94 (with transl. 95); Kealey, *Roger of Salisbury*, 258 (no. 22); (transl.) *VCH Berks.*, ii. 245

T(este) A(delelmo) th(esaurario). Apud Wintoniam.

The dating depends upon the identification of the witness as the royal treasurer, to which position Adelelm was appointed some time after Nigel the treasurer became bishop of Ely in 1133 (Richardson and Sayles, *Governance of Med. Eng.*, 220-1), and the arrest and death of Bishop Roger in 1139. According to van Caenegem, *Royal Writs*, 184 n. 5, the diplomatic of this act is that of a 'regency' writ.

179 *Confirmation by Jocelin [de Bohun], bishop of Salisbury, to Reading Abbey of 4s annually from the church of Sulham and 2s annually from the church of Purley [both Berks.]*   [1142 × 84]

A f 52r; B f 190r; C f 110r

Ego Iocelinus*a* dei gratia Sar(esburiensis) episcopus universis sancte Sar(esburiensis) ecclesie filiis, salutem et episcopalem benedictionem. Universitati vestre notificamus in presentia nostra fuisse probatum legitimarum*b* personarum sufficienti*c* testimonio quod ecclesia de Suleham ecclesie Rading(ensi) quatuor solidos annuatim debeat persolvere et ecclesia de Purleia duos. Ad hunc redditum faciendum antecessores nostri consenserunt*d* et nos, ne in posterum oblivioni tradatur, hoc confirmamus presentis carte testimonio et confirmando precipimus ut absque omni contradictione annuatim persolvantur.

a Om. in C	*b legittimarum B*
c Om. in B, C	*d consuerunt (sic) C*

The dating limits are those of Jocelin's pontificate.

180 *Confirmation by Jocelin [de Bohun], bishop of Salisbury, of Reading Abbey's possessions [in his diocese]—viz., Reading and Cholsey with churches and chapels, [East] Hendred, Blewbury, Thatcham, 1 hide at Underoure [Windsor], land formerly of Geoffrey Purcell in* Waletuna,[1] *the church of Wargrave, lands formerly of Herbert son of Fulcher in Marlborough and*

Payn of Moulsford, land given by Rannulf Grossus near Wallingford, 4 hides in Stratton [St Margaret] by gift of Richard de Marcy, 1 virgate given by Ralph of Ufton near Beenham—with all liberties granted by King Henry [*I*] [1144 × 84; ? 1144 × 54]

A f 52r; B f 190r; C f 110r

Iocelinus dei gratia Sar(esburiensis) episcopus omnibus fidelibus ad quos presens carta pervenerit, salutem. Ad episcopale spectat officium religiosos viros diligere et eorum in posterum tranquillitati providere. Hoc inducti rationis intuitu bona et possessiones quas dive memorie rex Henricus ecclesie Radingensi contulit et omnia nichilominus que eius tempore vel post eius decessum liberalitate regum, largitione*a* principum vel aliis iustis modis eadem ecclesia est adepta, vel in posterum poterit adipisci, prompto favore prosequimur et auctoritate episcopali communimus. Hec autem propriis nominibus duximus annotanda: videlicet, Rading(iam),*b* Chelseiam*c* cum ecclesiis, capellis et omnibus pertinentiis eorundem maneriorum, Henredam, Bleoberiam,*d* Techam*e* cum omnibus pertinentiis suis, hidam de Hunderora,*f* terram que fuit Gaufredi Purcelli in Waletuna,*g* ecclesiam de Waregrava*h* cum pertinentiis suis, terram que fuit Herberti filii Fulcherii apud Merleberga, terram que fuit Pagani*i* de Molesford, terram quam dedit Rannulfus Grossus iuxta Walengef(ordiam),*j* quatuor hidas in Strettona ex dona Ricardi de Marsi,*k* unam virgatam terre quam dedit Radulfus de Offentona*l* sub masrugia*m* iuxta Benham.*n* Ut autem hec omnia bona cum integritate omnium libertatum quas ecclesie Radingensi concessit rex Henricus firma semper eidem ecclesie et inconcussa perseverent et conserventur, presentis sigilli munimine et carte huius attestatione ea confirmamus.

a *A has* largiticione	*b* Radingas *B*
c Chauseiam *B*, Chaus' *C*	*d* Bleobir' *B*, *C*
e Tacheham *C*	*f* Underhor' *B*, *C*
g Walaton' *B*, Walton *C*	*h* Weregrave *B*, Weregrava *C*
i Page *C*	*j* Walingford' *B*, *C*
k Maysi *B*, *C*	*l* Uffenton' *B*, *C*
m marug' *C*	*n* Bienham *C*

Not earlier than 1144, the earliest date for Reading's tenure of Blewbury (see no. 667), and before the bishop's resignation in 1184; possibly, in view of the simple reference to King Henry, not later than 1154.

[1] This place has not been identified.

181 Confirmation by Robert [Chesney], bishop of Lincoln, addressed generally for Lincoln diocese, to Reading Abbey of its possessions [in that diocese]—viz., the churches of Stanton [Har-

court], Hanborough and Aston, and Wigston [Parva] in
Leicestershire   [1148 × 61]

A f 53r; B f 201v; C f 123r
Pd. Smith, *Lincoln I*, 144-5 (no. 230)

After the bishop's consecration, 19 Dec. 1148, and before 18 Apr. 1161, when Archbishop Theobald, who confirmed this act (no. 182), died. In *Lincoln I* Aston (Herts.)
is wrongly identified as Easton (Hunts.).

182 Confirmation by Theobald, archbishop of Canterbury, primate and legate, addressed generally, of Reading Abbey's ecclesiastical and temporal possessions—viz., Reading with its churches,
Thatcham, Cholsey, the churches of Cholsey and Wargrave, as witnessed by the charter of Henry I and the confirmation by William
[of Corbeil], archbishop of Canterbury, and the churches of Stanton
[Harcourt], Hanborough and Aston, and Wigstan [Parva], as confirmed by Robert [Chesney], bishop of Lincoln   [1150 × 61]

A f 50r; B f 188r-v; C ff 108v-109r
Pd. Saltman, *Theobald*, 437-8 (no. 215)

The dating limits are those of Theobald's period as legate.

183 Grant by Theobald, archbishop of Canterbury, primate and
legate, of an indulgence of twenty days to all who visit Reading
Abbey on the feast of the Invention or of the Exaltation of the Holy
Cross [3 May, 14 Sept.], a piece of which is contained
there   [1150 × 61]

A f 57v
Pd. Saltman, *Theobald*, 436-7 (no. 214)

Date as for no. 182

184 Grant by Theobald, archbishop of Canterbury, primate and
legate, of an indulgence of forty days to all who visit Reading Abbey
on the feast of St James, 25 July, whose hand is contained there, or
within the octave   [1155 × 61]

Original charter: BL Add. Ch. 19589
A f 57v
Pd. Saltman, *Theobald*, 436 (no. 213); (cal.) Hurry, *Reading Abbey*, 164

Endorsed: T' Cant' archiepiscopi de absolutione penitentium. In festo
sancti I(acobi) [*late 12th cent.*] .xl. d' [*13th cent.*]
Size: 220 × 175 mm
Seal: fragment in white wax on parchment tag, folded double,
through slit in fold at bottom

After the return of the Hand of St James to Reading in 1155 (Kemp, *Berks. Arch. Journ.*, lxv (1970), 2-3) and before Theobald's death.

185 Grant by Gilbert [Foliot], bishop of Hereford, of an indulgence of twenty days to all who visit Reading Abbey on the feast or within the octave of St James, whose relics are there, and make offerings [1155 × 63; prob. early 1163]

Original charter: BL Add. Ch. 19587
A f 58r-v
Pd. *Foliot Letters and Charters*, 390 (no. 339); (cal.) Hurry, *Reading Abbey*, 163

Endorsed: G.*ᵃ* Hereford' de absolutione penitentium in festo sancti I(acobi) [*12th cent.*] .xx. d' [*13th cent.*]
Size: 170 × 122 mm
Seal: in brown wax, much decayed and repaired, on tongue

ᵃ Gileb' *superscribed in later hand*

After the return of the Hand of St James (see no. 184 n.) and before Foliot's translation to London. Since he granted what was virtually a re-issue of this indulgence as bishop of London (no. 195), the present act may well have been granted shortly before his translation, in view of the impending dedication of Reading Abbey in 1164 (see also *Foliot Letters and Charters*, 389).

186 *Grant by Thomas [Becket], archbishop of Canterbury, following the example of Archbishop Theobald, of an indulgence of twenty days to all who visit Reading Abbey on the feast or within the octave of St James, whose hand is there* [prob. *c.* 19 Apr. 1164]

A f 57v

Thomas dei gratia Cantuariensis ecclesie minister humilis universis sancte matris ecclesie fidelibus, salutem. Domini et patris nostri pie memorie T(heobaldi) archiepiscopi vestigiis inherentes, ad honorem dei et reverentiam beati Iacobi cuius manus in ecclesia sancte virginis Marie apud Rading(iam) habetur, omnibus Christi fidelibus qui in eiusdem apostoli sollemnitate vel infra sollemnitatis oct(avas) eandem ecclesiam de Rading(ia) ob gloriosi apostoli venerationem pio affectu visitaverint de penitentia sibi iniuncta viginti dies indulgemus. Valete.

The outside dating limits are June 1162 × Nov. 1164, but this is most likely to have been granted on or near the date of the abbey's dedication by the archbishop, 19 Apr. 1164 (cf. no. 201).

187   *Grant by Robert, bishop of Bath, in imitation of the bishop of Salisbury,
of an indulgence of twenty days to all who visit Reading Abbey on the feast
of St James, whose relics are there, or within the eight days following*

[1155 × 66; prob. Apr. 1164]

A f 58v

Robertus dei gratia episcopus Bathon(iensis) universis sancte matris
ecclesie filiis, salutem. Cum universis sancte matris ecclesie filiis de-
bitores simus, eis obligatius tenemur astricti quos devotius crucem
domini baiulare, et vestigia eius sequi cognoverimus. Quoniam
itaque diligenti animadversione devotionem et religionem fratrum
de Rading(ia) consideramus, ut honor eis et veneratio debita impen-
datur elaborare debemus. Eapropter ad imitationem domini Sar(esburiensis) concedimus omnibus qui monasterium sancte Marie apud
Rading(iam) situm in festo beati Iacobi apostoli cuius reliquie ibi
recondite sunt vel in octo diebus sequentibus devote visitaverint, viginti dierum indulgentiam de penitentia sibi iniuncta et orationum et
beneficiorum ecclesie Bathoniensis participes eos esse statuimus.
Valeat fraternitas vestra in Christo pro nobis orans.

The outside dating limits are provided by the return of the Hand of St James to
Reading (see no. 184 n.) and the bishop's death, but the act was probably granted,
like the associated indulgences, on or near the date of the abbey's dedication (cf.
nos. 200–1).

188   Grant by Hilary, bishop of Chichester, with the assent of Jocelin the diocesan bishop, of an indulgence of fifteen days to all who
visit Reading Abbey between the vigil and octave of St James, whose
relics are there, and give alms   [1155 × 69; prob. Apr. 1164]

Original charter: BL Add. Ch. 19598
A ff 58v–59r
Pd. Mayr-Harting, *Acta of Chichester*, 108–9 (no. 45); (cal.) Hurry, *Reading Abbey*,
166

Endorsed: H. Cicestrensis episcopi de absolutione penitentium in festo
sancti Iacobi [*12th cent.*] .xv. d' [*13th cent.*]
Size: 107 × 155 mm
Seal: in brown wax, very worn, on tag

The outside dating limits are provided by the return of the Hand of St James and
the bishop's death, but the act dates probably from about the time of the abbey's
dedication. For further discussion, see Mayr-Harting, *Acta of Chichester*, 109.

189   *Grant by Richard [Peche], bishop of Coventry, of an indulgence of
twenty days to all who visit Reading Abbey on the feast or within the octave
of St James, whose relics are venerated there*

[1161 × 82; prob. Apr. 1164]

A f 59r

Universis sancte matris ecclesie filiis Ricardus humilis Coventr(ensis) ecclesie minister, salutem. Christiane religionis reverentia eos summo debet venerari studio quos in apostolica sublimitate constitutos re- demptoris humilitas nominavit amicos, et divina dispositione iudi- candi potestatem constat esse sortitos. Inde est quod devotionem vestram monemus atque exhortatione pia convenimus in domino quatinus pro salute animarum et venia delictorum ad sollennitatem beati Iacobi devote concurratis, cuius reliquias fratres Rading(enses) debito amplectuntur venerationis obsequio. Nos vero de dei miseri- cordia plenius confidentes omnibus qui in prescripta sollennitate ibidem convenerint aut infra oct(avas) ob honorem dei et beati apostoli Iacobi prefatum locum religiosa devotione adierint, de in- flicta sibi penitentia ex confessione sincera viginti dies remittimus et orationum ac beneficiorum Coventr(ensis) ecclesie participes eos ef- ficimus. Valete.

The outside dating limits are those of the bishop's pontificate, but the act was probably granted on or near the date of the abbey's dedication.

190 Grant by Hugh [du Puiset], bishop of Durham, of an indulg- ence of ten days to all who visit Reading Abbey on the feast of St James, whose relics are there, or within the eight days following, and make a gift [1155 × 95; prob. Apr. 1164]

A f 59r–v
Pd. G. V. Scammell, *Hugh du Puiset, Bishop of Durham* (Cambridge, 1956), 263–4 (no. 12)

The outside dating limits are provided by the return of the Hand of St James and the bishop's death, but the act was probably granted on or near the date of the abbey's dedication. The text is almost identical with nos. 191–2, 194, 196.

191 *Grant by Nigel, bishop of Ely, of an indulgence of twenty days to all who visit Readong Abbey on the feast of St James, whose relics are there, or within the eight days following, and make a gift*
[1155 × 69; prob. Apr. 1164]

A f 58v

Nigellus dei gratia Heliensis episcopus omnibus sancte matris ecclesie filiis, salutem. Loca sancta et religiosorum ac deo servientium viro- rum habitacula a fidelibus populis eo devotius visitanda et vener- anda sunt quod in eis sanctorum celebres existunt memorie, et reli- quie eorum venerabiles noscuntur esse recondite. Eapropter de dei confidentes misericordia concedimus omnibus qui ecclesiam beate

Marie apud Radingiam positam in festo beati Iacobi apostoli, cuius reliquie in ea creduntur esse reposite, vel in .viii. diebus sequentibus pia devotione et inpendende sanctissimis gloriosi apostoli reliquiis venerationis gratia adierint, visitaverint et ad honorem dei et apostoli sui reverentiam beneficium aliquod contulerint, viginti dierum remissionem de iniuncta sibi penitentia, et orationum ac beneficiorum Helyensis ecclesie participes esse concedimus. Valete.

The outside dating limits are as for no. 190, but the act probably dates from near the date of the abbey's dedication. The text is almost identical with nos. 190, 192, 194, 196.

192 Grant by Bartholomew, bishop of Exeter, of an indulgence of twenty days to all who visit Reading Abbey on the feast of St James, whose relics are there, or within the eight days following, and make a gift   [1161 × 84; prob. Apr. 1164]

Original charter: BL Add. Ch. 19605
A f 59r
Pd. Morey, *Bartholomew of Exeter*, 146 (no. 25); (cal.) Hurry, *Reading Abbey*, 170-1

Endorsed: B. Exoniensis episcopi de absolutione penitentium in festo sancti I(acobi) .xx. d' [*13th cent.*]

Size: 185 × 60 mm

Seal: good, in amber-coloured wax on tongue, with counterseal

The outside dating limits are those of the bishop's pontificate, but the act was probably granted on or near the date of the abbey's dedication. The text is almost identical with nos. 190-1, 194, 196. The original charter is unprepossessing and stained with damp.

193 Grant by Robert [Chesney], bishop of Lincoln, of an indulgence of twenty days to all who visit the relics of St James at Reading Abbey on his feast day and the eight days following, with some gift   [1155 × 66; prob. Apr. 1164]

A f 58v
Pd. Smith, *Lincoln I*, 145 (no. 231)

The outside dating limits are as for no. 190, but the act was probably granted on or near the date of the abbey's dedication.

194 *Grant by Nicholas [ap Gwrgant], bishop of Llandaff, of an indulgence of twenty days to all who visit Reading Abbey on the feast of St James, whose relics are there, or within the eight days following, and make a gift*
                                   [1155 × 83; prob. Apr. 1164]

A f 59v

Omnibus sancte ecclesie fidelibus Nicholaus dei gratia Landav(ensis) dictus episcopus, salutem. Loca sancta et religiosorum [*etc., as grant by Nigel of Ely (no. 191), concluding with the following slight variation*] ... et orationum ac beneficiorum Landav(ensis) ecclesie participes esse statuimus.

The outside dating limits are as for no. 190, but the grant was probably made on or near the date of the abbey's dedication. The text is almost identical with nos. 190-2, 196.

195 Grant by Gilbert [Foliot], bishop of London, of an indulgence of twenty days to all who visit Reading Abbey on the feast or within the octave of St James, whose relics are there, and make offerings [prob. 1163 × 64]

A f58r
Pd. (noted) *Foliot Letters and Charters*, 469 (no. 430)—variants from no. 185 above are noted *ibid.*, 390 (under no. 339)

This is a re-issue, in virtually identical terms, of Foliot's indulgence as bishop of Hereford (above, no. 185), printed *Foliot Letters and Charters*, 390. It was probably issued either shortly after his translation to London in 1163 or at about the time of the abbey's dedication in Apr. 1164.

196 *Grant by William [Turbe], bishop of Norwich, of an indulgence of twenty days to all who visit Reading Abbey on the feast of St James, whose relics are there, or within the eight days following, and make a gift* [1155 × 74; prob. Apr. 1164]

A f59r

Omnibus sancte ecclesie fidelibus Willelmus dei gratia Norwic(ensis) dictus episcopus, salutem. Loca sancta et religiosorum [*etc., as grant by Nigel of Ely (no. 191), omitting* populis *and concluding with the following slight variation*] ... et orationum ac beneficiorum Norwic(ensis) ecclesie participes esse statuimus.

The outside dating limits are as for no. 190, but the grant was probably made on or near the date of the abbey's dedication. The text is almost identical with nos. 190-2, 194.

197 *Grant by Godfrey, bishop of St Asaph, of an indulgence of fifteen days to all who visit Reading Abbey on the feast of St James, 25 July, whose relics are there, or within the eight days following, and make a gift* [1160 × 70; prob. Apr. 1164]

A f59v

Godefr(idus) dei gratia Lanelvensis episcopus universis sancte matris ecclesie filiis, salutem in Christo perpetuam. Pium est et animarum saluti valde pernecessarium locis sanctis devotam reverentiam et studiosam exhibere frequentiam, illis precipue in quibus sanctorum apostolorum vel martyrum aliorumve servorum et amicorum domini nostri Ihesu Christi sancte continentur reliquie, et religiosorum fratrum consistens conventus cotidiana deo pro suis benefactoribus offert cum orationibus devotis sacrificia. Quia igitur monasterium beate Marie de Rading(ia) et religioso monachorum inhabitatur conventu et pretiosis beati Iacobi apostoli et martiris fratris sancti Iohannis ewangeliste illustratur reliquiis, nos, confisi de misericordia dei et meritis sancti amici ipsius apostoli Iacobi aliorumque sanctorum quorum ibidem habentur venerande reliquie, relaxamus .xv. dies de penitentia sibi iniuncta omnibus illis qui in festo eiusdem apostoli, quod est .viii. kl' Augusti, sive infra octo dies proximos post festum prefate ecclesie Rading(ensi) piam visitationem cum fructu beneficii sui impenderint, eosque insuper orationum et beneficiorum nostrorum spiritualium participes facimus ante deum.

The outside dating limits are those of the bishop's consecration and suspension, but this act was probably granted on or near the date of the abbey's dedication.

198 *Grant by David [Fitz Gerald], bishop of St David's, of an indulgence of fifteen days to all who visit Reading Abbey on the feast of St James, whose relics are there, and make offerings* [1155 × 76; prob. Apr. 1164]

A f 59v

David dei gratia Menevensis episcopus universis sancte matris ecclesie filiis, salutem, gratiam et benedictionem. Non ignorat karitas vestra quam necessarie et quanta reverentia beatos apostolos venerari vos oporteat ut possitis promereri eos habere propitios quos in fine seculi scitis omnes vos secundum opera vestra iudicaturos. Inde est quod fraternitatem vestram pie in domino commonemus ut reliquias sancti Iacobi apostoli, quas fratres Rading(enses) summo fovent et venerantur obsequio, pia devotione requiratis ut vobis eius intercessione a domino peccatorum veniam et gratiam optineatis. Omnibus autem qui ad ecclesiam de Rading(ia) in eius sollennitate convenerint et honorem apostolo debitum oblationibus et orationibus sacris impenderint, nos de domini misericordia et beati apostoli confisi meritis quindecim dies de penitentia sua relaxamus.

The outside dating limits are as for no. 190, but the grant was probably made on or near the date of the abbey's dedication.

199 *Grant by Jocelin [de Bohun], bishop of Salisbury, of an indulgence of twenty-five days to all who visit Reading Abbey on the feast of St James, whose relics are there, or within the eight days following*

[1155 × 84; prob. Apr. 1164]

A f58r

Iocelinus dei gratia Sar(esburiensis) episcopus omnibus fidelibus per Sar(esburiensem) episcopatum constitutis, salutem et dei benedictionem. In ecclesiis benedicite deo domino de fontibus Israel, quia de Israel elegit sibi deus beatum Iacobum in quo habitaret fons aque vive salientis in vitam eternam. Quicumque igitur ad ecclesiam beate Marie de Rading(ia) pia devotione conveneritis in festo beati Iacobi apostoli, cuius reliquie in eadem ecclesia venerantur, universitatem vestram hortamur in domino ut non in ebrietatibus et luxuriosis conviviis, sed secundum prophetarum et apostolorum doctrinam in ecclesiis et locis religiosis reddatis laudem deo. Nos autem, de meritis beati Iacobi et religiosorum fratrum orationibus confisi, omnibus qui in festo sancti Iacobi et octo diebus sequentibus ecclesiam beate Marie de Rading(ia) pia devotione visitaverint, honorem ei et reverentiam exhibuerint .xxv. dies de penitentia sibi iniuncta relaxamus, et omnium orationum que in Sar(esburiensi) fiunt ecclesia participes eos esse concedimus.

After the return of the Hand of St James and before the bishop's resignation and death, but probably on or near the date of the abbey's dedication.

200 *Letter by Jocelin [de Bohun], bishop of Salisbury, to the bishops of England welcoming and confirming their grants of indulgence to Reading Abbey for the feast and octave of St James*

[prob. Apr. 1164]

A f6or

Venerabilibus dominis et fratribus clarissimis dei gratia episcopis per Angliam constitutis Iocelinus eadem gratia Sar(esburiensis) ecclesie humilis minister, salutem. Caritativum beneficii vestri munus quod monasterio beate dei genitricis Marie Rading(ensi) sanctitas vestra contulerit in festo beati Iacobi apostoli et in octo diebus sequentibus ad honorem eiusdem sancti, cuius pretiose reliquie ibidem reconduntur, nos et gratum collaudamus et ratum habemus. Valete.

Most probably shortly after the dedication of the abbey on 19 Apr. 1164. This letter strengthens the supposition that the group of indulgences for the feast of St James was granted at about the same time.

201   *Grant by Jocelin [de Bohun], bishop of Salisbury, of an indulgence of twenty days to all who visit Reading Abbey on the anniversary of its dedication [19 Apr.] or within the octave, and make an offering for the building*

[*c.*19 Apr. 1164]

A f6or

(I)ocelinus dei gratia Sar(esburiensis) episcopus omnibus Christi fidelibus per Sar(esburiensem) episcopatum constitutis, salutem et dei benedictionem. Innotuit satis universitati vestre quam pium sit et salubre venerabiles ac religiosos locos pia cum devotione et orationum fidelitate visitare. Inde est quod vestram rogamus attentius dilectionem et in domino exhortamur quatinus honestum ac religiosum locum de Rading(ia) in honore dei et beate dei genitricis virginis Marie et beatorum apostolorum Iohannis et Iacobi constructum die anniversarii dedicationis eius et per totas eiusdem diei oct(avas), devota cum humilitate, orationum sanctitate et elemosinarum vestrarum largitione, pro amore dei et salute animarum vestrarum visitare dignemini. Nos autem, de divina confisi clementia, omnibus qui ad predicti venerabilis loci de Rading(ia) incrementum ac constructionem de facultatibus suis aliquam benigne karitatis instinctu portionem contulerint, de iniuncta sibi penitentia .xx. dierum relaxationem indulgemus, predicantes vobis illam viginti dierum indulgentiam quam dominus T(homas) Cant(uariensis) et coepiscopi nostri eundem locum predictis diebus pie et caritative visitantibus concesserunt. Valete.

On or near the date of the abbey's dedication. The reference to the indulgences granted by Thomas Becket and the bishops is puzzling, since these in fact relate to the feast of St James and not to the abbey's dedication anniversary.

202   *Inspeximus and confirmation by Baldwin, archbishop of Canterbury and primate, of Archbishop Theobald's general confirmation to Reading Abbey [no. 182]*

[1185 × 90]

A f51r; B f188v; C f109r

Universis sancte matris ecclesie filiis ad quos presens scriptum pervenerit B(aldewinus) dei gratia Cant(uariensis) archiepiscopus totius Anglie primas, eternam in domino salutem. Ad notitiam vestram volumus pervenire nos scriptum bone memorie Theodbaldi predecessoris nostri in hec verba inspexisse. [*Here follows Theobald's confirmation,*[a] *above no. 182, printed by Saltman, 437–8 (no. 215), but Theobald is here called* totius Anglie primas.] Nos igitur, ut quod a memorato predecessore nostro iuste et rationabiliter ordinatum est et confirmatum firmam et perpetuam habeat stabilitatem, eandem confirmationem auctoritate qua fungimur communimus et sigilli nostri appositione roboramus. Hiis testibus:[b] magistro Silvestro, magistro R(adulfo) de Sancto Martino, magistro Edmundo, et multis aliis.

[a] *Quoted in full only in A*
[b] *B,C end with* et cetera

Baldwin was translated to Canterbury at the end of 1184 and left for the Third Crusade, on which he died, in Mar. 1190 (Landon, *Itin.*, 26).

203   *Grant by Hubert [Walter], bishop of Salisbury, for the health of the souls of, among others, Rannulf de Glanville and his wife Bertha who educated him, that the revenues of the chapel of St Laurence, Reading, may be assigned to the hospital there for the support of thirteen poor persons; the abbot and monks will make up any deficiency in the revenues and also support another thirteen poor persons from their own funds. The terms of service of the chaplain are defined*   [22 Oct. 1189 × Feb./Mar. 1190]

Original charter: BL Add. Ch. 19611
A ff 52v–53r; B f 191r–v; C f 111r
Pd. (cal.) Hurry, *Reading Abbey*, 172–3

Universis [a]sancte matris ecclesie filiis ad quos presens carta pervenerit, Hub(ertus) dei gratia Sar(esburiensis) episcopus eternam in domino salutem.[a] Nostri est officii que caritatis sunt fovere, que pietatis promovere. Hac siquidem inducti consideratione de assensu et coniventia dilecti filii nostri Galfr(edi) archidiaconi Berkess(ire)[b] concessimus et presentium auctoritate confirmavimus ut omnes fructus et obventiones capelle sancti Laurentii de Rading(ia) in usus et necessitates hospitalis eiusdem loci convertantur, ad sustentationem .xiii. pauperum, qui ibidem[c] pro salute anime nostre et antecessorum et successorum nostrorum, necnon et domini Rann(ulfi) de Glanvill(a) et domine Berte uxoris sue qui nos educarunt, et pro anima patris mei et matris mee et omnium parentum et benefactorum nostrorum perpetuo procurabuntur. Et si eiusdem capelle redditus ad id non suffecerint, dilecti filii nostri abbas et monachi de Rading(ia) quod defuerit ex condicto subministrabunt, preter alios .xiii. pauperes quos in eodem hospitali de suo specialiter exhibebunt.[d] Statuimus etiam ut capellanus ad predicti abbatis et monachorum presentationem in eadem pro tempore capella per nos institutus, quamdiu [e]ibidem per eosdem[e] ministraverit, canonicis mandatis nostris obediens existat, veruntamen[f] nec ad sinodum ob communem causam, nec ad capitulum extra villam Rading(ie) aliqua ratione tractus veniat, et ut ab omnibus consuetudinibus et omnibus que vel ab episcopo vel eius officialibus exigi solent immunis semper existat. Et si forte idem capellanus pecuniariter sit puniendus, pena eius cedat tantum in utilitatem memorati hospitalis. De suo dumtaxat ordine soli episcopo respondeat, abbati vero et monachis de ceteris omnibus que ad capelle et hospitalis pertinuerint administrationem. Is etiam honeste vite sit et opinionis integre, in hospitali manens eiusdem curam et animarum sollicite gerat, pauperes et peregrinos in mensa hospitalis secum cotidie a consanguineis et aliis secularibus semotus suscipiat, in usus preassignatos omnia quecumque perceperit ex integro convertat. Quod si secus quod absit egerit, post ammonitionem[g] diligenter exhibitam, si incorrigibilis extiterit, illum abbas amoveat, et alium idoneum episcopo ad idem officium representet. Si quis igitur hoc nostre concessionis statutum infringere vel minuere presumpserit, nostram maledictionem et divinam in corpore suo sentiat ultionem. Qui vero observaverit et manutenuerit, retribuat deus benedictionem pro benivolentia, gratiam pro gratia, vitam eternam pro boni operis beneficientia.[h] Testibus hiis:[i] prenominato Galfr(edo)[j] archidiacono, Azone archidiacono Sar(esburiensi), Bald(ewino) cancellario Sar(esburiensi),[k] magistro Vincentio vicearchidiacono[l] Wilt(esire), Roberto de Bellofago, magistro Simone de Scal(is), magistro Ricardo de Claie, magistro Alexandro capell(ano), Gautero capellano, Teodeb(aldo) Gauteri, et Bartholomeo fratre eius.

Endorsed: H. Saleburiensis episcopi de capella sancti Laurentii [*early 13th cent.*]

Size: 357 × 128 mm

Seal: large fragment of oval seal in white wax on tag; obverse: standing figure of bishop; on reverse complete counterseal with legend: H'TVS DEI GRATIA SARESBERIENSIS E[PI]SCOPVS

[a-a] et cetera *B,C*	[b] Berkesc' *A*, Berk' *B,C*
[c] ibi *A*	[d] exibebunt *A*
[e-e] per eosdem ibidem *B,C*	[f] verumptamen *B,C*
[g] amonitionem *A*	[h] benificientia *A*, beneficentia *C*
[i] his *A*; *B ends with* Hiis t', *C ends with* Hiis t' et cetera	
[j] Gaufr' *A*	[k] *A ends with* et multis aliis
[l] *Original charter has* archidiacono *with* vice *interlined*	

This act, which was entered in the original section of A, dates from the few months between Hubert's consecration and his departure for the Third Crusade (C.R. Cheney, *Hubert Walter* (1967), 32, 40; cf no. 224). The text has two odd features: it lapses into first person singular for *et pro anima patris mei et matris mee*, and it contains a sanctions clause of a type which was becoming rare and archaic by this time (cf no. 205). These may suggest that the act was either forged (on balance unlikely since the text was included in the original part of A composed in the early 1190s, i.e. during the bishop's tenure of the see) or, more likely, that it was composed by the Reading monks as beneficiaries rather than by the bishop's clerks. I am grateful to Prof. C.R. Cheney for valuable conversations on this point.

204 *Confirmation by Hubert [Walter], bishop of Salisbury, of Reading Abbey's ecclesiastical possessions [in the diocese] as held in the times of Bishops Roger and Jocelin and his own—viz., the school of Reading, pensions in the churches of Sulham, Purley and Englefield, and the churches of Cholsey, Wallingford St Rumwald, Wargrave, Tilehurst with the chapel of Sulhamstead [Abbots], Reading St Mary, Reading St Giles, Pangbourne and Beenham* [20 Apr. × 29 May 1193]

A f 71v; B ff 190v–191r; C ff 110v–111r

Universis sancte matris ecclesie filiis *ᵃ*ad quos presens scriptum pervenerit*ᵃ* H(ubertus) dei gratia Sar(esburiensis) episcopus, salutem *ᵇ*in eo qui est salus omnium.*ᵇ* Cum ex iniuncto nobis officio teneamur universis et singulis in suis petitionibus que ratione nituntur adesse, eorum tamen qui domino iugiter deserviunt debemus et volumus diligentius indempnitati prospicere et sollicitius negotiis intendere. Hoc igitur inducti rationis intuitu, venerabilibus et in Christo karissimis abbati et monachis de Rading(ia) concedimus et confirmamus scolas de Rading(ia), et .iiii. sol' de ecclesia de Suleham, et duos sol' de ecclesia de Purleia, et tres marcas de ecclesia de Englefeld annuatim percipiendas. Concedimus etiam eis et confirmamus ecclesiam de Causeia,*ᶜ* et ecclesiam sancti Rumbaldi de Walingef(ordia),*ᵈ* et ecclesiam de Weregrave, et ecclesiam de Tigeherste*ᵉ* cum capella de Silamestede,*ᶠ* et ecclesiam sancte Marie de Rading(ia), et ecclesiam sancti Egidii *ᵍ*in eadem villa,*ᵍ* et ecclesiam de Pangeburne, et ecclesiam de Bienham*ʰ* cum omni iure suo et pertinentiis, tenendas omni ea integritate et libertate qua eas tenuerunt temporibus bone memorie Rogerii [et]*ⁱ* Iocelini episcoporum Sar(esburiensium) predecessorum nostrorum et nostro. Quod ut in posterum firmum et inconcussum permaneat, presentis scripti testimonio et sigilli nostri appositione communimus. His testibus:*ʲ* Rann(ulfo) tesaur(ario) Sar(esburiensi), magistris S(imone) de Scales et Reinerio de Stanf(ordia), Gervasio, Roberto de Ruddebi, Gauterio de Stoct(ona), Iohanne clerico, Gregorio, Simone, canonicis Sar(esburiensis) ecclesie, Rog(erio) senescallo, Willelmo de Ruddebi, Guillelmo Cunseil, Rog(erio) de Cataine, Milone de Ruddef', et Gautero.

ᵃ⁻ᵃ Om. in B,C
ᶜ Chauseia B, Chaus' C
ᵉ Tyghelhurst' B,C
ᵍ⁻ᵍ Om. in B,C
ⁱ Om. in A, supplied from B,C

ᵇ⁻ᵇ Om. in B,C
ᵈ Walingf' B,C
ᶠ Silhamst' B, Silhamsted' C
ʰ Benham B
ʲ B,C end

The presence of Rannulf treasurer of Salisbury among the witnesses dates this act to after 20 Sept. 1192 (Cheney, *Hubert Walter*, 169), which, in conjunction with the English witness list, means that it dates from the weeks between Hubert Walter's return to England and his translation to Canterbury (*ibib.*, 38–9).

205 *Licence by Hubert [Walter], bishop of Salisbury, to Reading Abbey to appropriate the churches of Thatcham and Bucklebury, when they become vacant, to the use of the poor of the hospital before the abbey gate, lepers, pilgrims and other poor of Christ, saving sufficient provision for vicars*

[20 Apr. × 29 May 1193]

A f 71r–v; B f 191v; C f 111r–v; D f 57v
Pd. Barfield, *Thatcham*, ii. 50; (transl.) Humphreys, *Bucklebury*, 153–4

Hubertus dei gratia Sar(esburiensis) episcopus omnibus Christi fidelibus per episcopatum Sar(esburiensem) constitutis, salutem *a* in domino.*a* Quotiens que iusta sunt postulamur, moras ad concedendum facere nolumus, ne differre bona desideria que magis facienda sunt videamur. [*f 71v*] Quamobrem dilectorum ac religiosorum filiorum nostrorum monachorum de Rading(ia) precibus annuentes, ecclesias de Tacheam*b* et de Burghildebyri*c* cum omnibus pertinentiis suis, cum eas vacare contigerit, in usus pauperum hospitalis ante portam abbatie de Rading(ia), leprosorum in villa languentium, peregrinorum et aliorum Christi pauperum in perpetuum eis concedimus et presentis carte nostre munimine confirmamus, salva tamen sufficienti sustentatione vicariorum in predictis ecclesiis servientium. Et ut hec concessio nostra rata et inconcussa perseveret in posterum, eam sigilli nostri appositione roboramus. Si qua igitur ecclesiastica secularisve persona hanc nostre confirmationis cartam sciens infregerit aut contra eam temere venire presumpserit, secundo tertiove commonita si non congrue emendaverit, iram et maledictionem dei incurrat. Cunctis autem supradictorum pauperum Christi iura servantibus et eis bona facientibus sit pax et gratia domini nostri Iesu*d* Christi hic et in eternum. Amen.

a–a Om. *in B,C*
b Tacham *B,D*, Tacheham *C*
c Burchildebyr' *B*, Burghilb'i *C*, Burgildeb'r *D*
d Ihesu *B,C,D*

Despite its somewhat archaic features, this act probably dates from the same period as no. 204, which omits these two churches, for both were added to A at the same time immediately after its original composition. As was remarked above for no. 203, the sanctions clause and the 'Amen' may indicate composition by the abbey as beneficiary. The lepers referred to in this act and in no. 208 may have been in addition to those in the abbey's leper hospital of St Mary Magdalen (see no. 221).

206 *Signification by Hubert [Walter], archbishop of Canterbury and primate, addressed generally, that, although Reading Abbey has lent him its carts to convey a catapult to Marlborough, this shall not be to the prejudice of [the immunity of] the abbey in the future*   14 Feb. [1194]

A f 71v; B f 189r; C f 109v
Pd. *Memoranda Roll 1 John*, lxxiv

H(ubertus) dei gratia *a*Cantuar(iensis) archiepiscopus, totius Anglie primas, omnibus ad quos presens scriptum pervenerit, salutem. *a* Noverit universitas vestra quod abbas de Rading(ia) et monachi loci *b* eiusdem commodaverunt nobis solo petitionis nostre intuitu et dilectionis obtentu caretas suas ad deferendum unam petrariam ad Merleberg(am). Hoc ideo posteritati duximus significandum, *c* ne quod *b* liberalitate sola *d* nobis prestitum esse videtur ad consequentiam in posterum trahi posse in preiudicium prefate ecclesie iudicetur. *e* Teste Willelmo de Warenn(a). Apud Rading(iam), xiiii. die Februarii.

a-a et cetera *B,C*	*b* Interlined in A
c signandum *C (in error)*	*d* sua *C (in error)* *e* B,C end

For the date, see *Memoranda Roll 1 John*, lxxiv, where these letters of Hubert Walter acting as justiciar are discussed. The abbey's carts were needed to transport a catapult for the siege of the castle of Marlborough, which surrendered to the archbishop in March (Landon, *Itin.*, 84–5).

207 *Confirmation by Hubert [Walter], archbishop of Canterbury, primate and legate, of Reading Abbey's ecclesiastical possessions—viz., Reading with churches and chapels, namely, St Mary's parish church with the chapel of All Saints, and St Giles' church; the churches of Pangbourne, Beenham, Tilehurst with the chapel of Sulhamstead [Abbots]; the school of Reading; pensions from the churches of Sulham, Purley and Englefield; the churches of Cholsey, Wallingford St Rumwald, Wargrave, Hanborough, Stanton [Harcourt], Aston, Rowington; churches and chapels of Berkeley Hernesse; the churches of Eye and Leominster—and of its other possessions [unspecified]*
[Apr. 1195 × Feb. 1198]

A f 73r; B ff 188v–189r; C f 109r

H(ubertus) dei gratia Cant(uariensis) archiepiscopus, totius Anglie primas et apostolice sedis legatus universis sancte matris ecclesie filiis*a* ad quos presens scriptum pervenerit, salutem, gratiam et benedictionem. Quecumque pietatis intuitu religiosis locis*b* largitione regum sive principum seu quorumcumque fidelium oblatione *c* sub nostra iurisdictione in usus divinos cessisse *d* noscuntur, diocesani episcopi interveniente conniventia, nostri est officii illa roborare et nostre autoritatis *e* munimine stabilire. Inde est quod deo et beate

Marie et ecclesie de Rading(ia) et dilectis nobis in Christo filiis abbati et monachis eiusdem loci omnes possessiones et omnia bona tam ecclesiastica quam mundana que gloriose memorie Henricus rex nobilissimus Rading(ensis) ecclesie fundator primus eidem contulit ecclesie et carta sua confirmavit, scilicet Rading(iam) in qua eorum constructum*f* est monasterium cum ecclesiis et capellis eiusdem ville, scilicet ecclesiam beate Marie parochialem *g* cum capella omnium sanctorum cum omni alio iure suo, et ecclesiam sancti Egidii cum omni integritate sua. Ecclesiam etiam de Pangeb(urne), et ecclesiam de Benham,*h* et ecclesiam de Tigelhurst'*i* cum capella de Silamestede*j* confirmamus, et scolas de Rading(ia), et .iiii. sol' de ecclesia de Suleham,*k* et .ii. sol' *l*per annum*l* de ecclesia de Purlee, et tres marcas annuatim de ecclesia de Englefeld percipiendas, et ecclesiam de Chausie, et ecclesiam sancti Rumbaldi de Walingef(ordia),*m* et ecclesiam de Weregrava,*n* et ecclesiam de Haneberga, et ecclesiam de Stanton(a), et ecclesiam de Eston(a), et ecclesiam de Rochint(ona),*o* et omnes ecclesias et capellas de Berkelaihernes,*p* et ecclesiam de Eia, et ecclesiam de Leomenistria tenendam cum omnibus *q* predictis omni ea integritate, libertate et pace qua eas umquam *r* melius liberius ac *s* quietius tenuerunt temporibus nostris aut predecessorum nostrorum. Preterea quicquid in presenti canonice *t* possident seu in futuro rationabilibus modis adipisci poterunt nos quoque autoritate *u* nostra et scripti nostri testimonio confirmamus et in perpetuum possidenda concedimus. Quicumque ergo *v* adversus huius nostre confirmationis autoritatem *w* venire et predictorum fratrum possessiones turbare vel inquietare temere presumpserit, in districti iudicis examine omnipotentis dei maledictionem incurrat et iram. Cunctis autem predictorum fratrum iura servantibus et eisdem bona facientibus sit pax et gratia domini nostri Ihesu Christi hic et in perpetuum. Amen.

a *Interlined in A*
c *Om. in B,C*
e auctoritatis *B,C*
g parrochialem *B,C*
i Tyghelhurst *B,C*
k *Insert* per annum *B,C*
m Walingf' *B,C*
o Rokint' *B*, Rokynton' *C*
q *Om in C*
s aut *B,C*
u auctoritate *B,C*

b *A has here* pieta *marked for deletion*
d *A has* concessisse *with* con *erased*
f *A has* con *of* constructum *interlined*
h Bienham *C*
j Sylhamestede *B*, Silhamsted' *C*
l-l *Om. in B,C*
n Weregrave
p *A has* Berkelaihehernes
r unquam *B,C*
t *A has* canone
v igitur *B,C*   *w* auctoritatem *B,C*

While the archbishop exercised legatine authority, i.e. from shortly after his appointment as legate by Celestine III on 18 Mar. 1195 (*Epistolae Cantuarienses*, ed. W. Stubbs (RS, 1865), 368–9) to shortly after the lapsing of the appointment on the pope's death, 8 Jan. 1198. The archaic sanctions clause and 'Amen' suggest composition by Reading as beneficiary (see notes to nos. 203, 205).

208 *Licence by Hubert [Walter], archbishop of Canterbury, primate and legate, to Reading Abbey to appropriate to the use of the poor of the hospital before the abbey gate, lepers, pilgrims and other poor of Christ, the churches of Thatcham and Bucklebury, when they become vacant, saving sufficient provision for vicars; and grant, for the health of the souls of, among others, Rannulf de Glanville and his wife Bertha who educated him, that the revenues of the church of St Laurence, Reading, may be assigned to the same hospital for the support of thirteen poor persons* [Apr. 1195 × Feb. 1198]

A ff 72v–73r; B f 191v; C f 111v; D f 57r–v
Pd. Barfield, *Thatcham*, ii. 52; (transl.) Humphreys, *Bucklebury*, 158

H(ubertus) dei gratia Cant(uariensis) archiepiscopus, *a* totius Anglie primas et apostolice sedis legatus, universis sancte matris ecclesie filiis ad quos presens pagina pervenerit, salutem, gratiam et benedictionem. *a* Quotiens que iusta sunt *b* postulamur, ne bona desideria differre videamur, moras ad concedendum facere nolumus. Quocirca dilectorum nobis in Christo filiorum abbatis et monachorum de Rading(ia) precibus annuentes, ecclesias de þacham *c* et de Bukildeb(er)i *d* cum omnibus [*f 73r*] pertinentiis suis, cum eas vacare contigerit, in usus pauperum hospitalis ante portam abbatie de Rading(ia), leprosorum languentium in villa, peregrinorum et aliorum Christi pauperum in perpetuum eis concedimus et presentis carte nostre munimine confirmamus, salva tamen sufficienti sustentatione vicariorum in predictis ecclesiis servientium. *b* Concedimus etiam eis et confirmamus ut omnes fructus et obventiones ecclesie sancti Laurentii de Rading(ia) in usus et necessitates predicti hospitalis convertantur ad sustentationem .xiii. pauperum, qui ibidem pro salute anime nostre et antecessorum et successorum nostrorum, necnon et domini Rann(ulfi) de Glanvill(a) *e* et domine Berte uxoris sue qui nos educarunt, et pro anima patris nostri et matris nostre et omnium parentum et benefactorum nostrorum, perpetuo procurabuntur. Si qua igitur *f* ecclesiastica secularisve persona hanc nostre confirmationis paginam sciens infregerit aut contra eam temere venire presumpserit, *g* si non congrue emendaverit, maledictionem dei incurrat et nostram. Cunctis autem supradictorum pauperum Christi iura servantibus et eisdem *h* bona facientibus sit pax et gratia domini nostri Ihesu Christi hic et in eternum. Amen.

a–a et cetera *B,C*
b–b et cetera usque Et ut hec concessio *B,C, referring to Hubert Walter's act as bishop of Salisbury (no. 205)*
c Tacham *D*　　　　　　　　　　　*d* Burchildeb'i *D*
e Clanvilla *D*　　　　　　　　　　　*f B,C end with* et cetera
g A has presupserit　　　　　　　　　*h Both A and D have* eidem

Date as for no. 207. This confirms as archbishop Hubert's two acts as bishop of
Salisbury, nos. 203 and 205. Its archaic features suggest composition by Reading as
beneficiary (cf nos. 203, 205, 207).

209 *Notification by Hubert [Walter], archbishop of Canterbury, primate
and legate, addressed generally, concerning the case of a certain Brian and
Reading Abbey's judicial liberty to have cognizance of a charge of larceny
against him, despite the fact that the case involved other persons justiciable in
the king's court at Windsor, to which Abbot Hugh [II] of Reading sent Brian
on the archbishop's advice without prejudice to the abbey's rights in the
future*   [Apr. 1195 × Feb. 1198]

A ff 91v-92r; B f 189r; C f 109r-v

H(ubertus) dei gratia *Cant(uariensis) archiepiscopus, totius Anglie
primas et apostolice sedis legatus, omnibus ad quos presens scriptum
pervenerit,* salutem *b* in domino. *b* Noverit universitas vestra quod,
cum quidam nomine Brianus in curia abbatis de Rading(ia) detentus esset propter latrocinium posteaque in eadem curia confessus
esset se latrocinium illud quo detentus erat commisisse deberetque
ibidem secundum libertates quas domus de Rading(ia) habet ex eius
fundatoribus iudicium curie abbatis subire; quia idem Brianus post
confessionem suam quosdam retavit de foresta domini regis, ballivi
de Windesore *c* hoc audito venerunt et postulabant eundem Brianum
eis tradi ut prosequeretur *d* loquelam illam in curia domini regis
apud Windesor',*c* ad quam spectabant loquele de foresta domini
regis. Hugo vero, qui tunc temporis domui de Rading(ia) tanquam
abbas presidebat, *e* in hoc perplexus *f* erat, scilicet an posset per
confessionem suam ille Brianus non obstante exceptione aliqua con-
dempnari an curie de Windesor' *g* tradi, salvo iure et dignitate Rad-
ing(ensis) ecclesie in hoc casu. Et cum super hoc consilium nostrum
postularet quid esset ei faciendum, de consilio nostro idem abbas, ne
placita foreste usurpare videretur, eundem Brianum curie de Windesor', *g* tradidit, ibi prosecuturum appellationes quas fecerat contra
alios de foresta et inde ad curiam de Rading(ia), si alios vinceret,
rediturum et in eadem curia iudicium suum de [*f 92r*] furto *h* de quo
primum *i* retatus fuerat *j* recepturum. Hoc autem scriptum ei fecimus
ut protestemur illud quod a predicto H(ugone) abbate de predicto
Briano factum fuerat de nostro consilio factum esse, non ut ex hoc *k*
iuri et dignitati Rading(ensis) ecclesie aliquid in posterum deperiret.
Valete.

a-a et cetera *B,C*
c Windlesor' *B,C*
e *In A corrected from* presedebat
g Windl' *B,C*
i primo *B,C*

b-b *Om. in B,C*
d *A has* persequeretur
f *A has* proplexus
h *A has here* quod fecerat, *marked for deletion*
j fuit *B,C*   *k* *Interlined in A*

Date as for no. 207. Hubert Walter is here acting as justiciar. The text appears to imply that Hugh II (elected abbot of Cluny in 1199) was no longer abbot of Reading, but no such suggestion was intended.

210 *Confirmation by Herbert [Poore], bishop of Salisbury, of the grants of indulgences made by archbishops and bishops to Reading Abbey; and grant of an indulgence of twenty days to all who visit the Infirmary chapel, dedicated by the bishop on the octave of Easter [i.e., on 1 Apr.], on the anniversary or within the octave of that day, and confirmation of the indulgence of ten days for the same chapel on the same day granted by Eustace, bishop of Ely*

18 Apr. 1201

A f96r-v

Omnibus Christi fidelibus ad quos presens scriptum pervenerit Herb(ertus) dei gratia Sar(esburiensis) episcopus, salutem in domino. Inter omnes pastoralis officii sollicitudines ea precipue est commendanda diligentia que et Christi famulis in habitu religionis iugum obedientie portantibus pia subvenit provisione et fidelibus Christi loca eorum in orationum devotione et elemosinarum largitione visitantibus sarcinam pene pro peccatis inflicte paterna compassione studet mitigare, ut et locus religiosus et reliquie sanctorum ibidem divina voluntate reposite digne venerationis per frequentiam fidelium gaudeant obsequio, et pietas venerantium onus penitentiale sentiat alleviari. Attendentes igitur dilectorum nobis in Christo filiorum abbatis et conventus Rading(ensium) in sancta religione fervorem et in operibus misericordie gratiam hospitalitatis sepe etiam supra vires facultatum suarum omnibus impensam, de divine misericordie gratia et meritis sanctorum quorum reliquie in eorum monasterio continentur confisi, omnibus confessis et vere penitentibus predictum monasterium in orationum sacrificio et elemosinarum beneficio visitantibus relaxationes penitentiarum quas diebus et sollempnitatibus determinatis venerabiles patres archiepiscopi sive fratres nostri episcopi indulserunt, nosque auctoritate diocesana concedimus et cartis eorundem episcoporum super hec conscriptis quas inspici et legi fecimus pontificatus nostri assensum prebemus et confirmationem. Numerum etiam dierum secundum indulgentiam in eisdem cartis contentam, cum nominibus eorum qui inferius exprimendis sollempnitatibus indulserint, *a* certis duximus designare vocabulis. De indulgentia beati Th(ome) Cant(uariensis) archiepiscopi, qui ipsum monasterium in octav(is) Pasche dedicavit, ad festum dedicationis eiusdem, viginti dies. De indulgentia Iocelini Sar(esburiensis) episcopi, viginti quinque dies. De indulgentia G(ilberti) London(iensis) episcopi, .xx. dies. De indulgentia R(oberti) Baton(iensis) episcopi, .xx. dies. De indulgentia Roberti

Lincoln(iensis) episcopi, .xx. dies. De indulgentia Nigelli Eliensis
episcopi, .xx. dies. De indulgentia Godefr(idi) Lanelven(sis) episcopi, quindecim dies. De indulgentia G(ilberti) Hereford(ensis) episcopi, .xx. dies. De indulgentia David Meneven(sis) episcopi, quindecim dies. De indulgentia Nicolai Landav(ensis) episcopi, .xx. dies.
De indulgentia Hugonis Dunelmen(sis) episcopi, .x. dies. [*f96v*] De
indulgentia Bartholomei Exon(iensis) episcopi, viginti dies. De indulgentia R(icardi) Coventr(ensis) episcopi, .xx. dies. De indulgentia Hilarii Cicestr(ensis) episcopi, quindecim dies. De indulgentia
W(illelmi) Norwic(ensis) episcopi, .xx. dies. Ad festum sancti Philippi de indulgentia G(odefridi) Winton(iensis) episcopi, .xl. dies.
De indulgentia Iohannis Norwic(ensis) episcopi, .xl. dies. Ad festum
inventionis et exaltationis sancte crucis de indulgentia Theobaldi
Cant(uariensis) archiepiscopi, viginti dies. Nos quoque ad capellam
de infirmaria eiusdem monasterii, quam sancte et individue trinitati
in octavis Pasche dedicando consecravimus, omnibus confessis et
vere penitentibus qui eandem capellam eodem die vel per octavas
eius in orationibus vel beneficiis pie visitaverint, de misericordia vere
sempiterneque deitatis confisi, viginti dies de iniuncta penitentia
relaxamus et indulgentiam .x. dierum venerabilis fratris Eustachii
Eliensis episcopi ad prenominatam capellam eodem die factam auctoritate diocesana confirmamus. Et hoc totum cum presentis scripti
testimonio et sigilli nostri appositione duximus testificandum. Dat'
apud Suning(es) per manum Willelmi Raimundi, xiiii. kl' Maii,
pontificatus nostri anno septimo.

   ᵃ In MS corrected from indulgerint

211 *Confirmation by Herbert [Poore], bishop of Salisbury, of Reading
Abbey's tithes or pensions in its churches [in the diocese] with, where appro-
priate, details of the incomes of the perpetual vicars—viz., in the churches of
Reading St Mary, Reading St Giles, Wargrave, Beenham, Cholsey, Tilehurst,
Englefield, Bucklebury, Purley, Sulham, Pangbourne, Reading St Laurence,
Newbury, Wallingford St Rumwald, and the chapel of Sulhamstead
[Abbots]*   18 Apr. 1201

   A ff 96v–97v; (excerpt) D f 2or (passages marked *a–a, j–j, l–l* only)¹

ᵃOmnibus Christi fidelibus ad quos presens carta pervenerit
H(erebertus) ᵇ dei gratia Sar(esburiensis) episcopus, salutem in domino. Ne beneficia que a Christi fidelibus pio affectu et affectuosa
pietate locis religiosis et viris in eis iugem deo prestantibus famula-
tum misericorditer impenduntur, sive processu temporis sive malig-
nantium versutia, possit in posterum perturbari, episcopali decet ea
prospectione et protectione communiri. Attendentes igitur fervorem

religionis dilectorum nobis in Christo filiorum abbatis et conventus Rading(ensium) et hospitalitatis gratiam peregrinis et advenis et omnibus caritatis beneficium postulantibus impensam, eisdem monachis autoritate[c] pontificali confirmamus[a] in ecclesia beate Marie Rading' omnes decimationes plene et integre tam de blado quam de fabis et pisis et agnis extra burgum ad eandem ecclesiam pertinentes, ut eas in proprios usus secundum ordinationem domus sue convertant; omnes vero fructus et obventiones residuas ad eandem ecclesiam pertinentes quicumque pro tempore in eadem ecclesia ad presentationem eorundem monachorum a nobis vel successoribus nostris perpetuus fuerit vicarius institutus percipiet, reddendo prefatis monachis inde annuatim .lx. solidos et omnia[d] episcopalia [usitata][e] et consueta quantum ad vicariam suam pertinet sustinendo. Confirmamus etiam eisdem monachis in ecclesia beati Egidii Rading' omnes decimas plene et integre tam de blado quam de fabis et pisis et agnis extra burgum ad eandem ecclesiam pertinentes, ut eas simili modo in proprios usus convertant; omnes vero fructus et obventiones residuas ad eandem ecclesiam pertinentes quicumque pro tempore in eadem ecclesia ad presentationem eorundem monachorum a nobis vel successoribus nostris perpetuus fuerit vicarius institutus percipiet, reddendo annuatim prefatis monachis inde .xl. solidos et omnia[d] episcopalia usitata et consueta quantum ad vicariam suam pertinet sustinendo. Confirmamus quoque eisdem in ecclesia de Weregrave omnes decimas de blado et fabis et pisis ad eandem ecclesiam pertinentes; omnia vero alia ad eandem ecclesiam pertinentes quicumque pro tempore in eadem ecclesia ad presentationem eorundem monachorum a nobis vel successoribus nostris perpetuus fuerit vicarius institutus percipiet, reddendo inde nominatis monachis annuatim .xx. solidos et onera episcopalia usitata et consueta quantum ad vicariam suam pertinet sustinendo. Confirmamus etiam eisdem in ecclesia de Benh(am) omnes decimas ad eandem ecclesiam pertinentes [f97r], de blado scilicet exceptis decimis[f] de fabis et pisis et aliis leguminibus quas decimas videlicet de fabis et pisis et aliis leguminibus et omnia alia ad eandem ecclesiam pertinentia quicumque in ea perpetuus vicarius a nobis vel successoribus nostris ad presentationem eorundem monachorum fuerit institutus percipiet, reddendo inde annuatim memoratis monachis unam libram thuris et onera episcopalia usitata et consueta quantum ad vicariam suam pertinet sustinendo. Confirmamus etiam eisdem monachis in ecclesia de Chaus(eia)[g] omnes decimas[g] de blado ad eandem ecclesiam pertinentes, preter decimam de blado de Molesford quas decimas, videlicet de blado de Molesford, et omnes alias decimas tam in leguminibus quam in aliis rebus ad eandem ecclesiam pertinentibus et omnia alia ad eandem ecclesiam pertinentia percipiet perpetuus vi-

carius a nobis vel successoribus nostris ad presentationem eorundem
monachorum in eadem ecclesia institutus, reddendo inde annuatim
prefatis monachis quatuor marcas argenti, duas videlicet pro decimis
ortorum quas monachi quandoque perceperunt et alias duas pro
omnibus aliis rebus ad eandem ecclesiam pertinentibus; sustinebit
etiam idem vicarius quicumque in eadem ecclesia ad presentationem
eorundem monachorum a nobis vel successoribus nostris fuerit institutus omnia onera episcopalia consueta et usitata quantum ad vicariam suam pertinet. Confirmamus etiam eisdem monachis in ecclesia de Thigelhurst' omnes decimas de blado et agnis ad eandem
ecclesiam pertinentibus; perpetuus autem vicarius quicumque in
eadem ecclesia ad presentationem eorundem monachorum a nobis
vel successoribus nostris fuerit institutus omnia alia cum decimis
etiam de leguminibus ad eandem ecclesiam pertinentia percipiet,
reddendo inde annuatim prefatis monachis dimidiam marcam argenti et onera episcopalia quantum ad vicariam suam pertinet usitata et consueta sustinendo. Confirmamus etiam eisdem monachis in
ecclesia de Englefeld unam marcam per manum persone ad presentationem eorum a nobis vel successoribus nostris in eadem ecclesia
institute annuatim nomine pensionis percipiendam. [h] Ecclesiam de
Burghildeb(uria) cum triginta solidis de eadem per manum persone
a nobis vel successoribus nostris ad presentationem eorundem monachorum in eadem ecclesia institute annuatim percipiendis, cum
tribus etiam marcis de decimis de terra G(ilberti) Martell[2] ad eandem ecclesiam spectantibus per manum eiusdem persone annuatim
percipiendis. Confirmamus etiam eisdem monachis duos solidos de
[i] [ecclesia de] [i] Purleg(a) et quatuor solidos de ecclesia de Suleh(am),
salvo iure advocationis patronis earundem ecclesiarum, videlicet de
Purleg(a) et Suleh(am). Confirmamus etiam eisdem in ecclesia de
Pangeburn' .xxx. et duos solidos et .viii. denarios de eadem per
manum persone ad presentationem eorundem a nobis vel successoribus nostris institute in eadem ecclesia annuatim percipiendos. Confirmamus etiam eisdem [j]ecclesiam sancti Laurentii de Rading(ia)
cum omnibus obventionibus et pertinentiis suis ad usus pauperum
dei in hospitali quod iuxta eandem ecclesiam situm est collectorum;
ita quidem quod perpetuus vicarius ad presentationem eorundem
monachorum a nobis vel successoribus nostris institutus in eadem
ecclesia .xx. solidos annuatim de eisdem monachis ad indumenta sua
percipiet et panem et potum sicut monachus eiusdem monasterii et
septem denarios per ebdomadam pro compa[f97v]nagio et hospitium honestum et legata sua usque ad sex denarios et infra, supra
autem quod excreverit cum monachis dimidiabit; oblationem etiam
suam percipiet per quatuor sollempnitates anni; ipsi etiam monachi
diaconum propriis sumptibus invenient eidem ecclesie et capellano

ministrantem. Indulsimus quoque eidem vicario, quia infirmis et pauperibus in prefato hospitali oportet eum curam et diligentiam impendere, ut ad capitulum nisi in burgo Rading' venire non cogatur, set ad sinodum pro statutis ecclesie audiendis semel in anno cum aliis sacerdotibus et clericis conveniat, et tunc idem monachi capellano equum invenient. Et si forte episcopus in presentiam suam eundem capellanum pro excessu vel crimine suo vocaverit, ubi episcopus voluerit in episcopatu suo coram eo comparebit.^j Confirmamus etiam eisdem monachis in ecclesia de Niweb(uria) duos solidos; in ecclesia sancti Rumbaldi de Walingef(ordia) quatuor solidos. Confirmamus etiam eisdem monachis duas marcas et dimidiam argenti de capella de Silamst(ede) per manum perpetui vicarii a nobis vel successoribus nostris in eadem capella ad presentationem eorundem monachorum instituti annuatim percipiendas; et idem vicarius onera episcopalia consueta et usitata quantum ad vicariam suam pertinet sustinebit. In omnibus vero oneribus que ecclesias supradictas variis de causis contingere possunt, sicut vicarii vicinarum ecclesiarum, pro vicariis suis respondebunt. Abbas vero et conventus Rading(enses), sicut persone vicinarum ecclesiarum, plenarie respondebunt pro personatibus. Ut autem hec nostra concessio et indulgentia perpetue firmitatis robur obtineat, eas presenti carta et sigilli nostri munimine duximus confirmandas, salvis tamen in omnibus iure, auctoritate [et]^k dignitate ecclesie nostre et nostra et successorum nostrorum. ^l Dat' apud Suning(es) per manum Willelmi Raimundi, xiiii. kl' Maii, pontificatus nostri anno septimo. His testibus:^l magistris Hel(ia)³ de Chivel(e), H(ugone) de Gah(erste), R(adulfo) de Winesh(am), Th(oma) de Cabbeh(am), Abbrah(am), Bartholomeo, et magistro R(icardo) de Wdel(ege) capellanis, Iohanne de Wint(onia), R(ogero) de Hampt(ona) clericis, R(ogero)⁴ de camera, et multis aliis.

---

^{a-a} D f 20r   ^b Expansion from rubric of A; D has Hubertus (in error)
^c auctoritate D   ^d Probably either error for onera, or onera should be inserted
^e Supplied; cf. formula later in text   ^f decimis repeated in A
^{g-g} Altered in Ms from omnem decimam
^h Probably Confirmamus etiam eisdem should be inserted
ⁱ⁻ⁱ Supplied   ^{j-j} D f 20r
^k Supplied   ^{l-l} D f 20r

This general diocesan confirmation omits the church of Thatcham, which was dealt with in a separate act of the same date (no. 1114). However, by 1206 the bishop and the abbey were in conflict over the churches of Bucklebury and Thatcham (see no. 161) and difficulties seem to have continued in the time of R. bishop of Salisbury, either Richard Poore, 1217-28, or Robert Bingham, 1229-46 (*Sarum Charters and Documents*, 85, where the *R.* of the sources is expanded as *Ricardo* without warrant). Both churches were omitted from the diocesan confirmations of Hubert Walter and Robert Bingham (nos. 204, 212), although both as bishop and archbishop Hubert

gave licence for their appropriation to the poor of the hospital before the abbey gate
and others (nos. 205, 208), and his episcopal act was later inspected and confirmed
by Robert Bingham (no. 214; see also no. 215).

¹ The rubric of D (on f 19v) reads: *Hec carta excerpta est a carta generalis confirmationis
Huberti W.* [sic] *episcopi Sar'*.

² He was the lord of Marlston in the parish of Bucklebury. His name is usually
given as 'Geoffrey' (e.g. *VCH Berks.*, iii. 292), but there is no apparent authority for
this and 'Gilbert' is to be preferred. In the Reading charters he appears only as 'G.
Martel' (see also nos. 224, 294-6), but the abbey was in dispute with a *Gill'* Martel
in the 1190s (see no. 157) and a Gilbert Martel witnessed a charter relating to
Sheffield (in Burghfield) in 1197 × 8 (*Ancient Charters*, 106). The holder of Marlston in
1220 was certainly Geoffrey (*Fees*, i. 301), but in 1241, assuming him to be the same,
he was significantly said to be the son of Gilbert Martel (PRO JUST 1/37, m.18;
Humphreys, *Bucklebury*, 334).

³ For this and the following expansions, see *Sarum Charters and Documents*, index.

⁴ For this expansion, see nos. 617 and 844, the former identifying him as 'Roger of
the abbot's chamber'. He was clearly a witness from the abbey's side.

212 Confirmation by Robert [Bingham], bishop of Salisbury
[similar in general to no. 211], of Reading Abbey's tithes or pensions
in its churches [in the diocese] with, where appropriate, details of
the incomes and responsibilites of the perpetual vicars—viz., all
tithes in St Mary's church, Reading, both of corn and of beans,
peas, lambs, hay and mills, the perpetual vicar receiving all other
fruits of the church for an annual payment of 60s and discharging
episcopal, archidiaconal and other burdens; all tithes in St Giles'
church, Reading, both of corn and of beans, peas, lambs, hay and
mills, the perpetual vicar receiving all other fruits of the church for
an annual payment of 40s and discharging episcopal, archidiaconal
and other burdens; all tithes in the church of Wargrave (*Weregrave*)
of corn, beans, peas and hay, the perpetual vicar receiving all other
appurtenances for an annual payment of 20s and discharging episcopal, archidiaconal and other burdens; in the church of Beenham
(*Bienham*) *ᵃ* all tithes of corn and of the demesne hay, the perpetual
vicar receiving tithes of beans, peas and other legumes with other
appurtenances for an annual payment of 1 lb of incense and discharging episcopal, archidiaconal and other burdens; in the church
of Cholsey (*Chaus'*) the whole tithe of the abbey's demesne and of
the hay of Lollingdon (*Lolindune*) *ᵇ* and all tithes of corn, beans and
peas, except the tithes of Moulsford (*Molesford*) which, with all other
appurtenances, the perpetual vicar shall receive for an annual payment of 4 marks of silver, and he shall discharge episcopal, archidiaconal and other burdens; in the church of Tilehurst (*Tighelhurst*) *ᶜ*
all tithes of corn, beans, peas and mills of the parish and all tithes

of hay, except the tithes of hay of Theale (*la þele*) which, with all other appurtenances, the perpetual vicar shall receive, and he shall discharge episcopal, archidiaconal and other burdens;[1] in the church of Pangbourne (*Pangeburn'*) all greater and lesser tithes of the abbey's court of Bere (*la Bere*) and 32s 8d per annum from the parson; the church of St Laurence, Reading, appropriated to the use of the poor of the hospital built next to it, the perpetual vicar receiving annually from the abbey 20s for clothing, bread and ale as a monk, 7d per week for food, and worthy lodging, and having bequests up to 6d, anything above which he shall divide with the monks, and offerings on four feasts in the year, and a loaf and food each day for his servant; the vicar shall not be compelled to attend a [ruridecanal] chapter unless in Reading, but he shall attend synod once a year and, if called for offence before the bishop, shall appear before him wheresoever in the diocese; in the church of Sulhamstead [Abbots] (*Silhamstude*) *d* 40s per annum from the perpetual vicar, who shall discharge episcopal, archidiaconal and other burdens; in the church of St Rumwald, Wallingford (*Walingeford*) *e* 4s per annum; in the church of Englefield (*Englef'*) 1 mark of silver from the parson instituted on the presentation of the lord of the fee; in the church of Compton (*Cumptun'*) *f* 8s; in the church of Purley (*Purle*) 2s; and in the church of Sulham (*Suleham*) 4s, saving the right of advowson to the patrons of Englefield, Compton, Purley and Sulham

17 Apr. 1240

A ff 74r–75r; B ff 196r–197r; C ff 115r–116r

Dat' *g*apud Wodeford, xv. kl' Maii, *g* pontificatus nostri anno xi. Hiis testibus, et cetera.

a Benham *B*	*b* Lolindone *C*	
c Tighelherst *B,C*	*d* Silhamsted' *B,C*	
e Walingf' *B*, Walyngford' *C*	*f* Cumton' *B,C*	*g-g* Om. in *B,C*

This is basically an amplified version of no. 211 and shares the same *arenga*, but, while it adds the pension from Compton church (see no. 782), it omits reference to the church of Bucklebury and the pension from Newbury (see, respectively, nos. 698 and 815), and the items appear in a slightly different order towards the end of the list. All references to the patronage of the vicarages or rectories concerned are as in no. 211, except for Englefield rectory, whose patronage was altered by agreement in 1239 (see no. 800).

[1] No pension to the abbey from Tilehurst church is mentioned, but no. 211 gives ½ mark.

213 Inspeximus and confirmation of no. 212 by Robert, the dean, and the chapter of Salisbury   19 Apr. 1240

A ff 75v–76v; B f 197r; C f 116r

Dat' *a* per manum A(de) cancellarii nostri apud Sar(esburiam) xiii. kl' Maii, *a* anno gratie M.CC.xl. *b* Hiis testibus. *b*

a-a Om. in B,C
b-b Om. in C

The copy in A quotes the bishop's act in full apart from the witnesses; those in B and C give only its opening words.

214 Inspeximus and confirmation by Robert [Bingham], bishop of Salisbury, of the licence granted by Hubert [Walter], his predecessor, for the appropriation of the churches of Thatcham and Bucklebury, when they become vacant, to the poor of the hospital before the abbey gate and others [no. 205, the opening words and closing 'Amen' only quoted]. Witnesses [omitted]   [1229 × 46; ? *c.*1239]

B f 192r; C ff 111v–112r
Pd. Barfield, *Thatcham*, ii. 59

The outside dating limits are those of the bishop's pontificate, but, if this inspeximus relates somehow to no. 215, it would be of roughly the same date.

215 *Inspeximus and confirmation by Robert, the dean, and chapter of Salisbury, of the grant by Robert [Bingham], bishop of Salisbury, to Reading Abbey of the appropriation to its hospitality of the church of Bucklebury, a third part of the church of Thatcham and an annual pension of 9 marks from the other two parts of the same*   17 Aug. 1239

A f 111r (deleted by crossing through)

Universis sancte matris ecclesie filiis presens scriptum inspecturis vel audituris R(obertus) decanus et capitulum Sar(esburienses), salutem in salutis auctore. Litteras venerabilis patris nostri R(oberti) dei gratia Sar(esburiensis) episcopi inspeximus in hec verba.

Robertus dei gratia Sar(esburiensis) episcopus dilectis in Christo filiis R(icardo) eadem gratia abbati Rading(ensi) et eiusdem loci conventui, salutem, gratiam et benedictionem. Particeps mercedis efficitur qui bonorum operum se constituit adiutorem. Sane, cum facultates monasterii vestri ad hospitalitatis gratiam sectandam, a qua nullus cuiuscumque ordinis, etatis, sexus vel conditionis pro vestris beneficiis ad vos declinans se queritur alienum, noverimus minime sufficere, nos, ut de mercede vestra participium reportemus, ecclesiam de Burghildebir(ia) cum omnibus pertinentiis suis, salva vicaria in eadem auctoritate nostra taxata, cuius presentatio ad vos pertinebit; terciam partem preterea omnium terrarum, decimarum, fructuum et proventuum ecclesie de Thacham; item .ix. marcas annuas nomine pensionis de duabus reliquis portionibus eiusdem ecclesie percipiendas ab eiusdem ecclesie perpetuo vicario, patronatu eiusdem vicarie vobis salvo, ad hospitalitatis honera supportanda de assensu capituli nostri Sar(esburiensis) in vestros usus proprios et perpetuos duximus concedendas, auctoritate pontificali statuentes quod ecclesiam et pensionem supradictas cum prescriptis omnibus pacifice possideatis in posterum et inconcusse, salvis in omnibus iure, auctoritate et dignitate Sar(esburiensis) ecclesie et nostra et successorum nostrorum et archidiaconorum in quorum archidiaconatibus predicta sunt constituta. In huius rei testimonium presens scriptum sigillo nostro duximus muniendum. Hiis testibus: domino Egidio Berksyr' archidiacono, magistro Stephano de Manecest(re), Girardo de Wingeham, Petro de Cumba, Waltero de la Wile, Galf(re)do de Bedeford, canonicis Sar(esburiensibus), Petro de Winburne cappellano *a* Roberto de Wichampt(ona), Willelmo de Castellis, clericis nostris, et aliis. Dat' apud Sar(esburiam) xvi. kl' Septembris, pontificatus nostri anno xi.

Nos autem dictas venerabilis patris nostri ordinationem et concessionem ratas et gratas habentes, eas quantum in nobis est approbamus et sigilli nostri appositione confirmando corroboramus. Hiis testibus: dominis Roberto decano, Rogero precentore, Ada cancelario, *a* Henrico thesaurario, Thoma subdecano, Rogero succentore, et magistris Elia de Derham, Radulfo de Eboraco, Galf(re)do penitenciario, Ricardo de Knolle, Willelmo de Len, Willelmo de Leicest(re), et aliis. Dat' per manus A(de) cancellarii nostri, xvi. kl' Septembris, anno gratie M.CC.xxxix.

a Sic

The dates of the bishop's letters and of the inspeximus are the same. The document was deleted after entry in the earliest cartulary only, probably because, as far as Thatcham was concerned, it was superseded within the year by nos. 1116–18. It bears the same date as nos. 698–9, which relate to Bucklebury church only.

216   *Declaration by Giles, archdeacon of Berkshire, that, when he came on visitation to Reading Abbey on the morrow of St Hilary, 1246, after the death of Bishop Robert Bingham [of Salisbury], he testified that he did so by no other right than the authority of the vacant see*   [14 Jan. 1247]

A f86v

In nomine sancte et individue trinitatis. Amen. Cum anno gratie M.CC.xlvi. in crastino beati Hylarii ego Egidius archidiaconus Berksyr', vacante sede Sar(esb)u(riensi) per mortem pie memorie Roberti de Bingham episcopi, ad monasterium Rading(ense) causa visitationis descendissem, ne posset in posterum ab aliquibus in dubium devocari *a* an iure archidiaconali *b* an sedis auctoritate predicte tunc vacantis ad officium huiusmodi descenderem exequendum, ante ingressum capituli monasterii supradicti coram domino Ricardo tunc abbate et eiusdem loci conventu et aliis religiosis et secularibus tam viva voce quam per presentem scripturam publice protestabar quod nullo alio iure nisi auctoritate sedis predicte vacantis dumtaxat ad hoc officium processi, nec in aliquo predicto monasterio per visitationem huiusmodi preiudicare intendi, set ut libertas sedis predicte vacantis servaretur illesa. Et in huius rei *c* testimonium presenti scripture sigillum meum apposui. Hiis testibus: fratribus Alardo et Willelmo de ordine fratrum minorum, magistro Willelmo de Ledecumb' tunc officiali Berchsyr', magistro Ricardo de Benham canonico Sar(esburiensi), domino Henrico de Camel, domino Willelmo vicario de Aldremonston' tunc decano Radingensi, Henrico de la Stane clerico, et aliis.

217 *Lists of archiepiscopal and episcopal grants of indulgences to Reading Abbey for either the feast of St Philip,*[1] *or the feast of St James,*[2] *or the feast of each together,*[3] *or the whole year*[4]   [c. 1258 × 9]

  B ff 186v–187v

[*translation*]
On the feast of St Philip specifically (*In festo sancti Philippi specialiter*).[5]
Total: 176 [days].

	[No. of days][a]
John [Cumin], archbishop of Dublin [1182–c.1212]	40
Henry [of London], archbishop of Dublin [1213–28]	10
John [de Gray], bishop of Norwich [1200–14]	40
Ralph [Nevill], [bishop][b] of Chichester [1224–44]	13
Godfrey [de Lucy] of Winchester [1189–1204]	40
William [of Blois] of Lincoln [1203–06]	20
Walter [Mauclerc] of Carlisle [1223/4–46]	13

  [1] Presumably the feast of St Philip and St James the Less (1 May), but with emphasis on St Philip in Reading's case since it had a head relic of St Philip (see no. 49 n.).
  [2] The feast of St James the Great (25 July). For many of the grants listed here, see nos. 184–99.
  [3] Presumably grants for the two feasts of St Philip and St James, and of St James the Great.
  [4] This almost certainly means other feasts and anniversaries throughout the year, rather than the whole year, since at least two of the indulgences listed relate to a specific anniversary (see below p. 176 n. 8). This would also explain why two indulgences are listed for some prelates, presumably concerning different feasts.
  [5] See above n. 1.

Boniface[c] [of Savoy], archbishop of Canterbury
[1245-70][1]   40

On the feast of St James specifically (*In festo sancti Jacobi specialiter*).[2]
Total: 386 [days].

St Thomas [Becket], archbishop of Canterbury
[1162-70]   20
Theobald [of Bec], archbishop of Canterbury
[1139-61]   40
Henry [of London], archbishop of Dublin [1213-28]   20
Robert[d] [Chesney], bishop of Lincoln [1148-66]   20
Hugh [du Puiset], [bishop][b] of Durham [1153-95]   10
Gilbert [Foliot] of Hereford [1148-63]   20
Ralph [Nevill] of Chichester [1224-44]   13
Richard [Peche] of Coventry [1161-82]   20
Robert of Bath [1136-66]   20
Nicholas of Tusculum [1205-19][3]   20
Godfrey of St Asaph [1160-70/75]   15
David [Fitz Gerald] of St Davids [1148-76]   15
William [Turbe] of Norwich [1146-74]   20
Jocelin [de Bohun] of Salisbury [1142-84]   25
Hilary[e] of Chichester [1147-69]   15
Bartholomew of Exeter [1161-84]   20
Nigel of Ely [1133-69]   20
Walter [Mauclerc] of Carlisle [1223/4-46]   13
Gilbert [Foliot] of London [1163-87]   20
Nicholas [ap Gwrgant] of Llandaff [1148-83]   20
Boniface[c] [of Savoy], archbishop of Canterbury
[1245-70][4]   40

On the feast of each apostle together (*In festo utriusque apostoli communiter*).[5] Total: 174 [days].

Stephen [Langton], archbishop of Canterbury
[1207/13-28]   13
Albert [Suerbeer], archbishop of Armagh [1240-46]   15
William [of York], bishop of Salisbury [1247-56]   17

[1] An original indulgence of Archbishop Boniface survives, dated 2 March, 1254 (BL Add. Ch. 19624), but it cannot easily be identified with this or either of the other two indulgences listed here, since it grants 40 days indulgence for the Passion and Translation of St Thomas Becket.

[2] See above p. 174 n. 2.

[3] Cardinal bishop and papal legate to England at the end of the Interdict. A note of the 20-day indulgence was added to the table of contents in A (f 5v).

[4] See above n. 1.

[5] See above p. 174 n. 3.

Thomas, [bishop] *b* of Clonmacnois (*Cluanensis*)
[1236–*c*.1252, or 1252–78] [1]   10
Donatus of Killaloe (*Laoniensis*) [1221–*c*.1225, or
1231–52] [2]   10
Caducan of Bangor [1215–35/6]   20
Christian of Emly (*Ymilacensis*) [1238–49]   10
Navarus of Dax (*Aquensis*) [1239–72]   20
John [Collingham] of Emly (*Humil'*) [1228–36]   26
William of Llandaff [1186–91 × 1257–66] [3]   13
Gilbert of Ardfert (*Aerfertensis*) [1218–35]   20
[*f 187r*]

Throughout the year (*Per totum annum*).[4] Total: 1285 [days].

Richard, archbishop of Canterbury [1174–84, or
1229–31] [5]   20
Boniface [of Savoy], archbishop of Canterbury
[1245–70] [6]   20
William, archbishop of Bordeaux [1173–?1187, or
1207–27] [7]   20
Lucas [Netterville], archbishop of Armagh [1219–27]   30
Eugenius [mac Gille Uidhir], archbishop of Ar-
magh [1202–16]   41
Lucas [Netterville], archbishop of Armagh [1219–27]   20
Marianus [O Briain], archbishop of Cashel [1224–37]   20
Walter [de Gray], archbishop of York [1216–55]   40
Vincent *c* [de Pilmil], archbishop of Tours [1257–70]   30
Herbert [Poore], bishop of Salisbury [1194–1217] [8]   20
Richard [Poore] of Salisbury [1217–28]   25
Richard [Poore] of Salisbury [1217–28]   15
Robert [Bingham] of Salisbury [1229–46]   15
Robert [Bingham] of Salisbury [1229–46]   13
Albinus [O Maelmuidhe] of Ferns [*c*.1186–1223] [9]   13
Albinus [O Maelmuidhe] of Ferns [*c*.1186–1223]   5
John [of St John] of Ferns [1224–53]   20

[1] Either Thomas or Thomas O Cuinn.

[2] Either Donatus O h-Enni or Donatus O Cinneide.

[3] Either William of Saltmarsh (1186–91) or William de Goldcliff (1219–29) or
William de Burgh (1245–53) or William of Radnor (1257–66).

[4] See above p. 174 n. 4.

[5] Either Richard of Dover or Richard Grant.

[6] See above p. 175 n. 1.

[7] Either William the Templar, formerly abbot of Reading, or William Amanevi de
Geniès (*Gallia Christiana*, iii. 819–22).

[8] It is clear from no. 210 that the grant was for the anniversary of the dedication
of the Infirmary chapel or its octave.

[9] A note of this grant was added to the table of contents in A (f 5v).

William of Ely [1189–97, or 1255–56][1]	15
Eustace of Ely [1198–1215][2]	10
Hugh of Ely [1229–54, or 1257–86][3]	20
Hugh of Ely [1229–54, or 1257–86][4]	20
William of [?] Châlons-sur-Marne (*Cathalensis*) [1215–26][5]	10
William of [?] Châlons-sur-Marne (*Cathalensis*) [1215–26][6]	10
William of Leighlin (*Lechins'*) [1228–52]	20
William of Leighlin (*Lechins'*) [1228–52]	20
Alexander of [?] (*Lechin'*)[7]	13
Alexander of [?] (*Lechin'*)[8]	7
Simon [of Apulia] of Exeter [1214–23]	10
Simon [of Apulia] of Exeter [1214–23]	10
William [Briwere] of Exeter [1224–44]	20
Henry [Marshal] of Exeter [1194–1206]	20
Maurice [O Flaithbertaig] of Annadown (*Enach-dunensis*) [c.1202–41]	20
Thomas [O Mellaig] of Annadown [c.1242–47]	10
Ralph [of Bristol] of Kildare (*Dariensis*) [1223–32]	13
Ralph [of Bristol] of Kildare [1223–32]	10
Thomas of Clonmacnois (*Cluacensis*)[f] [1236–c.1252, or 1252–78][9]	40
Thomas of Clonmacnois (*Cloanensis*) [same date range]	20
Henry of Emly (*Ymilacensis*) [1212–27]	31
Christian of Emly [1238–49]	20
Maurice of [?] (*Menevens'*)[10]	15
Gervase of St Davids [1215–29]	15
Alexander of [?] (*Moramens'*)[11]	20

[1] Either William Longchamp or William of Kilkenny.

[2] See above p. 176 n. 8.

[3] Either Hugh of Northwold or Hugh Balsham.

[4] See previous note.

[5] These are the dates of William du Perche, bishop of Châlons-sur-Marne, but the identification of the bishopric is uncertain; possibly Caithness—William, bishop of Caithness, c.1250–61.

[6] See previous note.

[7] Bishopric unidentified; it appears to be Leighlin, but no bishop Alexander is listed (*Handbook of Brit. Chron.*).

[8] See previous note.

[9] See above p. 176 n. 1.

[10] Bishopric unidentified; if the cartulary scribe copied its name correctly, it would be St Davids, but no bishop Maurice is listed (*Handbook of Brit. Chron.*).

[11] Unidentified; possibly a mistake for either Andrew or Archibald, bishops of Moray (1223/4–42 and 1253–98), in which case the Latin should read *Moraviens'*.

Richard of Chichester [1215–17, or 1245–53] [1]	25
Richard of Chichester [same date range]	20
Simon [Fitz Robert] of Chichester [1204–07]	10
Edmund of Limerick (*Luminicensis*) [1215–22]	41
Robert [of Bedford] of Lismore [1219–23]	10
Henry [of Abergavenny] of Llandaff [1193–1218]	20
Fulk [Basset] of London [1244–59]	15
Jocelin [of Wells] of Bath [1206–42]	10
Raymond of Bayonne (*Baiocens'*) [f] [c.1217–56]	15
Walter of Waterford [1227–32]	20
Richard of Waterford [2]	15
Robert of Waterford [1200–04, or 1210–23] [3]	13
Hugh [of Beaulieu] of Carlisle (*Carleodensis*) [1219–23]	20
Hugh [of Beaulieu] of Carlisle [1219–23]	17
Caducan of Bangor [1215–35/6]	20
Richard of Bangor [1237–67]	10
William of [?] (*Ateradens'*) [4]	20
Thomas of Achonry (*Achadensis*) [(1227)–30, or 1251–65] [5]	13
Thomas [O Conchobhair], [archbishop] [g] of Tuam [1259–79]	20
[f 187v]	
Nicholas of Tusculum [1205–19] [6]	10
Raymond [de St Martin] of Aire (*Adurensis*) [1253–65]	40
John of Cambrai (*Cameracensis*) [1192–?1196] [7]	15
Henry of Ilium (*Magne Troie*) [c.1226–post 1231] [8]	10
Dionysius [O Mordha] of Elphin (*Elfinensis*) [ante 1226–29]	32
Maurice of Kilmacduagh (*Duanensis*) [1254–84]	13
Roger of Chester [1245–56, or 1258–95] [9]	20
Hugh of Hereford [1216–19, or 1219–34] [10]	20
Walter [Suffield] of Norwich [1245–57]	20

[1] Either Richard Poore or Richard Wich.

[2] No Richard appears in the list of bishops of Waterford before 1338.

[3] Either Robert I or Robert II.

[4] Bishopric unidentified; possibly Aire—William, bishop of Aire, c.1188–c.1194 (P. B. Gams, *Series Episcoporum Ecclesiae Catholicae* (reprinted, Leipzig, 1931), 480).

[5] Either Thomas O Ruadhan or Thomas O Maicin.

[6] See above p. 175 n. 3

[7] *Gallia Christiana*, iii. 32–3. He wrote a Life of Becket, with whom he had been 'joined in friendship' (*ibid.*).

[8] He acted as a suffragan bishop in the diocese of Liège from 1226 and in that of Coutances from 1231 (C. Eubel, *Hierarchia Catholica Medii Aevi*, i (2nd edn, Münster, 1913), 500, 'Trojan' n.1).

[9] Presumably either Roger Weseham or Roger Longespée, bishops of Coventry and Lichfield, and not Roger de Clinton, bishop of Chester 1129–48.

[10] Either Hugh de Mapenore or Hugh Foliot.

William of Llandaff [1186–91 × 1257–66] [1] 15
Milo [c] [O Conchobhair], bishop of Elphin
[1260–62] 20

[a] *The numbers of days are given in Roman numerals with* dies *after the first item and* d' *after the rest*

[b] episcopus *is om. for every bishop after the first in each section*

[c] *This item entered in slightly later hand, the days granted not being included in the total at the head of this section*

[d] *Ms has* 'Richard', *but see above, no. 193*

[e] *Ms has* 'Elias', *but see above, no. 188*

[f] *Sic*

[g] *Supplied, since not a bishop (cf. b)*

The list is to be dated *c.*1258 × 9, since, apart from the small number of later additions, it forms part of the original compilation of B and includes in the original hand Thomas [archbishop] of Tuam. Thomas, previously bishop of Elphin, was elected to Tuam after 17 July 1258, translated 23 Mar. 1259 and received temporalities 20 July 1259. The dates of prelates of the British Isles are supplied from *Handbook of Brit. Chron.* (3rd edn, 1986); those of continental prelates, unless otherwise stated, are taken from C. Eubel, *Hierarchia Catholica Medii Aevi,* i (2nd edn, Münster, 1913).

[1] See above p. 176 n. 3.

V ABBATIAL ACTS AND DOCUMENTS CONCERNING
THE ABBEY AS A COMMUNITY

218   *Charter of mutual* societas[1] *by Peter [the Venerable], abbot of Cluny, to Abbot Hugh [I] and the convent of Reading. On the death of the abbot of Reading, his successor shall be elected from the monks of that house or from the monks of Cluny, the prior of Cluny excepted*   [1123 × 30]

A f48v

Karissimo fratri nostro domno Hugoni Radingensi abbati eique commisso conventui frater Petrus fratrum Cluniacensium servus indignus, omnem in Christo pacis et societatis unitatem. Quoniam nobilissimus rex Anglorum Henricus benefactor noster egregius domum vestram quam noviter edificavit in ordine religionis monastice per fratres nostre congregationis fundare voluit, nos pro eiusdem regis gratia et petitione vestra vobis et successoribus vestris concedimus et in capitulo Cluniacensi presentes firmavimus ut quicumque abbas Radingensis monasterii fuerit capitulum in domo nostra et in ceteris domibus ad nos pertinentibus habeat et teneat, et fratres Rading(enses) ubicumque ad loca nostra venerint similiter ut nostri sint in capitul(o). Cum autem abbas Rading(ensis) quicumque ille fuerit ex hac vita migraverit, brevi ad nos perlato fiet ei officium consuetum et tricenarium. Fratribus vero prefati loci obeuntibus idipsum in conventu nostro et in omnibus locis nostris persolvendum statuimus quod nostris professis solvere solemus, eosque inter fratres nostros scribi in regula capituli annuatim recitandos decrevimus. Quod autem vobis vestrisque successoribus et conventui vestro tam presenti quam futuro concessimus idipsum nobis nostrisque successoribus et conventui nostro tam presenti quam futuro a vobis concedi et confirmari volumus, qui vos vestraque omnia parentes etiam vestros et benefactores tam defunctos quam vivos in orationibus et missis et elemosinis et omnibus bonis nostris suscipimus et matri misericordie commendamus. Statutum etiam est, in signum tante unitatis et ad maiorem Cluniacensis ordinis in domo Radingensi stabilitatem, ut abbate Radingensi ex hac vita migrante conventus eiusdem loci de propriis professis ecclesie sue non de alienis abbatem sibi eligant. Quod si inter eos persona idonea inventa non fuerit, tunc sibi eligant Radingenses de monachis Cluniac(ensibus) quemcumque ad hoc digniorem invenire potuerint, excepta persona prioris Cluniac(ensis). Electus autem eis sine contradictione abbas ordinetur. Hec instituta sunt voluntate et precepto domni regis Henrici et communi assensu tam ipsius quam nostro.

Rubric: Carta abbatis et conventus Cluniacensis super societate mutua

The dating limits are those of Hugh I's abbacy, but it probably dates earlier rather than later in the range. The cartulary notes another charter by the same concerning the same (*Item carta eorundem super eodem*). The charter presents problems, for not only does it end rather abruptly, but the abbot of Cluny's style is highly exceptional. To judge from his letters, he almost always styled himself *frater Petrus humilis Cluniacensium abbas* (see *The Letters of Peter the Venerable*, ed. G. Constable (Harvard, 1967), i, *passim*), very occasionally inserting *fratrum* after *humilis* (*ibid.*, 383, 423); and, although he once addressed his monks at Cluny as *eorum non tam abbas quam servus*, the circumstances were exceptional (*ibid.*, i. 334; ii. 187) and he appears not to have used *servus indignus* other than in the present charter. However, there is no reason to doubt the charter's basic authenticity, since its existence is otherwise well attested. It is clearly the *carta societatis* to which Abbot Hugh referred in some detail in 1138, when as archbishop of Rouen he settled a dispute between the abbots of Le Pin and Mortemer (*Recueil des historiens des Gaules et de la France*, xv. 695-6), and Pope Adrian IV later referred to a sealed *scriptum* of the abbot of Cluny affirming the *societas* and fraternity with Reading (above, no. 146). See also K. Leyser, 'Frederick Barbarossa, Henry II and the hand of St James', *EHR* xc (1975), 492 n.3.

[1] This expression is taken from the rubric.

219 *Grant by Peter [the Venerable], abbot of Cluny, to Abbot Anscher and the convent of Reading that the names of the latter's dead shall be written down with those of Cluny, and request for the continuation of reciprocal arrangements at Reading* [1130 × 35]

A ff 48v-49r

Venerabili et dilectissimo fratri nostro domino Ascherio abbati Radingensi universoque conventui frater Petrus abbas Cluniacensis, salutem et sinceram dilectionem. Licet universorum iustis petitionibus debeamus semper assensum prebere, specialiter [*f 49r*] tamen vestris non debemus ullatenus deesse, tum quia vos precipuo affectu diligimus, tum quia petitiones vestras mutue inter nos karitati augende et societati artius connectende in perpetuum non mediocriter valere perpendimus. Eapropter hortatu dilectissimi filii nostri Hugonis camerarii quod petitis libenter annuimus et ut vestra defunctorum nomina cum nostris professis mixtim scribantur precipimus, quamvis proprias abbatias nostras hanc nobiscum communionem non habere minime ignoremus. Vos quoque de nostris idem oportet facere, sicut et *a* facitis, sed ne oblivione seu neglegentia pretermittatur dignum duximus vestram fraternitatem commonere.

a Interlined

The dating limits are those of Anscher's abbacy. Peter the Venerable's style is unusual (see no. 218 n.), but not impossible.

220 *Confirmation by Abbot Hugh [IV] of Cluny to Abbot Hugh [II] and the convent of Reading of the charter of mutual* societas *granted by Abbot Peter [the Venerable]*   [1186]

A f 49r

Venerabili et karissimo fratri nostro domno Hugoni abbati Radingensi eidemque commisso sacro conventui frater Hugo humilis Cluniac(ensis) abbas, salutem et unitatis spiritum in vinculo pacis. Venientes ad nos karissimi fratres nostri Gervasius atque Willelmus exsecutores vestre electionis et interpretes regie voluntatis ut legationis sue facilius optinerent effectum, reverendi decessoris nostri domini abbatis Petri cartam pretenderunt, mutue societatis iura que inter Cluniacensem ecclesiam et vestram a fundationis sue exordio coaluit et sacri semper sumpsit incrementa vigoris indubitata serie protestante. Nos autem eiusdem patris vestigiis inherentes, ad predictorum fratrum petitionem prefatam societatem duximus innovandam, et presenti scripto sigilli nostri impressione munito retendendam, confirmantes ut abbas Radingensis quicumque fuerit capitulum habeat et teneat in domo nostra et in omnibus locis nostris. Fratres etiam Rading(enses) ubicumque ad loca nostra venerint similiter ut nostri sint in capitul(o). Pro defunctis etiam eorum in domibus nostris cum breve perlatum fuerit fiet eis quantum nostris professis et in regula scribentur cum nostris annuatim recitandis. Obeunte Radingensi abbate et brevi ad nos perlato, fiet apud nos officium pro eo consuetum et tricenarium. Quod autem vobis vestrisque successoribus et fratribus vestris presentibus ac futuris concedimus, idipsum nobis nostrisque successoribus ac fratribus nostris presentibus et futuris a vobis concedi et confirmari volumus. Statutum est etiam, in signum tante unitatis et ad maiorem Cluniacensis ordinis in domo Radingensi stabilitatem, ut obeunte abbate Radingensi conventus eiusdem loci de propriis professis ecclesie sue non de alienis abbatem sibi eligant. Quod si in aliquem suorum pacifico assensu convenire non potuerint, tunc sibi eligant Radingenses de monachis Cluniacensibus quemcumque ad hoc digniorem invenire potuerint, excepta persona prioris Cluniac(ensis). Electus autem sine contradictione abbas ordinetur. Hec instituta sunt voluntate et precepto domini Henrici illustris Anglorum regis, precipui benefactoris nostri, et tam nostro quam et conventus Cluniacensis sigillo firmata.

Shortly after the election of Abbot Hugh II of Reading in 1186. It is basically a re-issue of no. 218.

221 *Memorandum concerning the foundation by Abbot Anscher [of Reading]
of the leper house of St Mary Magdalen within the precinct of Reading Abbey
and the provisions assigned to the lepers*

[? late 13th cent.; Abbot Anscher 1130–35]

A f 11v; D f 38r
Pd. *Mon. Ang.*, iv. 43 (no. xiv)

Dompnus *ᵃ* abbas Ancherius constituit domum leprosorum ex devo-
cione sua in confinio Radyng(ensis) ecclesie que dicitur hospitale
sancte Marie Magdalene, ad quorum sustentacionem dantur singulis
diebus singuli cantelli *ᵇ*dimidium panem *ᵇ* habentes et dimid(ii) gal-
ones servicie *ᶜ* mediocris. Preterea singulis mensibus cuilibet eorum
dantur ab elemosinario .v. d' ad companag(ium) emendum. Preterea duas carectas feni cum uno equo cariando et pro eodem equo
sustentando a camerario habent, unam apud Estmed et aliam apud
Vobney. Capellano autem eiusdem loci dantur ad festum Michaelis
tantum sex ulne panni *ᵈ* de russet. Loco solidorum habet omnes
oblaciones per leprosos oblatas, nam reliquas *ᵉ* oblaciones dividit
cum leprosis. Habet etiam omnia emolumenta ex missis petitis et
tricenariis ibidem provenientia. Carectarius eorum habet a grane-
tario singulis diebus unum panem de orto, ab elemosinario vero
habet .xxxii. d' per annum ad duos terminos. Mulier ibidem serviens
panem habet sicut carectarius, ab elemosinario autem *ᵈ* .ii. s' per
annum.

ᵃ Dominus *D*   *ᵇ⁻ᵇ* dimid' panis *D*
ᶜ servisie *D*   *ᵈ* Om. in *D*
ᵉ Very uncertain reading in *D*

Both texts are in 14th-century hands; that in D was entered after most of the folio
had been filled, for it begins in a gap near the top of the folio, continues down the
right-hand margin and is completed at the bottom. A fuller, and presumably later,
account of provisions for the lepers is in D f 38r–v.

222 *Ordinance defining the punishments to be suffered by lepers who commit
offences, with regulations covering the absence of lepers from the house and
notes of the property assigned to the lepers*

[? mostly 1130 × 35; partly after 1165]

A f 12r

Audite iam fratres que sunt peccata pro quibus quisque frater si
forisfacit pati debet iusticiam. Si aliquis facit adulterium et probari
possit inde, domum omnino amittet et nullo modo potest reconciliari
nisi per consensum domini abbatis et conventus. Item si aliquis
percutit fratrem suum superbia vel ira vel odio, similiter domum

suam amittet. Item si aliquis dementiatur alium ira vel superbia, ieiunet per unum diem in pane et aqua, et cantellus suus et servisia sua eadem die debet poni super mensam magistri et sic distribuetur pro amore dei, et ieiunans debet sedere in area ante mensam et ibi commedere panem suum. Et si habet indignationem inde, secunda et tertia die consimiliter ieiunare [debet] *a*, quod si non emendaverit, domum suam amittet. Item si quis movet litem et magister domus precipit aliquem tacere, nisi taceat ad tertium iussum ieiunet per unum diem in pane et aqua ut supradictum est. Item non debet aliquis extra mansum ire sine socio nec moram facere ad portam seu ad crucem sine socio. Item si aliquis vult ire in negotio suo et moram facere per unam noctem vel plures, oportet habere licentiam totius conventus. Item si aliquis vult ire in negotio suo longe vel prope et si redierit eadem die, non debet ire sine licentia nec sine socio. Item predicti leprosi habebunt redditus de tenemento Grey in Erle et heriett(um) cum acciderit. Item duas acras terre in Spitelfeld ex dono W(illelmi) abbatis.

Iste Ancherius superius nominatus[1] propter enormitatem diversarum infirmitatum pauperum tunc temporis existentium, *b* cum voluntate et consensu confratrum, ob reverentiam dei pauperum pietate motus ordinavit ex mera devotione elemosinam supradictam, et cetera.

a Supplied   *b At this point a gap of 2 or 3 words filled by 3 dashes*

Entered in the same 14th-century hand as no. 221. These regulations appear to date from Abbot Anscher's time (1130-35), but Abbot William's gift to the lepers cannot be earlier than his abbacy (1165-73). A fuller set of regulations, without the references to property, is in D f 39r

[1] The reference is to the previous entry, no. 221.

223 *Precept by Abbot Roger [of Reading] concerning the weight of bread used daily in the monastery*   [1158 × 65]

A f 49r-v

Sciant presentes et futuri quod ego Rog(erius) abbas, rogatu et supplicatione totius conventus, hanc utramque libram panis, cotidiani videlicet .iiii. marcarum et dimidie, quadragesimal(is) vero .v. marcarum et trium solidorum, fieri precepi, et in perpetuo in hoc monasterio haberi, ne amodo subsequentium abbatum irrationabili potestate vel voluntate aut granetariorum mutatione hoc prenotatum pondus panis minuatur, nisi aliqua iusta et ma[*f 49v*]nifesta necessitate, quod tamen fiat voluntate et consensu totius conventus. Ne vero processu temporis hoc statutum ab aliqua persona cassetur et irritum fiat, voluntate et auctoritate totius conventus maledicti-

onem et anathematis sententiam in huius statuti violatores proferi-
mus; nichilominus predicti statuti amatoribus et conservatoribus
benedictionem nostram transmittimus.

The dating limits are those of Roger's abbacy.

224 *Notification by Abbot Hugh [II] and the convent of Reading of the
foundation of the hospital outside the gate [of the abbey]; and grant to it in
free alms, with the assent of Hubert Walter bishop of Salisbury, of the church
of St Laurence [Reading] for the maintenance of thirteen poor persons, the
abbey providing daily distribution of food to thirteen other poor brothers, and,
for the use of pilgrims, the profits of the fulling mill of Leominster and the
chapel of G(ilbert) Martel* [1189 × 93; ? 1191 × 93]

B f198r–v; C f117r–v; D f19v
Pd. *Mon. Ang.*, iv. 42–3 (no. xiii); Barfield, *Thatcham*, ii. 9–10; (cal.) Humphreys,
Bucklebury, 156

Universis Christi fidelibus *[ad quos presens scriptum pervenerit]*
frater H(ugo) Rading(ensis) ecclesie minister humilis et eiusdem loci
conventus, *[unanimis in domino]* salutem. Ad universitatis vestre
notitiam volumus pervenire excellentissimum quondam regem Anglorum Henricum primum domum Rading(ensem) fundasse ad sustentationem monachorum ibidem deo devote ac religiose servientium et ad susceptionem hospitum transeuntium, precipue tamen
pauperum Christi ac peregrinorum, *[f198v]* sicut ex ipsius carta
penes nos habita satis dilucide colligi* potest. Verum divitibus ut
ipse eorum timor exigit splendide ac honorifice ex more receptis,
pauperes et peregrini minus reverenter quam decuit et longe aliter
quam regia devotio disposuit in retroactis temporibus suscepti sunt.
Unde, cum ipsius elemosine non solum participes verum etiam pro-
curatores simus, ut in conspectu dei illam fideliter dispensemus, eam
in quantum sufficimus etiam pauperibus volumus esse communem.
Cuius rei causa ad relevandam pauperum inopiam et subsidium
peregrinorum hospitale quoddam extra portam construximus, ut qui
admissus non fuerit in hospitio superiori[1] ibi saltem quam reverenter
poterit suscipiatur. Unde, assensu et consensu diocesiani episcopi,
domini H(uberti) Walteri,* ut carta ipsius super eodem negotio apud
nos habita testatur,[2] ecclesiam beati Laurentii prefato hospitali in
perpetuam elemosinam concessimus ad sustentationem .xiii. pauperum in victu et vestitu et in aliis necessariis, aliis .xiii. pauperibus
fratribus consimilia alimenta ex cotidiana et consueta elemosina nostra subministrantes. Ad usum vero peregrinorum transeuntium concessimus omnes exitus molendini fulerez de Leomenistria* *et capellam G(ilberti) * Martel[3] cum omnibus decimis de dominio suo et de
terra rusticorum et cum aliis omnibus obventionibus maioribus et

minoribus.*f* Et ne hec donatio nostra lapsu temporis apud posteros in dubium veniat aut alicuius ausu temerario infringi et irritari attemptetur, eam sigillorum nostrorum appositione communire dignum duximus. Omnes autem quicumque predicte donationis fautores et defensores extiterint concedimus participes esse omnium bonorum que fiunt in domo nostra et in prefato hospitali. Si autem quis in contrarium venire presumpserit, conterat eum dominus in eternum.

a-a Om. in B,C; supplied from D
c perpendi D
e Leoministr' C
g For expansion, see no. 211 n.2

b-b As *a-a*
d Walterii D
f-f Om. in D

The outside dating limits are those of Hubert Walter's tenure of the see of Salisbury, but the reference to Gilbert Martel's chapel may date this deed to *c.*1191 × 93, to which period the settlement between Reading Abbey and the incumbent of Bucklebury, in which parish the chapel was situated, may possibly be dated (see no. 694). The same abbot's undertaking to Hubert Walter, bishop of Salisbury, to maintain 13 poor in the hospital, in addition to the 13 already maintained there, is in *Sarum Charters and Documents*, 46.

[1] Perhaps a reference to the guest-house of the abbey.
[2] See no. 203.
[3] In Bucklebury parish (see no. 694).

225   List of books in Reading Abbey   [*c.*1191 × *c.*1193]

A ff 8v–10v
Pd. S. Barfield, 'Lord Fingall's cartulary of Reading Abbey', *EHR*, iii (1888), 117–123;[1] (abridged) Coates, *Hist. of Reading*, Further Additions (no page nos.); (facsimile of f 8v) M. R. James, *Abbeys* (1925), pl. facing p. 82

Rubric: Hii sunt libri qui continentur in Radingensi ecclesia

The list is mainly contemporary with the original compilation of A, with a few near-contemporary additions (see *B. M. Cat. Add. Mss 1921–5*, 302–3). Of the donors and former owners of books mentioned in the text, Anselm the subprior occurs as late as 1185 × 6 (see no. 704). For the library of Reading Abbey in general, see N. R. Ker, *Medieval Libraries of Great Britain* (2nd edn, 1964), 154–8; Hurry, *Reading Abbey*, 103–26; J. R. L(iddell), 'Some notes on the library of Reading Abbey', *Bodleian Quarterly Record*, viii (1935–8), 47–54.

[1] This prints inaccurately the item *Gesta regis Henrici et ystoria Rading' in uno volumine* (see K. Leyser in *EHR*, xc(1975), 494).

226   List of books kept at Leominster Priory   [*c.*1191 × *c.*1193]

A f 12v
Pd. Barfield, *EHR*, iii (1888), 123–5

Rubric: Hii libri habentur in Leonensi ecclesia

Date as for no. 225. For the library of Leominster Priory in general, see Ker, *Medieval Libraries*, 114.

227 List of relics contained in Reading Abbey

[*c*.1191 × *c*.1193, with early 13th-cent. additions[1]]

A ff6v-8r

Rubric: He sunt reliquie que continentur in ecclesia Sancte Marie de Rading(ia)

Main date as for no. 225. The list is arranged in categories, beginning with relics of the Cross and Our Lord and continuing with those of the Virgin Mary, patriarchs and prophets, apostles, martyrs, confessors, and virgins. For discussion, see D. Bethell, 'The making of a twelfth-century relic collection', *Studies in Church History*, viii (1971), 61-72. It is planned to publish the list in full separately.

[1] The additions concern King John's gift of the Head of St Philip (see no. 49 n.; M. R. James, *A Descriptive Catalogue of the Manuscripts in the Library of Lambeth Palace* (Cambridge, 1932), 503) and the gift by Duke [William X] of Aquitaine to Henry I of a 'boy', i.e., a statue of the Christ Child which was kept at Reading and known later as the 'Child of Grace' (see Bethell, *ibid.*, 63 and n.2).

228 List of vestments and liturgical equipment in the custody of the keeper of copes [1226 × 38]

A f11r

Pd. Barfield, *EHR*, iii (1888), 116-17; Coates, *Hist. of Reading*, Further Additions (no page nos.); (transl.) Hurry, *Reading Abbey*, 75-6

Rubric: Hec sunt sub manu custodis capparum

This list is not entirely of one date, since as it stands it clearly incorporates slightly later additions, but it probably all dates from the time of Abbot Adam of Lathbury, 1226-38. The original parts are certainly after the death of Abbot Simon in 1226, since the pastoral staff which *was* his is included, and even among the additions Abbot Adam is nowhere referred to as though dead and no later abbot is mentioned. The additions to the list include the copes which came to the abbey with the burials of the son and daughter of Richard, earl of Cornwall, in 1232 and 1234, respectively (*Ann. Mon.*, i. 89, 93).

229 Grant by Abbot Adam [of Lathbury] and the convent of Reading to R.,[1] bishop of Salisbury, and his successors, and the dean and canons of Salisbury, that they and their men who hold of them in chief shall be quit of toll and other customs in the town (*villa*) of Reading and all the abbey's lands. Sealing with the abbot's and convent's seals [1226 × 38]

Original charter: Salisbury Chapter Muniments, Press II, Box 1/2

B f246r; Salisbury Chapter Muniments, 'Liber Evidentiarum C', p. 159; Wilts. Rec. Off. D1/1/2 ('Liber Evidentiarum B'), ff90v-91r; *ibid.* D1/1/3 ('Registrum Rubrum'), f46r-v (the last two formerly Salisbury Diocesan Registry)

Pd. *Sarum Charters and Documents*, 205 (from Salisbury registers)

*His testibus: R(adulfo) Cicestr(ensi), J(ocelino) Bathon(iensi) epis-
copis, Rad(ulfo) de Mortuo Mari, Willelmo de Sancto Johanne,
Roberto de Say, Mauricio de Gant, Roberto de Anvers,[2] Willelmo
de Sifreiwast, Thoma Huscarl', et multis aliis.*

Endorsed: De quieta clamantia theolonei apud Rading' [*13th cent.*];
   also post-medieval endorsement
Size: 154 × 152 mm
Seal: two tags through slits in fold at bottom. The convent's seal
   missing. That of the abbot oval in green wax, partially damaged; obverse, frontal standing figure of an abbot with pastoral
   staff in right hand; legend: .. DAM DEI G..TIA ..AS ..;
   counterseal, a hand with two fingers raised in blessing[3] between
   two scallops; legend: +ORA PRO NOB.. SANCTE JACOBE

   a-a Om. in B

The dating limits are those of Adam of Lathbury's abbacy, during which there were
two Bishops R. of Salisbury, Richard Poore (1217–28) and Robert Bingham (1229–
46).

   [1] *Sarum Charters* has *Ricardo*, for which there is no warrant.
   [2] The same has *Riveres* in error.
   [3] Clearly a depiction of the hand of St James and perhaps designed in imitation of
the actual reliquary. The same depiction appears on the seal of Abbots Richard I
and William II (below, no 800; Salisbury Chapter Muniments, Press II, Box 1/7).

230   *Letters obligatory by Abbot Robert [of Burgate], certain named obe-
dientiaries and the convent of Reading to John [of Darlington], archbishop of
Dublin, and Arditio, dean of Milan, collectors of the tenth in England, in
respect of £370 18s 11d of the tenth deposited in the abbey, mostly by Gerard
[de Grandson], bishop of Verdun, and the archbishop, and partly by the
archbishop with the consent of master Arditio. As pledges for the repayment of
this sum when required, they have placed a gold casket enriched with precious
stones given to the abbey by King John to contain the Head of St Philip, a
gold chalice and three precious Bibles in the custody of the prior, sacrist and
the monk, Thomas of Sherborne, under the archbishop's seal and a lock whose
key the archbishop has*   8 Dec. 1279

   B f 214v; C f 129r–v

Venerabili in Christo patri domino J(ohanni) dei gratia archiepiscopo Dublinensi et discreto viro magistro Ardicioni primicerio Mediolan' domini pape capellano, collectoribus decime terre sancte in
regno Anglie a sede apostolica deputatis, R(obertus) dei gratia
abbas, A. prior, A. supprior, J. precentor, J. sacrista, J(ohannes)*
camerarius, J. cellarius,[b] R. infirmarius, V. coquinarius, ordinis

sancti Benedicti de Rading', et eiusdem loci conventus, salutem cum
omni reverencia et honore. Tenore presencium vobis singnificamus^c
et de plano confitemur nos habere et penes nos et monasterium
nostrum esse in deposito trecentas et septuaginta libras, octodecim
solidos et undecim denarios sterlingorum de bona et legali pecunia
de denariis decime, que pecunia fuit penes nos deposita pro magna
parte per venerabilem patrem dominum G(erardum) episcopum
Virdunen(sem) et vos fratrem Johannem nunc archiepiscopum Dub-
lin(ensem), residuum autem nunc per vos archiepiscopum Dub-
lin(ensem) de consensu magistri Ardicionis socii vestri in deposito
recepimus, ita quod quinquaginta libras summe predicte sunt de
primo termino sex annorum, scilicet in festo Natalis domini, quas
preveniendo solvimus causa maioris securitatis. Ad totalem igitur
predicti depositi custodiam nos voluntarie obtulimus et fideliter
promittimus nos ipsum depositum vobis vel alteri vestrum integre et
sine difficultate cum omnibus expensis et dampnis restituros et soluturos. Et pro ipso deposito custodiendo et solvendo, subimus omne
periculum et casum incendii, ruine, violencie, furti, rapine et quemcumque alium casum et eventum qui aliquo modo evenire possent,
et renunciamus excepcioni non recepti depositi sive non recepte pecunie et omni alii excepcioni et defensioni, condicioni sine causa^d et
dolo et omni auxilio iuris et consuetudinis quo aliquo modo vel
ingenio contra predicta vel aliquod predictorum venire possemus.
Que omnia et singula etiam per fidem nostram inviolabiliter et ef-
ficaciter obligando omnia bona nostra pignori promittimus nos penitus observare et adimplere quandocumque per vos vel alterum vestrum vel aliquem certum nuncium sedis apostolice ad hoc
[deputatum]^e nos vel etiam aliquis nostrum fuerimus requisiti, ita
quod de requisicione credatur vestre vel alterius vestrum simplici
assercioni sine aliquo onere probacionis. Et insuper ne notabilis dif-
ficultas aut dilacio accidat solucionis aut restitucionis dicti depositi,
quedam vasa aurea et quosdam libros preciosos separatim posuimus
pro pignore sub custodia prioris, sacriste et domini Thome de Sire-
burn' auctoritate et ordinacione vestra, domine archiepiscope prefate, sub singno vestro ac sera cuius clavem penes vos habetis, videlicet unam capsulam auream lapidibus preciosis ornatam quam
contulit rex Johannes nostro monasterio ad reponendum capud
sancti Philippi apostoli, et unum calicem aureum, et tres Biblias,^f
duas in duobus voluminibus et terciam in tribus, ita quod si necesse
fuerit liceat vobis vel alteri vestrum seu cuicumque sedis apostolice
nuncio ad hoc deputato dictos libros et vasa pretacta apud merca-
tores vel alios pro^g summa premissi depositi inpignorare, et prenominati prior et alii duo monachi vel unus illorum si alii absentes
fuerint ea sine mora et absque aliquo impedimento per nos vel per

alios inferendo teneantur liberare. Et nichilominus supponimus nos censure ecclesiastice quam vobis liceat in nos exercere si in aliquo premissorum deficere nos contingat. In cuius rei testimonium et fidem huius obligacionis et promissionis presentes litteras fieri fecimus et eas duobus sigillis, scilicet abbatis nostri et communi sigillo conventus, fecimus sigillari. Dat' in capitulo nostro Rading' vi. idus Decembris, anno domini M.CC. septuagesimo nono. Hiis testibus: domino Anselmo Gubiu(n) canonico Dublin', magistro Stephano de Godon' rectore de E'achel',[h] domino Willelmo de Let canonico de Penbrit, Galfr(edo) de Prisa clerico, fratre Waltero de Cantebrigia ordinis predicatorum.

[a] *For expansion, see no. 132*
[c] *Sic in B*; significamus *C*
[e] *Supplied*
[g] *Om. in C*

[b] cellerarius *C*
[d] custodia *C*
[f] Blblias *in both copies*
[h] *Doubtful reading; ? rectius* Cachel'

For the consequences of these letters obligatory, see nos. 231–2. Although King John's gift of the Head of St Philip is well known (see no. 49 n.), this appears to be the only notice of his gift of a gold reliquary to contain it. Gerard de Grandson, appointed collector in 1275, died in 1278; Arditio was appointed collector in 1277 (W. E. Lunt, *Financial Relations of the Papacy with England to 1327* (Cambridge, Mass., 1939), 618–19).

231 *Notification by John [of Darlington], archbishop of Dublin, to James [Sabellus], cardinal deacon of St Mary in Cosmedin, that, although the preceding letter obligatory was sent in error to the latter with the final account of the sexennial tenth, the abbot and convent of Reading are not bound in the amount contained therein, since they have paid their share of the tenth in full; and request that the cardinal deacon indemnify the monks in this regard*

2 Mar. 1282[1]

B ff 215v–216r; C f 130v

Venerabili patri ac domino suo reverentissimo J(acobo) dei gratia Sancte Marie in Cosmed(in) et sacrosancte sedis apostolice diacono cardinali filiorum ac servorum suorum minimus indignus hominis utriusque prosperitatem cum sui recommendacione et votivos semper ad feliciora successus. Notum sit paternitati vestre quod nos, inspectis et examinatis rotulis et compoto collectorum a domino Ardicione nunc Mutinen(si) episcopo et a nobis fratre Johanne Dublinensi archiepiscopo in diocesibus Lincoln(iensi), Sarr(esburiensi),[a] Hereforden(si)[b] deputatorum, liquido invenimus quod viri religiosi abbas et conventus [*f 216r*] Rading(enses) ordinis Sancti Benedicti, Sarr(esburiensis)[a] diocesis, solverunt ad plenum totam decimam sex annorum de omnibus bonis suis temporalibus et spiritualibus in subsidium terre sancte deputatam collectoribus predictis, prout patet per litteras patentes dictorum collectorum que resident adhuc penes dictos religiosos. Et idem religiosi per neglegenciam^c sive oblivionem obmiserunt repetere a nobis litteram obligatoriam per quam confessi sunt se recepisse a domino Gerardo quondam Verdunen(si)^d episcopo et a nobis dicto fratre Johanne trecentas quinquaginta libras de predicta decima nomine depositi; et nos dictus frater J(ohannes) eandem litteram obligatoriam per manus domini Ardicionis una cum compoto nostro finali paternitati vestre transmisimus, credentes eos teneri in predicta summa pro eo quod illam litteram obligatoriam invenimus inter alias litteras obligatorias, cum tamen in nullo tenerentur nec teneantur. Quare supplicamus paternitati vestre humiliter et devote ut indempnitati dictorum religiosorum et eiusdem monasterii 'paternitate pietate^e super hoc providere velitis. Dominus vos conservet ecclesie sue sancte per tempora longiora. Dat' Lond'^{f} vi. non' Marcii, anno domini M.CC. octogesimo tercio.

Postscript: Istam litteram precedentem habemus de verbo ad verbum signatam sigillo fratris J(ohannis) de Derlinton' Dublin(ensis) archiepiscopi.

^{a} Sar' *C*	^{b} Herford' *C*
^{c} negligenciam *C*	^{d} Verdinen' *C*
$^{e-e}$ *Sic in both copies; ? rectius* paternitatis pietate	^{f} London' *C*

Although this notification states that the letter obligatory was in respect of £350, whereas the letter itself (no. 230) refers to £370 18s 11d, it is clear from no. 232 that the same letter is in question and that the archbishop, not having the text to hand, misremembered the correct figure. The account of this episode in Lunt, *Financial Relations*, 331, is inaccurate in some details.

[1] The year-date has been given as 1282 on the assumption that the year was held to begin on 25 March, but it is possible that 1283 is correct, since a rather ambiguous passage near the end of no. 232 may suggest that this notification was made after Arditio's departure from England, which occurred 1 July, 1282 (*ibid.*, 619).

232 *Exemplification by Geoffrey of Vezzano, canon of Cambrai, clerk of the papal chamber, nuncio and executor of the business touching the tenth in England, of his letter to Pope Honorius [IV] setting out the details of Reading Abbey's payment in full of its share of the tenth and explaining that, according to the abbot and convent, the misunderstanding over their letter obligatory arose because the collectors, not realizing that the sum contained therein was part of the abbey's contribution to the tenth, sent the letter to the apostolic see, whence it appears that the abbey still owes £370 18s 11d. Having inspected the rolls of collection and assessment and the final account of the tenth, Geoffrey has found errors concerning Reading's payments. He states that the late archbishop of Dublin, after the departure of Arditio, restored to the abbey the pledges mentioned in the letter, which itself he would have restored if he had it, and* *notified the pope, then cardinal, that the abbey had paid its tenth in full and that a mistake had occurred in the account, although the archbishop misremembered the sum contained in the letter as £350. Before proceeding further in this, Geoffrey awaits direction from the apostolic see*   5 July 1286

B f 215r–v; C ff 129v–130v

Noverint universi presentes litteras inspecturi quod nos Gifredus de Vezano, camere domini pape clericus, apostolice sedis nuncius et executor negociorum terre sancte super decima et aliis a dicta sede in Anglia deputatus, scripsimus domino nostro summo pontifici in hec verba.

Sanctissimo patri et domino, domino H(onorio) divina providencia summo pontifici, Gifredus de Vezano canonicus Cameracensis, camere sue humilis clericus, pedum obscula beatorum. Sanctitati vestre singnifico *ᵃ* quod postquam recepi mandatum apostolicum ut pecuniam decime in quibuscumque ecclesiis seu locis regni Anglie depositam reciperem et assignarem*ᵇ* certis sociis quatuor societatum mercatorum camere, inter alios religiosos scriptos*ᶜ* in compotis ad curiam destinatis, qui a me requisiti sunt super restitucione depositorum pecunie decime terre sancte, comparuerunt*ᵈ* abbas et conventus de Rading', Sarr(esburiensis)*ᵉ* diocesis, per duos de commonacis suis et ostendi eis litteras patentes ipsorum abbatis et conventus sigill(is) munitas continentes eos habere in deposito de pecunia decime trecentas septuaginta libras, decem et octo solidos et undecim denarios sterlingorum, et quod preter obligacionem eorum quedam pingnora sub sigillo bone memorie fratris Johannis Dublinensis archiepiscopi posuerunt, quarum litterarum tenor presentibus est annexus.[1] Ex parte vero ipsorum abbatis et conventus fuit expositum et per quietancias certas ostensum quod ipsi plenarie decimam eos contigentem solverant particulariter diversis collectoribus per diversas dioceses, videlicet, succentori Sarr(esburiensi)*ᵉ* et college suo collectoribus decime in episcopatu Sarr(esburiensi)*ᵉ* constitutis pro primo anno quadraginta libras, sex solidos; item cancellario Sarr(esburiensi)*ᵉ* et college suo collectoribus ipsius decime in dicto episcopatu deputatis centum nonaginta quatuor libras, quinque solidos, sex denarios; item tesaurario Hereford(ensi)*ᶠ* et college suo collectoribus decime in episcopatu Hereford(ensi)*ᶠ* quadraginta sex libras, tresdecim solidos, quatuor denarios; item fratri Warino tesaurario Novi Templi London' qui fuit collector London' pro primis duobus annis quinquaginta et octo libras; item domino Fulconi Lovel et college suo qui fuerunt collectores London' post dictum fratrem Warinum quinquaginta libras; item fratri Henrico Helyun camerario Sancti Petri Glovernie et college suo collectoribus in episcopatu Wygorn(iensi) tres libras, quatuordecim solidos, tres dena-

rios; item Johanni de Strodes et college suo collectoribus in episcopatu Roffen(si) tres libras, novem solidos, quatuor denarios, obolum;
item fratri Reynerio priori de Bello Loco et college suo collectoribus
Oxon' tres libras, decem et novem solidos, sex denarios; item Bartholomeo Marchi de Senis mercatori de societate filiorum Bon-
seg(no)ris de Senis ducentas libras; quarum particularum summa
ascendit ad sexcentas libras, septem solidos, undecim denarios,
obolum, que summa respondebat^g plenarie satisfaccioni decime con-
tingentis eorum monasterium, cuius bona tam temporalia quam
spiritualia ad valorem annuum mille librarum taxata esse dicebant
per dictum archiepiscopum et magistrum Raymundum de Nogeriis.
Et cum instancia requirebant predicti abbas et conventus sibi restitui
litteras supradictas, asserendo quod prefatus Dublinensis archiepiscopus et magister Hardicio primicerius Mediolan' nunc episcopus
Mutinen(sis) erraverunt ponendo in compoto quem miserunt ad
sedem apostolicam habere eos in deposito dictas CCC.lxx. libras,
xviii. solidos, xi. denarios, cum huiusmodi pecunia in eorum obli-
gacione contenta pro eorum decima fuerit de qua particulariter ut
predicitur satisfecerunt ad plenum. Ego vero, ad investigandam ver-
itatem super premissis rotulos collectorum per quos compotum predictis archiepiscopo et magistro Ardicioni reddiderunt et particulas
receptas a predicto Bartholomeo mercatore Senen(si) diligenter per-
scrutans, inveni a predictis collectoribus Sarr(esburiensibus),^{e} Here-
ford(ensibus),^{f} Lond(oniensibus), Wygorn(iensibus), Roffen(sibus)
et dicto Bartholomeo singulas quantita[$f215v$]tes que premittuntur
esse in dicto compoto computatas. Collectores vero Oxon' particulam quam receperant non repperi in eorum compoto computasse,
qui vocati, visa quietancia quam dederant, recognoverunt ipsam
particulam et de ipsa satisfecit unus ex eis. Inveni etiam in rotulis
taxacionum mihi a predicto magistro Ardicione dimissis bona temporalia et spiritualia spectantia ad monasterium Rading' taxata ad
mille libras. Et in uno de rotulis taxacionum scriptum est quod
debebant solvere Lond(onie). Et sicut mihi exposuit magister Jaco-
bus de Briga, publicus notarius, qui fuit clericus et notarius dicti
magistri Ardicionis et presens fuit in confectione et ordinacione compoti supradicti et ipsum compotum scripsit, propter verbum illud
quod debebant solvere Lond(onie) fuit erratum in ipso compoto
quia ordinantes compotum respexerunt solummodo quantitatem
contentam in litteris supradictis dictorum abbatis et conventus et
solucionem factam Bartholomeo Marchi et domino Fulconi Lovel et
college suo, que quantitates contente in litteris predictis et solute
dictis Bartholomeo et domino Fulconi ascendunt ad sexcentas viginti
libras, decem et septem solidos, xi. denarios. Et quia ordinatores
compoti inveniebant quod dicte particule excedebant^h decimam eos

contingentem iuxta predictam taxacionem, posuerunt excessum so-
lutum esse ultra taxacionem, sicut in scriptura inventa in libris mihi
a magistro Ardicione dimissis continente particulas de quibus prov-
enerunt ea que continentur in prefato compoto recepta per alios
quam per collectores et facta per manum dicti magistri* Jacobi in
presencia dicti magistri Ardicionis repperi contineri. Fui etiam presens ubi ex parte dictorum abbatis et conventus petebantur sibi
restitui littere supradicte a predictis archiepiscopo et magistro Ardicione. Set magister Ardicio, licet dominus archiepiscopus assereret
erratum esse, respondit quod missus erat compotus ad curiam et
nullo modo consentiret litteras restituere sede apostolica inconsulta,
ex quo in dicto compoto quantitas contenta in dictis litteris posita
fuerat in recepta et in liberata. Predictus vero archiepiscopus post
recessum dicti magistri Ardicionis restituit dictis religiosis pignora
que sub suo custodiebantur sigillo et litteras restituisset si penes eum
fuissent, ut credo. Et ante obitum suum in absencia mea litteras suas
patentes ad sanctitatem vestram dum eratis cardinalis pro ipsius
monasterii indempnitate fieri fecit, inter cetera continentes quod
abbas et conventus predicti decimam eos contingentem plene per-
solverant et erratum fuisse in compoto supradicto. Quantitas vero
pecunie quam continent obligatorie littere eius memorie totaliter
non occurrit, quod satis patere potest per tenorem litterarum suarum
hiis annexum,[2] quas diligenter vidi et inspexi trescentas et quinquaginta libras tantummodo continentes. Consideratis ergo premissis
videtur mihi quod error fuerit in compoto et ideo utrum eos compellere ad satisfaccionem an eisdem litteras obligatorias restituere
debeam expectare intendo apostolicum beneplacitum[k] et mandatum.

In cuius rei testimonium has litteras fieri fecimus patentes et nostri
sigilli munimine roborari. Dat' Lond' iii. non' Julii, anno domini
M.CC. octogesimo vi.

a Sic in B; significo *C*   *b* assignare *B,* assignar' *C*
c B has here et *marked for deletion, C has* et *not so marked*
d comparuerint *C*   *e* Sar' *C*
f Herford' *C*   *g* respondebit *C*
h Both copies have excedebat   *i-i Both copies have* per quam
j Both copies have this word after Jacobi *and marked for transposition*
k Interlined in B

Geoffrey of Vezzano had been a general papal collector in England since 1276 and
succeeded John of Darlington, archbishop of Dublin, as collector of the sexennial
tenth in Oct. 1283 (Lunt, *Financial Relations*, 619). See also *ibid.*, 331 (although this
account is erroneous in detail) and Lunt, 'A papal Tenth levied in the British Isles
from 1274 to 1280', *EHR*, xxxii (1917), 57.

¹ See no. 230.
² See no. 231. James Sabellus, cardinal deacon of St Mary in Cosmedin, became Pope Honorius IV in 1285.

233 Letters of quittance by *Salymb(enus)* *Allex'*, citizen and merchant of Siena, on behalf of himself and his fellow merchants, stating that he and William of Sutton, chamberlain of Reading [Abbey], computed all the debts which the abbey owed *Salymb(enus)* and his fellows and that all the debts have been satisfied, so that the abbey is as quit of any debt as it was before any loan was borrowed from them   9 Jan. 1287

B f 41r; C f 14r

Anno domini M.CC. octogesimo sexto, die jovis proxima post festum sancti Edwardi regis. Dat' London' die et anno quibus supra.

a-a *This passage appears at the beginning of the document, the rest at the end*

The date given here assumes that the feast of St Edward, king, is that of St Edward the Confessor, 5 Jan., in which case 1286 becomes in modern computation 1287. These letters were clearly part of the process of regularizing Reading's financial affairs and restoring the abbey to solvency which was taking place at this time (see nos. 92–3, 98–9).

234 *The case of the false Jewish bonds*   [1290]

B ff 216r–217v; C ff 131r–132v; F ff 85v–86v (not fully collated)

[*abridged translation*]

The sheriff [of Berkshire] was ordered that, whereas Reading Abbey was founded by the king's progenitors and he wishes to provide for the preservation of its possessions; and Gilbert Pincent (*Pinzon*) and Thomas *Hikon* showed to William of Sutton, chamberlain of the abbey, three bonds sealed with counterfeit seals similar to the seals of the abbot and convent, in which the abbot was bound to Jacob the Jew of Oxford, son of master Moses of London, and A. Sancte the Jew of Winchester in money and other goods and chattels to the value of £3,000, as the king understands from the abbot's complaint; he is to have the said Gilbert and Thomas with the said bonds *coram rege* on the day which the king appoints for the abbot.

On that day Gilbert and Thomas came, likewise the abbot. The abbot by attorney says that on Tuesday before Epiphany, 18 Edward I (3 Jan. 1290), in the house of Alice, widow of Alexander *de Estaus* at Wallingford the said Gilbert and Thomas showed to William the chamberlain the said three bonds sealed with seals utterly counterfeit in the manner of the abbot's and convent's seals.

Their tenor is as follows.

[1.] *Bond to A. Sancte, Jew of Winchester, for 400 quarters of wheat to be paid 29 Sept. 1276, in return for an advance of money, all the abbey's lands and chattels being mortgaged for this debt*

Omnibus Christi fidelibus presentes litteras inspecturis vel audituris conventus Rading', salutem in domino sempiternam. Noveritis nos teneri fide media A. Sancte judeo de Wynton' manenti apud Caversham in quatuor centum quarteriis frumenti, quarterium precii dimidie marce et quodlibet quarterium octo bussell(orum), reddendo predicto Sancte judeo in domo sua apud Kaversham ad festum sancti Michaelis, anno regni regis E(dwardi) quarto, faciendo eundem bladum sumptibus nostris propriis ibidem cariari vel denar(ium) prout judeo placuerit, videlicet pro quolibet*b* quarterio dimidiam marcam. Et si predictum Sancte propter nostrum defectum aliquos sumptus contingat facere, obligamus nos eidem Sancte sine aliqua contradictione satisfacere. Volumus eundem Sancte sine aliquo testimonio suo simplici verbo fore credendum. Volumus insuper et concedimus, si nos quoquo modo in predicta solucione defecerimus, aut in toto aut in parte, quod absit, quod vicecomes Oxon' et Berk' per omnes terras et catalla possit compescere donec predicto [*f216v*] judeo Sancte per plenum satisfecerimus. Et volumus quod Eadwardus*c* rex pro quolibet restrictu .x. libras habeat et vicecomes Oxon' .lx. s' et terra sancta .x. marcas, si nos in predicta solucione ad terminos statutos defecerimus. Et propter dictum debitum quod predicto judeo Sancte pro denariis pre manibus ab eodem receptis pro magno prodesse domus obligavimus et inpingnoravimus omnes terras et catalla mobilia et inmobilia quantascumque habuerimus vel possidere poterimus donec per plenum predicto iudeo satisfecerimus. Et resignemus omnimodas alias cavillaciones per quas predictum judeum*d* Sancte poterimus nocere. Et nos de die in diem posset facere excommunicare propter fidis fractionem cum candelis illuminatis et campanis pulsatis concedimus. In cuius rei testimonium huic scripto sigillum nostrum commune duximus apponendum.

[2.] *Receipt to Jacob the Jew of Oxford, son of master Moses of London, for £300 sterling and other valuables which the abbot will conceal from the king and queen and release to none but Jacob or his wife or a messenger carrying these letters*

Omnibus Christi fidelibus presentes litteras inspecturis vel audituris abbas de Rading', salutem in domino sempiternam. Noveritis nos per concensum nostri conventus recepimus in tesaur(iam) de Rading' in custodia de Jacobo judeo de Oxenford' filio magistri Mossy de London' .iii. C libras sterlingorum bonorum et legalium, et .xxx. li' [monet']*e* florines, et unum ciphum aureum pays .xiiii. li', et .xii.

coclearia aurea pays cuiuslibet .xxxii. d', et unum discum argenti de aumone pays .xx. li', et .ii. barell' barres^f de or de mugat. Et quod nos iuravimus in verbo dei quod nos solvemus eidem totum predictum tesaurum et celabimus versus regem et reginam. Et nos nullo modo neque pro excommunicacione neque pro iuramento deliberabimus nisi predicto Jacobo vel domine Henne femine sue vel certo nuncio istas litteras portanti. Et si aliter contingat nos facere quam per sacramentum iuravimus, concedimus nos excommunicari et numquam absolvi nisi per manus domini pape. In cuius rei testimonium sigillum nostrum una cum sigillo conventus nostri presentibus est appensum.

[3.] *Bond to the same for 100 sacks of wool for an advance of money, to be paid half on 29 Sept. 1277 and half on 17 Apr. 1278, all the abbey's lands and chattels being mortgaged for this debt*

Omnibus Christi fidelibus presentes litteras inspecturis vel audituris abbas de Rading' et conventus eiusdem loci, salutem in domino sempiternam. Noveritis nos teneri fide media Jacobo judeo de Oxon' filio magistri Mossi de London' in C. saccis bone lane et placabilis sine cot' et gard' pro certa summa pecunie quam nobis ad negocium et comodum conventus dederunt^g pre manibus precii cuiuslibet .x. li' sterlingorum bonorum et legalium, reddendo predicto judeo J(acobo) in domo sua apud London' ad festum sancti Michaelis anno regni regis E(dwardi) v. dimidiam et aliam dimidiam ad festum Pasche proximo sequens, faciendo eandem lanam propriis sumptibus nostris ibidem cariari vel denar(ium) prout judeo placuerit, videlicet pro quolibet sacco .x. li'. Et si predictum judeum propter nostrum defectum aliquos sumptus contingat facere, obligamus nos eidem J(acobo) sine aliqua contradictione satisfacere. Volumus eundem judeum sine aliquo testimonio suo simplici verbo fore credendum. Volumus insuper et concedimus, si nos quoquo modo defecerimus in predicta solucione, aut in toto aut in parte, quod absit, quod vicecomes Oxon' et de^h Berk' per omnes terras et catalla possit compellere donec predicto judeo J(acobo) per plenum satisfecerimus. Et volumus quod Eadwardus^c rex pro quolibet restrictu .x. li' habeat et vicecomes Oxon'.C.s' et terra sancta .x. marcas, si nos in predicta solucione ad terminos statutos defecerimus. Et propter predictum debitum quod predicto judeo pro denariis ab eodem pre manibus receptis obligavimus et inpingnoravimus omnes terras nostras et catalla mobilia et inmobilia quantascumque habuerimus et possidere poterimus donec per plenum predicto J(acobo) satisfecerimus. In cuius rei testimonium huic scripto sigillum nostrum una cum sigillo conventus nostri dignum duximus apponendum.

Afterwards, because the justices wished to be more certain about
the fact, they caused the said William of Sutton to come before
them. He says on oath that, on the feast of St James, 16 Edward I
(25 July, 1288), the said Gilbert Pincent came to him declaring that
the abbey was much in debt to the Jews and that the chamberlain
should remunerate him for his help and advice in relieving the
abbey, asking 40 marks for his aid and service. The chamberlain
told him that he could not deserve so much money for this affair.
Nevertheless, Gilbert showed him transcripts of two of the bonds.
Afterwards the chamberlain came to Wallingford on Tuesday before
Epiphany, 18 Edward I (3 Jan. 1290), to the house of Alice, widow
of Alexander *de Estaus*, where came Gilbert and Thomas *Hikon*, and
Thomas took out of his pocket a deed-box (*pixis*) in which were two
bonds sealed with the counterfeit seals, which bonds corresponded
with the transcripts Gilbert had shown the chamberlain previously.
The chamberlain asked if he had more deeds, upon which Thomas,
prompted by Gilbert, acknowledged that he had one, which he went
home to fetch and which he showed William in the said Alice's
lodging-house (*hospitium*).[1] They did not permit the chamberlain to
have or retain any of the sealed bonds, but kept them with them.
And on the fifth, sixth or eighth day following Brother Alan and
Peter the clerk went on the abbot of Reading's instruction to the
said Gilbert at Wallingford, where they were shown the same bonds
in the presence of the Jew, and Alan and Peter brought one bond
back with them to Reading to show the abbot, having given surety
to the Jew for its return. Alan returned it at Wallingford on the
following Sunday. Brother Alan says on oath that he and Peter the
clerk, on the abbot of Reading's instruction, went with the said
Gilbert to Wallingford on the 8th day after the said Tuesday (11
Jan. 1290), where he was shown the bonds in the Jew's presence,
and, at Gilbert's suggestion, brought one of them back to Reading
with surety for its return. He returned it at Wallingford on the
following Sunday (15 Jan.).

Peter the clerk on oath agrees with Alan.

Afterwards the justices caused the said Gilbert and Thomas to
come before them. Thomas says on oath that on a Tuesday after the
Circumcision [1 Jan.] last past, though whether it was the next after
he does not know, a certain Josce (*Joceus*) of Newbury (*Neubury*),
Jew, came to the house of Alice *Sauwiz* at Wallingford and handed
to him an unsealed deed-box in which were three bonds, whose
tenor he did not know. He handed them to William of Sutton and
John Gerard, monks of Reading, who took copies of them and returned them to him in the box, which he delivered to the said Josce.
On Wednesday in the following week Josce came again to Walling-

ford to the house of William *de la Wyke* and spoke with Alan, the abbot's chaplain, showing him the said bonds so that he might advise the abbot concerning them. Alan wished to take them away with him, but the Jew refused, handing him only one bond to take away on condition that it was returned to him on the following Sunday. Whether it was returned he does not know. Asked whether he received anything from the Jew for this business, he says not, but acted out of favour of the abbot, who is his lord and of whom he holds. Asked whether he knows the bonds to be true or false, he says false.

Gilbert on oath agrees with Thomas in substance, except that, whereas Thomas said previously that the Jew handed him three bonds, Gilbert says only two on one occasion and a third soon afterwards.

Since it is clear from the confession of Thomas and Gilbert that Thomas was in possession of the said bonds and received them from Josce of Newbury, and it is not yet clear to the court that he returned them to the Jew, wherefore the court considers him still seised of them; and because the said Gilbert was his partner in this affair; they are told to sue out a writ of arrest against the Jew that he be *coram rege* on the morrow of St John Baptist (25 June 1290). Meanwhile, Gilbert and Thomas are to be on bail. On that day Peter of Campden (*Campedene*), the abbot's attorney, comes and asks for a day that the abbot might prove the said bonds false by comparison of seals or in another way, and is given a day in 1 month from Michaelmas. The same day is given to William *de Carleton'*, acting for the king. Gilbert and Thomas, when asked how they wish to prove that they were not accomplices in the fabrication of the bonds, put themselves on the country. William *de Carleton'*, for the king, says that, although it might be established by the country whether the bonds were true or otherwise, the said Gilbert and Thomas were at fault in that they showed the bonds to the king and not to the country. He asks that it be allowed to the king for place and time. And Bartholomew of Northampton is told to sue out for the king a writ to summon twenty-four, etc.

*[a]*John of Tidmarsh (*Cedmers*) of the county of Berkshire, Gilbert of Kirkby (*Kirkeby*) of the county of Warwick, William of Fawley (*Faveleye*), master John of Lewknor (*Leukenor'*), William of Ufton (*Offinton'*) and Thomas *de Dauvers* of the county of Berkshire go bail for Gilbert Pincent and Thomas *Hikon* to be *coram rege* to answer to the king and the abbot of Reading on the plea of false bonds made under the name of the abbot and convent of Reading and sealed with a counterfeit seal.

[a] Eustaus *C*   *[b]* qualibet *C*

^c Edwardus C   *^d Om. in C, but space left blank*
^e Om. in B,C; supplied from F   *^f barrez F*
^g Sic in all copies; ? rectius dedit   *^h Om. in C*
ⁱ F omits the remainder, but continues with the trial of Josce of Newbury (see note)

This unsavoury affair came to court barely a year after the abbey had been restored
to solvency by the Crown's agent (see no. 98) and was heard in the year when
Edward I ordered the general expulsion of the Jews from England. The continuation
in F reveals that Josce of Newbury was found guilty of the forgery and that the case
against Gilbert Pincent and Thomas Hikon was apparently dropped (F ff86v-87r),
but the verdict on Josce was not easy. He was tried before at least two commissions,
one of gaol delivery at the Tower of London and one of justices appointed for the
custody of the Jews (*Cal. Pat. R. 1281-92*, 402, 405); the latter, sitting 23 Oct. 1290,
acquitted him on the verdict of a jury of Christians and Jews (F f86v), but the former
convicted him and the same verdict was also reached by other justices and king's
councillors (F ff 86v-87r). See also C. Roth, *The Jews of Medieval Oxford* (Oxford
Hist. Soc. n.s.ix, 1951), 80 n.1. Gilbert Pincent was a member of a prominent family
in and around Reading, and, if identical with the Gilbert Pincent who witnessed
many charters to the abbey and was a juror for Reading Hundred in 1269 (PRO
JUST 1/42, m.19), would seem unlikely to have become involved in an affair which
he knew to be fraudulent.

¹ Possibly an inn.

235   Form of appointment of a proctor for the abbot of Reading at
a provincial chapter [of the Black Monks in England]
[14th cent., after 1336]

B f226r

After 1336, when Pope Benedict XII created a single province for the English Black
Monks, the chapters were usually known as 'provincial' chapters, whereas the earlier
separate chapters of the provinces of Canterbury and York were known as 'general'
chapters (*Chapters of the English Black Monks*, ed. W. A. Pantin, i (Camden 3rd Ser.
xlv, 1931), p. v). The text in B is a late 14th-century addition, but its rubric reads
rather inconsistently: *Procuratorium pro generali capitulo.*

DOCUMENTS RELATING TO ENGLISH COUNTIES OTHER THAN BERKSHIRE

HOUGHTON CONQUEST

236 *Gift by Robert, earl of Leicester, to Reading Abbey, at the request of Albold, of 1½ hides at How End [in Houghton Conquest] which Albold held of his father and of him* [*c.* 26 Aug. 1127]

A f 36r; B f 100v; C f 51r

Ego Robertus comes Legr(ecestrie) concessi et dedi deo et beate Marie et monachis de Rading(ia) terram quam Albodus[a] tenuit de patre meo et de me, hoc est hidam et dimidiam de Hou.[b] Hoc donum feci presente domino meo H(enrico) rege, ipso idem concedente et donante, cum omnibus consuetudinibus et causis, libere et absolute, sicut sunt terre alie Radingensis ecclesie. Hoc donum feci propter preces ipsius Alboldi et per consilium uxoris mee [c]et baronum meorum, pro salute domini mei regis H(enrici) et mea et uxoris mee[c] et antecessorum et successorum meorum.[d] Huius donationis testes fuerunt: Willelmus de Tancardivilla, Gaufredus filius Pagani, Edwardus de Saresb(er)ia, Drogo de Munceio, Gaufredus de Turvilla, Hugo de Chahainnis, Willelmus Sorel. Apud Elingas. Signum Henrici regis. Signum Rogerii episcopi Sar(esburiensis). Signum Roberti comitis Legrecestrie. Signum Gaufredi cancellarii. Signum Willelmi de Tancardivill(a). Signum Nigelli thesaurarii.

[a] Alboldus *B,C*
[b] Hout' *B,C*
[c-c] *Om. in C (in error)*
[d] *B ends with* T' cum signis; *C ends*

Contemporary with Henry I's confirmation (no. 237). This land became the abbey's manor of How End in Houghton Conquest (*VCH Beds.*, iii. 293-4). The gift included lordship rights in the neighbouring vill of Shelton (in Marston Moretaine) which Albold had previously given to Lewes priory, Sussex. This is revealed by a deed of Abbot Hugh I of Reading, dated 1128, reciting the details of the gifts to Reading and Lewes and confirming the latter's tenure of Shelton in the same manner under Reading's lordship as previously under Albold's (*Cartl. Lewes*, iii. 33-4; *Regesta*, ii. 362). Dr David Crouch suggests that Albold may have been a member of the Turville family (see his *The Beaumont Twins* (Cambridge, 1986), 218-19).

237 *Notification by King Henry I to the sheriff and all his barons and faithful of Bedfordshire, of his confirmation of the preceding gift, and order*

*that the abbey shall hold it as freely as all its other lands given and conceded
by the king*   [*c.* 26 Aug. 1127]

A f 15r; B f 18v
Pd. *Regesta*, ii. 358 (no. cxcvi); (cal.) *ibid.*, 209 (no. 1506)

Henricus rex Angl(orum) vicecomiti et omnibus baronibus et fidelibus suis de Bedefordscira,*ᵃ* salutem. Sciatis quod concedo et confirmo donum Roberti comitis de Legrec(estria) quod fecit ecclesie de
Rading(ia), videlicet unam hidam et dimidiam terre de Hoct(ona)*ᵇ*
quam ipse ei dedit, sicut concedit per cartam suam. Et volo et
firmiter precipio quod bene et honorifice et libere teneat sicut tenet
omnes alias terras quas dedi ei et concessi per cartam meam. Testibus:*ᶜ* G(aufredo) cancellario, et Roberto de Oilli, et Gaufredo de
Clintona. Apud Eillingas.

ᵃ Bedefordsyr' *B*
ᵇ Hout' *B*
ᶜ *B ends*

When the king was at Eling (Hants) about to cross to Normandy in 1127 (Farrer,
Itin., 120; *Regesta*, ii, nos. 1496–1509). The text printed here is preferable to that in
Regesta, which is from B and lacks the witnesses. Cartulary A notes another charter
concerning the same.

238   Precept by King Stephen to W(illiam) Bacon, sheriff [of Bed-
fordshire], to allow Reading Abbey to hold its land of Houghton
[Conquest] as freely as in the time of Henry I and his own, as its
charters testify. Witnesses [omitted]   [1135 × 54]

B f 29v
Pd. *Regesta*, iii. 253 (no. 683)

The date cannot be fixed more precisely within Stephen's reign. This is the only
known reference to William Bacon as sheriff of Beds. (see *Regesta*, iii. 253).

239   *Final concord before the king's justices at Guildford between Reading
Abbey and Ralph son of Geoffrey of Houghton, by which the latter quitclaimed
to the abbey land in Houghton [Conquest] for 40 marks of silver*

13 Aug. 1179

B f 181r; C f 107r-v

Hec est finalis concordia facta anno post primam coronationem domini H(enrici)*ᵃ* regis Angl(orum) Henrici secundi xxv, die lune
ima ante assumptionem beate Marie, apud Guldeford' coram ius-
tic(iariis) domini regis Iohanne Norwic(ensi) episcopo, Hugone
Mordach, Michaele Belet, Ricardo del*ᵇ* Pek, Rad(ulfo) Briton', qui
tunc ibi aderant, inter abbatem de*ᶜ* Rading(ia) et conventum eiusdem loci et Rad(ulfu)m filium Gaufr(edi) de Hogtuna, de terra de

Hogtun(a), de qua placitum fuit inter eos in curia domini regis. Scilicet quod idem R(adulfus) remittit terram predictam de Hogtun(a) cum omnibus pertinentiis abbati et conventui de Rading(ia) et quiet(am)clamat de se et de*c* heredibus suis, et*c* totum ius suum quod in predicta terra clamabat abiuravit pro se et heredibus suis, et cartas suas quas inde habuit abbati et conventui de Rading(ia) reddidit. Pro hac autem remissione, concordia et abiuratione, dedit dominus abbas de Rading(ia) et conventus eiusdem loci Rad(ulf)o filio Gaufr(edi) .xl. marcas argenti.

a *This seems redundant*
b de *C*
c *Om. in C*

This final concord appears to conceal an amicable redemption by the abbey of an earlier grant of tenancy of its land at Houghton Conquest to Ralph or an ancestor of his.

240 Quitclaim by Robert son of Martin to Reading Abbey of all his right in the half-virgate of land with appurtenances which Martin, his father, sometime held in the vill of Houghton [Conquest] (*Hout'*). For this the abbey has given him 20s sterling. Sealing. Witnesses*a* [omitted] [13th cent.; not later than 1258]

B f 100v; C f 51r

a *Om. in C*

Dating very uncertain. The deed was not entered in A, but appears in the original section of B and is therefore not later than 1258.

241 Quitclaim by Gregory of Houghton (*Hout'*) to Reading Abbey of the half-virgate of land which David, his father, sometime held of the abbey in the vill of Houghton [Conquest], with houses, fields, pastures, meadow, wood and all other appurtenances. Sealing. Witnesses*a* [omitted] [13th cent.; not later than 1258]

B f 100v; C f 51r

a *Om. in C*

Date as for no. 240.

SHELTON (IN MARSTON MORETAINE)

242 *Gift in free alms by Nigel of Shelton to Reading Abbey of 2s annual rent in the vill of Shelton, to be received in perpetuity from William Haverun and his heirs* [prob. early 13th cent.; ? before 1219]

B ff 100v-101r; C f 51r

Omnibus Christi fidelibus ad quos presens scriptum pervenerit Nigellus de Selton', salutem. Sciatis me pro salute anime mee et pro animabus antecessorum et successorum meorum dedisse et concessisse et hac carta mea in liberam et puram et perpetuam elemosinam confirmasse deo et ecclesie conventuali de Rading(ia) et monachis ibidem deo servientibus et in perpetuum servituris duas solidatas annui redditus in villa de Selton' percipiendas in perpetuum a Willelmo Haverun et heredibus eius. Ita scilicet quod dictus W(illelmus) et heredes eius de cetero respondeant predictis monachis de predicto redditu ad duos terminos anni, videlicet ad festum sancti Michaelis de .xii. denariis et ad festum sancte*a* Marie in Marcio de .xii. denariis, ita plene et integre [*f 101r*] sicut mihi et heredibus meis respondere deberent si redditus ipse in manu nostra remansisset. Quare volo et concedo pro me et heredibus meis quod predicti monachi habeant et teneant predictum redditum in perpetuum plenarie et integre et ita libere et quiete sicut aliqua elemosina potest liberius et quietius possideri. Et ego Nigellus et heredes mei warantizabimus predictum redditum predictis monachis contra omnes homines et feminas in perpetuum. Quod ut perpetuum firmitatis robur optineat, presens scriptum sigilli mei appositione duxi roborandum. T(estibus).*a*

a Om. in C

Dating uncertain. The deed is not in A, but was entered in the original section of B and is therefore not later than 1258. However, Nigel of Shelton occurs in 1227 in a legal action which refers to a gift he made in Marston Moretaine to Simon of Lidlington in the time of war, i.e. late John or early Henry III (*Beds. Hist. Rec. Soc.*, iii. 11), and William Haverun was holding in Shelton as early as 1197 (*Fines sive Pedes Finium*, i. 8; *Feet of Fines 9 Richard I*, 53). Moreover, the abbey had immediate lordship of half a virgate in Shelton by 1219 (*Cur. Reg. R.*, viii. 96, 344), although whether this was identical with the tenement from which William Haverun was to pay the 2s rent is not clear.

243 Confirmation by Robert son of Nigel of Shelton (*Selton'*) of his father's gift in free alms to Reading Abbey of 2s annual rent in Shelton. Sealing. Witnesses*a* [omitted]. [? 1227 × 58]

B f 101r; C f 51v

a Om. in C

Not later than 1258, since it was entered in the original section of B, and presumably after the death of Nigel, who was still living in 1227 (see no. 242 n.). Possibly, however, contemporary with his father's gift.

CHEARSLEY

244 *Gift in free alms by Roger de Cressy to Reading Abbey of 13d annual rent in Chearsley on the feast of St James [25 July] to provide a light annually before the relics of St James* [1188/9 × 1246; ? early 13th cent.]

B f 94r; C f 48r

Universis sancte matris ecclesie filiis presens scriptum inspecturis Rogerus de Cressy, salutem in domino. Noveritis me karitatis intuitu et pro salute anime mee et animarum omnium antecessorum et successorum meorum dedisse et hac presenti carta mea confirmasse abbati de Rading(ia) et monachis eiusdem loci deo servientibus .xiii. nummatos redditus mei in Certeleia quos Willielmus filius Rad(ulf)i de Certel(eia) mihi solebat reddere per annum, habendos et percipiendos prefatis abbati et monachis ad festum sancti Jacobi apostoli in puram et perpetuam elemosinam ad usum annui luminarii coram reliquiis sancti Jacobi in eadem ecclesia repositis. Volo ergo et legaliter ac firmiter precipio quod, si prefatus W(illelmus) sive heredes sui defecerint in solutione prefati redditus ad prefatum terminum, liceat prefatis abbati et monachis distringere sufficienter per manus suas prefatum W(illelmum) sive heredes suos super tenementa que de me tenent quousque satisfecerint prefatis abbati et monachis de prefato redditu et de expensis suis circa prefatum redditum recuperandum factis. Et ego Rogerus et heredes mei warantizabimus prefatis abbati et monachis prefatum redditum contra omnes homines et feminas. Et in testimonium huius facti mei, presenti carte presens sigillum meum apposui. T(estibus).ᵃ

ᵃ *Om. in C*

The manor of Chearsley was held in the 12th and 13th centuries by the de Cressy family under the Honour of Giffard (*VCH Bucks.*, iv. 19). The outside dating limits of this deed are provided by the death of Roger's father, Hugh, in Mich. 1188 × Mich. 1189 and his own death in 1246 (Sanders, *English Baronies*, 16), but the fact that it was not entered in A and the slightly primitive air of some of the diplomatic suggest an early 13th-century date. The gift was clearly inspired by devotion to the Hand of St James.

CHESHAM

245 *Gift in free alms by Richard de Sifrewast to Reading Abbey of 100s*
worth of land in the vill of Chesham, for which the abbey has given him in his
great need 25 marks of silver   [1199 × 1252; ? early 13th cent.]

A f 77r; B f 92v; C f 47r-v

Sciant presentes et futuri quod ego Ricardus de Siffreiwast,[a] per
assensum et voluntatem heredis mei, dedi et concessi et presenti
carta mea confirmavi deo et beate Marie et beatis apostolis Johanni
et Jacobo et abbati et conventui de Rading(ia), pro salute mea et
uxoris mee et liberorum meorum et omnium antecessorum et successorum meorum, centum solidatas terre in villa de Cestresham,
videlicet terras et tenementa subscripta cum omnibus hominibus
eorundem tenementorum et cum tota eorum prole et sequela, quantum iuris in eis habui, et cum omnibus pertinentiis suis. Scilicet,
terram G(regorii)[b] capellani, mesuagium[c] Hugonis Coci iuxta mes-
agium[d] dicti capellani, terram Thurstani Basset, terram Thome de
Berchamsted',[e] terram Johannis filii Joc(elini), terram Bald(ewini)
de Blakewelle, terram Hardingi de Aqua, terram Ricardi filii Rogeri, terram Azonis, terram Alani filii Geroldi, terram Seberni, terram Symonis de Blakewelle, et totam partem quam habui in terra
de Berges; terras etiam quas Willelmus de Murieslade, Rogerus
Buckemaister,[f] Ailwinus Buckemaister, Hugo Buckem(aister) et All-
marus[g] de la Dene tenuerunt de me in essarto quod Willelmus filius
Rad(ulfi) tenuit de me iuxta boscum de Hokerugge. Totam vero
predictam terram cum omnibus hominibus terre illius sicut predictum est et cum omnibus pertinentiis suis assignavi predictis abbati
et conventui pro centum solidatis terre habendam et tenendam iure
perpetuo in liberam puram et perpetuam elemosinam, quam ego et
heredes mei eis warantizabimus contra omnes homines et [h]contra
omnes[h] feminas. Et ego et heredes mei adquietabimus[i] eos et omnes
homines suos de scutagio et de warda de Windleshor'[j] et de omnibus
ad scutagium et ad wardam pertinentibus, quantum pertinet ad
terram illam. Habeant etiam[k] et teneant omnia predicta libere et
quiete et absolute absque omni seculari servitio, exactione et demanda que eis fieri possit a me vel ab heredibus meis. Si vero
predicte terre non valuerint per annum centum sol(idatas) vel quod
ego et heredes mei non potuerimus eis warantizare predictas terras
et redditus, faciemus eis rationabile escambium in eadem villa ad
valentiam eorum que eis defuerint vel que warantizare non poterimus. Quod si totam terram de Cestresham perdiderimus ego vel
heredes mei, unde ipsi predictam[l] retinere non possint, vel quod ego
aut heredes mei aliam terram in eadem villa ad valentiam eis[m]

escambire non possimus, reddemus eis sine mora et absque omni difficultate .xxv. marcas argenti quas ab eis in maxima necessitate percepimus cum custo quod posuerint super nos et nostros in cibo et potu per considerationem legalium hominum, et reddemus eis cartam quam de ipsis habui; et ipsi reddent mihi vel heredibus meis cartam quam habuerunt de me quam cito habuerint .xxv. marcas argenti et cetera, sicut predictum est. Et ut hec mea donatio et concessio rata et stabilis perseveret, illam presenti scripto et sigilli mei appositione roboravi.[n] Hiis testibus.

[a] Siffrewast *C*	[b] *Expansion from B,C:* Greg'
[c] mesagium *B*	[d] mesuagium *C*
[e] Berkhamst' *B*, Berkhamsted' *C*	[f] Buckemaistre *B,C*
[g] Ailm' *B,C*	[h-h] *Om. in B,C*
[i] acquietabimus *B,C*	[j] Windlesor' *B,C*
[k] *Om. in C*	[l] *Insert* terram *B,C*
[m] *Om. in B,C*	[n] *B ends with* T', *C ends*

The gift was made in the Sifrewast manor in Chesham known by the 15th century as Chesham Bury. The deed was not entered in the original parts of A, but among 13th-century additions. A Richard de Sifrewast succeeded his father, Robert, in the manor in 1199 and seems in turn to have been followed by his son and heir, Richard, who in 1252 subinfeudated the manor to his brother, Roger (*VCH Bucks.*, iii. 209-10). The outside dating limits are thus 1199 and 1252, but the somewhat long-winded and unsophisticated diplomatic of the later clauses of the deed suggests an earlier rather than a later date. The William son of Ralph mentioned in the deed may be the William son of Ralph of Berkhamstead with whom Richard de Sifrewast made a final concord concerning land in Chesham in 1200 (*Bucks. Feet of Fines*, 19). An undated charter by William *de Muresled'* gives to Gilbert *de Greinwile* 6 acres in *Esselee* (in Chesham), next the land which belonged to Elwin *Buchemeister*, at an annual rent to the abbot of Reading of 4s (*Early Bucks. Charters*, ed. H. G. Fowler and J. G. Jenkins (Bucks. Archaeol. Soc. Recs. Branch, iii, 1939), 11). Thurstan Basset witnessed a Chesham charter in 1190 × 94 (*Cartl. Missenden*, ii. 1).

246 Quitclaim by Ralph the painter (*le peintur*) to Reading Abbey of all his right in 31½ acres of land in the vill of Chesham (*Cestresham*) which he claimed by the king's writ of right in the abbot's court against William *de Murislad'*,[a] Alfwin *pot(er)*,[b] Roger *pot(er)*[b] and John son of Jocelin. Neither he nor his heirs shall claim or be able to claim anything against the abbey or against the others holding the said land of the abbey. For this the abbey has given him 20s sterling. Sealing. Witnesses[c] [omitted]

[13th cent.; not later than 1258]

B f93r; C f47v

[a] Murieslad' *C*
[b] port' *C*
[c] *Om. in C*

Not later than 1258, since the deed was entered in the original section of B; probably not very long after no. 245, since William *de Murislad'* and John son of Jocelin appear in both and Alfwin *poter* and Roger *poter* in the present deed may be the same as the Ailwin and Roger *Buckemaister* of no. 245.

GRENDON UNDERWOOD

247 Gift in free alms by John of Hanney (*Hanneya*), chaplain, to Reading Abbey of ½ hide and ½ virgate of land with appurtenances in Grendon [Underwood] (*Grendon'*) and the service of Cicely, his sister, and her heirs from 1 virgate of land in the same vill, and the service of Emma, his sister, and her heirs from ½ virgate of land in the same vill, as was conceded to them by his father and by him. To be held in free alms, saving the foreign service which the abbey shall do to the lords of the fee from the land given to it, the donor's sisters discharging the foreign service pertaining to their lands. For this the abbey has accepted the donor for sufficient maintenance, as is confirmed in its charter to him. Witnesses*a* [omitted]

[? *c.* 1200 × 38]

B f 93v; C f 47v

a Om. in C

Dating uncertain. The deed was not entered in A, suggesting a date after the 12th century, and is earlier than no. 248, which can be dated certainly earlier than 1253 and possibly before 1238. The abbey's land in Grendon Underwood was later reckoned at 1 hide held under the manor, which in the 13th century was held of the earl of Cornwall (*VCH Bucks.*, iv. 51).

248 Notification by Henry *de Scaccario* that he and his heirs are bound to render annually to Reading Abbey 5s sterling for all service belonging to it, viz., 2s 6d each at the Annunciation and at Michaelmas, for the land which they hold of the abbey in Grendon [Underwood] (*Grendon'*), which the abbey has by gift in free alms of John the chaplain. Sealing. Witnesses*a* [omitted]

[before 1253; ? before 1238]

B f 93v; C f 48r

a Om. in C

After no. 247 and certainly earlier than Jan. 1253, when Ralph de Scaccario gave the land to Robert of Grendon, clerk, who was holding in 1254–5 (*Bucks. Feet of Fines*, 99; *Rot. Hund.*, i. 24; *VCH Bucks.*, iv. 53). Henry de Scaccario witnessed a Reading Abbey agreement in 1219 (no. 779) and was under-sheriff of Berkshire in 1217 and sheriff in 1220–26 and 1229–32 (*List of Sheriffs*, 6). He was still living 26 June, 1237 (*Close Rolls 1234–37*, 539), but was possibly dead in 1238, when Petronilla, his wife, appointed another as her attorney (*ibid. 1237–42*, 126).

LENBOROUGH

249 *Confirmation by Ernulf of Chelsfield of the gift to Reading Abbey by Alan son of Robert of Lenborough of 3½ hides in Lenborough* [1138 × 48]

A f42v; B f9ov; C f46r

Arnulfus*ᵃ* de Chelesfeld' omnibus amicis suis Francis et Anglicis tam presentibus quam futuris, salutem. Sciatis quod ego et heres meus concedimus et sigillo confirmamus donationem quam Alanus filius Roberti de Lithingeberga*ᵇ* fecit deo et sancte Marie et monachis de Rading(ia) de terra patris sui de Lithingeberga,*ᵇ* scilicet tres hidas et dimidiam. Et ita libere et quiete eam teneant sicut eam liberius et quietius pater eius tenuit. Hec*ᶜ* autem huius rei facio gratia quatinus orationum et elemosinarum et omnium beneficiorum ecclesie Rading(ensis) participes efficiamur.*ᵈ* Testes sunt huius conventionis et concessionis Siwardus sacerdos, et tres filii predicti Arnulfi, Simon scilicet et Helyas et Hugo, Simon de Godintona, et Willelmus filius eius, et multi alii.

ᵃ Ernulfus *C*	*ᵇ* Liþingeberg' *B,C*
ᶜ Hoc *B,C*	*ᵈ* *B ends with* T', *C ends*

The date is derived from the confirmation by Gilbert, earl of Pembroke (no. 250). The gift was included in Pope Eugenius III's general confirmation to Reading (no. 143). The land amounted to half the Domesday manor of Lenborough held by Ernulf de Hesding of the bishop of Bayeux (*VCH Bucks.*, iii. 484), but the *VCH* is clearly incorrect in stating that the earliest authenticated date for Reading's acquiring land in Lenborough is 1202 (*ibid.*). For the marginal note which appears alongside this deed in A, see no. 260 n.

249a Note of a charter by Alan son of Robert (*Robricti*) concerning 3½ hides of land in Lenborough (*Liþingeberg'*)   [1138 × 48]

B f9ov

Date as for no. 249. It is odd that none of the Reading cartularies, especially A, bothered to transcribe this deed.

250 *Confirmation by Gilbert [Fitz Gilbert], earl of Pembroke, of the same gift as conceded by Ernulf of Chelsfield*   [1138 × 48]

A f42v; B f9ov; C f46r

Comes Gilebertus de Penbroc*ᵃ* omnibus amicis suis et hominibus Francis et Anglicis, salutem. Sciatis quod ego concedo et grahanto donationem quam Alanus filius Roberti de Lithingeberga fecit deo et sancte Marie et monachis de Rading(ia) de terra patris sui de Lithingeberg(a), videlicet de tribus hidis et dimidia, sicut Arnulfus*ᵇ* de Chelesfeld illud iure concedit. Quare volo et firmiter precipio quod monachi predicti terram illam in bene et in pace teneant.*c* Testibus:*d* Philippo de Humez, Pagano de Cumip', Willelmo dapifero.

a Pembr' *B*, Pembrok' *C*   *b* Ernulfus *B,C*
c C ends   *d .B ends*

The dating limits are those of Gilbert's earldom. This confirmation reveals that the Domesday overlordship of the bishop of Bayeaux had by now come to the earl of Pembroke, although there appears to be no other notice of this.

251 *Confirmation by Simon of Chelsfield of the gift by his father, Ernulf, to Reading Abbey of 3½ hides in Lenborough; they are to be quit of all service while the war lasts, but when peace comes his service will be reserved. Roaldus shall perform to the monks the service owed to Simon, and the monks shall perform no service to Girard de Lucy or anyone else apart from Simon and his heirs*   [1138 × 53]

A ff 42v–43r; B f 90v; C f 46r

Sciant omnes sancte matris ecclesie filii quod ego Symon de Chelesf(eld) donationem quam pater meus Arnulfus*a* fecit ecclesie sancte Marie de Rading(ia) et monachis ibidem deo servientibus et sigillo confirmavit, scilicet tres hidas et dimidiam in Lingeberga, granto et concedo et, ut firmius roboretur, sigillo meo confirmo, cum pax venerit, salvo meo servitio, quia dum guerra duraverit volo terram quietam esse ab omni servitio. Volo etiam quod Rualdus*b* servitium suum exhibeat monachis quod mihi debetur, et monachi prefati nullum servitium faciant Girardo de Luci nec alicui alii nisi mihi in vita mea, de cuius feudo*c* terra illa est, et me defuncto heredibus meis.*d* Testibus:*e* Rogero medico, Lodowico presbitero, Gocelino filio eius, Hilboldo sellario, et [*f 43r*] multis aliis.

a Ernulfus *B,C*   *b* Roaldus *B,C*
c feodo *B,C*   *d C ends*
e B ends

After no. 249 and before the end of the 'war' of Stephen's reign. This deed hints at the difficulties and uncertainties in tenures and services that might arise under Stephen. It probably provides the background for the agreement between Roaldus and the abbey (no. 252). How Girard de Lucy might have become involved is unknown.

252 *Notification by Roaldus that he has received 3½ hides in Lenborough at annual farm from Reading Abbey for an annual rent of 60s, to be held for as long as the abbey pleases, after which the tenement shall return to it with its buildings and cultivated lands. Both Roaldus and his son, Elias, have sworn to keep this agreement*   [1138 × 53]

B f 91r; C f 46v

Noverint fideles ad quoscumque presens scriptum pervenerit quod ego Roaldus suscepi tres hidas et dimidiam in Liþingeberga de abbate et conventu de Rading(ia) ad firmam annuam, reddendo .xxx. solidos annuatim ad ^asanctum Michaelem^a et .xxx. solidos ad Pascha. Tenebo autem hoc tenementum de anno in annum quamdiu placuerit predicto abbati et monachis, ita ut cum prefatum tenementum rehabere voluerint, absque omni difficultate eis restituam sicut tenementum in quo nullum ius clamare possum nec aliquis per me nisi per voluntatem eorum, cum domibus et terris excultis quas mihi tradiderunt, scilicet aulam et talamum et coquinam et duo horrea et berkeriam et boveriam bene parata et .xii. acras de ivernagio et .xviii. acras de tramesio. Hanc vero conventionem fideliter observandam ego Roaldus et Hel(ias) filius meus iuravimus super sanctum evangelium, et quod non queremus artem vel ingenium quo de rehabendo predicto tenemento aliquantulum prefati monachi vexentur. T(estibus).^b

^{a-a} festum Michaelis *C*
^b *Om. in C*

Date as for no. 251.

253 *Precept by King Henry II to the sheriff of Buckinghamshire to do right to Reading Abbey concerning Elias of Lenborough, who, the abbey complains, has unjustly mown the meadows and harvested the corn of Hugh, its man* [1173 × 88; ? 1179]

A f 26r-v; B f 27r
Pd. (in part) van Caenegem, *Royal Writs*, 202 n. 4

Henricus dei gratia rex Anglie ^aet dux Norm(annie) et Aquit(anie) et comes Andeg(avie)^a vicecomiti de Bukinhamsc(ira),^b salutem. Precipio tibi quod [*f 26v*] sine dilatione plenum rectum teneas abbati et monachis de Rading(ia) de Elia^c de Lingeberga, de quo queruntur quod ipse iniuste falcavit prata et messuit blada Hugonis hominis illorum et asportavit ea postquam idem Hugo fecit eis homagium, et iniuriam inde eis fecit. Et nisi feceris, iusticie mee de partibus illis faciant, ne amplius inde clamorem audiam pro penuria recti. T(este)^d Rannulfo de Glanvill(a). Apud Bruhull'.

^{a-a} et cetera *B*   ^b Bukingh'sir' *B*
^c Hel' *B*   ^d *B ends*

The inclusion of *dei gratia* in the royal style, on which Cartulary A seems generally to be scrupulous, dates this writ not earlier than 1173. It was given at Brill (Bucks.) and must therefore be earlier than July, 1188, when the king left England for the last time (Eyton, 288). Eyton suggests that he was at Brill in the summer of 1179 (*ibid.*, 227).

253a Note of a charter by Payn de Mandubleil (*Mandublel*)^a to Elias son of Roaldus concerning land at Lenborough (*Lingeberga*)^b   [1155 × 70]

A f 43v; B f 91v

^a Mandubel *B*   ^b Liþingeberg' *B*

The existence of this charter adds further to the evidence of confusion in the tenure of Lenborough. Payn de Mandubleil was the great-grandson of the Domesday holder of Lenborough, Ernulf de Hesding, being descended from the latter's daughter, Matilda. He succeeded his father, Patrick II de Chaworth, in the honour of Kempsford (Glos.) in 1155 and died in 1170 (Sanders, *English Baronies*, 125). Since he cannot have had any claim to Lenborough other than through his father, this charter is probably not earlier than 1155. Any claim in Lenborough would, however, conflict with that of his relatives, the Chelsfields, unless it involved an overlordship, as may perhaps be inferred from the *carta* of Payn in 1166, which stated that among his knights of ancient enfeoffment Simon of Chelsfield held 5 knights' fees (*Red Bk. Exch.*, i. 297).

254 *Quitclaim, in the king's court at Westminster, by Elias son of Roaldus of Lenborough to Reading Abbey of 3½ hides of land in Lenborough which he had unjustly occupied and withheld against its will; for this the abbey has given him 15 marks of silver and a palfrey*   [1190 × 95]

A f 43r; (noted) B f 91v

Helias filius Roaldi de Lingeberga omnibus ad quos littere presentes pervenerint, salutem. Noverit universitas vestra me in curia domini regis apud Westmon(asterium), coram H(ugone) Dunelm(ensi) et Willelmo Eliensi et H(ugone) Coventrensi episcopis et Iocelino Cicestr(ensi) archidiacono et Rogero filio Reinfredi et magistro Thoma de Husseburna et Michaele Belet et Simone de Pateshelle tunc iusticiariis et aliis baronibus et fidelibus domini regis qui tunc ibi aderant, recognovisse et quietas clamasse in perpetuum tres hidas et dimidiam terre in Lingeberga cum bosco et plano et cum omnibus aliis pertinentiis suis abbati et conventui de Rading(ia) cum omnibus pertinentiis suis^a sicut ius eorum, quas iniuste occupaveram et ipsis reclamantibus diu detinueram, liberas et quietas de me et heredibus meis in perpetuum ab omni vexatione et calumpnia, sicut illas in quibus unquam nullum ius habui. Et pro hac recognitione et quieta clamantia, predicti abbas et conventus dederunt michi .xv. marcas argenti et unum palefridum. Et ad maiorem eorum securitatem, hoc eis me fideliter observaturum sacramento prestito confirmavi et sigilli mei appositione corroboravi.

^a *Sic*

After the consecration of William Longchamp, bishop of Ely, on 31 Dec. 1189, and before the death of Hugh du Puiset, bishop of Durham, on 3 Mar. 1195.

255 *Quitclaim largely identical to the preceding, but including a reference to the original lease of the land to Elias and his father, and the statement that the abbey's payment to Elias is in respect of the quitclaim and the costs expended by him on buildings and cultivation* [1190 × 95]

B f 91r-v; C f 46v

Helyas filius Roaldi de Liþingeberg(a) omnibus ad quos littere presentes pervenerint, salutem. Noverit universitas vestra me in curia domini regis apud Westm(onasterium), coram H(ugone) Dunelm(ensi) et W(illelmo) Elyen(si) et H(ugone) Coventr(ensi) episcopis et Iocelino Cicestr(ensi) archidiacono et Rogero filio Rainfr(edi) et magistro Th(oma) de Husseb(urna) et Michaele Belet et Symone de Pateshull' tunc iustic(iariis) et aliis baronibus et fidelibus domini regis qui tunc ibi aderant, recognovisse et quiet(as) clamasse in perpetuum [f 91v] tres hydas et dimidiam terre in Liþingeberg(a) cum bosco et plano et cum omnibus aliis pertinentiis suis abbati et conventui de Rading(ia), sicut ius eorum, quas iniuste occupaveram et ipsis reclamantibus contra iusiurandum quod ego et pater meus fecimus in capitulo de Rading(ia) cum predictam terram ad firmam annuam susciperet diu detinueram, liberas et quietas de me et heredibus meis ab omni vexatione et calumpnia, sicut illas in quibus nullum ius unquam habui. Et pro hac quieta clamantia et pro costiamento quod in domibus et culturis expenderam, predicti abbas et conventus dederunt mihi .xv. marcas argenti et unum palefridum. Et ad maiorem eorum securitatem, hoc eis me fideliter observaturum sacramento prestito confirmavi et sigilli mei appositione corroboravi.

Date as for no. 254. The original lease is no. 252.

255a Note of a charter by Elias son of Roaldus to Muriel concerning $\frac{1}{2}$ virgate of land in Lenborough (*Liþingeberg'*) [before 1195]

B f 91v

Before the latest possible date for nos. 254-5.

256 *Final concord in the king's court at Westminster between Roger de Bosco and Emma, his wife, and Reading Abbey, by which the former quitclaimed to the latter the third part of $3\frac{1}{2}$ hides of land in Lenborough, which Emma claimed as dower by gift of her late husband, Elias of Lenborough; for this the abbey gave them 5 marks of silver and 5s* 18 Mar. 1196

B f 181v; C f 107v

Hec est finalis concordia facta in curia domini regis apud
Westm(onasterium), die lune proxima ante festum sancti Benedicti
[*21 Mar.*] anno regni regis Ricardi septimo, coram H(uberto) Can-
tuar(iensi) archiepiscopo, R(icardo) London(iensi) episcopo,
R(icardo) Elyensi archidiacono, Osb(erto) filio Herv(ei), Symone
de Pateshull', Ricardo de Herierd' tunc iustic(iariis) et aliis fidelibus
domini regis tunc ibi presentibus, inter Rogerum de Bosco et
Emmam uxorem eius, petentes per ipsum Rogerum positum loco
ipsius Emme ad lucrandum vel perdendum, et H(ugonem) abbatem
et conventum de Rading(ia), tenentes per Walterum clericum ipsius
abbatis positum loco eorum ad lucrandum vel perdendum, de tertia
parte trium hydarum et dimidie terre cum pertinentiis omnibus in
Lengeberg(a), quam tertiam partem terre predicta Emma clamavit
in dotem suam ex dono Helye de Lengeberg(a) quondam viri sui, et
unde placitum fuit inter eos in prefata curia. Scilicet quod predictus
Rogerus et E(mma) quiet'clamaverunt totum ius et clamium quod
habuerunt in predicta tertia parte[a] terre cum pertinentiis de eis
predictis abbati et conventui de Rading(ia) et successoribus eorum
in perpetuum. Et pro hoc fine et concordia et quiet'clamio, predicti
abbas et conventus dederunt prefatis R(ogero) et E(mme) .v. marcas
argenti et .v. solidos.

[a] *B has here* tertia *marked for deletion*

See also *Rot. Cur. Reg.*, i. 7; *Cur. Reg. R.*, i. 15.

257 *Confirmation by Gilbert de la Pomeray and Letia, his wife, of Alan son
of Robert's gift to Reading Abbey of 3½ hides of land in Lenborough, as the
charters by Ernulf of Chelsfield and Simon of Chelsfield testify; and gift of the
homage of William Boistard and the service of ½ mark and the whole service
which he owed them for one of the said hides. The abbey shall pay to Gilbert
and Letia at Chelsfield the annual ½ mark, which shall be accounted to the
abbey as the king's service in castle-guard at Rochester pertaining to the said
land*   [later 12th cent.; before 1194]

A f 43r; B ff 90v-91r; C f 46v

Sciant presentes et futuri quod ego Gilebertus de la Pumerai[a] et
uxor mea Letia concessimus et presenti carta confirmavimus deo et
sancte Marie de Rading(ia) et monachis ibidem deo servientibus,
pro animabus antecessorum nostrorum et omnium fidelium et salute
nostra et heredum nostrorum, tres hidas terre et dimidiam in Lingeberga[b] quas Alanus filius Robricti[c] predictis monachis dedit, tenendas de nobis et heredibus nostris ita libere et quiete, integre et
finabiliter sicut unquam quietius et melius Robrictus pater predicti
Alani tenuit et sicut carta domini Arnulfi[d] de Chelesfeld eis testatur

et sicut carta domini Simonis de Chelesfeld eis testatur; scilicet in hominibus et redditibus, in bosco, in plano, in pratis et pascuis,[e] aquis et aliis libertatibus et in omnibus ad predictas hidas pertinentibus, salvo servitio domini regis quod ad dimidium militem pertinet. Preterea dedimus et concessimus predictis monachis homagium Willelmi Boistard[f] et dimidiam marcam argenti quam nobis debebat de servitio annuatim et totum servitium eius quod nobis debebat. Et predictus Willelmus et heredes eius facient predictis monachis predictum servitium pro una predictarum hidarum quam de nobis tenuit. Ita quod prefati monachi singulis annis nobis et heredibus nostris dimidiam marcam argenti ad festum sancti Michaelis persolvant apud Chelesfeld, quam nobis predictus Willelmus Boistard[g] de prenominata hida reddere solebat annuatim. Hec autem dimidia marca argenti computabitur monachis in servitium domini regis in warda de Rovecestria[h] et in omnibus aliis servitiis ad predictam terram[g] pertinentibus.[i] His testibus: Ricardo capellano, Henrico de Lundenestun(a), Nicholao Duchet, Laurentio homine eius, Reginaldo Flemeng, Stephano Bono Christiano, Adam Ascali, Helya clerico, Sansone, et multis aliis.

[a] Pomeria B,C   [b] Liþingeberg B,C
[c] Roberti C   [d] Ernulfi B,C
[e] pasturis B,C   [f] Boistard' B,C
[g] Omitted in B,C   [h] Rovecestr' B, Rovecestre C
[i] B ends with T', C ends

After no. 251, the confirmation by Simon of Chelsfield, whose daughter Letia was (*Kent Feet of Fines*, 9-10), and certainly before 20 Oct. 1197, when Letia was already married to her second husband, Philip de Dammartin (*ibid.*, 8), but, since it was entered in the orignal section of A, not later than 1193. This is the earliest of Reading's Lenborough deeds which refers to castle-guard at Rochester.

258 Confirmation and gift, in terms identical to those of the preceding, by Philip de Dammartin (*Danmartin*) and Leticia, his wife, to Reading Abbey   [end of 12th cent.]

A f 90v; (noted) B f 91r

His testibus: Ricardo capellano, Henrico de Lundenestan(a), Nicolao Duket, Laurentio homine eius, Stephano Bono Christiano, et Andrea senescallo de Radinges, Mauricio de Pereces, Iohanne de Rameseia, Roberto Brand, et multis aliis.

Though not in the original section of A, this was added in a very similar hand soon afterwards. The first five witnesses also witnessed no. 257. Letia, or Leticia, daughter of Simon of Chelsfield, married successively Gilbert de la Pomeray and (by 20 Oct. 1197) Philip de Dammartin, and with each husband she confirmed Alan son of Robert's gift to Reading and gave the service of William Boistard. Though not the eldest daughter of Simon of Chelsfield, she clearly received Chelsfield and mesne lordship of Lenborough. From the evidence of 3 final concords of 1197–8, not involving Reading (*Kent Feet of Fines*, 8–10), and that of the Reading charters, the family tree of the Chelsfields can be partially reconstructed as follows:

Ernulf of Chelsfield

Simon of Chelsfield = Juliana		Elias	Hugh
Alice	Letia of Chelsfield		Sara
	= (i) Gilbert de la Pomeray		
Thomas Escollant	= (ii) Philip de Dammartin		Philip de Dine

This deed presumably ante-dates the final concord of 1201 (no. 259).

259 *Final concord in the king's court at Westminster between Philip de Dammartin and Letia, his wife, and Abbot Elias of Reading, by which the former quitclaimed to the latter the service of 20½d which they were demanding from 3½ hides of land in Lenborough, and conceded the said land to the abbot in perpetuity for an annual farm of ½ mark and 4s 3½d for castle-guard at Rochester; for this the abbot gave them 20s*   2 Dec. 1201

B f 181v; C f 107v
Pd. *Fines sive Pedes Finium*, i. 200–1; (cal.) *Bucks. Feet of Fines*, 21 (both from PRO foot: CP 25(1)/14/5/16)

Hec est finalis concordia facta in curia domini regis apud Westm(onasterium) a die sancti Martini in tres septimanas, anno regni regis Iohannis tertio, coram G(aufredo) filio Petri, Symone de Pateshull', Iohanne de Gestling',ᵃ Godefr(ido) de Insul(a), Waltero de Creping' iustic(iariis) et aliis fidelibus domini regis ibidem tunc presentibus, inter Phil(ippum) de Da(m)martin et Letiam uxorem suam, petentes, et Helyam abbatem de Rading(ia), tenentem per Gaufr(edum) de Norwic' positum loco suo ad lucrandum vel perdendum, de servitio trium hydarum terre et dimidie cum pertinentiis in Liþingeberg(a), unde placitum fuit inter eos in prefata curia et unde predicti Ph(ilippus) et Let(ia) exigebant .xx. denarios et obolum de servitio quos predictus abbas non cognovit se debere. Scilicet quod predictus Ph(ilippus) et Let(ia) quiet'clamaverunt pro se et heredibus suis predicto abbati totam demandam quam habuerunt in dicto servitio .xx. denariorum et oboli in perpetuum. Et idem Ph(ilippus) et Let(ia) concesserunt predicto abbati et successoribus eius totam predictam terram cum pertinentiis tenendam de se et heredibus ipsius Let(ie) in perpetuum per servitium dimidie marce argenti per annum de firma et .iiii. solidorum et .iii. denariorum et .i. oboli pro warda castelli de Rovecestr(ia), pro omni servitio salvo forinseco servitio, reddendeᵇ ad festum sancti Michaelis ad Chelesfeld. Et pro hac concessione, fine et concordia, predictus abbas dedit predictis[c] Ph(ilippo) et Let(ie) .xx. solidos sterlingorum.

[a] Gesteling' C   [b] Sic in B,C and PRO foot
[c] Om. in C

This presumably superseded no. 258, q.v. with n.

260   *Gift by Simon of Chelsfield to Reading Abbey of the entire service of Alice of Kimble from the tenement which she held of him in Lenborough; and confirmation of the 3½ hides of land in Lenborough which the abbey already held of him and from which it was accustomed to pay him 11s 1½d annually, but which shall now be free of all exactions including castle-guard and scutage; for all this the abbey has given him 55 marks of silver*

[13th cent., before 1243]

A f 109r; B ff 91v–92r; C f 47r

Sciant presentes et futuri quod ego Simon de Chelefeld[a] dedi et concessi et[b] presenti carta mea confirmavi deo et ecclesie sancte Marie de Rading' et abbati et monachis ibidem deo servientibus totum et integrum servitium Alicie de Kenebell' et heredum suorum de tenemento quod dicta Alicia de me tenuit in Lithingeburch[c] sine omni retinemento. Habendum et tenendum dictis abbati et monachis Rading' prefatum servitium prenominate Alicie et heredum suorum cum omnibus pertinentiis et cum omnibus rebus que ad tenementum predicte Alicie quod de me tenuit in predicta villa et heredum suorum pertinent, vel aliquo casu possint pertinere, libere et quiete, plenarie et integre, bene et in pace, sicut melius et liberius et quietius tenent aliqua tenementa sua et sicut aliqua[d] elemosina potest esse magis libera et ab omni seculari servitio et exactione magis quieta et absoluta. Ita quod nec ego Simon nec heredes mei quicquam exigemus nec exigere poterimus a dictis abbate et monachis, nec a dicta Alicia nec ab heredibus suis, ratione illius tenementi nec occasione alicuius rei quod ad ipsum tenementum pertineat vel possit pertinere, set sint dicta Alicia et heredes sui de dicto tenemento suo et de omnibus servitiis et de omnibus rebus ad ipsum tenementum pertinentibus soli abbati et monachis de Rading' respondentes et de omnibus intendentes. Et ego Simon et heredes mei warentizabimus[e] dictis abbati et monachis de Rading' prefatum tenementum cum pertinentiis et ipsum tenementum adquietabimus[f] et defendemus de warda et scutagio et omni seculari servitio et omni exactione et de omnibus rebus. Concessi etiam et confirmavi abbati et monachis de Rading' tres hidas terre et dimidiam cum pertinentiis in Lithingeburch[c] quas prius de me tenuerunt et unde[g] soliti fuerunt reddere michi[h] undecim solidos et tres obolos per annum. Habendas et tenendas ipsis abbati et monachis libere quietas et absolutas ab omni seculari servitio et omni redditu et omni exactione in perpertuum. Ita quod nec ego Simon nec heredes mei in dictis tribus hidis terre et dimidia cum pertinentiis nec in dicto redditu nec in aliquibus que ad ipsam terram pertineant vel pertinere possint quicquam clamabimus nec quicquam exigemus nec clamare vel exigere poterimus, set ego Simon et heredes mei prefatas tres hidas terre et dimidiam cum pertinentiis dictis abbati et monachis contra omnes gentes warentizabimus,[e] et de warda et scutagio et omni seculari servitio et omni exactione et de omnibus rebus adquietabimus[f] et defendemus. Pro[i] supradictis itaque meis donationibus, concessionibus et confirmationibus, warentizatione,[j] adquietatione[k] et defensione, dederunt[l] dicti abbas et monachi triginta quinque marcas argenti.[m] Hiis testibus.

[a] Chelesfeld *B,C*	[b] *Insert* hac *B,C*
[c] Liþingeberg' *B,C*	[d] *Illegible deletion in A*
[e] warantizabimus *B,C*	[f] acquietabimus *B,C*
[g] *A has* inde	[h] *Insert* .xi. mihi *C(in error)*
[i] *A has* hac *deleted*	[j] warantizatione *B,C*
[k] acquietatione *B,C*	[l] *Insert* mihi *B,C*
[m] *B ends with* T', *C ends*	

After no. 259, dated 1201, and before the notice in 1242–3 that Robert *Bostart* and Alice of Kimble each held half a knight's fee in Lenborough of the abbot of Reading, the latter holding of the heirs of Chelsfield (*Fees*, ii. 871). However, Simon of Chelsfield was still alive then, being recorded as holding at Chelsfield in Kent (*ibid.*, 668). In 1254–5 Robert *Boistard* and Richard of Kimble each held 3½ hides of the abbot in Lenborough (*Rot. Hund.*, i. 29). It is clear, therefore, that Alice of Kimble held 3½ hides in Lenborough and that, when Simon of Chelsfield gave her service to Reading Abbey, he was re-uniting under Reading's lordship the 7-hide manor held in 1086 by Ernulf de Hesding under the bishop of Bayeaux (see no. 249 n.). This deed by Simon of Chelsfield superseded all previous agreements regarding the service due from the 3½ hides which Reading already held in Lenborough, as is pointed out by a marginal note in A f 42v, alongside the original deed by Ernulf of Chelsfield (no. 249), which reads: *Iste sex carte de Lithingeb' subscripte transmutate sunt per innovationem carte Symonis de Chelesfeld', sicut per eam plenius patere poterit. Quere eam in fine libri.* The 6 charters referred to are nos. 249, 250–1, 254, 257 and 261, the last in fact not being concerned with this tenement.

261 *Gift in free alms by Ralph de Langetot to Reading Abbey of 1 hide of land in Lenborough, with the consent of his mother, Cecily, of whose dower the land is*   [*c.* 1130 × 53]

A f 42v; B f 90v; C f 46r

Sciant omnes christiani tam presentes quam futuri quod ego Radulfus de Langetot dono et concedo deo et sancte Marie et monachis de Rading(ia) unam hidam terre in Lingeberga cum omnibus appendiciis suis in pratis et hominibus, pro anima patris mei Rad(ulfi) et mea et pro salute omnium antecessorum meorum, in perpetuam elemosinam solam*a* et quietam ab omni seculari servitio. Et hoc facio consilio et concessu matris mee Cecilie, de cuius duario terra ipsa est.*b* Testibus:*c* Willelmo de Caisne, et Roberto de Caisne, et Hugone de Caisn(e), et Milone de Langetot, et Geraldo de Normanvilla, et Adeliza de Caisn(e), et Cecilia matre mea, et Emma sorore mea.

a Sic in A; B,C have solutam
b C ends
c B ends

Before July, 1153, since it was included in Pope Eugenius III's general confirmation to Reading (no. 143), and probably not earlier than 1130, since the land was not among the possessions confirmed to Reading by Innocent II in 1130 × 35 (no. 141). The gift was made out of the second Domesday manor in Lenborough, consisting of 3 hides, which was held of Walter Giffard by a certain Ralph, with whom it is tempting to identify the father of the present donor. The de Langetot family was still in possession in the 13th and 14th centuries (see *VCH Bucks.*, iii. 483).

262 Record of a plea *quare cepit* brought against Abbot [William III] of Reading by Edmund Giffard, who, by his attorney Simon of Kilby (*Kylby*), alleges that on Monday before the feast of St Martin [11 Nov.], 36 Edward III, at a place called *Hay* in the vill of Lenborough (*Lethingebergh'*)*a* the abbot took and unjustly detained 6 oxen, 6 cows and 4 pack-animals (*iumenta*) belonging to him, causing him loss to the value of £40. The abbot, by his attorney John *Straton,b* defends the action and claims that the seizure of the cattle took place within the manor of Lenborough (*Lethingbergh'*)*a* and not at the place called *Hay*; and, in order to obtain their return, he says that a certain Robert *de Etone* holds of the abbot by right of Reading Abbey a messuage and 3½ hides of land in the vill of Lenborough (*Lethyngbergh'*),*a* of which the place cited by the abbot is a parcel and which constitute the manor of Lenborough, by homage and fealty, scutage at the rate of 10s for a 40s-scutage and the service of 63s 4d annually, viz., in equal portions on the feast of St James [25 July] and on the feast of St Martin, of which services the late abbot of Reading, Henry [of Appleford], the present abbot's predecessor, was seised by the hand of the said Robert as his true tenant; and, because the said rent was 2½ years in arrears by the day of the seizure of the cattle, the cattle were taken for the rent of the first year in the said place in the abbot's fee. Edmund [Giffard] repeats his claim that the seizure took place at *Hay*. Both parties put themselves on a jury*c* for the octave of Holy Trinity. Afterwards, the case having been adjourned to the quindene of Michaelmas, 38 Edward III, unless justices of assize should take assizes in the county, the justices came before then to [High] Wycombe (*Wycomb'*) on

Tuesday before the feast of St Margaret [20 July]. In the quindene of Michaelmas the abbot came by his said attorney and the said justices of assize sent their record, namely, that the abbot came before Robert *de Thorp*' and John *Knyvet*, justices of assize, and Edmund Giffard, though solemnly summoned, did not. Therefore the latter is judged to be in mercy, and the abbot is *sine die* and is to have return of the said cattle. Afterwards, in the quindene of Michaelmas, 39 Edward III, the abbot came by his attorney, John *de Denton*', and the sheriff sent word (*mandavit*) that he had caused the said cattle to be returned to the abbot, which the abbot acknowledged   1364–5

B f 185r-v; (in part) B f 92r

Rubric: De termino Pasche anno xxxviii, rotulo Cxxxi

a Lethyngburgh' *B f 92r*
b de Stratone *B f 92r*
c *B f 92r ends here*

This was a Common Pleas action, the full text being a copy of the record on the roll of that court for Easter term, 38 Edward III (PRO CP 40/417, rot. 131d). The alleged offence took place on 7 Nov. 1362, but the case was heard in 1364 and finally cleared in 1365. The only Abbot Henry of Reading was Henry of Appleford, abbot 1342–61.

FINCHINGFIELD

263 *Gift by Roger Bigod, earl of Norfolk, to Reading Abbey of 3 marks annual rent in the church of Finchingfield, to be expended during the donor's life on the repair of the shrines, reliquaries and other requirements of the high altar in the abbey and, after his death, on his anniversary there. The earl retains the advowson and will present each new parson to the diocesan bishop in the presence of Reading monks, in order to safeguard payment of the rent*   [1189 × 98; prob. 1193 × 98]

A f 92v

Universis sancte matris ecclesie filiis Rog(erus) Bigot comes Norfolch(ie), salutem eternam in domino. Ad publicam volo pervenire notitiam quod ego, pro anima patris mei et matris mee et pro salute anime mee et Ide comitisse uxoris mee et omnium filiorum et antecessorum et successorum meorum, dedi et hac carta mea confirmavi deo et monachis de Rading(ia) .iii. marcatas redditus annuatim percipiendas in ecclesia de Fingingefeld. Ego autem semper decedente persona prefate ecclesie personam presentabo episcopo diocesano coram monachis de Rading(ia) ad hoc in presentatione predicta vocandis, ut cautionem sufficientem coram episcopo de solutione predictarum trium marcarum annuarum de persona instituenda suscipiant, nec aliquid amplius in prefata ecclesia quam .iii. marcas exigere valeant per manum persone institute. Has autem tres marcas ita dedi ut dum vixero per manus vel per consilium Roberti monachi et Rad(ulfi) fratris eius de Norfolch expendantur in reparatione feretrorum et philacteriorum et in ceteris que necessaria fuerint principalis altaris Rading(ensis) ornatui. Cum autem decessero, de predicto redditu fiet anniversarium meum in conventu Rading(ensi). Hanc autem elemosinam .iii. marcarum libere et quiete et perpetuo possidendam prefatis monachis ita dedi ut mihi et heredibus meis semper presentatio predicte ecclesie permaneat. T(estibus).

After the earl's creation in 1189 and, since Finchingfield church has clearly not yet been given to Thetford priory, before no. 264, which is to be dated not later than Feb. 1198. However, since this deed was not entered in the original section of A, it is probably not earlier than 1193. The earl had slightly earlier given to Reading 3 marks rent annually from his mills in Walton (? Norfolk), to be held until he should assign the same amount in Finchingfield church or another church (see no. 485).

264 *Notification by Prior Martin and the convent of Thetford [St Mary, Norfolk] that they are bound to pay to Reading Abbey 40s annually, until they shall assign this amount in a specific rent. If the church of Finchingfield, given to them by Earl Roger Bigod their patron, shall become vacant before this has been done, they will assign the rent as a portion of that church or elsewhere*   [1189 × 98; prob. 1193 × 98]

A f 91v

Universis sancte matris ecclesie filiis ad quos presens scriptum pervenerit Martinus prior Theodfordie eiusdemque loci conventus, salutem in domino. Noverit universitas vestra nos debere monasterio de Rading(ia) eiusdemque loci conventui .xl. solidos annuatim solvendos eis apud Rading(iam) vel custodi domorum suarum apud Lundon(iam) ad Pascha, quousque in certo competenti et securo redditu ubi eis et nobis commodius visum fuerit illos eis assignemus. Quod si ecclesiam de Finchelefeld', quam nobis nobilis comes Rog(erus) Bigot advocatus noster in elemosinam concessit, a persona Rad(ulf)o de Diceto vacare contigerit antequam eis isdem redditus competenter assignetur, tunc in certa portione eiusdem ecclesie vel alibi dictum redditum eis assignabimus. Ita quod ipsi nichil aliud in eadem ecclesia possint vendicare nisi predictos .xl. solidos ibi vel in alio loco congruo eis assignatos, quos per assignationem nostram de elemosina comitis Rog(eri) annuatim debent percipere. Hiis testibus: Ricardo de Cadomo, Rog(ero) filio Osb(ert)i, Milone Lenveise, Rog(ero) de Braham', Roberto capellano, Michaele capellano, Rann(ulfo) de Sahinges, Waltero de Cadomo, Hugone de Braham, Matheo clerico, Willelmo filio Guidonis, Iohanne filio Turstani,[a] Willelmo camerario abbatis de Rading(ia), et pluribus aliis.

  [a] *Ms* Turstano

After no. 263 and before Hubert Walter's confirmation (no. 266), which is to be dated not later than Feb. 1198; but, since the deed was not entered in the original section of A, probably not earlier than 1193.

265 *Notification by Roger Bigod, earl of Norfolk, that, at the instance of Prior Martin and the convent of Thetford [St Mary, Norfolk], he has gone surety for them in respect of their payment to Reading Abbey of 3 marks annually under the terms of the preceding deed*
          [1189 × 98; prob. 1193 × 98]

A f 91v

Omnibus ad quos presens scriptum pervenerit Rog(erus) Bigod comes Norf(olchie), salutem. Noverit universitas vestra quod ego, ad instantiam Martini prioris de Theodf(ordia) eiusdemque loci con-

ventus, posui me plegium eorum versus monachos de Rading(ia) de
solutione trium marcarum annuatim persolvendarum prefatis monachis de Rading(ia) ad Pascha apud Rading(iam) vel custodi domorum suarum apud Lond(oniam), quousque ecclesiam de Finchelefeld', quam predicto priori et monachis in elemosinam contuli, a
persona Rad(ulfo) de Diceto vacare contigerit, ut tunc in certa portione eiusdem ecclesie vel alibi illas ad commodum ipsorum percipiant, si tamen prius eis alias super hoc satisfactum non fuerit. Quod
si forte prefati monachi de Theodford(ia) predictam conventionem
non tenuerint, ego vel heredes mei illos tenere compellam et predictis
monachis de Rading(ia) satisfieri faciam. Test(ibus).

Date as for no. 264.

266 *Confirmation by Hubert* [*Walter*], *archbishop of Canterbury, primate
and legate, of the arrangement contained in the preceding two deeds*
[Apr. 1195 × Feb. 1198]

A f 94v; B f 202v; C f 123v

H(ubertus) dei gratia Cantuariensis archiepiscopus *a*totius Anglie
primas et apostolice sedis legatus, omnibus sancte matris ecclesie
filiis ad quos presens scriptum pervenerit, eternam in domino*a* salutem. Ex officii nostri debito securitati et paci virorum religiosorum
duximus ut tenemur intendere, et tam res quam redditus eorum
rationabiliter obtentos*b* auctoritatis nostre munimine confirmare et
protegere. Eapropter ad omnium volumus notitiam pervenire nos,
ex continentia cartarum dilectorum filiorum nostrorum Martini
tunc tempore prioris*c* Theford(ie)*d* et *e*eiusdem loci conventus,*e* necnon Rog(eri) Bigot comitis Norfol(chie), quas inspeximus, manifes-
tius advertisse eosdem monachos de Theford(ia)*f* debere monasterio
Rading(ensi) eiusdemque*g* loci conventui .xl. solidos annuatim solvendos eis apud Radinges vel custodi domorum suarum apud Lon-
don(iam) ad Pascha, quousque in certo competenti et securo redditu
ubi utrique parti commodius visum fuerit illos eis assignent. Quod
si ecclesiam de Finchelefeld',*h* quam eisdem monachis de The-
ford(ia)*f* memoratus comes Rog(erus) Bigot*i* eorum patronus in elemosinam concessit, a persona Rad(ulf)o de Diceto vacare contigerit
antequam monasterio Rading(ensi) et conventui loci eiusdem prefatus redditus competenter assignetur, tunc in certa portione eiusdem ecclesie vel alibi predicti monachi de Theford(ia)*f* conventui de
Rading(es) dictum redditum assignabunt. Ita quod idem conventus
de Rading(es) nichil aliud in eadem ecclesia possit vendicare nisi
predictos .xl. solidos si ibi fuerint assignati. Et de hoc prefatus comes
Rog(erus) fideiussorem se constituit versus monachos de Rading(es),

sicut in carta sua quam prememoravimus noscitur contineri. Ut igitur hec in posterum nulli veniant in dubium, immo ex testimonio et confirmatione nostra maius optineant firmamentum, ea sicut rationabiliter expressa sunt et confirmata presentis scripti serie et sigilli nostri appositione quantum in nobis est *j*duximus confirmare*j* et communire. His*k* testibus.

a-a et cetera *B,C*
c *Om. in* C
e-e conventus eiusdem loci *B,C*
g *A has* eiusd'; *B,C have* eiusdemque
i *Om. in* B,C
k Hiis *B,C*

b optentos *B,C*
d Theod'ford' *B,C*
f Theodf *B,C*
h Finchingefeld' *B,C*
j-j confirmare duximus *B,C*

While the archbishop exercised legatine authority (see no. 207 n.). This confirmation was the only one of the deeds relating to Finchingfield to be copied into cartularies B and C. In fact, it seems likely that the earl's gift in the church of Finchingfield did not take permanent effect, since, although his obit was entered in the calendar in the almoner's cartulary (D f 14v), Reading had no financial interest in the church in 1291 (*Taxatio*, 18).

BERKELEY

267 Gift in free alms by Empress Matilda, daughter of King Henry and lady of the English, to Reading Abbey, for the souls of among others her father and mother, King Henry I and Queen Matilda, anf for the health and safety of among others her husband (*dominus*), Geoffrey duke of Normandy, and for the stability and peace of the kingdom of England, of the church of Berkeley with its appurtenances, viz., what the clerks there have, churches, chapels and tithes appurtenant to it   [1144 × 47]

A f 15v; B f 19r-v
Pd. *Regesta*, iii. 259 (no. 702)

Testibus:*a* Roberto comite Gloecestr(ie), et Unfr(edo) de Buhun dapifero, et Iohanne filio Gisleberti, et Willelmo Diffublato, et Gocelino Baillolo. Apud Divisas.

a B ends

After Geoffrey became duke of Normandy, 23 Apr. 1144, and before the death of Robert, earl of Gloucester, 31 Oct. 1147. Cartulary A notes another charter by the same concerning the same. The history of the churches of Berkeley and its Hernesse in Stephen's reign is beset with complications (see B. R. Kemp, 'The churches of Berkeley Hernesse', *Trans. Bristol and Glos. Archaeol. Soc.*, lxxxvii (1968), 96–110), but it is likely that this gift did not originate with the Empress but with Queen Adeliza and her clerk, Serlo (see nos. 268, 270).

268 *Notification by Queen Adeliza to Simon, bishop of Worcester, and all her ministers and all clergy and laity of Berkeley Hernesse, of her gift in free alms to Reading Abbey of the churches of Berkeley Hernesse, viz., the church of Berkeley with the prebends appurtenant to it and the prebends of two nuns, and the churches of Cam, Arlingham, Wotton[-under-Edge], Beverston and Almondsbury, with chapels, lands and tithes*   [1147 × 50]

A f 16v; B ff 20v-21r
Pd. *Mon. Ang.*, iv. 42 (no. ix)

Adeleid(is) dei gratia regina Simoni eadem gratia Wigorn(iensi) episcopo et omnibus fidelibus suis ministris et omnibus clericis et laicis *a*tam Francis quam Angl(is)*a* de Berchelayhern(es),*b* salutem. Sciatis me concessisse et dedisse ecclesie de Rading(ia) et monachis ibidem deo servientibus in elemosina in perpetuum, pro anima domini mei regis Henrici et pro anima Godefridi ducis patris mei et matris mee et omnium parentum meorum et pro salute domini mei Willelmi comitis Cicestr(ie) et pro salute anime mee filiorumque[c] meorum omniumque fidelium vivorum et defunctorum, ecclesias de Berkel(ay)hernes,[d] scilicet ecclesiam de Berkel(ay) cum prebendis eidem ecclesie pertinentibus et prebendis duarum monialium, et ecclesiam de Chamma et ecclesiam de Elingeham[e] et ecclesiam de Wottona et ecclesiam de Beverstan et ecclesiam de Almodesbur(ia)[f] cum capellis et terris et decimis, tam de dominio quam de cuiuscumque tenemento, et cum omnibus rebus et consuetudinibus et libertatibus eisdem ecclesiis pertinentibus. Quare volo et firmiter precipio ut ea bene et in pace et honorifice et libere teneant. Testibus:[g] episcopo Hilario Cicestr(ensi), et magistro Edwardo canonico Cicestr(ensi), et Osberto capellano episcopi Wigorn(iensis), magistro Serlone, et multis aliis.

[a-a] tam Anglis quam Francis B		[b] Berkelayhern' B
[c] et filiorum B		[d] Berkel'hern' B
[e] Erlingeham B	[f] Almodesbir' B	[g] B ends

After the consecration of Hilary of Chichester, 3 Aug. 1147, and before the death of Simon, bishop of Worcester, 20 Mar. 1150. For the prebends and the nuns' prebends in Berkeley church, see Kemp, 'Berkeley Hernesse', 101–3.

269 Notification by William [d'Aubigny], earl of Chichester, to Theobald, archbishop of Canterbury, primate and legate, that he has given and conceded to Reading Abbey in free alms, by the hand of Simon, bishop of Worcester, the church of Berkeley with all churches of the demesne of Berkeley Hernesse, viz., the churches of Cam, Arlingham, Beverston, Wotton[-under-Edge] and Almondsbury, with appurtenances, chapels and tithes   [prob. 1147 × 50]

B f 200v; C ff 118v–119r
Pd. Saltman, *Theobald*, 442

Testibus: Francone capellano, et magistro Serlone, et cetera.

Probably a confirmation of, and contemporary with, the gift of his wife, Queen Adeliza (no. 268).

270 Notification by master Serlo to Simon, bishop of Worcester, that, with the assent of his lady Queen Adeliza, he has conceded in alms to Reading Abbey all the churches of Berkeley Hernesse, as the bishop gave them to him; and request that the bishop deliver to the abbey the church of Cam, which Gloucester Abbey has occupied against him, and the prebend of the church of Berkeley which Roger of Berkeley gave to Reginald son of Walter of Cam without the

bishop's or his assent after he had been seised of it, as Theobald
archbishop of Canterbury has ordered the bishop to do*

[1147 × 50; ? 1147 × 48]

B f 200v; C f 119r
Pd. Saltman, *Theobald*, 442

T(estibus): Aalid(e) regina, et cetera.

ᵃ C ends

In general, probably contemporary with no. 268, but, if of the same time as a letter
from Gilbert Foliot, abbot of Gloucester, to Abbot Edward of Reading referring to
the church of Cam and Reginald's prebend in the church of Berkeley (*Foliot Letters
and Charters*, 107), on which see Kemp, 'Berkeley Hernesse,' 105, before or not long
after Foliot's consecration as bishop of Hereford, 5 Sept. 1148.

270a Note of four charters concerning the churches of Berkeley
previously granted to master Serlo, viz., by Th(eobald) archbishop
of Canterbury, Simon bishop of Worcester, Empress Matilda, and
Queen Adeliza

B f 200v; (also note of Queen Adeliza's only) B f 21r
Pd. Saltman, *Theobald*, 441

271 *Gift in free alms by Simon, bishop of Worcester, to Reading Abbey, at
the request and assent of Queen Adeliza, of all the churches of Berkeley
Hernesse, viz., the churches of Berkeley, Cam, Arlingham, Wotton[-under-
Edge], Beverston and Almondsbury with all their appurtenances, and the
prebends formerly of two nuns in the church of Berkeley* [1147 × 50]

A f 53r-v; C ff 119v-120r

Simon humilis dei gratia Wigorn(iensis) ecclesie minister universis
sancte dei ecclesie fidelibus, salutem. Quoniam precedentium parit
oblivionem et temporum diuturnitas et memorie labentis infirmitas,
gesta nostri temporis tanquam litterarum manu porrigere posteritati
curavimus. Dignum itaque duximus notificari presentibus atque futuris clericis et laicis nos, assensu et petitione domine nostre Aelidis
regine, concessisse et in perpetuam elemosinam dedisse ecclesie de
Rading(ia) et monachis ibidem deo militantibus omnes ecclesias de
Berkeleiahernes,ᵃ videlicet ipsam ecclesiam de Berkel(eia) cum omnibus appendiciis suis, et ecclesiam de Chammaᵇ cum omnibus appendiciis suis, et ecclesiam de Erlingeham et ecclesiam de Wottona
cum omnibus ap[*f 53v*]pendiciis suis, et ecclesiam de Beverstan et
ecclesiam de Almodesburiaᶜ cum omnibus appendiciis suis, et insuper duas prebendas quas due moniales optinere solebant in predicta
ecclesia de Berkel(eia) cum omnibus consuetudinibus et pertinentiis

pretaxatis ecclesiis adiacentibus. Volumus igitur et auctoritate episcopali precipimus ut prenominata ecclesia de Rading(ia) prelibatas
ecclesias cum prebendis sanctimonialium bene et in pace et honorifice, salvo in omnibus episcopali iure et personarum canonice recep-
tarum, teneat*d* et inconcusse possideat.*e* Testibus: Hilario Ci-
cestr(ensi) episcopo, et Ricardo decano de Cicestr(ia), Warino
canonico de Arundel, et multis aliis.

a Berkeleihern' *C*   *b* Camma *C*
c Almodesburi *C*   *d* *A and C have* teneant *and* possideant
e *C ends*

Date as for no. 268.

272 Confirmation by King Stephen, addressed generally, of the
gift by Queen Adeliza to Reading Abbey of the churches of
Berkeley   [1147 × 50]

A f 19r; B f 30r; C f 6r
Pd. *Regesta*, iii. 256-7 (no. 695)

Testibus:*a* Roberto de Ver, et Willelmo Mart(el), et Rein(aldo) de
Warenn(a), et Gaufr(edo) de Ver. Apud Sanctum Edmundum.

a *B,C end*

Probably contemporary with no. 268.

273 Gift in free alms by Henry, duke of Normandy, to Reading
Abbey of the church of Berkeley, to be held as freely as the abbey
holds any gift of his grandfather, King Henry I
                                                      [1150 × 7 Sept. 1151]

A f 20r; B f 25r
Pd. *Regesta*, iii. 260 (no. 706)

Testibus:*a* Willelmo canc(ellario), Alexandro de Bohun*b* dapifero,
Willelmo de Crevecuer, Willelmo de Ansgervill(a). Apud Faleseiam.

a *B ends*
b *A has* Bohum

After Henry became duke of Normandy and before he succeded as count of Anjou.

274 Notification by Henry, duke of Normandy, to Theobald, archbishop of Canterbury and legate, that he has given to Reading
Abbey the church of Berkeley with all appurtenances; and request,
since he has heard that his gift displeases his farmer, Roger of Ber-

keley, that the archbishop should prevent him from disturbing the abbey, if the need should arise [1150 × 7 Sept. 1151]

A f 20r; B f 25r-v
Pd. *Regesta*, iii. 260-1 (no. 707); Saltman, *Theobald*, 442-3

T(este):*ª* Willelmo canc(ellario). Apud Falesiam.

ª B ends

Date as for no. 273. For discussion, see Kemp, *art. cit.*, 104.

275 Mandate and precept by Henry, duke of Normandy, to Roger of Berkeley to allow Reading Abbey to have in peace the church of Berkeley, which the Empress, his mother, and he have given to it [1150 × 7 Sept. 1151]

B f 200v; C f 118v
Pd. *Regesta*, iii. 261 (no. 708)

T(este): W(illelmo) canc(ellario).

Date as for no. 273.

276 Mandate and precept by Henry, duke of Normandy and Aquitaine and count of Anjou, to Abbot R(eginald) and the convent of Reading to abide by the agreement made in his presence regarding the church of Berkeley. Earl Reginald [of Cornwall], who acts for the duke in England, will assign to the abbey 25 librates of land promised from the duke's demesne, which the abbey shall accept without objection [Apr. x Dec. 1154]

A f 26r; B f 25v
Pd. *Regesta*, iii. 261 (no. 709); Richardson and Sayles, *Governance of Med. Eng.*, 256 n. 2; (transl.) *ibid.*, 256

Testibus:*ª* Reginaldo comite Cornubie, et Roberto de Dunstanvill(a). Apud Augum.

ª B ends

While Henry was duke of Aquitaine and in Normandy; he left Barfleur for England 7 Dec. 1154 (Eyton, 1). The agreement did not take effect and the abbey did not receive the 25 librates of land.

277 *Notification by Robert [Foliot], bishop of Hereford, and Simon, abbot of St Albans, judges-delegate of Pope Alexander III, of the settlement before them of the action brought by Reading Abbey against Bristol Abbey concerning the churches of Berkeley Hernesse. Bristol shall hold the churches in the name of Reading and shall pay Reading 20 marks annually, and the two abbeys* *shall co-operate in recovering from Gloucester Abbey what has been withheld from the same,[1] and shall share equally between them the acquisitions they may secure. King Henry II shall so provide that, while Henry archdeacon of Exeter[2] is alive, Reading Abbey shall receive the 20 marks without difficulty*

18 Oct. 1175

A ff 53v-54r; C f 119r

Robertus dei gratia Herfordensis[a] episcopus et Simon abbas Sancti Albani universis sancte matris ecclesie[b] filiis presentibus et futuris, salutem. Ad publicam notitiam volumus devenire quod, cum dominus papa Alexander tertius causam quam abbas et monachi Rading(enses) abbati et canonicis sancti Augustini de Brist(olda)[c] super ecclesiis de Berkel'hernesse[d] movebant nobis cognoscendam commisisset et fine debito terminandam, partibus in nostra presentia constitutis, domino rege Henrico .ii. ad pacem studiosius operam dante, inter ipsos sub hac pacis forma convenit. Videlicet quod iamdicti canonici prescriptas ecclesias de Berkel'hernes,[d] cum universis ad eas pertinentibus que ipsi canonici tempore inite transactionis vel aliquis eorum nomine possidebat, perpetuo nomine monachorum Rading(ensium)[e] possidebunt, solvendo monachis pro illis ecclesiis annuas .xx. marcas in perpetuum, .x. ad Pascha et .x. ad festum sancti Michaelis. Cum autem de assensu utriusque partis fuerit ut ea que a monachis Gloecestrie vel a quibuslibet aliis detinentur, sive ecclesie sint sive alia beneficia de Berkel'hernes,[d] mediante iustitia revocentur, ad eorum revocationem sumptus pro equis portionibus debebunt ab utraque partium ministrari. Et quicquid per sententiam evincere vel pace interveniente recuperare poterunt[f] in usus communes tam monachorum quam canonicorum pro mediis portionibus cedet. Ad hec sciendum quod dominus rex predictus de solutione iamdictarum .xx. marcarum quoad Henricus Exoniensis archidiaconus vixerit ita provisurus est quod et monachi Rading(enses) eas a canonicis prenominatis annis singulis sine difficultate percipient [*f 54r*] et canonicorum indempnitati providebitur. Celebrata autem fuit hec transactio anno dominice incarnationis M.C.lxxv, die festo sancti Luce evangeliste, apud Londoniam. His testibus: Henrico .ii. rege Anglorum, Ricardo Cant(uariensi) archiepiscopo, Gisleberto Lond(oniensi) episcopo, Ricardo episcopo Wint(oniensi),[g] [Roberto episcopo Herf(ordensi), Bartholomeo episcopo Exon(iensi), Gaufr(edo) episcopo Elyensi, Symone abbate Sancti Albani, et cetera].

---

[a] Heref' C
[b] Om. in C
[c] Bristoll' C
[d] Berkeleihern' C
[e] Radyngie C
[f] potuerint C
[g] *A ends with* et multis aliis, *the remainder being supplied from C*

On this law-suit and that over the church of Cam (no. 284), see Kemp, 'Berkeley Hernesse', 107–8; also Richardson and Sayles, *Governance of Med. Eng.*, 316–17; H. Mayr-Harting, 'Henry II and the Papacy, 1170–1189', *JEH*, xvi (1965), 41–2.

¹ Mainly the church of Cam and the third prebend of Berkeley (Kemp, 'Berkeley Hernesse', 107–8).

² Son of Robert fitz Harding, who gave him the churches of Berkeley in *c.* 1153 when he was serving as Duke Henry's treasurer (*ibid.*, 101); he later became archdeacon of Exeter (Morey, *Bartholomew of Exeter*, 119–20).

278 *Confirmation by Richard [of Dover], archbishop of Canterbury, primate and legate, of the preceding*   [*c.* 18 Oct.] 1175

A ff 50v-51r; C f 119v

Ricardus dei gratia Cant(uariensis) archiepiscopus totius Anglie primas et apostolice sedis legatus universis Christi fidelibus, salutem. Causa que inter monachos de*ª* Rading(ia) et canonicos de Bristold'*ᵇ* ad Sanctum Augustinum apostolica fuit auctoritate venerabili fratri nostro R(oberto) Herford(ensi)*ᶜ* episcopo et dilecto filio S(imoni) abbati Sancti Albani commissa, eisdem fratribus assidentibus sub presentia domini regis Henrici secundi et nostra et aliorum quamplurium religiosorum virorum, sub hac transactionis forma conquievit. Videlicet quod iamdicti canonici Sancti Augustini de Bristold'*ᵇ* ecclesias de Berkelaihernesse,*ᵈ* cum universis ad eas pertinentibus que ipsi canonici tempore inite transactionis vel aliquis eorum nomine possidebat, nomine monachorum de Rading(ia) perpetuo possidebunt, solvendo monachis pro ipsis ecclesiis annuas .xx. marcas in perpetuum, .x. ad Pascha et .x. ad festum sancti Michaelis. Cum autem de assensu utriusque partis fuerit ut ea que a monachis de*ª* Gloec(estria) vel aliis, sive ecclesie sint sive alia beneficia de Berkelaihernesse,*ᵈ* mediante iustitia revocentur, ad eorum revocationem sumptus pro equis portionibus debebunt ab utraque partium ministrari. Et quicquid per sententiam evincere vel pace interveniente potuerint revocare, in usus communes tam monachorum quam canonicorum pro mediis portionibus cedet. Ad hec sciendum quod memoratus dominus rex de solutione iamdictarum .xx. marcarum quoad Henricus Exoniensis archidiaconus vixerit ita provisurus est quod et monachi de Rading(ia) singulis annis*ª* a prenominatis canonicis*ᵉ* sine difficultate eas percipient et canonicorum indempnitati providebitur. Hec autem transactio facta fuit anno *ᶠ*dominice incarnationis*ᶠ* M.C.lxxv. Sicut igitur a predictis fratribus [*f 51r*] nostris Herfordensi*ᵍ* episcopo et abbate Sancti Albani apostolica auctoritate qua fungebantur et scripto eorum auctentico*ʰ* quod oculis nostris perspeximus eadem transactio fuit confirmata, sicut etiam in presentia nostra eam fuisse factam recolimus, auctoritate qua fungimur eam communimus et corroboramus quatinus, tantorum testimoniorum vallata presidiis, nullis in posterum possit perversionibus perturbari.*Testibus: magistro Gerardo, domino* Roberto de Novo Burgo, Walerano archidiacono Baioc(ensi), Amico archidiacono Rothom(agensi), et aliis multis.

a Om. in C	*b Bristoll' C*
c Hereford' C	*d Berkeleihern' C*
e A repeats here singulis annis	*f-f domini C*
d Heref' E	*h autentico C*
i C ends	*j A has domno*

Probably soon after no. 277, but, since the archbishop says *eam fuisse factam recolimus*, not on the same day. A late medieval marginal note in A reads: *nota istam cartam*.

279   *Confirmation by King Henry II of the same settlement*
[*c.* 18 Oct. 1175]

A ff 23v-24r; B f 25v; Berkeley Castle Muniments, Bristol cartulary f 19r (not fully collated)

Henricus*a* rex Anglie *b*et dux Norm(annie) et Aquit(anie) et comes Andeg(avie) archiepiscopis, episcopis, abbatibus, comitibus, baronibus, iustic(iariis), vicecomitibus et omnibus ministris et fidelibus suis Francis et Anglis totius Anglie, salutem.*b* Sciatis me concessisse et presenti carta confirmasse conventionem et concordiam que rationabiliter facta fuit, coram me et iudicibus delegatis R(oberto) episcopo Herford(ensi)*c* et Simone Sancti*d* Albani abbate et pluribus aliis personis qui*e* aderant, inter monachos de Rading(ia) et canonicos Sancti Augustini de Brist(olda) de ecclesiis de Berkelaihernesse.*f* Hanc scilicet quod canonici Sancti Augustini de Brist(olda) perpetuo possidebunt nomine monachorum de Rading(ia) ecclesias de Berkel(ai)hern(esse),*g* cum omnibus ad eas pertinentibus que ipsi canonici vel aliquis eorum nomine possidebat die qua inter eos concordia facta fuit de illis*h* ecclesiis, solvendo monachis annuatim pro illis ecclesiis .xx. marcas, .x. ad Pascha et .x. ad festum sancti Michaelis. Si autem ecclesias vel alia ecclesiastica bona ad Berkelaih(ernesse)*g* pertinentia monachi et canonici predicti perquirere potuerint, equalibus expensis adquirere debebunt et inter se equaliter partiri. Quare volo et firmiter precipio quod hec conventio et concordia firmiter et inconcusse inter eos teneatur sicut coram me et personis qui*e* aderant facta fuit et utrobique concessa et sicut carte quas inde habent testantur. Testibus:*i* R(icardo) Cant(uariensi) [*f 24r*] archiepiscopo, G(ileberto) London(iensi), R(icardo) Vint(oniensi), G(aufredo) Heliensi, B(artholomeo) Exon(iensi), Iohanne Norwic(ensi), R(oberto) Herford(ensi) episcopis, Simone abbate Sancti Albani, comite Willelmo de Mand(avilla), Ricardo de Luci, Willelmo filio Audel(ini)*j* dapifero,*k* Reginaldo de Curtenai, Thoma Basset, Willelmo de

Stut(evilla), Hugone de Creissi, et Roberto filio Bernardi, et Thoma
fratre suo. Apud Westmonasterium.

<table>
<tr><td>^a Insert dei gratia B, Bristol cart.</td><td>^{b-b} et cetera B</td></tr>
<tr><td>^c Heref B</td><td>^d Interlined in A</td></tr>
<tr><td>^e que B, Brist. cart.</td><td>^f Berkeleihern' B</td></tr>
<tr><td>^g Berkel'hern' B</td><td>^h eisdem B, Brist. cart.</td></tr>
<tr><td>ⁱ B, Brist. cart. end</td><td>^j A has Andel'</td></tr>
<tr><td>^k A has dapiferi</td><td></td></tr>
</table>

On or near the date of no. 277.

280 *Notification by Abbot Richard [of Warwick] and the convent of Bristol
of the same settlement between themselves and Reading Abbey, listing the
churches of Berkeley Hernesse as Berkeley, Wotton[-under-Edge], Beverston,
Almondsbury, Ashleworth and Cromhall, and naming as the alienated parts of
the spiritualities the churches of Cam and Arlingham, but without reference to
Gloucester Abbey's involvement*   18 Oct. 1175

A ff 47v-48r

Ricardus dictus abbas Sancti Augustini Bristold(e) totusque eiusdem
loci conventus universis sancte ecclesie filiis, salutem. Ad publicam
volumus notitiam devenire quod causa que inter monachos de Rad-
ing(ia) et nos super ecclesia de Berkelaia aliquandiu ventilata est
coram domino Roberto Herford(ensi) episcopo et domino*a* Simone
abbate Sancti Albani, qui in eadem causa a domino*a* papa Alexandro .iii. iudices fuerant delegati, presente domino rege H(enrico) .ii.
et ad pacem plurimum operam dante, sub apostolica auctoritate
qua in his dicti iudices fungebantur tali compositione mediante terminata est. Videlicet quod nos ecclesias de Berkel(eia)hernesse,*b* scilicet ecclesiam de Berkel(eia) et de Wttuna et de Beverstana et de
Almodesb(er)ia et de Esseleswrd(a) et de Cromhala singulas cum
suis pertinentiis, nomine monachorum de [f 48r] Rading(ia) perpetuo possidebimus solvendo annuatim ecclesie Rading(ensi) .xx. marcas, .x. ad Pascha et .x. ad festum sancti Michaelis. Si vero alia que
ab aliis quacumque iniuria detinentur, nominatim ecclesiam de
Chamma et ecclesiam de Erlingeham aut quecumque alia ecclesiastica bona ad ecclesias de Berkel(eia)hernesse*b* pertinentia, predictis
monachis et nobis de communi consilio revocare placuerit, ad hoc
ab illis et a nobis sumptus ex equo dabuntur et quecumque assequi
potuerimus inter nos et illos equis portionibus dividentur. Dominus
etiam rex predictus pro desiderio pacis id adiecit se ita provisurum
quod, quamdiu tenuerit H(enricus) Exon(iensis) archidiaconus, et
monachi suam a nobis annuatim percipient pensionem et nos tamen
indempnes existemus. Celebrata est autem hec transactio anno
incarnationis dominice M.C.lxxv,*c* die sancti Luce, apud

Lond(oniam), papante domino Alexandro*d* .iii., regnante H(enrico)
.ii. His testibus: Ricardo Cant(uariensi) archiepiscopo, Gileberto
Lond(oniensi) episcopo, Ricardo Wint(oniensi) episcopo, Roberto
Herford(ensi)   episcopo,   Bartholomeo   Exon(iensi)   episcopo,
Gaufr(edo) Elyensi episcopo, Simone abbate Sancti Albani, Mauri-
cio de Berkel(eia), Roberto et Ricardo filiis eius.

a Ms domno
b Expansion from rubric in Ms
c Ms M.C.Lxxxv; the correct date is given in Bristol cartulary (see note)
d Ms Aex'

The complementary act by Abbot Joseph and the convent of Reading, in the same
terms and with the same witnesses, is Bristol cartulary (Berkeley Castle Muniments)
f 64v.

281   Confirmation by Pope Alexander III, addressed to the abbot
and convent of Reading, of the settlement between Reading and
Bristol abbeys over the church of Berkeley and its appurtenances,
made by the judges–delegate, the bishop of Hereford and the abbot
of St Albans   [Oct. 1175 × Aug. 1181]

A ff 69v-70r
Pd. Holtzmann, *Papsturkunden*, iii. 434 (no. 319)

After the settlement and before the pope's death.

282   Confirmation by Pope Alexander III of the assignment by
Abbot Joseph of Reading to the monks of Reading, for their victuals,
of the payment which the church of Berkeley makes annually to the
abbey   [Oct. 1175 × Aug. 1181]

A f 70r
Pd. Holtzmann, *Papsturkunden*, iii. 405-6 (no. 279)

Rubric: Item carta eiusdem de confirmatione viginti marcarum ad
coquinam fratrum Rading' de eadem ecclesia

The rubric places it beyond doubt that the payment concerned was the 20 marks
provided for in the 1175 settlement. Date therefore as for no. 281.

283   *Request and mandate by King Henry II to Bartholomew, bishop of
Exeter, and John [of Greenford], bishop of Chichester, to uphold the right of
the king and of Reading Abbey in its dispute with Gloucester Abbey over the
church of Cam, which Gloucester holds presumptuously by gift of Roger of
Berkeley, since the church is of the king's gift and Roger had no right in it
other than as farmer of the fee*   [May 1175 × July 1177]

A f 103r

H(enricus) dei gratia rex Angl(ie), dominus Hybernie, dux Norm(annie) et Aquit(anie) et comes Andeg(avie) dilectis episcopis et patribus B(artholomeo) Exon(iensi) et I(ohanni) Cicestr(ensi), salutem. Pro abbatia de Rading(ia) et monachis ibidem deo servientibus preces porrigo vobis affectuosas, rogans attentius quatinus intuitu caritatis et pro dilectione et prece mea loco mei sitis et promotioni sue intendatis in causa que vertitur inter eos et monachos Gloec(estrenses) de ecclesia de Camma, quia pro certo habeatis quod ecclesia illa de iure meo et de donatione mea est et Rog(erus) de Berkel(eia) nichil iuris in ea habuit nisi qualem firmarius habere potest. Ipse enim firmarius meus erat de feudo illo in quo ecclesia ipsa fundata est. Quapropter mando vobis ut ius meum in ea observetis et promotioni cause sue tam diligentem operam adhibeatis quod et ego et ipsi ius nostrum de ipsa adipiscamur, cum ipsi monachi Gloc(estrenses) presumptuose eam ipsis detineant per concessionem prefati Rogeri eis inde iniuriose et irrationabiliter factam. Tantum itaque eis inde faciatis quod sentiant et gratulentur preces meas erga vos sibi profuisse, ut tenear inde vobis uberrimas grates referre, et libentius in negotiis et petitionibus vestris vos exaudire. Teste me ipso apud Merleb(ergam).

As it stands this document is suspicious in two respects. Both the inclusion of 'Lord of Ireland' in the king's style and the form of the attestation clause (*Teste me ipso*) are extremely unlikely for Henry II, though standard for Henry III (on *Teste me ipso*, see Tout, *Chapters*, i. 135-6 n. 3), but, on the other hand, the bishops are unquestionably those who acted as papal judges-delegate in the dispute over the church of Cam in 1177 (see no. 287). The document appears only in A, where it was entered not among other acts of Henry II in the original compilation of the cartulary, but among additions of Henry III's reign. It seems unlikely to be a complete forgery, however, since there is no obvious reason why it should have been fabricated in the 13th century when the abbey's position in the church of Cam was sufficiently fortified by other deeds, and, in view of the consistent use of first person singular, it is better regarded as, at worst, a modified version of a genuine original, the text of which may only have reached the abbey in the 13th century without the king's full title and attestation clause. It dates after the king's return to England following the consecration of John of Greenford as bishop of Chichester (6 Oct. 1174), and before the final *actum* of the judges-delegate in the case (28 July 1177).

284 *Record of the settlement before King Henry II of the dispute between the abbeys of Reading and Gloucester over the church of Cam, namely, that Gloucester shall pay annually to Reading a pension of 6 marks from the church, half of which will be handed over by Reading to Bristol Abbey, and Reading shall assist Gloucester in the recovery of alienated appurtenances of the church* [prob. mid-June] 1177

B 172r; C f 102r-v

Ex subscriptis innotescat quod controversia que inter monachos
Rading(enses) et monachos Glouc(estrie)[a] super ecclesia de Camma
vertebatur in presentia domini regis Henrici secundi compositionis
fine ita conquievit, ut, videlicet, monachi Glouc(estrie)[a] monachis
Rading(ensibus) de ecclesia prenominata .vi. marcas annuatim in
pensionem persolvant, tres ad festum sancti Michaelis et tres ad
Pascha, in perpetuum possidentes ecclesiam predictam cum omnibus
pertinentiis suis. Id etiam compositionis tenori adiectum est ut, ad
prescripte ecclesie pertinentias revocandas que ei subtracte sunt aut
a quibuscumque detente, monachis Glouc(estrie)[a] Rading(enses)
monachi consilium et auxilium caritative et[b] socialiter impendant.
Pensionis vero prescripte[c] partem mediam ad terminos predictos
canonici Sancti Augustini de Brist(olda)[d] per manum[e] monachorum
Rading(ensium) annuatim percipient, iuxta tenorem rescripti quod
de ecclesiis de Berkeleihern(esse) in aliis inter eos constitutum est.
Huius rei testes sunt: dominus rex Henricus .ii., et cetera. Act(um)
apud Wdestok(am)[f] anno domini M.C.lxxvii.

[a] Gloucestrie C	[b] Om. in C
[c] Interlined in B	[d] Bristol' C
[e] manus C	[f] Wodestok' C

In 1177 and before no. 287, during which time the king was at Woodstock c. 14–18
June (Eyton, 216).

285 *Confirmation by King Henry II of the settlement before Bartholomew,*
bishop of Exeter, and John [of Greenford], bishop of Chichester, judges-
delegate of Pope Alexander III, of the dispute between the abbeys of Reading
and Gloucester, with Bristol Abbey assisting Reading, over the church of Cam.
Gloucester shall hold the church of the king in chief and pay Reading 6 marks
of silver annually, half of which Reading shall hand over to Bristol. Reading,
with the assistance of Bristol, shall advise and aid Gloucester in the recovery
of alienated appurtenances of the said church   [prob. mid-June, 1177]

Original charter: BL Add. Ch. 19606 (damaged)
A f 24r; B ff 24v–25r
Pd. *Arch. Journ.*, xx. 295; *Trans. Royal Soc. Lit.*, 2nd ser., xi. 328–9; (cal.) Hurry,
    Reading Abbey, 169–70

[Henricus][a] dei gratia rex Angl(orum) [b]et dux Norm(annorum) et
Aquit(anorum) et comes And(egavorum) archiepiscopis, episcopis,
ab[batibus],[a] comitibus, baronibus, iustic(iariis), vicecomitibus,
ministris et omnibus fidelibus suis Francis et Angl(is) totius Anglie,
[salutem].[a] [b]Sciatis me concessisse et presenti carta mea confirmasse
pacem et finem factum coram B(artholomeo) et I(ohanne)
Exon(iensi) et Cicestr(ensi) episcopis inter monasterium et monachos
de Rading(ia) et monasterium et monachos Gloec(estrie) de con-

troversia et lite que assistentibus canonicis Sancti Augustini de Bris-
tow(a)^c et aliis competitoribus monachorum de Rading(ia) vertebatur inter eadem monasteria et eosdem monachos de ecclesia de
Camma^d et omnibus eius pertinentiis. Videlicet quod, assensu meo
et predictorum episcoporum qui ex mandato domini pape Alexandri
tertii in controversia illa fuerant iudices delegati, inter predicta monasteria et monachos in eis deo servientes ita convenit quod monasterium Gloec(estrie), pro bono pacis et nomine transactionis pro
memorata controversia et querela perpetuo terminanda, solvet annuatim monasterio de Rading(ia) sex [marcas]^a argenti, tres ad
Pascha et tres ad festum sancti Michaelis, quarum medietatem
perci[pient]^a ca[nonici]^a [Sanc]ti^a Augustini de Bristowa^c per
manus monachorum de Rading(ia). Tenebit autem^e mo[nasterium
Gloecestrie]^a predictam ecclesiam de Camma cum omnibus pertinentiis suis de me in capite sicut propriam elemosinam meam, salva
monachis de Rading(ia) predicta sex marcarum solutione a monasterio Gloec(estrie) facienda, ita quod et monachi de Rading(ia) sex
illas marcas tanquam propriam elemosinam meam perpetuo percipiant et possideant. Id etiam compositionis tenori adiectum est ut,
ad prenominate ecclesie de Camma pertinentias revocandas que ei
subtracte sunt aut a quibuscumque detente, monachi de Rading(ia)
coadiuvantibus^f canonicis Sancti Augustini consilium et auxilium
monachis Gloec(estrie) karitative^g et sociali[ter impen]^{a}dant. Debent etiam monachi Gloec(estrie) predictorum canonicorum Sancti
Augustini de Bristow(a)^h super m[emo]^{a}rata compositione quantum
in eis est fideliter firmiterque servanda cartam confirmationis [ha-
bere].^{a} Quare volo et firmiter precipio quod hec pax et concordia et
finis factus inter supradicta m[onasteria]^a et monachos de prefata
ecclesia de Camma et omnibus pertinentiis suis stabilis sit et incon-
[cusse teneat]ur.^{a} Testibus:^{i} comite Willelmo de Mann(avilla),^{j}
Roberto comite Legr(ecestrie), Fulcone Paienell(o),^{k} Rogero de
St[utevilla, Ro]^{a}berto [de]^a Stut(evilla), Willelmo [de]^a Stut(evilla),
Gaufr(edo) Pertic', Willelmo filio Ald(elini) dapifero. Apud [Wod-
est(ocam)].^{a}

Endorsed: Carta regis H. secundi de pace et fine inter monachos
Rading' et monachos Gloecestrie super ecclesia de Chamma et
eius pertinentiis [*12th cent.*]
Size: 162 × 220 mm
Seal: fragment of great seal in light brown wax on plaited green and
red cords

^{a} *Original charter damaged, supplied from A* $^{b-b}$ et cetera *B*
^{c} Bristold' *A*, Brist' *B* ^{d} Chamma *A*
^{e} *Insert* predictum *A* ^{f} coadivantibus *A*
^{g} caritative *B* ^{h} Brist' *A,B*

i B ends   *j* Mand' *A*
k Painell' *A*

Date as for no. 284. This charter raises a difficulty, for, although it states that the
settlement was reached before the judges–delegate, there is no other indication that
they were present at Woodstock and they issued no other document relating to the
case (at least, none has survived) apart from their confirmation of the settlement
given at Wilton just over a month later (no. 287).

286 *Notification by Abbot Hamelin and the convent of Gloucester of the
same settlement over the church of Cam*   [*c.* mid-June] 1177

A f 48r-v; C f 120r-v

Hamelinus dei gratia dictus abbas Gloecestr(ie)*a* et illius loci conventus universis sancte matris ecclesie fidelibus, salutem in domino.
Notum sit universitati vestre quod, cum inter monasterium Radingense et nostrum, canonicis Sancti Augustini de Bristold(a)*b* assistentibus et competitoribus monachorum Radingensium, controversia
verteretur super ecclesia de Camma et omnibus pertinentiis eius,
amicis intervenientibus et illustris regis H(enrici) .ii. auctoritate et
assensu, necnon et Bartholomei Exoniensis et Iohannis Cicestrensis
episcoporum, qui ex mandato domini Alexandri pape .iii. in ea
fuerant iudices delegati, sub hac pacis forma tandem lis tota in
perpetuum sopita est. Monasterium nostrum, pro bono pacis et nomine transactionis pro memorata querela perpetuo terminanda, solvet
annuatim monasterio Rading(ensi) .vi. marcas argenti, tres ad Pascha et tres ad festum sancti Michaelis, quarum medietatem percipient canonici Sancti Augustini de Bristold(a)*b* per manus monachorum Radingensium. Tenebit autem monasterium nostrum
predictam ecclesiam de Camma cum omnibus pertinentiis suis de
rege in capite sicuti propriam ipsius elemosinam, salva monachis
Radingensibus predicta .vi. marcarum solutione a monasterio nostro
facienda, ita ut et monachi Rading(enses) sex illas marcas tanquam
propriam domini regis elemosinam perpetuo percipiant et possideant. Id etiam compositionis tenori adiectum est ut, [ad]*c* prescripte ecclesie pertinentias revocandas que ei subtracte sunt aut a
quibuscumque detente, Radingenses*d* monachi, coadiuvantibus canonicis Sancti Augustini, nobis consilium et auxilium karitative*e* et
socialiter impendant. Debemus etiam nos eorundem canonicorum
super memorata compositione quantum in eis est fideliter firmiterque servanda cartam confirmationis habere. Acta sunt hec*f* apud
Wudestokam in presentia domini nostri regis Henrici secundi, anno
ab incarnatione domini M.C.lxxvii.*g h* His testibus: domino nostro
rege Henrico secundo, Hugone abbate de Mucheleneia, Widone
Extraneo tunc vicecomite Salopesb(erie), Willelmo filio Rad(ulfi)

tunc vicecomite de Notingeham. Hii[i] interfuerunt et assensum pre-
buerunt: Willelmus tunc prior, Willelmus tunc cam(erarius) Sancti
Augustini [f 48v] de Bristold(a), Edwardus tunc prior, Rog(erus)
tunc cam(erarius), Reginaldus tunc baiulus abbatis Rading(ensis),
Willelmus de Sancto Oswaldo, Alexander tunc prior Stanleie, et
Alexander tunc baiulus abbatis Gloecestrie.

[a] Glouc' C	[b] Bristoll' C
[c] Om. in A, supplied from C	[d] Radyngie C
[e] caritative C	[f] Interlined in A, om. in C
[g] M.C.lxxv C	[h] C ends
[i] A has His	

The form of the attestation clauses leaves some doubt as to whether this was actually
given at Woodstock, but it must in any case be of nearly the same date as nos. 284–
5. It is to be noted that this notification does not explicitly state that the judges-
delegate were present at Woodstock, although the king clearly was (see no. 285 n.).

287 Notification by Bartholomew, bishop of Exeter, and John [of
Greenford], bishop of Chichester, judges–delegate of Pope Alexander
III, that the dispute over the church of Cam between the abbeys of
Reading and Gloucester, with Bristol Abbey assisting Reading, has
been settled [details of the settlement as in no. 285]. This settlement
was reached in the presence of King Henry II at Woodstock and is
now confirmed by the judges–delegate at Wilton   28 July 1177

A f 54r; C f 120r; C f 154r
Pd. Morey, *Bartholomew of Exeter*, 140–1; Mayr-Harting, *Acta of Chichester*, 128–9

Hanc etiam nostre confirmationis paginam super prescripta compositione in presentia domini nostri illustris regis H(enrici) secundi
apud Wodestoc(am)[a] facta, anno ab incarnatione domini
M.C.lxxvii,[b] v. kl' Augusti apud Wilt(onam)[c] indulsimus. His testibus:[d] Reg(inaldo) Bat(honiensi) episcopo, Henrico abbate de Wav-
erl(eia), Baldewino abbate Fordensi,[e][f] [Stephano priore Sancte
Trinitatis que est Lond(onie), Iohanne priore de Ferle, Sefredo decano Cicestr(ensi), Waltero precentore Sar(esburiensi), Symone archidiacono Wygorn(iensi), Rog(ero) archidiacono de Berdestapel',
Ricardo Lupello, Roberto priore de Kenildeworth', magistro Thoma
de Husleburne, magistro Vincentio, Petro et Gaufr(edo) clericis
domini Exon(iensis), Edmundo et Ph(ilipp)o de Lond(onia) clericis
domini Cicestr(ensis)].

[a] Wodestok' C f 120r; Wodestoke C f 154r
[b] M.C.lxxv C f 120r
[c] Wiltone C f 120r; Wilton' C f 154r
[d] C f 120r ends
[e] Forde C f 154r
[f] A ends with et multis aliis, the remainder being supplied from C f 154r

The witness-list printed here is much longer than those printed by Morey and Mayr-Harting, each of whom takes his text only from A. This confirmation, and especially the sentence immediately preceding the attestation clause, supports the view that the judges–delegate had not been present when the settlement was reached before the king at Woodstock, probably in mid-June, despite the wording of no. 285. The king was not still at Woodstock at the time of this confirmation, but at Winchester (Eyton, 218). It seems likely, then, that the judges–delegate did no more than confirm the settlement, in which no doubt their advice and authority were heeded, and that my earlier account of this case (Kemp, 'Berkeley Hernesse', 107) needs correcting in this respect.

288 Confirmation by Pope Alexander III, addressed to the abbot and monks of Reading, of the settlement between Reading and Gloucester abbeys over the church of Cam made by the judges–delegate, the bishop of Hereford and the abbot of St Albans

[July, 1177 × Aug. 1181]

A f 71r

Pd. Holtzmann, *Papsturkunden*, iii. 431 (no. 314)

After the settlement and before the pope's death. The text wrongly names as the judges–delegate those who in fact acted in the 1175 settlement between Reading and Bristol over the churches of Berkeley Hernesse (no. 277), but there can be no doubt that the bishops of Exeter and Chichester are intended.

289 *Notification by Abbot John and the convent of Bristol that they have assumed Gloucester Abbey's obligation to pay annually to Reading Abbey 6 marks from the church of Cam, in accordance with the agreement before William [de Vere], bishop of Hereford, Richard, abbot of Cirencester, and Geoffrey [of Henlawe], prior of Llanthony, judges–delegate of Pope Clement III in the dispute between the three abbeys over the third prebend of Berkeley. However, during the life-time of Walter, dean of Cam, Bristol shall pay Reading 3 marks only, and after his death 6 marks*   [c. 1189 × 91]

A f 92r; C f 120v

Omnibus Christi fidelibus ad quos presens scriptum pervenerit Iohannes dei gratia abbas Sancti Augustini de Bristollo*ᵃ* et totus eiusdem loci conventus, eternam in domino salutem. Noverit universitas vestra nos obligationem .vi. marcarum quas monachi de Gloecestr(ia)*ᵇ* 'monachis de Rading(ia)*ᶜ* annuatim de ecclesia de Camma persolvebant in nosmet ipsos suscepisse. Et pro memoratis monachis de Gloecest(ria)*ᵈ* predictis monachis de Rading(ia), prout in amicabili compositione in scripturam redacta super tertia prebenda de Berchelai,*ᵉ* coram venerabili*ᶠ* W(illelmo) dei gratia Hereford(ensi) episcopo et R(icardo) eadem gratia abbate Cirencest(rensi) et G(alfredo) priore de Lanton(ia) confecta, quibus cause ventilatio que vertebatur inter H(ugonem) dei gratia abbatem et monachos de Rading(ia) et T(homam) eadem gratia abbatem et monachos *g*de Gloecest(ria)*g* et nos super tertia prebenda de Berchelai*h* autoritate domini pape Clementis tertii fuerat commissa, nos predictarum .vi. marcarum quantitatem soluturos constituisse. Ita scilicet ut in vita Walteri decani de Camma .iii. tantummodo marcas nomine monachorum de Gloecest(ria)*d* monachis de Rading(ia) annuatim ad Pascha persolvamus. Post decessum vero prefati W(alteri) de .iii. marcis residuis prenominatis monachis de Rading(ia) nomine monachorum de Gloecest(ria)*i* annuatim ad festum sancti Michaelis respondebimus. Et ut hec obligatio perpetue firmitatis robur optineat et in recidive dubitationis scrupulum nequeat devenire, presentis scripti munimine et sigilli nostri*j* appositione corroboravimus.

a Bristoll' *C*	*b* Gloucestria *C*
c-c Om. in *C*	*d* Glouc' *C*
e Berkeleia *C*	*f* venerabilibus *C*
g-g Gloucestrie *C*	*h* Berkel'*C*
i Gloucestr' *C*	*j* mei *C* (in error)

Either during the pontificate of Clement III, 20 Dec. 1187– late Mar. 1191, or not long after his death; possibly not earlier than 1189, when Geoffrey of Henlawe may have become prior of Llanthony (*Heads of Relig. Houses*, 172). The act was not included in the original compilation of A. For discussion, see Kemp, 'Berkeley Hernesse', 108–9.

290 *Remission by Abbot Hugh [II] and the convent of Reading to Gloucester Abbey of the annual pension of 6 marks due from the church of Cam, in accordance with the agreement before the judges–delegate [as in no. 289] in the dispute between the abbeys of Gloucester and Bristol over the third prebend of Berkeley, so that, during the life-time of [Walter] of Cam, Gloucester and Bristol shall each pay 3 marks annually to Reading, and after Walter's death Bristol shall pay the full 6 marks annually* [*c.* 1189 × 91]

C f 154v

Universis sancte matris ecclesie filiis ad quos presens scriptum pervenerit H(ugo) dei gratia abbas Radyng(ensis) et eiusdem loci conventus, salutem in eo qui est salus omnium. Ad universitatis vestre volumus notitiam pervenire nos pensionem sex marcarum quas monachi Gloucestr(ie) nobis annuatim nomine ecclesie de Camme persolvere tenebantur predictis monachis Glouc(estrie), prout in amicabili compositione super tertia prebenda de Berkeleya inter Thomam et Iohannem eadem gratia de Glouc(estria) et de Bristoll' abbates et eorundem locorum*a* conventus coram venerabilibus W(illelmo) dei gratia Herefordensi episcopo et Ricardo eadem gratia abbate de Cirencestr(ia) et Gaufrido priore de Lanton(ia),*b* quibus cause ventilatio a domino papa Clemente tertio super predicta

prebenda de Berkeleya fuerat commissa, confecta continetur, in perpetuum remisisse. Ita scilicet ut in vita [Walteri][c] de Camme monachi de Glouc(estria) tres tantummodo marcas de predicta pensione
nobis annuatim ad festum sancti Michaelis persolvant; canonici vero
de Bristoll' de tribus marcis residuis vivente predicto Waltero ad
Pascha nobis annuatim respondebunt. Post decessum vero Walteri
idem canonici de Bristoll' pro predictis monachis de Glouc(estria)
integras sex marcas predictas nobis annuatim se soluturos constituerunt, tres videlicet ad festum sancti Michaelis et tres ad Pascha, et
inde nobis cartam suam fecerunt. Quod ratum habentes et gratum
predictos monachos Glouc(estrie) super hac liberatione et immunitate scripto auctentico sigilli nostri appositione corroborato[d] dignum
duximus communiendos. Hiis testibus: magistris Willelmo et Daniele
de Radyng(ia), et aliis.

<table>
<tr><td>[a] locorum repeated</td><td>[b] Ms Lonton'</td></tr>
<tr><td>[c] Om. in Ms</td><td>[d] cor of corroborato interlined in Ms</td></tr>
</table>

Date as for no. 289.

291 *Concession by Abbot Simon and the convent of Reading to Bristol Abbey*
of the churches of Berkeley Hernesse, viz., the churches of Berkeley,
Wotton[-under-Edge], Almondsbury and Ashleworth, to be held in the name
of Reading Abbey for an annual payment of 20 marks. Concerning the pension
from the church of Beverston, about which there has been conflict between the
two abbeys, Bristol shall pay Reading 2 marks of the 5 marks which it receives
annually from that church, and if more can be acquired it shall be divided
equally between the two abbeys. If other ecclesiastical appurtenances of the
churches of the Hernesse, viz., the churches of Cam, Arlingham and Cromhall,
can be recovered, they shall be equally divided likewise   [1213 × 26]

C f 119r-v

Omnibus sancte matris ecclesie filiis ad quos presens scriptum pervenerit frater Symon abbas Radyng(ensis) et eiusdem loci conventus,
salutem in domino. Ad innovationem preteritorum et cautelam fu-
turorum universitatem vestram scire volumus nos unanimi voluntate
et assensu [dedisse][a] et concessisse deo et canonicis de Bristoll' ecclesias de Berkeleihern(esse), videlicet ecclesiam de Berkel(eia), de Wot-
ton(a), de Almodesb(ur)i, de Aisseleswrth', singulas cum pertinentiis
suis nomine nostro possidendas, reddendo annuatim monasterio Ra-
dyng(ensi) .xx. marcas, .x. ad Pascha et .x. ad festum sancti Michaelis. [f 119v] Nomine autem ecclesie de Beverstan', de cuius pensione inter nos questio mota fuerat, dicti canonici nobis annuatim
duas marcas de .v. marcis quas de dicta ecclesia percipiunt supradictis terminis persolvent. Si vero quidam[b] supra .v. marcas illas liti-
gando vel componendo potuerint adquirere, communibus sumptibus

adquiratur et equis portionibus inter nos dividatur. Si autem alia que ab aliis quacumque iniuria detinentur, nominatim ecclesiam de Camma et ecclesiam de Cromhal' et ecclesiam de Erlingeham aut quecumque alia ecclesiastica bona ad ecclesias de Berkeleihern(esse) pertinentia, utrisque placuerit partibus revocare, equis sumptibus utriusque partis hoc fiet, et quecumque inde assequi potuerint equis portionibus dividunt. Insuper dicti canonici dictum redditum ad monasterium Radyngie deduci facient, ita tamen quod, si per .xv. dies vel per tres septimanas post dictos terminos hoc non fecerint, inde occasio litigandi aut malignandi non assumatur. Ad maiorem autem utriusque partis securitatem, sub interminatione anathematis in utroque capitulo specialiter est inhibitum ne quis contra compositionem inter nos super dictis ecclesiis initam vel presens scriptum venire presumens maliciose et iniuste litem suscitet vel molestiam. Et ut huius scripti firmitas illibata perpetuo perseveret, utriusque capituli sigillorum appositione est roborata. Teste utroque capitulo.

a Om. in Ms, but some such word is needed   *b* Reading uncertain

The dating limits are those of Simon's abbacy. The cartulary rubric describes this act as a chirograph. For discussion, see Kemp, 'Berkeley Hernesse', 109.

292 Record of the action brought by the abbot of Reading [in the Exchequer] against the abbot of Gloucester for £18 arrears in the annual payment of 6 marks which Reading ought to receive from Gloucester. Reading's attorney proffers before the barons the deed by Abbot Hamelin and the convent of Gloucester [above, no. 286] and the confirmation of the same by King Henry II [above, no. 285]. Gloucester's attorney is unable to deny the obligation. The court orders Gloucester to pay the arrears and to be in mercy for unjust detention, etc.   [1288, before 16 Oct.]

B f 214r; C f 129r

Date shortly before that of no. 294. The arrears amounted to 4½ years non-payment. This and the following case took place during the period when the Crown's agent was restoring Reading Abbey to solvency (see nos. 92, 98).

293 Record of the action brought by the abbot of Reading [in the Exchequer] against the abbot of Bristol for 42 marks arrears in an annual pension of 20 marks. Reading's attorney proffers before the barons a certain deed of obligation witnessing to this [? no. 280], and Bristol's attorney recognizes the debt. The court decides, etc.   [1288, before 16 Oct.]

B f 214r; C f 129r

Date as for no. 292. The arrears amounted to over 2 years non-payment.

294 Precept by King Edward I to the sheriff of Gloucestershire to levy from the goods and chattels of the abbot of Bristol 42 marks owed to the abbot of Reading, and from the goods and chattels of the abbot of Gloucester £18 owed to the abbot of Reading, which the latter recently recovered against them in the king's court before the barons of the Exchequer by the custom of the court, as is clear to the king by inspection of the rolls of the Exchequer, and which they have not yet paid to him. The sheriff is to have the money at the Exchequer at Westminster in the quindene of St Martin [11 Nov.], to be paid to the abbot of Reading   16 Oct. 1288

B f 214r; C f 129r

T(este) J(ohanne) de Cobbeham. Apud Westm(onasterium) xvi. die Octobris, anno regni nostri xvi.

BODDINGTON

295 *Gift in free alms by Henry FitzGerold to Reading Abbey of the 6 marks of silver which Robert de Mucegros used to pay him annually from the farm of Boddington. He gives his body after his death for burial in Reading Abbey at the feet of his father and next to his brother*   [1216 × c.1231]

A f 76v; B f 119v; C f 65r

Sciant presentes et futuri quod ego Henricus filius Geroldi dedi et concessi et hac presenti carta mea confirmavi deo et sancte Marie et ecclesie de Rading(ia) et abbati et monachis ibidem deo servienti-bus, pro salute anime mee et omnium antecessorum et successorum meorum et domini mei Willelmi Marescalli, in liberam puram et perpetuam elemosinam illas sex marcas argenti quas Robertus de Muchegros mihi annuatim de firma de Botintun(a)ᵃ reddere solebat ad quatuor terminos anni, scilicet ad festum sancti Michaelis .xx. solidos, ad Natale domini .xx. solidos, ad Pascha .xx. solidos et ad festum sancti Johannis Baptiste .xx. solidos. Habendas et tenendas predictis abbati et monachis in perpetuum ᵇ[libere et quiete, integre et plen(arie), bene et in pace, sicut ego unquam liberius et melius eas tenui ac tenere debui],ᵇ reddendo inde annuatim mihiᶜ et here-dibus meis pro omni servitio unam libram piperis ad festum sancti Michaelis. Et ego Henricus filius Geroldi et heredes mei predictas .vi. marcasᵈ redditus predictis abbati et monachis contra omnes gentes warantizabimus ᵉ[et defendemus].ᵉ Ego vero, cum de hac vita deo volente decessero, do corpus meum ecclesie Rading(ensi) sepe-liendum ad pedes patris mei iuxta fratrem meum. Et ut hec mea donatio et concessio rata et stabilis in perpetuum perseveret, eam sigilli mei impressione roboravi.ᶠ Hiis testibus.

^a Botinton' B,C   ^{b-b} Om. in A, supplied from B,C
^c michi C   ^d marcatas B,C
^{e-e} As b-b   ^f B ends with T', C ends

The donor's brother, referred to near the end of this deed, was Warin FitzGerold, who died in July, 1216 (*EYC*, iii. 471). The donor died *c.* 1231 (Farrer, *Honors and Knights' Fees*, iii. 171). Henry FitzGerold acquired, with his wife Ermentrude Talbot, that half of the manor of Kemerton (Glos.) to which the Mucegros estate in Boddington was appurtenant, and was in possession by Sept. 1218 (*VCH Glos.*, viii. 211). William Marshal is probably the first of that name, earl of Pembroke, whom Henry served as an intimate familiar (S. Painter, *William Marshal* (Baltimore, 1933), 142, 276, etc.); if this deed was made after Marshal's death, it would date after 14 May 1219 (see no. 1056 n.). The rubrics of texts B and C state that three forms of this charter existed, but that this, with a cross, was the best. However, in view of the differences between the text in A and that in B and C, they may be copies of different originals. For the burials of the donor's father, Henry FitzGerold, and his brother, Warin, in Reading Abbey, see no. 393.

296 Inspeximus and confirmation by Warin FitzGerold, son of Henry FitzGerold, of his father's gift to Reading Abbey in Boddington (*Botint(una)*) [no. 295], saving to himself and his heirs the annual payment of 1 lb of pepper. Warranty and sealing. Witnesses^a [omitted]   [? *c.* 1231]

A ff 76v-77r; B f 119v; C f 65v

^a Om. in C

Probably soon after Henry FitzGerold's death in *c.* 1231 (see no. 295 n.). The rubrics of texts B and C state that two forms of this charter existed, but that this, with a cross, was the better. It should be noted, however, that the text in A and that in B and C quote respectively the text of Henry's charter that each cartulary has previously entered (see no. 295 n.), although B and C give only its opening words and refer the reader to the preceding entry.

GLOUCESTER

297 Gift by Walter Mason (*Meyzonarius*) of Gloucester (*Glouc'*), with the assent of Alice his wife, to John *le Sureys*, his brother, of all his land with houses, buildings and appurtenances outside the north gate of Gloucester between the land of John *le Blund* and that of the donor, which has been measured by good men (*probi homines*). It is 7½ yards wide at the front, 8½ further back, and 55 yards long, measuring with an inch interposed between yards (*Continet de latitudine in fronte septem virgas ulnarias et dimidiam cum pollice interposito, residua vero pars continet de latitudine octo virgas ulnarias et dimidiam cum pollice interposito. In profunditate continet quinquaginta et quinque virgas* *ulnarias cum pollice interposito*).[1] To be held freely by hereditary right in perpetuity, by rendering annually to the donor and his heirs 1d at Easter; to Richard *le Blund* and his heirs or assigns 1 mark of silver at the four established terms of the year; to the abbot of Reading 2s; and to the king $7\frac{1}{2}$d at Hockday, for all service, exaction and demand. For this John has given him in his great business (*ingens negocium*) $8\frac{1}{2}$ marks of silver, and to Alice his wife $\frac{1}{2}$ mark and a mantle. Warranty. Alice has sworn on the Gospels not to disturb John concerning the said land. Sealing with the seals of the donor and his wife Alice. Witnesses [omitted]   [? *c.* 1258 × 90]

B f 135r; C ff 77v-78r

Presumably not earlier than 1258, since not entered in the original section of B, and before *Quia emptores* (1290). A Walter Mason occurs in 1301 (W. H. Stevenson, *Calendar of Records of the Corporation of Gloucester* (Gloucester, 1893), 295); John *le Sureys*, alias *le Sutherne*, in 1260 × 1 and 1287 × 8 (*ibid.*, 234, 280); John *le Blund* from *c.* 1250 to 1275 × 6 and, if alias *le White*, down to 1309 (*ibid.*, 191, 261, 303); and Richard *le Blund* certainly from 1252 × 3 to 1275 × 6 (*ibid.*, 208, 260).

[1] For the use of the term *virga ulnaria* for a yard at Gloucester, see *ibid.*, 80 n. 5. For the practice at Gloucester and elsewhere of measuring lengths by placing a thumb (equalling an inch) between each yard measured, see *ibid.*, vi-vii; P. Grierson, *English Linear Measures* (Reading, 1972), 19.

298   Sale and quitclaim by Edith, widow of [?][a] *pollart*[1] of Gloucester (*Glouc'*), with the assent of Robert her son, to Richard of Maisemore (*Maysmor'*), burgess of Gloucester, of all her land in the parish of St Oswald, Gloucester, viz., that lying between the land of Robert Rich (*Dives*) and that of Roger son of Simon, for 20s 4d sterling which Richard has paid her for her most urgent business (*urgentissimum negocium*). To be held by Richard and his heirs or assigns freely and in perpetuity, by rendering annually to the archbishop of York 5d less $\frac{1}{4}$d as land-gavel at Hockday, and to the abbot of Reading 18d rent at the Purification for all services and demands, as the vendor used to render. Warranty and sealing with the seals of the vendor and her son Robert. Witnesses[b] [omitted]

[? later 13th cent.]

B f 135v; C f 78r

[a] *Name om. in both texts*
[b] *Om. in C*

Dating very uncertain, but both this and no. 297 were entered in B at the same time and in the same hand. A Richard of Maisemore occurs in 1280 (*Historia et Cartularium Monasterii ... Gloucestriae*, ed. W. H. Hart (RS, 1863-7), ii. 210-11).

[1] Possibly the name Pollard, members of which family occur in Gloucester in the 13th century (see Stevenson, *op. cit.*, 122, 200, etc.).

BOYATT

299 Gift in free alms by Reginald FitzPeter to Reading Abbey, for the health of the souls of, among others, himself, Peter FitzHerbert his father, and Herbert his brother, of the 40s annual rent which the abbot and monks of Waverley (*Waverlegh'*) used to pay to him and to Herbert his brother for the land of Boyatt (*Boveyate*) on the feast of the Nativity of St Mary [8 Sept.]. Reading Abbey may distrain on the abbot and monks of Waverley at Boyatt in the event of non-payment of the rent. Warranty and sealing. Witnesses[a] [omitted]   [*c.* May 1248]

B f 115r; C ff 61v/63r (see no. 300 n.)

[a] *Om. in C*

This rent was bequeathed to Reading in Herbert FitzPeter's testament, which was made before 24 May, 1248, by which date he had clearly died (see no. 324). Waverley Abbey had been in possession of Boyatt since at least 1189 (*VCH Hants.*, iii. 442).

300 Memorandum that distraint for the 40s rent [given in no. 299], in the event of non-payment, might be made (*iacet*) in the field called *Wydelond'* in Boyatt (*Boveyate*) along with a sheepfold (*bercaria*) and a croft lying at the northern end of the field, containing 109 acres of land, and in 15 acres of wood on the western side lying alongside the said field   [? late 13th x early 14th cent.]

C f 62v; (in margin) B f 115r; C f 63r

C f 62 is a narrow strip of parchment bound into the cartulary after the main text had been written, in order to provide room for this memorandum on its reverse; this accounts for the fact that C's text of no. 299 is begun, according to the current foliation, on f 61v and concluded on f 63r. This memorandum was first entered in the margin of B against the text of no. 299 in a late 13th- or early 14th-century hand, and copied in this position in the original section of C, but in each case the text of the memorandum has been mutilated by subsequent trimming of the folios.

SOUTHAMPTON

301 *Precept by King Henry I to William de Pont [de l'Arche] and Payn, reeve of Southampton, that Reading Abbey is to hold the land which Robert the priest gave to it as well and honourably as Robert held it, and as the king ordered by his other writ*   [1123 × 33; ? 1133]

A f 15r; B f 18v
Pd. *Regesta*, ii. 379 (no. cclxxvi); (cal.) *ibid.*, 269 (no. 1797)

Henricus rex Angl(orum) W(illelmo) de Pont(e) et Pagano preposito[a] Hamt(one), salutem. Precipio quod abbas et monachi de Rading(ia) teneant terram quam Robertus presbiter dedit et concessit ecclesie de Rading(ia) ita bene et in pace et iuste et honorifice sicut idem Robertus melius tenuit et sicut precepi per aliud breve meum. Testibus:[b] G(alfredo) filio Pag(ani), et Unfr(edo) de Buhun. Apud Rading(iam).

[a] prepositis *B*
[b] *B ends*

After the appointment of the first abbot of Reading and before the king's last crossing to Normandy (2 Aug. 1133). The editors of *Regesta*, ii, suggest 1133. The text printed here is preferable to that printed by *Regesta*, which is from B and lacks the witnesses.

302 Precept by King Henry I to Baldwin de Redvers and Payn, reeve of Southampton, in terms very similar to the preceding, but adding the name of Ketellus, Robert the priest's ancestor, who also held the land. Witnesses [omitted]   [1123 × 33; ? 1133]

B f 18v; (noted) A f 15r
Pd. *Regesta*, ii. 379 (no. cclxxv); (cal.) *ibid.*, 269 (no. 1796)

Date as for no. 301.

SOUTH CHARFORD

303 *Gift in free alms by Hugh de Chernet to Reading Abbey of 6 acres of meadow in [South] Charford*   [c. mid-12th cent.]

A f 41v; B f 115v; C f 63r

Sciant presentes et futuri sancte ecclesie filii quod ego Hugo de Carnet dedi deo et sancte Marie de Rading(ia) et monachis ibidem [deo][a] servientibus .vi. acras prati apud Cerdifordiam in perpetuam elemosinam et liberam et quietam ab omni servitio, pro anima mea et pro animabus patris et matris mee et uxoris mee et filiorum et fratrum meorum et omnium parentum meorum. Volo itaque hanc donationem meam firmam esse et stabilem.[b] Ideoque eam confirmo sigillo meo.[c] His testibus: Cristina uxore mea, Waleranno de Carnet fratre meo, Edmundo de Benam, et multis aliis.

[a] *Om. in A, supplied from B,C*
[b] stabibilem *A, with the second* bi *marked for deletion*
[c] *B ends with* T', *C ends with* et cetera

Dating very uncertain, but in 1086 the manor of South Charford was held of Hugh de Port by William de Chernet (*VCH Hants.*, i. 478) and in 1166 Hugh de Chernet (presumably the present donor) was recorded among the military tenants of John de Port in Hampshire (*Red Bk. Exch.*, i. 208). At least one generation separated Hugh from the Domesday holder, for an original deed by Hugh to Breamore priory confirms a gift made by his father, Ingelram (PRO E326/9228), the latter being possibly the Ingelram Apostolicus who became a monk at Reading and gave the abbey the manor of Whitsbury (see no. 307).

SOUTH WARNBOROUGH

304 *Gift in free alms by Alan de Creon to Reading Abbey of [? one] hide of land at Crowdale [in South Warnborough]¹ with pasture rights for 12 oxen and 100 sheep in winter* [1121 × c.1150]

A f44r

Sciatis*ᵃ* omnes homines mei Franci et Anglici de Warneburne ego Alanus de Creun me*ᵇ* dedisse [?]omnem*ᶜ* hidam terre a Crudeshole que fuit Liveno(n) sancte Marie de Rading(ia), pro anima patris mei et matris mee et omnium fidelium defunctorum, solam et quietam, in bosco et in plano et in pascuis, et in hieme .xii. boves et .c. oves cum meis, in elemosinam. Testibus: Ernulfo capellano, et Anfrido clerico, et Thoma milite, et multis aliis.

ᵃ Ms has Sciatis *with the a apparently erased*
ᵇ The syntax ineptly changes at this point
ᶜ Ms reads ⊖., which is very like the European form of the Arabic zero, which is clearly impossible; it may be a deletion, but, if not, the best reading, while not certainly correct, is omnem (*cf. A. Cappelli,* Dizionario di Abbreviature Latine ed Italiane (*4th edn, Milan 1949*), 244)

After the arrival of the first monks at Reading in June, 1121, and before Alan de Creon's death, which, although he was grandson of the Domesday holder of South Warnborough (*VHC Hants.*, iii. 378), occurred not earlier than 1143—see BL Add. Ms 32101 (Pedwardyn family cartulary) f89v, pd. *Mon. Ang.*, iv. 125-6, which is a charter by Alan to Freiston priory, Lincs., witnessed by Edward abbot of Crowland, 1143-73. The present gift to Reading seems not to have taken effect, and the charter was accordingly not copied into the abbey's later cartularies.

¹ *Crudeshole* appears also in that form in Alan's charter to Freiston priory (see above), and in the 16th century as *Crowdale* alias *Crowdishole* (*L. and P. For. and Dom.*, *Hen. VIII*, xviii(2), 56).

STRATFIELD SAYE

305 Gift in free alms by Robert de Say and Alice, his wife, to Reading Abbey of 13s 4d rent in the manor of Stratfield [Saye] (*Stratfeld*), viz., from John of Marlow (*Merlaue*) 5s, from William of

Grazeley (*Greysull'*) 3s 6d, from Ivetta the widow 6d, from Henry
the butler (*pincerna*) 2s, and from Ralph *de Wike* 4d; and gift of
Adam *de Scheta*, their villein (*nativus*), with all his progeny (*sequela*)
and with the croft whence Adam and his own after him are due to
pay the abbey 2s [? annually]; and grant of full suit of their men
whom they may or shall place (*assedere*) there. Warranty, under pain
of 5 marks, and sealing with the donors' seals   [*c.* 1220 × 58]

B f57r; C ff24v–25r

Robert de Say occurs in a dispute with Reading Abbey in 1225 (PRO JUST 1/36,
m.2), in 1227 (*VCH Hants.*, iv. 58) and in 1242–3 when he was recorded as holding
1 knight's fee in Stratfield (Hants.) of John de Stuteville (*Fees*, ii. 705). In fact, he
acquired the manor by marriage to Alice de Stuteville earlier in the century (*VCH
Hants.*, iv. 58). John of Marlow occurs in 1241 and 1248 (PRO JUST 1/37, m. 25B
d; Clanchy, *Berks. Eyre of 1248*, 172). This deed was entered in the original section of
B and is therefore not later than 1258. It appears, with no. 306, under Berkshire at
the end of deeds relating to Stratfield Mortimer, presumably because it was administered with the abbey's land there.

306 Gift and quitclaim in free alms by Robert de Say, with the
assent of Alice de Stuteville, his wife, to Reading Abbey of Adam *de
la Schete* with all his issue and all his suit. Sealing. Witnesses
[omitted]   [*c.* 1220 × 58]

B f57r; C f25r

Date as for no. 305.

WHITSBURY

307 *Notification by King Henry I to the bishop of Salisbury and the sheriff,
barons and faithful of Wiltshire that he has given in perpetuity to Reading
Abbey the land and church of Whitsbury as Ingelram Apostolicus, monk of
Reading, gave them and as freely as he held them*   [1130 × July 1133]

A f15r; B f18r–v
Pd. *Regesta*, ii. 383 (no. ccxcvii); (cal.) *ibid.*, 281 (no. 1862)

Henricus rex Angl(orum) *ᵃ*episcopo Sar(esburiensi) et vicecomiti et
omnibus baronibus et fidelibus suis de Wiltescir(a), salutem.*ᵃ* Sciatis me *ᵇ*dedisse et*ᵇ* concessisse deo et ecclesie Rading(ensi) in perpetuum terram Ingelrami Apostolici, monachi ipsius ecclesie, de Wic-
cheberia*ᶜ* cum ecclesia eiusdem*ᵈ* ville et hominibus et omnibus rebus
ei pertinentibus, sicut Ingelramus eas ei dedit et concessit, et sicut
ipse melius habuit et liberius dum eam tenuit. Et volo et firmiter*ᵉ*
precipio quod bene et in pace et libere teneat ecclesia Rading(ensis)
in eadem libertate qua alias suas tenuras tenet.*ᶠ* Testibus:*ᵍ*

W(illelmo) comite Warenn(e), et G(alfredo) filio Pagani, et Drogone de Monci. Apud Windr(esores).

a-a et cetera *B*	*b-b* *Om. in B*
c Wichebir' *B*	*d* ipsius *B*
e *Om. in B*	*f* habet *B*
g *B ends*	

Not earlier than 1130, when Ingelram still held Whitsbury, being excused Danegeld of 8s in Wiltshire (*PR 31 Henry I*, 23); and before the king's final crossing to Normandy on 2 Aug. 1133. The text printed here is fuller than that printed by *Regesta*, but see also no. 308 n. Whitsbury was in Wiltshire until 1895 (*VCH Hants.*, iv. 594).

308   *Further notification by the same concerning the same*

[1130 × July 1133]

B f 18r; (noted) A f 15r[1]

H(enricus) rex Angl(orum) episcopo Sar(esburiensi) et vicecomiti et omnibus baronibus et fidelibus suis de Wiltesir(a), salutem. Sciatis me dedisse et concessisse deo et ecclesie Rading(ensi) in perpetuum terram Ingelrami Apostolici, monachi ipsius ecclesie, de Wichebir(ia) cum ecclesia ipsius ville et hominibus et omnibus rebus ei pertinentibus, sicut Ingelramus eam quietius et liberius tenuit. Et volo et firmiter precipio quod bene et in pace et libere teneat in eadem libertate qua suas alias tenuras tenet. T(estibus).

Date as for no. 307. The two charters are very similar. One text only was entered in A and two in B, but the text in A shares some features with one of those in B and some with the other, so that one cannot be certain that the association of texts adopted here is the correct one.

[1] The rubric for no. 307 in A adds: *Hec duplex est.*

309   Confirmation by King Stephen to Read:ng Abbey of the land of Whitsbury formerly belonging to Ingelram Apostolicus, monk of the abbey, and given by King Henry I. To be held with all liberties with which the abbey holds its other lands, and as King Henry's charter testifies

[1136 × June 1139]

A f 19r; B f 29v
Pd. *Regesta*, iii. 253 (no. 685)

Testibus:*a* H(enrico) episcopo Wint(oniensi), et R(ogero) episcopo Sar(esburiensi), et*b* A(lexandro) episcopo Linc(olniensi), et R(oberto) de Ver, et A(lberico) de Ver, et W(illelmo) Mart(el). Apud Oxen(efordiam).

a *B ends*	*b* *A repeats* et

Before the arrest of the bishops, 24 June 1139. King Stephen cannot have been in Oxford before 1136.

310   Precept by King Stephen to Walter of Salisbury and his ministers that the land and men of the abbot of Reading at Whitsbury are to be quit of pleas, plaints, hundreds, shires, sheriff's aids, etc., as in the time of King Henry I, and as King Henry's and his own charters testify   [1136 × 40]

A f 19v; B f 29v
Pd. *Regesta*, iii. 253 (no. 684)

T(este):*ᵃ* A(lberico) de Ver. Apud Ferham.

ᵃ B ends

Stephen is unlikely to have been in Fareham before 1136. Aubrey de Vere I died May, 1141, and Aubrey de Vere II joined the Empress in 1141. Stephen was at Lincoln from Christmas, 1140, until his capture on 2 Feb. 1141 (see *Regesta*, iii, no. 684 n.). It is noteworthy that, while the charters of Henry I (nos. 307-8) included the church of Whitsbury, the acts of Stephen (309-10) did not. This was probably because a dispute existed between Reading and Breamore priory (Hants.) over this church, which Ingelram had given to Breamore before his gift to Reading (*Regesta*, ii, no.1810; *Cal. Chart. R.*, iv. 262). The problem was solved in 1164 when Abbot Roger and the convent of Reading conceded the church to Breamore, to be held of the abbey for 5 lbs of incense annually (PRO Exchequer Chartae Antiquae, E315/vol. 53, no. 223).

311   Gift by Hugh of Godshill (*Godeshull'*) to Reading Abbey of 12½ acres of meadow in *Thistelesmor'*,*ᵃ* viz., all the meadow which he had between the old animal pound (*pundfalda*) and the meadow of Richard de Cardeville (*Cardunvill'*)*ᵇ* which lies between the ditch [running] from the animal pound northwards, with the whole ditch, and again from the pound as far as the ditch of the prior of Breamore (*Brummor'*) to the west, and from the same ditch as far as the aforesaid ditch of Richard de Cardeville. To be held freely by rendering annually to the donor and his heirs 2s at Michaelmas for all service, exaction and demand. Also grant that the abbey may enclose and improve the meadow. Warranty and sealing, and delivery of seisin. For this the abbey has given him 16 marks of silver. Witnesses*ᶜ* [omitted]   [13th cent., before 1248]

A f 106r-v; B f 116v; C f 63r-v

ᵃ Thistlemore C
ᵇ A has Cardunvvill'
ᶜ Om. in C

This deed was entered among 13th-century additions in A, but in the original section of B. The donor, who took his name from Godshill in the parish of Fordingbridge, Hants. (*VCH Hants.*, iv. 572), occurs in 1208 in Wiltshire in a forest context associated with the New Forest (*PR 10 John*, 205). In 1212 he was recorded as holding 1 carucate in Linwood, Hants., and one of the four bailiwicks in the New Forest (*Fees*, i. 76); in 1242-3 he held in Ibsley, Hants. (*ibid.*, ii. 694); and in 1242 he gave land to Maiden Bradley priory in Over Burgate, in Fordingbridge (*VCH Hants.*, iv. 570). He was still living in 1251 (*Close Rolls 1247-51*, 461; *Cal. Chart. R.*, i. 364), but was dead by Aug. 1256 (*Close Rolls 1254-6*, 435). For his gifts of meadow in this area to Beaulieu Abbey, see *The Beaulieu Cartulary*, ed. S. F. Hockey (Southampton Rec. ser., xvii, 1974), 148-50 (cf. *ibid.*, 118-20, 188). Richard de Cardeville was dead in 1247 (*Excerpta e rot. fin.*, ii. 15). 'Thistlemore' has not been certainly identified, but, although the rubric of B describes it as being in Whitsbury, the bounds given in nos. 313-14 suggest that it lay in Fordingbridge parish (cf. *Cartl. Beaulieu*, 148); the rubric probably means that, on acquiring the meadow, Reading Abbey administered it with the manor of Whitsbury. However, a presumably different meadow called 'Thistlemore' also belonging to Hugh of Godshill appears to have existed in Milton, Hants. (*ibid.*, 119-20, 156).

312 Gift by Hugh of Godshill (*Godeshulle*) to Reading Abbey of 7½ acres of meadow in *Thysteslmore,*[a] extending in length from the gate in the new ditch and the ditch which encloses the meadow to the meadow of Richard de Cardeville (*Kardunvill'*),[b] and in breadth from the said new ditch to the meadow which the abbey previously had from him. To be enclosed and held freely by rendering annually to the donor and his heirs 12d at Easter for all service, custom, exaction and demand. Warranty with provision for reasonable exchange to the same value in the same meadow of *Thystelmor',*[c] if warranty is not possible. For this the abbey has given him 10 marks of silver. Witnesses[d] [omitted]   [13th cent., before 1248]

A f 102v; B ff 116v-117r; C f 63v

[a] Thistelmor' *B*, Thistelesmor *C*   [b] Cardunvill' *B,C*
[c] Thistelmor' *B*, Thistelmore *C*   [d] *Om. in C*

Date as for no. 311. The rubric of B describes the meadow as being at Whitsbury.

313 Gift by Hugh of Godshill (*Godeshull'*) to Reading Abbey of the entire meadow in *Thistelmor'* which is between the old ditch and the wood of Godshill and between the Drove-road (*Drava*)[1] and the bank of the [River] Avon (*Avene*), with the entire embankment (*crista*) of the said ditch. To be held freely by rendering annually to him and his heirs 2s sterling at Michaelmas for all service, exaction, custom, etc. Also grant that the abbey may enclose, ditch and hedge the said meadow, and repair the ditch between the hedge in the meadow and the wood of Godshill or make a new ditch and enclose the said hedge. Warranty with provision for reasonable exchange to the full value either in meadows or in lands, if warranty is not possible. For this the abbey has given him 33 marks of silver in his great need, viz., 20 marks to acquit himself against the Jews of Winchester (*Wint'*) and 13 marks to acquit himself against Peter, *serviens* of Downton [Wilts.] (*Dunton'*); and the abbey has given to

Ivetta, his wife, 1 palfrey worth 2 marks. Sealing. Witnesses[a]
[omitted]   [? c.1220 × 56]

B f117r; C ff63v–64r

[a] Om. in C

Dating uncertain. The deed was not entered in A, suggesting that it may date some
time after nos. 311–12; Hugh of Godshill was dead by Aug. 1256 (*Close Rolls 1254–6*,
435). Peter, *serviens* of Downton, may be the same as the Peter of Downton (*Duding-
ton*') who occurs in 1249 (*Civil Pleas of the Wiltshire Eyre 1249*, ed. M. T. Clanchy
(Wilts. Rec. Soc., 1971), 94).

¹ Cf. 'la Drane', *Cartl. Beaulieu*, 148.

314 Confirmation by Hugh of Godshill (*Godesh(ulle)*) to Reading
Abbey of the three meadows in *Thistelesmor*'[a] which he had previously given, viz., 12½ acres for 2s annually at Michaelmas, 7½ acres
for 12d annually at Michaelmas,¹ and the meadow between the old
ditch and the wood of Godshill and between the Drove-road and
the bank of the [River] Avon for 2s annually at Michaelmas. However, for the health of his soul and those of Juetta his wife and
others, the abbey will now pay only 3s annually for the said three
meadows instead of the 5s which it used to pay. Warranty with
provision for reasonable exchange to the full value either in meadows
or in lands, if warranty is not possible. Sealing. Witnesses[b] [omitted]
                                                [? c.1220 × 56]

B f117r–v; C f64r

[a] Thistelmore C
[b] Om. in C

Date as for no. 313, but this is rather later.

¹ This rent was previously payable at Easter (see no. 312).

315 Grant in free alms by Hugh of Godshill (*Godeshull*') to Reading
Abbey that it may have 20 beasts (*averia*) in the pasture of the New
Forest, the bailiwick and keeping of which belonged to him and his
heirs, with free entry and exit, to remain in the pasture in accord-
ance with the wishes of the abbey or of its bailiffs of Whitsbury
(*Wichebir*'). Sealing. Witnesses[a] [omitted]   [? c. 1220 × 56]

B f117v; C f64v

[a] Om. in C

Date as for no. 313. Hugh was one of the four bailiffs in the New Forest (see no. 311
n.).

315a   Notes of the following:

(i) charter between the same Hugh and Peter of Downton (*Don-ton*') concerning a certain meadow in Whitsbury (*Wichebir*');

(ii) another between the same.   [before Aug. 1256]

B f117v; C f64v

Before Hugh of Godshill's death (see no. 313 n.).

316   *Quitclaim by Henry son of Robert del Hif to Reading Abbey of all the land which he sometime held of it in Whitsbury for 20s annually. For this the abbey has given him in his great need 4 marks of silver to redeem himself from the Jews and has granted to him for life food and clothing in the monastery as one of the abbot's servants or, if illness or other cause prevents him from serving, specified provisions*   [13th cent., not later than 1258]

B ff117v–118r; C f64v

Sciant presentes et futuri quod ego Henricus filius Roberti del Hif dedi, concessi et quiet'clamavi*ᵃ* abbati et conventui de Rading(ia) totam terram cum pertinentiis suis quam aliquando de eis tenui in Wichebir(ia) pro .xx. solidis annuis, habendam et tenendam predictis abbati et monachis libere et quiete, bene et in pace in perpetuum. Pro hac donatione, concessione et quiet'clamatione,*ᵇ* dederunt mihi predicti abbas et conventus .iiii. marcas argenti in magnis necessitatibus meis ad redimendum me de iudaismo. Concesserunt etiam mihi omnibus diebus vite mee victum et vestitum in domo Rading(ensi) sicut uni ex servientibus [*f118r*] domini abbatis dum in servitio eorum fuero. Si autem contigerit quod, propter egritudinem vel aliam causam, servire nequivero, concesserunt mihi singulis diebus vite mee unum simenellum de Chaus(eia) et unam suram micham et unum galonem de cervisia conventus et alterum de cervisia mixta et companag(ium) singulis diebus tam ad prandium quam ad cenam, sicut uni ex servientibus domini abbatis, et annuatim unam marcam argenti pro omnibus rebus ad vestituram et ad calciaturam spectantibus. Ego autem Henricus et heredes mei hanc donationem, concessionem et quiet'clamationem predictis abbati et monachis contra omnes homines et feminas warantizabimus. Et ut hec mea donatio, concessio et quiet'clamatio stabilis et inconcussa perseveret, presens scriptum sigilli mei appositione roboravi. T(estibus).*ᶜ*

ᵃ quietumclamavi C
ᵇ quietacl' C
ᶜ Om. in C

Dating uncertain, but the deed was not entered in A and was included in the original section of B. The text has been printed here in full on account of its interesting details regarding provisions for servants of the abbot of Reading.

316a   Note of a charter by the same Henry to William *Havel* [concerning land] *at Whitsbury (*Whychebyr'*)*

[13th cent., not later than 1258]

B f118r

a–a Apparently added later

Date as for no. 316, but rather earlier.

317   Gift in free alms by William *Havel* to Reading Abbey of all the land which he sometime held of Henry son of Robert *de Ywa* in Whitsbury (*Wichebir'*). Sealing (*presentem cartam sigillo meo munitam*[a] *prefatis abbati et conventui reliqui in testimonium*). Witnesses[b] [omitted]

[13th cent., not later than 1258]

B f118r; C f64v

a B has this word before meo *and marked for transposition*
b Om. in C

Date as for no. 316.

318   Notification by Henry son of Robert *del Hyf* that, having inspected the charter of gift by William *Havel* to Reading Abbey in Whitsbury (*Wichebir'*), and knowing it to be lawful, he has confirmed the same. Sealing. Witnesses[a] [omitted]

[13th cent., not later than 1258]

B f118r; C f65r

a Om. in C

Date as for no. 316. Clearly *del Hyf* is equivalent to *de Ywa* in no. 317.

319   Memorandum concerning dues paid at the Exchequer for the meadow of Whitsbury (*Wychebir'*). In roll 54 the abbot of Reading rendered account for 40s to retain a meadow of 24 acres, as is contained in roll 45, and for £6 for previous years. In the treasury £4 by two tallies, and the abbot owes £4, for which W(illiam) the sheriff ought to acquit him, as he recognized and as is contained in the memoranda

[1270]

B f6r

The rolls referred to are Pipe Rolls of Henry III's reign. The sheriff concerned was William le Dun, sheriff of Wiltshire from 23 Nov. 1267 to 18 May, 1270 (*List of Sheriffs*, 152).

320 *Memorandum concerning the annual farm of 40s owed to the Crown by the abbot of Reading for a 24-acre meadow at Whitsbury in the New Forest. It was first paid to the king's Exchequer in 1251, following the Forest Eyre of Robert Passelewe—extract from Pipe Roll 35 Henry III quoted. After the New Forest was assigned by Henry III to Eleanor [of Castile], wife of the future Edward I, the latter as king instructed the abbot to pay the sum to her and, in 1276, ordered the Exchequer to make allowance to the abbot accordingly—letters close quoted. On the same day the sum was first paid into the Queen's Wardrobe at Westminster, the abbey receiving letters patent to that effect from the Queen* [prob. late 1276]

B f2v

Memorandum quod firma .xl. solidorum de prato de Wychebiry quod est in Nova Foresta primo intravit in pipam, sive in magnum rotulum domini regis ad scaccarium, anno coronationis H(enrici) regis patris domini E(dwardi) regis tricesimo quinto. Et tunc primo soluta fuit ad scaccarium illa firma .xl. solidorum post itinerationem vel iter Roberti Passelewe de foresta. Et continetur in eodem rotulo sub hiis verbis:

Abbas Rading' debet solvere annuatim .xl. solidos pro retinendo quodam prato*a* .xxiiii. acrarum de feudo domini regis in Nova Foresta. 1251

Et preceptum est per litteras domini E(dwardi) regis, anno eiusdem .iiii. in festo sancti Michaelis, *b*baronibus de scaccario*b* quod de cetero solvatur dicta firma .xl. solidorum domine A(lianore) consorti domini regis tanquam pertinens ad Novam Forestam, per breve regis sub hac forma:

E(dwardus) dei gratia, et cetera, baronibus suis de scaccario, salutem. Cum dominus H(enricus) rex pater noster dudum dedisset et concessisset karissime consorti nostre Alianore regine Anglie Novam Forestam cum omnibus ad eam spectantibus habendam prout in carta predicti patris nostri plenius continetur,[1] per quod mandavimus dilecto nobis in Christo abbati de Radinges quod illos .xl. solidos quos idem abbas ad dictum scaccarium prius solvere consuevit pro .xxiiii. acris prati in foresta predicta et ad eandem forestam spectantibus eidem consorti nostre solvat iuxta concessionem predictam, vobis mandamus quod dictos .xl. solidos eidem abbati singulis annis allocetis quam diu dicta foresta fuerit in manu consortis nostre predicte. Teste me ipso. Apud Westmonasterium, xx. die Octobris, anno regni nostri quarto.[2] 20 Oct. 1276

Et memorandum quod eodem die primo soluti fuerunt dicti .xl. solidi Henrico de Wodestok' apud Westmonasterium in warderoba domine regine ad*c* opus suum per manus Pagani tunc camerarii

Radingie. Unde habemus litteram patentem a domina regina de dicta solutione tali modo sibi facta.

^a *Ms has this word before* quodam *and marked for transposition*
^{b-b} *Interlined*
^c *Reading uncertain*

This memorandum appears to have been compiled at about the time of the first payment to Queen Eleanor, 20 Oct. 1276. In a later hand there follows a note referring the reader to the other side of the folio (f2r) for notice of the abbot's quittance of pannage and herbage for his beasts in the New Forest (see no. 321).

¹ *Cal. Chart. R.*, ii. 143, dated 26 May 1270.
² *Cal. Close R. 1272–79*, 313.

320a   Note of a concession by King Edward I concerning the payment to the Queen of the 40s for meadow in the New Forest
[? 1276 or 1306]

C f225v

This probably refers either to the letters close quoted in no. 320 or to letters patent, dated 20 Jan. 1306, ordering the abbey to pay 40s for a tenement in the New Forest to Queen Margaret, Edward I's second wife (*Cal. Pat. R. 1301–7*, 413).

321   Memorandum that it is enrolled in the rental of Lyndhurst (*Lyndhurst*), concerning the rent of the bailiwick of Godshill (*Gody-shulle*), that the abbot of Reading by virtue of his meadow should have all his beasts (*averia*) grazing in the New Forest quit of pannage and herbage dues throughout the year. The enrolment was made at Salisbury (*Sarr'*) on Saturday after the octave of the Purification [2 Feb.], 19 Edward I, in the presence of master Ralph of Ivinghoe (*Yvyngho*), master Henry *Huse* and the others assigned by the king to correct the excesses of the Queen's bailiffs in the New Forest
[*c.* 10 Feb. 1291]

B f2r

Presumably of approximately the same date as the enrolment. Queen Eleanor died 25 Nov. 1290, and soon afterwards Ralph of Ivinghoe, chancellor of St Paul's, and others were appointed to hear and settle complaints against her bailiffs and ministers (cf. *Cal. Close R. 1288–96*, 225; *Cal. Pat. R. 1281–92*, 484).

WINCHESTER

322   *Gift by Hugh de Mortimer [the younger] to Reginald Lamb of land in Winchester, to be held for an annual payment of 1 lb of pepper*
[before 1181]

A f36v

Sciant omnes tam presentes quam futuri quod ego Hugo de Mortuomari dedi in civitate Wintonie, pro servitio suo, Reginaldo Agno et heredibus suis terram quandam de me et de meis heredibus tenendam. Et ille et heredes sui mihi et heredibus meis dabunt singulis annis in recognitione unam libram piperis. Cuius rei testes isti sunt: Stephanus filius Pagani, Willelmus filius Baldewini, prepositi Wint(onie), Benedictus clericus, Petrus clericus, Haim*a* clericus vicecom(itis), Ernoldus Herefost, Iohanne filius Radulfi, et multi alii.

a Sic; ? rectius Hamo

The donor was Hugh de Mortimer the younger, the eldest son and heir of Hugh de Mortimer (died 1180-1), who predeceased his father leaving no progeny (*Complete Peerage*, ix. 272). The rent from this land was no doubt the rent, or part of it, which the same donor gave to Reading Abbey (see no. 1069). Reginald Lamb occurs as a witness to three deeds in Reading and one in Whitley between 1158 and 1199 (nos. 824, 827, 838, 1212).

323 *Grant by Richard [of Ilchester], bishop of Winchester, to Reading Abbey and the men living on its demesne lands of quittance of tolls in the bishop's fairs at Winchester. The abbey has admitted him to confraternity and will celebrate the anniversary of his death as for an abbot* [1174 × 88]

A f 53r; B f 114v; C f 61v

Universis sancte matris ecclesie filiis ad quos presens scriptum pervenerit Ricardus miseratione divina Wint(oniensis) ecclesie minister, salutem in domino. Noverit universitas vestra nos, divino intuitu et pro salute nostra et predecessorum et successorum nostrorum episcoporum Wint(oniensium), dedisse et concessisse monasterio de Rading(ia) et monachis ibidem*a* deo servientibus et familie sue, necnon et omnibus hominibus in dominicis terris eorum degentibus, quitantiam ab omni tollo in nundinis nostris Wint(onie), tam in emptionibus quam*b* venditionibus eorum. Et ipsi admiserunt nos misericorditer in fraternitatem domus sue et omnium orationum, elemosinarum et beneficiorum que fient in perpetuum in loco predicto et domibus religiosis ad ipsum pertinentibus participes constituerunt. Repromiserunt nichilominus in verbo veritatis quod in obitus nostri die sollemne*c* pro nobis anniversarium tanquam pro abbate suo in perpetuum de cetero celebrabunt. Quocirca volumus atque statuimus in futurum ut prefati monachi, una cum familia sua et hominibus eorum in dominicis ipsorum terris manentibus, in memoratis nundinis Wint(onie) prescripta quietantia gaudeant et libertate. Quod ut stabile perseveret et firmum, illud scripto presenti nostroque sigillo duximus roborandum.*d* His testibus: Herberto

Cant(uariensi) archidiacono, magistris Ham(one) et Hugone medico, et multis aliis.

^a *A has* ibidem *twice, the first deleted*   ^b *Insert in B,C*
^c sollempne *B,C*   ^d *B ends with* T', *C ends*

The dating limits are those of the bishop's pontificate. Herbert archdeacon of Canterbury was Herbert Poore who held that office from 1174 until his appointment as
bishop of Salisbury in 1194. Bishop Richard died 22 Dec. 1188. Whether the abbey
kept his obit is unknown, since December is unfortunately missing from the calendar
in the Almoner's Cartulary (D ff 11v–16v).

324 *Notification by brothers Richard* de Fissacr' *and Henry* de
Lamwrth', *O.P.*, *Walter FitzPeter, Sir Reginald FitzPeter, Walter* de
Nimet *and John son of Alexander, executors of the testament of Herbert
FitzPeter, of his bequests to Reading Abbey in free alms, with his body, in
Winchester and Boyatt*   24 May 1248

B ff 114v–115r; C f 61v

In nomine domini nostri Jhesu Christi nos frater Ricardus de Fissacr', frater Henricus de Lamwrth', ordinis predicatorum, Walterus
filius Petri, dominus Reginaldus filius Petri, Walterus de Nimet,
Johannes filius Alexandri, executores testamenti Herberti filii Petri,
notum facimus universis Christi fidelibus quod dictus Herbertus filius Petri dedit, concessit et in testamento suo cum corpore suo legavit
et assignavit monasterio de Rading(ia) et abbati et monachis ibidem
deo servientibus, in puram et perpetuam elemosinam, totam illam
curiam que vocatur la Parok' cum edificiis, capella et omnibus pertinentiis extra portam occidentalem civitatis Winton(ie); et sex marcatas redditus et .xviii. denaratos singulis annis ad Nativitatem beate
Marie [8 Sept.] percipiendas, videlicet, extra burgum Wint(onie) de
terra Bukok' .iiii. solidos, de terra quam Willelmus Delwede tenet
.ii. s', de terra quam Johannes Alured'^a tenet .ii. s', de Ysemaine .ii.
d', item infra burgum Wint(onie) de terra Johannis Martin' in alto
vico ad piscariam unam marcam, item in alto vico de terra
Gaufr(edi) Barun .xx. s', item de monachis de Waverl(eia) pro terra
de Boveyete^b .xl. s' percipiendos annuatim in die Nativitatis beate
Marie ad dictam curiam de la Parok'. Que omnia prefatus Here-
bertus^c predictis abbati et monachis in testamento ipsius sigillo suo
signato dedit et assignavit.[1] Et in huius rei testimonium et maiorem
securitatem [*f 115r*] huic scripto sigilla nostra apponi fecimus. Dat'
apud Rading(iam) die dominica proxima ante Ascensionem domini
[28 May], anno gratie M.CC.xlviii.

^a Aluredus *C*
^b Boveyte *C*
^c Herbertus *C*

For Reginald FitzPeter's gift of the 40s rent from Boyatt, made in consequence of his brother's bequest, see no. 299.

[1] This sentence is cited and discussed by M. M. Sheehan, *The Will in Medieval England* (Toronto, 1963), 189 n. 97.

BRIMFIELD

325 Notification by Empress Matilda, daughter of King Henry and lady of the English, to R(obert) [de Bethune], bishop of Hereford, and Miles of Gloucester and all barons and faithful of Herefordshire, that she has given to the monks of Reading and Leominster the manor of Brimfield which Ulger the huntsman held, as the right of the church of Leominster; and precept that they shall hold the manor as freely as they hold Leominster, which is the *caput* of that manor, with all the customs and liberties with which they hold their other lands [8 Apr. × 25 July 1141]

A f63r
Pd. *Regesta*, iii. 259 (no. 701)

Testibus: A(lexandro) episcopo Linc(olniensi) et canc(ellario), et Roberto de Oilli. Apud Oxoneford.

After the Empress became 'Lady of the English' and before Miles of Gloucester was created earl of Hereford. This charter was entered in the original hand of A, but not with other acts of the Empress, and was included in the contemporary table of contents at the beginning of the cartulary. The gift appears to have been ineffective, for the charter was not entered in the later cartularies nor in the Leominster cartulary. Brimfield had been one of the 'members' of Leominster in 1066 (*VCH Herefs.*, i. 314), but was apparently detached and made into a forest serjeanty by Henry I, presumably before the foundation of Reading Abbey, since in 1212 Hugh son of Robert was said to hold Brimfield by forest serjeanty in Shropshire by gift of Henry I (*Fees*, i. 102). Ulger the huntsman was probably therefore a predecessor of Hugh son of Robert.

BROADFIELD

326 *Notification by Robert [de Bethune], bishop of Hereford, of the agreement reached in his presence in the synod of Hereford between the monks of Leominster and Miles the Constable over the parish of the men of Broadfield. Leominster shall receive from Broadfield* scrifcorn, *the crop of 2 acres of the demesne in August, and Peter's Pence, as previously, but the church of Bodenham shall bury the dead and receive the remaining benefits* [1131 × 37]

A f56v; E f60r

Volumus ad notitiam posterorum pervenire concordiam factam de disceptatione qua inter se invicem contendebant monachi de Leoministr(ia) et Milo Conestabulus pro parrochia hominum de Bradefeld' quos predicti monachi ad parrochiam de*a* Leoministr(ia)*b* dicebant pertinere et Milo defendebat. Concordati sunt autem eo tenore ut monachi*c* Leoministr(ie) haberent de predicta villa Bradefeld' scrifcorn sicut antea habuerant, et in Augusto .ii. acras bladi de dominio, unam videlicet frumenti et alteram avene, quia has antea quoque habuerant, et romescot reciperent sicut etiam prius receperant; et corpora defunctorum ecclesia de Bodeham sepeliat et cetera beneficia recipiat. Acta sunt hec in synodo Herford(ensi)*d* nobis presentibus *'*Roberto episcopo Herford(ensi) et abbatibus Waltero Glow(cestrensi), Godefrido Wichilec(umbensi), Herberto Salop(esberiensi), et multis aliis.*'*

a *Om. in* E   *b* Leomen' E
c *Insert* de E   *d* Heref' E
e-e episcopo Heref' Rob' et cetera E

After the bishop's consecration, 28 June, 1131, and before the death of Godfrey abbot of Winchcombe, 6 Mar. 1137 (*Heads of Relig. Houses*, 79). The rubric of A mistakenly refers to *Bradeford*, i.e., Broadward (see nos. 327-32). For *scrifcorn*, see no. 358 and n. The present agreement illustrates how a place which was still regarded in 1123 as in the *parochia* of Leominster (see no. 354) could be largely lost to a neighbouring church outside the *parochia*, in this case Bodenham, which had itself already been given to Brecon Priory (*Mon. Ang.*, iii. 264); cf. the chapel/church of Humber (no. 348).

BROADWARD

327 *Quitclaim by Hugh of Kilpeck to Roger, earl of Hereford, of the hamlet of Broadward, in order that the earl may give it in free alms to Reading Abbey. In exchange he has received Kingstone, which the earl has released from the claim of Robert Brito* [1154 × 55]

Original charter: BL Add. Ch. 19588
A f45v; B f121r; C f66v; E f78r
Pd. *Arch. Journ.*, xxii. 155-6; (cal.) Hurry, *Reading Abbey*, 163-4

Sciant omnes fideles sancte ecclesie quod ego Hugo de Chilpeet*a* clamavi quietam de me et de omnibus heredibus meis in perpetuum villulam de Bradeford cum omnibus appendiciis suis Rogero comiti de Hereford*b* ut det eam in perpetuam elemosinam ecclesie sancte Marie de Radingis et monachis ibidem deo servientibus. Pro hac terra accepi escambium ab eodem comite secundum voluntatem meam, *'*id est*c* Kingestun,*d* quam predictus comes adquietavit*e* de Rodberto*f* Britone,*g* et eam mihi libere et quiete dedit propter *h*terram predictam.*h* Et ideo nichil iuris clamabimus in ea nec egc nec heredes mei post me usque in sempiternum.*i* Huius rei testc sunt: G(ilebertus) episcopus Herefordensis,*b* Radulfus decanus, Petrus archidiaconus,[j] Walterus archidiaconus, et Gislebertus cantor, cum toto capitulo Herefordie, Baderun de Munemue, Walterius de Clifford, Rodbertus de Candos, Henricus frater comitis, Herebertus de Castello Helgot, Ricardus de Cormeiles, Mauricius vicecomes, et de civibus Herefordie Herebertus filius Fucaldi, Rodbertus filius Walteri, Radulfus filius Iwein, et multi alii.

Endorsed: Hugo de Clipeet de Brad' [*12th cent.*] Manerium ac vill' de Bradeford' Leom' in com' Hereford' [*14th cent.*]

Size: 139 × 163 mm

Seal: missing, parchment tag remaining

[a] Chilpeec *A*, Kilpeec *B,C*	[b] Herford' *A*
[c-c] i. *B,C,E*	[d] Kingeston' *A*
[e] acquietavit *A*	[f] Roberto *A,C*
[g] Brittone *A*	[h-h] predictam terram *A*

[i] *B,E end with* T', *C ends*

[j] *A ends with* Gilebertus cantor, cum toto capitulo, et multis aliis

The outside dating limits are provided by the consecration of Gilbert Foliot and the death of Earl Roger, but no. 330 shows that it is of the same date as nos. 328-9. Hugh of Kilpeck already held 2 hides in Kingstone, his tenure dating back to *c.*1128-39, at which date another 2 hides were held by Miles the Constable, Earl Roger's father (*Herefs. Domesday*, 78, 127). The latter 2 hides were presumably now given to Hugh, thus putting him in possession of all 4 hides making up Kingstone in 1086 (*VCH Herefs.*, i. 312).

328 Gift in free alms by Roger, earl of Hereford, to Reading Abbey of his manor of Broadward as it was held by Hugh the Forester, who has quitclaimed it to him in exchange for Kingstone. The earl has made this gift for the health of his soul [etc.] and as reparation for the damage done to the abbey's men and possessions by the earl and his men during the war   [1154 × 55]

A f45v; B f120v; C f66r; E f78r-v
Pd. Walker, 'Hereford Charters', 23-4 (no. 25)

[a]Huius rei testes sunt: G(ilebertus) episcopus Herford(ensis), Radulfus decanus, Petrus archidiaconus, Walterus archidiaconus, et multi alii.

[a] *B ends with* T'; *C ends*; *E ends with* Test'

The war referred to in this charter is the 'Anarchy' of Stephen's reign, which is clearly now in the past. The earl rebelled unsuccessfully against Henry II in Mar. 1155, became a monk soon after at Gloucester and died within the year (Walker, *ibid.*, 9).

329 Notification by Roger, earl of Hereford, to Gilbert [Foliot], bishop of Hereford, and the chapter of Hereford, that he has given in free alms to the convent of Reading and Leominster the land of Broadward, which Hugh the Forester quitclaimed to him for an exchange [1154 × 55]

A f45v; B f120v; C f66r
Pd. Walker, 'Hereford Charters', 24 (no. 26)

De hac autem donatione testes sunt: Henricus frater meus, Nicho-laus[b] Basset dapifer, Alanus filius Mein, Oliver de Merlem', et multi alii.

[a] B ends with T', *C ends*
[b] A has Nochol'

Date as for no. 328.

330 Notification by Gilbert [Foliot], bishop of Hereford, that Roger, earl of Hereford, has given in free alms to Reading Abbey the hamlet of Broadward, which he acquired from Hugh of Kilpeck by exchange for the vill of Kingstone, which the earl released from the claim of Robert Brito. In the bishop's presence in the chapter of Hereford the earl gave Hugh seisin of Kingstone, Hugh gave the earl seisin of Broadward, and then the earl gave Reading Abbey seisin of Broadward [1154 × 55]

A f55r; B ff120v–121r; C f66v
Pd. *Foliot Letters and Charters*, 389 (no. 338)

*Huius donationis isti sunt testes: ego G(ilebertus) episcopus Herf(ordensis) cum toto capitulo nostro, Baderun de Munemue, Walterus de Clifford, et multi alii.

[a] B ends with T', *C ends*

Date as for no. 328. This act shows that nos. 327–30 are all of the same date.

331 Precept by Empress Matilda, daughter of King Henry, on her own part and that of her son King Henry II, to Maurice of Hereford not to allow the monks of Reading to be impleaded concerning their chattels or lands, and especially of Broadward, of which they were seised when the king last crossed to Normandy, until he returns to England [1159 × 60]

A f94v; B ff19v–20r
Pd. *Regesta*, iii. 261–2 (no. 711); *Memoranda Roll 1 John*, lxviii–lxix

T(este)*[a] Huberto de Wallibus. Apud Pratum.

[a] B ends

This is clearly addressed to Maurice as sheriff of Herefordshire, a position he held only in 1154–5 and 1159–60 (*List of Sheriffs*, 59). It was only in the second of these periods that Henry II was abroad, Aug. 1158–Dec.1162 (Eyton, 40, 58). The editors of *Regesta*, iii, suggest that, since the Empress is here apparently acting as regent while in Normandy (at Notre-Dame du Pré, Rouen), the precept may date from the time of Henry II's expedition to Toulouse, June–Sept. 1159

332 *Final concord in the king's court at Westminster between Abbot Hugh [II] and the convent of Reading and John of Kilpeck, by which the latter recognized half the vill of Broadward, excluding the capital messuage and adjacent alder-grove, to be the right of the former; in return the abbot and convent leased to John and his heirs in perpetuity half the mill of Broadward for an annual rent of 10s, and paid him 18 marks of silver. If John or his heirs can recover from the heirs of Roger, earl of Hereford, the exchange which the latter gave to Hugh of Kilpeck, John's grandfather, in Kingstone or elsewhere, the whole vill of Broadward shall remain to the abbot and convent, and John or his heirs shall repay the 18 marks of silver*   23 Oct. 1197

B f 182v; C ff 107v–108r

Hec est finalis concordia facta in curia domini regis apud Westm(onasterium) die iovis proxima post festum sancti Luce ewangeliste, anno regni regis Ricardi ix, coram G(odefrido) episcopo Wint(oniensi), Her(berto) episcopo Sar(esburiensi), Hugone Bard(ulf), Rad(ulfo) Hereford(ensi), Ricardo Elyensi archidiaconis, magistro Thoma de Husseburn', Ricardo de Heriet', Symone de Pat(es)hull', Osb(erto) filio Hervei,[a] iustic(iariis), et aliis fidelibus domini regis ibidem tunc presentibus, inter H(ugonem) abbatem et conventum ecclesie Rading(ensis), petentes, et Iohannem de Kylpec,[b] tenentem, de tota villa de Bradeford' cum pertinentiis, unde placitum fuit inter eos in prefata curia. Scilicet quod predictus Iohannes recognovit et concessit medietatem illius ville cum pertinentiis esse ius[c] ecclesie de Rading(ia) in perpetuum, preter capitale mesuagium et alnetum quod est iuxta illud mesuagium. Et pro hoc fine et concordia et recognitione predicti Hugo abbas et conventus concesserunt et dimiserunt prenominato I(ohanni) et heredibus suis medietatem molendini illius ville que ad eos pertinet, tenendam de[d] ecclesia de Rading(ia) ipse et heredes sui in perpetuum per liberum servitium .x. solidorum per annum pro omni servitio ad Annuntiationem beate Marie et ad festum sancti Michaelis persolvendorum, et preterea Hugo abbas et conventus de Rading(ia) dederunt prenominato I(ohanni) .xviii. marcas argenti. Ita quod si predictus I(ohannes) vel heredes sui cum auxilio predicti abbatis et conventus vel sine eorum auxilio possint recuperare de heredibus R(ogeri) comitis de[d] Heref(ordia) escambiam quam idem R(ogerus) comes dedit Hugoni de Kylpec[b] avo predicti Iohannis in Kingestun', vel si alibi quam in Kingest(un') escambiam recuperare possint, tota villa cum pertinentiis, scilicet Bradef(ord'), remanet predictis abbati et conventui in perpetuum; et prenominatus I(ohannes) vel heredes sui solvent predictis abbati et conventui .xviii. marcas argenti, et escambia quam idem I(ohannes) vel heredes sui recuperare poterint permanebit eis, scilicet Iohanni et heredibus suis.

 a ? Ern' *C*   *b* Kylpek *C*
c Insert ipsius abbatis et *C*   *d Om. in C*

The foot of this fine has not survived.

EYE

333 Licence by Hugh [de Mapenore], bishop of Hereford, to Reading Abbey to appropriate the church of Eye with all its chapels, saving a competent vicarage of 100s. The vicar shall bear episcopal and archidiaconal burdens, and the chapels shall be properly served [Dec. 1216 × Dec. 1218]

A ff 97v–98r; E f 67r–v
Pd. B. R. Kemp, 'Hereditary benefices in the medieval English Church: a Herefordshire example', *BIHR*, xliii (1970), 13

Hiis testibus:*a* Th(oma) decano, W(illelmo) precentore, H(elia) thesaurario, A(lbino) cancellario, W(illelmo) archidiacono Heref(ordie), H(ugone) archidiacono Salopesire, Gregorio, Roberto capellano, Nicolao Turri, clericis, Hugone de Fulef(ord'), et multis aliis.

a E ends with et cetera

The identity of the bishop is established by the fact that the act was inspected and confirmed by the legate, Guala, who left England in Dec. 1218 (see no. 335). The bishop was consecrated 18 Dec. 1216.

334 Notification by the same that, Roger formerly vicar of Eye having resigned the church, the bishop has admitted and instituted Reading Abbey as parson in the same, saving the assignment of a perpetual vicarage for the vicar who shall serve there
[Dec. 1216 × Apr. 1219; ? before Dec. 1218]

A f 100v; E f 67v
Pd. Kemp, 'Hereditary benefices', 13–14

Hiis testibus:*a* Thoma decano Hereford, W(illelmo) archidiacono Heref', H(ugone) archidiacono Salopesbir', magistro Albino cancellario Hereford, magistro Nicholao de Wlverehamt(ona), Willelmo le Poher, domino R. Celler', et multis aliis.

a E ends with et cetera

The outside dating limits are those of Hugh de Mapenore's pontificate (Hugh archdeacon of Shropshire succeeding him as bishop of Hereford), but the act may well be
of the same date as no. 333. Although Roger resigned, he was instituted to the new
vicarage by the same bishop on the abbey's presentation (see Kemp, *ibid.*, 6-7, 14).

335 Confirmation by Pope Honorius III to the abbot and convent
of Reading, at their request, of the bishop of Hereford's grant of the
church of Eye (*Eya*) with its chapels, of which the pope has learnt
from the letters of G(uala), then cardinal priest of St Martin, and
from the abbot and convent   8 July 1219

A f 79r; E f 70r

Dat' Reate viii. idus Julii, pontificatus nostri anno tertio.

Guala, papal legate, left England in Dec. 1218 (H. G. Richardson, 'Letters of the
legate Guala,' *EHR*, xlviii (1933), 250-1). His inspeximus and confirmation of no.
333 is E f 72r-v, which, if it is contemporary with another inspeximus for Reading
(see no. 361 n.), may date to 18 Nov. 1218. No. 333 was also inspected and confirmed
by Hugh Foliot and Ralph Maidstone, bishops of Hereford (E f 68v, f 69v), and
confirmed by Edmund Rich, archbishop of Canterbury, the legate Otto and Pope
Alexander IV (E f 72r, ff 72v-73r, f 104v).

336 *Record of the dispute between Philip of Eye and the abbot of Reading
over the advowson of the church of Eye*   1281-86

B ff 219r-221r; C ff 132v-135r

[1] Writ *Quod permittat* by King Edward I to the sheriff of Herefordshire, to order the abbot of Reading to permit Philip of Eye
(*Eya*) to present to the church of Eye, vacant and of his gift, as he
says, which the abbot is unjustly preventing; or, if he refuses, to
summon the abbot before the justices at Westminster in the quindene of Michaelmas.

Teste me ipso apud Westm(onasterium) xxvii. die Junii, anno
regni nostri ix.   27 June 1281

[2] The abbot was summoned to answer to Philip of Eye on a
plea that he permit him to present to the church of Eye, vacant, etc.
Philip claims that a certain Osbert, who held the manor of Eye to
which the advowson belonged, in the time of King Richard I
presented a certain Roger son of Osbert, clerk, who was admitted
and instituted; that the church is now vacant by his death; and that,
because Philip now holds the manor, the presentation belongs to
him. The abbot says that he cannot answer to this writ, since the
church is full by the abbot and convent, who hold it in appropriation of their own advowson and so held it for 20 years before
the writ was obtained. Philip replies that this exception ought not
to be admitted and claims that the abbot never had the church by

gift of anyone nor presented any clerk to it, but had entry to the church only by the said Roger son of Osbert, parson of the church, who demised it for a term of years; and the abbot shows no deed of enfeoffment in the advowson. Philip therefore seeks judgement as to whether the exception ought to be admitted in this case.

Afterwards, in the quindene of Michaelmas [1283] Philip and the abbot come [before the justices of the Common Bench] at Westminster, and the same arguments are put by the parties. Philip further maintains that in this case an inquest on plenarty should not be held by the ordinary, since the abbot shows no enfeoffment in the advowson and says only that the church is full by himself and the convent. After a day's adjournment the abbot proffers certifications of divers archbishops and bishops stating that the abbot and convent hold the church in appropriation. Asked by the justices if he has anything from a layman concerning the advowson, the abbot, after a further day's adjournment, proffers a charter of King Henry I giving the abbot and convent in free alms Leominster with its appurtenances, churches, chapels, cemeteries, offerings and tithes. Philip says that this charter should not now be of advantage to the abbot, since he did not proffer it earlier, though asked several times. The case is adjourned to the quindene of St Martin, and then to the quindene of St Hilary [1284].

[3] [Attempt to transfer the case *coram rege*]
Mandate by King Edward I to the justices [of the Common Bench] to send to him in the quindene of St Hilary, wherever he should be in England, the record and process of the case, since Philip of Eye has complained to the king of too much delay in the action hitherto.

Teste me ipso apud Gridelington' v. die Januarii, anno regni nostri xii.   5 Jan. 1284

In the quindene of St Hilary the abbot essoins himself by William *Dun*, who is told to inform the abbot that the case is to be *coram rege*.

Writ to the [sheriff of] Hereford to summon the abbot of Reading to be before the king or his *locum tenens* in the quindene of Easter, wherever he should be in England, to hear judgement in the case which was before the justices of the Bench and which the king has adjourned *coram rege*.

Teste R(adulfo) de Hengeh(am), apud Lincoln(iam) vii. die Februarii, anno regni nostri duodecimo.   7 Feb. 1284

In the quindene of Easter the abbot's attorneys were essoined to the quindene of Holy Trinity.

In the quindene of Holy Trintiy, the abbot having cited Magna

Carta that common pleas should not follow the king's court but be
held in a fixed place, etc., the parties are given a day for judgement
on this point *coram rege* in three weeks from Michaelmas. On that
day the abbot's attorneys were essoined to the quindene of St Hilary
[1285], on which day both Philip and the abbot appeared by attorneys *coram rege* at Bristol, where they were given a day on the morrow
of the close of Easter at Westminster before R(alph) de Hengham
and his fellows, because judgement was not yet made. There they
were given a day before the justices of the Bench on the morrow of
the Ascension [3 May].

[4] [Resumption of the case in the Common Bench, 4 May 1285]
On that day both parties appeared by attorneys. The court decides
that, since the plea is one of possession only, and the abbot is ready
to verify that the church is full of himself and the convent holding
it in appropriation of their own advowson, and the abbot proffered
a charter of Henry I concerning the advowson, there should be an
inquest in the ecclesiastical court as to whether or not the church is
vacant.

Mandate by King Edward I to R(ichard) [Swinfield], bishop of
Hereford, to hold an inquest as to whether the church of Eye is
vacant, and, if not, by whose presentation and from what time it
has been full, the result to be notified to the justices at Westminster
in one month from Holy Trinity.

Teste T(homa) Weilond' apud Westm(onasterium) xii. die Maii,
anno regni nostri xiii.   12 May 1285

In one month from Holy Trinity, the abbot being present by
attorney and Philip essoined, the bishop notified the justices by his
letters that, as a result of the inquest held in response to the king's
mandate, he has found that the church of Eye is not vacant, because
the abbot and convent of Reading are incumbent, but from what
time and by whose presentation he could not know for certain,
although several believe that they have it by gift of King Henry I,
while others believe that Osbert, grandfather of Philip, presented a
certain Roger, who was admitted to the church.

Dat' apud Sugwas vi. idus Junii, anno domini M.CC. octogesimo
quinto.   8 June 1285[1]

The parties are given a day in the quindene of Michaelmas, when,
because the bishop's reply was inadequate in not stating from what
time the church was full, he is ordered to make further enquiry.

Mandate by King Edward I to the same bishop of Hereford, in
the light of the earlier mandate and of the bishop's reply, to inform
the justices at Westminster distinctly and clearly in the quindene of

St Hilary at whose presentation and from what time the church has been full.

Teste T(homa) de Weilond' apud Westm(onasterium) viii. die Novembris, anno regni nostri xiii. 8 Nov. 1285

In the quindene of St Hilary [1286] the bishop's fuller reply was received, but, Philip of Eye being essoined, the case was adjourned to the quindene of Easter. On that day the bishop's letters reported that the church of Eye is full of the abbot and convent of Reading, and has been so time out of mind, by gift of King Henry I and by confirmation and appropriation of bishops and chapters of Hereford and archbishops of Canterbury, as is contained in the charters of the said King Henry and other kings of England and in letters of archbishops of Canterbury, viz., St Thomas the martyr and St Edmund the confessor and others, which the bishop has seen.

Dat' apud Arleye die conversionis sancti Pauli apostoli, anno domini M. ducentesimo octogesimo quinto. 25 Jan. 1286

Therefore the court decides in favour of the abbot *sine die*, and Philip is in mercy for false claim.

For discussion, see Kemp, 'Hereditary benefices ...', 7. This interesting case illustrates the interaction of the king's and the bishop's jurisdictions in settling advowson disputes. For the same in a slightly earlier period, see J. W. Gray, 'The *ius praesentandi* in England from the Constitutions of Clarendon to Bracton', *EHR*, lxvii (1952), esp. 494–502.

[1] The bishop's letters are printed from his register in *Reg. Swinfield*, 46–7.

337 *Record of the inquest held in Leominster Priory on the king's mandate concerning the vacancy of the church of Eye* 7 June 1285

B ff 221v-223r; C ff 135r-136v

Inquisicio facta in cappella beate Marie in ecclesia conventuali Leom' die jovis proxima ante festum sancti Barnabe apostoli [11 June], anno domini M.CC. octogesimo quinto, super vacacione ecclesie de Eye, ad mandatum regis secundum tenorem eiusdem qui talis: Edwardus dei gratia, et cetera.[1]

Quidam Walterus iuratus et examinatus diligenter et in primo interrogatus[a] utrum ecclesia de Eya sit vacans vel non, dicit quod non est vacans quia prior Leom' recipit fructus et incumbit possessioni. Requisitus de causa scientie, dicit quod talis est fama patrie. Requisitus si testis qui loquitur habeat noticiam parcium inter quas questio agitatur, dicit quod sic. Requisitus a quo tempore, dicit quod a quadraginta annis[b] et supra. Dicit etiam quod nec odio vel amore vel speciali gracia dicit ea que deponit, nec aliquid recipit[c] nec sperat recipere pro testimonio ferendo. Et est iste qui loquitur plus-

quam sexagenarius. Dicit etiam quod manerium Leom' cum appendiciis[d] suis fuit concessum abbati et conventui Rading' et causam
scientie dicit per hoc quod instrumenta eorum super hoc confecta
vidit et audivit. Requisitus si ecclesia[e] Leom' cum capellis sit concessa dictis religiosis in proprios usus, dicit quod dicta ecclesia cum
omnibus cappellis concessa est in proprios usus excepto quod nescit
aliquid dicere de Bromfeld et de Eye. Requisitus quomodo ista sciat,
dicit per hoc quod recipiunt fructus de eisdem, et de hoc fama est in
patria. Et aliquando vidit quod de dictis duabus fructus non receperit, scilicet[f] de Brumfeld et de Eye. Requisitus qui tunc receperit
fructus, dicit quod in capella de Brumfeld quidam magister Adam
dictus de Brumfeld recepit fructus in eisdem,[g] et quidam Rogerus in
ecclesia de Eya. Requisitus quomodo sciat ista, dicit quod ista vidit
et audivit eos nominare rectores. Requisitus si tenementum quod
Ph(ilippus) de Eya tenet ibidem fuerit de appendiciis pertinencibus
ad manerium de Leom', dicit quod nescit. Requisitus si dictum
tenementum quod Ph(ilippus) de Eya tenet fuit in manibus dictorum religiosorum virorum, dicit quod nescit. Requisitus si dictam
ecclesiam possiderunt per C. annos, dicit quod a .xxx. annis et
parum supra tenuerunt et non multum amplius. Requisitus si ecclesie de Leom' et de Eya cum capellis fuerint appropriate dictis religiosis, dicit quod sic, et de hoc est fama, et ab eo tempore receperunt
fructus. Requisitus quis appropriavit eisdem dictas ecclesias, dicit
quod non recolit. Requisitus utrum tenuerunt eas appropriatas, dicit
quod sic. Requisitus de causa scientie, dicit per hoc quod fructus
perceperunt.[h] Requisitus quis ultimo fuit ibi rector, dicit quod quidam Rogerus avus Ph(ilipp)i de quo agitur. Requisitus si fuit rector
vel vicarius, dicit quod habebatur pro rectore. Requisitus quis presentavit ad eandem, dicit quod nescit quia fuit dominus et rector.
Dicit etiam quod numquam vidit dictum Osb(ertum) nec novit[i] si
ad eandem ecclesiam presentavit an non, nec novit cui presentacio
fuit facta, nec quis erat episcopus tunc temporis, nec etiam utrum
fuit institutus per episcopum. Requisitus per cuius presentacionem
vel collacionem habuerunt prefati religiosi ecclesiam de Eya, dicit
quod nescit. Requisitus a quo tempore fuerit plena, dicit quod triginta annis ut supra dicit textus qui loquitur.

Quidam Ph(ilippus) iuratus et examinatus et requisitus utrum
dicta ecclesia de Eya sit vacans, concordat cum prefato W(altero)
supraexaminato, et reddit causam scientie quia percipiunt dictos
fructus et iste qui loquitur emit partem de dictis fructibus. Et novit
partes litigantes a .x. annis, nec odio vel amore perhibet testimonium, nec aliquid recipit vel recipere sperat pro testimonio ferendo.
Et est iste qui loquitur triginta annorum, ut dicit. Et quod manerium Leom' cum appendiciis fuit concessum abbati et conventui Rad-

ing' per H(enricum) quartum*j* regem Anglie. Et hoc novit per cartam domini regis quam vidit et audivit. Audivit*k* etiam et
instrumenta*l* vidit per que videtur appropriata dictis religiosis, et
hoc scit per predicta instrumenta, nec recolit de tempore in quo
fructus non perceperunt dicte ecclesie [*f222r*] de Eya. Requisitus per
quantum tempus, dicit quod nescit nisi prout audivit per instrumenta dictorum religiosorum. Requisitus ad cuius presentacionem
vel collacionem est plena de dictis religiosis, dicit quod per collacionem H. et per litteras sigillatas sigillo episcopi Johannis[2] habent
dictum manerium cum appendiciis. Requisitus si tenementum de
Eya una cum advocacione de Eya sit pendens vel appendicium ad
dictam ecclesiam de Eya, dicit quod nescit. Requisitus si unquam
vidit ibi aliquem alium rectorem, dicit quod non. Audivit tamen
quod quidam Rogerus fuit ibidem qui se fecit vocare rectorem, por-
rectas tamen litteras*k* audivit cuiusdam iudicis delegati in quibus
vicarius nominatur. Requisitus si vidit aliquem patronum presentare
ad dictam ecclesiam, dicit quod non.

Quidam Radulphus iuratus et examinatus et requisitus, dicit quod
ecclesia de Eya non vacat, quia prior Leom' recipit fructus et incumbit possessioni, ad cuius presentacionem ignorat, quia ingressum habuerunt per regem. Et de causa scientie, dicit quod per hoc quod*k*
audivit cartas regis. Requisitus a quo tempore tenuerunt ecclesiam,
dicit quod numquam vidit eos extra ecclesiam. Requisitus si Rogerus
de quo supra fit mencio fuerit rector dicte ecclesie vel firmarius, dicit
quod fuit firmarius perpetuus, prout in quibusdam litteris videbatur
contineri, et per alias litteras nominatus est vicarius. Requisitus ad
cuius presentacionem, dicit quod ignorat nec cui episcopo fuit presentatus nec per quem admissus. Dicit quod novit litigantes a sex
annis, nec prece vel*m* precio, odio*k* vel amore perhibet testimonium.
Et dicit quod manerium de Leom' cum appendic(iis) datum est
dictis religiosis per regem H(enricum) prefatum, prout apparet per
litteras eiusdem, et quod*n* ecclesia de Eya appropriata est eisdem,
prout apparet per litteras Johannis episcopi et per confirmaciones
quorundam diocesanorum quas audivit, ut dicit.

Quidam Johannes iuratus et examinatus et requisitus, dicit quod
ecclesia de Eya non est vacans, set est plena de abbate et conventu
Rading', qui fructus dicte ecclesie percipiunt et possessioni incumbunt tanquam rectores eiusdem. Requisitus de causa scientie, dicit
quod fama patrie talis est. Requisitus ad cuius presentacionem, dicit
quod ignorat. Requisitus de tempore a quo plena est de ipsis, dicit
quod a .xx. annis et citra. Requisitus de causa scientie, dicit quod
fuit scolaris Leom' et hoc vidit et audivit. Requisitus utrum Rogerus
prenominatus fuerit rector eiusdem ecclesie vel vicarius, dicit quod
nescit, nec si fuit admissus, nec ad cuius presentacionem, nec cui

episcopo. De appropriacione nichil scit,[o] ut dicit. In aliis concordat cum preiurato suo.

Quidam R. interrogatus et examinatus et requisitus super primo articulo, scilicet utrum ecclesia de Eya sit vacans vel non, dicit quod non vacat. Requisitus quomodo scit, dicit[k] quod abbas et conventus Rading' incumbunt possessioni, nescit tamen ad cuius presentacionem vel a quo tempore. Item requisitus quomodo scit hoc, dicit quod notorium est per patriam. Requisitus si manerium de Leom' fuerit concessum abbati et conventui de[k] Rading' cum appendiciis et si ecclesia de Leom' cum capellis fuerit concessa eisdem in proprios usus, dicit quod sic. Requisitus quomodo scit, respondet quod[k] per famam patrie. Requisitus quid sit fama, dicit quod fama est commune dictum tocius patrie. Requisitus si tenementum quod Ph(ilippus) de Eye tenet fuerit de appendiciis et pertinentiis manerii de Leom' et si tenementum illud fuit aliquo tempore in manu dictorum abbatis et conventus tanquam appendicium manerii de Leom', dicit quod nescit. Requisitus si dicti abbas et conventus teneant ecclesiam de Eya in proprios usus vel umquam tenuerunt, dicit quod nescit; scit tamen quod eam tenent, ut prius. Requisitus quanto tempore dicti religiosi possiderunt ecclesiam de Eya, dicit quod nescit. Requisitus si ecclesie de Leom' et de Eye fuerint appropriate dictis religiosis Rading', dicit quod sic. Requisitus quomodo scit, dicit quod per famam et instrumenta eorum super hoc confecta que aliquando vidit;[p] tamen non recolit de nominibus concedencium. Interrogatus si unquam vidit alium rectorem in ecclesia de Eya nisi abbatem, dicit quod non; dicit tamen [f 222v] quod audivit pluries et a pluribus quod quidam nomine Rogerus tenuit dictam ecclesiam et gerebat se pro rectore et quod vocatus fuit rector. De aliis nichil scit.

Quidam H. interrogatus et examinatus de primo articulo, qui in hoc concordat cum primo teste. Requisitus ad cuius presentacionem et a quo tempore, dicit quod nescit. Requisitus[q] de predicto Rogero, de quo concordat cum priore; dicit tamen quod contrarium credit propter instrumenta que vidit.

Quidam R. interrogatus et examinatus diligenter, dicit quod nichil scit de interrogatis.

Quidam R. interrogatus et examinatus de primo articulo, dicit quod incumbunt possessioni, nescit tamen ad cuius presentacionem nec a quo tempore. Requisitus si unquam fuit ibi alius rector preter abbatem, dicit quod nescit; audivit tamen ab aliquibus quod quidam nomine Rogerus tenuit dictam ecclesiam de Eye et vocabatur a pluribus rector. De aliis nichil scit.

Quidam R. interrogatus et examinatus, in primo articulo concordat cum predictis, dicens quod abbas et conventus Rading' incum-

bunt possessioni ecclesie de Eye, nescit tamen ad cuius presentacionem nec a quo tempore, addens quod audivit a multis quod
quidam Osb(ertus) dominus de Eye presentavit ad[k] dictam ecclesiam de Eye quendam Rogerum filium et quod dictus[r] R(ogerus)
tenuit dictam ecclesiam tanquam rector. Requisitus de forma pre-
sentacionis et cui presentatus et per quem institutus, dicit quod
nescit, et hec didicit per relata set neminem vidit de illis. Credit
tamen quod ea que dicta sunt de Rogero falsa esse[s] propter instrumenta que audivit. De aliis nichil scit[o] nisi quatenus intellexit per
recitacionem instrumentorum.

Quidam[t] interrogatus et examinatus, dicit quod abbas et conventus Rading' incumbunt possessioni ecclesie de Eye, nescit tamen ad
cuius presentacionem nec [a][u] quo tempore. Requisitus si dicta ecclesia fuit unquam concessa dictis religiosis in proprios usus, dicit
quod nescit. Requisitus de dicto Rogero, dicit quod audivit quod
idem Rogerus tenuit aliquo tempore dictam ecclesiam tanquam rector. Requisitus an fuerit presentatus et per quem, dicit quod nescit;
magis tamen credit quod non fuerit verus rector propter instrumenta
que vidit. Audivit tamen quod dictus[r] Rogerus tenuit ecclesiam de
Eye multo tempore et obiit circiter triginta annos.

Quidam R. interrogatus et examinatus, dicit quod ecclesia de Eye
non vacat eo quod abbas et conventus Rading' incumbunt possessioni eiusdem, set ad cuius presentacionem vel a quo tempore nescit.
Item dicit quod audivit quod quidam Rogerus aliquando tenuit
dictam ecclesiam et fecit se vocari rectorem, propter quod dictus
abbas contra ipsum in foro ecclesiastico est expertus.[3] Dicit tamen
quod non credit ipsum fuisse rectorem. De aliis nichil scit.[o]

Quidam Nicholaus dicit quod religiosi incumbunt possessioni ecclesie de Eye, set ad cuius presentacionem vel a quo tempore nescit,
addens quod audivit a quodam quod quidam Rogerus tenuit dictam
ecclesiam de Eye aliquo tempore tanquam rector, set nescit si rector
fuerat vel non, quia de presentacione seu admissione eiusdem nullam
scit[v] certitudinem.

Quidam Th(omas) interrogatus et examinatus, dicit quod abbas
et conventus Rading' incumbunt possessioni dicte ecclesie de Eye,
set ad cuius presentacionem vel a quo tempore nescit, addens quod
vidit ibi tres vicarios, scilicet Willelmum, Ricardum et Adam, qui
nunc est,[4] institutos ad presentacionem abbatis et conventus Rading'
in ecclesia de Eye, unde sibi videtur quod ipsi sint veri rectores.
Interrogatus de dicto Rogero, dicit quod vidit eum tenere dictam
ecclesiam multo tempore, set nescit qualem ingressum habuit
ad dictam ecclesiam de Eya, nec si fuit rector vel non. De aliis
nichil scit[o] nisi quatenus audivit per recitacionem instrumentorum
abbatis.

[a] interogatus *C throughout*	[b] *Both texts repeat* annis
[c] recepit *C, and sometimes later*	[d] appendenc' *C throughout*
[e] *Both texts have* ecclesie	[f] set *C*
[g] *Sic in both texts; ? rectius* eadem	[h] receperunt *C*
[i] movit/monit *? C, and sometimes later*	[j] *Sic in both texts*
[k] *Om. in C*	[l] instrumentum *C*
[m] nec *C*	[n] quia *C*
[o] sit *C*	[p] *Insert* et *C*
[q] *Insert* si *C*	[r] predictus *C*
[s] *Sic in both texts; ? rectius* sunt	[t] *Name om.*
[u] *Supplied*	[v] fecit *C*

For discussion, see Kemp, 'Hereditary benefices . . .', 7–8.

[1] Referring to the mandate, dated 12 May 1285, quoted in no. 336.
[2] John Breton, bishop of Hereford 1269–75.
[3] Probably referring to the abbey's appeal against Roger to the pope in 1246, the case being delegated to the prior of Wallingford, before whom it was heard in 1251 (E f 7or–v; pd. Kemp, 'Hereditary benefices,' 14; discussed *ibid.*, 8–9).
[4] Adam was instituted 23 Mar. 1283 (*Reg. Swinfield*, 524).

338 *Record of the inquest held on the bishop of Hereford's mandate by the dean and clergy of the [rural] deanery of Leominster concerning the church of Eye*   7 June 1285

B f 223r; C f 136v

Inquisicio facta ad mandatum domini Hereford(ensis)[a] episcopi per decanum et clerum decanatus Leom' super ecclesia de Eye in ecclesia conventuali Leom' die iovis proxima ante festum beati Barnabe apostoli [11 June], anno domini M.CC. octogesimo quinto. Utrum dicta ecclesia vacet, dicit quod non est vacans eo quod religiosi viri abbas et conventus Rading' incumbunt possessioni dicte ecclesie. Et dicit quod iidem abbas et conventus sunt veri patroni eo quod Henricus rex eis terras et tenementa cum ecclesiis et capellis Leom' et Eye [dedit],[b] ut patet per instrumenta eorumdem super hiis confecta. Quem ultimo ad eandem presentavit nescimus. Litigiosa est quod dominus Bogo de Clar' clericus se opponit contra dictos abbatem et conventum de dicta ecclesia. Non est pensionata. Et dicit quod persona presentata ydonea est et in multis[c] aliis locis beneficiatus.

[a] Herford' *C*   [b] *Supplied*
[c] certis *C*

This inquest was held on the same day as no. 337, but, though related to it, was distinct in origin and purpose. It appears to be either a draft report of an inquest *de iure patronatus* or an abridged version of the same. Such inquests normally followed presentations to benefices and, although the vicarage of Eye was not vacant in 1285 (see *Reg. Swinfield*, 524, 529), it is possible that this inquest was held in response to a presentation of Bogo de Clare, who was certainly much beneficed elsewhere, by Philip of Eye, even though the latter was then in dispute with Reading Abbey over the advowson. For Bogo de Clare, see A. H. Thompson, 'Pluralism in the medieval Church', *Assoc. Archit. Soc. Reports and Papers*, xxxiii (1915-16), 53-7.

EYWOOD (?)

339 Notification of the settlement in the presence of Gilbert [Foliot], bishop of Hereford, and the chapter, between Leominster Priory and Serlo, priest of Kinnersley, over the chapel and tithes of *Ewda*.[a] Serlo has admitted that the chapel does not belong of right to his church but to the church in whose territory it is known to be, and has withdrawn his church's claim to it, but, by the bishop's mediation and with the permission of Leominster Priory, the chapel has been assigned to his care for his life for an annual pension of 5s. Witnesses [omitted]   [1148 × 63]

A f 56r; E f 61v
Pd. *Foliot Letters and Charters*, 391 (no. 341)

[a] Eiwda *E*

The dating limits are those of Foliot's pontificate of Hereford. *Ewda* is possibly Eywood in Titley parish, some 7 miles north of Kinnersley, but there is no trace of a chapel there. In 1130 × 35 Abbot Anscher of Reading made a grant of the wood called *Eiwde*, retaining the tithes in his hand (E f 118r-v). Kinnersley was reckoned to be in the *parochia* of Leominster in 1123 (see no. 354), but there is no evidence that it remained so thereafter. The portion of 6s 8d in Kinnersley church due to Leominster Priory in 1291 (*Taxatio*, 160) possibly derived from a later revision of the present settlement.

FORD AND HAMPTON (? MAPPENORE)

340 *Mandate by William [of Corbeil], archbishop of Canterbury and legate, to Peter, archdeacon of Hereford, and his ministers to remove the clerks whom they have intruded into the chapels of Ford and Hampton,[1] belonging to the church of Leominster, without the knowledge or consent of Abbot Hugh [I] of Reading*   [1126 × 30; ? after 15 Aug. 1127]

C f 121r

Willelmus dei gratia Cant(uariensis) archiepiscopus et sedis apostolice legatus, P(etro) Herford(ensi) archidiacono et ministris suis, salutem. Dominus Hugo Radyng(ensis) abbas conqueritur quod in capellis Forde et Hamtun(e) ad ecclesiam Leom(inistrie) pertinentibus, ipso abbate nesciente nec concedente nec assentiente, clericos intromisistis, quod nequaquam sic facere debueratis. Mandamus itaque super hoc vobis quatinus hoc citius emendetur clericos inde removendo, donec per abbatem fiat quicquid inde fiet. Quod nisi feceritis et clamorem inde audiam, quod ad me pertinuerint[a] faciam sicut de negligentibus et obedire refugientibus ad ea que per auctoritatis apostolice manum firmata cognovimus. Valete.

^a Sic; ? rectius pertinuerit

After the archbishop became legate and before Abbot Hugh became archbishop of Rouen, but possibly during the vacancy in the see of Hereford, 15 Aug. 1127—28 June, 1131 (see Z.N. and C.N.L. Brooke, 'Hereford cathedral dignitaries in the 12th and 13th centuries', *Cambridge Hist. Journ.*, viii (1944), 15). Both places were listed as in the *parochia* of Leominster in 1123 (see no. 354).

¹ Probably Hampton Mappenore (see no. 342), since no chapel is recorded at Hampton Ricardi (now Hampton Court) and none at Hampton Wafer before 1186 × 98 (see no. 346 n.).

HAMNISH

341 *Notification by Walter de Clifford that he has received from Reading Abbey 24 acres, including a spring, stream and small wood, to enlarge his park of Hamnish, for 2s and a white doe-skin annually*   [c. 1135 × c. 1170]

A f 46r; E f 78r

Sciant presentes et futuri quod ego Walt(erus) de Clifford accepi de abbate Rading(ensi) et conventu eiusdem loci ad ampliandum parcum meum de Hamenesse .xxiiii. acras de virgata[a] quam[b] tenuit Ailrich[c] filius Ordive cum fonte et rivo quem fons facit et grava parva que in eadem terra habentur, pro .ii. solidis et pelle damme alba annuatim ecclesie Leom(inistrie) persolvendis, ego et heredes mei ad festum apostolorum Petri et Pauli. Hec quoque donatio rata erit et stabilis quamdiu predictum censum ego et heredes mei bene reddiderimus et memorata terra in manu nostra fuerit. Si autem aliquo casu aut mutatione aliqua ad aliud dominium transierit, terra monachorum absque omni contradictione ad ipsos libera revertetur. Ego vero Walt(erus) homagium feci abbati et fidelitatem iuravi.[d] His testibus: W. de Braosa, Radulfo de Baskervilla, Hugone de Sai, Gaufredo presbitero, et multis aliis.

^a A has here terre marked for deletion
^b Insert tunc E
^c A has Ailvrich with v marked for deletion
^d E ends with Test'

Walter succeeded to the Clifford estates in c.1138 and died in 1190 (Sanders, *English Baronies*, 35). Hamnish was held under the manor of Leominster T.R.E., and in 1086 by Drew fitz Ponz (*VCH Herefs.*, i. 316). By c.1128 × 39 it had descended to his nephew Walter de Clifford (*Herefs. Domesday*, 78), but by the middle of Henry II's reign, possibly *c.*1160 × 70, Walter had subinfeudated the manor to a certain Peter (*ibid.*, 14), after which it continued to be held of the Honour of Clifford (*Fees*, ii. 799; *Aids*, ii. 381, 398). The land here conceded to Walter may have been in the abbey's adjacent lordship of Stockton, or the abbey may have retained possession of a small part of Hamnish now transferred to him. By a separate deed Walter gave Leominster the tithes of Hamnish in return for the grant of a chapel there (E f 77r–v).

HAMPTON MAPPENORE

342 Notification by Gilbert [Foliot], bishop of Hereford, that at the request and will of the abbot of Reading he has consecrated a cemetery at Hampton [Mappenore], whose lord, Peter of Mappenore, has granted to the mother church of Leominster the chapel within the cemetery, 40 acres of his land and all tithe of his demesne and of his men with all parochial right   [1148 × 63]

A f 55v; E f 62r
Pd. *Foliot Letters and Charters*, 388–9 (no. 337)

The dating limits are those of Foliot's pontificate of Hereford. Hampton Mappenore was probably next to Hampton Ricardi (now Hampton Court) in Hope-under-Dinmore (*Herefs. Domesday*, 86).

HAMPTON RICARDI

343 Notification by Gilbert [Foliot], bishop of Hereford, to the clergy and people of the diocese that the dispute between the abbot of Reading and Gilbert of Hampton over the tithes of Hampton [Ricardi], which belonged of old by right to the church of Leominster and which Gilbert violently withheld in the time of war, has been settled. In the presence of the bishop and chapter of Hereford the abbot proved by the oath of clergy and laity that the entire parochial right belonged to Leominster, and received possession of the same   [1154 × 63]

A f 56r–v
Pd. *Foliot Letters and Charters*, 391–2 (no. 342)

While Foliot was bishop of Hereford and, since the reference to 'the time of war' suggests that the 'Anarchy' of Stephen's reign was over, not earlier than 1154. Gilbert of Hampton was alias Gilbert of Bacton, who at this time held Hampton Ricardi (now Hampton Court) in Hope-under-Dinmore (*Herefs. Domesday*, 12, 85–6) as well as Bacton (*ibid.*, 42).

344 *Notification by Robert [Foliot], bishop-elect of Hereford, acting as papal judge–delegate, of the settlement of the case between Roger son of*

*Maurice and Abbot Joseph and the monks of Reading over the demesne tithes
of Hampton [Ricardi], which Roger claimed as appurtenant to his church of
Bacton. Roger has renounced the tithes into the bishop-elect's hand as appurtenant to the church of Leominster, and the bishop-elect has consigned them to
the abbot and monks, who in turn have granted them to Roger for life for an
annual pension of 1 gold coin*   [Apr. 1173 × 6 Oct. 1174]

A f55v; A f56v; E ff59v–6or

Robertus dei gratia Herford(ensis)*[a]* ecclesie electus universis sancte
matris ecclesie filiis, salutem eternam in domino. Noverit universitas
vestra causam que vertebatur inter Rog(eru)m filium Mauricii et
Ioseph abbatem et monachos de Rading(ia) super decimationibus
totius dominii de Hamtona,*[b]* quas idem Rog(erus) ex mandato domini pape quod nobis super his*[c]* cognoscendum*[d]* attulerat ad ius ecclesie sue de Bakintun(a)*[e]* pertinere contendebat, amicabili interveniente compositione coram nobis fuisse sopitam. Modus autem
compositionis talis est. Memoratus Rogerus*[f]* cessit iuri quod videbatur habere in predictis decimationibus et eas tanquam ad ius
ecclesie de Leominist(ria)*[g]* pertinentes in manu nostra refutavit. Nos
itaque auctoritate domini pape qua in hac parte functi sumus me-
moratas decimationes iamdicto abbati et monachis quietas et absolutas resignavimus. Abbas vero de voluntate et consilio conventus
pretaxatas*[h]* decimationes iamdicto Rogero*[i]* in tota vita sua concessit
habendas sub unius aurei pensione singulis annis infra oct(avas)
sancti Michaelis persolvendi. Ne ergo in posterum alicuius versutia
posset*[j]* ista compositio dissolvi et in irritum revocari, eam litterarum
nostrarum attestatione et sigilli nostri appositione auctoritate domini
pape qua freti sumus curavimus roborare.

[a] Hereford' *E*	*[b]* Hamt' *E*
[c] hiis *E*	*[d]* cognoscendis *E*
[e] *A f55v has* Rokintun' (*in error*); Bakint' *A f56v;* Bachintun' *E*	
[f] *Insert* de voluntate sua *E*	*[g]* Leomen' *E*
[h] *A f55v has* pretaxas	*[i]* Rogerio *A f56v*
[j] possit *E*	

While Robert Foliot was bishop-elect. Joseph became abbot in 1173. The text in A
f55v runs on directly from no. 342 without a separate rubric or large initial at the
beginning; it was thus missed by the compiler of the contemporary table of contents
at the beginning of the cartulary, where it ought to have appeared on f5v. That the
Hampton of this act is Hampton Ricardi is established by (i) the reference to Bacton
church, both Hampton Ricardi and Bacton having been held earlier by Gilbert of
Bacton, alias of Hampton (see no. 343 n.), and (ii) by the naming of the place in no.
345 as Hampton Gilberti, referring to the earlier tenure by the same Gilbert. Moreover, both nos. 343 and 344 were together confirmed by Giles de Braose, bishop of
Hereford 1200–15, when Roger son of Maurice surrendered the tithes through the
bishop to Leominster Priory (E f65r–v).

345 *Notification of the settlement of the case between Abbot Joseph and the convent of Reading and Roger son of Maurice over the demesne tithes of Hampton Ricardi,*[1] *which Roger claimed as appurtenant to his church of Bacton. In the chapter of Reading Roger acknowledged the abbey's right in return for a grant to him of the tithes for life for an annual pension of 1 bezant*

[1173 × 74]

A f46r; C f121r

Notum sit tam presentibus quam futuris quod causa que inter ecclesiam Rading(ensem) et Rog(eru)m filium Maur(icii) super decimationibus totius dominii de Hamtona Gileberti,*a* quas idem Rog(erus) tanquam ad ecclesiam suam de Bachint(una) de iure pertinentes vendicabat, in hunc modum amicali*b* interveniente compositione terminata est. Predictus siquidem Rog(erus) in presentia domni Ioseph abbatis et totius conventus in capitulo Rading(ensi) plenum ius ecclesie Rading(ensis) in eisdem decimationibus*c* recognovit et iuri suo si quod in eis habuerat tactis sacrosanctis evangeliis renuntiavit. Domnus autem abbas Ioseph voluntate et consensu*d* totius conventus concessit eidem Rog(ero) predictas decimationes tota vita sua tenendas de ecclesia Rading(ensi) pro annua pensione unius bisantii*e* infra oct(avas) sancti Michaelis persolvendi. Hec autem conventio rata erit*f* quamdiu idem Rog(erus) ecclesie Radingie*g* fidelis extiterit et predictum bisantium*h* bene solverit.

a Gilberti C	*b* amicabili C
c decimis C	*d* consilio C
e baisantii C	*f* *Insert* et stabilis C
g Radyng' C	*h* baisant' C

Contemporary with, or very soon after, no. 344, although this deed was probably made at Reading.

[1] Hampton Gilberti in the text is the same as Hampton Ricardi (see no. 344 n.).

HAMPTON WAFER

346 Notification by Gilbert [Foliot], bishop of Hereford, that, at the request of Robert of Hampton and with the assent of the monks of Leominster, he has consecrated a cemetery at Hampton [Wafer] as a sanctuary (*ad refugium*) for Robert's men; and that Robert has given the monks in free alms all the tithe of his demesne and of his men in his fee of Hampton [Wafer], with 30 acres of land, and has promised to pay the ½ mark of silver annually which he anciently owed to the priory and had unjustly detained. The agreement was confirmed by Elias de Ponte, burgess of Hereford, who then held the

land of Robert in pledge (*in vadium*) and promised to pay the rent
on his behalf   [1148 × 63; ? 1148 × 54]

A f55r-v; E f62r
Pd. *Foliot Letters and Charters*, 387-8 (no. 335)

... apud Leoministriam presentibus et audientibus his testibus:*
Waltero Foliot archidiacono de Salopesb(eria), Waltero de Clune
capellano episcopi, Hugone nepote episcopi, et multis aliis.

a *E ends with* et cetera

The outside dating limits are those of the bishop's pontificate, but the consecration
of a cemetery for sanctuary may suggest the troubled times of Stephen's reign (cf. no.
368). The identification of the place as Hampton Wafer rests on the identity of
Robert of Hampton with the Robert *Wafre* who held the manor in Henry II's reign
(*Herefs. Domesday*, 12, 85). No chapel is mentioned in this agreement, but one was
certainly in existence by 1186 × 98, when its advowson was in dispute between the
prior of Leominster and Simon *le Wafre* (E f64r, f111r). A cemetery *ad refugium* did
not constitute a burial ground—cf. 'Cartl. Brecon', *Arch. Cambrensis*, 4th Ser. xiv. 228,
where there is a reference to *cimiterium ... sine omni sepultura ad refugium pauperum tempore
hostilitatis si ita contigerit* (date: 1179 × 89, for which see *Heads of Relig. Houses*, 91 and
n. 3).

HATFIELD

347 Confirmation by Theobald, archbishop of Canterbury and
primate, of the arrangements made by Robert [de Bethune] and
Gilbert [Foliot], bishops of Hereford, regarding the consecration of
a cemetery at Hatfield for the benefit of Leominster Priory, namely,
that it shall be regarded as an augmentation of the cemetery of
Leominster, on condition that the offerings for those buried at Hatfield or their dying bequests shall go to the monks of Leominster as
if they were buried at Leominster. The clerk serving in the chapel
of Hatfield shall ensure to the monks the preservation of this right,
and in those matters which concern the diocesan bishop the chapel
shall be treated as a chapel and not as a mother church (*mater
ecclesia*)   [1148 × 61]

A f54v; E ff71v-72r
Pd. Saltman, *Theobald*, 440-1 (no. 217)

After the consecration of Foliot as bishop of Hereford, and before Theobald's death.
The absence from the archbishop's style of the legatine title, which he acquired in
1150 (Saltman, 30-1), is not sufficient to date it earlier, since the archbishop's acts
while he was legate frequently omit it (*ibid.*, 191-2). The acts by Bishops Robert and
Gilbert, which this confirms, are E f60r-v and f61r.

HUMBER

348 Notification by Gilbert [Foliot], bishop of Hereford, to the faithful of his diocese that Walter del Mans and Agnes, his wife, have in the bishop's presence given in free alms to Leominster Priory the virgate and meadow in *Purtlint(ona)*[a] which William son of Symer holds for 4s annually, and 12d from the rent of the mill which Hugh the miller son of Edwin holds; and that, with the consent of Edward, abbot of Reading, and at the request of the monks of Leominster, the bishop has consecrated a cemetery for Walter and his wife at their chapel of Humber, on condition that one body only is buried there, the rest with their bequests being taken to Leominster as previously   [1148 × 54]

A f56r; E f61v
Pd. *Foliot Letters and Charters*, 386-7 (no. 334)

[b]Huius rei testes sunt ex parte monachorum: Walt(erius) Foliot archidiaconus Salopesb(erie), Hugo nepos episcopi, W(alterius) de Clun' capellanus episcopi, Adam de Eya decanus Leom(inistrie), G. capellanus de Humbre, Ailbricth vicarius eius, P(etrus) de Mapp(enora), R. frater eius, Herew' filius Alwardi, Hugo de Leomin(istria), Walclinus dapifer; ex parte Walterii: Matheus filius eius, W. nepos eius, et multi alii.

[a] Portlinton' E
[b] E ends with T' et cetera

After Foliot became bishop of Hereford and while Edward was abbot of Reading, which he had ceased to be before the end of 1154. Walter and Agnes subsequently, and not later than 1155, gave the 'church' of Humber to Brecon Priory ('Cartl. Brecon', *Arch. Cambrensis*, 4th Ser. xix. 33), the gift being confirmed by Roger, earl of Hereford, who died in 1155 (*ibid.*, 149) and by Gilbert Foliot (*Foliot Letters and Charters*, 355, no. 291). Humber was thus, like Broadfield (no. 326), another place which, though included in the *parochia* of Leominster in 1123 (see no. 354), was later lost for the most part into the hands of another religious house.

HURSTLEY

349 *Delivery of seisin by Roger, abbot of Reading, to Roger of Letton of the land of Hurstley which his grandfather had held and to which he proved his title against Robert of Brobury in the abbey's court of Reading*
                                                                 [1158 × 65]

Original charter: BL Add. Ch. 19594
C f139v; E f118v
Pd. (cal.) Hurry, *Reading Abbey*, 116

Sciant presentes et futuri sancte ecclesie filii quod ego Rog(erius) abbas Rading(ensis) assensu et *consilio conventus* seaisivi*b* Rog(erium) de Leituna de terra de Hurteslega*c* quam avus ipsius tenuerat, et quam dirainavit*d* adversus Rodbertum*e* de*f* Brogberia*g* in curia nostra de Rading(ia). Et concessi ut eandem terram teneat pro eodem servitio quod predictus Rodbertus*h* nobis*i* inde annuatim reddere solebat ad festum beatorum apostolorum Petri et Pauli, scilicet pro dimidia marca argenti ad eundem terminum persolvenda.*j* His testibus: Hugone dapifero, Aimone*k* de Coddebroc,*l* Raimundo,*m* Lewino portario, Walterio coco, Hugone clerico.

CYROGRAPHUM

Endorsed: Contra Rogerium de Leituna [*13th cent.*]
    De diversis locis in Berksire¹ [*14th cent.*]
Size: 108 × 112 mm
Seal: no sign of sealing

a-a concilio et conventus *C*	*b* seisiavi *E*
c Hurthesleg' *E*	*d* direinavit *E*
e 'Robertum *C,E*	*f* Om. in *C*
g Brogebir' *E*	*h* Robertus *C,E*
i Om. in *E*	*j* *E ends with* Test'
k Simone *C* (*in error*)	*l* Cotebrok' *C*
m Ramundo *C*	

The dating limits are those of Roger's abbacy. Hurstley, in Letton, about 11 miles S.W. of Leominster, was not mentioned in Domesday Book, but may have come to Reading with the manor of Leominster, since the evidence of this deed allows the abbey's lordship to be dated back probably to Henry I's time. Roger of Letton, grandson of Reading's earlier tenant, was probably lord of Letton and a predecessor of the Adam who held Letton later in Henry II's reign (*Herefs. Domesday*, 47). However, possibly during Stephen's reign, Hurstley had been occupied by Robert of Brobury, lord of Brobury (*ibid.*, 48), who had nevertheless held it of the abbey. Both Letton and Brobury were held of the Lacy family. In a deed of 1173 × 86 Abbot Joseph of Reading described Hurstley as 'our land' (E f 120v).

¹ The later endorsement is clearly erroneous, and the same mistake is evident in the copying of the charter into the 14th-century cartulary C among Berkshire deeds, with the rubric: *Carta Rog' abbatis de terra in Hurteley*, i.e. mistaking Hurstley for Hartley, near Reading (cf. *Berks. Place-Names*, i. 104).

LA MORE

350 Gift in free alms by John de St Aubin (*de Sancto Albino*)*a*, lord of *La Mora*, to Reading Abbey of his whole manor of *La More*,*b* *Westintone* and *Witesy* with houses, gardens, meadows, pastures, moors and all appurtenances, and with the rents and services of

Margery, his mother, and Margery, widow of John de St Aubin, and after their deaths the lands and tenements which they hold in dower, and with the rents, services and homages of all other men and their tenements in *La More*; with courts, pleas. homages, reliefs, wardships, marriages, escheats and all other things pertaining to the lordship from them and their tenements; and with all right and claim that the donor or his heirs have or could have in the said manor, rents, dowers, tenements, services and all other appurtenances; except the messuage and 15 acres of land which Roger White (*Albus*) and Alice his wife held for their lives in *Westin(tone)*. To be held freely by the abbey, by doing to the lords of the fee the due and customary services. Warranty and sealing. Witnesses [omitted]   [1261 × 91; ? c.1280 × 90]

B f 206v; C ff 124v–125r; E f 176r–v

a Insert: 'son of William de St Aubin' *E*   *b* La Mora *C*

After 1261, when the donor was under-age, since in that year Simon *de Halton'* sold to Reading Abbey for 5 years his right in the lands formerly of William de St Aubin in *La Mora* and the marriage of William's son and heir, John (E ff 175v–176r); and before 1291, when the prior of Leominster held 2 carucates at *Mora* (*Taxatio,* 173); however, the form of reference to 'the lords of the fee' suggests a date not long before *Quia emptores* (1290) and the text in B is in a late 13th-century hand. There are good grounds for identifying *La More* with the Middleton (in Kimbolton) which was held T.R.E. under the manor of Leominster and in 1086 by Durand the sheriff (*VCH Herefs.*, i. 316). In Henry II's reign Middleton was held by John Pichard, from whom it descended to his heirs (*Herefs. Domesday*, 14, 87). In 1242-3 John de St Aubin (grandfather of the present donor—see no. 352 n.) held Middleton of Roger Pichard as a fifth of a knight's fee (*Fees*, ii. 799) and in 1346 the abbot of Reading held a fifth of a knight's fee in *La More* (*Aids*, ii. 399). Since the present donor conveyed his whole manor to the abbey, the later *La More* seems to be identical with the Middleton of 1242-3. Moreover, in the 13th century the chaplain of Middleton received tithes from *inter alia* the demesne of *La More* and the land of Thomas *de Wytese* (E f 104r).

351 Quitclaim by John de St Aubin, son of William de St Aubin, to Reading Abbey of all his right in the manor of *La More* with houses [etc.] and with the rents and services of Margery, his mother, and Margery, widow of John de St Aubin, and the lands and tenements which they hold or held in dower, and with the rents and services of all his other men and tenants in the manor, except the messuage and 15 acres of land which Roger White (*Albus*) and Alice his wife held for their lives in *Westintun'*.*a* Sealing. Witnesses*b* [omitted]   [1261 × 91; c.1280 × 90]

B ff 206v–207r; C f 125r; E f 177r

a Westinton' *E*   *b Om. in* C,E

Date as for no. 350.

352   Confirmation by Roger Pichard of Ystradwy *(Stratdewy)*[a] to Reading Abbey of the whole manor of *La More* in the liberty of Leominster, which the abbey has of his fee, as contained in the charter of gift by John de St Aubin, son and heir of William de St Aubin, in perpetuity with the dowers of Margery, widow of the said William, and Margery, widow of John, father of the said William. For this the abbey has given him 20 marks of silver and has agreed to pay him and his heirs ½ mark at Michaelmas annually at Leominster in perpetuity for all secular demands, suits of courts and royal services. Warranty and sealing   [1261 × 91; ? c.1280 × 90]

B f 207r; C f 125r; E ff 178v-179r

[a] Stradeuwy ? *E*

Date as for no. 350. From the details of this confirmation and the evidence in no. 350 n., the following family tree can be drawn:

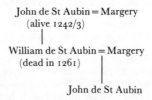

John de St Aubin = Margery
(alive 1242/3)

William de St Aubin = Margery
(dead in 1261)

John de St Aubin

The first Margery may not have been William's mother but a second wife of John the elder, since John the younger does not call her his grandmother.

353   Quitclaim in free alms by Roger Pichard, lord of Ystradwy *(Stradewey)*[a] to Reading Abbey and the monks at Leominster of the ½ mark which they owed him annually at Michaelmas for the manor of *La More* or by reason of the tenement of *La More* sometime held of him, along with all his right in the said manor. The abbey and the monks of Leominster may convert the ½ mark to any use they wish. Warranty of the said manor and sealing. Witnesses[b] [omitted]   [? late 13th cent.]

B f 207r-v; C f 125r-v; E f 178r-v

[a] Stradewiy *E*
[b] *Om. in E*

This is clearly later than no. 352, and is entered in B in a different hand from that of nos. 350-2. Roger Pichard was still living 13 July, 1297 *(Cal. Close R. 1296-1302,* 44), but had certainly died by May, 1306, when John Pichard, the next lord of Ystradwy, was dead *(Cal. Inq. P. M..*, iv. 233).

LEOMINSTER

354 *Grant and confirmation by Richard [de Capella], bishop of Hereford, to Reading Abbey and Abbot Hugh [I], of the church of Leominster with all its appurtenant parish, viz.*, *of Broadward*, Ach,[1] *Monkland, both Dilwyns, Luntley, Kinnersley, Woonton, both Sarnesfields, Titley, Hope[-under-Din-more], Wharton, Newton, Gattertop, Stoke [Prior], both Hatfields,[2] Risbury, Humber, Edvin [Ralph], Butterley, Broadfield, both Hamptons,[3] Ford, Hen-nor, Eaton,[4] Hampton [Wafer], Stockton, Ashton[-in-Eye],[4] Brimfield, Upton, Middleton, Drayton, Hamnish, While, Pudleston, Brockmanton, Forde [in Pudleston],[4] Luston, Eye and Croft. Old and reliable men have testified to these in the bishop's presence, but, on account of exceeding antiquity, they did not name many places which were anciently in the parish of Leominster*   1123 [after 15 Apr.]

A ff 54v–55r; E f 59v
Pd. *Mon. Ang.*, iv. 56 (no. ii)

Ego dei gratia Herford(ensis)[a] episcopus Ricardus manu propria mea concessi et confirmavi ecclesie Rading(ensi) et eius abbati primo domino Hugoni ecclesiam sancti Petri de Leoministria cum omni ad ipsam pertinente parrochia, scilicet de Bradeford', et de Ach, et de Leena, et de Diliga prima et secunda que ambe magis proxime sunt Leomin(istrie),[b] et de Luntelega,[c] et Kinardeslega,[d] et de Winne-tuna, et de utraque Sernesfelda, et de Titelega,[e] de Hopa quoque et de Wavertuna, et de Niwetuna, et de Gatredehopa, de Stokes quo-que et de utraque Hethfeld', et de Risebiria, et Humbra, et Gedes-fenna, et Buterlega,[f] et Bradesfelda, et utraque Hamtona, et Forda, et Henoura,[g] et Eatuna, et Heentuna, de Stoctuna[h] quoque et Es-setuna,[i] et Brumesfelda,[j] et Uptuna, et Michlatuna,[k] et Dreituna, et [*f 55r*] Hamenesce,[l] et Wihale,[m] et Putlesduna, et Brocmanetuna, et Forda, de Lustuna quoque et Eya,[n] et Croftona.[o] Hec antiqui et auctentici[p] viri in presentia mea attestati sunt, et plurima que anti-quitus de parrochia Leomin(istrie) fuerunt pro vetustate nimia se tacuisse dixerunt. Nos vero ea que suprascripta sunt ecclesie Rad-ing(ensi) et tius abbati confirmamus, salva iustitia quam unicuique servare debemus. [q]Actum est anno verbi incarnati M.C.xxiii, reg-nante Henrico rege feliciter regnante.[q]

[a] Hereford' *E*   [b] Leomenistrie *E*   [c] Lunthelega *E*
[d] *A has* Kinardardeslega *with* dar *marked for deletion*; Chinardeslega *E*
[e] Titellega *E*   [f] Butterlega *E*   [g] Heanoura *E*
[h] Stochtuna *E*   [i] Esscetun' *E*   [j] Bremesfeld' *E*
[k] Miclatun' *E*   [l] Hamenessce *E*   [m] Whiale *E*
[n] Heya *E*   [o] Crofta *E*   [p] autentici *E*
[q-q] Act' anno domini M.C.xxiii *E*

After Hugh became abbot of Reading (see above, p 15). This important act, giving the extent of the *parochia* of Leominster in 1123, is discussed by R. Lennard, *Rural England 1086-1135* (Oxford, 1959), 400-1, and by B. R. Kemp, 'The Foundation of Reading Abbey ...', unpubl. Ph.D. thesis, Reading 1966, 151-7.

[1] Unidentified, but it appears in Domesday Book as *Alac (VCH Herefs.*, i. 316; *Herefs. Domesday*, 14) and in *c.*1220 as *Akes* (E ff 111r-112r).
[2] Hatfield Magna and Hatfield Parva.
[3] Hampton Mappenore and Hampton Ricardi (now Hampton Court), both in Hope-under-Dinmore.
[4] Probabable identification.

355 *Mandate by William [of Corbeil], archbishop of Canterbury and legate, to Peter, archdeacon of Hereford, and his ministers to cause to be paid to the church of Leominster the tithes of all lands in its parish, namely, of Broadward, Wharton, Newton, Gattertop,* Achis,[1] *Eaton,*[2] *Hamnish, Hatfield, the other Hatfield,*[3] *Hampton,*[4] *Risbury and Broadfield*

[1126 × 36; ? 1127 × 31]

A f93v; C f120v

W(illelmus) dei gratia Cant(uariensis) archiepiscopus et sancte Romane ecclesie legatus P(etro) Hereford(ensi)[a] archidiacono et ministris suis, salutem. Mando vobis ut[b] ecclesie Leomenist(rie) viriliter reddi faciatis decimas de omnibus terris que in parochia supradicte ecclesie sunt,[c] et nominatim de Bradeford, et de Wauretun', et de Niwetun', et Gatredeopa,[d] et Achis, et Etona,[e] et Hameschis,[f] et Hetfeld',[g] et alia Hetfeld',[g] et Heamton',[h] et Riseberia,[i] et Bradefeld'. Quod si reddere noluerint, ecclesiastice non dormiat severitas iustitie. [Valete].[j]

[a] Herford' *C*	[b] et *C (in error)*
[c] sint *C*	[d] Gatredehopa *C*
[e] Etuna *C*	[f] Hameness' *C*
[g] Hethfeld' *C*	[h] Heamtun' *C*
[i] Riseburi *C*	[j] *Om. in A, supplied from C*

While the archbishop was legate, but possibly during the vacancy in the see of Hereford, 1127-31 (Z.N. and C.N.L. Brooke, *Cambridge Hist. Journ.*, viii. 15), and, if contemporary with no. 340 above, before Abbot Hugh I of Reading became archbishop of Rouen in 1130.

[1] Unidentified, but probably the same as *Ach* in no. 354.
[2] Probable identification.
[3] Hatfield Magna and Hatfield Parva.
[4] Probably Hampton Mappenore (see no. 340 n.1).

356 Confirmation by Gilbert [Foliot], bishop of Hereford, to Abbot Roger and the abbey of Reading, of the grant and confirmation made by Richard [de Capella], bishop of Hereford, to Abbot

Hugh [I], of the church of Leominster with all its appurtenant parish, viz., of Broadward [etc., as in no. 354], as contained in Bishop Richard's charter [1158 × 61]

A f 55r; E ff 60v–61r
Pd. *Foliot Letters and Charters*, 392–3 (no. 343)

After Roger became abbot of Reading and, since this act is mentioned in Archbishop Theobald's confirmation (no. 357), before his death, 18 Apr. 1161.

357 Confirmation by Theobald, archbishop of Canterbury and primate, to Abbot Roger and the monks of Reading, of the gift to Abbot Hugh [I] of the church of Leominster with all appurtenances and the *parrochia* of Broadward, of *Ach* [etc., listing the places as in no. 354], following the charters of G(ilbert) [Foliot], bishop of Hereford, and his predecessor, Richard [de Capella] [1158 × 61]

A f 54r–v; E f 71v
Pd. Saltman, *Theobald*, 439–40 (no. 216)

After Roger became abbot of Reading and before Theobald's death.

358 *Notification by William [de Vere], bishop of Hereford, that, when the vacant vicarage of the monastery of Leominster was in his custody pending the presentation of a vicar, he learnt that the vicars serving in the monastery were accustomed to receive 12 sheaves annually from each virgate cultivated by the parishioners, called 'scrifcorn', for a pension of ½ mark; and that in the collection of these sheaves the tithes appropriated to the monks were threatened with loss by unlawful seizure. Therefore, after discussion with his officials and others the bishop has allowed the monks to appropriate the said sheaves, and the monks have assigned in compensation a portion equal in value to the said 'scrifcorn' in accordance with the wishes of the vicar presented to him. The vicar declared publicly that he was content with the vicarage as then ordained to bear episcopal customs* [1186 × 93]

A ff 56v–57r; E f 62v

Universis Christi fidelibus ad quos presentes littere perveniunt[a] Willelmus dei gratia Herford(ensis)[b] episcopus, salutem in domino. Cum vicariam monasterii de Leom(inistria)[c] vacantem usque ad idonei vicarii presentationem ex officio episcopali nobis iniuncto in custodia nostra tenuissemus, ex officialium nostrorum inquisitione et de monachorum iamdicti [*f 57r*] loci indubitata relatione[d] cognovimus vicarios in iamdicto monasterio ministrantes .xii. garbas de singulis virgatis terre a parrochianis exculte que scrifcorn[e] vulgaliter[f] appellabantur sub pensione dimidie marce annuatim solere percipere; et ex hac garbarum[g] perceptione, generali consuetudini ecclesie incognita, collectioni decimarum ad usum monachorum pertinentium nacta occasione malignandi enorme dispendium consuevit imminere.[h]. Colligentes etenim[i] iamdictas garbas usurpata quadam immunitate delinquendi prescriptas [decimas][j] monachorum ut dicebatur impudenter dissipare et impune distraere[k] consueverunt. Nos itaque indempnitati memorati monasterii providere volentes, et utilitatem prelibate vicarie conservare disponentes, cum officialibus nostris et viris discretis super hoc habito tractatu, monachis supradictas[l] garbas in usus proprios convertendi immunitatem[m] indulsimus, ab eisdem monachis in compensationem iamdicti scrifcorn[e] alia portione non minorem commoditatem continente, secundum arbitrium vicarii nobis presentati, perpetuo assignata; ita quod idem vicarius illa vicaria sicut tunc temporis fuit ordinata ad sustinendas episcopales consuetudines se fuisse contentum publice est confessus. Quod ne de cetero cuiuslibet calliditate in ambiguitatem vel altercationem possit revocari, illud presentis pagine inscriptione et sigilli nostri appositione confirmare curavimus. His testibus:[n] Willelmo de Stok' vice-archidiacono, magistro Iohanne de Colecestr(ia), Martino clerico, et multis aliis.

[a] *Sic in A, but almost certainly error for* pervenerint, *as in E*
[b] Heref' E
[c] Leomenistr' E
[d] *A has* religione (*in error*)
[e] scrifcorn E
[f] wlgariter E
[g] *A has* decimarum (*in error*)
[h] iminere E
[i] vero E
[j] *Om. in A, supplied from E*
[k] subtrahere E
[l] suprascriptas E
[m] *Reading from E; A has* immutionem
[n] *E ends with* et cetera

After William became bishop of Hereford and, since the act is entered in the original section of A, not later than 1193. *Scrifcorn*, or *scriftcorn*, was a customary ecclesiastical render in corn in the *parochia* of Leominster, where it seems to have replaced the similar and more normal churchscot, which is never mentioned there. Its earliest recorded occurrence is in 1131 × 37 in connection with Broadfield in the *parochia* (see no. 326), but it was clearly of much older origin. See also B.R. Kemp, 'The Foundation of Reading Abbey . . .', 182–9.

359 *Inspeximus and confirmation by William [de Vere], bishop of Hereford, of an agreement between Gervase, dean of the monastery of Leominster, and Walter of Stockton, perpetual vicar of the same place, over 'scrifcorn', the agreement being in the form of a grant by Abbot Hugh [II] of Reading to Walter of the perpetual vicarage of Leominster called 'ad crucem' with the appurtenances which his predecessor, William, held [and] the vicarage of Hope[-under-Dinmore] for ½ mark annually. Walter shall have three chaplains until he is ordained, on account of the scattered nature of the parishes, and their and his rights in the offerings are specified. Because of the seizure of Leominster's tithes under cover of 'scrifcorn' in the time of William, it is*

*agreed between Gervase the dean and the said Walter that all tithe of corn
shall remain entirely to Leominster Priory, and for the sale of the 'scrifcorn'
the dean will give Walter ½ mark annually* [1186 × 93]

A f57r-v; E f63r

Universis sancte matris ecclesie filiis ad quos presentes littere pervenerint W(illelmus) dei gratia Herford(ensis)[a] episcopus, salutem‾
in domino. Universitati vestre significamus nos instrumentum transactionis super blado quod dicitur scrifcorn[b] inter Gervasium decanum monasterii de Leoministr(ia) et Walt(eru)m perpetuum vicarium eiusdem loci formate in hec verba inspexisse.

Sciant presentes et futuri quod ego H(ugo)[c] abbas Rading(ensis)
ex assensu fratrum concessi Waltero clerico de Stoctuna[d] perpetuam
vicariam Leoministr(ie)[e] que dicitur ad crucem cum omnibus[f] suis
pertinentiis quas predecessor eius Willelmus tenuit [et][g] vicariam[f]
de Hope pro dimidia marca annuatim solvenda ecclesie de Leo-
ministr(ia) ad festum sancti Michaelis. Serviet autem predictus
W(alterus) hoc modo ut tres habeat capellanos donec ipse ordinetur,
propter parrochiarum[h] dispersionem, qui de singulis missis unum et
non amplius si eum deus donaverit[i] denarium percipient, et secundas
divisas rationabiles circa morientes, et panem et cervisiam que ex
devotione fidelium ad altare deferuntur, sive Leoministr(ie) sive
Hope, exceptis precipuis festivitatibus in quibus [j]amplius nichil[j]
quam suum denarium percipient. Que festivitates sunt iste: dies natalis domini, Parasceve, Pasche et Pentecostes, et[f] festivitates sancte
Marie et[f] apostolorum Petri et Pauli, et[f] Reliquiarum, et omnium
sanctorum. Quicquid autem ex tricenariis vel ex confessione fidelium
in Quadragesima provenerit, quod non sit loco decime, in usus predicti Walt(eri) cedet. Sed quia in diebus Willelmi per occasionem
illius bladi quod vocatur scrifcorn[b] decime Leoministr(ie) solebant
surripi et defraudari, convenit inter Gervasium decanum
Leom(inistrie) et nominatum Walt(eru)m ut omnis decima bladi
ubique integra maneat ad opus ecclesie Leoministrie, ut capellanis
auferatur omnis occasio malignandi vel male agendi. Dabitque decanus Leoministr(ie) Waltero annuatim dimidiam marcam pro ven-
ditione bladi illius. [*f57v*] Hanc conditionem et conventionem
iuravit ipse W(alterus) in capitulo Leom(inistrie) se fideliter
observaturum et nichil amplius exacturum, tacto sacro evangelio.[k]
Iurabunt etiam hoc ipsum qui sub nomine ipsius[l] alicubi ministra-
bunt, et episcopo et suis de episcopalibus respondebunt. [m]His testibus: Hugone de Kinardesl', Willelmo pincerna, Rad(ulfo) de Stok',
R. fratre eius.[m]

Quod ne processu temporis in dubium vel irritum venire possit,
presentis pagine inscriptione et sigilli nostri appositione illud corro-

borare et confirmare curavimus. His testibus:[n] magistro Iohanne[o] de
Gloec(estria), magistro Iohanne de Calne.

[a] Heref' E	[b] scriftcorn E
[c] Hugo E	[d] Stocht' E
[e] Leomen' E	[f] Om. in E
[g] Supplied conjecturally	[h] parrochianorum E
[i] dederit E	[j-j] nichil amplius E
[k] ew(angelio) E	[l] illius E
[m-m] T' et cetera E	[n] E ends with et cetera
[o] A has this name before magistro and marked for transposition	

Date as for no. 358. In Leominster Priory the titles 'dean' and 'prior' were inter-
changeable (see B. R. Kemp, 'The monastic dean of Leominster', *EHR*, lxxxiii (1968),
505-15). Gervase was thus in the position of prior and is to be identified with the 'G.
prior of Leominster' who occurs in an agreement dating from Bishop William de
Vere's time concerning the chapel of Hampton Wafer (E f 111r). For *scrifcorn*, see no.
358 n.

360 *Licence by William [de Vere], bishop of Hereford, to the monks of
Leominster to appropriate the vicarage called 'ad crucem' of Leominster and
the chapel of Hope[-under-Dinmore]. The chaplains who shall celebrate divine
service for the people shall be in the monks' mensa, answering to the bishop
in spirituals and to the monks in temporalities. With the assent of Walter of
Stockton [the vicar]*   [1186 × 98; ? c.1193 × 98]

A f 93v; E ff 63v-64r

Omnibus sancte matris ecclesie filiis [a]ad quos presens scriptum pervenerit[a] W(illelmus) [b]dei miseratione Hereford(ensis) ecclesie minister humilis, eternam in domino salutem.[b] Quoniam religiosorum
loca [c]pio semper et benigno favore sunt promovenda, illorum pro-
pensius religiosorum necessitatibus relevandis quodam favoris privilegio tenemur assistere qui indigentium honera[d] et advenientium
sarcinas misericorditer et benigne noscuntur sustinere.[c] Attendentes
igitur dilectorum in domino filiorum monachorum de Leomin-
ist(ria)[e] hospitalitatis gratiam quam in relevandis pauperum indi-
gentiis et communicandis affluentium sarcinis supra vires facultatum
suarum ipsos scimus et novimus inpendisse,[f] volumus et autoritate[g]
nostra episcopali concedimus ut liberum sit et licitum predictis monachis vicariam que dicitur ad crucem Leomen(istrie)[e] et capellam
de Hopa pertinere[h] in usus suos convertere et omnia ad ipsam pertinentia percipere. Capellanos autem qui populo divina celebrabunt
quales noverint sibi idoneos in mensa sua habeant, qui nobis et
successoribus nostris de spiritualibus respondeant et predictis monachis de temporalibus satisfaciant. Et quia hanc concessionem nostram, assensu et voluntate Walteri clerici [i]de Stoctun(a)[i] legitime[j]

factam, perpetuam et firmam volumus permanere, eam presenti
scripto et sigillo nostro confirmare curavimus.[k]

[a-a] Om. in E   [b-b] Heref' episcopus salutem E
[c-c] et cetera ut supra E, referring to preceding entry (see note)
[d] lonera (sic) A   [e] Lem' E
[f] impendisse E   [g] auctoritate E
[h] Sic in both texts; prob. error for pertinentem
[i-i] Om. in E   [j] legittime E
[k] E adds T' et cetera

The outside dating limits are those of the bishop's pontificate, but, since the act was
not entered in the original section of A, it may well be not earlier than c.1193. There
is another and fuller version of this licence in E f63v, immediately preceding E's text
of the present version, stating that the act has been made for the health of the souls
among others of Henry I and Queen Adeliza, who nurtured the bishop, and at the
request of Abbot Hugh [II] of Reading and of Richard the dean and William the
precentor and other canons of Hereford; it also states that Walter of Stockton was
the vicar and that he resigned the vicarage into the bishop's hands.

361 *Notification by Hugh [de Mapenore], bishop of Hereford, that,
whereas the manor and church of Leominster were given to Reading Abbey at its
foundation, and the abbots have since then had control of monastic affairs at
Leominster and have at their discretion appointed and removed the deans and
monks deputed to keep the said manor and church, the bishop has now confirmed
to Reading Abbey the power of appointing and removing the monks deputed to
keep the same, and its ancient and established control of monastic affairs there,
saving the dignity of the church of Hereford*   [Dec. 1216 × Dec. 1218]

A f98r; B ff182v-183r; C f108r; E ff66v-67r; F 78r-v
Pd. *Mon. Ang.*, iv. 56-7 (no. viii); *Reg. Swinfield*, 30 (inspeximus by the legate
     Guala), 100 (inspeximus by the bishop)

Omnibus [a]sancte matris ecclesie filiis presens scriptum inspecturis
Hugo dei gratia Hereford(ensis)[b] episcopus, eternam in domino salutem.[a] Cum in fundacione Radingensis monasterii manerium de
Leoministr(ia)[c] cum omnibus pertinenciis suis et ecclesia eiusdem
loci cum omnibus ad eam spectantibus ad sustentacionem dicti monasterii de Rading(ia) essent collata, et abbates Radingenses ab ipsa
fundacione monasterii sui liberam habuerint facultatem ordinandi
et disponendi de omnibus que ad ordinem monachicum spectant
apud Leoministr(iam), necnon pro arbitrio suo decanos et monachos
quoscumque ad custodiam manerii et ecclesie deputatos prout eis et
monasterio Rading(ensi) visum fuerat[d] expedire constituere et amovere consueverint, volentes iura eorum in omnibus illesa conservari,
auctoritate pontificali de consensu tocius capituli nostri unanimi, ad
perpetuam confederacionem inter ecclesiam de Hereford(ia)[b] et
monasterium Rading(ense), concedimus et confirmamus quod abbas

et conventus Rading(enses) 'in perpetuum' possessione sua in dictis
disposicionibus et consuetudinibus pacifice gaudentes liberam habeant facultatem constituendi et amovendi monachos quoscumque
ad custodiam manerii et ecclesie de Leoministr(ia)ᶜ deputatos, et
alios secundum antiquas et usitatas consuetudines suas substituendi,
etᶠ ordinandi et disponendi de omnibus que ad ordinem monachicum spectant ibidem, salva in aliis dignitate Hereford(ensis) ecclesie.
Et ut hec nostra confirmacio perpetuam firmitatem obtineat,ᵍ eam
presenti scripto et tam sigilli nostri quam sigilli capituli nostri ap-
posicione communire curavimus.ʰ Hiis testibus: Thoma decano, Willelmo precentore, Hel(ia) thesaurario, Albino cancellario, Willelmo
archidiacono Hereford(ie),ᵇ Gregorio, Roberto, capellanis, Nicholao, Theoder(ico),ⁱ clericis, et multis aliis.

ᵃ⁻ᵃ et cetera E	ᵇ Herford' C
ᶜ Leomen' F	ᵈ fuerit E
ᵉ⁻ᵉ Om. in B,C	ᶠ Om. in C
ᵍ optineat C,E	ʰ E ends with T' et cetera
ⁱ Theodor' B,C	

That the bishop is Hugh de Mapenore (1216-19) is established by the fact that the
act was inspected and confirmed by the legate, Guala, who left England in Dec. 1218
(E f 73r; *Reg. Swinfield*, 30). The latter was given at Reading on 18 Nov., probably
1218 (Z.N. and C.N.L. Brooke, *Cambridge Hist. Journ.*, viii. 5). The number of cartulary copies of the present act indicates the importance attached to it; for this reason
it has been printed here in full, since, although it is in print elsewhere, the texts in
Swinfield's Register differ slightly from the Reading texts, and the *Monasticon* text is
taken from the shortened version in E. For further discussion, see Kemp, 'The monastic dean of Leominster', 508-9.

362　*Confirmation of the same by Pope Honorius III*　　8 July 1219

A f 79r; B f 183r; C f 108r-v; E f 67r; F f 78v
Pd. *Mon. Ang.*, iv. 57 (no. ix)

Honorius episcopus servus servorum dei dilectis filiis abbati et conventui monasterii de Rading(ia), salutem et apostolicam benedictionem. Cum a nobis petitur quod iustum est ᵃet honestumᵃ tam vigor
equitatis quam ordo exigit rationis, ut id per sollicitudinem officii
nostri ad debitum perducatur effectum. Ex litteris sane dilecti filii
nostri G(uale) tunc temporis Sancti Martini presbiteri cardinalis, et
vobis referentibus, intelleximus quod, cum monasterium vestrum ab
ipsa sui fundacione manerium et ecclesiam de Leoministr(ia)ᵇ Herefordensis diocesis cum omnibus eorum pertinenciis obtinuerit,ᶜ et
monasterii predicti abbates ordinandi et disponendi de omnibus que
apud Leoministr(iam)ᵈ ad ordinem monasticum pertinent liberam
habuerint facultatem et ad custodiam manerii et ecclesie predictorum deputare quosdam qui decani dicuntur et monachos libere con-

sueverint et etiam ammovere,^{e} venerabilis frater noster episcopus et capitulum Hereforden(ses) vos uti huiusmodi disposicionibus, libertatibus et consuetudinibus concesserunt. Eapropter, dilecti in domino filii, vestris iustis precibus inclinati concessionem huiusmodi, sicut provide ac utiliter facta est [ut]^f in eorundem episcopi et capituli litteris dicitur contineri, ^{g}auctoritate apostolica confirmamus^g et presentis scripti patrocinio communimus. Nulli ergo omnino hominum liceat hanc paginam nostre confirmacionis infringere vel ei ausu temerario contraire. Siquis autem hoc attemptare presumpserit, indignacionem omnipotentis dei et beatorum Petri et Pauli apostolorum eius se noverit incursurum. Dat' Reate viii. idus Julii, pontificatus nostri anno tertio.

$^{a-a}$ Om. in E ^{b} Leomen' F
^{c} optinuerit E ^{d} Leomenistr' F
^{e} amovere C,E,F ^{f} Om. in A,B,C, supplied from E; F has et
$^{g-g}$ auctoritate confirmamus apostolica B,C

363 Inspeximus and confirmation of no. 361 by Hugh Foliot, bishop of Hereford. Sealing   [1219 × 34]

C ff 120v–121r

The dating limits are those of the bishop's pontificate. The cartulary text gives no indication as to whether the original had witnesses.

364 *Inspeximus and confirmation by Hugh Foliot, bishop of Hereford, of the gift in free alms by Abbot Adam [of Lathbury] and the convent of Reading to Henry of Burton, chaplain, of the vicarage of Leominster 'ad crucem' and of Hope[-under-Dinmore] with specified assigned revenues, for an annual pension of ½ mark of silver. The abbot and convent's letters were brought to the bishop for confirmation by Thomas, dean of Leominster, as proctor*
[1226 × 34]

A f 11v; E f 69r

(U)niversis Christi fidelibus ^{a}ad quos presens carta pervenerit H(ugo) Foliot divina permissione Hereford(ensis) ecclesie minister [humilis],^{b} eternam in domino salutem.^{a} Universitati vestre notum facimus nos cartam domini abbatis Rading(ensis) et eiusdem loci conventus in hec verba inspexisse.

Sciant presentes et futuri quod ego A(dam) dei gratia abbas Rad(ingensis) et eiusdem loci conventus unanimis dedimus et concessimus Henrico de Burton'^{c} capellano vicariam Leom(inistrie) que dicitur ad crucem et de Hop(a) cum omnibus pertinentiis suis in perpetuam elemosinam possidendam hoc modo, ut in propria persona ministret et de singulis missis unum si deus dederit et non amplius percipiat*d* denarium, et secundas divisas rationabiles circa morientes que tales sint et esse debent, quod primas non excedant, et totum panem et cervisiam que ex oblatione fidelium provenerit sive Leom' sive Hop'; et quicquid ex tricenariis vel ex confessione fidelium in Quadragesima provenerit, quod non sit loco decime, percipiet, et etiam denarii de sponsalibus qui offeruntur super libr(o) in ostio monasterii. Volumus etiam et concedimus quod predictus Henricus et successores sui vicarii Leom(inistrie) percipiant annuatim de bursa nostra Leom(inistrie) .xl. solidos hoc modo assignatos, videlicet in festo sancti Michaelis .x. solidos et ad Natale domini .x. solidos et ad Pascha .x. solidos et in festo sancti Johannis Baptiste .x. solidos, et dabit nobis predictus Henricus annuatim dimidiam marcam argenti in festo sancti Michaelis nomine pensionis pro predicta vicaria.

Nos autem dictam taxationem prefate vicarie ratam habentes et acceptam, fratre Th(oma) decano Leom(inistrie) coram nobis per litteras dictorum abbatis et conventus ad predictam vicariam taxandam procuratore constituto, eam presenti scripto et sigilli nostri testimonio in perpetuum confirmamus.*e* Hiis testibus, et cetera.

Rubric: there is no rubric in A, but that in E reads: Idem de presentacione Henrici de Burcht' ad vicariam Leom', et de taxatione eiusdem vicarie

a-a et cetera E   *b* Om. in A, but prob. in original
c Burcht' E   *d* percipiet E
e E ends with T'

After Adam became abbot of Reading, and before the bishop's death. Thomas, dean or prior of Leominster, occurs as late as 1239 (Kemp, 'The monastic dean of Leominster', 507).

365 Gift by Roger, earl of Hereford, to Adam of Middleton of the amount of meadow which the earl has near Leominster, on condition that the monks receive Adam and maintain him for life. Wherefore, the earl wills and orders that the monks shall hold the said meadow freely by the said agreement and similarly after Adam's death

[1143 × 55]

A f 45v
Pd. Walker, 'Hereford Charters', 34 (no. 52)

Testibus: Willelmo Torel, Nic(holao) de Magen', et R. de Mapp(enora), et Nic(holao) filio Maur(icii), et pluribus aliis quorum nomina tarde est mihi numerare.

The dating limits are those of Roger, earl of Hereford, who here appears to be providing for Adam's old age by arranging a corrody at Leominster (Walker, *ibid.*,

34 n.1). Since the deed was entered only in A, it may not have taken permanent effect.

366   Quitclaim in perpetuity by John ᵃcalled *Godard* of Leominsterᵃ to Abbot Robert [of Burgate] and the convent of Reading, of all his right in 30 selions of arable land in *Werefurlong*ᵇ by Leominster on the south, between the abbot and convent's demesne and the land of Thomas *de la Bache*, and extending from the said demesne to the water called *Argye*; also in 20 selions lying on *la Stockinge* within the demesne of the abbot and convent. These lands he bought from John, son of Hugh the miller, and for greater security has handed over to the abbot all the deeds he had concerning the lands. Warranty and sealing. Witnessesᶜ [omitted]   [1269 × 90]

B f 120r; C ff 65v–66r; E f 144v

ᵃ⁻ᵃ 'Godard called of Leominster' *E*
ᵇ *B,C have* Werefulong, *E has* Werfurlong
ᶜ *Om. in C,E*

The dating limits are those of Abbot Robert.

366a   Note of a charter by John, son of Hugh the miller, to John *Godard* concerning the same lands

B f 120r; C f 66r

This charter is entered in E ff 143v–144r. John Godard is given 30 selions in *le Wereforlong* lying between the land of the prior of Leominster and that of Thomas *de la Bache*, and 20 selions on *le Stockinge* within the demesne of the prior. John will pay annually to Leominster Priory 10s on behalf of the donor and his heirs, to Philip *de Fonte* and heirs ½d, and to the donor and heirs 1 rose.

366b   Note of a charter by Hugh the miller to John, his son, concerning the same lands

B f 120r; C f 66r

This charter is entered in E f 144r. It is a quitclaim by Hugh son of Richard the miller of Hope, and describes the lands as in no. 366a n.

366c   Note of a charter by Philip *de Fonte* to John, son of Hugh the miller, concerning the same lands

B f 120r; C f 66r

LUCTON AND STOCKTON

367 Gift and quitclaim in free alms by Hugh[a] son of Alan[1] to Abbot R(ichard) [I] and the convent of Reading, of all his right in two messuages and 2 virgates of land which sometime belonged to John son of Rener[b] in Lucton (*Luctune*);[c] and in all the lands which sometime belonged to Alice daughter of Thomas of Eyton (*Eytune*),[d] his uncle, in the vill of Stockton (*Stoctune*)[e] which could come to him by reason of the said Alice; saving to him and his heirs all the land, with woods, meadows and all appurtenances, which sometime belonged to Thomas of Eyton (*Eyton'*),[f] his uncle, in Eyton[f] and Luston (*Lustone*)[g] according to the charter which the said Thomas had from Reading Abbey. Sealing. Witnesses[h] [omitted]   [1238 × 58]

A f84v; B f120v; C f66r; E f95r

[a] *Om. in* B,C (*in error*)	[b] Reyner B,C; Reiner E
[c] Lucton' B,C,E	[d] Eyton' B,C
[e] Stocton' B, Stokton' C	[f] Eytun' E
[g] Lustun' E	[h] *Om. in* C

Since this charter is entered among the later additions in A and in the original section of B, the abbot must be Richard I (of Chichester), 1238-62. The messuages and virgates in Lucton had been leased to John son of Reiner by Abbot Elias, 1200-1213 (E f125r-v). The land, etc., which Hugh was to retain in Eyton and Luston may have been the property leased by the same abbot to Thomas of Eyton (E f124r-v).

[1] The rubrics of B and C call him 'Hugh *Walensis* son of Alan'.

RISBURY

368 Notification by Gilbert [Foliot], bishop of Hereford, to all faithful of his diocese that he has consecrated a cemetery at Risbury in the land of the monks of Leominster as a sanctuary for their men and those of Nicholas of Maund, at the request of Nicholas and with the monks' consent. Nicholas has given the monks the full tithe of his men's land and 2 acres from each virgate, and from his own demesne 12 acres and half his tithe during his life, the whole after his death   [1148 × 63; ? 1148 × 54]

A ff55v-56r; E f61r-v
Pd. *Foliot Letters and Charters*, 388 (no. 336)

Huius rei testes sunt:[a] Walt(erus) Foliot archidiaconus Salopesb(erie), Hugo nepos episcopi, et multi alii.

[a] E *ends with* et cetera

The outside dating limits are those of Foliot's pontificate of Hereford, but the consecration of a cemetery for sanctuary may suggest the troubles of Stephen's reign (cf. no. 346). Nicholas of Maund occurs a little earlier as lord of the manor of Risbury (*Herefs. Domesday*, 78). Risbury lay in the *parochia* of Leominster (see no. 354). There was no church or chapel there until Robert Malherbe, lord of the manor later in Henry II's reign (*Herefs. Domesday*, 13), was allowed a private chapel by Reading Abbey (E f 8or).

369 *Notification by the abbots of Thame and Notley and William prior of Hurley, judges–delegate of Pope Honorius III, of the settlement before them, with the assent of the prior of Brecon, of the dispute between Reading Abbey and Adam, dean and vicar of Humber, over the suit of the men of the fee of Adam Malherbe in Risbury. Reading Abbey has conceded that the men shall attend the chapel of Humber with their offerings, saving to the abbey all tithes of Risbury and to the mother church of Leominster bequests and the burial of the dead. The vicar and his successors shall pay Reading 3s annually on the feast of St Peter and St Paul, when all the said men of Risbury shall come with their offerings to the church of Leominster as its parishioners*

[? late 1217 × 18]

A ff 104v–105r; C f 121r–v
Pd. 'Cartl. Brecon', 229–30 (from 18th-cent. copy, from unknown source, in Oxford, Bodl., Carte 108)

Omnibus presens scriptum inspecturis de Thame et de Nutleia*ᵃ* abbates et Willelmus prior de Hurlea, *ᵇ*eternam in domino*ᵇ* salutem. Mandatum domini pape suscepimus in hec verba.

Honorius episcopus servus servorum *ᶜ*dei dilectis filiis de Tham(e) et de Nuthleia abbatibus et priori de Hurleia, Lincoln(iensis) et Sar(esburiensis) diocesum, salutem et apostolicam benedictionem. Dilecti filii abbas et conventus Rading(enses) suam ad nos transmisere querelam quod prior Maioris Malvern(e), R. rector ecclesie de Strettun' et quidam alii Wigorn(iensis), Herefordensis et Lincoln(iensis) diocesum super quibusdam capellis, decimis, sepulturis et rebus aliis iniuriantur eisdem. Quo circa discretioni vestre per apostolica scripta mandamus quatinus partibus convocatis audiatis causam et appelatione remota mediante iusticia terminetis, facientes quod statueritis per censuram ecclesiasticam firmiter observari. Testes autem qui fuerunt nominati, si se gratia, odio vel timore subtraxerint, per censuram eandem cessante appelatione cogatis veritati testimonium perhibere. Quod, si non omnes hiis exequendis potueritis*ᵈ* interesse, duo vestrum ea nichilominus exequantur. Dat' Anagn(ie) xv. kl' Julii, pontificatus nostri anno primo.*ᵉ*

Cum igitur auctoritate istarum literarum lis mota esset inter dictos abbatem et conventum Rading(enses) ex una parte et Adam decanum et vicarium de Humbr' ex *ᶜ*alia parte*ᵉ* super sequela quorundam hominum de Risebir(ia), tandem partibus convocatis et in iure constitutis, consensu prioris de Breckenneu,^{f} hoc fine lis conquievit. Videlicet quod dicti abbas et conventus Rading(enses) concesserunt omnibus hominibus de feudo^g Ade Malherbe de Risebir(ia) quod adeant et sequantur capellam de Humbr' cum omnibus debitis^h oblationibus suis ad divinum officium ibi ^{i}celebrandum et^i audiendum et ad spiritualia ibidem percipienda, salvis abbati et conventui Rading(ensibus) omnibus decimis de Risebir(ia) tam minutis quam omnibus aliis, et salvis testamentis eorum et successorum eorum^j que^k primo et principaliter fieri debent ecclesie de Leoministr(ia) et eorundem corporibus que ad matrem ecclesiam de Leoministr(ia) debent deferri, et salvis abbati et conventui Rading(ensibus), vel quicumque^l loco eorum fuerit apud Leoministr(iam), omnibus que de prefatis hominibus percipiunt et semper hactenus percipere consueverunt. Dictus vero Adam et successores sui in perpetuum reddent singulis annis abbati et conventui Rading(ensibus) ad recognicionem dicte sequele tres solidos sterlingorum die sanctorum apostolorum Petri et Pauli, et eadem die venient omnes dicti homines de Risebir(ia) ad ecclesiam de Leoministra^m singulis annis cum debitis oblacionibus suis ut eiusdem ecclesie parochiani.^{n} Nos vero^o auctoritate nostra de communi consensu partium super hiis perpetuata precipimus suprascriptam formam ab omnibus inviolabiliter observari. Ita quod non liceat uncquam^p ulli hominum hanc composicionis for[f $105r$]mam infringere vel ei ausu temerario contraire. Valete in domino.

^{a} Nutle C	$^{b-b}$ *Om. in C*
$^{c-c}$ et cetera C	^{d} *A repeats* potueritis
$^{e-e}$ altera C	^{f} Breckeneu C
^{g} feodo C	^{h} *Insert* et C
$^{i-i}$ *Om. in C*	^{j} suorum C
^{k} qui C	^{l} *Sic in both texts; ? rectius* cuicumque
^{m} *Sic in A*; Leom' *in C*	^{n} parrochiani C
^{o} autem C	^{p} unquam C

Probably not long after Honorius III's commission, dated 17 June 1217. Brecon Priory had an interest, since it held the church/chapel of Humber (see no. 348 n.), and confirmed the present settlement (E f 96r). Adam Malherbe was lord of Risbury, where the family held one eighth of a knight's fee (*Fees*, i. 101; ii. 799).

ASTON

370 *Gift by Queen Adeliza to Reading Abbey, on the first anniversary of the death of King Henry I, her late husband, of the manor of Aston with its church* [1 Dec. 1136]

Original charter: in the possession of the Malcolmson family[1]
A f16r; B f20r
Pd. *Mon. Ang.*, iv. 41-2 (no. vii); *Trans. East Herts. Arch. Soc.*, i (1900), 129-30 (with facsimile and transl.); (facsimile) *Antiquaries Journ.*, xiv (1934), pl. 1

Notum sit omnibus fidelibus sancte ecclesie totius Anglie atque Normannie quod ego Adelidis[a] regina uxor nobillissimi[b] regis Henrici et filia[c] Godefridi ducis Lotharingie concessi et perpetualiter dedi deo et ecclesie sancte Marie de Rading(ia) pro salute et redemptione anime domini mei nobilissimi regis Henrici et mea,[d] pro salute etiam domini nostri Stephani dei gratia regis Anglorum, et uxoris eius Mathildis[e] regine, et totius progeniei nobilissimi regis Henrici, et patris et matris mee, et parentum meorum tam vivorum quam defunctorum, omniumque fidelium Christianorum vivorum et defunctorum, Eastonam manerium meum quod dedit mihi dominus meus nobilissimus rex Henricus ut regine et sponse sue in [f]Hertforda schira[f] cum omnibus ei pertinentibus ita libere et quiete tenendum sicut ego ipsa unquam melius in dominio meo dono domini mei nobilissimi regis Henrici tenebam, scilicet cum socho[g] et sacha[h] et tol[i] et theam et [j]infangene ðief,[j] cum ecclesia et dominio, cum hominibus liberis et villanis, cum bosco et plano, cum pratis et pascuis,[k] cum aquis et molendinis, cum viis et semitis, cum omnibus consuetudinibus et libertatibus cum quibus dominus meus illud tenuit in dominio suo, et mihi dedit. Hanc autem donationem feci in primo anniversario domini mei nobilissimi regis Henrici in eadem ecclesia per quoddam pallium quod super altare posui. Testibus[l] subscriptis: scilicet Rogero episcopo Salesb(er)ie,[m] Symone episcopo Wigornie, Ingulfo abbate de Abend(onia), Waltero abbate de Egenesham, Bernardo abbate de Monte Sancti Michaelis, Warino priore de Wigornia, Nicholao priore Sancti Martini de Bello, Radulfo priore de Oseneia, Hermanno capellano regine, magistro Serlone clerico regine, Adam et Rodberto filio Walteri canonicis de Waltham, Radulfo, Teodbaldo, Rogero clericis episcopi Salesberie,[m] Symone nepote episcopi Wigornie, [n]Gervasio, Bertranno clericis episcopi Wigornie,[n] Ioscelino fratre eiusdem regine, Peurello de Bellocampo, Milone de Bellocampo, Ricardo de Bellocampo, Stephano de Bellocampo, Hugone de Cramanvilla, Mauricio de Windlesora,*º et Rainaldo fratre eius, Gausfredo de Tresgoz, Rodberto de Tresgoz, Iohanne de Falesia, Rodberto de Calz, Francone de Bruscella, Gozone conestabulario eiusdem regine, Engelberto de atrio, Willelmo de Harafleot,* Willelmo de Berchelai, Waltero de Dena, Baldewino dispensatore, Vitale aquario, Warino de Blancbuissun. Apud Rading(iam).

Endorsed: de Estona. Adelaidis regine [*12th cent.*]; *also post-medieval endorsement*

Size: 280 × 315 mm

Seal: fine and almost complete impression of the queen's seal (adapted from Queen Matilda's seal) in white wax on leather tag; legend: .. SIGILLVM AALIDIS ... GRACIA*q* REGINAE ANGLIE

a Adeleidis *A*	*b* nobilissimi *A,B*
c Om. in B	*d* Insert et B
e Matild' *B*	*f-f* Herefordschir' (sic) *A*, Hertf'syra *B*
g soccha *A*, soco *B*	*h* saccha *A*, saca *B*
i toll *A*, toll' *B*	*j-j* infangenetheof *A,B*
k paschuis *A*	*l* B ends
m Sar' *A*	*n-n* Omitted in A
o Windr' *A*	*p* Arafleot *A*
q Only the lower parts of GRA survive	

The gift was made on the first anniversary of Henry I's death. The original charter with its seal is very fine. For King Stephen's confirmation of the gift, see no. 13.

1 In 1900 the charter was among the Aston deeds in the possession of the Abel Smith family of Watton-at-Stone, Herts. (*Trans. East Herts. Arch. Soc.*, i. 129). It remained so until at least 1930, but by 1932 had passed to the Malcolmson family, who had acquired the Aston estate (*Antiquaries Journ.*, xiv. 7). Although the Abel Smith and Malcolmson deeds were deposited in the Hertford Record Office after the Second World War, the present charter was retained by the Malcolmson family. I am greatly indebted to the kindness of Mr. I. C. Malcolmson for permission to inspect the charter.

371 *Confirmation in free alms by William [d'Aubigny], earl of Lincoln, of the gifts to Reading Abbey by Queen Adeliza, his wife, of the manor and church of Aston and 100s worth of land in Stanton [Harcourt, Oxon.] and the church of that vill*   [Dec. 1139 × 1141]

Original charter: BL Add. Ch. 19586
A ff 43v–44r; B f 97v; C f 49r–v
Pd. Warner and Ellis, i, no. 14 (with facsimile); *Arch. Journ.*, xxii. 153; (in part)
    Trans. East Herts. Arch. Soc., i. 135; (cal.) Hurry, *Reading Abbey*, 158–9

Notum sit presentibus et futuris omnibus ecclesie catholice filiis quod ego Willelmus comes Lincolnie concessi et per kartam*a* meam confirmavi in perpetuam elemosinam deo et ecclesie sancte Marie de Radingis[b] et abbati et monachis ibidem deo servientibus manerium meum de Estona in 'Hertforda schira[c] cum terris et ecclesia et hominibus et omnibus rebus et consuetudinibus ad illud pertinentibus quod regina Adeleidis sponsa mea eis dedit pro anima nobilissimi regis Heinrici[d] et pro salute et redemptione anime ipsius et mee et omnium parentum nostrorum tam vivorum quam defunctorum, et preter hoc centum solidas[e] terre in Stantona[f] in [g]Oxeneforda schira[g] ad procurationem conventus et religiosarum personarum illuc convenientium in termino anniversarii domini mei nobilissimi regis Heinrici,[d] et insuper ecclesiam eiusdem ville cum omnibus rebus eidem ecclesie pertinentibus ad continua luminaria ante corpus domini nostri Ihesu Christi et ante corpus nobilissimi regis H(ein)rici.[d] Et volo atque precipio ut libere et honorifice et quiete teneant cum omnibus liberalibus consuetudinibus cum quibus idem nobilissimus rex H(einricus)[d] ea in dominio tenuit et regine dedit.[h] Testibus:[i] Hermanno capellano, et Rad(ulfo) capellano, et Rogerio[j] capellano, et magistro Serllone,[k] [l]et Heudone filio Alani, et Adelardo Flandr(ensi), et Gaufrido Tresgot, et Roberto de Calz, et Pag'n de Vilers, et Alano Pilot, et Willelmo de Cuini, et Willelmo Revel, et Milone Basset, et Nicholao de Asinis, et Rotardo camerario, et Reginaldo de Windlesores, et Morello[m] de Merlei.

Endorsed: Willelmi comitis Lincoln(ie) de Estuna et de .C. solidatis terre in Stantona et de ecclesia eiusdem manerii [*12th cent.*]
Size: 227 × 266 mm
Seal: missing, slit for tag in fold at bottom

[a] cartam *A,B,C*
[b] Rading' *A,B*; Radyng' *C*
[c-c] Herfordsc' *A*, Hertford'syr' *B*, Hertfordsyr' *C*
[d] Henrici *or* Henricus, *as appropriate, A,B,C*
[e] *Sic in original charter*; sol' *A,C*; solid' *B*
[f] Staunton' *C*
[g-g] Oxonef'sc' *A*, Oxon'f'syr' *B*, Oxenf'schire *C*
[h] *C ends*
[i] *B ends*
[j] Rogero *A*
[k] Serlone *A*
[l] *A ends with* et multis aliis
[m] *Original charter has* Mauritio *marked for deletion*, Morello *interlined*

Probably contemporary with no. 535, in view of the similarity in the witness lists, and certainly before William d'Aubigny ceased to be earl of Lincoln in or before 1141.

372 *Confirmation by King Henry II to Reading Abbey of his manor of Aston with its church. The men of the vill shall have the same liberty that the men of Reading and Cholsey have* [Jan. 1156 × Apr. 1157]

Original charter: BL Add. Ch. 19593
A f 22v; B ff 25v–26r
Pd. *Arch. Journ.*, xx. 296; *Trans. Royal Soc. Lit.*, 2nd ser., xi. 315; *Trans. East Herts.*
Arch. Soc., i. 134; *Cal. Chart. R.*, iii. 279 (from inspeximus of Edward II—see no.
102); (cal.) Hurry, *Reading Abbey*, 166

H(enricus) rex Angl(orum) *ᵃ*dux Norm(annorum) et Aquit-
(anorum)*ᵇ* et comes And(egavorum) archiepiscopis, episcopis, abbatibus, comitibus, baronibus, iustic(iariis), vicecomitibus et omnibus
ministris et fidelibus suis Francis et Anglis, salutem.*ᵃ* Sciatis me
pro animabus Henrici regis illustris avi mei eiusque uxoris
Matil(dis)*ᶜ* regine avie mee et omnium antecessorum et successorum
meorum et mea in perpetuam elemosinam presenti carta confirmasse
deo et sancte Marie et monachis meis de Rading(ia) Eston(am)
manerium meum in Herfordsir(a)*ᵈ* cum omnibus appendiciis suis et
cum ecclesia eiusdem ville ita bene et in pace et libere et quiete et
honorifice et plenarie tenendum, in boscis et planis et pasturis, in
stagnis et aquis, piscariis et molendinis et omnibus aliis rebus ad
idem manerium pertinentibus, sicut melius et liberius et quietius
aliquid tenent ex dono Henrici regis avi mei et meo. Sintque homines eiusdem ville liberi et quieti de siris*ᵉ* et hundredis et omnibus
placitis et querelis, de auxiliis et careagiis*ᶠ* et omnibus exactionibus,
de theloneis et passagiis et omnibus aliis consuetudinibus. Habeantque omnem libertatem quam habent vel habere debent homines
de Rading(ia) vel Ceals(eia)*ᵍ* ex concessione Henrici regis avi mei
vel mea. Testibus: domina Imperatrice,*ʰ* Philippo Baioc(ensi) episcopo, Reginaldo comite, Roberto de Novo Burgo, Manaser Biset
dapifero, Iocelino de Balliolo, Roberto de Curci, Thoma de Sancto
Iohanne, Driu de Munci, Willelmo de Crevecuer, Willelmo de An-
gervilla, et G(alfredo) filio Pag(ani). Apud Rothomagum.

Endorsed: Carta regis H. secundi de confirmatione manerii de Estona
et de libertate hominum eiusdem ville [*12th cent.*]
Size: 185 × 138 mm
Seal: portion of great seal on plaited cords.

ᵃ⁻ᵃ et cetera B	*ᵇ* Aquitanie A
ᶜ Math' A, Matill' B	*ᵈ* Herfordsch' A
ᵉ schiris A, syr' B	*ᶠ* cariag' B
ᵍ Chealseia A, Cheals' B	*ʰ* B ends with et cetera

Before the death of Robert de Courci, who was slain during the king's invasion of
North Wales in July, 1157 (Eyton, 28). Before that time the king was on the Continent from Jan. 1156 to early Apr. 1157 (*ibid.*, 16, 25). He was certainly at Rouen on
2 Feb. 1156 (*ibid.*, 16). This charter is no doubt contemporary with the king's general
confirmations, which omit Aston (nos. 18–19).

373 *Precept by King Henry II to the justice, sheriff and ministers of Hertfordshire that the abbot of Reading's men of Aston shall be quit of shires,
hundreds, pleas and other plaints as in the time of King I, and that no-one
shall demand aids or works from them beyond what they used to do*

[1155 × 58]

A f 26r; B f 26r
Pd. *Trans. East Herts. Arch. Soc.*, i. 134

Henricus rex Angl(orum) *^a*et dux Norm(annorum) et Aquit-
(anorum) et comes Andeg(avorum)*^a* iustic(iario) et vicecomiti et
ministris suis de Hertford'sc(ira),*^b* salutem. Precipio quod homines abbatis Rading(ensis) de Estona sint quieti de scir(is) et
hundred(is) et placitis et aliis querelis, sicut fuerunt tempore regis
H(enrici) avi mei, sicut carta regis H(enrici) testatur, ne quis super
hoc eis iniuriam vel contumeliam faciat, nec*^c* ab eis auxilia vel
operationes aliquas exigat, nisi quas facere solent et debent. T(este)*^d*
Thoma cancellario. Apud Dunest(aplum).

^{a-a} et cetera *B*   *^b* Hereford'sc' *in A*; Hertfordsir' *B*
^c vel *B*   *^d* *B ends*

Before Thomas Becket, the chancellor, became archbishop of Canterbury in 1162,
and while the king was in England, i.e. either 1155 × Jan. 1156 or Apr. 1157 × Aug.
1158. In the clause of address *iustic'* has been here expanded in the singular, since,
given the early date, it is likely that a local justice is involved (see Stenton, *English
Justice*, 29, 68).

374 Notification by Theobald, archbishop of Canterbury,*^a* that the
dispute between Gilbert, nephew of Amfrey, and Abbot Roger of
Reading concerning certain land at Aston and certain deeds which,
according to Gilbert, had been violently removed from him, which
dispute was delegated by Pope Adrian IV to the archbishop for
settlement, has been terminated. Having heard the arguments on
both sides, the archbishop has acquitted the abbot of Gilbert's
complaint   [1158 × 59]

B ff 97v–98r; C f 49v
Pd. Saltman, *Theobald*, 435 (no. 212)

^a *Both texts have* et cetera *at this point*

After Roger became abbot of Reading in 1158, and before or not long after Pope
Adrian IV's death on 1 Sept. 1159. Amfrey was the rector of Aston who, with his
nephew Gilbert, had recently been in dispute with the abbot of St Albans over,
respectively, the church of Shephall and land at *Hanleia* (see no. 691).

375 *Release and quitclaim by Hamo son of William to Reading Abbey of
all the land which he held of it in the new assart of Aston, as 13½ acres, and*

renunciation of all right in the same which he or his heirs or successors had or could have by virtue of any gift or concession. For this the abbey has given him 100s   [? early 13th cent.]

Original charter: Hertford County Record Office, D/E AS 109
B f 97v; C f 49v

Sciant presentes et futuri quod ego Hamo filius Willelmi reddidi, remisi et *ᵃquietam clammavi*ᵃ de me et de omnibus heredibus et successoribus meis in perpetuum deo et ecclesie beate Marie de Radinges et abbati et monachis ibidem deo servientibus totam terram quam habui in novo assarto de Estona cum omnibus pertinentiis suis quam de eis tenui pro tredecim acris et dimidia. Habendam et tenendam dictis abbati et conventui de Radinges in perpetuum libere et quiete, integre, pacifice et plenarie ut ius ecclesie sue, ita quod nec ego Hamo nec heredes mei nec aliquis ex parte nostra aliquo tempore vel aliquo modo aliquid iuris in predicta terra vel eius pertinentiis habere vel clammare*ᵇ* poterimus, quia totum ius et clammium*ᶜ* quod ego vel heredes aut successores mei in predicta terra vel eius pertinentiis ratione alicuius concessionis vel donationis habuimus vel habere possemus, ego Hamo pro me et pro heredibus et pro omnibus successoribus meis dictis abbati et conventui de Radinges resignavi et in perpetuum *ᵈquietum clammavi.*ᵈ Et ad maiorem eorum securitatem plenariam saisinam eis*ᵉ* inde feci et cartam quam de dicto abbate et conventu inde habui eis reddidi et omnia predicta presenti carta mea confirmavi. Pro hac autem concessione, remissione, confirmatione et *ᶠquieta clammantia,*ᶠ dederunt michi dicti abbas et conventus centum solidos estelingorum.*ᵍ* *ʰHiis testibus: Johanne filio Gaufr(edi), Radulfo de la Rivere, Johanne de Westwich, Gaufr(edo) de Mundene, Nicholao de Muchlefeld, Henrico de Camel, Waltero de Bachamton', Helya de Scaccario, Philippo de Stocton', Henrico clerico, Ricardo Marescallo, et multis aliis.

Endorsed: Carta Hamonis filii Willelmi de terra de Estona [*13th cent.*]

Size: 171 × 91 mm

Seal: fragment in pale red wax on tag; circular with design of foliated cross in a lozenge; legend: ...NIS . FIL. WILLI

ᵃ⁻ᵃ quiet'cl' *B*, quietcl' *C*   ᵇ clamare *B,C*
ᶜ clamium *B,C*   ᵈ⁻ᵈ quiet'cl' *B*, quietumclam' *C*
ᵉ *B has this word after* feci *and marked for transposition; C has it after* feci *without transposition mark*
ᶠ⁻ᶠ quiet'cl' *B*, quietaclamacione *C*
ᵍ sterling' *B*, sterlingorum *C*   ʰ *B ends with* T', *C ends*

It seems likely that Hamo son of William is identical with the Hamo of Aston who was a free tenant of the abbey in Hertfordshire in ? 1208–13 (*Fees*, i. 628). A Hamo son of William witnessed a deed to the abbey in Sulhamstead Abbots, certainly not later than 1184 (no. 1076), but he may well be a different person. Although the present deed was not entered in A, its diplomatic has certain primitive features supporting a fairly early date. I am indebted to the kindness of Mr R. M. Abel Smith for permission to print from the originals of nos. 375-9 and from the contemporary copy of no. 380.

376 Quitclaim by John son of Robert Humphrey (*Humfr'*) of Stevenage (*Stiðenhach'*)*ᵃ* to Reading Abbey of warranty of the land which he formerly held of it in the vill of Aston (*Aston'*) for 2s annual rent, which land he sold to Walter, rector of the church of Aston, and concerning which he vouched the abbot to warranty in the king's court. Sealing [? *c.* 1260]

Original charter: Hertford County Record Office, D/E AS 105
B f 98r; C f 49v

*ᵇ*Hiis testibus:*ᶜ* Roberto de Gravel', Adam filio Bernardi, Laurencio de Hypegrave, Johanne de Watton', Roberto Jordan', Petro de Bedewell', Nicholao filio Rogeri, Willelmo Brun, Andrea Pedef(er), Willelmo Hamfrey, Waltero Gernun, Johanne de la Hull', et aliis.

Endorsed: Carta Johannis filii Roberti Hunf' de Stivenhach' de quietaclam' warantye de dimidia virgata terre in Eston' [*13th cent.*]
Size: 177 × 89 mm
Seal: fragment of small pointed oval seal in green wax on tag; legend: ... FIL'I. ROBER. ...

ᵃ Stivenhach' *B,C*
ᵇ *C ends*
ᶜ *B ends*

Not in the original section of B, but entered very soon afterwards. A Walter was rector of Aston in 1240 (PRO E42/384); Thomas Griffin was rector in 1214 (PRO E40/14535), and subsequently, before 1235, Henry de Kamel was instituted (*Rot. Hug. de Welles*, i. 93). Another deed concerning the same with largely the same witness-list, but made slightly earlier when John still held the land himself, is Hertford Co. Record Office, D/E AS 106. It was not copied into the cartularies, but it has a nearly perfect impression of John's seal.

377 Gift in free alms by Walter son of William of Graveley (*Gravele*) to Reading Abbey of ½ virgate of land which he held of John son of Robert Humphrey (*Hunfray*)*ᵃ* of Stevenage (*Stythenache*)*ᵇ* in the vill of Aston (*Estone*). Warranty and sealing [? *c.* 1260]

Original charter: Hertford County Record Office, D/E AS 103
B f 98r; C ff 49v-50r

*ᶜ*Hiis testibus:*ᵈ* domino Alexandro de Andevill', Philippo de Merdeley, Roberto Jordan, Andrea Pedefer, Willelmo le Escot, Willelmo Anfray, Stephano le Marchand, et aliis.

Endorsed: Carta Walteri filii Willelmi de Gravel' de dimidia virgata
terre in Eston' [*13th cent.*]
Size: 196 × 80 mm
Seal: missing; tag through slit in fold at bottom

^a Hunfr' *B*, Humfr' *C*   ^b Stichenhach' *C*
^c *C ends*   ^d *B ends*

Date as for no. 376 and certainly earlier than 29 Sept. 1269, when the abbey leased
this land to him for life (Hertford Co. Record Office, D/E AS 102). A William of
Graveley occurs in the late 12th century and may have been in possession of the
manor of Graveley (*VCH Herts.*, iii. 87).

378   Confirmation and quitclaim by John son of Robert Humphrey
(*Hunfray*)^a of Stevenage (*Stythenache*)^b to Reading Abbey of the ½
virgate of land in the vill of Aston (*Estone*) which Walter son of
William of Graveley (*Gravele*) formerly held of him for an annual
rent of 1d at Easter and which Walter has given to the abbey in
free alms. Also gift and quitclaim in free alms of the same 1d annual
rent. Warranty and sealing   [? *c.* 1260]

Original charter: Hertford County Record Office, D/E AS 104
B f 98r; C f 50r

'Hiis testibus:^d domino Alexandro de Andevill', domino Ivone de
Hamle, Roberto de Gravel', Roberto Jordan, Philippo de Merdel',
Roberto de Brochole, Willelmo Amfray, et aliis.

Endorsed: Confirmacio Johannis filii Roberti Hunfr' de dimidia vir-
gata terre et uno denar' redditus in Eston' [*13th cent.*]
Size: 217 × 136 mm
Seal: missing; tag through slit in fold at bottom

^a Hunfr' *B*, Humfr' *C*   ^b Stichenhach' *C*
^c *C ends*   ^d *B ends*

Contemporary with no. 377.

379   Gift and quitclaim by Geoffrey son of John of [?] Ashwell
(*Eyswell'*)^a to Reading Abbey of the entire tenement which he sometime held of it in the vill and territory of Aston (*Eston'*) with messuage, gardens, rents, easements and all appurtenances. Warranty.
For this the abbey has given him 34 marks sterling. Sealing
                                                             [? *c.* 1260]

Original charter: Hertford County Record Office, D/E AS 108
B f 98v; C f 50r–v

Testibus:^b domino Waltero de Gravel' tunc rectore ecclesie eiusdem
ville, Philippo de Mardel', Thoma de Sysseverne, Roberto de Ardes,

Galfrido de Brochole, Roberto et Johanne filiis eiusdem Galfridi, Andrea pe de fer, Galfrido capellano, Stephano de Benintone, et multis aliis.

Endorsed: Carta Galfr' filii Johannis de quodam tenemento in Eston' [*13th cent.*]
Size: 267 × 130 mm
Seal: well-preserved circular seal (diameter 30 mm) in green wax on tag; design of head-and-shoulders profile of tonsured priest holding small hammer or ? tuning fork; legend: +S' GALFRIDI CANTORIS FERNENSIS^c

a Eyswelle *B*
b B,C end
c *The first letter of this word may be* S

This deed was entered in B in the same hand as nos. 376-8 and is certainly earlier than 29 Sept. 1269, when the land was leased for life to Walter son of William of Graveley (Hertford Co. Record Office, D/E AS 102). The latter deed calls the present donor Geoffrey *de Essewell'* and describes the land as having been formerly of Lucy of Gaddesden (*Gatesden'*).

380 Mandate by King Edward III to William Trussel, escheator this side of the Trent, that, since King Henry II confirmed the manor and church of Aston (*Eston'*) in Hertfordshire to Reading Abbey in perpetual alms by a charter[1] confirmed by a charter of King Edward II,[2] and since it is clear from an inquest held by the escheator at the king's order and returned into Chancery that the abbot of Reading and his predecessors have held the said manor without render or making any chantries or alms, and the manor is held of the king in chief by the service of praying for the king and his progenitors and successors, the escheator is to allow the abbot to hold it in this way and to cease any further disturbance of the abbot in his possession of the manor   5 Mar. 1337

B ff 98v-99r; C f 50v; Hertford County Record Office, D/E AS 3[3]
Pd. (cal.) *Cal. Close R. 1337-39*, 5-6 (from Close Roll)

Teste me ipso apud Westmon(asterium) quinto die Marcii, anno regni nostri undecimo.

[1] No. 372.
[2] No. 102.
[3] This is not the original writ but a contemporary copy, beginning *Rex dilecto et fideli suo* and with no evidence of sealing. It is endorsed in the same hand: 'Et si contingat quod aliquis escaetor domini regis onerare velid [*sic*] manerium abbatis Radyng' de Astone in comitatu Hertf' ad aliquas elemosinas faciendas, mittendum est ad cancelar' domini regis et in rotul' eiusdem cancelar' primo termino scilicet in Marcio anno regni regis Edwardi tercii a Conquestu undecimo invenietur quod predictum manerium de quibuscumque elemosinis tribuendis exoneratur.'

BERKHAMSTEAD

381   *Gift in free alms by Philip son of William of Berkhamstead to Reading Abbey, with his brother John who has become a monk at Reading, of three plots of land in Berkhamstead, two of which were sometime held of Philip and afterwards of the abbey by Philip's brother, Robert, and all of which are to be held for annual rents. Also confirmation of the gift by his brother, Robert, of a forinsec stall in front of the monastery*   [? early 13th cent.]

A f 106r; B f 160v; C ff 95v–96r; D f 33r–v (with omissions)

Sciant presentes et futuri quod ego Philippus filius Willelmi de Berkhamsted'*ᵃ* dedi et concessi et hac presenti carta mea confirmavi deo
et sancte Marie et abbati et conventui de Rading(ia), pro anima
patris mei et pro salute mea*ᵇ* et omnium antecessorum meorum et
successorum, *ᶜ*cum Iohanne fratre meo, qui in ecclesia de Rading(ia)
monachatus est,*ᶜ* totam terram in burgo de Berchamsted'*ᵈ* que iacet
inter terram que fuit Willelmi de la Strecchelane*ᵉ* et terram que fuit
Aliz Lelle, que extenditur a regali via usque ad terram Lamberti le
Flemeng,*ᶠ* cum omnibus pertinentiis suis, in puram et perpetuam
elemosinam, *ᵍ*quam Robertus frater meus aliquando tenuit de me et
postea de domo Rading(ensi), sed totam terram illam et totum ius
quod in ea habuit predicto abbati et conventui de Rading(ia) resignavit et quietum clamavit,*ᵍ* tenendam de me et heredibus meis libere
[et]*ʰ* quiete, reddendo inde annuatim mihi et heredibus meis duodecim denarios pro omni servitio quos ego et heredes mei reddere
debemus domino feodi*ⁱ* ad .iiii. terminos, videlicet, ad festum sancti
Michaelis tres denarios, ad Natale domini tres denarios, ad Pascha
tres denarios, ad Advincula sancti Petri tres denarios. Concessi etiam
eis totam terram in eodem burgo*ʲ* que iacet inter terram que fuit
Gaufridi Bodin et terram que fuit Rogeri Slupie, cum omnibus pertinentiis suis, *ᵏ*quam etiam predictus Robertus frater meus aliquando
tenuit de me et postea de domo Rading(ensi), sed totam terram
illam et totum ius quod in ea habuit predicto abbati et conventui
similiter resignavit et quietum clamavit,*ᵏ* quam terram in perpetuum
possidebunt predicti abbas et conventus, reddendo inde annuatim
mihi et heredibus meis duodecim denarios pro omni servitio quos
ego et heredes mei reddere debemus domino feodi*ⁱ* ad*ˡ* .iiii. terminos,
*ᵐ*videlicet, ad festum sancti Michaelis tres denarios, ad Natale domini tres denarios, ad Pascha tres denarios, ad Advincula sancti Petri
tres denarios.*ᵐ* Preterea dedi eis *ⁿ*in halimoth de*ⁿ* Berchamsted'*ᵃ*
totam terram que iacet inter terram que fuit Radulfi pistoris et
terram que fuit Brichtgive,*ᵒ* cum omnibus pertinentiis suis, in puram
et perpetuam elemosinam, tenendam in dominico suo vel sicut eis
placuerit de me et heredibus meis, reddendo inde annuatim mihi et

heredibus meis quatuordecim denarios pro omni servitio quos ego et heredes mei persolvere debemus pro eodem feodo[p] ad quatuor terminos, videlicet, ad festum sancti Michaelis tres denarios et obolum, ad Natale tres denarios et obolum, ad Pascha[q] tres denarios et obolum, ad Advincula [r]sancti Petri[r] tres denarios et obolum. Hanc autem conventionem,[s] donationem et concessionem ego et heredes mei domui de Rading(ia) contra omnes homines et [t]contra omnes[t] feminas warantizabimus. Insuper concessi et confirmavi prefatis abbati et conventui de Rading(ia) donum Roberti fratris mei quod eis fecit simili intuitu, videlicet, forinsecam seldam ante monasterium versus austrum. Et [ad][h] hanc donationem et concessionem fideliter roborandam, presens scriptum sigilli mei appositione roboravi. Hiis testibus.

Additional note (B,C only): Item alie due eiusdem de eodem et fere eisdem verbis, sed ista melior est, quia plenior et per innovationem istius transmutantur ille due.

[a] Berkhamested' *B*, Berkhamsted' *C*, Berkamsted' *D*
[b] *Om. in D*
[c-c] *Om. in D*
[d] Burkhamsted' *B*, Burkhamsted' *C*, Berkamsted' *D*
[e] Strechelane *B,C*
[f] Flemming *D*
[g-g] *Om. in D*
[h] *Om. in A, supplied from other copies*
[i] feudi *D*
[j] *A has* burco
[k-k] *Om. in D*
[l] *Insert* predictos *D*
[m-m] *Om. in D*
[n-n] in halimot de *B*, halimot in *C*
[o] Brichgive *B,C,D*
[p] feudo *D*
[q] *A has* Pasca
[r-r] *Om. in B*
[s] *Om. in B,C,D*
[t-t] *Om. in B,C,D*

This is not entered in the original section of A, but among additions of the early 13th century. In view of the important omissions from the text in D, it is likely that this is one of the less satisfactory versions mentioned in the note in B and C, in which case D is earlier than A, B, C, and also earlier than no. 382 (q.v. for further discussion).

382 *Release and quitclaim by Robert son of William of Berkhamstead to Reading Abbey of the land which he held of it in the borough of Berkhamstead, either through the abbey or through his brother, Philip* [? early 13th cent.]

B f161r; C f96r; D f32r-v

Sciant [a]presentes et futuri[a] quod ego Robertus filius Willelmi de Berkhamested'[b] resignavi et reddidi abbati et conventui de Rading(ia) in portimot[c] de Berkhamested'[b] totam terram quam de eis tenui in burgo de Berkhamested'[b] et quietum eis clamavi totum ius quod in terra illa habui sive per illos sive per Ph(ilippum) fratrem meum aliquando et quicquid in ea habui quocumque modo. Videlicet, totam terram que iacet inter terram que fuit Willelmi de la

Strecchelane et terram que fuit Aliz Lelle, que extenditur a regali via usque ad terram Lamberti le Flemeng,*d* cum omnibus pertinentiis suis; et totam terram illam in eodem burgo que iacet inter terram que fuit Gaufr(edi) Bodin et terram que fuit Rogeri Slupie cum omnibus pertinentiis suis. Ut totam terram illam et totum ius quod ad illam pertinet habeant et possideant predicti abbas et monachi in dominico suo vel sicut eis melius placuerit absque omni demanda et calumpnia que eis fieri possit per me vel per heredes meos. Et quod nullam in posterum inde vexationem vel molestiam habere*e* possint, predictam*f* resignationem et quietamclamationem presenti scripto et sigilli mei appositione fideliter roboravi. Hiis testibus.

a–a et cetera *D*
c portemoth *D*
e sustinere *D*
b Berkhamsted' *C*, Berkamstede *D*
d Flemyng' *C*, Flemmeng *D*
f prefatam *D*

Earlier than the final version of no. 381. It is clear from these two deeds that Philip was the eldest brother. One of his brothers, Robert, held of him certain lands in Berkhamstead. When the third brother, John, became a monk at Reading, Philip gave the abbey the lands and service of Robert with Robert as tenant. Robert subsequently quitclaimed the lands in question to the abbey by the present deed.

383 *Gift in free alms by Robert son of William of Berkhamstead to Reading Abbey of a forinsec stall in front of the monastery [? in Berkhamstead]*

[? early 13th cent.]

A f 107r–v; B f 161r; C f 96v; D f 32r

Sciant presentes et futuri quod ego Robertus filius Willelmi de Berchamstede*a* dedi et concessi et hac presenti carta mea confirmavi deo et sancte Marie et abbati et conventui de Radinges, pro anima patris mei et pro salute mea et omnium antecessorum et successorum meorum, forinsecam seldam ante monasterium versus austrum, in puram et perpetuam elemosinam, quam Willelmus filius Symonis tenuit de me per servitium sex solidorum per annum. Quam seldam et quod servitium assignavi et dedi predictis abbati et conventui de Radinges tenendum de me et de heredibus meis iure perpetuo, reddendo inde annuatim mihi*b* et heredibus meis duodecim denarios pro omni servitio ad quatuor terminos, videlicet, ad festum sancti Michaelis tres denarios, ad [*f 107v*] Natale domini tres denarios, ad Pasca*c* tres denarios, et ad Vincula sancti Petri tres denarios. Hanc autem donationem et concessionem ego*d* et heredes mei ecclesie de Rading(es) contra omnes homines*e* warantizabimus.*f* Hiis testibus.

a Berkh' *B*, Berkhamsted' *C*, Berkamstede *D*
c Pascha *B,C,D*
e *Insert* et feminas *B,C*
b michi *C,D*
d *Insert* Robertus *D*
f *Insert* in perpetuum *B,C*

Earlier than no. 381, which confirms this gift. The location of the stall is uncertain. The text does not state that it was in the town and there was never a monastery *sensu stricto* there, but the rubrics of B and C say 'in Berkhamstead' and the gift was confirmed by Philip of Berkhamstead.

384 Gift in free alms by William *del Boys* to Reading Abbey of 12d annual rent in the borough of Berkhamstead (*Berkhamsted*)[a] from the messuage which William *le Fainel* holds of him, between the tenement which belonged to William *le Flemeng*[b] and that which belonged to Robert *Scoche*, to be paid by William *le Fainel* at the same terms as he was due to pay the rent to the donor. Warranty and sealing. Witnesses [omitted]   [? *c.* 1230 × 50]

A f111v; D ff32v–33r

[a] Berkamstede *D*
[b] Flameng *D*

Date uncertain, but it was entered in A in the same hand as ac act of 1240 (no. 1116) and in the original section of D. Curiously this deed was not entered in B and C.

385 Gift by Robert Battle (*Bataille*) of Berkhamstead (*Berkh*(*amested*))[a] to Reading Abbey of all the land between his gate and the main street (*vicus regalis*) which was the frontage of his house (*qui fuit frons domus eiusdem Roberti*), viz., all the land which Richard *Barun* held of him for an annual service of 2s; and all the land which Geoffrey the steward (*dispensator*) held of him by a similar annual service of 2s. [To be held] by rendering annually to the donor and his heirs 1d for all service, viz., $\frac{1}{4}$d each at Michaelmas, Christmas, East er and St Peter Advincula. Also gift of all the land between the land which belonged to Peter, nephew of the dean, and that which belonged to William son of Uthred (*Uctredus*),[b] viz., all the land which Robert *Brid* held of him, for which the abbey shall pay him annually 12d for all service, viz., 3d each at Michaelmas, Christmas, Easter and St Peter Advincula. Warranty. For this the abbey has given him 2 marks of silver. Witnesses [omitted]
                        [13th cent., not later than 1258]

B f161r–v; C f96v; D f32v

[a] *Expansion from rubric;* Berkhamsted' *C*, Berkamstede *D*
[b] Utred' *C*

Impossible to date precisely, but it was not entered in A and appears in the original section of B. The donor witnessed six Berkhamstead charters to Missenden Abbey, four of which are dated by the editor to *c.* 1225 (*Cartl. Missenden*, ii. 47, 58, 64, 67).

HERTFORD

386   *Release and quitclaim by William Cane to Abbot Simon and the convent of Reading of the tenement which he had of them in the parish of St Andrew, Hertford. In the full court of Aston*   [1213 × 26]

B f98v; C f50r

Sciant presentes et futuri quod ego Willelmus Cane resignavi et quiet'clamavi,[a] dedi et concessi et hac presenti carta mea confirmavi deo et beate Marie et abbati et conventui de Rading(ia) totum tenementum quod de eis habui in villa de Hertford(ia) cum omnibus pertinentiis suis, videlicet, totum tenementum cum edificiis et omnibus aliis pertinentiis quod iacet in parrochia[b] sancti Andree iuxta terram Johannis Toutlond'. Habendum et tenendum libere, quiete et absolute secundum quod eis placuerit iure perpetuo, sicut ius et feudum ecclesie Rading(ensis), absque omni calumpnia, exactione et demanda que eis unquam a me vel a meis inde fieri possit. Et propter hanc resignationem et quiet'clamationem,[c] donationem, concessionem et carte mee confirmationem, dederunt mihi predicti abbas et conventus de Rading(ia) unam marcam argenti. Quod ut firmum et stabile sit in perpetuum, presenti scripto sigillum meum apposui et domino Symoni abbati nomine ecclesie de Rading(ia) in plenaria curia de Estun(a) plenariam saisinam perpetuo duraturam inde feci. T(estibus).[d]

[a] quietumclamavi C	[b] parochia C
[c] quietamclamationem C	[d] Om. in C

The dating limits are those of Simon's abbacy. In ? 1208–13 William son of Cane, who was probably the same as the present donor, was among the abbot's free tenants in Hertfordshire, probably in Aston (*Fees*, i. 628). There is no record of an original gift to the abbey in Hertford and the details of this quitclaim suggest that this tenement may have been an appurtenance of the manor of Aston.

SAWBRIDGEWORTH

387   *Gift by Henry FitzGerold, the king's chamberlain, to Reading Abbey of 1¼ virgates of land in Sawbridgeworth producing an annual rent of 26s 0½d, with the men dwelling there and their progeny*   [1174 × 5]

A f38r; B f95v; C f48r

Henricus filius Geroldi, domini regis camerarius, uxori sue M(atildi) de Caisne filiisque suis et omnibus hominibus atque fidelibus suis, salutem. Notum sit vobis omnibus quod ego, pro salute anime mee, concessi et dedi et presenti scripto et sigilli mei testimonio confirmavi

deo et ecclesie sancte Marie de Rading(ia) et monachis ibidem deo
servientibus unam virgatam terre et quartam partem virgate in manerio de Sabrictheswrð(a),ᵃ reddentes annuatim .xxvi. solidos et
obolum, cum hominibus supra eandem terram manentibus cum fu-
tura eorum prole. Et volo et heredibus meis precipio ut, quantum
ad illos pertinet, tam libere et quiete habeant et teneant sicut alias
possessiones suas habent, cum pratis et pasturis et omnibus aliis
pertinentiis.ᵇ Testibus:ᶜ Radulfo capellano de Wichurchia, Walerano
de Crichel', Roberto filio Henrici, et multis aliis.

ᵃ Sebrichteswrþe B,C
ᵇ C ends
ᶜ B ends

This gift was made on his death-bed (see no. 389). He died in 1174–5 (Farrer, *Honors
and Knights' Fees*, iii. 169) and was buried in Reading Abbey (see no. 393). The donor
was hereditary chamberlain of the Exchequer of Receipt (E. Kimball, *Serjeanty Tenure
in Medieval England* (New Haven, 1936), 91; J.H. Round, *The Commune of London*
(Westminster, 1899), 83), and made this gift out of the 74 librates in Sawbridgeworth
with which Geoffrey de Mandeville had enfeoffed his elder brother, whose heir he
was, before 1166 (*Red Bk. Exch.*, i. 356) and which were later known as the manor of
Pishiobury (*VCH Herts.*, iii. 336). The remainder of Sawbridgeworth continued in the
Mandeville demesne and was later called the manor of Sayesbury (*ibid.*, 335). Reading Abbey's land, with later additions (nos. 392–3, 395), became the manor of Groves
(*ibid.*, 339).

388 *Confirmation by Warin son of Henry FitzGerold, the king's chamberlain, of the preceding gift* [1174/5 × 1216; poss. 1193 × 1216]

A f95r; B f95v; C f48r

Sciant presentes et futuri quod ego Warinus filius Henrici filii Ger-
aldi,ᵃ domini regis camerarius, pro amore dei et salute anime mee
et anima patris mei et matris mee et omnium antecessorum meorumᵇ
et successorum meorum, dono et concedo et sigilli mei attestatione
confirmo deo et ecclesie sancte Marie de Rading(ia) et monachis
ibidem deo servientibus ᶜterram illam totamᶜ quam pater meus illis
dedit in Sebricthewrtheᵈ cum omnibus libertatibus et consuetudinibus suis, sicut in carta patris mei continetur.ᵉ Hiis testibus.

ᵃ Geroldi C
ᶜ⁻ᶜ totam terram illam B,C
ᵉ B ends with T', C ends

ᵇ Om. in B,C
ᵈ Sebrichteswrþe B,C

After no. 387 and before Warin's death in 1216 (*EYC*, iii. 471). Since it was not
entered in the original section of A, possibly not earlier than 1193.

389 *Notification by William de Mandeville, earl of Essex, that he has
received from Abbot Joseph and the convent of Reading the land which Henry*

FitzGerold gave them in Sawbridgeworth, which he and his heirs by his wife shall hold for 1 lb of incense annually. If he has no legitimate heirs, the abbey shall recover possession as freely as he or his ancestors possessed it

[1174/5 × 80; ? 1175]

A f41r; (noted) B f96r

Sciant presentes et futuri quod ego Willelmus de Mandevilla, comes Estsexie, recepi a Ioseph abbate Rading(ensi) et eiusdem loci conventu terram quam Henricus filius Geroldi moriturus concessit domui de Rading(ia) in manerio de Sabrihteswrð(a), scilicet terram Rannulfi que reddit .xi. solidos et .v. denarios, et terram Herewardi reddentem .v. solidos et .viii. denarios et obolum, terram Ordgari reddentem .v. solidos, et terram Ernisi reddentem .iii. solidos et .xi. denarios. Tenebo autem eam terram ego et heredes mei post me quos habuero de coniuge mea post nuptias genitos, pro libra una incensi annuatim solvenda ecclesie de Rading(ia) ad festum Assumptionis sancte Marie virginis [*15 Aug.*]. Si non habuero de coniuge propria heredes legitimos, recipient prefati monachi prefatam terram tam libere et quiete possidendam perpetuo quam libere et quiete ego vel antecessores mei eam unquam possederunt. His testibus: Rogero Bigot, Hugone Talebot, Gileberto de Veir, et multis aliis.

After no. 387 and, since the earl appears not yet to be married, before his marriage in Jan. 1179/80 (*Complete Peerage*, v. 118). The witnesses are the same as the first three who witnessed another charter by the earl, probably in 1175 (no. 1073).

390 *Certification by Warin FitzGerold to the justices-in-eyre in Hertfordshire that his father, Henry, gave to Reading Abbey 2 marks worth of land in Sawbridgeworth, which now, as he hears, Geoffrey de Say is withholding from the abbey, and that the land does not belong to that part of the manor which belonged to William de Mandeville, earl [of Essex], since Henry held it for long after the partition until his death. Therefore, he requests the justices to deliver the land to the abbey* [prob. 1190]

B f95v; C f48r–v

Iustitiis domini regis itinerantibus in Hertfortsyr'ᵃ War(inus) filius Ger(oldi), salutem. Sciatis quod Henricus pater meus dedit monachis de Rading(ia) in perpetuam elemosinam duas marcatas terre in Sebrichteswrþe, quas sicut audivi Gaufr(edus) de Say modo predictis monachis difforciat. Unde quia ego elemosinam patris mei teneor garantizare, vos precor attentius quatinus prefatam terram prefatis monachis deliberetis pro amore dei et domini regis et nostra. Pro certo autem quod illa pars terre non pertinet ad partem predicti manerii que fuit Willelmi comitis de Mandevill(a), quia multo tempore post partitionem illam pater meus tenuit illam et usque ad finem vite sue. Valete.

a Hertfordschyr' *C*

After the death of William de Mandeville, 12 Dec. 1189 (see *Handbook of Brit. Chron.*), and, since there is no reference to Geoffrey FitzPeter who had a life interest in the land from *c.* 1193 at the latest, and probably from 1190 (see no. 391), probably not later than 1190. When William de Mandeville died without legitimate issue, his rights passed to his aunt, Beatrice de Mandeville, who had married William de Say (d. 1144), and her heirs. A complicated inheritance dispute ensued between Geoffrey de Say, Beatrice's younger son, and Geoffrey FitzPeter, who married Beatrice de Say, daughter of Beatrice de Mandeville's elder son (Sanders, *English Baronies*, 71). Geoffrey de Say appears to have succeeded to the Mandeville inheritance for a time, but to have lost it to Geoffrey FitzPeter by Sept. 1190 (*PR 2 Richard I*, 111), although he appears to have retained the Mandeville manor in Sawbridgeworth (the later manor of Sayesbury)—see, e.g., *Fees*, i. 123. By virtue of that, and probably because William de Mandeville had leased Reading Abbey's land (no. 389), Geoffrey de Say seized the latter. By the present certification Warin FitzGerold, tenant of the later manor of Pishiobury, assures the justices in effect that Reading's land was not part of Sayesbury (i.e. that part of Sawbridgworth which belonged to William de Mandeville after the partition—which can refer only to the enfeoffment of FitzGerold before 1166, as in no. 387 n.), but part of Pishiobury, and that therefore Geoffrey de Say can have no claim to it. I am indebted to the kindness of Professor J. C. Holt for valuable help on these points.

391 *Notification by Geoffrey FitzPeter that he has received from Reading Abbey a lease for life of its land in Sawbridgeworth, formerly held of it by William [de Mandeville], earl of Essex, for an annual rent of 1 mark, payment of which he assigns out of the rents of his mills in his manor of Amersham [Bucks]*   [1190 × 93; prob. 1190]

A f45r (deleted); (noted) B f96r[1]

Sciant presentes et posteri quod ego Gaufredus filius Petri accepi ab abbate Rading(ensi) et monachis eiusdem loci terram suam in Sabrichteswrda quam Willelmus comes Essexie de eis tenuit per unam libram incensi, tenendam tantum in vita mea solvendo annuatim eis pro ea marcam unam argenti, dimidiam marcam ad Pascha et dimidiam ad festum sancti Michaelis. Hunc autem redditum eis assignavi in manerio meo Agmodesham de redditibus molendinorum meorum. Quod si aliquo casu contigerit de molendinis eos non posse habere redditum suum, baillivus meus de eadem villa eis perficiet redditum illum ad terminos statutos. Nullus autem heredum vel successorum meorum aliquid iuris sibi vendicent*a* in predicta terra de Sabrichteswrd(a), quia post dies meos eam tanquam propriam tenere debent abbas et monachi de Rading(ia). His testibus: Simone de Pateshella, Hel(ia) capellano, Willelmo clerico de Bukinham, et pluribus aliis.

a Sic; *? rectius* vendicet

Certainly after the death of William de Mandeville, 12 Dec. 1189, and before Geoffrey was styled earl of Essex in 1199, but, since the deed was entered in the original section of A, it is not later than 1193. Although Geoffrey acquired the bulk of the Mandeville inheritance in 1190 (*PR 2 Richard I*, 111), he appears not to have secured the Mandeville manor in Sawbridgeworth (see no. 390 n.). This deed is not of itself evidence that he did so, since Reading's land was not part of that manor (no. 390), although it does suggest that he had an interest in it, which he is most likely to have had after securing the main Mandeville inheritance in 1190. This wuld also have been a useful time for Reading to assert the independence of its own land Accordingly, the date 1190 has been suggested for this lease. The deed ws entered only in A and there crossed through, evidently deleted when it was nullified by Geoffrey's death in 1213.

[1] The note reads: *Carte due Gaufr(edi) filii Petri de firma terre de Sebrichteswrpe.*

392 *Gift in free alms by Warin FitzGerold, the king's chamberlain, to Reading Abbey of 24 acres of land in Sawbridgeworth with tenants*

[1204 × 15]

A f 104r-v; B ff 95v-96r; C f 48v

Sciant presentes et futuri quod ego Warinus filius Geroldi, domini regis camerarius, dedi et concessi et hac presenti carta mea confirmavi, pro salute anime mee et omnium antecessorum et successorum meorum, deo et sancte Marie et beato Iacobo de Rading(ia) octo acras terre in villa de Sebricteswrthe*a* quas Rogerus [*f 104v*] le bedel tenuit de me reddendo mihi annuatim duos solidos, et octo acras terre quas Walterus filius Radulfi*b* tenuit de me in eadem villa reddendo mihi annuatim quinque solidos, similiter octo acras quas Walterus filius Ernys tenuit de me in prenominata villa annuatim reddendo mihi duos solidos. Has autem predictas terras cum omnibus pertinentiis et hominibus predictis et tota eorum posteritate et catallis et possessionibus ipsorum habebunt et possidebunt prefati monachi de Rading(ia) in pace, libere et quiete, sine omni servitio seculari et aliqua exactione, sicut puram et perpetuam elemosinam. Ut autem hec mea donatio rata et inconcussa permaneat, sigilli mei appositione duxi roborandam.*c* Hiis testibus: Thoma Basset, Alano Basset, Waltero Foliot, Iohanne vicecomite de Berkes(ira), Ricardo Morin, Hugone de Bixe, Rad(ulfo) Bruncoste, Willelmo de Brioma, et Silvestro fratre eius, Willelmo de Huntercumbe, Alano vinetario, Hugone filio Raimundi, Gilleberto fratre eius, Ricardo Bulloc, et multis aliis.

a Sebricht'wrþe *B*, Sebrichtwrþe *C*
b Rand(ulf)i *B,C*
c *B ends with* T', *C ends*

While John de Wickenholt was *custos* or sheriff of Berkshire (*List of Sheriffs*, 6). The donor was the son of Henry FitzGerold and died in 1216 (see no. 388 and n.).

393 *Gift in free alms by Warin FitzGerold to Reading Abbey, with his body for burial in the abbey at the feet of his father, of 3 marks worth of land in Sawbridgeworth* [prob. *c.* July 1216]

A f 98r; B f 96r; C f 48v

Sciant presentes et futuri quod ego Gwarinus*a* filius Geroldi reddidi corpus meum apud Rading(iam) sepelliendum*b* ad pedes patris mei cum in fata concessero et, cum corpore meo, pro salute anime mee et pro anima patris mei et matris mee et omnium antecessorum et successorum meorum, concessi et dedi et hac presenti carta mea confirmavi deo et beate Marie et sancto Iacobo de Rading(ia) et monachis ibidem deo servientibus in puram et perpetuam elemosinam tres marchatas*c* terre in villa de Sebrichteswrd(a)*d* hoc modo assignatas. Videlicet, unam virgatam terre quam Willelmus filius Helie et Rad(ulfus) de la Lega tenent reddendo inde annuatim viginti solidos, et triginta acras terre arabilis que vocantur Godmundesfeld', cum parvo prato quod solebat mihi reddere quatuor denarios, pro aliis*e* viginti solidis. Habendas et tenendas plene et integre, libere et quiete et honorifice, liberas et quietas ab omni exactione et demanda et seculari servitio, sicut liberius et quietius tenent et possident alia tenementa sua. Et ut hec mea donatio rata sit et stabilis, eam sigilli mei appositione roboravi.*f* Hiis testibus: Willelmo Marescallo comite de Pembroc, Henrico filio Geroldi, Thoma Basseth, Alano Basset, Petro de la Mar', Rog(ero) Foliot, Waltero de Bachamton', Galfrido clerico, Nigello Bonvalat, Rad(ulfo) Bruncoste, Willelmo de Huntescumbe, Roberto de Sideham, Nicholao de Michlefeld, et multis aliis.

a Warinus *B,C*   *b* sepeliendum *B,C*
c marcatas *B,C*   *d* Sebricht'wrþe *B*, Sebrichtwrþe *C*
e *B,C repeat* pro aliis (*sic*)   *f* *B ends with* T', *C ends*

Probably shortly before he died in July, 1216 (*EYC*, iii. 471).

394 Confirmation by Margaret*a* de Ripariis, in her widowhood, to Abbot Adam [of Lathbury] and the monks of Reading of all the lands given by Henry FitzGerold [no. 387]; the arable land called *Godmundefeld* and a meadow which rendered 4d [see no. 393]; and all the lands with villeins, suit and services which Warin FitzGerold, her father, gave [no. 392]. To be held by the abbot and monks in free alms. They and their men of Sawbridgeworth (*Sebrithewrthe*)*b*

shall be quit of all suit, custom, tallage, aid, work and secular exaction of Margaret or her heirs. Witnesses[c] [omitted].   [1226 × 38]

A f 109v; B f 96r–v; C ff 48v–49r

[a] *All texts have* 'Margery'
[b] Sebricht'wrþe *B*, Sebrithwrþe *C*
[c] *Om. in C*

The dating limits are those of Adam of Lathbury's abbacy. Margaret was the daughter and heir of Warin FitzGerold (d. 1216). She married firstly Baldwin de Redvers
of Plympton (d. 1216) and secondly Fawkes de Breauté, whose estates were forfeited
in 1224 and who died in 1226 (Sanders, *English Baronies*, 137–8, 143; *VCH Herts.*, iii.
337; *DNB*, vi. 251). She died in 1252 (Sanders, 144).

395   Gift by Margaret[a] de Ripariis, in her widowhood, to Reading
Abbey of 50 shillings worth of land and rents in Sawbridgeworth
(*Sebrithewrthe*),[b] viz., 34½ acres of land from her demesne for 23s
annually, of which 11½ acres lie in the field of *Barlingedone*[c] nearest
the land of Geoffrey de Say, 11½ acres in the field of *Kamesfeld*
nearest the land of Geoffrey de Say, and 11½ acres in the field of
Witenhale towards the Cross nearest the land of Geoffrey de Say; the
entire service of William son of Roger and his heirs from a tenement
for which he used to pay 11s annually in commutation of scutage,
carriage and 8 boon-reapings (*bedripp'*), but for which he has agreed
to pay the abbey 13s annually; William the reeve (*prepositus*) with
his land and progeny for 8s; and a pasture extending from the Cross
along *Godmundesfeld*,[d] which Walter *le Frere* sometime held, for 6s
annually. Also confirmation of the entire arable land of *Godmundefeld*[d]
and of the road in the same. All to be held as freely as the abbey
holds any of its tenements. Warranty. For this the abbey has given
her 50 marks of silver to help her to pay off her debts to the king for
the recovery of her land in England, which the king had caused to
be taken into his hand.[e]   [1226 × 30]

A ff 109v–110r; B ff 96v–97r; C f 49r

Hiis testibus: Roberto de Walteham, Gaufrido clerico, Hugone de
Fuleford', Alano de Englefeld', Thoma Huscarl, Willelmo Morin,
Roberto de Chincham, Ricardo Neire Nuit, Ricardo de la Mare,
Willelmo de Hoctone, Simone de Latebire, et multis aliis.

[a] *All texts have* 'Margery'   [b] Sebricht'wrþe *B*, Sebrichtwrþe *C*
[c] Barlindon' *B,C*   [d] Godmundfeld' *C*
[e] *B ends with* T', *C ends*

After the death of her second husband, Fawkes de Breauté, in 1226, and before the
death of Geoffrey de Say in 1230 (Sanders, *English Baronies*, 98). Margaret was in
process of recovering her dower lands in 1225 (*Excerpta e rot. fin.*, i. 126).

HOO

In this section nos. 402–39 are given mainly in the order in which they appear in B and C, with the insertion of relevant final concords.

396 *Writ* Liberate *by King Henry II to Robert, earl of Leicester, and the barons of the Exchequer for 40 marks of silver annually to Reading Abbey from the king's rent at Hoo, until the king shall assign 40 marks rent in a definite place* [prob. May × July 1164]

A f24v; B f27v
Pd. *Memoranda Roll 1 John*, lxxvi n. 2; van Caenegem, *Royal Writs*, 192

Henricus rex Angl(orum) *ᵃet dux Norm(annorum) et Aquit-(anorum) et comes Andeg(avorum) R(oberto)ᵃ* comiti Legr-(ecestrie) et baronibus scaccarii,ᵇ salutem. Liberate de redditu meo de Hou abbati et monachis meis de Rading(ia) .xl. marcas arg-enti singulis annis ad duos terminos, ad festum sancti Michaelis et ad Pascha, donec assignem eis certo loco .xl. marcatas redditus. T(este)ᶜ Gaufredo archidiacono Cant(uariensi). Apud Wigorn(iam).

ᵃ⁻ᵃ *et cetera* B
ᵇ *A has* scaccarum
ᶜ *B ends*

The king made the gift at the time of the abbey's dedication, 19 Apr. 1164 (see no. 398; *PR 15 Henry II*, 161) and probably issued this writ while he was in Worcestershire in the summer (Eyton, 72). It is an early writ *Liberate*. For discussion, see van Caenegem, *Royal Writs*, 192, 185 n. 3; *Memoranda Roll 1 John*, lxxvi n. 2, lxiv n. 7.

397 *Writ* Liberate *by King Richard I to the barons of the Exchequer for the same, as the writ of King Henry II witnesses* 18 Sept. [1189]

A f28r–v; B f32v; C f8r
Pd. *Memoranda Roll 1 John*, lxiv

Ricardus dei gratia rex Anglie *ᵃdux Norm(annie) Aquit(anie) comes Andeg(avie)ᵃ* baronibus scaccarii, salutem. Liberate de redditu meo de Hou abbati et monachis [*f28v*] meis de Rading(ia) .xl. marcas argenti singulis annis ad duos terminos, ad festum sancti Michaelis et ad Pascha, donec assignem eis certo loco .xl. marcatas redditus, sicut breve patris nostri regis H(enrici) quod habent testatur. T(este)ᵇ Roberto de Witefeld. Apud Dodeford, xviii. die Septembris.

ᵃ⁻ᵃ *et cetera* B,C
ᵇ *B,C end*

This was given at Dodford (Northants.) a few days after the king's several acts in favour of Reading given on 12 Sept. 1199 at Geddington (Northants.)—see, e.g., nos. 34–7; also Landon, *Itin.*, 8.

398   *Notification by Robert Bardulf that he and his heirs are obliged to pay annually to Reading Abbey 40 marks of silver from the farm of his manor of Hoo, as given by King Henry II at the dedication of the abbey, and as confirmed by King Richard I*   [Nov. 1203 × Feb. 1205]

B f 102r; C f 52r

Omnibus sancte matris ecclesie filiis Robertus Bardulf, salutem. Noverit universitas vestra quod ego et heredes mei tenemur annuatim solvere abbati de Rading(ia) et monachis ibidem deo servientibus .xl. marcas argenti de firma manerii mei de Hou, quas Henricus rex bone memorie filius M(atildis) imperatricis in dedicatione monasterii Rading(ensis) eidem monasterio in dotem dedit et concessit, et filius eius rex Ricardus in predicto manerio de Hou percipiendas confirmavit. Et ut hoc ratum et inconcussum permaneat, presens scriptum sigilli mei appositione roboravi. T(estibus).*a*

a Om. in C

After 10 Nov. 1203, when King John confirmed to Robert Bardulf Hoo and his other lands (*Rot. Chart.*, 112), which had been held by his brother, Hugh, who died in that year (*PR 1 John*, 69; *PR 5 John*, 103; *EYC*, vi. 266 n. 4); and before no. 400, which assigns certain lands in place of the annual payment. Payment of the 40 marks had disappeared from the Pipe Rolls after 1189 (see *Memoranda Roll 1 John*, lxiv n. 7) and the precise wording of the present deed suggests strongly that in Richard I's reign the money had been received directly from Hoo and not at the Exchequer, as was certainly now to be the case (see no. 399).

399   *Precept by Robert Bardulf to his bailiffs of Hoo to pay the farm which he is due to pay annually to Reading Abbey, viz., 20 marks each at Easter and Michaelmas*   [Nov. 1203 × Feb. 1205]

B f 102r; C f 52r

Robertus Bardulf baillivis*a* suis de Hou, salutem. Precipio vobis quod illi qui vobis litteras istas patentes detulerit sine omni molestia et dilatione liberetis firmam quam teneor annuatim solvere monachis ecclesie Rading(ensis), scilicet .xx. marcas ad Pascha et .xx. marcas ad festum sancti Michaelis.

a ballivis C

Date as for no. 398.

400   *Assignment by Robert Bardulf to Reading Abbey, at the request of King John, of the 40 marks worth of silver, given by King Henry II, in land in the* *manor of Hoo. Namely, all tenants belonging to the parish of Allhallows with their progeny, rents and tenements, viz., 8 sulings, and half a yoke[1] held by Alan and* Berdeis, *with two crofts called* Oxenegars *in the parish of St Mary's Hoo;* 2½ *sulings in the parish of St Mary's Hoo held by a number of named tenants; and in the parish of St Werburgh* [*i.e., the modern parish of Hoo*] *half a yoke and 9 acres next to* Edgareslawe *held by Henry of Cobham for* ½ *mark annually. To be held as the king's free alms. The abbey's men shall come only to three hundred-courts annually, called law-days, and then merely to afforce Robert's court, on pain of compulsion by the abbot or his bailiff; and Reading Abbey shall have all legal rights over the said tenants and lands in accordance with its liberties* [*c.* 8 Feb. 1205]

A f 101r; B ff 101v–102r; C f 51v

Sciant presentes et futuri quod ego Robertus Bardulf, ad voluntatem et petitionem domini Iohannis regis Anglie, assignavi ecclesie Rading(ensi) et abbati et conventui eiusdem loci in manerio de Hou annuas quadraginta marcatas argenti in terra, quas[a] dominus rex Henricus pater domini regis Iohannis dedit in dotem eidem ecclesie Rading(ensi) in die dedicationis illius percipiendas de eodem manerio. Cuius assignationis ista est forma: omnes videlicet tenentes qui pertinent ad parochiam[b] Omnium Sanctorum et sequelas et redditus et tenementa ipsorum in eadem parochia,[c] scilicet octo sullingas cum omnibus pertinentiis suis et cum dimidio iugo quod Alanus et Berdeis[d] tenent et cum duobus croftis qui[e] vocantur Oxenegars in parochia[c] Sancte Marie que sunt aiugata cum predictis .viii. sullingis; et preterea duas sullingas et dimidiam cum omnibus pertinentiis suis in predicta parochia[c] Sancte Marie quas tenent isti: Adam Berd et participes ipsius tenent duo iuga et dimidium, David Heþene[f] et participes eius duo iuga, Hugo[g] Pereur[h] et participes eius dimidium iugum, Hagenild duo iuga .x. acras minus, Hugo de Cumba dimidium iugum et decem acras que etiam participes eorum tenent cum illis, et iugum Andrielde quod Alanus et participes eius tenent, Henricus filius Edwardi et participes ipsius tenent .iiii. iuga, Erny et participes eius iugum et dimidium, et iugum Yoklede quod heredes Gaufr(edi) Taleboth[i] tenent; et in parochia[c] Sancte Werburge[j] dimidium iugum et novem acras iuxta Edgareslawe que Henricus de[k] Cobbeham tenet reddendo annuatim dimidiam marcam. Omnes vero predictas terras, homines, redditus et tenementa, cum omnibus pertinentiis suis, iure perpetuo habebunt et possidebunt predicti abbas et monachi de Rading(ia) libere et quiete, bene et in pace, integre,[l] plenarie et honorifice, sicut liberam, puram et perpetuam elemosinam domini regis, sicut liberius et melius tenent alibi terras suas per concessiones regum Anglie quieta et absoluta ab omni consuetudine et exactione et ab omnibus hundredis et sectis et ab omnibus placitis et^k querelis et ab omnibus omnino rebus de me et de omnibus heredibus meis^m et successoribus meis in perpetuum. Homines quidem ipsorum de prefato tenemento venient solummodo ad tria hundreda per annum, que vocantur lagedayes,^{n} pro nulla alia re nisi solummodo pro curia mea efforcianda. Qui si venire neglexerint, abbas tantum per se vel per ballivum^o suum eos venire compellet, ita quidem quod ibi non vexentur nec trahantur in placitum, nec aliquid omnino ab eis exigatur. Placita enim omnia et omnes causas et querelas et attachiamenta etiam omnia, et omnes exitus quocumque modo provenerint, habebunt ipsi abbas et monachi de Rading(ia) in curia sua secundum libertates quas habent per concessiones regum Anglie. Omnia etiam forisfacta et amerciamenta et omnia que de predictis terris et tenementis et hominibus suis provenire quoquomodo poterunt, ipsorum sint in perpetuum absque ulla vexatione vel calumpnia. Ut autem hec^p assignatio et^k concessio rata et stabilis in perpetuum permaneat, eam presenti scripto et sigilli mei appositione bono animo et devoto corroboravi.^{q} Hiis testibus: domino H(uberto) Cantuar(iensi) archiepiscopo, domino I(ohanne) Norwic(ensi) aepiscopo, domino G(alfredo) filio Petri comite Essex(ie), domino W(illelmo) Marescallo comite de Penbrok, domino W(illelmo) Briwerr', domino G(alfredo) de Boklond', domino S(imone) de Pateshill', domino H(enrico) maiore de Lond(onia), domino Henrico de Cobbeh(am).

^{a} quam B,C	^{b} parrochiam B,C	^{c} parrochia B,C
^{d} Berdeys B,C	^{e} *Sic in all texts; not impossible, but ? rectius* que	
^{f} Heþne C	^{g} Henr(icus) B,C	^{h} Perur C
^{i} Talebot B,C	^{j} Wereburge B,C	^{k} *Om. in* C
^{l} *Insert* et C	^{m} *Om. in* B,C	^{n} laghedayes B,C
^{o} baillivum B,C	^{p} *Insert* mea B,C	^{q} *B ends with* T', *C ends*

The distinguished witness list suggests a date approximately the same as that of King John's confirmation (no. 401), three of the witnesses being common to both. This assignment of lands to Reading was made in the manor of Hoo, to which the hundred of Hoo was annexed and which included the three later parishes of Allhallows, St Mary's Hoo and Hoo, the first two of these being named from their churches' dedications. The *caput* of the manor was at Hoo, whose church, originally the mother church of the others, was dedicated to St Werburgh (Hasted, *History of Kent*, iv. 4, 13). Although Reading Abbey acquired by this charter lands in all three later parishes, its main estate, later known as the manor of Windhill, lay in Allhallows (*ibid.*, 28). By the terms of the charter the abbey also acquired part of the hundred of Hoo (see below, no. 444).

[1] From the details in this charter it is clear that in this part of Kent a 'yoke' was a sixth part of a suling.

401 Confirmation by King John of the assignment made to Reading Abbey by Robert *Bardulf*, in lands and men in the manor of

Hoo (*Hou*), of the 40 marks worth of silver given to the abbey on the day of its dedication by King Henry II. To be held by the abbey as the free alms of King Henry and of himself   8 Feb. 1205

A f31r; B f35v; C f10v
Pd. *Rot. Chart.*, 141 (from Charter Roll)

Testibus:[a] G(alfredo) filio Petri comite Essex(ie), Willelmo Mares-callo comite Penbroc, Willelmo Briwerr', Hugone de Nevill', Thoma Basset, Thoma de Sanford, Petro de Stok', Willelmo de Cantilupo, Ricardo de Argenton', Iohanne filio Hugonis. Dat' per manum Ios-celini de Well(es) apud Wudestok(am) octavo die Februarii, anno regni nostri sexto.

[a] *B,C end*

402   Gift by Ralph *Paynel* to Reading Abbey of 46s worth of rent in the manor of Hoo (*Hou*), viz., from William *Beluncle* for his own hereditary land 25s 3¾d; from the same William for the land which he had with Amice, his wife, of the tenement of William of Grain (*Grene*) 18s 6¼d; and from Andrew son of Bruning, Wulfnoth *de Fraxino*, Adam son of Roger, Robert son of Stephen and *Wlnor'* daughter of *Eylrich* for 10½ acres which they held of the donor 26d. To be held freely in perpetuity with homages, fines, amercements, reliefs, escheats, suits and all things which could come to the donor or his heirs, either in demesne or in services. Warranty with provision for reasonable exchange in lands, men and rents from the donor's inheritance in the same manor. For this the abbey has given him 40 marks of silver. Sealing Witnesses[a] [omitted]   [1225 × 37]

B f102r-v; C f52r

[a] *Om. in C*

Ralph Paynel was one of the co-heirs of Robert Bardulf, by virtue of which he acquired a quarter of a knight's fee in Hoo in July, 1225; he died before 15 May, 1237 (*EYC*, vi. 266–7). The rent here conveyed to Reading may have been in the parish of St Werburgh, Hoo, since Beluncle was a manor in that parish which in 1225 was acquired by Jordan Foliot, another of Robert Bardulf's co-heirs (Hasted, *History of Kent*, iv. 8; *Rot. Lit. Claus.*, ii. 47; *Cur. Reg. R.*, xiii. 7).

403   Gift by Hugh of Dagenham [or Dagnam] (*Dakeham*) to Reading Abbey, with the consent of his wife and heirs, of 9½ acres of land in the field called *Havedland*, from the vill of Windhill (*Windhill'*)[a] to his own messuage. To be held freely by rendering annually to him and his heirs 2d at Michaelmas. For this the abbey has given him

for his great need 6 marks of silver and has acquitted him of all
service belonging to the land. Sealing. Witnesses[b] [omitted]

[1205 × 58]

B f 102v; C f 52r–v

[a] Windhull' *C*
[b] *Om. in C*

After the abbey first received land in Hoo (see no. 400) and, since the deed was
entered in the original section of B, not later than 1258; since it was not entered in
A, it may well be later than no. 404. Dagenham is now Dagenham Farm in Allhallows.

404 *Gift by Hugh of Dagenham [or Dagnam] to Reading Abbey of 5½
acres of land in Aisfeld, in return for which the abbey has remitted gavelet of
his land, which he has incurred through default in his rent, and has acquitted
him and his heirs of the 13d annual rent belonging to the same land. He and
his heirs shall be responsible for all other things, such as pontage at Rochester
and all else belonging to the king or his bailiffs. For this the abbey has given
him 33s* [1205 × *c.* 1230]

A f 107r; B f 102v; C f 52v

Sciant presentes et futuri quod ego Hugo de Dakenham[a] dedi et
concessi et[b] presenti carta mea confirmavi deo et beate Marie et
ecclesie de Rading(ia) et abbati et conventui eiusdem loci quinque
acras terre et dimidiam cum pertinentiis in Aisfeld. Habendas et
tenendas iure perpetuo libere et quiete per hoc quod idem abbas et
conventus remiserunt mihi gavelettum terre mee in quod incidi ex
defectu redditus mei, et clamaverunt me et heredes meos quietos de
annuo redditu ad eandem terram pertinente, scilicet de tredecim
denariis per annum, et de donis et auxiliis que ad predictos[c] perti-
nebunt de tanta terra. Ego autem et heredes mei adquietabimus[d]
predictas quinque acras et dimidiam cum pertinentiis de omnibus
aliis rebus, ut de pontagio de Roffec(estria) et de omnibus rebus ad
dominum regem et ad baillivos[e] suos pertinentibus, et illas contra
omnes homines et [f]contra omnes[f] feminas in perpetuum warantizabimus predictis abbati et conventui. Et propter hanc donationem et
concessionem dederunt mihi predicti abbas et conventus triginta tres
solidos. Et ut hec concessio et donatio firma et stabilis [g]et perpetua[g]
permaneat, presens scriptum sigillo meo confirmavi.[h] Hiis testibus.

[a] Dakeham *B,C*
[c] ipsos *B,C*
[e] ballivos *C*
[g-g] *Om. in B,C*
[b] *Insert* hac *B,C*
[d] acquietabimus *B,C*
[f-f] *Om. in B,C*
[h] *B ends with* T', *C ends*

After no. 400 and entered in A with 13th-century documents of before *c.* 1230. For
Dagenham, see no. 403 n.

405 Virtually identical to the preceding, except that the amount of land given in *Aisfeld* is 5 acres. Witnesses [omitted]

[1205 × *c.* 1230]

A f 105r; (noted) B f 102v; C f 52v[1]

Date as for no. 404. This is entered only in A, and was probably either an earlier version of no. 404, superseded by the addition of an extra ½ acre, or an incorrect version of the same.

[1] The rubrics in B and C for no. 404 add: *Hec duplex est.*

406 Gift in free alms by Isabella Tregoz to the canons of Flitcham (*Flicham*) [Norfolk], for the support of a chaplain for the souls of her father and ancestors, of all her land in *Estlande* in Hoo (*Hoe*), with all appurtenances in lordships, homages, marshes and pastures, which William *Aguilun*, her father, gave her in free marriage-portion. To be held freely, saving the foreign service. Sealing. Witnesses [omitted]

[1244 × *c.* 1250]

A f 88r; (noted) B f 103r

After the death of William Aguillun (see below) and probably not later than *c.* 1250, since the deed was entered in A, with nos. 407-8, in the same hand as no. 411, which is datable to 1246. The deed by Flitcham priory to Reading (no. 408) locates the land in Allhallows. The donor was a member of one branch of the Aguillun family, on which in general see L. F. Salzman, 'The family of Aguillon', *Sussex Archaeol. Collections*, lxxix (1938), 45-60; her branch is discussed by T. Stapleton, *Liber de Antiquis Legibus* (Camden Soc., 1846), ix-lxxxiii. She was the daughter of William Aguillun, who died in 1244 (*Excerpta e rot. fin.*, i. 424; Stapleton, xvi), and sister of the latter's successor, Robert Aguillun, later a prominent loyalist and sheriff of Surrey and Sussex in 1267 (see no. 407; Salzman, 57; *List of Sheriffs*, 135). In 1217 William Aguillun was in possession of lands in Kent, including Stoke, near Hoo, in right of his wife (*Bracton's Note Book*, iii. 309), and these no doubt included the estate in Allhallows which Robert Aguillun held of the abbot of Reading at his death in 1286 (*Cal. Inq. P. M.*, ii. 361) and from which the present gift was made. Isabella's surname suggests that she married a member of the Tregoz family, but I have been unable to trace the marriage and she does not appear in L. F. Salzman's account of the family—'Tregoz', *Sussex Archaeol. Coll.*, xciii (1955), 34-58. The connections between the various branches of the Aguillun family are not always clear (see, e.g., Salzman, 'Aguillon', 59), but Isabella's gift to Flitcham priory establishes a link between her branch and that which descended from another Robert Aguillun, who is presumed to have founded the priory early in Henry III's reign (F. Blomefield, *Hist. of Norfolk* (2nd edn, 1805-10), viii. 418; *VCH Norfolk*, ii. 380; Knowles and Hadcock, 157).

407 Confirmation by Robert *Aguilon* to the priory of St Mary ad Fontes of Flitcham (*Flicham*) of the whole tenement in *Estlande* in Hoo (*Ho*), as his sister Isabella gave it for the support of a canon for

the souls of herself and her ancestors. To be held in free alms.
Sealing. Witnesses [omitted]   [1244 × c. 1250]

A f 88r; (noted) B f 103r

Date as for no. 406.

408 Release and quitclaim by Prior Philip and the canons of the
priory of St Mary ad Fontes of Flitcham (*Flicham*) to Reading Abbey
of all their right in the whole tenement which Isabella Tregoz gave
them from her marriage-portion in *Estlond*[a] in the vill of Hoo (*Ho*)[b]
in the parish of All Saints, viz., in homages, lands, rents, pastures,
marshes and stock, with all appurtenances. For this the abbey has
given them 70 marks of silver. Sealing. Witnesses[c] [omitted]
                                                    [1244 × c. 1250]

A f 88r; B ff 102v-103r; C f 52v

[a] Estlonde B, Estlond' C   [b] Hou B,C
[c] Om. in C

Outside dating limits as for no. 406, but this is somewhat later than nos. 406-7.
Philip, the first known prior of Flitcham, occurs in 1256 (*VCH Norfolk*, ii. 381). The
rubric of B says that there were two copies of this deed (*Hec duplex est*).

409 Final concord in the king's court at Marlborough (*Merleberg'*)
on the morrow of St Martin, 31 Henry III, before the king himself,
William of York provost of Beverley, William de Cantilupe, Ralph
FitzNicholas, John of Lexington (*Lexint'*) steward of the king, Jere-
miah of Caxton (*Caxton'*) and others, between the abbot of Reading,
plaintiff, and the abbot of Boxley (*Boxle*), defending by W(illiam)[a]
of Blockley (*Blokle*) as attorney, concerning 80 acres of land in Hoo
(*Ho*). The abbot of Reading complained that, against the king's
prohibition, the abbot of Boxley had invaded this land and his fee
of Hoo, which King John gave to Reading Abbey in free alms. In
settlement the abbot of Boxley recognized the land to be the right
of the abbot and abbey of Reading, and quitclaimed all right in the
same. For this the abbot of Reading gave the abbot of Boxley £80
sterling. It is to be understood that the abbot of Reading shall
perform to the other chief lords of the fee the service belonging to
the land, and all other due and customary services   12 Nov. 1246

B f 178r; C f 106r
Pd. (cal.) *Kent Feet of Fines*, 405 (from PRO foot: CP 25(1)/284/18/68)

[a] *Expansion from PRO foot*

410 Final concord in the king's court, before Roger of Thirkleby
(*Turkebi*) and others, etc., [identical to the preceding, but omitting

the final sentence relating to the performance of service due from the land]   [c. 1246]

A f 88v; (noted) B f 178r; C f 106r[1]

Clearly not before the same justices as no. 409, but probably of approximately the same time. The foot appears not to survive.

[1] The rubrics in B and C for no. 409 read: *Hec duplex est.*

411 Quitclaim by Abbot Simon and the convent of Boxley (*Boxl'*)[a] to Reading Abbey of the whole land [b]and pasture[b] and all right in the tenement of *Estlond,*[c] viz., a fourth part of the tenement in the parish of All Saints in Hoo (*Ho*),[d] which part Henry *Malemeyns,* knight, sold to Boxley, as his charter, which Boxley now hands over to Reading, witnesses. Reading Abbey shall render annually to Henry and his heirs 1 pair of spurs or 6d at Easter for all service. For this Reading Abbey has given Boxley Abbey £80 sterling. Sealing. Witnesses[e] [omitted]   [1246]

A f 88r-v; B f 103r; C f 52v

[a] Boxle *B,C*	[b-b] *Om. in B,C*	[c] Estlande *B,C*
[d] Hou *B,C*	[e] *Om. in C*	

Contemporary with the final concord (no. 409). For the manor of the Malemeins family in Allhallows, see Hasted, *History of Kent,* iv. 39. Henry held in Hoo in 1235-6 and 1242-3 (*Fees,* i. 570; ii. 666); he was still living in 1262 (*Cal. Inq. P. M.,* i. 155), but was presumably dead in 1266, when Thomas Malemeins was apparently in possession (*Cal. Misc. Inq.,* i. 225).

411a Note of a charter by Henry *Malemeins* to the monks of Boxley (*Boxle*) concerning a certain tenement in Hoo (*Hou*)   [before 1246]

B f 103r

Before no. 409.

412 Gift, quitclaim and confirmation by Henry *Malemeins* of the sale which the abbot and convent of Boxley (*Boxle*) have made to Reading Abbey of his tenement in the parish of All Saints, Hoo (*Hou*) [i.e. in Allhallows], so that he and his heirs shall be able to claim no right in the tenement save 6d annually at Easter as quit-rent (*forgabulum*) for all service. For this Reading Abbey has given him 15s sterling. Sealing. Witnesses[a] [omitted]   [c. late 1246]

B f 103r; C ff 52v-53r

[a] *Om. in C*

Probably soon after no. 409.

413 Gift in free alms by Henry *Malemeins* to Reading Abbey of the 6d [annual] rent which the abbot and convent of Boxley (*Boxle*) used to pay him from the tenement of *Estlonde*. Sealing. Witnesses[a] [omitted]   [1246 × 58; ? *c*. late 1246]

B f103r–v; C f53r

[a] *Om. in C*

After no. 412 and, since it is in the original section of B, not later than 1258. Henry was still living in 1262 (see no. 411 n.). The deed is, however, possibly contemporary with no. 412 or slightly later.

414 *Gift by Dionisia, daughter of Stephen* Treisius, *to Reading Abbey of all her land in the field called* Suthdune *lying against the vill of Windhill [in Allhallows], for which the abbey has given her 12s 6d* [1205 × *c*. 1220]

A f99v; B f103v; C f53r

Sciant presentes et futuri quod ego Dionisia filia Stephani Treisii dedi et concessi et hac presenti carta mea confirmavi deo et sancte Marie et abbati et conventui de Radinges totam terram meam quam habui in campo qui dicitur Suthdune,[a] scilicet unam acram et virgatam et paulo plus que iacet contra vicum de Windh(u)lle[b] ex parte meridionali, inter terram Edwardi filii Vuiat et Elicie vidue. Tenendam et possidendam in perpetuum libere [c]et quiete[c] absque omni calumpnia et demanda que uncquam[d] fieri possit a me vel heredibus meis, reddendo inde annuatim mihi et heredibus meis unum obolum ad festum sancti Michaelis. Pro hac autem concessione, dederunt mihi predictus abbas et conventus ad magnam necessitatem meam duodecim solidos et sex denarios argenti, et quietam me clamaverunt ab omni servitio ad predictam terram pertinente.[e] Et ut hec concessio rata sit et stabilis, eam sigilli mei appositione roboravi.[f] Hiis testibus: domino Henrico capellano, Roberto filio Thome, Hugone de Dakeham, Edwardo filio Vuiat', Willelmo serviente domini abbatis, et multis aliis.

[a] Suthedun' *B,C*	[b] Windhull' *B,C*
[c-c] *Om. in C*	[d] unquam *B,C*
[e] *A has* pertinente(m)	[f] *B ends with* T', *C ends*

After the abbey first acquired land in Hoo (no. 400); the deed is entered in A with other deeds in the same hand which date not later than *c*. 1220. The rubrics of B and C locate the land at Hoo, i.e. Allhallows. For Windhill, see no. 400 n.

415 Gift by Richard son of Joseph of [?] Hever (*Evere*)[a] to Reading Abbey of all his land of *Paddukeslande* [in Hoo, ? Allhallows] with the marsh appurtenant to it. To be held freely in perpetuity by rendering annually to him and his heirs 1d at Michaelmas. For this the abbey has given him 4½ marks of silver and has acquitted [him] of all service belonging to the tenement. Sealing. Witnesses[b] [omitted]   [1205 × c. 1240]

A f83v; B f103v; C f53r

[a] *A* has Ruere (*in error*); *B,C* have Evere (*cf., witness list of no. 416*)
[b] *Om. in C*

After the abbey first acquired land in Hoo (no. 400); the deed is entered in A with other deeds in the same hand which appear to date mostly from the 1220s and 1230s and which are immediately followed in a different hand by nos. 1202–3, dating from early 1241. The date of the present deed is possibly *c.* 1220 × 40. The rubrics of B and C locate the land at Hoo, and, since the donor was clearly already a tenant of the abbey, it was probably in Allhallows.

416 *Demise by Robert son of Eilric of [?] Hever to Reading Abbey of all his land and marsh of Paddockeslonde [in Hoo, ? Allhallows], viz., a third part of 8 acres and of pasture for 10 sheep on the marsh. The abbey has given him 16s*   [1205 × c. 1230]

A f108v; B f103v; C f53r–v

Sciant presentes et futuri quod ego Robertus filius Eilrici de Evere dimisi et concessi et hac presenti cartha mea confirmavi deo et sancte Marie et abbati et conventui de Rading(ia) totam terram meam et totum meum mariscum de Paddockeslonde,[a] scilicet tertiam partem octo acrarum terre defensabilis cum tertia parte pasture decem ovium in marischo.[b] Tenendam et habendam in perpetuum libere et quiete absque omni calumpnia et demanda que unquam fieri posset[c] a me vel heredibus meis, reddendo inde annuatim mihi et heredibus meis unum obulum ad festum sancti Michaelis pagandum.[d] Pro hac autem concessione et dimissione dederunt mihi predictus abbas et conventus Rading' ad meam magnam necessitatem sexdecim solidos sterlingorum, et quietos clamaverunt me et heredes meos ab omni servitio ad predictam terram pertinente. Et ut hec mea concessio rata sit et stabilis, eam sigilli mei appositione roboravi.[e] Hiis testibus: Henrico capellano, Roberto filio Thome, Roberto de la Dene, Willelmo de Windh(u)ll' bailivo, Edwardo filio Vuiat, Willelmo Pede, Willelmo filio Elfwen, Alexandro et Radul(fo) fil(iis) Juvetti, Ricardo de Evere, Alexandro et Willelmo fil(iis) Radulfi, et multis aliis.

[a] Paddok'lande *B*, Paddokeslande *C*
[b] marisco *B,C*
[c] possit *B,C*
[d] pacandum *B,C*
[e] *B ends with* T', *C ends*

After the abbey first acquired land in Hoo; the deed is entered in A with 13th-century documents of before *c.* 1230, but, since three of the witnesses are common also to no. 414, the two deeds may be of roughly the same date. For the location, see no. 415 n.

417   Gift by Luke (*Lucasius*) son of William of Frindsbury (*Frendes-bur*')|and Avicia|daughter of Roger of Hoo (*Ho*),[a] his wife, to Reading Abbey of 8 acres of land, pasture for 28 sheep in the marsh of Hoo,[b] and 4d rent, [c]viz., in the parish of All Saints, Hoo[c] [i.e., Allhallows]. To be held freely by rendering annually to them and their heirs 1 pair of gloves worth 1d, or 1d, at Easter for all secular service, exaction and demand. For this the abbey has given them 20 marks of silver. Warranty and sealing. Witnesses[d] [omitted]

[early July 1247]

A f88v; B f104r; C f53v

[a] Hou *B,C*
[b] *Insert* 'viz., in the parish of All Saints, Hoo' *B,C*
[c-c] 'in the same vill of Hoo' *B,C*
[d] *Om. in C*

The date is approximately that of the final concord (no. 418).

418   Final concord in the king's court at Westminster in the quindene of St John Baptist, 31 Henry III, before Henry of Bath (*Bathon*'), Alan of Wassand (*Watsand*')[a] and William of Wilton (*Wylton*'), justices, and others, between Abbot Richard [I] of Reading, plaintiff by Ernald of Boynton (*Boynt*') as attorney, and Luke (*Lucas*) son of William and Avicia, his wife, defending, concerning 8 acres of land, 4d rent and pasture for 28 sheep in Hoo (*Ho*). Plea of warranty of charter. Luke and Avicia recognized the same to be the right of the abbot and abbey of Reading by their own gift, to be held of them and the heirs of Avicia in free alms by rendering annually to them 1d at Easter for all service, custom and exaction. Warranty by them and the heirs of Avicia. For this the abbot gave them 20 marks of silver   8 July 1247

B f179r; C f107r
Pd. (cal.) *Kent Feet of Fines*, 195 (from PRO foot: CP 25(1)/96/29/504)

[a] Watesand' *C*

Comparison with no. 417 suggests that this was a fictitious action designed to strengthen the gift.

419   Demise and quitclaim by Robert son of Thomas to Reading Abbey of the whole mill [at Hoo] which he bought from the heirs of Edward *de Gosepett*', with the site where it stands and the road belonging to it, as is contained in the charters which he had from the heirs of the said Edward, with all suit belonging to the mill. To be held freely by rendering annually to the said heirs 3d. For this the abbey has given him 100s sterling. Witnesses[a] [omitted]

[1205 × 58]

B f 104r; C ff 53v–54r

[a] *Om. in C*

After the abbey first received land in Hoo and, since the deed was entered in the original section of B, not later than 1258. The rubrics of B and C locate the mill in Hoo.

419a Note of three charters to the same Robert concerning the same mill by Henry and John sons of Edward *de Gosepett'* and by John, their brother   [not later than 1256]

B f 104r

Before no. 419.

420 Sale by David son of Edward to Reading Abbey of 4s rent which William of Grain (*Gren*), son of John, owes him from 2 acres of land and pasture for 25 sheep which he holds of him in Grain, to be paid to the abbey at four terms of the year, viz., 12d each on the vigil of St Thomas the apostle before Christmas [21 Dec.], the vigil of Easter, the vigil of St John Baptist and the vigil of Michaelmas. The abbey shall hold the rent freely in perpetuity by rendering annually to the vendor and his heirs 1d on the vigil of Michaelmas as recognition. Warranty. For this the abbot has given him 32s sterling as entry-fine. Witnesses[a] [omitted]   [1205 × 58]

B f 104r–v; C f 54r

[a] *Om. in C*

Date as for no. 419. The property concerned was in the Isle of Grain.

421 Quitclaim by Ailwin son of Edward of Windhill (*Windhull'*) to Reading Abbey of 3 acres and 1 perch of land at Windhill [in Hoo, Allhallows], [viz.] in *Westfeld* 2½ acres extending eastwards from the western ditch and 3 perches below the same land towards the water. To be held freely in perpetuity by rendering annually to him and his heirs 1d at Michaelmas for all service, exaction and demand. The abbey shall answer for (*defendere*) all things appurtaining to the land. Warranty and sealing. For this the abbey has given him for

his great need 4 marks and 16d, and a tunic each to him and his
wife. Witnesses[a] [omitted]   [1205 × 58]

B f104v; C f54r

[a] *Om. in C*

Date as for no. 419. The rubrics of B and C locate this land at Hoo, and the reference
to Windhill places it in Allhallows. The details given in this deed reveal that in this
region the perch was a measure of land area and equal to one quarter of an acre
(but cf. no. 436).

422   Gift in free alms by Ornorth *Taleboth* to Reading Abbey of
1½d rent which Henry *Malemeins* used annually to pay to the abbey
for a road (*iter*) by the house of Alan the sacrist and leading to
Homstale. To be held freely in perpetuity of Ornorth and his heirs.
Warranty and sealing. Witnesses[a] [omitted]   [1205 × 58]

B f104v; C f54r–v

[a] *Om. in C*

Date as for no. 419. For Henry Malemeins, see no. 411 n.

423   *Demise by Christiana, daughter of Stephen* Treis, *to Reading Abbey of*
6d annual rent in Allhallows. The abbey has given her 3s   [1205 × c. 1230]

A f108r; B ff104v–105r; C f54v

Sciant presentes et futuri quod ego Christiana[a] filia Stephani Treis
dimisi et concessi et hac presenti cartha[b] mea confirmavi deo et
sancte Marie et abbati et conventui de Rading(ia) annualem[c] redditum sex denariorum annuatim percipiendum de Alexandro et
Willelmo filiis Rad(ulfi) de Babroc[d] quos mihi debebant annuatim
propter terram quam habui in parochia[e] Omnium Sanctorum de
Hoo, secundum quod carthe[f] quas dicti Alexander et Willelmus de
me habent testantur, cum omnibus pertinentiis et contingentiis que
ad me et ad meos heredes de predicto denariorum redditu pertinere
vel contingere posset. Tenend(um) et habend(um) in perpetuum
libere et[g] quiete et integre absque ullo retinemento et absque omni
calumpnia[h] que unquam fieri possit a me vel heredibus meis,
[i][reddendo inde mihi et heredibus meis annuatim unum obolum ad
festum sancti Michaelis pacandum].[i] Pro hac dimissione et concessione, dederunt mihi predictus abbas et conventus de Rading(ia) ad
meam magnam necessitatem tres solidos sterlingorum. Et ut hec
mea[j] dimissio rata et inconcussa permaneat, huic scripto sigillum
meum apposui.[k] Hiis testibus: Henrico capellano, Willelmo bailivo
domini abbatis, Roberto filio Thome, Edwardo filio Vuiat, Willelmo

filio Elfwen, Willelmo Pede, Alexandro et Willelmo filiis Radulfi, Johanne de Estlande, Thoma de Dakeham, Stephano et Thoma filiis Merwen, Gurberto*l* filio Gos, Roberto filio Wulwardi, Rand(ulfo) de Evere, Johanne clerico, Alexandro et Radulfo filiis Juvet', et multis aliis.

a Christina *B,C*	*b* c. *B*, carta *C*
c *A has* annuales	*d* Babbroc *B,C*
e parrochia *C*	*f* c. *B*, carte *C*
g *Om. in B,C*	*h* *Insert* et demanda *B,C*
i-i *Om. in A, supplied from B,C (see note)*	*j* *Insert* concessio et *B,C*
k *B ends with* T', *C ends*	*l* *Reading uncertain, possibly* Turberto

After the abbey first acquired land in Hoo (see no. 400); entered in A with 13th-century deeds of before *c.* 1230 (cf. nos. 404, 416, 428). Several of the witnesses are common to no. 414 and/or no. 416. The rubric of B states that there were two versions (*Hec duplex est*); in view of the variants between the text in A and that in B and C, it is likely that the two texts represent the two versions, of which that in B and C is the fuller with the clause concerning the abbey's payment of ½d rent to the donor.

424 Gift by William *de Hare* to Reading Abbey of 4 acres of land of the land *Wif* [at Hoo], with pasture for 4 sheep, which he bought from Richard *de Dene*. To be held in perpetuity by rendering annually to him and his heirs or assigns 1d rent at Michaelmas for all service, to be paid in the abbot's court at Windhill (*Windhill'*).*a* The abbey shall answer for the land in all things. Warranty. For this the abbot, with the advice of the whole convent, has given him 2 marks of silver as entry-fine. Witnesses*b* [omitted]   [1205 × 58]

B f 105r; C f 54v

a Windhull' *C*
b *Om. in C*

Date as for no. 419. The rubrics of B and C locate the land in Hoo, which, in view of the reference to Windhill, probably means Allhallows.

425 Demise by Stephen son of William *de Ecclesia* to Reading Abbey of 3 acres and 16 day-works (*daywerc*) of arable land and pasture [at Hoo], for 30s sterling. To be held freely in perpetuity for 1d to be rendered annually to him and his heirs at Michaelmas for all services. The abbey shall answer for the said land for all services. Warranty and sealing. Witnesses*a* [omitted]   [1205 × 58]

B f 105r; C f 54v

a *Om. in C*

Date as for no. 419. The rubrics of B and C locate the land at Hoo.

426 Gift by Stephen *de Ecclesia* to Reading Abbey of 2 acres and 4 day-works (*daywerc*) of his land in the field called *Thornfeld* [in Hoo], extending in length from the eastern dike (*fovea*) westwards for 34 perches. To be held freely in perpetuity in fee. The abbey shall answer for the land for such service as belongs to it, and shall give him and his heirs annually 1d as quit-rent (*forgabulum*) at Michaelmas. Warranty and sealing. For this the abbot has given him 17s 10d as entry-fine. Witnesses[a] [omitted] [1205 × 58]

B f 105r-v; C ff 54v-55r

[a] *Om. in C*

Date as for no. 419. The rubrics of B and C locate the land at Hoo.

427 Gift by Thomas *de Ecclesia* to Reading Abbey of 3 acres of his land in the field called *Thornfeld* [in Hoo], next to the dike (*fovea*) on the north in front of the parson's entrance (*janua*), lying in length from west to east. To be held freely in perpetuity in fee. The abbey shall answer for the land for such service as belongs to it, and shall give him and his heirs annually 1d as quit-rent (*forgabulum*) at Michaelmas. Warranty and sealing. For this the abbot has given him 25s as entry-fine. Witnesses[a] [omitted] [1205 × 58]

B f 105v; C f 55r

[a] *Om. in C*

Date as for no. 419. The rubrics locate the land at Hoo.

428 *Demise by Stephen son of Payn of* Babbroc *to Reading Abbey of 2 acres of land in the field called* Sutdone *lying against the vill of Windhill [in Allhallows], for which the abbey has given him 20s* [1205 × c. 1230]

A f 108v; B f 105v; C f 55r

Sciant presentes et futuri quod ego Stephanus filius Pagani de Babbroc[a] dimisi et concessi et hac presenti cartha[b] mea confirmavi deo et beate[c] Marie et abbati et conventui de Rading(ia) duas acras terre quas habui in campo qui dicitur Sutdone,[d] que iacent contra vicum de Windh(u)lle[e] ex parte meridionali proxime et continuate terre Alexandri et Willelmi filiorum Rad(ulfi) de Babbroc.[a] Tenendam et habendam in perpetuum libere et[f] quiete[g] absque omni calumpnia et demanda que unquam fieri posset[h] a me vel heredibus meis, reddendo inde annuatim mihi et heredibus meis unum obulum[i] ad festum sancti Michaelis pagandum.[j] Pro hac autem concessione dederunt mihi[k] predictus abbas et conventus de Rading(ia) ad meam magnam necessitatem viginti solidos sterlingorum, et quietos

clamaverunt me et heredes meos ab omni servitio ad predictam
terram pertinente. Et ut hec mea concessio rata sit et stabilis, eam
sigilli mei appositione roboravi.[l] Hiis testibus: Henrico capellano,
Roberto filio Thome, Roberto de la Dene, Willelmo bailivo, Edwardo filio Vuiat, Willelmo filio Elfwen, Willelmo Pede, Alexandro
et Radulfo filiis[m] Juvett', Ricardo de Evre, Thoma et Stephano
fil(iis) Merwen, Scotlando de Ecclesia, Willelmo filio Elfwini, Philippo de Fraxino, et multis aliis.

[a] Balbroc C	[b] c. B, car. C
[c] sancte B,C	[d] Suthdune B, Suthdun' C
[e] Windhull' C	[f] Om. in B,C
[g] Insert et C	[h] possit B,C
[i] Sic in A; ob' B,C	[j] pacandum B,C
[k] Om. in B	[l] B ends with T', C ends
[m] A has filii	

Date as for no. 423. The rubrics of B and C locate the land at Hoo, i.e. Allhallows
(cf. no. 414 and n.).

429 *Gift by Ailmar son of Edward of Windhill to Reading Abbey of 1 acre
of land in* Wthfeld [*in Hoo, ? Allhallows*], *for which the abbey has given
him 11s 6d*   [1205 × c. 1220]

A f 100r–v; B ff 105v–106r; C f 55r–v

Sciant presentes et futuri quod ego Ailmarus filius Edwardi de Wind-
helle[a] dedi et concessi et hac presenti carta mea confirmavi deo et
sancte Marie et abbati et conventui de Rading(ia) unam acram
terre mee cum pertinentiis in Wthfeld,[b] cuius una medietas iacet
contra vicum de Windeshull(e)[c] ex parte aquilonari et altera media-
tas iacet in eodem campo proxima terre Hugonis de Dakeham que
dicitur Havelande,[d] pertingens usque ad[e] Wthfelde.[f] Tenendam et
habendam in perpetuum libere et quiete absque omni calumpnia
[*f 100v*] et demanda que uncquam[g] fieri possit a me vel heredibus
meis, reddendo inde annuatim mihi et heredibus meis unum obolum
ad festum sancti Michaelis. Pro hac concessione dederunt mihi predictus abbas et conventus ad magnam necessitatem meam undecim
solidos et sex denarios argenti, et quietum me clamaverunt ab omni
servitio ad eandem terram pertinente.[h] Et ut hec concessio rata sit
et stabilis, eam sigilli mei appositione roboravi.[i] Hiis testibus: domino Henrico capellano, Roberto filio Thome, Hugone de Dakeham,
Edwardo filio Vuiat, Willelmo serviente domini abbatis, Alexandro
et Ricardo[j] filiis Juvetti,[k] et multis aliis.

[a] Windh(u)lle B, Windhull' C	[b] Wstfeld' B, Westfeld' C
[c] Windh(u)lle B, Windhullu C	[d] Havedland' B,C
[e] Om. in C	[f] Pettfeld' B,C

g unquam *B,C*   *h A has* pertinente(m)

i B ends with T', *C ends*   *j Sic in A, but in other deeds called Ralph (e.g., no. 428)*

k A has Luvetti, *but cf. nos. 423, 428*

After the abbey first acquired land in Hoo; the deed was entered in A with other deeds in the same hand which date from not later than *c.* 1220 (cf. no. 414). The rubrics of B and C locate the land in Hoo, which, in view of the reference to Hugh of Dagenham (see nos. 403–5) and of the fact that Ailmar was clearly already a tenant of the abbey, probably means Allhallows.

430 *Gift by Alexander son of Edward of Windhill to Reading Abbey of 1 acre of land in* Wstfelde [*in Hoo, ? Allhallows*], *for which the abbey has given him 9s*   [1205 × *c.* 1220]

A f 100v; B f 106r; C f 55v

Sciant presentes et futuri quod ego Alexander filius Edwardi de Windhulle dedi et concessi et hac presenti carta mea confirmavi deo et sancte Marie et abbati et conventui de Radinges unam acram terre mee in Wstfelde*a* que iacet a curia domini abbatis versus Wthfeld.*b* Habendam et possidendam in perpetuum libere et quiete absque*c* omni calumpnia et demanda que uncquam*d* fieri possit a me vel heredibus meis, reddendo inde annuatim mihi et heredibus meis unum obolum ad festum sancti Michaelis. Pro hac autem concessione dederunt mihi*e* predictus abbas et conventus ad magnam necessitatem meam novem solidos sterlingorum, et quietum me clamaverunt ab omni servitio ad dictam terram pertinente.*f* Et ut hec concessio rata sit et stabilis, eam sigilli mei appositione roboravi.*g* Hiis testibus: domino Henrico capellano, Roberto filio Thome, Bartholomeo baillivo de Hou, Hugone de Dakahm,*h* Edwardo filio Vuiat, Willelmo serviente domini abbatis, Roberto palmario, Alexandro et Willelmo fil(iis) Rad(ulfi), et multis aliis.

a Westfeld' *B,C*   *b* Petfeld *B,C*

c ab *B,C*   *d* unquam *B,C*

e michi *C*   *f A has* pertinente(m)

g B ends with T', *C ends*   *h Sic in A, ? rectius* Dakaham

Date as for no. 429. The rubrics of B and C locate the land at Hoo, and the field concerned is clearly the same as that in no. 429.

431 Sale by Ralph of [?] Hever (*Evere*) to Abbot Adam [of Lathbury] of Reading, for great need, of 3 acres of arable land in the field called *la Dene* [in Hoo], next to the ditch on the south. To be held freely in perpetuity, saving to him and his heirs 1d annually at Michaelmas for all things which could accrue to him or his heirs.

Warranty. For this the abbot has given him 33s sterling. Sealing.
Witnesses[a] [omitted]   [1226 × 38]

B f 106r; C f 55v

[a] *Om. in C*

The dating limits are those of Adam of Lathbury's abbacy. The rubrics locate the
land at Hoo.

432 Sale by Richard *Strakeberd*, for great need, to Abbot Adam [of
Lathbury] of Reading, for 48s, of 6½ acres of land in the field called
Middelfeld towards the south in the manor of Hoo (*Hou*). To be held
freely in perpetuity, saving to him and his heirs 1d annually at
Michaelmas for all things which could accrue to him or his heirs.
Warranty. Witnesses[a] [omitted]   [1226 × 38]

B f 106r; C f 55v

[a] *Om. in C*

The dating limits are those of Adam of Lathbury's abbacy.

433 Demise by Richard *Strakeberd* to Reading Abbey of 3½ acres of
his land in the field called *Middelfeld* [in Hoo], next to the other
land which he demised to it to the north, and extending in length
from east to west. To be held freely in perpetuity in fee. The abbey
shall answer for the land for such service as belongs to it, and shall
give him and his heirs annually 1d as quit-rent (*forgabulum*) at
Michaelmas. Warranty. For this the abbot has given him 39s as
entry-fine. Sealing. Witnesses[a] [omitted]   [1226 × 58]

B f 106v; C ff 55v–56r

[a] *Om. in C*

After no. 432 and, since the deed was entered in the original section of B, not later
than 1258.

434 Gift in free alms by Henry son of Solomon (*Salemon*)[a] to Reading Abbey of 10 acres of his land and pasture for 15 sheep [at Hoo].
To be held by rendering annually to him and his heirs 12d, viz., 6d
each at Michaelmas and the feast of St Thomas [21 Dec.]. The
abbey shall answer to all lords of the fee for all demands and customs
which the land owes. For this the abbey has received him in all
masses and prayers in Reading Abbey for ever. Witnesses[b]
[omitted]   [1205 × c. 1240]

A f 83v; B f 106v; C f 56r

^a Salemun *B,C*   ^b *Om. in C*

Date as for no. 415. The rubrics of B and C locate the land at Hoo.

435 Gift by Robert and Hugh, sons of Thomas palmer (*palmer'*),^a to Reading Abbey of three pastures for sheep in the tenure of the abbey in Allhallows (*Hou*), lying ^bin common in the marsh^b of G. of Dagenham (*Dagham*),^c Godfrey his brother, Alexander Palmer (*Palmerus*),^d Adam *de Fraxino* and Reading Abbey. To be held freely in perpetuity by rendering annually to them and their heirs 1 costard (*pom' costard*) as quit-rent (*forgabulum*) at Michaelmas for all services due. Warranty. For this the abbey has given them 7s sterling as entry-fine. Witnesses^e [omitted]   [1205 × 58]

B f 106v; C f 56r

^a palmere *C*
^{b–b} *Or* 'in the common marsh'; *B has* in communi in marisco, *C has* in communi marisco   ^c Dakeham *C*
^d Palm' *C*   ^e *Om. in C*

Date as for no. 419. The references to the abbey's tenure and to G. of Dagenham show that these marshes were in Allhallows.

436 Demise by Mabel, daughter of David *de Fraxino*, to Reading Abbey of 4 acres of her land and pasture for 4 sheep in her marsh [in Allhallows] with their appurtenances and houses, whereof 3 virgates of land lie in the field called *Eisfeld'* next to the king's highway (*regale keminum*) running west–east; 2 acres less 1 virgate lie in the field called *Westfeld* next to the dike towards the west and extending south–north; 1 acre lies in the field called *Suthfeld*, half among the parts of land of her sisters extending west–east, and the other half in the same parts of land extending south–north; and ½ acre lies in the field called *Herdelond* next to the dike towards the west and extending south–north. To be held freely by hereditary right, by rendering annually to her and her heirs ½d at Michaelmas, payable at the abbot's court, for all services and customs. The abbey shall acquit the land against the court of Windhill (*Windh(u)lle*)^a in everything appurtaining to the land. Warranty. For this the abbey has given her 50s sterling as entry-fine. Witnesses^b [omitted]   [1205 × 58]

B ff 106v–107r; C f 56r–v

^a Windhulle *C*   ^b *Om. in C*

Date as for no. 419. The reference to the court of Windhill and the field names establish that the land lay in Allhallows (cf. nos. 404,, 414, 421). The details given in this deed reveal that here a virgate was reckoned at one quarter of an acre (but cf. no. 421).

437 *Gift by William* Babbe *to Abbot Simon and the convent of Reading, for 1 mark sterling as entry-fine, of 1 half-load of corn of the toll-corn of the mill of* Homstall' [*at Hoo*] [1213 × 26]

B f 107r; C f 56v

Sciant presentes et futuri quod ego Willelmus Babbe dedi et concessi et hac presenti carta mea confirmavi abbati et conventui de Rading(ia) unam dimidiam summam bladi, scilicet de tolcorn de molendino de Homstall'. Tenend(am) et habend(am) de me et heredibus meis dicto abbati et conventui quamdiu stat in loco illo ubi stetit quando vendidi predictum bladum, libere, quiete, bene*a* in pace hered(itarie) sine omni calumpnia, reddendo inde annuatim dictus abbas et conventus unum obolum de redditu ad festum sancti Michaelis mihi et heredibus meis pro omnibus servitiis inde debitis. Et ego W(illelmus) et heredes mei warantizabimus dictum bladum de predicto molendino dicto abbati et conventui contra omnes homines et feminas et omnes calumpnias. Pro hac autem donatione et concessione et hac presenti carta mea confirmatione, warantizatione et sigilli mei impressione, dederunt mihi predicti S(imon)*b* abbas et conventus de Rading(ia) unam marcam sterlingorum in gersumam. T(estibus).*c*

a *Insert* et C
b *Possibly* scilicet; *lower case* s *in B, upper case in* C
c *Om. in* C

The dating limits are those of Simon's abbacy (but see textual note *b*). The rubrics locate the mill at Hoo.

437a Note of a charter between Richard Butler (*le Butiller*) and James of Caversham (*Kaveresham*) concerning 1 acre of land and 2 day-works (*daiwerc*) at Hoo (*Hou*) [not later than 1258]

B f 107r

Entered in the original section of B.

438 Gift by John *de Prato* of Essex to Reading Abbey of 22s annual rent in the parish of St Mary's Hoo (*Hou*), viz., from the rent which Robert *le Jevene* owed him for a marsh and pasture for 20 sheep in *Wellingenemerse* and for a marsh and pasture for 12 sheep in *Plotmerse*, which rent the heirs of the said Robert shall pay to the abbey at two terms of the year, viz., half each at the Nativity of St John Baptist and at Michaelmas. To be held freely with escheats, wardships, reliefs and all profits which could accrue to him or his heirs, by rendering annually to him and his heirs 1 clove at Michaelmas for all secular service, exaction and demand. For this the abbey has given him 22 marks of silver. Warranty and sealing. Witnesses [omitted]   [? *c.* 1260]

B f 107v; C f 56v

Not in the original section of B, but entered very soon afterwards in the same hand as nos. 376–9.

439 Gift in free alms by John *de Prato* of Stanford (*Stanford'*) of Essex to Reading Abbey of the same annual rent. [Identical to the preceding, but omitting the abbey's obligation to pay 1 clove annually and stating that the gift is to be held in free alms.] Warranty and sealing. Witnesses [omitted]   [? *c.* 1260]

B f 107v; C f 57r

Date as for no. 438, but presumably after it.

440 Final concord in the king's court at Westminster in the octave of Michaelmas, 27 Henry III, before Robert of Lexington (*Lexint'*), Roger of Thirkleby (*Turkeby*), Jollan *de Nevill'* and Gilbert of Preston (*Preston'*), justices, and others, between Abbot Richard [I] of Reading, plaintiff by Ernald (*Ernid'*)[a] of Boynton (*Boynton'*) as attorney, and John *Pade*, defendant, concerning the customs and services which the abbot was demanding from John for the free tenement which he holds of the abbot in Hoo (*Ho*), namely, that he should pay annually 8s 5¼d, that he should do suit of the abbot's court in Hoo every three weeks, and that he should pay a relief after the death of any woman who had dower from the said tenement, all of which John did not acknowledge. In settlement John recognized and granted, for himself and his heirs, that they would pay 8s 5¼d at four terms of the year, viz., on the feast of St Thomas the apostle [21 Dec.] 33¾d, on Palm Sunday 22½d, on the Nativity of St John Baptist 22½d and at Michaelmas 22½d; that they would do suit at the said court every three weeks; and that they would pay a relief of 25d on the death of himself and any of his heirs for all service and exaction. For this the abbot quitclaimed all right to any relief after the death of any woman who had dower from the tenement, and all arrears of the said service and all damages up to the date of this agreement   6 Oct. 1243

B f 178r–v; C f 106r–v
Pd. (cal.) *Kent Feet of Fines*, 178 (from PRO foot: CP 25(1)/96/27/453)

[a] *PRO foot has* Ernulfum

441 Final concord in the king's court at Westminster in the octave of Michaelmas, 27 Henry III, before the same justices, between Abbot Richard [I] of Reading, plaintiff by Ernald (*Ernl'*)^a of Boynton (*Boynt'*) as attorney, and Roger of Alkham (*Halkham*) and Lauretta his wife, defendants, concerning the customs and services which the abbot was demanding from them for the free tenement which they hold of the abbot in Hoo (*Ho*), namely, that they should pay annually 25s 3¾d at the abbot's court in Hoo, and that they should do suit of that court every three weeks, all of which they did not acknowledge. In settlement Roger and Lauretta recognized and granted, for themselves and the heirs of Lauretta, that they would pay annually 25s 3¾d in the said court at four terms of the year, viz., on the feast of St Thomas the apostle 8s 5¼d, on Palm Sunday 5s 7½d, on the feast of St John Baptist 5s 7½d and at Michaelmas 5s 7½d; and that they would do suit of the said court every three weeks. Moreover, they gave the abbot 20s sterling for their arrears. For this the abbot quitclaimed to them and the heirs of Lauretta all arrears of the said service and all damages up to the date of this agreement   6 Oct. 1243

B f 178v; C f 106v
Pd. (cal.) *Kent Feet of Fines*, 178–9 (from PRO foot: CP 25(1)/96/27/463)

^{a} *PRO foot has* Ernulfum

442 Final concord in the king's court at Westminster in 3 weeks from Holy Trinity, 28 Henry III, before Jollan *de Nevill'* and John of Cobham (*Cobeham*), justices, and others, between Abbot Richard [I] of Reading, plaintiff by Ernald of Boynton (*Boynt'*) as attorney, and Henry *le Bret* and Matilda his wife, defendants, concerning 32 acres of land, 18d rent and pasture for 32 sheep in Hoo (*Ho*). Fine levied, viz., that Henry and Matilda recognized the land, rent and pasture to be the right of the abbot and abbey of Reading, and quitclaimed the same for themselves and the heirs of Matilda. For this the abbot gave them 30 marks of silver   19 June 1244

B f 179r; C ff 106v–107r
Pd. (cal.) *Kent Feet of Fines*, 182 (from PRO foot: CP 25(1)/96/27/468)

443 Grant by King Henry III to Reading Abbey of a weekly market on Tuesday at its manor of Hoo (*Hou*) [i.e., in Allhallows] in the county of Kent, and of an annual fair there to last for three days from the vigil to the morrow of All Saints, unless the market and fair should be to the damage of neighbouring markets and fairs
20 Aug. 1271

B f 108r; C f 57r
Pd. *Mon. Ang.*, iv. 45 (no. xxvii); (cal.) *Cal. Chart. R.*, ii. 175 (from Charter Roll)

Hiis testibus: Elya de Rabayne, Stephano de Eddeworth', Willelmo de Sancta Eremina, Gaufrido de Percy, Willelmo Ernaud, Petro Evera(r)d,*a* Rogero de Wanton', et aliis. Data per manum nostram apud Westimonasterium*b* vicesimo die Augusti, anno regni nostri quinquagesimo quinto.

a Everard' *C*   *b* Westmonasterium *C*

444   Record of an action *Quod permittat* brought at Rochester, before master Roger of Seaton (*Seyton'*) and his fellow justices-in-eyre in Kent, on the fourth day in the quindene of St John Baptist, 55 [Henry III], by John de Grey (*Grei*) and Nicholas Poynz against Abbot Robert [of Burgate] of Reading, namely, that he should permit them to take down a gallows in the vill of All Saints, Hoo (*Hou*) [i.e., Allhallows], which Richard, late abbot of Reading, unjustly erected to the detriment of their free tenement in Hoo. The abbot does not come and is to be attached to be before the justices at Westminster in the octave of Michaelmas, etc.

Record also of another action *Quod permittat* brought on the same day by the same John and Nicholas against the same abbot, namely, that he should permit them to take down a tumbrel in the vill of All Saints, Hoo, which Richard, late abbot of Reading, unjustly erected to the detriment of their free tenement in Hoo. The abbot does not come and is to be attached to be before the justices at Westminster in the octave of Michaelmas, etc.   11 July 1271

B f 245v

In 1274-5 it was recorded that the hundred of Hoo was divided between the abbot of Reading, Hugh Poynz and Henry de Grey, and that the abbot had for eight years past erected a gallows in the hundred and given justice of life and limb (*Rot. Hund.*, i. 220). The abbot Richard named in the present action was, therefore, Richard II (1262-9). The families of Poynz and Grey were the eventual successors to Robert Bardulf in that part of the hundred not acquired by Reading Abbey (see above, no. 400 n.; Hasted, *History of Kent*, iv. 4-5). Nicholas Poynz died in 1273 (Sanders, *English Baronies*, 39).

445   *Quo warranto proceedings concerning the liberties of Hugh Poynz, the abbot of Reading and Henry de Grey in Hoo*   [Apr. × Nov. 1293]

B f 14v
Pd. (in part) *Placita de Quo Warranto*, 361 (from Eyre Roll)

[The text follows the printed version, the only major differences being: (i) after *Regis* (pd. para. 2, line 4) add *patris domini Regis*;

(ii) delete last sentence of printed text, *Ideo ... etc.*, and continue as follows.]

De libertatibus dicunt quod abbas de Rading' clamat habere returnum brevium, wreccum maris, visum franci plegii et que ad visum pertinent, et infangenethef, utfangenethef in manerio suo de Hou, nesciunt quo waranto. *Et abbas per atturnatum suum venit et dicit quod abbas de Rading' et omnes predecessores sui a tempore fundationis abbathie predicte, quo ad returnum brevium, dominus rex est in seisina, et similiter de placito vetiti namii.* Et vicecomes hoc idem testatur. Et quo ad alias libertates dicit quod ipse et predecessores sui abbates et monachi de Rading' habent de hominibus suis et de tota possessione sua, et de alienis in ea forisfacientibus vel ibi cum forisfacto interceptis, hundreda et omnia placita cum scotto et lotto, tholl et theam, infangenethef, utfangenethef in omnibus locis cum omnibus causis que sunt vel esse possunt, et cetera, per cartam domini H(enrici) regis patris, et cetera, quam profert et que hoc idem testatur, et cetera.

a–a *This sentence is clearly corrupt, possibly owing to an omission*

These proceedings were heard in the Canterbury sessions of the 1293-4 Kent eyre, for which see Crook, *General Eyre*, 176. The passage printed here in full is not included in the existing edition, but it clearly forms part of the same entry in B. See also no. 130.

446 Quo warranto proceedings concerning the abbot of Reading's 40 marks rent in the manor of Hoo (*Hou*)   [Apr. × Nov. 1293]

B f 15r
Pd. *Placita de Quo Warranto*, 365-6 (from Eyre Roll)[1]

Date as for no. 445.

[1] The entry on the Eyre Roll concerns the king's claim against Hugh de Poynz and Henry de Grey, for half the manor of Hoo each, and against the abbot of Reading for the 40 marks rent. The entry in B is a shortened, selective version of this, comprising those parts of the enrolment which relate to the abbot of Reading.

447 *Quo warranto proceedings in Kent concerning the abbot of Reading's liberties in his manor of Windhill in Hoo [i.e., Allhallows]*
[Nov.] 1313 × [June] 1314

B ff 136r-137v; C ff 78r-79v
Pd. (in part) *Placita de Quo Warranto*, 316-17 (from Eyre Roll); *Year Books of Eyre of Kent 6 & 7 Edward II*, iii (Selden Soc. xxix, 1913), 191-2 (from Year Books)[1]

[The text follows the first four paragraphs of the text printed in *Placita de Quo Warranto*, with no significant variations, and continues as follows.]

Jurati presentant quod manerium de Hoo quod valet per annum Cx. libras fuit aliquo temporo manerium regis Ricardi, qui quidem rex dedit illud manerium cuidam Hugoni Bardolf'. Et Ricardus de Grey, Hugo filius et heres Nicholai Poinz et abbas de Rading' modo tenent manerium predictum, nesciunt quo waranto. Ideo preceptum est vicecomiti quod venire faciat eos, et cetera. Postea venit predictus Ricardus per attornatum suum et bene cognoscit quod predictus Hugo Bardolf' habuit predictum manerium de Hoo de dono predicti regis Ricardi et quod idem Hugo obiit seisitus de eodem manerio. Et dicit quod post mortem predicti Hugonis predictum manerium de Hoo, simul cum aliis terris et tenementis que fuerunt eiusdem Hugonis, descenderunt quibusdam Beatrici, Matill(i), Isolde, Juliane et Cecilie, filiabus et heredibus predicti Hugonis, et dicit quod predictum manerium de Hoo, quod accidit in propartem predictarum Isolde et Juliane parti[*f 137r*]tum fuit inter eas. Et dicit quod de predicta Isolda exivit quidam Ricardus, et de ipso Ricardo quidam Johannes, et de ipso Johanne quidam Henricus de Grey, et de ipso Henrico idem Ricardus de Grei qui nunc tenet medietatem predicti manerii, et cetera. Et de predicta Juliana exivit quidam Hugo, et de eodem Hugone quidam Nicholaus Poinz, et de ipso Nicholao predictus Hugo Poinz qui tenet aliam medietatem predicti manerii et est infra etatem et in custodia domini regis. Ideo remaneat usque ad etatem, et cetera.

Et predictus abbas per attornatum suum venit et dicit quod dominus H(enricus) rex pater domini Johannis regis dedit in dotem predicte ecclesie de Rading' quadraginta marcatas[a] annui redditus percipiend(as) de manerio suo de Hoo. Et dicit quod predictum manerium postea devenit ad manus cuiusdam Roberti Bardolf', qui quidem Robertus concessit et assignavit cuidam abbati et conventui ecclesie predicte de Rading' et successoribus suis quasdam terras et homines in predicto manerio de Hoo redditum predictarum quadraginta marcarum, quam quidem concessionem et assignacionem Johannes rex consanguineus domini regis nunc concessit et carta sua confirmavit predicte ecclesie de Rading', abbati et conventui eiusdem loci, videlicet concessionem et assignacionem quam Robertus Bardolf' eis fecit in certo redditu in terris et hominibus in manerio de Hoo de annuis quadraginta marcatis argenti quas dominus H(enricus) rex pater eiusdem domini J(ohannis) regis dedit in dotem eidem ecclesie de Rading', et quod voluit et firmiter precepit quod predicti abbates et monachi de Reding' haberent et tenerent predictas terras assignatas, homines, redditus et tenementa cum pertinenciis suis iure perpetuo, bene et in pace, libere, quiete, integre et plenarie in omnibus locis et rebus, sicut puram et perpetuam elemosinam predicti domini H(enrici) regis patris sui. Et profert cartam predicti domini Johannis regis que hoc testatur. Item de libertatibus dicunt quod abbas de Reding' clamat habere visum franci plegii, emend(ationes) assise panis et cervisie fracte de tenentibus suis in Hoo, et retornum brevium, wreccum maris et infangenethef, nesciunt quo waranto. Et predictus abbas per attornatum suum venit et, quo ad retornum brevium et wreccum maris, dicit quod ipse nichil inde clamat. Ideo remaneat [*f 137v*] domino regi. Et quo ad alias libertates Galfr(ed)us de Hertepol,*b* qui sequitur pro domino rege, dicit quod ipse sequitur versus eum per breve de eisdem libertatibus. Ideo nichil inde hic.

[The text continues with paragraph 5 in the printed version, which is its last paragraph, omitting the first two sentences, *Et Galfr's . . . jurata, etc.*; and then concludes as follows.]

Et dicunt jurati quod ipse abbas alias coram Johanne de Berewik' et sociis suis justic(iariis) ultimo itinerantibus in comitatu isto² implacitatus fuit de predictis quadraginta marc(atis) redditus. Et inde coram eisdem justic(iariis) recessit*c* quietus per iudicium. Et quesitis rotulis compertum est in eisdem quod recessit inde sine die. Ideo idem abbas nunc sine die, salvo jure, et cetera.

Rubric: De itinere justic' in comitatu Kanc' anno regni regis Edwardi filii regis Edwardi septimo

*Marginal note (C f 78v only):*³ Nota hic quod per homines non intelliguntur solum nati(vi) sicut per legisperitos nunc supponitur, cum Kancia tota sit libera a servi(tu)te.

---

a marcas C   *b* Herteypol C   *c* Insert et C (in error)

For the dates of the justices' sessions at Rochester in 7 Edward II, see Crook, *General Eyre*, 181. The version in the Reading cartularies is clearly much fuller than the printed texts.

¹ The passages included in the Year Books are the same as those in *Placita de Quo Warranto.*
² In 1293 (Crook, *ibid.*, 176).
³ This note appears in C alongside the passage which includes the word *hominibus* (*Placita de Quo Warranto*, p. 316, col. 2, last line).

448 Writ *Certiorari* by King Edward III to Nicholas *Heryng'*, his escheator in Kent, to inform the king in Chancery of the reason for the escheator's having seized into the king's hand the abbot of Reading's manor of Windhill (*Wyndhull'*) in Hoo (*Hoo*), and of the value of the same manor   11 Mar. 1373¹

B f 110v

Teste me ipso, apud Westm(onasterium) xi. die Marcii,*a* anno regni
nostri Anglie quadragesimo septimo, regni vero nostri Francie tricesimo quarto.

a Ms has Maii (*see note* 1)

¹ The date given in the text is 11 May, but, in view of the date of the escheator's
inquest (no. 449), this must be an error for 11 March.

449 Record, indented, of the inquest held at Rochester, Kent, before Nicholas *Heryng'*, the king's escheator in Kent, 8 April, 47 Edward III, by the oath of Robert *Grigge*, etc., who say that Henry
[of Appleford], late abbot of Reading, and the chapter on 16 May,
26 Edward III [1352], demised their manor of Windhill (*Wyndhull'*),
which is held of the king in chief in free alms, to Thomas of Grain
(*Grean*) and his heirs for 15 years or to Thomas for life, if he survived
the 15 years, at an annual rent of £36, without the king's licence;
that in 32 Edward III [1358-9], within the said term of 15 years,
Thomas of Grain demised his estate in the manor to Thomas *de
Pympe*, knight, without the king's licence; that both Thomas of Grain
and Thomas *de Pympe* died within the said term of 15 years; and
that the manor is worth £38 annually. Sealing with the jurors' seals
alternatim   8 Apr. 1373

B f 110v
Pd. (cal.) *Cal. Misc. Inq.*, iii. 340

450 Precept by King Edward III to Nicholas *Heryng'*, his escheator
in Kent, that, whereas the king's court and other experts of his
council, on being informed by the inquest, held before the escheator
and returned into Chancery, of the reason for the seizure into the
king's hand of the manor of Windhill (*Wyndhull'*) [details of the
inquest quoted as in no. 449], did not consider the reason sufficient
to justify such seizure, and the king being unwilling that the abbey
should be wrongly oppressed, the escheator is to remove the king's
hand from the manor and to deliver to the abbot of Reading any
profits he has taken from it immediately. Witness, etc.

[*c.* Apr. 1373]

B ff 110v-111r

Probably soon after no. 449.

WIGSTON PARVA

451 Notification by King Stephen to the bishop of Lincoln, and the justice, sheriff and barons of Leicestershire, of his gift in free alms to Reading Abbey of the land of Wigston [Parva] held by William, the king's almsman (*elemosinarius*), who has become a monk of Reading; and precept that the abbey shall hold it with all the liberties with which it holds its other lands 1137

A f 18v; B f 30r; C f 6r
Pd. *Regesta*, iii. 252 (no. 681)

*a*Testibus:*b* Rogero episcopo Sar(esburiensi), et Ricardo episcopo Baioc(ensi), et multis aliis. Apud Westm(onasterium), anno incarnationis dominice MCxxxvii.

a C ends
b B ends

452 Precept by King Stephen to the sheriff of Leicestershire that the king's alms of Wigston [Parva], which William his almsman gave to Reading Abbey with his permission, shall be as free and quit of pleas, plaints and other causes as are the abbey's other lands; and that he is not to allow the men of Arnald de Bosco or of anyone else to exact any forfeiture (*quicquam ei forisfaciant*). Witnesses [omitted] [*c.* 1137]

B f 30r; C f 6r; (noted) A f 18v
Pd. *Regesta*, iii. 252 (no. 682)

Probably contemporary with no. 451. This date differs from that suggested by *Regesta* (1148 × 54). The land concerned in nos. 451-2 is to be identified with the 2 carucates of land in Wigston, belonging to Sharnford, which were held in 1086 by Aluric the priest of the king's alms (*VCH Leics.*, i. 311; Nichols, *History Leics.*, iv. 124). The association with the neighbouring manor of Sharnford probably explains Arnald de Bosco's claims in Wigston Parva. In 1086 2 carucates in Sharnford, the largest of the Domesday holdings there, were held by Hugh de Grandmesnil (*VCH Leics.*, i. 314), whose estates came by mortgage into the hands of Robert de Beaumont, count of Meulan, in 1101 (L. Fox, 'The honor and earldom of Leicester', *EHR*, liv (1939), 386-7). The latter's successor, Robert earl of Leicester, inherited the lordship of Sharnford, where, it is most likely, Arnald de Bosco was his tenant and whence he laid claim to Wigston at the time of the gift to Reading.

452a   Note of a charter by King Stephen to W(illiam) the almsman concerning the land of Wigston [Parva] (*Wigestana*)   [1135 × 37]

A f18v; B f30v

After the king's accession and before no. 451.

453   *Confirmation by Robert, earl of Leicester, of the agreement between Abbot Edward and the convent of Reading, and Arnald de Bosco, concerning the land of Wigston [Parva] for 30s annually*   [1137 × 54]

A f44r; B f121v; C f66v

Robertus comes Legrecestrie*a* Edwardo dei gratia abbati Radingensi totique fratrum conventui, salutem. Noscat fraternitas vestra et sine dubitatione teneat quod ego concedo pactionem quam Arnaldus de Bosco fecit vobiscum de terra de Wigestana pro .xxx. solidis per annum, et pactionem in manu capio ita quod, si Ernaldus*b* in aliquo deficeret, ego facerem quod Ernaldus*b* eam plenarie teneret.*c* T(este)*d* G(alfredo) Abbate.

a Leyc' B,C
b Arn' B, Arnaldus C
c C ends
d B ends

After no. 451 and while Edward was abbot of Reading. This agreement apparently settled the difficulties alluded to in King Stephen's writ (no. 452).

454   *Release by Arnald de Bosco to the abbot and convent of Reading of their land of Wigston [Parva], which he held of them during pleasure, in return for the goodwill of the abbey which they have granted to him*   [1148 × 55]

A f44r; B f121v; C f66v

Sciant presentes et futuri quod ego Ernaldus*a* de Bosco reddidi abbati Rading(ensi) et conventui terram suam de Wigestana liberam et quietam de me et de omnibus heredibus meis, pro beneficio ecclesie sue quod mihi concesserunt, quam terram de eis tenui quamdiu eis placuit.*b* Huius rei sunt testes: Robertus comes Legrec(estrie), et Robertus de Belemia prior de Bermundeseia, et multi alii.

a Arnaldus B,C
b B ends with T', C ends

Robert de Belesme was prior of Bermondsey 1148-55 (*Heads of Relig. Houses*, 115). This deed ended the agreement between Arnald de Bosco and Reading confirmed by Robert earl of Leicester (no. 453), and cannot easily be regarded as a solution to the difficulties alluded to in Stephen's writ (no. 452), as supposed by *Regesta*, iii. 252.

455   *Gift and quitclaim by Peter of Belgrave to Reading Abbey of the whole vill of Wigston [Parva] after the death of Eustace, his nephew, to whom he gave the said vill to be held of the abbey for life for 30s annually*

[? early 13th cent.]

B f121v; C ff66v–67r

Notum sit omnibus tam presentibus quam futuris quod ego Petrus de Belegrave dedi et quietamclamavi et hac presenti carta confirmavi de me et heredibus meis totam villam de Wigestan(a) cum omnibus pertinentiis, pro salute anime mee et antecessorum meorum, deo et abbatie*ᵃ* de Rading(ia) et monachis ibidem deo servientibus in perpetuum, scilicet post obitum Eustachii nepotis mei, cui predictam villam dedi et confirmavi habendam et tenendam de predicta abbatia*ᵇ* et monachis omnibus diebus vite sue, reddendo inde annuatim predicte abbatie*ᵃ* et monachis .xxx. solidos pro omnibus. Et ut hec donatio et quiet'clamatio firma sit et stabilis, eam sigilli mei appositione roboravi. T'.*ᶜ*

ᵃ abbathie *C*
ᵇ abbathia *C*
ᶜ *Omitted in C*

Date uncertain. Possibly after the late 12th century, since not in A; and presumably before no. 456.

456   Final concord in the king's court at Westminster, Wednesday after the Conversion of St Paul [25 Jan.], 11 Henry III, before the king himself, between Petronella*ᵃ* of Belgrave (*Belegrave*), seeking, and Abbot Adam [of Lathbury] of Reading, holding, concerning the manor of Wigston [Parva] (*Wiggestan*')*ᵇ* with appurtenances. Assize of mort d'ancestor. Petronella*ᵃ* quitclaimed for herself and her heirs to the abbot and his successors all her right in the manor in perpetuity, for which the abbot gave her 60 marks of silver

27 Jan. 1227

B f177v; C f106r

ᵃ *PRO foot has* Petronilla
ᵇ Wigestan' *C*

The foot of this fine is PRO CP 25(1)/284/18/15. It is one of five fines exceptionally made before the king alone shortly after he declared himself to be of age (*List of Various Common-Law Records*, Lists and Indexes 1970, 37–8). Cf. no. 128.

457   Release and quitclaim by Ralph *de Arraby* to Reading Abbey of the whole windmill (*molendinum ad ventum*) which Peter of Belgrave (*Belegrave*) sometime granted to him, situated in the field of Wigston

[Parva] (*Wigestan'*), with the site and all suit belonging to the mill.
For greater security he has given the abbey full seisin and has surrendered the charter which he had from Peter of Belgrave and all
his muniments concerning the mill. For this the abbey has given
him 20 marks of silver. Witnesses[a] [omitted]   [? before *c.* 1230]

B ff 121v–122r; C f 67r

[a] *Om. in* C

Certainly not later than 1258, since entered in the original section of B, but possibly
before *c.* 1230, since (a) it may perhaps be inferred from nos. 455–6 that the abbey
was recalling its possessions in Wigston Parva into demesne in the early part of the
13th century, in which case this deed, by which it recovered the mill, may be of the
same period; (b) a Ralph de Araby occurs in the Curia Regis Rolls from 1200 to
1230, often as an attorney for others (*Rot. Cur. Reg.*, ii. 194; *Cur. Reg. R.*, ix. 247; x.
71; xii. 352; xiv. 117), and may be the same as the present Ralph. In 1284–5 the
abbot of Reading held in Wigston 16 virgates of land in villeinage and 1 windmill of
the king in chief (*Aids*, iii. 104).

457a   Note of a charter by Peter of Belgrave (*Belegrave*) to Ralph
de Arraby concerning the same mill   [? early 13th cent.]

B f 122r

Before no. 457.

458   Mandate and precept by Pope Alexander III to the bishops
of London and Chichester that, whereas the church of Wigston
[Parva] from before the time of hostility had a cemetery and baptism
rights (*baptismus*) and was subject to no church other than the cathedral (*ecclesia episcopalis*), and the men of the place, seeing that it was
too poor to support a priest, began to pay their tithes to the church
of Claybrooke until they might have their own priest; and since the
said men are now prohibited by the rector of Claybrooke from
rebuilding their church and restoring it to its former status, the
bishops are to prohibit the rector from making any such prohibition
contrary to justice   [1159 × 81]

A ff 70v–71r
Pd. Holtzmann, *Papsturkunden*, iii. 423 (no. 302)

The dating limits are those of Alexander III's pontificate. Contrary to Holtzmann's
assertion (*ibid.*), Reading Abbey did not hold the church of Wigston Parva. The
papal mandate makes no mention of Reading, but it would have been of interest to
the abbey as a substantial landholder in the parish, and was probably for this reason
entered in A. The 'time of hostility' referred to by the pope is no doubt the 'Anarchy'
of Stephen's reign.

459 *Gift by Queen Adeliza to Reading Abbey of 100s annually at Christmas from her hithe in London, for the celebration of the anniversary of her husband, King Henry I* [prob. *c.* 1 Dec. 1136]

A f17r; B f20r
Pd. *Mon. Ang.*, iv. 42 (no. viii)

Sciant presentes et futuri quod ego Adel(eidis) dei gratia Anglorum regina dedi ecclesie de*ᵃ* Rading(ia) unoquoque anno in Natali domini .C. solidos de heda mea Lund(onie)*ᵇ* ad faciendum anniversarium domini mei regis Henrici. Et volo et firmiter precipio quod ipsi sint primi centum solidi qui singulis annis exierint et haberi poterint de predicta heda mea Lundonie.*ᶜ* Testibus:*ᵈ* Rogero episcopo Sar(esburiensi), Bernardo de Sancto David, Simone Wigorn(iensi), Rogero Cicestr(ensi) episcopis, Ingulfo abbate Abend(onie), Waltero [abbate]*ᵉ* de Eglesh(am), et multis aliis.

ᵃ Om. in B	*ᵇ Londonie B*	*ᶜ London' B*
ᵈ B ends	*ᵉ Supplied*	

The witnesses and the provision for Henry I's anniversary suggest that this gift was made on the same occasion as the queen's gift of the manor of Aston, Herts. (no. 370).

460 *Confirmation in free alms by William de Turville to Reading Abbey of three messuages in London previously given by his father [Geoffrey]* [1124 × *c.* 1150]

A f40r; B f111v; C f59r

Sciant presentes et futuri quod ego Willelmus de Turvilla, pro me et pro anima patris mei et matris mee et antecessorum meorum, concedo in elemosinam tres mansuras terre in Lundonia*ᵃ* ecclesie sancte Marie de Rading(ia) et monachis ibidem deo servientibus habere perpetuo iure liberas et quietas, sicut pater meus unquam melius habuit, qui illas ante me illis dedit. Mansuras istas tenuit Walt(erius)*ᵇ* Tortus Nasus de patre meo et post eum Werno filius eius. Quicquid illi de patre meo tenuerunt, et ipse Werno de me postea, concedo predictis monachis ut totum firmiter et absolute possideant.*ᶜ* Testibus:*ᵈ* Radulfo fratre meo, et Herberto et Gervasio hominibus meis, et multis aliis.

ᵃ London' B,C	*ᵇ Walterius B*
ᶜ C ends	*ᵈ B ends*

The terms of this deed suggest that the father's gift had not taken immediate effect, since the second tenant named had continued to hold of William. The dating of members of the Turville family in the twelfth century is uncertain, but recent work by Dr David Crouch, set out in his *The Beaumont Twins* (Cambridge, 1986), 116–20, 218–19), shows that G. H. Fowler's reconstruction of the family tree in *Beds. Hist. Rec. Soc.*, vii (1923), 204–7, can no longer be accepted. The present charter can be dated not later than *c.* 1150, since it was confirmed by the earl of Leicester by that date (no. 461). For this and other reasons Dr Crouch concludes that the present William's father was Geoffrey I de Turville, who was blinded for treason in 1124 by order of Henry I (Orderic Vitalis, vi. 352); he is presumed to have died soon afterwards, since it was apparently his eldest son, Geoffrey II, who was in attendance on Robert earl of Leicester in 1127 (see no. 236) and who held most of the family lands in England by 1130, when he was excused Danegeld in four counties (*PR 31 Henry I*, 46, 85, 102, 106). Moreover, since William de Turville appears to have been a younger brother of Geoffrey II (*Cartl. Missenden*, i. 187) and to have inherited some of the elder Geoffrey's English possessions, including the London property, the present charter cannot be earlier than 1124. William was certainly dead by 1163, at which date his former manor of Helmdon (Northants.) was held by his brother, Geoffrey II (*VCH Northants.*, i. 369; *PR 9 Henry II*, 41). I am grateful to the kindness of Dr Crouch for help on these points and for allowing me to see the text of his book before it went to press.

461 *Confirmation by Robert, earl of Leicester, to Reading Abbey of three messuages in London given in free alms by Geoffrey de Turville and Adeliza, his wife, and afterwards confirmed by William, their son* [1124 × c. 1150]

A f 40r-v; A f 104r; B f 111v; C ff 58v-59r

Sciant presentes et futuri quod ego Robertus*[a]* comes de Legrecestria*[b]* concedo ecclesie sancte Marie de Rading(ia) et monachis ibidem deo servientibus tres mansuras in Lond(onia) quas Gaufredus*[c]* de Turvilla*[d]* et Adaleis*[e]* uxor eius eisdem monachis in elemosinam dederunt, et Willelmus filius eorum post eos concessit et per cartam suam confirmavit. Has mansuras tenuit Walt(erius) Tortus Nasus de Gaufredo de Turvilla,*[d]* et post eum [*f 40v*] Werno filius eius. Quas ego concedo predictis*[f]* monachis pro anima mea et omnium antecessorum meorum liberas et quietas perpetuo possidendas sicut elemosinam.*[g]* Testibus:*[h]* Willelmo filio Roberti, et Ernaldo de Bosco, et Rainaldo filio Walterii, et Gulberto capellano. Apud Lundoniam.

[a] Rodb' *B*
[c] Galfredus *A f 104r*
[e] Adeleis *B*, Adelis' *C*
[g] *A f 104r and C end*

[b] Leicestria *A f 104r*, Leecestr' *B,C*
[d] Turevilla *A f 104r*
[f] eisdem *A f 104r*
[h] *B ends*

After no. 460 and not later than *c.* 1150, when the first witness William fitz Robert, or William de Harcourt, who was still living in 1149, appears to have died (see Crouch, *The Beaumont Twins*, 126, 220). The rubrics of B and C state that there were two copies of this confirmation (*Hec duplex est*) and in the margin of A f 40v there is a note of another charter by the same concerning the same; in view of the variants between A f 104r and the other texts, it is possible that it is the other copy.

462 *Lease by Abbot G. and the convent of Westminster to Azo and Alice, his maternal aunt, and his heirs, of the land which his father, Alfred, held in London near the cemetery of St Laurence on Thames, for an annual rent of 2s* [? 1138 × c. 1157]

A f48v; B f113r; C f6ov

G.[a] abbas Westmon(asterii) et totus conventus eiusdem loci[b] concedunt Azoni et Aliz matertere sue et heredibus ipsius terram quam Alvredus[c] pater ipsius Azonis tenuit in Lundonia[d] prope cimiterium sancti Laurentii super Tamisiam. Et volumus ut eam bene et in pace teneant eo tenore quo predictus Alvredus[c] tenuit, scilicet .ii. solidos reddendo per annum, ad Pascha .xii. denarios et ad festum sancti Michaelis .xii. denarios.[e] His testibus.

[a] *Om. in C*
[b] *A has* salutem, *marked for deletion*
[c] *A has* Alwredus *with second element of* w *marked for deletion*
[d] London' *B,C*
[e] *B ends with* T', *C ends*

The suggested dating limits are those of Abbot Gervase of Westminster, the last Abbot G. before the 15th century, but the abbot concerned may possibly be Gilbert Grispin, ?1085-1117/8. The text cannot be in its original form, since it moves from a third-person verb in the first sentence to a first-person verb in the second. It has the nature of a contemporary abstract, but, despite this, it clearly has features in common with surviving original charters of Abbot Gervase (cf. P. Chaplais, 'The original charters of Herbert and Gervase, abbots of Westminster', *Med. Misc. for D. M. Stenton*, 101-2). How the deed came to Reading is unknown, but, since it was entered in the original section of A, it must have been acquired by 1193. The parish of St Laurence on Thames, or St Laurence Pountney (C. N. L. Brooke and G. Keir, *London 800-1216: the Shaping of a City* (1975), 123), was close to Candlewick Street, now Cannon Street (E. Ekwall, *Street Names of the City of London* (Oxford, 1954), 79), and was in the 13th century known as St Laurence Candlewick. In 1291 the abbot of Reading had property in the parish of St Laurence Candlewick worth 4s per annum (*Taxatio*, 11).

463 *Letter by Hugh [of Amiens], archbishop of Rouen, to the city of London, expressing gratification at its support of King Stephen and testifying that, [when he was abbot of Reading], Algar the priest, with the assent of his brother Baldwin, gave to the abbey his house and land [in London], concerning which a dispute has recently arisen between Algar and the abbey, as he has heard* [1141 × 44]

A f49v; B f113r-v; C f6ov

Hugo dei gratia Rothomagensis archiepiscopus senatoribus inclitis, civibus honoratis et omnibus communie[a] Londoniensis, concordie gratiam, salutem eternam. Deo et vobis agimus gratias pro vestra fidelitate stabili et certa domino nostro[b] regi Stephano iugiter impensa. Inde per regiones nota est vestra nobilitas, virtus et potestas. Fiducia igitur accepta de vestra liberalitate atque iustitia, dignum duximus ad vos perpaucis scribere de causa illa que, ut audivimus, inter Radingensem ecclesiam et Algarum presbiterum noviter orta est, pro domo scilicet*c* et terra ipsius Algari. Recordantur sane nobiscum fratres nostri quia, postquam querelas nostras prout ipse voluit dimisimus illi,*d* tandem sponte sua idem Algarus ad nos rediit et, assentiente Baldewino fratre suo, libera donatione nobis, ecclesie scilicet*e* Rading(ensi), in capitulo fratribus presetibus prefatam domum suam et terram perpetuo possidendam donavit, ita tamen ut in vita sua eam teneret et pro recognitione .ix. solidos annis singulis vite sue ecclesie Radingensi persolveret. Post decessum vero suum libera et quieta ad Radingense monasterium pertinens remaneret. Hoc ita vobis mandamus quos iustitie defensores esse cognovimus. Oportet igitur vos*f* defensare et tueri iustitiam ecclesie Rading(ensis), ut per virtutem vestram pax ecclesie conservata coram deo appareat, qui pro his*g* et aliis bonis vestris et vos in presenti pacatos et victores efficiat et in futuro benedictionem impendat. Amen.

a commune B,C   *b* Om. in C
c Placed before pro B,C   *d* ei B,C
e Placed before ecclesie B,C   *f* Placed before igitur C
g hiis B,C

The archbishop sent a letter of similar import to Robert, bishop of London, which cannot be earlier than 1141 (no. 464). He would not have referred to Stephen as 'our king' after the loss of Rouen to Geoffrey, count of Anjou, in Apr. 1144. For comment on this letter, and especially on its reference to the commune of London, see J. H. Round, *Geoffrey de Mandeville* (1892), 116, where the first three sentences are printed.

464   *Letter by Hugh [of Amiens], archbishop of Rouen, to Robert [de Sigillo], bishop of London, intimating the same*   [1141 × 44]

A f 49v

Reverendo patri et amico suo in Christo R(oberto) Lundoniensi episcopo H(ugo) Rothomag(ensis) sacerdos, salutem et pacem. Sanctitati vestre dignum duximus intimare quia Algarus presbiter, omissa querela que inter nos et ipsum versabatur de domo sua, tandem venit ad nos Radingiam et sponte sua, prout*a* recordamur, domum suam cum terra concessit nobis, ita ut singulis annis inde redderet nobis .ix. solidos in vita sua. Hanc itaque donationem nobis ab eo factam pontificali auctoritate vestra precipite ut maneat, ne sacerdos ille, qui doctor veritatis in plebe debet apparere, super hoc diabolo fallente mendacium teneat pro veritate. Commendo me

precibus et meritis vestris ut nos deus eruat a malis, karissime pater
et domine.

^a *Ms has here* nos *marked for deletion*

It is clear from no. 463 that this letter dates from before King Stephen lost the duchy
of Normandy in 1144. The only R. bishop of London after Hugh became archbishop
of Rouen and before 1144 was Robert de Sigillo, 1141–50. He had been master of
the writing chamber in Henry I's last years and subsequently, according to John of
Hexham, had become a monk at Reading (see *Regesta*, iii, pp. x–xi).

465 Notification by King Stephen to the justice, sheriff and barons
of London that Hugh [of Amiens], archbishop of Rouen, testifies
that, when he was abbot of Reading, Algar the priest and Baldwin
his brother gave their lands and houses in London in free alms to
Reading Abbey; and precept that the abbey shall accordingly hold
the same in peace   [1141 × 44]

A f 19r; B f 29r
Pd. *Regesta*, iii. 255–6 (no. 693)

T(este)^a Roberto de Ver. Apud Windr(esores).

^a *B ends*

Contemporary with nos. 463–4.

465a Note of another [act by the same] to the bishop of London
concerning the same   [1141 × 44]

B f 29r; (?) A f 19r[1]

Date as for no. 465.

[1] After the text of no. 465, A adds: *Item carta eiusdem de eodem.*

466 Precept by Queen Eleanor [acting as regent for King Henry
II] to John fitz Ralph, sheriff of London, to enquire into the complaint made to her by the monks of Reading that they have been
unjustly disseised of lands in London, given to them by Richard son
of B. when he became a monk, viz.,^a from the tenures of the abbot
of Westminster and the abbot of St Augustine's, Canterbury; and,
if he find this to be true, to reseise the monks, saving the right of the
said abbots in those lands   [Jan. 1156 × Apr. 1157]

B f 113v; C f 60v
Pd. van Caenegem, *Royal Writs*, 460 (no. 93) (with transl.)

^a *The Mss have* s. *for* scilicet, *and not for* suis *as printed by van Caenegem*

John fitz Ralph was a sheriff of London 1154-7 (S. Reynolds, 'Rulers of London in the twelfth century', *History* lvii (1972), 355), during which period the king was abroad Jan. 1156—Apr. 1157 (Eyton, 16, 25). This writ is cited by van Caenegem as an early writ of reseisin (*op. cit.*, 279, 301 n. 3).

467   Mandate and precept by Queen Eleanor [acting as regent for King Henry II] to John fitz Ralph, sheriff of London, to compel John *Bucont* to warrant to the monks[a] of Reading 40s worth of land which he gave them in London, or an exchange to the same value   [Jan. 1156 × Apr. 1157]

Bf113v; Cff6ov-61r
Pd. *Memoranda Roll 1 John*, lxviii; van Caenegem, *Royal Writs*, 480 (no. 127) (with transl.)

T(este) M(atheo) canc(ellario).

   [a] monach' *B*, monachis *C*; *the printed texts have* monachos *incorrectly* (*van Caenegem's text is taken from Memoranda Roll 1 John*)

Date as for no. 466. John *Bucont* is to be identified with the John Bucuinte who was a sheriff of London 1169-72 (Reynolds, 'Rulers of London', 355) and who was closely involved in the London money market and money-lending in the city (Brooke and Keir, *London 800-1216*, 214, 221, 229; H. Jenkinson, 'A money-lender's bonds of the twelfth century', *Essays in History presented to R. L. Poole*, ed. H. W. C. Davis (Oxford, 1927), 196, 207 (no. iv), 209 (no. vii)). Either he or another of the same name was a sheriff of London 1190-1 (Reynolds, 355) and had some connection with the royal courts (Stenton, *English Justive*, 150). I am grateful to the kindness of Miss J. M. Boorman for help on these points.

468   *Agreement between Reading Abbey and Aumary, goldsmith of London, and Joan his wife, by which the latter shall pay annually 1 mark of silver for a messuage in the parish of St Leonard Eastcheap, London, increasing their rent by 16d, in return for remission by the abbey of arrears of rent up to ½ mark*   [late 12th × early 13th cent.]

   Af100v; Bf112r; Cf59v

Hec est conventio inter abbatem et conventum Rading', ex una parte, et Almericum aurifabrum London(ie) et Iohannam uxorem suam, ex altera parte, de uno mesagio[a] cum pertinentiis apud London(iam) in Estchep in parochia[b] Sancti Leonardi. Videlicet, quod idem Almaricus[c] et eadem Iohanna et heredes sui reddent de predicto tenemento dictis abbati et conventui Rading' annuatim unam marcam argenti, scilicet, ad Pascha dimidiam marcam et ad sanctum Michaelem dimidiam marcam, de quo tenemento accrescunt redditum suum de sexdecim denariis pro relaxatione reragii redditus quam ei fecerunt dicti abbas et conventus usque ad dimidiam marcam. Et ad hoc fideliter observandum pro se et pro uxore sua et pro heredibus suis idem Almaricus[c] iuravit tactis sacrosanctis evangeliis,[d] et hanc conventionem fideliter confirmavit tam sacramento quam sigillo suo et sigillo uxoris sue, ita quod, si detineant redditum suum ultra quindecim dies post diem quo debent reddere redditum suum, dabunt de pena unum bisantium[e] pro trespasso suo.

[a] mesuagio B,C	[b] parrochia B
[c] Almericus B,C	[d] ewangeliis C
[e] baisantium C	

Not in the original section of A, but entered in a hand of the early 13th century with other deeds down to c. 1220. In 1291 the abbot of Reading had property in the parish of St Leonard Eastcheap worth 12s per annum (*Taxatio*, 11), i.e., the amount which this messuage paid before the 16d increase in rent.

469 *Lease by Abbot Elias and the convent of Reading to Walter Ilefostre, citizen of London, and his heirs of their houses in the parish of St Benet [Sherehog], London, viz., what they have there between St Benet and St Antonin, for an annual rent of 2½ marks. The lessees shall pay for all repairs without reduction of rent, and the abbot and monks of Reading and their household shall have lodging in these houses when in London. Walter has given an entry-fine of 5 marks and, to the convent, a chasuble worth 2½ marks* [1200 × 1213]

B ff 112v–113r; C f 6or

Sciant presentes et futuri quod ego Hel(ias) dei gratia abbas Rading(ensis) et eiusdem loci conventus concessimus et tradidimus Waltero Ilefostre civi Lond(onie) domos nostras in Lond(onia) que sunt in parrochia[a] Sancti Benedicti cum omnibus pertinentiis, videlicet, quicquid ibidem habemus inter Sanctum Benedictum et Sanctum Antonium[b] in domibus et terris sine aliquo retinemento, tenendas de nobis iure hereditario pro .ii. marcis et dimidia annuatim reddendis ecclesie Rading(ensi) ad duos terminos, ad festum sancti Michaelis .xvi. solidos et octo denarios et ad Pascha .xvi. solidos et .viii. denarios. Tenebunt autem predictus Walterus et heredes sui prefatas domos cum pertinentiis tali conditione quod omnem earum emendationem et restaurationem de suo facient sine redditus predicti diminutione. Abbas etiam Rading(ensis) et omnes monachi Rading(enses) et familia eorum in eisdem domibus, quotiens London(iam) venerint et voluerint, hospitium habebunt. Hanc autem conventionem eis debemus warantizare contra omnes gentes. Pro hac autem concessione dedit nobis [f 113r] prefatus W(alterus) quinque marcas argenti in gersumam et quandam casulam dedit conventui pro salute anime sue de pretio duarum marcarum et dimidie. Hanc conventionem prefatus W(alterus) iuravit super textum evan(geliorum) in capitulo Rading(ensi) se perpetuo sine fraude servaturum. T(estibus).*c*

a parochia C
b *Sic, rectius* Antoninum; Anntonium C
c *Om. in* C

The dating limits are those of Elias's abbacy. The rubrics call this deed a chirograph. The property lay in the parish of St Benet Sherehog, south of Cheapside, adjacent on the south to the parish of St Antonin. The cartulary texts say St Anthony, but there was no such parish in medieval London. In 1291 the abbot of Reading had property in the parish of St Benet Sherehog worth annually £1 13s 4d, i.e. 2½ marks (*Taxatio*, 11).

470 *Notification by Walter* Ilefostre *that he has received the same from Abbot Elias and the convent of Reading for an annual rent of 2½ marks and with the same conditions*   [1200 × 1213]

B f 112v; C ff 59v–60r

Sciant presentes et futuri quod ego Walt(erus) Ilefostre civis London(ie) accepi ab Hel(ia) abbate et conventu*a* Rading' domos suas in London(ia) que sunt in parrochia*b* Sancti Benedicti cum omnibus pertinentiis, videlicet, quicquid ibidem habent inter Sanctum Benedictum et Sanctum Antonium,*c* tenendas de eis iure hereditario pro duabus marcis et dimidia annuatim reddendis ecclesie Rading(ensi) ad duos terminos, ad festum sancti Michaelis .xvi. solidos et octo denarios et ad Pascha .xvi. solidos et octo denarios. Ego autem et heredes mei tenebimus prefatas domos cum pertinentiis tali conditione quod omnem earum emendationem et restaurationem de nostro faciemus sine redditus predicti diminutione. Abbas etiam Rading(ensis) et omnes monachi Rading(enses) et familia eorum in eisdem domibus, quotiens London(iam) venerint et voluerint, hospitium habebunt. Pro hac autem concessione dedi eis .v. marcas argenti in gersumam, et quandam casulam dedi conventui de pretio duarum marcarum et dimidie pro salute anime mee. Hanc conventionem iuravi super textum evan(geliorum) in capitulo Rading(ensi) me perpetuo sine fraude servaturum. Volo etiam quod omnes heredes mei qui mihi in predicto tenemento succedent faciant idem sacramentum et fidelitatem in capitulo Rading(ensi) quam ego feci. T(estibus).*d*

a conventui C (*in error*)
b parochia C
c *Sic, rectius* Antoninum (*see no. 469, n.*)
d *Om. in* C

Contemporary with no1 469. A 14th-century marginal note in B reads: *ten' Ricardi de Lincoln'*.

471 *Acknowledgement by Cecily and Lucy, daughters of Waleran son of Meillealm, that they and their heirs owe annually to Reading Abbey 2 marks for the lands which the said Waleran held of it in the parish of All Hallows [? Fenchurch, London]; and grant that distress may be taken throughout these lands in the event of non-payment of the rent* [not later than 1258]

B f112r–v; C f59v

Omnibus ad quos presens scriptum pervenerit Cecilia et Lucia, filie Waleranni filii Meillealmi, salutem. Litteris presentibus testificamur quod nos et heredes nostri reddere tenemur annuatim monachis de Rading(ia) .ii. marcas argenti duobus terminis anni, videlicet, infra oct(avas) Pasche unam marcam et infra octo dies post festum sancti Michaelis .i. marcam [f112v], pro terris quas dictus Walerannus tenuit de dictis monachis in parrochia*a* Omnium Sanctorum ubi fenum venditur. Quare concessimus pro nobis et heredibus nostris quod predicti monachi sive eorum attornati in London(ia) namia capiant in omnibus locis predictarum terrarum quibus inventa fuerint distringenda usque ad plenam solutionem, si predictus redditus prenominatis terminis solutus non fuerit. Et in huius rei testimonium huic scripto sigilla nostra apposuimus. T(estibus).*b*

a parochia C
b Om. in C

Impossible to date narrowly, but not later than 1258, since it was entered in the original section of B. A 14th-century marginal note in B reads: *ten' J. de Prestone.* In 1291 the abbot of Reading had property in the parish of All Hallows *ad fenum* worth annually £1 6s 8d, i.e., 2 marks (*Taxatio*, 11). It seems that the parish concerned must be All Hallows Fenchurch (later St Gabriel Fenchurch), although Ekwall discounts the derivation of Fenchurch from the Latin *fenum*, 'hay' (*Street Names London*, 96).

472 *Gift by Thomas le Perrer, son of Peter the goldsmith, to Reading Abbey of land with buildings in the parish of Holy Innocents outside London, for an annual service to him and his heirs of 1d, and to the nuns of Kilburn of 5s 4d on his behalf. For this the abbey has given him 12 marks of silver* [1213 × 26]

B f111v; C f59r

Sciant presentes et futuri quod ego Thomas le Perrer filius Petri aurifabri dedi et concessi et*a* presenti carta mea confirmavi deo et beate Marie et beatis apostolis Iohanni et Iacobo et abbati et conventui de Rading(ia) totam terram cum edificiis et omnibus pertinentiis suis que iacet inter terram quam Willelmus filius Reineri et Serlo filius Henrici tenent*b* et terram Gunnilde Brekebred in parrochia*c* Sanctorum Innocentium extra London(iam). Habend(am) et

tenend(am) predictis abbati et conventui in feudo et hereditate et
iure perpetuo libere, quiete, plenarie et pacifice de me et heredibus
meis per liberum servitium unius denarii in festo sancti Michaelis
mihi et heredibus meis super eodem tenemento reddendi, et faciendo
pre me monialibus de Keleburne servitium .v. solidorum et .iiii.
denariorum per annum ad terminos statutos pro omnibus servitiis,
consuetudinibus, auxiliis et omnibus demandis. Et ego et heredes
mei warantizabimus predictis abbati et conventui totam predictam
terram cum omnibus pertinentiis suis contra omnes homines et feminas in perpetuum per predictum servitium. Pro hac autem donatione, concessione, confirmatione et warantizatione dederunt mihi
supradicti abbas et conventus .xii. marcas argenti. Et ut hec mea
donatio, concessio et warantizatio rata et stabilis in perpetuum permaneat, presenti scripto et sigilli mei appositione roboravi.
T(estibus).*d*

a Insert hac C	*b Both texts have* tenet
c parochia C	*d Om. in* C

The dating limits are those of Simon's abbacy, he having been abbot when this land
was acquired (see no. 473). B adds a note of another deed by the same in the same
words.

473 *Quitclaim, in the full county court of Middlesex, by Bartholomew son
of William to Abbot Simon and the monks of Reading of all right in the land
which they bought from Thomas son of Peter, his kinsman, concerning which
there was sometime a plea between Bartholomew and the abbey in the county
court of Middlesex on the king's writ of right*   [1213 × 26]

B f 112r; C f 59r–v

Sciant presentes et futuri quod ego Bartholomeus filius Willelmi
remisi et quiet'clamavi de me et de heredibus meis Symoni abbati
de Rading(ia) et monachis eiusdem loci et eorum successoribus in
perpetuum totum ius et clamium quod habui vel habere potui in
tota terra cum omnibus pertinentiis suis quam idem abbas et monachi emerunt de Thoma filio Petri, consanguineo meo, et in qua
predicti abbas et monachi edificia sua construxerunt et unde aliquando placitum fuit inter nos in comitatu Middelsex' per breve
domini regis de recto. Ita quod nec ego nec heredes mei vel*a* aliquis
alius per nos vel pro nobis de terra illa cum pertinentiis aliquid*b*
unquam clamare vel exigere poterimus. Et ut hec mea remissio,
quiet'clamatio*c* stabilis permaneat, presens scriptum sigilli mei appositione munivi. Pro hac autem remissione et*d* quiet'clamatione*e*
dederunt mihi predicti abbas et monachi centum solidos sterlingorum. Hoc quidem factum fuit in pleno comitatu Middelsex'.
T(estibus).*d*

| ^{a} nec C | ^{b} aliquod C | ^{c} quietaclam' C |
| ^{d} Om. in C | ^{e} quietaclamacione C | |

The dating limits are those of Simon's abbacy.

474 Final concord in the king's court at Westminster, the morrow of St Simon and St Jude [28 Oct.], 7 Henry III, before Martin of Pattishall (*Pateshull'*), Ralph *Harang*,^{a} Stephen of Seagrave (*Segrave*), Thomas *de Hayden'*, Robert of Lexington (*Lexint'*), justices, and others, between Bartholomew son of William, seeking by Philip of Stockton (*Stocton'*) as attorney, and Abbot Simon of Reading, holding by G(eoffrey)^b *de Frowik* as attorney, concerning a messuage and garden in the vill (*vicus*) of Westminster. Bartholomew quitclaimed to the abbot and abbey of Reading all his right in the same, for which the abbot gave him 20s sterling   29 Oct. 1222

B f 180v; C f 107r

Pd. (cal.) *A Calendar to the Feet of Fines for London and Middlesex*, ed. W.J. Hardy and W. Page (1892–3), i. 16 (from PRO foot: CP 25(1)/146/6/50)

^{a} Hareng' C
^{b} Expansion from PRO foot

474a Notes of the following:
(i) charter by Alexander son of Gilbert to John son of Thomas concerning land at London (*London'*);
(ii) chirograph between Clementia, widow of Peter the goldsmith, and John of Windsor (*Windlesor'*)^a concerning the same land at London   [not later than 1258]

B f 112r; C f 59v

^{a} Windesor' C

These cannot be later than 1258, since they were noted in the original section of B, but they may well be much earlier in the century. Peter the goldsmith in (ii) may be the Peter the goldsmith, father of Thomas *le Perrer* in no. 472.

475 *List of the abbot of Reading's rents in London*   [1291]

B f 111r

[*translation*]

In the parish of St Martin Candlewick Street (*Candelwykstret*)[1]	6s
In the parish of St Benet Gracechurch (*de Grescherch'*)	9s
In the parish of St Laurence Candlewick Street[2]	4s
In the parish of St Leonard Eastcheap (*Estchepe*)[3]	12s
In the parish of St Peter Broad Street (*Bredstret*)	6s

In the parish of St Benet Sherehog (*Schorhog*)[4]   33s 4d
In the parish of St Mary Woolchurch (*Wolcherchehawe*)[5]   13s 4d
In the parish of St Martin Ottewich (*Oteswych'*)   2s
In the parish of All Hallows Fenchurch (*ad fenum*)[6]   26s 8d
In the parish of St Michael Candlewick Street[7]   10s
In the parish of St Stephen Walbrook (*Walebrok'*)   10s
Total of a tenth: 13s 2½d

This is almost identical with the entry in the Taxation of Pope Nicholas IV of 1291 under the heading, *Bona abbatis de Redyng in parochiis*, in the section relating to temporalities in the archdeaconry of London (*Taxatio*, 11–12), where, however, the amount in All Hallows Fenchurch is given as £1 6s 4d (£1 6s 8d, the amount in B, being a variant reading in other copies) and the tenth as 13s 2¼d.

1 Probably the parish more commonly known as St Martin Orgar, since it was the only medieval parish of St Martin on Candlewick Street, now Cannon Street.
2 More commonly St Laurence Pountney (see no. 462 n.).
3 See no. 468.
4 See nos. 469–70.
5 See no. 481.
6 See no. 471 and n.
7 Probably St Michael towards the Bridge, or St Michael Crooked Lane, since it was the only medieval parish of St Michael on or near Candlewick Street, now Cannon Street.

476   Record of assize of novel disseisin *[held before the coroner and sheriffs of London, Saturday before St Nicholas [6 Dec.], 35 Edward I],* between Abbot Nicholas [of Whaplode] of Reading and Gilbert of Ashingdon (*Asschendon'*). The abbot complains that, whereas Gilbert held of him a messuage in London for the service of 2½ marks annually and of providing lodging for the abbot and monks and their household in that tenement when they come to London at the abbot's expense, Henry of Lenton (*Lenton'*), monk of Reading, came to the tenement on Friday before the feast of St Edmund the king [20 Nov.], 34 Edward I, distrained on the same for the said rent and took lodging in the tenement, but Gilbert had the distresses replevied and contested the rent, and he ejected Henry and his household from the tenement by force, thereby disseising them. Gilbert replies that the assize does not lie in these causes, since pleas involving replevin of distresses belong by city custom to the Husting, and, because the lodging is not a free tenement, it ought not to be the subject of an assize. On the first point, since pleas of replevin belong to the Husting, the abbot loses his case. On the second point Gilbert says nothing whereby the assize ought not to proceed, but, since it is the time of Advent (*propter instans tempus adventus domini*) and because the court is not licensed by the bishop to take assizes,[1] it is respited to the octave [? of St Hilary].[2] Afterwards, on Saturday before the Conversion of St Paul [25 Jan.], 35 Edward I, the jury, John of Guildford (*Geldeford*),[b] etc., say that the abbot, through his monk, was seised of the lodging as a free tenement and had been unlawfully disseised by Gilbert. Accordingly the court orders the abbot's reseisin and damages of 20s against Gilbert, who is in mercy 3 Dec. 1306; 21 Jan. 1307

B ff 113v–114r; C f61r

Rubric: Assise nove disseisine et mortis antecessoris capte coram coron(atore) et vic(ecomitibus) London' die sabbati proxima ante festum sancti Nicholai, anno regni regis E(dwardi) xxxv.

a-a Supplied from rubric
b Guldeford' C

The offence took place on 19 Nov. 1305. The tenement concerned was in the parish of St Benet Sherehog (see no. 469) and lay to the east of St Sithes Lane (*ex inf.* D. Crouch and J. Stedman, of the Social and Economic Study of Medieval London). In 1277 it was held of the abbey by Robert of Ashingdon and was described as the abbey's 'capital house' in the city (*Calendar of Letter-Books of the City of London*, A, ed. R. R. Sharpe (1899), 14).

[1] In 1306 Advent began on 27 November. The period from Advent to the octave of Epiphany was traditionally one of those during which the hearing of pleas was prohibited. In 1275 Edward I asked the bishops to relax this rule for petty assizes, but no general concession was forthcoming, although individual bishops sometimes granted temporary dispensations (*Handbook of Dates*, 66). Clearly in this case the bishop of London had not done so.

[2] This bracketed passage is not in the text, but some such addition is required, since the mere octave of 3 Dec. would still be in Advent and therefore impossible for the taking of the assize. Moreover, the octave of St Hilary as a return day includes 21 Jan., the day when the present case resumed.

477 Record of assize of novel disseisin *a*[brought before Hervey*b* of Stanton (*Stantone*) and his fellow justices-in-eyre at the Tower of London, 14 Edward II],*a* by the abbot of Reading against John son of William of Hannington (*Hanyngton*') chaplain, Adam of Bury (*Bury*), Hervey*b* of Bury, and Gervase and Elias, servants of John *de Triple*, who, the abbot complains, disseised him of his free tenement of 10s rent in London. John, Adam and Hervey come, the others not, but John answers for them as bailiff, etc. On their behalf John, and similarly Adam and Hervey, state that they have and claim nothing in the rent and have made no injury or disseisin. For himself John says that the tenements from which the abbot claims the rent are not of the fee or demesne of the abbot. The abbot, by attorney, replies that John holds the tenements for an annual rent of 10s, of which the abbot was seised as of a free tenement until John and the others unjustly disseised him. John answers that the assize ought not to be made, because Thomas of Chigwell (*Chikewelle*)^c and Agatha his wife hold three shops of the same tenements and held them on the day when the abbot's writ was obtained, namely 24 May, 14 Edward II, but are not named in the writ. The jury declare on oath on this point that Thomas and Agatha did hold the shops on 24 May, and therefore the court decides on this writ against the abbot, who is in mercy for false claim   [24 May × 4 July] 1321

B f223r–v; C f136v

Rubric: Placita coram Hervico^d de Stantone et sociis suis justiciariis domini regis itinerantibus apud Turrim Lond', anno regni regis Edwardi filii regis Edwardi quartodecimo

^{a–a} *Supplied from rubric*   ^b *C has* 'Henry' *throughout*
^c Checkewell' *C*   ^d Henrico *C*

After the date of the writ and before the end of the eyre (Crook, *General Eyre*, 181).

478   Record of further assize of novel disseisin in the same case, before the same justices, naming as defendants all those named in no. 477 and Thomas of Chigwell (*Chykewelle*) and Agatha his wife. John, Thomas, Agatha, Adam and Hervey come, the others not, but Hervey answers for them as bailiff, saying that neither he nor the absentees have or claim anything in the rent, or have made any injury or disseisin. Adam, as tenant of part of the tenements concerned, namely, a cellar, chamber and garden, says that he holds those tenements by right of his wife Rose, who is not named in the writ, wherefore he seeks judgement on the writ; in any case he has made no injury or disseisin. John, as tenant of part of the tenements concerned, namely, a gate, chamber and kitchen, likewise denies injury or disseisin. Thomas and Agatha, tenants of three shops of the said tenements, deny injury or disseisin. All place themselves on the assize. The abbot of Reading, in answering Adam's exception, says that, when the previous writ was quashed in the present eyre, Adam said that he had nothing in the said rent and had caused no injury or disseisin, and the writ was quashed because of the exception made by John son of William over the omission of Thomas and Agatha from the list of defendants; and the abbot seeks judgement as to whether the present writ, obtained immediately after the quashing of the earlier writ, ought to fail because of Adam's exception. Adam says that the garden now placed in view in the present writ was not included in the quashed writ. Both Adam and the abbot seek judgement of the assize. The jury declare that the garden and all the said tenements now in view were in view in the previous writ, and that John son of William did unjustly disseise the abbot of the rent of 10s, but Thomas, Agatha, Adam, Hervey, Gervase and Elias were not parties to the disseisin. The court accordingly awards reseisin to the abbot and 5 marks damages; and John is in mercy for false claim against Thomas and the others   [24 May × 7 July] 1321

B f223v; C f137r

After no. 477, but within the same dating limits.

479 Licence by King Edward III, at the request of John of Stonor (*Stonore*), to Robert of Abingdon (*Abyndon*') to alienate in mortmain to Reading Abbey four messuages and a stone quay in London, which are held of the king in chief, to find two secular chaplains to celebrate divine service daily in the Lady Chapel of Reading Abbey for the souls of master Richard of Abingdon, his successors and heirs and all faithful deceased for ever. Licence also to the abbot and convent to receive and hold the same   18 Oct. 1327

C f226r
Pd. (cal.) *Cal. Pat. R. 1327-30*, 183 (from Patent Roll)

Teste me ipso apud Notungham, decimo octavo die Octobris, anno regni nostri primo.[a]

[a] *Ms adds in the same hand:* scilicet Edwardi tercii post Conquestum

480 Demise in free alms by Robert of Abingdon (*Habyndon*') to Reading Abbey of all the tenements and a stone quay in London which formerly belonged to master Richard of Abingdon (*Abyndon*'), his uncle, whose heir he is. The abbey shall find two secular chaplains to celebrate divine service daily in the Lady Chapel of Reading Abbey for the souls of master Richard, his successors and heirs and all faithful deceased for ever. Sealing   26 Dec. 1327

C f228r

Hiis testibus: domino Hamone de Chykewell' maiore London(ie), Johanne de Oxon', Willelmo Prodhomme, Waltero Turk', Roberto de Ely, et aliis. Dat' apud Redyng' die sabbati[a] in festo sancti Stephani prothomartiris, anno regni regis Edwardi tercii a Conquestu primo.

[a] *Ms has* sabati

481 Record of assize of novel disseisin [a][brought before Robert Girdler (*Girdelere*) and Adam Wymondham, sheriffs, and William of Hockley (*Hockele*), coroner, of London, Saturday the feast of St

Catherine the Virgin, 42 Edward III].*a* Abbot William [III] of Reading, by his attorney Thomas of St Albans (*de Sancto Albano*), complains that Benedict Cornwall (*Cornewaille*), palmer,*b* and Agnes his wife, on Monday after the Translation of St Thomas the Martyr [7 July], 42 Edward III, disseised him of 13s rent in the parish of St Mary Woolchurch (*Wollech(erch)ehawe*), London. The defendants, by Robert of Watlington (*Watlyngton'*) as their bailiff, deny the charge, claiming that the abbot was never in seisin of the rent. Both parties put themselves on the assize. The abbot's attorney is asked by the court to show the cause of the disseisin and says that, when he went to the tenement of the defendants to distrain for the said rent being in arrears, they prevented distraint and illegally recovered the distresses (*fecerunt ... rescussum et vetit(um), et cetera*). The jury—Thomas *Averay*, John *Helescompe*, William Derby (*Derbi*), John Daniel (*Danyel*), Nicholas *Maichamet*, William Sonning (*Sunnyng'*), Thomas of Ware (*Ware*), Thomas *Roket*, Richard Dorset (*Dorsete*), Thomas *de Same*, Robert *Hunyforde*, Geoffrey Woking (*Wokkyng'*)—declare on oath that the abbot was seised of the said rent, as had been Abbot Henry [of Appleford][1] and Abbot Nicholas [of Whaplode][2] and all their predecessors time out of mind and before the Statute of Mortmain. Abbot Hugh[3] was seised of the rent long before the Statute in the time of King Henry.[4] Therefore, the defendants did disseise the abbot to damages of 10 marks. Asked whether the disseisin was by force and arms, the jury say not. Accordingly the court awards the abbot reseisin of the rent and 10 marks damages, the latter of which the abbot's attorney remits, and Benedict and Agatha are in mercy. Henry *Traynel*, serjeant (*serviens*), is ordered to deliver seisin of the rent to the abbot, which he does in the court   25 Nov. 1368

B f 141r–v

Rubric: Assise nove disseisine et mortis antecessoris capte coram Roberto Girdelere et Adam Wymondham vic(ecomitibus) London' et Willelmo de Hockele coron(atore) eiusdem civitatis die sabati in festo sancte Katerine virginis, anno regni regis E(dwardi) tercii post Conquestum quadragesimo secundo

a-a Supplied from rubric
b Uncertain; Ms pamiar'

The disseisin took place on 10 July 1368.

[1] Abbot 1342–61.   [2] Abbot 1305–28.
[3] Either Hugh I (1123–30) or Hugh II (1186–99).
[4] Either Henry I or Henry II.

QUIDENHAM

482 *Gift in free alms by William d'Aubigny, earl of Sussex, to Reading Abbey of 1 mark's worth of rent in Quidenham, viz., the land held by Ralph Magnus, to provide a pittance on the anniversary of Jocelin [of Louvain], his uncle* [c. 1186 × 89]

Original charter: BL Add. Ch. 19604
A f41r; A f103r; (noted) B f100r
Pd. *Arch. Journ.*, xxii. 154; (cal.) Hurry, *Reading Abbey*, 170

Sciant presentes et futuri quod ego Willelmus de Albeni^a comes Susexie^b dedi deo et ecclesie de Rading(ia) unam marcatam redditus in Quiddenham,^c scilicet terram quam Rad(ulfus) cognomento Magnus tenet, in liberam et perpetuam elemosinam pro anima regine Adelize matris mee et pro anima patris mei et Ioc(elini) castellani avunculi mei et omnium antecessorum et successorum meorum et mea, ut inde fiat refectio conventui in anniversario Ioc(elini) avunculi mei.^d Hiis^e testibus: Reinerio fratre meo, Gileberto de Norfolke,^f Ricardo Aguillun, Willelmo de Alta Ripa, Willelmo de Elnestede.

Endorsed: Carta Willelmi de Aubeni de redditu unius marce in Quiddenham. Est alia melior de eodem [*late 12th × early 13th cent.*]
Size: 140 × 66 mm
Seal: missing; tag for seal

^a Aubeni *A f103r*	^b Sussex' *A f103r*	^c Quidenham *A f41r, A f103r*
^d *A f103r ends with* T'	^e His *A f41r*	^f Norfolkia *A f41r*

The donor was the son of Queen Adeliza and her second husband, William d'Aubigny, earl of Arundel. He was styled earl by Christmas 1186, and his present gift was included in Richard I's general confirmation to Reading, dated 12 Sept. 1189 (no. 34). The estate from which this gift was made was held of Roger Bigod by three free men in 1086 (*VCH Norfolk*, ii. 106). On the marriage of William d'Aubigny, grandfather of the present donor and father of the first earl of Arundel, to Matilda, daughter of Roger Bigod (*Complete Peerage*, i. 233), he was enfeoffed with 10 knights of the latter's fee (*Red Bk. Exch.*, i. 395, 397-8), which seem to have included the land at Quidenham.

483 *Gift in free alms by the same concerning the same land, with additional gift of common of pasture* [c. 1186 × 93]

Original charter: BL Add. Ch. 19603
A f92v; B f100r; C f50v
Pd. *Arch. Journ.*, xxii. 155; (cal.) Hurry, *Reading Abbey*, 170

Sciant presentes et futuri quod ego Willelmus de Albeni comes Susexie*a* dedi deo et ecclesie de Rading(ia) et monachis ibidem*b* servientibus unam marcatam redditus in Quidenham,*c* scilicet totam
terram quam Rad(ulfus) cognomento Magnus tenet, cum omnibus
ad terram illam pertinentibus. Dedi etiam eis communionem pasture
et exitus in mea que circumiacet terra, ut sit terra quam eis dedi in
liberam*d* et perpetuam elemosinam et homines in ea manentes, pro
salute anime mee et omnium antecessorum et successorum meorum,
ut inde fiat refectio conventui in anniversario Ioc(elini) avunculi
mei.*e* Testibus:*f* Reinerio fratre meo, Gileberto de Norfolche, Willelmo de Alta Ripa, Willelmo de Elnestede, Osberno Verrer,
Rog(erio) de Sacristia Rading(ie), et multis aliis.

Endorsed: Wll' com' Susexie de redditu .i. marce [*12th cent.*] in Quidenham cum pertinentiis [*13th cent.*]

Size: 120 × 97 mm

Seal: large fragment in white wax on tag; obverse: mounted knight;
on reverse counterseal, lion passant reguardant (see *B.M. Cat.
Seals,* ii. 236–7)

a Sussex' B,C	*b* *Insert* deo B,C	*c* Quidenam C
d *Insert* puram C	*e* *C ends*	*f* A,B, *end*

The donor was styled earl by Christmas 1186 and died 24 or 25 Dec. 1193. This deed
may be contemporary with, or slightly later than, no. 482, but, since it was not
entered in the original section of A with no. 482, it may date from shortly before the
earl's death.

484   *Confirmation by William d'Aubigny, earl of Sussex, son of the preceding, of his father's gift in free alms to Reading Abbey in Quidenham*

[1193 × 1221]

A f95r; B f100r; C f50v

Sciant*a* presentes et*b* futuri quod ego Willelmus de Albeni comes de
Sussex(ia), filius Willelmi de Albeni comitis, concessi et presenti
carta mea confirmavi deo et ecclesie Rading(ensi) donationem quam
pater meus eidem ecclesie fecit, scilicet unam marcatam redditus in
Quidenham,*c* scilicet terram quam Rad(ulfus) cognomine Magnus
tenuit, in liberam et perpetuam elemosinam pro anima Alicie*d* regine
avie mee et pro anima patris mei et avi mei et omnium antecessorum
meorum*e* et successorum meorum et mea, sicut carta patris mei
testatur.*f* Hiis testibus.

a *Insert* tam B,C	*b* quam B,C	*c* Quidenam C
d Alitie B	*e* *Om. in* B,C	*f* B *ends with* T', C *ends*

This William d'Aubigny was the 3rd earl of Arundel, 1193–1221.

WALTON

485 *Gift in free alms by Roger Bigod, earl of Norfolk, to Reading Abbey of 3 marks worth of rent. The abbey shall receive this annually from his mills in Walton, until he shall assign the same amount in the church of Finchingfield [Essex] or in another church* [1189 × 93]

A f41r

Sciant presentes et futuri quod ego Rog(erus) Bigot comes Norfolch(ie) dedi et hac carta confirmavi tres marcatas redditus deo et monachis de Rading(ia) pro salute anime mee et Ide comitisse uxoris mee et omnium filiorum et antecessorum et successorum meorum in liberam et perpetuam elemoninam. Has tres marcas annuatim percipient monachi prefati de molendinis meis in Waletuna ad duos terminos, scilicet ad festum sancti Michaelis .xx. solidos et .xx. solidos ad Pascha, donec illas assignavero et assignatas firmiter habere fecero in ecclesia de Finchingefeld vel in aliqua alia ubi eis commodius videbitur. Quod cum fecero, quietus ero de solutione .xl. solidorum quos de molendinis meis percipere solebant, et cartam meam mihi vel heredibus meis reddent contenti prefato prefate ecclesie redditu, sicut predictum est. Hos .xl. solidos ad predictos terminos serviens meus de Waletuna annuatim persolvet custodi domorum monachorum de Rading(ia) in domibus eorum apud London(iam). Testibus: Roberto capellano meo, Michaele de Waketun(a), Eustachio de Braham, Godefr(ido) de Bello Monte, Ricardo Buzi, Radulfo Ruffo, Waltero de Terstuna, et multis aliis.

After the earl's creation on 25 Nov. 1189 and, since the charter was entered in the original section of A, not later than 1193. The charter was not entered in Reading's later cartularies, because it was superseded by the same earl's gift of 3 marks annually in Finchingfield church (no. 263), when, in accordance with its terms, it was presumably returned to him. The identification of Walton is uncertain, but it is possibly East Walton, Norfolk, where a small estate was held in 1086 of Roger Bigod by Robert de Vals (*VCH Norfolk*, ii. 95). However, although the cartulary has *Norfok'* in the margin against this charter, the Reading monks appear to have used 'Norfolk' to include places in Suffolk as well, since charters concerning Dunwich (nos. 546–7) are classed as being in Norfolk both in the margins of A and in the folio headings of B. It is possible, therefore, that the present place is Walton, Suffolk, where in 1086 a certain Norman held the manor of Roger Bigod (*VCH Suffolk*, i. 476).

ADWELL

486 Final concord in the king's court at Westminster in the quindene of Easter, 14 Henry III, before Thomas of Moulton (*Muleton'*),
Stephen of Seagrave (*Segrave*), William of Raleigh (*Ralegh'*), Robert
of Lexington (*Lexinton'*), William of London (*Lond'*)*ᵃ* and master
Robert of Shardlow (*Sherdelawe*), justices, and others, between Abbot
Adam [of Lathbury] of Reading, seeking by Hugh of Fulford (*Fule-
ford'*) as attorney, and Aumary son of Robert, whom William son of
Aumary called to warranty and who warranted to him concerning
8½ virgates of land in Carswell (*Kersewell'*)*ᵇ* [Berks.]. The abbot
quitclaimed all his right in the said land to Aumary and his heirs.
In return Aumary gave and quitclaimed to the abbot and abbey of
Reading the homage and full service of William son of Richard and
his heirs from the tenement which he held of Aumary in Adwell
(*Adewell'*),*ᶜ* viz., 2 marks annually and the foreign service appurtaining to the tenement. This concord was made in the presence of the
said William, who acknowledged that he owed that service.

21 Apr. 1230

B f 174r; C f 103r–v

ᵃ London' *C*   *ᵇ* Kereswell' *C*   *ᶜ* Aldewell' *C*

The foot of this fine is PRO CP 25(1)/7/10/3. It is correctly classed as a Berkshire
fine, but is placed here under Oxfordshire as in the cartularies, since by it the abbey
acquired its interest in Adwell. Aumary son of Robert was lord of the manor of
Adwell (*VCH Oxon.*, viii. 8). Reading Abbey had acquired its land in Carswell (in
Buckland), probably in 1185 × 86, from Aumary son of Ralph, his grandfather (no.
769; *Cur. Reg. R.*, vi. 288), who had also held Adwell (*VCH Oxon.*, viii. 8). As is clear
from nos. 487–9, the tenement in Adwell whose lordship the abbey now acquired was
the mill and 11 acres of land.

487 Grant by Aumary son of Robert that William son of Richard
shall hold of Reading Abbey the mill of Adwell (*Aldewelle*) which he
formerly held of Aumary, and that all his men of Adwell shall do
suit of the mill. Whoever shall hold the mill shall have the whole
grinding (*molta*) of Aumary's house and of his heirs, with all fisheries
and water-courses belonging to the mill and all ways of access to
repair or improve the mill and its pond. Aumary and his heirs shall
not build nor cause or permit to be built a corn mill (*molendinum ad*

molendum) in the vill of Adwell or outside, nor alter the water-courses to the detriment of the mill. Those coming to the mill or pond shall have free access and exit through his land. Sealing. Witnesses[a] [omitted] [Apr. 1230]

B f 81v; C ff 40v-41r

[a] *Om. in C*

Contemporary with the final concord (no. 486).

488 Gift by Aumary son of Robert to Reading Abbey of the entire service of William son of Richard of Adwell (*Aldewell*') and his heirs, and of whatever Aumary used to receive from him for the mill and 11 acres of land in Adwell. To be held by the abbey freely and quit of all custom, exaction and secular service. Also grant that whoever shall hold the mill and 11 acres shall have free water-course to and from the mill and free pond, with all suit of the mill and the whole grinding (*molta*) of Aumary's house and of his heirs in the vill of Adwell. Warranty. Witnesses[a] [omitted] [Apr. 1230]

B ff 81v-82r; C f 41r

[a] *Om. in C*

Contemporary with nos. 486-7.

489 Notification by William son of Richard that he and his heirs are due to render annually to Reading Abbey at Reading 2 marks of silver for the mill of Adwell (*Aldewell*') at four terms of the year, viz., $\frac{1}{2}$ mark each at the Annunciation of St Mary, the Nativity of St John Baptist, Michaelmas and the feast of St Thomas the Apostle, for the faithful payment of which he has done homage to the abbot. Sealing. Witnesses[a] [omitted] [prob. Apr. 1230]

B f 82r; C f 41r

[a] *Om. in C*

Probably contemporary with nos. 486-8.

BOLNEY (IN HARPSDEN)

490 Gift in free alms by Richard son of Henry son of Alan *Blundus* of Bolney (*Bulehud*'),[a] at the instance of Walter almoner of Reading, to the almonry of Reading of the $\frac{1}{2}$ virgate of land in Bolney which his father Henry held by gift of the latter's father, Alan *Blundus*. To be held freely[b] by rendering annually to the lord of the fee or his

heirs 6d, viz., 3d each at the Annunciation of St Mary and Michaelmas, for all service and secular exaction, saving the king's service.
For this the almoner and his successors will provide him with food
and clothing in the hospital or elsewhere for life. Sealing. For greater
security Richard has delivered to the almonry the charter which his
father Henry had concerning the said ½ virgate, and has quitclaimed
all his right in the same. Witnesses [omitted].   [? *c.* 1220 × 31]

B f 158r; C ff 94v–95r; D f 46r (incomplete)

a Bulehude *C*, Bulehutha *D*   *b* *D omits all the following*

Dating very approximate and based on the occurrence of Walter, almoner of Reading, in or before 1231 (no. 710) and the probable succession of two other almoners
before 1240 (see no. 712 n.). This gift was made in the manor of Bolney held at this
time by Reginald de Blancmuster of the Honour of Giffard (see no. 493 n.).

490a   Note of a charter by Alan *Blundus* to Henry, his son, concerning land at Bolney (*Bulehud'*)   [*c.* early 13th cent.]

B f 158r

This was the charter handed over to Reading Abbey in no. 490.

491   Confirmation by Randulf*a* *Alein* to the almonry of Reading of
the preceding gift by Richard son of Henry of Bolney (*Bulehud'*)*b* in
Bolney. To be held*c* freely by rendering annually to him and his
heirs 6d, viz., 3d each at the Annunciation of St Mary and Michaelmas, for all service and secular exaction, saving the king's service.
Sealing. Witnesses*d* [omitted]   [? *c.* 1220 × 31]

B f 158v; C f 95r; D f 46r (incomplete)

a Rad' *D*   *b* Bulehude *C*, Bulehutha *D*
c *D omits all the following*   *d* *Om. in C*

Probably contemporary with no. 490 and certainly before June, 1247, when Rannulf
Aleyn was dead (*Oxon. Feet of Fines*, 135).

491a   Notes of the following:
  (i) charter by Matilda, widow of the same Randulf, concerning
       her dower of the same land;
  (ii) charter by Adam of Spaldington (*Spaudlinton'*) concerning the
       same;
  (iii) charter by Walter Giffard and Matilda, his wife, concerning
       the same land;
  (iv) charter by Albrea, widow of Henry son of Alan *Blundus*, con-
       cerning her dower of the same land   [not later than 1258]

B f 158v

Entered in the original section of B. The first two charters noted here suggest that Adam of Spaldington married Randulf Alein's widow; he certainly occurs with his wife, Matilda, from Apr. 1241 (*Oxon. Feet of Fines*, 115, 116, 134), but in June, 1247, he received by final concord land and rent in Bolney from Walter Aleyn in the presence of Matilda, widow of Rannulf Aleyn, who quitclaimed her dower right in the same (*ibid.*, 135).

492　Gift in free alms by Randulf *Alein* of Bolney (*Bulehud'*), with the assent of M(atilda) his wife, to the almonry of Reading of a croft in Bolney called *la Redecrofte*. Warranty and sealing. Witnesses[a] [omitted]　　　　　　　　　　　　　　　　[before June 1247]

B f 158v; C f 95r

[a] *Om. in C*

The donor was dead at the latest by June, 1247 (see no. 491 n.).

492a　Note of a charter by the same to Walter, his son, concerning the same land　　　　　　　　　　　　　　[before June 1247]

B f 158v

Date as for no. 492.

493　Confirmation in free alms by Reginald *de Blancmuster* of the gifts to the almonry of Reading by Randulf *Alein* of Bolney (*Bulehud'*)[a] and Richard son of Henry of, respectively, the croft called *la Readecrofte*[b] and ½ virgate of land, both in Bolney. For this the almoner of Reading has given him 20s sterling. Sealing. Witnesses[c] [omitted]　　　　　　　　　　　　　　[prob. before June 1247]

B ff 158v–159r; C f 95v

[a] *Bulehude C*　　　　　　[b] *Redecrofte C*　　　　　　[c] *Om. in C*

This confirms nos. 490 and 492, both of which are certainly before June 1247, when Randulf Alein was dead. In 1235–6 Reginald Blancmuster (*alias* de Albo Monasterio, *alias* of Whitchurch) held 1 knight's fee in Bolney of the Marshal portion of the Honour of Giffard (*Fees*, i. 446), the Honour having been divided in 1189 (Sanders, *English Baronies*, 62). He held this in right of his wife, Alice, one of the two daughters and co-heirs of Nicholas of Bolney, the other being Margery, wife of Alan of Farnham, all of whom occur in final concords in Bolney in 1237, 1241 and 1242 (*Oxon. Feet of Fines*, 235, 112–13, 237). In 1242–3 Reginald was said to hold of Matthew *de Culuber'*, who held of the Earl Marshal (*Fees*, ii, 828). He also held in a number of places in Berkshire (*VCH Berks.*, iii. 424; iv. 63, 513, 533) and was living as late as 1248 (Clanchy, *Berks. Eyre of 1248*, 38, 355–6).

HANBOROUGH

494 *Notification by King Henry I to the bishop of Lincoln and the sheriff, barons and faithful of Oxfordshire that he has given the church of Hanborough to Reading Abbey in free alms; and precept that the abbey shall hold it as well as it holds his other alms*   [c. 1130 × July 1133]

A f 14v; B ff 17v–18r
Pd. *Mon. Ang.*, iv. 41 (no. v); (cal.) *Regesta*, ii. 282 (no. 1863)

Henricus rex Angl(orum) episcopo Linc(olniensi) et vicecomiti et omnibus baronibus et fidelibus suis de Oxonefordsira, salutem. Sciatis me dedisse et concessisse in elemosinam deo et ecclesie *ª*de Rading(ia)*ª* ecclesiam meam de Haneberga cum terris et domibus et decimis et omnibus rectitudinibus illius ecclesie. Et volo et precipio quod bene et in pace et quiete teneat, sicut tenet alias elemosinas meas. Testibus:*b* W(illelmo) comite Warenn(e), et G(ervasio)*c* filio Rogeri, et Drogone de Monci. Apud Windr(esores).

ª–ª Rading' *B*
b *B ends*
c *See Regesta ii, loc. cit.*

The witnesses and place date suggest strongly that this was given at approximately the same time as no. 307. A note in B f 17v states that there were two copies (*Hec duplex est*). In 1086 Hanborough was held by Gilbert de Gant of the king in chief (*VCH Oxon.*, i. 419–20). He died *c.* 1095 (Sanders, *English Baronies*, 46) and was succeeded by his son Walter, from whom, according to a disclaimer of 1242 × 50, Henry I took Hanborough and two other manors and gave them for life to Walter's sister, the king's mistress (*Fees*, ii. 1158). It was no doubt while the manor was thus in the king's control that he detached the church (not mentioned in Domesday Book) and conveyed it to Reading.

495 *Gift in free alms by Simon de St Liz [III], earl of Northampton, to Reading Abbey of the church of Hanborough, as King Henry gave it*
[? 1156 × 57 *or* 1165 × 76]

A f 43v; B f 204v; C f 124v
Pd. Kennett, *Parochial Antiquities*, i. 140, 150

Simon de Senliz comes Norhamt(onie) episcopo Lincolnie, archid(iaconis), baronibus, iusticiariis, vicecomitibus, ministris, clericis, laicis et omnibus sancte ecclesie filiis per Oxonef(ord)sc(iram)*ª* constitutis, salutem. Sciant omnes tam presentes quam futuri me dedisse et concessisse et in perpetue possessionis elemosinam confirmasse deo et ecclesie sancte Marie de Rading(ia), pro salute anime mee et parentum meorum, ecclesiam de Haneberga*b* cum terris et decimis et omnibus ecclesie pertinentibus, sicut rex Henricus dedit et concessit in vita sua. Unde volo et precipio quod ecclesia de

Rading(ia) et monachi eam in perpetuum possideant et in pace teneant. Hi*ᶜ* sunt testes huius carte: Ricardus de Camvilla,*ᵈ* *ᵉ*Milo de Baalum, Hugo capellanus, Eustachius de Frisenvilla, Simon filius Rad(ulfi), Alexander de Arden, Willelmus de Insula.

ᵃ Oxenef˙syram *B*, Oxenef˙syram *C*
ᵇ Haneberhga *B*   *ᶜ* Hii *B,C*
ᵈ Canvill' *B,C*   *ᵉ* *B,C end with* et cetera

Dating uncertain, but the earl must be Simon de St Liz III, since an interest in the Gant manor of Hanborough can only have arisen from this earl's marriage to Alice, daughter and heir of Gilbert de Gant, earl of Lincoln, who died in 1156 (*Complete Peerage*, vi. 645; vii. 672). The marriage took place in 1156 (Robert of Torigny, 189) and Simon, son and heir of Simon de St Liz II, earl of Northampton and Huntingdon (d. 1153), was probably recognized as earl of Northampton 1156-7, but not thereafter until 1165 (*Complete Peerage*, ix. 664; *PR 11 Henry II*, 49, *12 Henry II*, 39). He was certainly earl of Northampton and Huntingdon from 1174 until his death in 1184 (*Complete Peerage*, vi. 645; ix. 664 and note *c*). For the problems involved in the identification and dating of the earls of Northampton and Huntingdon in the 12th century, see *Sir Christopher Hatton's Book of Seals*, 239. The first witness of the present charter is probably the Richard de Camville who died in 1176 rather than his son of the same name (*PR 3 and 4 Richard I*, xxv-xxvi). On the whole, the earlier of the suggested dating limits seems preferable, since Henry I was not infrequently called simply 'King Henry' in the early years of Henry II' reign. Moreover, although the disclaimer of 1242 × 50 shows that the manor of Hanborough did not follow the Gant descent after its removal by Henry I, it also states that the lady to whom he gave it for life died in Henry II's reign (*Fees*, ii. 1158), so that at the beginning of the reign there was still the possibility of its coming to Simon de St Liz after her death.

496 Precept by King Edward III to John of Eastbury (*Estbury*), his escheator in Oxfordshire and Berkshire, that, since it has been granted by royal charters that during an abbatial vacancy every possession of Reading Abbey shall remain to the prior and convent, he is to allow them in his bailiwick all possessions of the abbey now vacant by the death of Abbot Henry of Appleford (*Appulford*). If he has taken any issues from these possessions since the abbot's death, he is to restore them to the prior and monks   29 July 1361

B ff 184v-185r
Pd. (cal.) *Cal. Close R. 1360-64*, 197 (from Close Roll)[1]

Teste me ipso apud Swalewefeld' xxix. die mensis Julii, anno regni nostri tricesimo quinto.

[1] The Close Roll calls John of Eastbury escheator in Oxon., Berks. and Wilts. It notes similar letters to the escheators in Herefordshire, Warwickshire, Hertfordshire, Bedfordshire, Kent and Sussex. The precept has been located here under Hanborough, since in the cartulary it immediately follows no. 497, to which it has an obvious relevance.

497 Record of a plea *Quod permittat* brought by King Edward III against the abbot of Reading in respect of the church of Hanborough (*Hanebergh'*). Michael *Skyllyng'*, acting for the king, claims the king's right to present to the church by virtue of royal custody of the abbey, since after the death of Robert of Wardington (*Wardynton*), who was instituted on the presentation of Henry [of Appleford], late abbot of Reading, the church remained vacant until the vacancy of the abbey by the death of the said Abbot Henry. The abbot's attorney, John of Denton (*Denton'*), cites a charter by King John[1] confirming the privileges of the abbey as granted by King Henry I,[2] including the provision that on the death of an abbot every possession of the abbey should remain entirely to the prior and convent, since the abbot does not have his own revenues distinct from those of the convent; and he cites a confirmation of the same by the present king, dated 6 Edward III.[3] He further claims that the abbey has enjoyed this privilege since the time of Henry I's charter and at each vacancy has had the king's writ to his escheator in the said county to remove the king's hand, etc. The Crown replies that, since after each vacancy the new abbot applied for restitution of the abbey's temporalities, this admitted royal custody during vacancies as in the case of other abbeys of the king's patronage in England. Moreover, the charter by Henry I contains no express statement that the prior and convent should have advowsons and presentations during an abbatial vacancy, and the abbot does not claim that they had. The abbot answers that *omnis possessio* in Henry I's charter included all possessions, and that it is not alleged for the king that he or any of his progenitors ever had the presentation to any of Reading's churches during an abbatial vacancy since the making of that charter. In the recent vacancy the present king ordered by his writ, dated Swallowfield (*Swalewfeld'*) 29 July, 35 Edward III [1361],[4] and sent the tenor of the same to his justices, that the prior and convent should have every possession during that vacancy, by virtue of which writ the escheator delivered to the prior and convent all the possessions of the abbey in his bailiwick. Furthermore, the church of Hanborough was not vacant during the abbatial vacancy, and neither the present king nor any of his progenitors ever had the presentation to that church during an abbatial vacancy after the making of Henry I's charter. Both parties seek judgement. Judgment is given *ad presens* in favour of the abbot, saving the king's right, etc.   Michaelmas Term 1365

B ff 183v–184v

Rubric: De termino sancti Michaelis anno regni regis Edwardi tercii a Conquestu xxxix. Rotulo xxxvi.

The date of Abbot Henry of Appleford's death is unknown, but it had certainly taken place by 29 July, 1361 (see no. 496). Royal assent to the election of his successor, William of Dumbleton, was given on 15 Aug. 1361 (*Cal. Pat. R. 1361-64*, 52) and the relevant escheators were ordered to deliver the abbey's temporalities to him on 7 Sept. (*ibid.*, 58). However, also on 15 Aug. the king presented to the church of Hanborough by reason of the voidance of the abbey (*ibid.*, 53) and subsequently, on 7 Apr. 1365, presented again to the church by reason of the late voidance of the abbey (*Cal. Pat. R. 1364-67*, 102).

[1] No. 48.

[2] See no. 1.

[3] This is probably an error for 8 Edward III, the date of Edward III's inspeximus which ultimately confirmed King John's charter (no. 109), since no such confirmation in 6 Edward III is known.

[4] No. 496.

LASHBROOK (IN SHIPLAKE)

498   *Gift in free alms by Michael de Baseville to Reading Abbey of $\frac{1}{2}$ virgate of land and a strip of cultivated land in Lashbrook*   [prob. 1156 × 89]

A f 38r; B f 157v; C f 94r

Sciant presentes et futuri quod ego Michael de Basevilla[a] dedi et concessi deo et sancte Marie de Rading(ia) in liberam[b] et perpetuam elemosinam dimidiam virgatam terre quam Hardingus tenet in Lechebroch,[c] et totam illam culturam que est inter illam semitam que tendit de Winsisheche[d] ad vadum de Lechebroch,[e] cum curtillagiis[f] que sunt inter vadum et domum Estmundi, cum pratis et pasturis et omnibus ad prefatam terram pertinentibus, pro salute anime mee et omnium antecessorum et successorum meorum. Testibus:[g] Iurdano de Basevill(a), domina Ysabella de Sifrewast uxore mea, Gileberto de Basevilla nepote meo, Roberto de Basevill(a), et multis aliis.

[a] Baseville C	[b] *Insert* puram B,C
[c] Lechebrok B, Lechebroc C	[d] Winsishege B,C
[e] Lechebroc B, Lechebrok' C	[f] curtilagiis C
[g] B,C *end with* et cetera	

This gift was included in Richard I's general confirmation to Reading in Sept. 1189 (no. 34), but not in those of Henry II in 1156 × 57 (nos. 18-19). The origin of Michael de Baseville's tenure in Lashbrook is unclear, although a Gilbert de Baseville, who may be his nephew witnessing here, later acquired an interest in Shiplake by marriage (see no. 499, n.) and witnessed a deed concerning Sheffield, in Burghfield (Berks.), in 1197-8 (*Ancient Charters*, 107). Moreover, in 1175-6 Michael was certainly in possession of an estate at Whitley, near Reading (Berks.), a few miles away from Shiplake (*PR 21 Henry II*, 136, *22 Henry II*, 132). In 1194 he occurs with his wife Isabella (presumably Isabella de Sifrewast—cf. no. 819 n.) in a dower suit in Dorset (*Rot. Cur. Reg.*, i. 81-2).

499 Notification by Gilbert de Baseville (*Basevill'*)[a] that he and his heirs are bound to pay to Reading Abbey 26d annually at Michaelmas for the use and support of the poor; and, in order that the abbey may receive this sum more freely and certainly, appointment of Richard *de Fraxino* and his successors to pay the same annually to the almoner of Reading at the said term from the land which he held of Gilbert and his heirs in Lashbrook (*Lechebroc*).[b] The 26d will be allocated to Richard and his successors in their rent due to Gilbert and his heirs. In the event of non-payment of the 26d, the almoner may distrain on the chattels or tenement of Richard and his successors[c] [*c.* 1220 × 58]

> Original charter: BL Add. Ch. 19612
> B f 157v; C f 94r-v; D f 33v
> Pd. *Arch. Journ.*, xxii. 160; (cal.) Hurry, *Reading Abbey*, 173

His[d] testibus:[e] Simone vicario de Ssiplake, Joelo de Sancto Germano, Toma de Englefeld,[f] Gileberto Warino, Hugone de Fuleford, Henrico clerico, Roberto Wille, et multis aliis.

Endorsed: Carta Gileberti Basevill' de redditu .xxvi. d' apud Lechebroc de Ricardo de Fraxino percipiend' [*13th cent.*]
Size: 274 × 90 mm
Seal: large fragment of circular seal in white wax on tag; obverse: shield of arms (? Baseville); on reverse faint impression of counterseal.

[a] Basevile *D*	[b] Lechebrok' *C*, Lecchebroc *D*
[c] B,C end with T'	[d] Hiis *D*
[e] D ends	[f] *Original charter has* Englefelf

Entered in the original section of B. Simon vicar of Shiplake occurs in *c.* 1230, 1235 × 37 (as 'dean' of Shiplake) and 1242 (*Cartl. Missenden*, iii. 92-4, 85, 96) and in the period 1213 × 35 (*Rot. Hug. de Welles*, i. 178). The donor of the present charter is thus Gilbert de Baseville II, whose father Gilbert de Baseville I died on 18 May, 1212 (*Ann. Mon.*, ii. 273). For Gilbert II see *The 1235 Surrey Eyre*, ed. C. A. F. Meekings, i (Surrey Rec. Soc., xxxi, 1979), 167-8. His date of death is unknown, but he was apparently elderly in 1252, when he secured exemption for life from being placed on assizes, juries or recognitions (*Cal. Pat. R. 1247-58*, 151), and a reference to his heirs in Jan. 1259 suggests that he was by then dead (*Cal. Inq. P. M.*, i. 126). The problem is complicated by his being succeeded by his son, also called Gilbert, who died apparently in 1265 (*1235 Surrey Eyre*, i. 168). Of the other witnesses to this charter, Hugh of Fulford served as the abbot of Reading's attorney in 1227 and 1230 (see nos. 511, 486) and witnessed charters in 1226 × 30 and 1231 (nos. 395, 532), so that a date after *c.* 1220 seems likely. Although Gilbert II's main possessions were in Surrey and Sussex, he had an interest in Lashbrook probably via his father's marriage to Alice de Dunstanville, one of the daughters and eventual co-heirs of Alan de Dunstanville and Muriel de Langetot, daughter and co-heir of Emma de Langetot in the manor of Shiplake (*1235 Surrey Eyre*, i. 167; Farrer, *Honors and Knights' Fees*, iii. 38; *VCH Sussex*, iv. 41; *Cartl. Missenden*, iii. 83-88). Emma de Langetot was possibly the sister of Ralph de Langetot who witnessed the latter's charter to Reading in Lenborough (no. 261).

499a Note of a charter by Robert son of Rand(ulf) to W(illiam) son of Richard concerning *Hedhapeldorecroft* in Lashbrook (*Lechebroc*). [not later than 1258]

B f 157v

Entered in the original section of B.

500 Gift in free alms by William son of Richard *de Esenton*'[a] to the almonry of Reading of a croft called *Hedhapeldurecrofte* in Lashbrook (*Lachebroc*)[b] with a broad cart-track next to the fence of G. into the vill, as defined by fences on each side (*cum una lata via ad carettam iuxta sepem G. in vicum sicut sepes undique proportant*). To be held freely by rendering annually to Robert son of Rann(ulf) of Lashbrook (*Lechebroc*) and his heirs 12d, viz., 6d each at the Annunciation and Michaelmas, for all custom, demand and secular service, saving the king's service. Warranty and sealing. Witnesses[c] [omitted]
[not later than 1258]

B ff 157v–158r; C f 94v

[a] *Esentone C*   [b] *Lechbrok' C*   [c] *Om. in C*

Entered in the original section of B.

501 Confirmation by Robert son of Rand(ulf) of Lashbrook (*Lechebroc*) of the preceding gift, for the same annual rent to himself and his heirs and saving the king's service. Sealing. Witnesses[a] [omitted]
[not later than 1258]

B f 158r; C f 94v

[a] *Om. in C*

Probably contemporary with no. 500. Entered in the original section of B.

502 Lease, in chirograph form, by Abbot Richard [I] and the convent of Reading to Peter of Barrow (*Barue*) and Isabella, his wife, of $\frac{1}{2}$ virgate of land and a croft called *Redecroft* in Bolney (*Bulehud*'), which the abbey had by gift of Richard son of Henry and Randulf son of Alan,[1] and a croft called *Heieapeldorecroft* in Lashbrook (*Lachebroc*),[a] which William son of Richard gave to the abbey.[2] To be held freely by Peter and Isabella and their heirs in perpetuity by rendering annually to the almonry of Reading 5s, viz., 2s 6d each at

Michaelmas and Easter, for all custom, demand and secular service. The lessees shall acquit the lands against the chief lords for all dues, services and suits. In the event of non-payment of the rent, the abbey may distrain on the tenements and all chattels of the lessees and their heirs. For this Peter has given the abbey 1 mark of silver as entry-fine. Warranty and sealing, each party sealing with their seals the other's part. Witnesses [omitted]   [1238 × 58]

B f 159r; C f 95v

a Lachebrok' *C*

Since this is entered in the original section of B, the abbot is Richard I (of Chichester), 1238–62.

¹ See nos. 490, 492. Randulf son of Alan is clearly the same as Randulf *Alein.*
² See no. 500.

NEWNHAM MURREN

503 Bequest by Richard *Morin* to Reading Abbey of his body for burial there and, with it, gift in free alms, with the consent of his heir, of the following: all the land which Richard *Bertram* held of him; all the land which belonged to Roger *Prudhume*ᵃ which William *Wulurich*ᵇ held of the donor; 60 acres of arable land which were of his demesne, viz., 36 acres lying by Grim's Ditch (*Grimesdich*), whose heads adjoin the way called Tidgeon Way (*Tuddingweie*) and extend westward from it, 16 acres on the other side of the way extending on its eastern side from south to north, and 8 acres next that land towards the hospital¹ extending eastward from the way; 2 acres in his meadow of Newnham [Murren] (*Niweham*)ᶜ at the northern end next to *Waldich*, measured by the legal perch (*pertica*); 2 messuages which Ralph *de Ottevile* and Robert the porter (*portarius*) held of him, with 2 acres appurtenant to them and lying between them and the meadow; pasture in the same meadow for 1 plough-team of oxen (*carucata boum*) when the meadow is exposed to the oxen of the lord of the vill, and in other pasture appurtenant to the vill; and access to their land to plough [etc.], and to reach their land for any purpose. Also quitclaim of all right which the abbey claimed in half the water of the Thames along the length of his land between Mongewell (*Mungewelle*) and Wallingford Bridge (*pons de Walengeford*ᵈ), concerning which there has been a dispute between him and the abbey, and gift of the other half of that water, so that the abbey shall have the whole of the wter quit of all exaction and vexation; the abbey's fishermen are to have free access to the same with their nets over his meadow. Warranty and sealing.ᵉ

[prob. Jan. × Feb. 1219]

Original charter: BL Add. Ch. 19615
B ff 85v-86r; C ff 43v-44r
Pd. *Arch. Journ.*, xxii. 156–7; *Pal. Soc. Facs.*, 1st ser., pl. 216 (with facsimile); (cal.)
Hurry, *Reading Abbey*, 174

Hiis testibus: domino Ricardo Sar(esburiensi) episcopo, domino Johanne de Munemuþe, Ricardo filio domini regis Johannis, Henrico de Scacario, Walt(ero) Foliot', Henrico Foliot, Roberto de Braci, Hugone de Colverdune, Johanne de Wikenholte, Gaufr(edo) Marmiun, Hugone de Bixe, Nicholao de Chauseia, Hugone Morin, Ricardo Bertram, Willelmo de Huntescumbe, Hugone vinitario, Roberto filio Willelmi, et multis aliis.

Endorsed: Carta legacionis Ricardi Morin [*13th cent.*] de Niwenham [*later 13th cent.*]
Size: 224 × 211 mm
Seal: missing, three holes remaining in fold at bottom for cords

a Prudhumme *B*, Prudehumme *C*   *b* Wlurich *B,C*
c Niwenham *C*   *d* Walingford' *B,C*
e B ends with T', *C ends*

Richard Morin entered a monastery, presumably Reading, before 25 May, 1221 (*Excerpta e rot. fin.*, i. 65), but, since three of the witnesses including Richard Poore, bishop of Salisbury, were justices-in-eyre in Berkshire in 1219, the charter was almost certainly given during the main session of the eyre at Reading (see Clanchy, *Berks. Eyre of 1248*, xciii; and cf. no. 779, which was made at the same time and also concerned the water of the Thames). Richard Morin held 1 knight's fee of the Honour of Wallingford in 1201, 1201 × 12 and 1212 (*Rot. de Ob. et Fin.*, 150; *Red Bk. Exch.*, i. 145; *Fees*, i. 119).

1 The hospital of Crowmarsh Gifford, Oxon. (see below, nos. 507–8).

504 Quitclaim by Richard *Morin* to Reading Abbey of all the right which the abbey claimed in half the water of the Thames along the length of his land between Mongewell (*Mungewell'*) and Wallingford Bridge (*pons de Walingf'*), concerning which there has been a dispute between him and the abbey; and gift in free alms, with the consent of his heir, of the other half of that water; the abbey shall have the whole of the water quit of all exaction by him and his heirs. The abbey's fishermen shall have free access to the same with their nets over his meadow. Witnesses*a* [omitted]   [prob. Jan. × Feb. 1219]

B f 86r; C f 44r

a Om. in C

Probably contemporary with no. 503, whose text on the water of the Thames it follows closely.

505 Confirmation by William *Morin*, son of Richard *Morin*, to Reading Abbey of all his father's bequest, grant and gift in lands, waters, fisheries, meadows, pastures, messuages and all other things, as his father's charter witnesses. Warranty and sealing. Witnesses[a] [omitted]   [*c.* 1219 × 22]

B f 85v; C f 43v

[a] *Om. in C*

After no. 503 and before 23 June, 1222, by which time William Morin was dead (*Excerpta e rot. fin.*, i. 88). He may have died while on a pilgrimage to the Holy Land (see no. 507), and probably without heirs of his body (see no. 511 n.). It seems likely that he was the surviving younger son of Richard Morin (*ibid.*).

506 Notification by William *Morin* that he has handed over to Abbot S(imon) and the convent of Reading the rent of 5s from the land of Geoffrey English (*le Engleis*[a]) in the vill of Newnham [Murren] (*Neuham*)[b] as security (*vadium*) for the ½ mark of silver which the abbey has lent him in his great need, to be held until the debt is repaid. Witnesses[c] [omitted]   [*c.* 1219 × 22]

B f 85r; C f 43r

[a] Engleys *C*   [b] New(en)ham *C*   [c] *Om. in C*

Date as for no. 505.

507 Gift in free alms by William *Morin* to Reading Abbey of 61 acres of arable land of his demesne in the field of Newnham [Murren] (*Niwenham*),[a] viz., 16 acres in *Bechfurlang* extending northward from Grim's Ditch (*Grimesdich*), 5 acres at the head of these extending to the Icknield Way (*via que dicitur Ykenhilda*), 14 acres next to the land of William *Godday* in *Middelfurlang* in *Northfeld*, 6 acres extending from the said 21[1] acres as far as Icknield (*Ikenhilda*) by the land of William *Godday*, 10 acres in *Middelfurlang* next to the land which the abbey had from Richard *Morin*, the donor's father, and below that land towards the Thames in the south field, and 10 acres below Tidgeon Way (*Tudingeweya*) next to the crofts nearest the hospital of Crowmarsh [Gifford] (*Craumers*) and below the land which the abbey had from his father on the other side of the road; also of 1 acre of meadow in Newnham [Murren] next to the meadow which the abbey had from his father towards the south. Also grant that, by reason both of this land and of that given by his father, the abbey shall have all appurtenant right and easement in all the demesne pastures and common pastures of the vill. Warranty. For this the abbot and monks have given him, as their brother (*sicut* *fratri suo*), in his great need, 10½ marks of silver for his journey to the Holy Land. Witnesses[b] [omitted]   [*c.* 1219 × 22]

B f 85r; C f 43r

[a] Newenham *C*
[b] *Om. in C*

Date as for no. 505.

[1] Presumably the first two specified items of 16 acres and 5 acres.

508 Sale by William *Morin* to Reading Abbey of the corn crop growing on (*inbladatio et tota vestitura de*) the 10 acres next to the crofts nearest the hospital of Crowmarsh [Gifford] (*Craumers*) beside the road, which with other lands he has given to the abbey. For this and other things the abbey has given him 60s sterling. Sealing. Witnesses[a] [omitted]   [*c.* 1219 × 22]

B f 85r-v; C f 43r

[a] *Om. in C*

Date as for no. 505.

509 Notification by William *Morin* that on the Sunday in the middle of Lent (*dominica medie Quadragesime*) he received 60s from Reading Abbey by the hand of Richard son of Henry and W. son of Andrew for lands and the growing corn (*inbladatio*) of certain lands. The abbey was thus quit of all debts owed to him then and previously. Witnesses[a] [omitted]   [*c.* 1219 × 22]

B f 85v; C f 43r

[a] *Om. in C*

Date as for no. 505.

509a Note of a charter by Felicity, widow of Richard *Morin*, concerning her dower in Newnham [Murren] (*Nyweham*)

[? *c.* 1221 × *c.* 1230]

B f 86v

Probably not long after Richard Morin entered religion (see no. 503 n.), since, to judge from the terms of no. 503, he may well have been infirm and have died soon afterwards.

510 Quitclaim by Walter Bacon (*Bacun*) and Felicity [his wife],[a] widow of Richard *Morin*, to Reading Abbey of all Felicity's dower right in the land, rent and meadow of the free tenement of her late husband in the vill of Newnham [Murren] (*Neweham*),[b] which the abbey had by gift of the said Richard; also in 30 acres of land in Newnham [Murren], which the abbey had by gift of Nicholas of Cholsey (*Chels'*); all of which they claimed from the abbey and Nicholas by the king's writ of right in the court of Wallingford (*Walingf'*).*c* For this the abbey has given them 40s sterling. Swearing of faith (*affidavimus*) and sealing with their seals. Witnesses*d* [omitted]   [? *c.* 1221 × *c.* 1230]

B f 86v; C f 44r-v

a Not in text, supplied from rubrics   *b* Newenham C
c Walyngford' C   *d Om. in C*

Date in general as for no. 509a, but probably later than it.

511 Final concord in the king's court at Westminster in the quindene of Holy Trinity, 11 Henry III, before Hubert de Burgh (*Burgo*) earl of Kent and justiciar of England, Martin of Pattishall (*Pateshull'*),*a* Thomas of Moulton (*Mulet'*)*b* Thomas *de Haydene*, justices, and others, between Abbot Adam [of Lathbury] of Reading, plaintiff by Hugh of Fulford (*Fuleford'*) as attorney, and Ralph *Sansaver* and Matilda his wife, defending by the same Ralph as Matilda's attorney, concerning 6½ marks rent in Newnham [Murren] (*Neuham*)*c* which the abbot claimed from them for 140 acres of land, 3 acres of meadow and 18s 4d rent which they held of him in that vill by a fine made between them in the king's court at Westminster, which rent they were detaining. Settlement by fine, viz., that Ralph and Matilda recognized that the land, meadow and rent were the right of the abbot, and for this the abbot leased the same to them, except the fees and services of Richard *Bertram* and Richard *Produm'*d* and their heirs which are to remain to the abbot and abbey of Reading for ever. Ralph and Matilda and the heirs of Matilda shall render annually for the remainder 5 marks of silver instead of 6½ marks, viz., 16s 8d each at the Nativity of St John Baptist, Michaelmas, Christmas and Easter. Distraining clause for the abbot in the event of non-payment. Ralph and Matilda shall acquit their land, meadow and rent against the chief lords of the fee regarding all other services, customs and exactions, allowance being made to them for the foreign service of the fees of Richard *Bertram* and Richard *Prodom*.*d* In all other respects the previous fine between the parties is to remain in force   20 June 1227

A f 85r-v; B f 173v; C f 103r
Pd. (cal.) *Oxon. Feet of Fines*, 233 (from PRO foot: CP 25(1)/284/18/37)

a Pat'hill' *B*   *b* Muleton' *B,C*
c Niweham *B*, Nywenham *C*   *d* Prosdom *B,C and PRO foot*

The earlier fine between the parties (the abbot being Simon) was made in Jan. 1223 (*Oxon. Feet of Fines*, 67) and was presumably not entered in the Reading cartularies since it was superseded by the present fine. According to the 1223 fine, Richard son of Geoffrey Morin, Matilda's brother, was present and quitclaimed all his right to her and Ralph Sanzaver. In a case before the king's court in 1230, which involved Ralph and Matilda by voucher to warranty, reference was made to Richard Morin, Matilda's grandfather, and to Richard Morin, her brother, the latter of whom had given the manor of Newnham to Ralph Sanzaver with Matilda in free marriage (*Cur. Reg. R.*, xiv. 163-4); the charter of gift was inspected and confirmed by Henry III in May, 1231 (*Cal. Chart. R.*, i. 132). Moreover, in 1229 Ralph Sanzaver's wife (unnamed) was described as the grand-daughter and heir of the Richard Morin of King John's time (*Excerpta e rot. fin.*, i. 190). It is clear, therefore, that the younger Richard, who made the gift to Ralph and Matilda, was the grandson of the elder Richard, but it is equally clear that his (and Matilda's) father was not William Morin but Geoffrey Morin. When in 1222, following the death of William Morin, the latter's land came to the younger Richard, it came to him not as William's son, but significantly *tamquam filio primogeniti filii Ricardi Morin avi sui* (*ibid.*, 88). All this can mean no other than that Geoffrey Morin had been the elder son of the elder Richard Morin, but that William, the younger son, had succeeded his father, very possibly because Geoffrey had already died, and confirmed the father's bequests to Reading (no. 505). If, as seems likely, William died without heirs of his body, an opportunity then arose for the son of the elder brother successfully to assert his claim. From these details the following genealogy may be suggested:

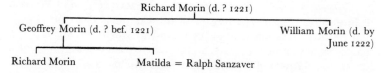

Richard Morin (d. ? 1221)

Geoffrey Morin (d. ? bef. 1221)   William Morin (d. by June 1222)

Richard Morin   Matilda = Ralph Sanzaver

If this reconstruction is correct, it is a further example of the primacy of a younger son's claim over that of the son of a predeceased elder son (cf. the succession to William de Mandeville, earl of Essex, in 1189, above, no. 390 n.).

512 Concession by Walter of Huntercombe (*Huntercumb'*),[a] knight, to Abbot R(obert) [of Burgate] and the convent of Reading of 5 marks annual rent from the tenement which Ralph *Sanzaver* and Matilda his wife sometime held of them in Newnham [Murren] (*Newenham*) outside Wallingford (*Walingford*), viz., 16s 8d each at Christmas, Easter,[b] the Nativity of St John Baptist and Michaelmas. If Walter or his heirs default in payment, the abbot and convent may distrain on all their movable and immovable goods in the same vill. He and his heirs or assigns are bound to do fealty to the abbot and his successors for the said tenement on succeeding to the tenancy. Sealing   31 Oct. 1278

B f 84v; C f 42v

Hiis testibus: dominis Alano filio Roaldi, Rolando de Erle,[c] Olivero de Punchardun, et Johanne de Chaus(eie),[d] militibus, domino Roberto Fuk', Willelmo de Bleobur', Johanne Lill', Thoma Huscarl', Nigello de Maundevil',ᵉ Adam de Burchild', Roberto de Preston', Reginaldo Aungevin,ᶠ Gileberto de Mulesham, et aliis. Dat' apud Westm(onasterium) die lune in vigilia Omnium Sanctorum, anno regni regis Edwardi sexto.

ᵃ Huntercumbe C
ᵇ B has Michaelmas with Pasche added later above; C has festum Pasche
ᶜ Erlee C   ᵈ Chause C
ᵉ Maundevill' C   ƒ? Aungevun' C

Walter of Huntercombe was recorded in 1278-9 as lord of the vill of Newnham, which he held of the Honour of Wallingford, and as owing Reading Abbey 5 marks annually as rent of assise (*Rot. Hund.*, ii. 777). For his involvement in the abbey's tenement, see no. 515. The Huntercombes had had an earlier interest in Newnham, however, since before 1219 a William of Huntercombe married Gunnora, niece of the elder Richard Morin (the donor to Reading in no. 503), who gave them 32s rent in Newnham as a marriage-portion (*Cur. Reg. R.*, xiv. 163-4; see also *The Sandford Cartulary*, ed. A. M. Leys (Oxfordshire Rec. Soc., xix, xxii, 1938-41), i. 29-33).

513 Memorandum that on the vigil of All Saints, 6 Edward I, Walter of Huntercombe (*Huntercumbe*) acknowledged before Thomas de Weylonde, John de Luvetot, Roger of Leicester (*Leyc'*) and William of Brompton (*Brumpton'*), justices of the Common Pleas (*de Banco*), that he owes Reading Abbey 15 marks, of which he will repay 5 marks each year for 3 years at the rate of 16s 8d at Christmas, Easter, the Nativity of St John Baptist and Michaelmas

31 Oct. 1278

B f 2v

This is clearly related to no. 512, which bears the same date, but precisely how is uncertain.

514 Notification by William of Barford (*Bereford'*), knight, that Abbot Nicholas [of Whaplode] and the convent of Reading have satisfied him, up to the date of these presents, in respect of all arrears of an annual rent of 5 marks which they have conceded to him by their bond (*scriptum obligatorium*), viz., to retain to himself by their assent the 5 marks which he owed them annually for the tenements he held of them in Newnham [Murren] (*Newenham*), in allocation of the said annual rent conceded to him by them. Given at Reading, Monday the feast of St Martin the bishop, 19 Edward II

11 Nov. 1325

B f 84v

Sir William of Barford was chief justice of the Common Pleas, 1309-26 (*DNB*, iv. 324-5). Following his death in 1326, the inquest post mortem, dated 2 Sept., stated that he held of Reading Abbey 80 acres of arable in Newnham at fee farm for an annual service of 5 marks (*Cal. Inq. P. M.*, vi. 471).

515 *An account of the history of Reading Abbey's land in Newnham* [*Murren*] *from its acquisition to the third quarter of the 14th century, with a description of its location* [1326 × 55]

B f 80r

Ricardus Moryn dedit centum acras arabiles et duas acras prati de manerio de Newnham abbati et conventui Rading' imperpetuam elemosinam tempore regis Johannis, et postea predictus abbas et conventus illas centum acras terre et duas acras prati eidem Ricardo et heredibus suis vendidit,[a] tenendo de predictis abbate et conventu et successoribus suis reddendo annuatim sibi et successoribus suis ad festum sancti Michaelis archangeli quinque marcas argenti. Predictus Ricardus tenuit predictam terram ad totam vitam suam et annuatim solvit predictum redditum predictis abbati et conventui. Et post decessum suum Willelmus Moryn filius suus et heres totam predictam terram et pratum pro eodem redditu tenuit et fideliter solvit per totam vitam suam. Et postea Radulphus[b] Sanzaver duxit in uxorem filiam predicti Ricardi Moryn sororem et heredem dicti Willelmi, qui totam terram et pratum Ricardi tenuit et fideliter predictum redditum solvit annuatim abbati et conventui. Et postea idem Radulphus vendidit predictam terram et pratum Henrico filio Ricardi. Henricus filius Ricardi vendidit eandem terram et pratum Andegero Sanzaver. Et idem Andigerus vendidit eandem terram et pratum Waltero Mouclerk' episcopo Cardeliensi,[1] qui dedit totam illam terram et pratum Willelmo de Huntercombe, qui quidem Willelmus et Willelmus filius suus et Walterus filius Willelmi predictam terram et pratum tenuerunt. Hii et omnes alii predicti predictum redditum predictis abbati et conventui annuatim fideliter solverunt. Et predictus Walterus vendidit totam predictam terram et pratum domino Rogero de Drayton', rectori ecclesie de Harewell'. Et modo predicte centum acre terre et pratum sunt in manus[a] domini Edmundi de Bereford. Iste centum acre terre iacent in quatuor particulis. Una particula iacet in uno le3 et extendit versus orientem in Techingwey. Et altera pars iacet versus Mongewell. Et tercia pars extendit versus occidentem. Et quarta particula sub Hykenyldewey et extendit versus austrum in Cirthwey, aliud capud super dominium domini extendens versus borialem. Et duo[a] acre prati iacent inter pratum comitis Oxon' et pratum domini et extendit in Tamis(iam).

[a] *Sic*   [b] *Ms has* Radulpus

This account was written during the tenancy of Sir Edmund of Barford, who succeeded his father William in 1326 and died 26 Sept. 1354 (*Cal. Inq. P. M.*, vi. 471; x. 213). It is obvious from the charters printed above that the early portion of this history is highly inaccurate; neither its genealogical details nor its dating can be trusted.

¹ Walter Mauclerc, bishop of Carlisle 1223/4–46.

OXFORD

516 Gift in free alms by Peter fitz Herbert, with the consent of Herbert his heir, to Reading Abbey, with his body, of his whole tenement (*curia*) with garden in Oxford (*Oxon'*). Sealing. Witnesses*a* [omitted]   [1204 × 35; ? 1235]

    B f 8ov; C f 4or

    a *Om. in C*

The donor was the son and heir of Herbert fitz Herbert, who died in 1204, and died himself in 1235 (Sanders, *English Baronies*, 8–9). The reference to his body makes it likely that this was a death-bed gift. The property had certainly come to the abbey by 5 Nov. 1235, when the king ordered that 'the messuage in the town of Oxford which Peter fitz Herbert gave to the abbot of Reading', having been taken into the king's hand for default in the payment of murage for which it was liable, should be restored to the abbot (*Close Rolls 1234–37*, 204).

517 Confirmation by Reginald fitz Peter to Reading Abbey of the gift by his father, Peter fitz Herbert, in Oxford [the original quoted his father's charter, but the cartularies have only: *Sciant presentes et futuri, et cetera ut supra*]; and gift of the right of advowson and patronage of the church of St John Baptist situated in the tenement (*in fundo eiusdem curie*). Warranty. Witnesses [omitted]   [? 1255]

    B f 8ov; C f 4ov

Probably contemporary with no. 518. Reginald was the younger son of Peter fitz Herbert and succeeded his elder brother, Herbert fitz Peter, in 1248 (Sanders, *English Baronies*, 9; cf. no. 299).

518 *Notification by Reginald fitz Peter, knight, to Henry [Lexington], bishop of Lincoln, that he has confirmed to Reading Abbey the gift by his father, Peter fitz Herbert, of his tenement with garden in Oxford; and has given in free alms the right of patronage of the church of St John Baptist in the tenement; with request that the bishop shall admit to that church whom the monks present as true patrons*   20 June 1255

    B ff 8ov-81r; C f 4ov

Venerabili in Christo patri H(enrico) dei gratia Linc(olniensi) episcopo suus*a* R(eginaldus) filius Petri, miles, salutem in domino.

Sancte paternitati vestre significamus quod, cum olim bone memorie P(etrus) filius Herberti, pater noster, quandam curiam cum gardino quam habuit in villa Oxon(ie) deo et beate Marie et monasterio Rading(ensi) monachisque ibidem deo servientibus cum corpore suo totaliter per cartam suam contulisset, nos dictam donationem ratam habentes ipsam predictis monasterio et monachis in perpetuum confirmavimus. Et insuper ius patronatus ecclesie Sancti Johannis Baptiste que sita est in eadem curia sive in eodem fundo, quod ad antecessores nostros et nos aliquando de iure spectabat, pro salute anime nostre et antecessorum nostrorum et successorum in puram et perpetuam elemosinam deo et beate Marie et predictis monasterio et monachis Rading(ensibus) pro nobis et successoribus nostris in perpetuum donavimus, concessimus et per cartam nostram confirmavimus. Quibus donationi, concessioni et confirmationi vestrum paternum implorantes assensum, rogamus et devote supplicamus quatinus presentatum ab eisdem ad dictam ecclesiam Sancti Johannis utpote a veris patronis et in posterum [*f 81r*] presentandos paterna sollicitudine admittere velitis. In huius rei testimonium presentes litteras nostras vobis et successoribus vestris ad perpetuam rei memoriam transmittimus patentes eisdem monasterio et monachis Rading(ensibus) ad eorum munimen perpetuum, si placet, remittendas. Hoc idem successoribus vestris quibuscumque presentibus litteris perpetuo valituris significamus. Dat' apud Crocham[b] anno gratie M.CC. lv, die dominica proxima ante festum Nativitatis sancti Johannis Baptiste. Valete.

[a] *Om. in C*
[b] Crokham *C*

The use of first person plural in this deed is notable. The abbey presented to the church of St John, Oxford, in 1265 (*Rotuli Ricardi Gravesend Diocesis Lincolniensis*, ed. F. N. Davis *et al.* (Canterbury and York Soc., 1925), 218). However, in 1266 the abbey conveyed its Oxford property to Walter de Merton and his heirs or assigns in perpetuity for an annual rent of 3s (*Merton Muniments*, ed. P. S. Allen and H. W. Garrod (Oxford, 1928), 18 with facsimile pl. IIIa) and it became the site of Merton College. The deed describes the property as follows: 'our whole tenement ... in the parish of the church of St John Baptist in Oxford, viz., our whole plot on the western side of the same church, formerly built upon but now vacant, to which tenement belongs the advowson of the said church.' See also *VCH Oxon.*, iii. 95. In 1279 the warden and scholars of Merton Hall held in demesne a *curia* in the parish of St John, Oxford, by gift of the abbot of Reading; they held from him as mesne lord for 3s annually and from the prior of St Frideswide's in chief for ½d annually (*Rot. Hund.*, ii. 801).

SHOWELL
(in Little Tew, formerly in Swerford)

519   *Final concord in the king's court at Westminster by which John Mar-*
shal quitclaimed to Reading Abbey his right in $1\frac{1}{4}$ virgates of land in Showell,
for which the abbey gave him 3s   28 Oct. 1195

B f 174v; C f 104r
Pd. (cal.) *Feet of Fines, Henry II and Richard I* (PRS, xvii, 1894), 42 (from PRO foot:
CP 25(1)/282/2/14)

Hec est finalis concordia facta in curia domini regis die festo Symonis
et Iude, anno regni regis Ricardi vii, apud Westm(onasterium),
coram   H(uberto)   Cant(uariensi)   archiepiscopo,   R(icardo)
Lond(oniensi) et G(ilberto) Roff(ensi) episcopis, R(adulfo) Here-
ford(ensi) et R(icardo) Elyensi archidiaconis, W(illelmo) de War-
end', H(enrico) de Cast(illione), Symone de Pateshill',[a] Ricardo de
Herierd', Osb(erto) filio Hervic(ii) et aliis fidelibus domini regis tunc
ibi presentibus, inter Iohannem Marescallum, petentem, et abbatem
et conventum de Rading(ia), tenentes per Robertum camerarium
positum loco abbatis et conventus ad lucrandum vel perdendum, de
una virgata terre et quarta parte unius virgate terre in Sevewell',
unde placitum fuit inter eos in prefata curia. Videlicet quod predictus Iohannes quiet(um)clamavit totum ius et clamium quod habuit
in terra illa prefatis abbati et conventui eius de se et heredibus suis
in perpetuum. Et pro hac quiet(a)clamatione predicti abbas et conventus dederunt prefato Iohanni tres solidos.[b]

[a] Patishull' *C*
[b] *PRO foot adds* argenti

This John Marshal appears to be identifiable with the probably illegitimate son of
John Marshal (d.s.p.l. 1194), elder brother of William Marshal, earl of Pembroke.
Being illegitimate he did not succeed to the Marshal estates. He died before 27 June
1235 (see *Complete Peerage*, viii. 525 n.*b*, 526; x. 360 and Appendix G, 96). Showell,
now represented by Showell Farm, was formerly a detached part of Swerford parish,
but since 1932 has been in the parish of Little Tew (see *VCH Oxon.*, xi. 247).

520   *Gift by Henry of Peasenhall and Mabel, his wife, to Reading Abbey*
of all their land in Showell, viz., $5\frac{1}{2}$ virgates, to be held of Adam de Sim-
plingeford', lord of the fee, as a quarter of a knight's fee, for which the
abbey has given them 34 marks, and to Adam 20s   [c. Oct. 1207]

A f 105r-v; B ff 83v-84r; C f 42r

Sciant presentes et futuri quod ego Henricus de Pesehale et Mabilia
uxor mea, pro magna necessitate et utilitate nostra et heredum et
infantum nostrorum, dedimus et[a] concessimus et presenti carta nos-

tra confirmavimus domui de Rading(ia) et abbati et conventui eiusdem loci totam terram nostram [*f 105v*] de Sevewelle cum omnibus
pertinentiis suis, videlicet quinque virgatas terre*b* et dimidiam cum
pratis et pasturis, cum hominibus nostris de eadem villa et tota
progenie sua et sequela, et omnibus aliis rebus ad predictam terram
et ad predictos homines pertinentibus. Habendum et tenendum iure
perpetuo de Adam de Simplingeford',*c* domino feodi, libere et
quiete, integre et plenarie, per regale servitium quod nos eidem Ade
facere consuevimus, videlicet*d* per quartam partem feodi unius militis, pro omni servitio et exactione, absque omni calumpnia et demanda que eis a nobis vel heredibus aut successoribus nostris uncquam*e* fieri possit. Hoc autem tactis sacrosanctis evangeliis*f* tam ego
Henricus quam Mabilia uxor mea fideliter tenendum*g* iuravimus, et
totam predictam terram cum omnibus pertinentiis a nobis adiura-
tam*h* predictis abbati et conventui de Rading(ia) quietam clamavi-
mus de nobis et de omnibus heredibus et successoribus nostris in
perpetuum, et plenariam saisinam eis inde fecimus. Hanc etiam
terram cum omnibus predictis contra omnes homines et *i*contra
omnes*i* feminas et*a* nos et heredes nostri predictis abbati et conventui
in perpetuum warantizabimus. Et ad hoc fideliter observandum ego
Henricus et Mabilia uxor mea presenti scripto sigilla nostra apposuimus. Pro hac autem donatione, concessione, conventione et confirmatione dederunt nobis predicti abbas et monachi de Rading(ia)
triginta et quatuor marcas argenti, et Ade de Simplingeford',*c* domino feodi, viginti solidos sterlingorum pro concessione et confirmatione sua.*j* Hiis testibus.

a Om. in C	*b* Om. in B,C
c Simplingf' B, Simplingford' C	*d* scilicet B,C
e unquam B,C	*f* ewangeliis C
g A has tenendam	*h* abiuratam B,C
i-i Om. in B,C	*j* B ends with T', C ends

Probably contemporary with, or a little before, the final concord (no. 522). Mabel
appears to have been a relative of Adam de Simplingford, for she is probably the
Mabel daughter of Robert de Simplingford who in 1197 received by final concord
from Hugh de Simplingford and Adam, his son, 5½ virgates in Showell to be held as
a quarter of a knight's fee (*Feet of Fines, 9 Richard I*, 74–5 (no. 105); *Oxon. Feet of Fines*,
3).

521 *Confirmation of the same by Adam* de Simplingeford, [*and grant*]
*that the abbot shall acquit him and his heirs against the king for the foreign
service of a quarter of a knight's fee, for which the abbey has given him 20s*
[*c.* Oct. 1207]

A f 105v; B f 83v; C f 43v

Sciant presentes et futuri quod ego Adam*a* de Simplingeford*b* concessi et presenti carta mea confirmavi abbati et conventui de Rading(ia) donationem et concessionem quam Henricus de Pesehale et Mabilia uxor sua eis fecerunt de tota terra sua in Sevewell'*c* quam de me tenuerunt, videlicet de quinque virgatis terre et dimidia, cum pratis et pasturis et omnibus pertinentiis suis. Tenendas de me et de heredibus meis iure perpetuo libere et quiete, integre et plenarie*d* per servitium regale, videlicet per quartam partem feodi*e* unius militis, pro omni servitio, demanda et exactione. Ita videlicet quod idem abbas et successores sui quietabunt me et heredes meos de predicto forinseco servitio versus dominum regem. Et ego et heredes mei predictam terram cum omnibus pertinentiis suis predicto abbati et ecclesie de Rading(ia) contra omnes homines et *f*contra omnes*f* feminas in perpetuum warantizabimus. Et pro hac concessione et confirmatione dederunt mihi predicti abbas et monachi de Rading(ia) viginti solidos sterlingorum.*g* Hiis testibus.

a Interlined in A	*b* Simplingford B,C
c Sewell' B	*d* plene C
e feudi B,C	*f-f* Om. in B,C
g B ends with T', C ends	

Probably contemporary with no. 520. Adam *de Simplinges* held half a knight's fee of the king in chief in Oxfordshire in 1212 (*Fees*, i. 104). See also *Red Bk. Exch.*, i. 176.

522 Final concord in the king's court at Westminster in the octave of Michaelmas, 9 John, before Geoffrey Fitz Peter earl of Essex, master Eustace de Fauconberg (*Falcobergio*), John *de Gestleng'*, Walter of Creeping (*Crepping'*),*a* justices, and others, between Abbot Elias of Reading, by the monk Simon as attorney, and Henry of Peasenhall and Mabel his wife, concerning $5\frac{1}{2}$ virgates of land in Showell. Plea of warranty of charter. Henry and Mabel recognized the land to be the right of the abbot and abbey of Reading and conceded the same, to be held of Adam *de Simplingeford'*,*b* chief lord of the fee, and his heirs for the foreign service of a quarter of a knight's fee. Warranty. For this the abbot gave them 34 marks. Adam was present and granted this, and further granted that the abbot and his successors should acquit the said land of the foreign service to the king on behalf of Adam and his heirs. Warranty by Adam and his heirs. For this the abbot gave Adam 20s sterling   6 Oct. 1207

B f 174r-v; C ff 103v-104r

Pd. (excl. justices' names) *Oxon. Feet of Fines*, 38-9 (from PRO foot: CP 25 (1)/187/2/84)

a B,C have Cressing' (*in error*); *PRO foot has* Crepping
b Simplingford' C

This is clearly a judicial fortification of nos. 520-1. See also *Cur. Reg. R.*, v. 87, 92.

522a Note of a charter by Henry of Peasenhall[a] to John son of William concerning 1 virgate of land in Showell (*Sewell'*)

[1197 × 1207]

B f 84r; C f 42r

[a] *The note has* eiusdem, *but, since it follows no. 520, perhaps Henry and Mabel his wife are intended*

After the fine of 1197 (see no. 520 n.) and before no. 520.

523 *Gift in free alms by William* de Pikeshulle *and Alice, his wife, to Reading Abbey of all their land in Showell, viz., 6 virgates, of which 2 virgates shall be in the abbey's demesne or otherwise as it pleases, and the other 4 shall be held at rent by the donors and their heirs* [1200 × 1213]

A f 105v; B f 83r; C f 42r

Sciant presentes et futuri quod ego[a] Willelmus de Pikeshulle[b] et Aliz uxor mea dedimus et concessimus et presenti carta nostra confirmavimus deo et sancte Marie et abbati et monachis de Rading(ia) totam terram nostram de Sevewell',[c] videlicet sex virgatas terre cum omnibus pertinentiis suis, in liberam et[d] puram et[a] perpetuam elemosinam. Ita quod habeant et teneant inde duas virgatas cum[e] pertinentiis libere et absolute in dominico suo, vel sicut eis melius placuerit, illas scilicet quas Ricardus de Cimiterio et Gillebertus filius Godwini tenuerunt, et nos et heredes nostri tenebimus de predictis abbate et monachis reliquas quatuor virgatas, reddendo inde eis annuatim quatuor solidos pro omni servitio, salvo servitio domini regis, ad duos terminos, videlicet ad festum sancti Martini duos solidos et ad festum sancti Iohannis Baptiste duos solidos. Et nos et heredes nostri warantizabimus predictam terram prefatis abbati et conventui[f] contra omnes homines et [g]contra omnes[g] feminas. Et ut hec concessio nostra firma et stabilis in perpetuum permaneat, eam presenti scripto et sigillorum nostrorum appositione roboravimus.[h] Hiis testibus.

[a] *Om. in C*	[b] Pik'hull' *B*, Pikhull' *C*
[c] Sewell' *B,C*	[d] *Om. in B*
[e] *Insert* omnibus *C*	[f] monachis *B,C*
[g-g] *Om. in B,C*	[h] *B ends with* T', *C ends*

The dating limits are those of Elias's abbacy (see no. 523a).

523a Note of a charter by Abbot Elias to the same W(illiam) concerning 4 virgates of land in Showell (*Sewell'*) [1200 × 1213]

B f 83r

This is presumably the grant of the lease of 4 virgates provided for in no. 523.

524 *Confirmation by Adam* de Simplingeford *to Reading Abbey of the gift by William* de Pik'hull' *and Alice, his wife, of 6 virgates of land in Showell, of his fee, and grant that the abbey shall acquit him and his heirs against the king for the royal service of a quarter of a knight's fee on that land*   [1200 × 1213]

B f 83r-v; C f 42r

Sciant presentes et futuri quod ego Adam de Simpling'ford'[a] concessi et presenti carta mea confirmavi donationem et concessionem W(illelmi) de Pik'hull'[b] et Aliz(e) uxoris sue quam fecerunt deo et sancte Marie et abbati et monachis de Rading(ia) de tota terra sua de Sewell',[c] que est de feodo meo, videlicet de sex virgatis terre cum omnibus pertinentiis suis, [*f 83v*] habendas et tenendas in liberam, puram et perpetuam elemosinam, sicut carta predictorum W(illelmi) et Alize testatur. Concessi etiam quod predicti abbas et monachi adquietent me et heredes meos versus dominum regem de servitio regali quod est super terram illam, scilicet de quarta parte feudi unius militis, ita quod nec ego nec heredes mei aliquam demandam faciemus alicui de prefata terra, set libera et quieta et absoluta sit in manibus predictorum abbatis et monachorum de Rading(ia) in perpetuum. T(estibus).[d]

[a] Simplingford' *C*   [b] Pikhull' *C*
[c] Sewelle *C*   [d] *Om. in C*

Contemporary with no. 523, which it confirms. Since Adam held half a knight's fee in Oxfordshire in 1212 (see no. 521 n.), the effect of nos. 520 and 523 was to place the whole amount in the hands of Reading Abbey (cf. no. 528).

525 *Confirmation by John son of William* de Picheshulle *of his parents' gift to Reading Abbey of 6 virgates of land in Showell*
          [prob. early 13th cent.]

A f 106v; B f 83r; C f 41v

Sciant presentes et futuri quod ego Iohannes filius Willelmi de Picheshull'[a] concessi et presenti carta mea confirmavi donationem et concessionem Willelmi patris mei et Alice[b] matris mee quam fecerunt deo et sancte Marie et abbati et monachis de Radinges de tota terra sua de Sevewell',[c] videlicet de sex virgatis terre cum omnibus pertinentiis suis, habendas et tenendas in puram et perpetuam elemosinam, sicut carta patris mei et matris mee testatur.[d] Hiis testibus.

[a] Pik'hull' *B*, Pikhulle *C*   [b] Alize *B,C*
[c] Sewell' *B,C*   [d] *B ends with* T', *C ends*

This deed is entered in A with 13th-century deeds of before *c.* 1230, including nos. 520, 521 and 523. It cannot be earlier than the earliest date for no. 523.

525a Note of a charter by the same to Muriel [*de Vernun*]¹ concerning 1 virgate of land in Showell (*Sewell'*)   [? *c.* 1220]

B f 83r; C f 41v

Possibly of about the same time as his chirograph with Reading Abbey (see no. 526 n.).

¹ For her name, see no. 526.

526 Release and quitclaim by Hugh de Bosco, son of John *de Pik'hull'*,ᵃ to Reading Abbey of the 4 virgates of land in Showell (*Sevewelle*) which Adam *de Fenne*, Geoffrey of Rollright (*Rollendrith*), Gilbert son of *Goldeya* and Alexander *ante portam* sometime held of him; and confirmation and quitclaim of 1 virgate of land in Showell which Muriel *de Vernun* sometime held. Warranty, saving 6s rent annually from the abbey to Alan son of William *de Pik'hull'*.ᵇ For this the abbey has given Hugh in his great need 15 marks sterling, a robe and a rouncey worth 20s. Sealing. Witnessesᶜ [omitted]
[? 1227 × 58]

B f 84r; C f 42v

ᵃ Pikhull' *C*   ᵇ Pikhulle *C*   ᶜ *Om. in C*

On 10 Aug. 1220 Hugh's father, John son of William *de Pikeshull'*, demised to Reading Abbey for 7 years all his land of Showell, viz., 5 virgates, of which 2 he had in demesne and 3 were held of him. The abbey was to hold this land with all rights, including the crops, in addition to the crop of 38 acres which John had earlier sold to the abbey with meadow and hay. After the 7 years, the land would return to John and his heirs. No rent wss specified, but the abbey gave John £7 sterling in his great need to recover his inheritance elsewhere (BL Add. Ch. 19613). The agreement was not entered in the abbey's cartularies. However, although the date of John's death is unknown, the termination of this agreement in Aug. 1227 provides the earlier terminus for the present release and quitclaim. The later terminus is derived from the fact that the latter was entered in the original section of B.

526a Notes of the following:
(i)   charter by Adam *de Simplingford'* to Alan son of W(illiam) *de Pik'hull'* concerning 4 virgates of land in Showell (*Sewell'*);
(ii) confirmation by William son of Adam to the same Alan concerning the same land

B f 84r

From the details in nos. 525–526a the following genealogy may be suggested:

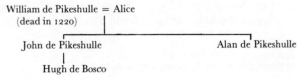

527   *Grant by Eleanor, countess of Salisbury, to Reading Abbey and its men of Showell of quittance of the hundred of Wootton*

[prob. 1205 × 33; poss. *c.* 1205 × 1213]

A f 100v; B f 84r; C f 42v

Sciant presentes et futuri quod ego Alienora comitissa de*ᵃ* Sar(esburia) dedi et*ᵃ* concessi et hac presenti carta*ᵇᶜ* confirmavi, pro salute mea et omnium antecessorum et successorum meorum, abbati et conventui de*ᵃ* Rading(ia) et omnibus hominibus suis de Sevewell' omnimodam libertatem et quietantiam de hundredo et de omnimodis sectis hundredi mei de Wutton',*ᵈ* et de hidagiis et wardis, et de visu *ᵉ*franci pleggii,*ᵉ* et de omnibus ad hundredum et ad predictum visum pertinentibus, et*ᶠ* auxiliis et*ᵍ* exactionibus, demandis et de omnibus omnino rebus ad me et ad meos*ʰ* spectantibus de terris et tenementis, rebus et catallis et omnibus hominibus suis de Sevewell'. Et ut hec mea concessio firma sit et stabilis, eam presenti scripto *ⁱ*meo et*ⁱ* sigilli mei appositione roboravi.*ʲ* Hiis testibus: Roberto Porchet, Reginaldo de Valle, Willelmo Pippard, Hugone de Didenham, et multis aliis.

ᵃ Om. in C	*ᵇ Om. in B*
ᶜ Insert mea *C*	*ᵈ A has* (?) Winton'; *B, C have* Wtton'
ᵉ⁻ᵉ francplegii *B,* franciplegii *C*	*ᶠ Insert* de *B,C*
ᵍ Om. in B,C	*ʰ* nos *C*
ⁱ⁻ⁱ et *B; om. in C*	*ʲ B ends with* T', *C ends*

The grantor was the widow of William fitz Patrick, earl of Salisbury, her third husband, who died in 1196. She married fourthly, by 1198, Gilbert de Malesmains and died between 31 May 1232 and 12 Aug. 1233 (*Complete Peerage*, xi. 378–9). The manor and hundred of Wootton were part of her dower from her first marriage to William Paynel (*Fees*, i. 11; *VCH Oxon.*, xi. 3, 265), and after her fourth husband's defection to France in 1205 she held it and her other possessions in England (*Complete Peerage*, xi. 378; *Rot. Lit. Claus.*, i. 285). The charter probably dates, therefore, not earlier than 1205 and possibly to the time of Reading Abbey's main acquisitions in Showll (nos. 520, 523).

528   Mandate by King Henry III to the barons of the Exchequer that, whereas it is granted by the charters of previous kings that Reading Abbey shall be quit of scutage in lands already acquired and yet to be acquired, and although it may not have enjoyed this liberty in lands acquired after that grant, nevertheless of the king's special grace the liberty is now confirmed and the abbey is to be quit of the scutage which is being demanded by summons of the Exchequer for half a knight's fee in Showell (*Sevewell'*)

20 July 1232[1]

A f 33v; B f 38v; C f 12v
Pd. *Close Rolls 1231–34*, 88 (from Close Roll)

Teste me ipso apud Lamehuth', xx. die Julii, anno regni nostri xvi.*
*Per dominum Karl(eolensem).

a All cartularies have xv, *but see note 1*
b Insert Dat' *B,C*

¹ The year-date is that given on the Close Roll, whereas the cartularies have 1231. The latter cannot be correct, however, since on 20 July, 1231, the king was in Gloucester (*Close Rolls 1227–31*, 531–2).

529 *Gift by John des Préaux to Hugh de Strepini of 12 acres of meadow between Little Tew and Showell, nearest on the eastern side to the plot of meadow which Rannulf [de Blundeville], earl of Chester, gave to Hugh de Colonces* [c. 1206 × 1231]

A f 105r; (noted) B f 82v; C f 41r¹

Sciant presentes et futuri quod ego Iohannes de Pratellis dedi et concessi et hac presenti carta mea confirmavi Hugoni de Strepenni, pro humagio et servitio suo, duodecim acras de prato meo que sunt inter Parvam Tywam et Sevewell' proximas ex parte orientali illi parti prati quam R(annulfus) comes Cestrie dedit Hugoni de Culvunches, in longitudine vero extensas a semita que dirigitur a Parva Thiwa ad Sevewelle usque ad torrentem qui currit ex parte australi prati mei. Tenendas de me et de heredibus meis ipsi et suis quos in heredes facere voluerit libere et quiete, pro omni servitio et pro omni exactione reddendo annuatim mihi vel heredibus meis dimidiam libram piperis ad Nativitatem sancti Iohannis Baptiste. Ego autem et heredes mei warantizabimus predictas duodecim acras predicto Hugoni et heredibus quos mihi* fecerit contra omnes homines. Hiis testibus.

a Sic

Not earlier than *c.* 1206, when Rannulf earl of Chester gave the larger part of Great Tew to John des Préaux (*VCH Oxon.*, xi. 229), and certainly before Nov. 1231 (see no. 532); however, since it is also earlier than nos. 530–1, probably well before 1231. The meadow was in Little Tew but appurtenant to the lordship of Great Tew (see no. 532 n.).

¹ The note in B and C refers to two charters by John to Hugh concerning these 12 acres of meadow.

529a Note of a confirmation by Rannulf [de Blundeville], earl of Chester, to Hugh *Strepinni* concerning 12 acres of meadow in Showell (*Sevewell'*) [c. 1206 × 1231]

B f 84r

Date as for no. 529.

530 *Gift by Hugh de Strepini to Reading Abbey, with his body, of 12 acres of meadow between Little Tew and Showell, which John des Préaux gave him*   [*c.* 1206 × 1231]

A f 104r; B f 82v; C f 41r

Sciant presentes et futuri quod ego Hugo de Streppinni,[a] intuitu dei et pro salute anime mee, dedi et concessi et presenti carta mea confirmavi deo et sancte Marie et ecclesie de Rading(ia), cum corpore meo, duodecim acras prati inter Parvam Tywam et Sevewell',[b] quas dominus meus Iohannes de Prawes[c] dedit mihi pro servitio meo. Habendas et tenendas abbati et conventui de Rading(ia) iure perpetuo per servitium dimidie libre piperis predicto Iohanni et heredibus suis annuatim solvendum ad festum sancti Iohannis Baptiste pro omni servitio.[d] Hiis testibus: Iohanne filio Hugonis, Iohanne de Wekenholt, Hugone paupere, Willelmo de Barton', Alexandro decano de Swereford, Alexandro filio ipsius, Rad(ulfo) de Wocton', Roberto del Broc, et multis aliis.

[a] Strepinni *B*, Strepenn' *C*	[b] Sevewellam *B,C*
[c] Parawes *C*	[d] *B ends with* T', *C ends with* et cetera

Date as for no. 529, but possibly not later than *c.* 1220. John de Wickenholt was sheriff of Berkshire 1204–15 and a justice-in-eyre there in 1219. Alexander dean of Swerford witnessed a charter to Osney Abbey in 1189 (*Cartl. Oseney*, iv. 375; *Ann. Mon.*, iv. 43) and a Reading Abbey deed concerning Showell in 1220 (BL Add. Ch. 19613); he may be the Alexander of Swerford who was archdeacon of Salop, Lichfield diocese, in 1221 and 1232 (J. Le Neve, *Fasti Ecclesiae Anglicanae*, ed. T. D. Hardy (Oxford, 1854), i. 573) and sheriff of Berkshire in 1232 (*List of Sheriffs*, 6). For Hugh Paupere at dates between 1205 and *c.* 1220, see *Cartl. Oseney*, v. 210; iv. 212 etc.; vi. 18 etc.

531 *Confirmation by John des Préaux of the same in free alms for the annual render of ½ lb of pepper. The abbey and its men shall have reasonable access over his meadow and common of pasture in his whole meadow between Little Tew and Showell after the hay has been removed. For this the abbey has received him into special confraternity*   [*c.* 1206 × 1231]

A f 104r; B f 82v; C f 41v

Sciant presentes et futuri quod ego Iohannes de Pratellis concessi et presenti carta mea confirmavi deo et beate Marie et abbati et conventui de[a] Rading(es) donationem quam Hugo de Streppeni[b] eis fecit de duodecim acris prati quas dedi et concessi et carta mea confirmavi eidem Hugoni pro servitio quod fecerat mihi et antecessoribus meis, illas videlicet que sunt inter Parvam Tywam et Sevewell'[c] proximas ex parte orientali illi[d] parti prati quam Rannulfus comes Cestrie dedit Hugoni de Culunches, in longitudine vero extensas a semita que dirigitur a Parva Tywa ad Sevewell' usque ad torrentem qui currit ex parte australi prati mei. Et volo et finaliter concedo quod predicti abbas et conventus de Radinges habeant et teneant totum*e* predictum pratum cum omnibus que ad predictum pratum pertinere possunt omni tempore tancquam*f* de dono meo iure perpetuo et in liberam, puram et perpetuam elemosinam. Ipsi tamen, in recognitionem advocationis mee, reddent mihi et heredibus vel successoribus meis dimidiam libram piperis annuatim ad festum sancti Iohannis Baptiste pro omnibus rebus que uncquam*g* ad me vel ad successores meos pertinere vel a predicto tenemento exigi poterunt. Concessi etiam predictis abbati et conventui et suis quod habeant rationabilem introitum et exitum super pratum meum ad eundum et veniendum et ad attrahendum fenum suum, et quod habeant communem pasturam in toto prato meo quod est inter Parvam Tywam et Sevewell'*h* quando fenum asportatum fuerit. Ego autem et heredes et successores mei warantizabimus predictis abbati et conventui predictas duodecim acras cum omnibus pertinentiis contra omnes homines et contra*i* omnes feminas. Predicti vero abbas et conventus receperunt me in specialem fraternitatem domus Rading(ensis) et concesserunt michi et omnibus antecessoribus et successoribus et omnibus meis communionem omnium spiritualium bonorum que fiunt vel fieri poterunt in ecclesia sua in perpetuum.*j* Hiis testibus: Alexandro decano de Suereford, Alexandro de Mildecumb', Willelmo de Barton', Iacobo de Bissech', Henrico de Covintria, Rog(ero) Iugelett', Waltero filio Alani, Symone de Pratell(is), Roberto Russell', Roberto de Berler', Reinaldo senescallo, Henrico de Camel, Roberto de Sideham, Roberto pincerna, et multis aliis.

a Om. in C   *b* Strepinni B,C   *c* Sewell' B,C
d A had originally illi(us), the us abbreviation being then erased
e Om. in B,C   *f* tanquam B,C   *g* unquam B,C
h Sevewelle C   *i* Om. in C   *j* B ends with T', C ends

Date in general as for no. 530. Roger Jugelet held $\frac{1}{2}$ hide in Great Tew by gift of Rannulf, earl of Chester, probably from before *c.* 1206 (*VCH Oxon.*, xi. 236; cf. *The English Register of Godstow*, ed. A. Clark (Early English Text Soc., 1905–11), 550–1). Reginald the steward witnessed Reading Abbey deeds in 1186 × 1213 and 1204 × 20 (nos. 842, 892); also Henry de Camel in 1204 × 20 (no. 892); and Robert de Sideham in 1204 × 20, 1213 × 15 and 1216 (nos. 892, 778, 393).

532 *Notification by John des Préaux that, whereas he had sometime confirmed to Reading Abbey 12 acres of meadow between Little Tew and Showell, extending from the path between Little Tew and Showell to the stream running to the south of his own meadow, and because that path is often moved on account of uncertainty about its location, at the request of Abbot Adam [of Lathbury] he has with his own hands set up definite stone boundary marks by the view of his men of Tew and the men of Showell. All meadow within these*

*bounds the abbey shall hold for the ½ lb of pepper which it renders to him and
his heirs and successors on the feast of St John Baptist* 2 Nov. 1231

B ff 82v-83r; C f 41v

Sciant presentes et futuri quod, cum^a ego Johannes de Pratell(is)
aliquando concessissem et per cartam meam confirmassem abbati et
conventui Rading' .xii. acras prati inter Parvam Tywam et Sewell'
proximas ex parte orientali illi parti prati quam Rann(ulfus) comes
Cestr(ie) dedit Hugoni de Cunches et in longitudine extensas a semita que dirigitur a Parva Tywa ad Sewell' usque ad torrentem
[f 83r] qui currit ex parte australi prati mei, quia semita illa sepius
removetur de loco in locum propter incertitudinem semite ad petitionem domini Ade tunc abbatis Rading(ensis)^b per visum et considerationem proborum hominum meorum de Tywa et hominum de
Sewell' manibus meis petras posui ipsasque certas metas constitui.
Quare volo et pro omnibus heredibus et successoribus meis firmiter
precipio quod abbas et monachi de Rading(ia) quiete et in pace et
cum omnibus libertatibus habeant et teneant totum et integrum in
longitudine et latitudine pratum suum infra metas illas comprehen-
sum pro dimidia libra piperis quam nobis reddent annuatim ad
festum sancti Johannis Baptiste pro omnibus rebus. Et ego Johannes
et heredes mei warantizabimus abbati et monachis de Rading(ia)
totum predictum pratum contra omnes homines et feminas. Actum
est hoc in crastino Omnium Sanctorum apud Sewell' anno regni
regis H(enrici) filii regis J(ohannis) xvi, coram Henrico de Sancto
Yvon(e), tunc camerario Rading(ie), Hugone de Fuleford', Roberto
de Brok', et cetera.

^{a} *Om. in* C
^{b} Radyngie C

The meadow was located in Little Tew (*Taxatio*, 43), but, since it was appurtenant
to the lordship of Great Tew (*VCH Oxon.*, xi. 252), it was sometimes described as
being in Great Tew—e.g. in 1250 and 1279, on the latter occasion with the name
Inmed (*Close Rolls 1247-51*, 367; *Rot. Hund.*, ii. 845).

SOUTH LEIGH

533 *Gift in free alms by Richard de Camville to Reading Abbey, at the
request of Milicent his wife and of Robert Marmion her son, of the chapel of
[South] Leigh with 2 virgates of land and other land to make a cemetery*
[1143/4 × 76; ? before 1170]

A f 93r-v; B f 204v; C f 124v
Pd. Kennett, *Parochial Antiquities*, i. 140

Notum sit universis sancte ecclesie *filiis atque* fidelibus quod ego Ricardus de Canvile,[b] voluntate et petitione Milesent uxoris mee et Roberti Marmionis filii sui, donavi et in perpetuam elemosinam concessi deo et sancte Marie de Rading(ia) et monachis ibidem deo servientibus capellam de Leya cum duabus virgatis terre, quarum una fuit de dominio nostro, altera de terra hominum de Leya tam nostrorum quam aliorum hominum ville, et preter illas terram ad cimiterium faciendum. Et volumus et concedimus *ut eas* liberas omnino et ab omni servitio nobis pertinenti[d] et[e] consuetudine seculari quietas teneant et habeant, pro salute et incolumitate mea et uxoris mee Milesent et Roberti filii sui et pro anima Roberti Marmionis et pro animabus omnium antecessorum[f] nostrorum, ut sint participes omnium beneficiorum domus [f 93v] de Rading(ia) in eternum, in quibus abbas et conventus nos receperunt tanquam speciales fratres domus Rading(ensis). Test(ibus).[g]

a-a Om. *in C*	[b] Canvill' *B,C*
c-c A has eas ut, *marked for transposition*	
[d] pertinente *B,C*	[e] *Interlined in A*
[f] *Om. in B,C*	[g] *Om. in C*

After 1143/4, when Robert Marmion, Milicent's first husband, died (*Complete Peerage,* viii. 506–7); before 1176, when Richard de Camville died (*PR 3 and 4 Richard I,* xxv–xxvi). Milicent was clearly alive at the time of this gift and, since she may have been dead in 1170 (*Sir Christopher Hatton's Book of Seals,* 29), the gift may perhaps be before that date. In 1291 the chapel of South Leigh was assessed with the church of Stanton Harcourt (*Taxatio,* 31), and it was probably because South Leigh was anciently in the *parochia* of Stanton Harcourt, whose church Reading Abbey had already acquired (no. 535), that this gift was made.

STANTON HARCOURT

534 *Gift by Queen Adeliza to Reading Abbey of 100s worth of land in her manor of Stanton [Harcourt], which her husband King Henry I gave her, namely that of Reginald the forester, in order to make provision for the convent and religious persons attending the abbey on the king's anniversary*

[prob. *c.* 1 Dec. 1136]

A f 16v; B f 20r-v
Pd. Kennett, *Parochial Antiquities,* i. 132, 153

Aelidis[a] dei gratia regina presentibus et futuris omnibus ecclesie dei catholice filiis, salutem. Notum vobis facio me concessisse et dedisse deo et ecclesie sancte Marie de Rading(ia) et fratribus ibidem deo servientibus centum solidatas terre in manerio meo Stant(one) in Oxonefordschir(a)[b] quod dominus meus rex H(enricus) mihi dedit, cum omnibus rebus eidem terre pertinentibus, et nominatim Rein-aldi forestarii. Et hoc ad procurationem conventus et religiosarum personarum illuc convenientium in termino anniversarii domini mei regis Henrici, pro salute anime ipsius et anime mee omniumque parentum nostrorum tam vivorum quam defunctorum, ita libere et quiete sicut unquam idem dominus meus rex H(enricus) idem manerium tenuit et mihi dedit. Testibus:[c] Simone episcopo Wigorn(iensi), et Waltero abbate de Egenesham, et multis aliis. Apud Rading(iam).

[a] A. B
[b] Oxonef'sir' B
[c] B ends

Probably of approximately the same date as the queen's gift of the manor of Aston (no. 370). The two named witnesses also witnessed that gift at Reading and the queen's gift in London (no. 459), which probably passed on the same occasion. The land in Stanton Harcourt did not become a permanent possession of Reading Abbey (see no. 536 n.).

535 *Gift by Queen Adeliza, widow of King Henry I, to Reading Abbey of 100s worth of land in Stanton [Harcourt], to make provision for the convent and religious persons attending the abbey on the king's anniversary, and of the church of that manor to provide lights continuously before the Holy Sacrament and before the tomb of King Henry*   [Dec. 1139 × 1141]

Original charter: B.L. Add. Ch. 19573
A f 16v; B f 20v
Pd. *Arch. Journ.*, xx. 287–8; Kennett, *Parochial Antiquities*, i. 153–4; (in part) *ibid.*, 132; (cal.) Hurry, *Reading Abbey*, 158

Notum sit presentibus et futuris omnibus ecclesie catholice filiis quod ego Aelidis[a] regina uxor nobilissimi regis Henrici concessi et dedi deo et ecclesie sancte Marie de Radingis et fratribus ibidem deo servientibus centum solidatas terre in manerio meo de Stantona in [b] Oxeneforda schira,[b] ad procurationem conventus et religiosarum personarum illuc convenientium in termino anniversarii domini mei nobilissimi regis Henrici, et preter illas centum solidatas terre concessi eis et dedi ecclesiam eiusdem manerii Stantone cum omnibus rebus eidem ecclesie pertinentibus. Et volo atque[c] precipio ut in pace et libere et quiete teneant cum omnibus liberalibus consuetudinibus cum quibus dominus meus nobilissimus rex Henricus ea in dominio suo tenuit et mihi dedit. Notumque sit quod eandem ecclesiam concessi ad continua luminaria ante corpus domini nostri Ihesu Christi et ante corpus domini mei nobilissimi regis Henrici. Testibus:[d] Hermagno capellano, et Alluredo[e] capellano, et Francone capellano, et magistro Serlone, et Eudone filio Alani, et Aalardo Flandr(ensi), et Gaufrido de Tresgoz, et Raginaldo de Windr(esores), et Roberto[f] de Chalz,[g] et Roberto de alta ripa, et Rotardo cam(erario), et Warino cam(erario), et Godeschalco[h] conestab(ulario),[i] et Waltero Crabbe.

Endorsed: Adelaidis regine de .c. solidatis terre in Stantona et ecclesia eiusdem manerii [*12th cent.*]

Size: 216 × 191 mm

Seal: on leather tag, oval of white wax (now brown) with frontal standing figure of a queen, legend now indecipherable (but see *Arch. Journ.*, xx. 288)

[a] Adel' *B*	[b-b] Oxonefordscira *A*, Oxon'f'syre *B*
[c] et *A*	[d] *B ends*
[e] Aluredo *A*	[f] Rodberto *A*
[g] Calz *A*	[h] Godescalco *A*
[i] conestabulo *A*	

Probably after the death on 11 Dec. 1139 of Roger bishop of Salisbury, who appears to have held the church (see no. 536), and before the queen's second husband, William d'Aubigny, ceased to be earl of Lincoln in or before 1141, since he confirmed his wife's gifts with that title (no. 371).

536 *Notification by Queen Adeliza to Alexander bishop of Lincoln that she divided her manor of Stanton [Harcourt] and gave one part to Reading Abbey, another to the Templars, another to Milicent her cousin, wife of Robert Marmion, and another to William of Harfleur; and that, although she retained in her hand the church and all that the bishop of Salisbury held of her, she has now given the church in free alms to Reading Abbey*

[Dec. 1139 × 44; ? 1139 × 41]

B f 20v

Pd. Kennett, *Parochial Antiquities*, i. 154; (in part) *ibid.*, 132

A(elidis) dei gratia regina A(lexandro) episcopo Linc(olniensi) amico suo karissimo, salutem et amicitias. Sciat dilectio vestra quod manerium meum de Stanton(a) partim divisi et concessi sancte Marie et conventui de Rading(ia) pro anima regis H(enrici) domini mei, et partim concessi fratribus de Templo de Iherusalem, et partim concessi Milesendi cognate mee uxori Roberti Marmiun, et partim concessi Willelmo de Harefluctu pro servitio suo. Attamen omni tempore ecclesiam de Stanton(a) et omnia que episcopus Sar(esburiensis) avunculus [vester][a] in Stanton(a) de me tenebat in manu mea detinui. Et nunc sciatis me concessisse beneficia eiusdem ecclesie de Stanton(a) conventui de Rading(ia) in elemosinam pro anima H(enrici) regis domini mei et pro animabus omnium fidelium defunctorum, et represento vobis dominum abbatem de Rading(ia)

cum monachis suis, ut pro amore dei et meo benigne eos recipiatis
et quod vestrum est eis voluntarie faciatis. T(estibus).

^a *Supplied*

The bishop of Salisbury referred to here must be Roger (d. 11 Dec. 1139), since the
gift of the church to Reading was confirmed by Adeliza's second husband as earl of
Lincoln, a title which he abandoned in or before 1141, the earliest possible date for
the next bishop of Salisbury; moreover, Bishop Roger was Alexander of Lincoln's
uncle. This deed is therefore probably after 11 Dec. 1139. It is also not later than
1144, the latest possible date for the death of Robert Marmion (see no. 533 n.), but
it may be contemporary with no. 535. The queen also gave 1 hide in Stanton to
Eynsham Abbey (*Eynsham Cartulary*, ed. H. E. Salter (Oxford Hist. Soc., 1907–8), ii.
172). Reading did not permanently retain its part of the manor, despite confirmations
of Adeliza's gift by her second husband and by King Stephen and the Empress (nos.
371, 13, 537). Henry II's general confirmations to Reading specify only the church
of Stanton Harcourt (nos. 18–19) and there is no later evidence that the abbey held
temporalities there. In fact, it seems likely that the 100s worth of land held by
Reginald the forester which Adeliza gave to Reading (no. 534) constituted what later
appears as a forest or quasi-forest serjeanty at Stanton Harcourt given by Richard I
to Henry de la Wade in *c.* 1192 in fulfilment of that king's undertaking to provide
him with 100s worth of rent (A. L. Poole, *Obligations of Society in the XII and XIII
Centuries* (Oxford, 1946), 69; *PR 4 Richard I*, 213). In 1212 the serjeanty was described
as having duties involving the king's beasts at Woodstock and of cutting a meadow
of hay in the park of Woodstock (A. L. Poole, 69, citing *Fees*, i. 103). If this serjeanty
is to be identified with the land given by Adeliza to Reading, the Crown had clearly
recovered it by Richard I's time, but of how that came about there is no evidence.
A further interesting complication arose in *c.* 1219 when William de Harcourt, guardian of Henry de la Wade's heir, claimed the advowson of Stanton Harcourt from
the abbot of Reading, but withdrew his suit (*Fees*, i. 253; *Rot. Hug. de Welles*, i. 31).

536a Note of a charter by Queen Adeliza concerning a tenth part
of the manor of Stanton [Harcourt] (*Stanton'*) given to W(illiam) of
Harfleur (*de Harefluctu*)   [1136 × 44]

B f 21r

This is clearly the gift referred to in no. 536, although why the charter should have
come to Reading is unclear. It must date before the latest terminus for no. 536 and
may be as early as Adeliza's original gift to Reading in 1136 (no. 534).

537 Notification by Empress Matilda, daughter of King Henry, to
A(lexander), bishop of Lincoln, and all barons of Oxfordshire, that
she has given in alms to Reading Abbey the church of Stanton
[Harcourt], as Queen Adeliza and William [d'Aubigny] her hus-
gand gave and confirmed it; and precept that the abbey shall hold
it as well as it holds its other possessions (*res*)^a

[2 Feb. × 7 Apr. 1141]

Original charter: BL Add. Ch. 19578
A f 15v; B f 19r

Pd. Warner and Ellis, i, no. 20 (with facsimile); Kennett, *Parochial Antiquities*, i. 132; *Arch. Journ.*, xx. 290; *Journ B.A.A.*, xxxi. 391–2; *Regesta*, iii. 257 (no. 697); (cal.) Hurry, *Reading Abbey*, 160

His testibus: B(ernardo) episcopo de Sancto David, et R(oberto) comite de Gloec(estria), et Hunf(rido) de Buun*b* dapifero. Apud Rading(iam).

Endorsed: Mathill' Imperatricis de ecclesia de Stant' et omnibus ad eandem ecclesiam pertinentibus [*12th cent.*]

Size: 193 × 82 mm

Seal: missing; leather tag remaining, sewn on to fold, which is lacking the small part formerly below the slit.

 a B ends with T'
 b Buhun *A*

After the battle of Lincoln (2 Feb. 1141) and before the Empress assumed the title *Domina Anglorum* (7/8 Apr. 1141)—see *Regesta*, iii. 257.

538 *Mandate by Queen Adeliza to Abbot Edward and the convent of Reading not to place the church of Stanton [Harcourt] or anything else of her alms outside their demesne* [1139 × 51]

 Original charter: BL Add. Ch. 19574
 B f 20v
 Pd. *Arch. Journ.*, xx. 288; Kennett, *Parochial Antiquities*, i. 154; (cal.) Hurry, *Reading Abbey*, 159

A(elidis) dei gratia regina E(dwardo) abbati et toto*a* conventui de Rading(ia), salutem. Audivi a quibusdam quod vultis ecclesiam de Stant(ona) extra dominium vestrum et manum ponere. Quare mando vobis quod nolo ut*b* illam vel aliquod*c* aliud de elemosina mea extra manum vestram ponatis. T(este)*d* Rein(aldo) de Windr(esores). Apud Arondell(am).

Endorsed: Adeleidis regine ne ecclesia de Stantona mittatur extra dominium nostrum [*12th cent.*]

Size: 142 × 52 mm

Seal: large fragment of oval seal in white wax on tongue

 a toti *B*
 b Interlined in original charter
 c Sic in original charter and *B*
 d B ends

After the gift of the church to Reading, which probably took place after Dec. 1139 (no. 535), and before the queen's death in 1151. Edward was abbot of Reading 1136–1151/4.

539 Mandate and precept by King Stephen to A(lexander), bishop of Lincoln, and Walter, archdeacon of Oxford, not to deprive the abbot of Reading of any holding whereof the church of Stanton [Harcourt] was seised in the time of King Henry I and his own, and especially Northmoor (*Mora*). The abbot is not to be impleaded in this matter without the king's express order, and there shall be no chapel at Northmoor until title to it has been proved (*donec dirationata fuerit*). Witnesses [omitted]   [1139 × 48]

B f 3or; C f 6r
Pd. Kennett, *Parochial Antiquities*, i. 154; *Regesta*, iii. 252 (no. 680); (in part) van Caenegem, *Royal Writs*, 215 n. 4

After Adeliza's gift of the church of Stanton Harcourt to Reading (no. 535) and before the death of Alexander, bishop of Lincoln, on 20 Feb. 1148. It is probably also earlier than Archbishop Theobald's settlement of the dispute over Northmoor (no. 540).

540 Notification by Theobald, archbishop of Canterbury and primate, to A(lexander), bishop of Lincoln, and all faithful of Holy Church, that the dispute between the abbey of St Denis [Paris] and Reading Abbey over the 'parish' of Northmoor (*Mora*) has been settled in his presence. St Denis shall build a chapel with cemetery at Northmoor and shall hold it, with the parishioners and tithes, of Reading Abbey by paying annually to the mother church of Stanton [Harcourt] 1 mark of silver, half each at Michaelmas and Easter, in recognition of subjection. Neither abbey shall decrease or increase this annual payment, which shall be paid by the possessor of the chapel   [May 1145 × Feb. 1148]

A f 5or-v; (noted) B f 2o2r[1]
Pd. Saltman, *Theobald*, 433-4;[2] F. M. Stenton, 'Acta Episcoporum', *Cambridge Hist. Journ.*, iii (1929-31), 3-4

Hec ut diximus pacis concordia in nostra presentia Cantuarie facta est, assistentibus et cooperantibus nobis atque attestantibus venerabilibus fratribus et coepiscopis nostris Roberto Herford(ensi), Simone Wigorn(iensi), Iocelino Sar(esburiensi), Roberto Baton(iensi), Rogero Cestr(ensi), et multis aliis abbatibus et clericis diverse dignitatis et ordinis. Valete.

After Theobald became primate (Holtzmann, *Papsturkunden*, ii. 191) and before the death of Alexander of Lincoln. At an earlier stage of the dispute, but also after Theobald's appointment as primate, Gilbert Foliot, abbot of Gloucester, and other ecclesiastics had been instructed by the archbishop to settle it, but had been prevented from doing so by the prior of Reading's appealing to the pope (*Foliot Letters and Charters*, 101). It is clear from Foliot's letter to Theobald that the abbey of St Denis claimed Northmoor as appurtenant to its church of Taynton (Oxon.).

541 Virtually identical to the preceding, except that the cartulary rubrics state that the original was sealed with the seal of the abbey of St Denis. Witnesses the same[a] [May 1145 × Feb. 1148]

A f 50v; B ff 201v-202r; C f 123r
Pd. (noted) Saltman, *Theobald*, 434

[a] *B,C end after Robert bishop of Bath with* et cetera

Date as for no. 540. It is clear that one of the acts was sealed with the archbishop's seal, the other with that of St Denis.

542 *Concession by Hugh [of Wells], bishop of Lincoln, to Reading Abbey of 20 marks annually from the church of Stanton [Harcourt], viz., 10 marks newly conceded by the bishop and 10 marks which the abbey previously had, to be received from the parson, Thomas de Camel, and his successors, who shall bear all ordinary burdens of the church* 31 Mar. 1220

A f 107v; B f 201v; C ff 122v-123r
Pd. Kennett, *Parochial Antiquities*, i. 194

Omnibus Christi fidelibus ad quos presens scriptum pervenerit Hugo dei gratia Linc(olniensis) episcopus, salutem in domino. Noverit universitas vestra nos divine pietatis intuitu, de assensu Rog(eri) dechani[a] et capituli nostri Linc(olniensis), concessisse dilectis in Christo abbati et conventui Rading' viginti marchas[b] annuas de ecclesia de Stantune,[c] scilicet decem marchas[b] eis de novo per nos concessas et alias decem quas prius habuerunt, per manum Thome de Kammel[d] persone eiusdem ecclesie et successorum suorum nomine perpetui beneficii percipiendas. Idem autem Thomas et successores sui omnia onera ordinaria ipsius ecclesie debita et consueta sustinebunt, salvis in omnibus episcopalibus consuetudinibus et Linc(olniensis) ecclesie dignitate. Quod ut perpetuam obtineat firmitatem, presenti scripto sigillum nostrum una cum sigillo predicti capituli nostri Linc(olniensis) duximus apponendum. Hiis testibus:[e] Rogero dechano, Galf(redo) precentore, Giliberto thesaurario, Roberto Norh(amtoniensi), Johanne Bedeford(ensi), Willelmo Buking(hamensi), et Roberto Huntigd(onensi)[f] archidiaconis, Johanne subdecano, Hugone archidiacono Stowe, magistris Willelmo filio Fulconis et Ada de Sancto Edmundo, Walt(ero) Blundo, Rog(ero) de Bristoll(o) et Roberto de Wassingburne,[g] Petro de Hungar', Petro de Bathon(ia) et Petro de Cheuremunt, canonicis Linc(olniensibus),

et Olivero de Chedneto clerico. Dat' per manum Thome de Fisker-
tone capellani, canonici Linc(olniensis), in capitulo Linc(olniensi)
apud Linc(olniam) pridie kalend' Aprilis, pontificatus nostri anno
undecimo.

^a decani *B,C*   ^b marcas *B,C*   ^c Staunt' *C*
^d Camel *B,C*   ^e *B,C end*
^f *A originally had* Huntind', *the penultimate letter being altered to* g
^g *Sic in A; ? rectius* Bassingburne

That the bishop concerned is Hugh of Wells is established by the principal witnesses
and by the notice in his register that he conceded the annual 20 marks in his eleventh
year (*Rot. Hug. de Welles*, iii. 96). This concession represented a doubling of the
pension formerly payable from Stanton Harcourt church, but a little earlier doubts
had been raised as to whether the original 10 marks pension claimed by Reading was
due and ancient, and, when Thomas de Camel had been instituted by the bishop at
Reading on the presentation of the abbot and convent in *c.* 1219, he had been
inhibited by the bishop from paying the pension until its antiquity had been established (*ibid.*, i. 31).

543 Admission and institution by Hugh [of Wells], bishop of Lincoln, of Thomas de Camel, clerk, as parson of Stanton [Harcourt]
(*Stanton'*)^a on the presentation of the abbot and convent of Reading,
the patrons, saving 20 marks annually to the abbot and convent
from the church by the hand of Thomas and his successors, who
shall bear all due and customary burdens of the same. Witnesses^b
[omitted]   [*c.* 31 Mar. 1220]

B f 202r; C f 123r
Pd. Kennett, *Parochial Antiquities*, i. 194

^a Staunton' *C*
^b *Om. in C*

Probably contemporary with the bishop's concession of the increased pension (no.
542), since Thomas de Camel had already been instituted in *c.* 1219 pending clarifi-
cation of the pension (no. 542 n.).

544 *Promise and obligation by Thomas de Camel, parson of Stanton [Har-
court], that he and his successors will pay annually to Reading Abbey a total
pension of 20 marks from the church of Stanton [Harcourt]. This was made
in the chapter of Lincoln in the presence of Hugh [of Wells], the bishop, and
before Roger the dean and the canons; and he later swore to observe it in the
chapter of Reading and renewed it in the local [rural] chapter before the
official of the archdeacon of Oxford*   [prob. 1220]

B f 202r; C f 123r-v

Sciant presentes et futuri quod ego Th(omas) de Kamel, persona de
Stant(one),^a spontanea voluntate et mera devotione quam habeo ad

domum de[b] Rading(ia) et ad dominos meos abbatem et conventum eiusdem loci, bona fide promisi et meipsum obligavi in presentia domini Hugonis Linc(olniensis) episcopi, coram Rogero decano Linc(olniensi) et canonicis suis in capitulo Linc(olniensi), ad solven-dum annuatim predictis abbati et conventui Rading' .x. marcas annuas eisdem concessas de gratia domini Linc(olniensis) episcopi et capituli sui de ecclesia de Stant(one)[a] de assensu et bona voluntate mea, preter alias decem marcas annuas quas prius percipere con-sueverunt de antiqua pensione eiusdem ecclesie, quas etiam ipsis persolvam cum aliis .x. marcis predictis secundum quod[c] illis con-cessum est et confirmatum per cartam dicti episcopi Linc(olniensis) et capituli sui. Has igitur .xx. marcas fideliter dictis dominis meis reddam, sicut et successores mei facere debebunt, ad .iiii. terminos anni, ad Pascha scilicet .v. marcas, ad festum beati Johannis Baptiste .v. marcas, ad festum Omnium Sanctorum .v. marcas, et ad Purifi-cationem .v. marcas, sine omni difficultate vel contradictione vel vexatione predictorum abbatis et conventus Rading'. Et ad hoc faciendum, tam de solutione quam de terminorum observatione, meipsum bona fide obligavi in capitulo Rading(ensi) sacramento corporaliter prestito super sancta evangelia. Et eandem obligati-onem innovavi in capitulo loci coram officiali domini archidiaconi Oxon(iensis) presentibus et hoc videntibus capellanis et aliis multis qui eidem capitulo interfuerunt. Ut autem hec mea obligatio rata et stabilis in posterum permaneat, eam sigilli mei appositione roboravi. T(estibus).[b]

[a] Staunton' C
[b] Om. in C
[c] Interlined in B

Probably soon after no. 542.

545 Grant by Pope Honorius III to the abbot and convent of Reading of papal protection for themselves, their abbey and all the goods (*bona*) which they rightly possess at present or shall acquire in the future, and especially for the render of 20 marks which they declare they have at Stanton [Harcourt] (*Staunt(one)*)) and which the pope confirms to them   11 Dec. [prob. 1220]

A f 78v

Dat' Lateran', iii. idus Decembris.

The outside dating limits are 1220, when the increased pension was conceded, and 1226, since the pope died in March, 1227. However, it probably dates from the year of Hugh of Wells's concession (no. 542).

DUNWICH

546 *Gift by John, count of Mortain, to Reading Abbey of a burgage which belonged to William son of William son of Anand in Dunwich, to be held by the service of 3s 4d annually*   28 Aug. 1192

A ff 90v-91r; B f 35r; C f 10r-v

Iohannes comes Moreton(ii) omnibus hominibus *et amicis suis Francis et Angl(is) presentibus et futuris, salutem.* Sciatis me dedisse et hac mea carta confirmasse deo et ecclesie sancti Iacobi de Rad-ing(ia) et monachis ibidem deo servientibus unum burgagium cum edificiis et pertinentiis quod fuit Willelmi filii Willelmi filii Anandi et in Dunewico, tenendum in perpetuum de me et heredibus meis per servitium .iii. solidorum et .iiii. denariorum per annum pro omni servitio et consuetudine. Quare volo et firmiter precipio quod prefati monachi eandem domum cum pertinentiis habeant et teneant in perpetuum per predictum servitium libere et quiete, bene et in pace, absque omni molestia et impedimento quod eis inde fieri possit. Testibus:*b* Stephano Ridel cancellario meo, Willelmo comite Sar(esburie), Willelmo Briwere, Galfr(edo) filio Petri, Ingera(m) de Pratell(is), magistro Petro Canuto. Apud Rading(iam) [*f 91r*] xxviii. die Augusti, regni regis Ricardi anno iii.

a-a et cetera *B,C*
b *B,C end*

A has in the margin *Norhfolkia*, but clearly the place concerned was in Suffolk. John's description of Reading Abbey as 'the church of St James' is interesting, particularly in the light of his gift in the same year of 1 mark of gold annually, inspired by the Hand of St James there (no. 42).

547 *Release and quitclaim by Robert son of Walter of Westleton to Reading Abbey of the tenement which belonged to Anund Bonspere in the suburb of Dunwich, for which the abbey has given him 13s*   [? early 13th cent.]

A f 103r; B f 99v; C f 50v

Sciant presentes et futuri quod ego Robertus filius Walteri de Wes-tletun(a)*a* reddidi abbati et conventui de Rading(ia), sicut ius suum, totum tenementum cum pertinentiis quod fuit Hanundi*b* Bonspere in suburbio de Dunwic(o) quietum de me et heredibus meis in perpetuum. Ita quod nec ego nec heredes mei*c* aliquo tempore ali-

quam habere poterimus reclamationem. Pro hac autem quietacla-
matione et huius carte mee confirmatione dederunt mihi prefati
abbas et conventus de Rading(ia) .xiii. solidos argenti. In cuius rei
testimonium huic scripto sigillum meum apposui.*d* Hiis testibus.

a Westlestun' *B,C*
b *A has* Hamundi; Anundi *B*, Anand' *C*
c *Insert* inde *B*; *insert* in *C*
d *B ends with* T', *C ends*

Dating very uncertain, but the deed is entered among 13th-century additions in A
and *Anund* may be identifiable with *Anand* in no. 546. A has in the margin 'Norfolk',
and in B the deed is entered under the folio-heading 'Norfolk', but the county
concerned was Suffolk.

CATSHILL (IN GODALMING) AND CHIDDINGFOLD

548 *Precept by King Henry I to Richard Basset and Aubrey de Vere and the sheriff and all his burgesses of Guildford that the men of Geoffrey Purcell, his usher, of Catshill and Chiddingfold are to be as free from toll and custom as they were in the time of Geoffrey's father* [1129 × 33; ? 1130]

Original charter: BL Add. Ch. 19572
B f 18v
Pd. *Arch. Journ.*, xx. 287; *Pal. Soc. Facs.*, 1st ser., pl. 192 (2) (with facsimile); *Journ. B. A. A.*, xxix. 260; (cal.) Hurry, *Reading Abbey*, 158; Farrer, *Itin.*, 131-2 (no. 612), reprinted from *EHR* xxxiv (1919), 555-6; *Regesta*, ii. 240-1 (no. 1655)

H(enricus) rex Angl(orum) Ricardo Basset et A(lberico) de Ver et vicecomiti et omnibus burgensibus suis de Geldefort,^a salutem. Precipio quod homines Gaufr(edi) Purcelli hostiar(ii) mei de Chatishilla^b et de Chedelingefolt^c sint ita bene et iuste in pace de theloneo et omni consuetudine sicut fuerunt tempore patris sui. T(este)^d Milone Gloec(estrie). Apud Winton(iam).

Endorsed: Henr' regis primi^e de Cateshella [*12th cent.*]
Size: 155 × 72 mm
Seal: fragment of fourth seal of Henry I on tongue

^a Geldeford' *B* ^b Chateshill' *B* ^c Chedelingefold *B* ^d *B ends* ^e *Inserted above the line*

After Geoffrey succeeded his father in 1129-30 (*PR 31 Henry I*, 50) and before Henry I left England for the last time in Aug. 1133. Farrer dated it to 1130 (*Itin.*, 131) and this is followed by *Regesta*, ii. 240. For the gift of Geoffrey's land in Catshill to Reading Abbey, see nos. 11-12, 17.

GUILDFORD

549 *Final concord in the king's court at Westminster at the Exchequer by which the abbot of Reading leased to John Alecok of Guildford for life, and after his death to his wife for life, 4s worth of rent from land in Guildford for 4s annually; after both their deaths the rent shall remain to the abbey quit of their heirs in perpetuity* 21 Oct. 1191

B f 173r; C f 102v

Hec est finalis concordia facta in curia domini regis apud Westm(onasterium) ad scaccarium die lune proxima post festum sancti Luce evangeliste [18 Oct.], anno regni regis Ricardi iii., coram domino Waltero Rothom(agensi) archiepiscopo et Godefr(ido)*a* Wint(oniensi) et Ricardo Lond(oniensi) episcopis, et Willelmo Maresc(allo)*b* et Gaufr(edo) filio Petri et Rog(ero) filio Reinfr(idi) et Roberto de Wittefeld' et Osb(erto) filio Hervei et magistro Thoma de Husseburn', iustic(iariis) domini regis, et multis aliis domini regis fidelibus ibidem tunc presentibus, inter abbatem Rading(ensem), petentem per W. capellanum positum loco predicti abbatis in curia domini regis ad lucrandum vel perdendum, et Iohannem Alecok de Guldef(ordia), tenentem, de quatuor solidis redditus terre in Guldef(ordia), unde placitum fuit inter eos in curia prefata. Scilicet quod predictus abbas de Rading(ia) concessit predicto I(ohanni) tenere de illo et de conventu de*c* Rading(ia) in tota vita predicti I(ohannis) predictos .iiii. solidos redditus per .iiii. solidos per annum. Et post decessum predicti Iohannis uxor eius tenebit predictum redditum in tota vita sua de predicto abbate et conventu per .iiii. solidos per annum, scilicet duos solidos ad Pascha et .ii. solidos ad festum sancti Michaelis. Et post decessum utriusque, scilicet predicti Iohannis et uxoris eius, predicti .iiii. solidi redditus remanebunt quieti in perpetuum predicto abbati et conventui de heredibus prenominati Iohannis et uxoris sue.

a Godfr' *C* *b* Mareschal' *C* *c* Om. in *C*

HONOUR OF PETWORTH

550 Gift in free alms by Jocelin [of Louvain], brother of Queen Adeliza, to Reading Abbey, for the souls of King Henry I, Godfrey duke [of Louvain] his father, William earl of Chichester, Queen Adeliza and others, of 100s worth of rent in the Honour of Petworth, viz., the land which Robert of Diddlesfold held with a piggery of 10 sows and 1 boar, the land which Theodoric of Diddlesfold held, and the land which Edwin *Hunte* held, with free pannage for the demesne pigs   [*c.* 1140 × 51]

A f 37r; B f 108v; C f 57v
Pd. *EYC*, xi. 359 (no. 289)

a Testibus:*b* Hermanno capellano, et magistro Serlone, et magistro Reginaldo de Windresor(es), et multis aliis.

a C ends
b B ends

After the donor's brother-in-law, William d'Aubigny, became earl of Chichester (or Arundel), and before the death of Queen Adeliza. The rubric of A describes the charter as 'concerning the land of Diddlesfold' (A f 36v), a place now represented by Diddlesfold Farm in the parish of Lurgashall (A. Mawer *et al.*, *The Place-Names of Sussex* (English Place-Name Soc., vi–vii, 1929–30), i. 112). It formed part of the Honour of Petworth, which was given to Jocelin of Louvain by William d'Aubigny and Queen Adeliza as a tenancy of the Honour of Arundel (Farrer, *Honors and Knights' Fees*, iii. 17–18; *EYC*, xi. 357–8).

551 Notification by Jocelin [of Louvain], brother of Queen Adeliza, to Hilary, bishop of Chichester, that he gave to Reading Abbey the lands of Robert of Diddlesfold, Theodoric and Edwin *Hunte* in the vill of Petworth, with a piggery of 10 sows and 1 boar and free pannage [i.e., as in no. 550]; and further that, when he was at Reading for the burial of his sister, Queen Adeliza, he gave to the abbey the assarts which these three men had occupied on his demesne, whence they were doing no service to him or to the monks, and 1 virgate of land and the right to have 40 pigs with his own pigs in his parks and enclosures between the feasts of St Martin and St Thomas [11 Nov.–21 Dec.]   [1151 × 57; ? 1151]

A f 37r-v; B f 108v; C f 57r-v
Pd. *EYC*, xi. 359–60 (no. 290)

*His testibus: Iohanne episcopo Wigornie, Ingulfo abbate de Abendonia, Gileberto abbate de Waverleia, Bernardo presbitero, Francone capellano, et multis aliis.

a B ends with T', *C ends*

After the death of Queen Adeliza and before the death of John of Pagham, bishop of Worcester, 31 Mar. 1157, but possibly on or shortly after the occasion of the queen's funeral at Reading in 1151.

552 Gift in free alms by Jocelin [of Louvain], brother of Queen Adeliza, to Reading Abbey, for the souls of King Henry I and Queen Adeliza and others, and for the health of King Henry II and his sons, of the land of Fernhurst which belonged to Heyshott and the mill of Sutton [1154 × 80; ? 1176 × 80]

A f 37r; B ff 108v-109r; C f 57v
Pd. *EYC*, xi. 360 (no. 291)

Testibus:^b^ Willelmo de Aubeni, Arnulfo persona de Pettewrda, Willelmo de Einesford, et multis aliis.

a C ends   *b B ends*

After the accession of Henry II and before the donor's death in late 1179 or early 1180 (Farrer, *Honors and Knights' Fees*, iii. 18). On the grounds that the first witness is not styled earl nor called 'son of the earl', Sir Charles Clay suggested the possibility of a date not earlier than 1176 (*EYC*, xi. 360). The land of Fernhurst belonged to that part of Heyshott which belonged to the Honour of Petworth (Farrer, i. 27).

553 *Confirmation by Henry de Percy of the whole tenement which his father, Jocelin [of Louvain], gave to Reading Abbey, viz., the lands of Robert of Diddlesfold, Theodoric and Edwin Hunte; the assarts made by these men on his father's demesne; 1 virgate of land of Chneppe which Andrew holds; all the land of Fernhurst which belonged to Heyshott; the mill of Sutton with its customary suit and appurtenances; the right to have in the tenement a piggery of 10 sows and 1 boar with free pannage; and the right to have 40 pigs with his own pigs in his parks and enclosures quit of pannage between the feasts of St Martin and St Thomas. Reading Abbey has given him 25 marks in his need* [1 Jan.] × 2 Sept. 1190

A f 37v; B f 109r-v; C f 58r

Sciant presentes et futuri quod ego Henricus de Perci^a^ concedo et confirmo deo et monachis de Rading(ia), pro anima patris mei et matris mee et pro salute anime mee et omnium antecessorum et successorum meorum, totum tenementum quod pater meus Iocelinus eis dedit, scilicet, totam terram que fuit Roberti de Dudelesfald,^b^ et totam terram Theod(er)ici,^c^ et totam terram que fuit Edwini Hunte, cum omnibus ad easdem terras pertinentibus; et preter hec essarta que tres prefati homines occupaverant de dominio patris mei; et unam virgatam terre de Chneppe*d* quam Andreas tenet; et totam terram de Fernhurst que pertinuit ad Essiethe*e* cum omnibus in eadem terra manentibus vel ad illam pertinentibus; et molendinum de Suttuna*f* cum solita*g* sequela et terris et stagnis et omnibus eius pertinentiis quas hactenus habuit. Concessi etiam prefatis monachis ut unam habeant in prefato tenemento porcariam de .x. suibus et de*h* uno verre et pannagium quietum de eadem porcaria et de nutritura eiusdem, et .xl. porcos cum propriis porcis meis vel aliis, si quos ibidem ad pannagium habuero, in parcis et in defensis meis a festo sancti Martini usque ad festum sancti Thome apostoli quietos et sine pannagio. Volo igitur et omnibus fidelibus meis firmiter precipio ut prefati monachi hec omnia libere et in pace, honorifice et quiete *i*in perpetuum*i* ab omni seculari servitio et exactione teneant in terris et aquis et stagnis et pratis et*h* boscis et pasturis, tam dominicis quam communibus, et in omnibus rebus et locis. Et omnes homines in prefatis tenementis manentes liberos habeant exitus et quietos sibi et pecoribus suis et peculiis in omni communi pastura cum pecoribus hominum meorum in tota tenura de Pettewrda.*j* Prefati vero monachi, necessitati mee subvenientes, .xxv. marcas dederunt, et ex hoc benivolentiam meam sibi merito etiam*k* in aliis in quibus rationabiliter potero comparaverunt. Testibus: *l*Hugone et Willelmo et Willelmo Dunelmensi et Elyensi et Herfordensi episcopis, Bertranno de Verdun, Roberto de Withefeld, Iocelino archidiacono, et multis aliis.*l* *m*[Apud Westm(onasterium) coram iust(iciariis) domini regis Ricardi regni ipsius anno primo.]*m*

a Percy *B,C*	*b* Dudlesfald' *C*
c Theod(ri)ci *B,C*	*d* Chneppa *B,C*
e Esshiete *B,C*	*f* Sutton's *B*, Sottone *C*
g tota *C*	*h* Om. in *C*
i-i imperpetuum *C*	*j* Pettewrþa *B,C*
k et *C*	*l-l* et cetera *B,C*
m-m Om. in *A, supplied from B,C*	

After the consecration of William Longchamp as bishop of Ely, 31 Dec. 1189, and before the end of 1 Richard I, 2 Sept. 1190. This charter, which is noticed in *EYC*, xi. 361, confirms nos. 550-2. The un-named virgate in no. 551 is here described as 'of *Chneppe* which Andrew holds'.

554 Grant by Henry de Percy to Reading Abbey that, if he shall change his seal, he will freely and without payment seal again the charter which the abbey has from him concerning the tenement which his father gave   [1190 × 93; poss. *c.* 1190]

A f 37v (deleted)
Pd. *EYC*, xi. 361 (no. 292)

Testibus: Willelmo de Alta Ripa, et Willelmo de Dudeham, et Willelmo filio Arturi.

This deed appears only in A, where it is deleted by crossing through. It is certainly after no. 553, which it follows in A, and before Michaelmas 1198, by which time Henry de Percy was dead (*Complete Peerage*, x. 449), but, since it appears in the original section of A, it is to be dated not later than 1193 and may possibly be roughly contemporary with no. 553.

555 *Gift in free alms by Henry de Percy to Reading Abbey of half a virgate of land in* Scheldefald', *which Godwin Ruffus held, in return for the abbey's quitclaim to him and his heirs of the piggery of 10 sows and 1 boar and the right to have 40 pigs in his enclosures and parks quit of pannage dues*

[1190 × 98; ? 1193 × 98]

A f 90r; B f 109v; C f 58r-v

Sciant presentes et futuri quod ego Henricus de*ᵃ* Perci*ᵇ* dedi et concessi et hac carta mea confirmavi deo et sancte Marie de Rading(ia) et monachis ibidem deo servientibus, pro anima patris mei et mea et omnium antecessorum et successorum meorum, dimidiam virgatam terre*ᶜ* de Scheldefald' quam Godwinus Ruffus*ᵈ* tenuit, cum ipso homine in ea manente cum omnibus ad eandem terram pertinentibus in bosco, in*ᵉ* plano et in omnibus locis in liberam et*ᵃ* puram*ᶠ* elemosinam. Volo igitur et omnibus fidelibus meis firmiter precipio ut predicti monachi hanc prefatam terram libere et in pace, honorifice et quiete*ᵍ* teneant ab omni seculari servitio et exactione quietam; et ut homo in prefata terra manens liberos habeat et quietos exitus sibi et pecoribus suis et peculiis in omni communi pastura cum pecoribus hominum meorum in tota tenura de Puttew'th(a),*ʰ* sicut in carta patris mei et mea continetur. Prefati vero monachi pro hac donatione mea clamaverunt quietam mihi et heredibus meis porcariam de decem suibus et uno verre et nutritura eorundem et .xl. porcos quos, sicut in carta patris mei et mea*ⁱ* continetur, habere debuerant in defensis et parcis meis a festo sancti Martini usque ad festum sancti Thome apostoli de pasnagio quietos.*ʲ* Hiis testibus: Willelmo de Alta Ripa, Urso de Lhinces, Rad(ulfo) de Budeh(am), Rad(ulfo) de Stopeh(am), Willelmo de Perci, Roberto de Alta Ripa, Waltero de Suttun(a), et Simone de Waura, Willelmo filio Arturi sen(escallo), Thoma de Dedelesfald', Alardo de Suttun(a), Roberto et Ricardo clericis, et aliis satis.

ᵃ Om. in C
ᶜ Om. in B,C
ᵉ et B,C
ᵍ quietam C
ⁱ A has mee

ᵇ Percy B,C
ᵈ Rufus B,C
ᶠ Insert et perpetuam C
ʰ Pettewrþa B,C
ʲ B ends with T', C ends

After no. 553 and before Michaelmas 1198, when Henry de Percy was dead (see no. 554 n.), but, since the charter was not entered in the original section of A, possibly not earlier than 1193. The rubrics of B and C describe the land as 'in Petworth', meaning probably the Honour of Petworth. Reading's quitclaim of the piggery and pannage rights is printed in *Percy Chartulary*, ed. M. T. Martin (Surtees Soc., 1909), 414 (no. 976); and *EYC*, xi. 361–2 (no. 293).

556 *Confirmation by William [d'Aubigny III], earl of Sussex, of the gifts to Reading Abbey by Jocelin [of Louvain], brother of Queen Adeliza, and Henry de Percy, his son, including the half-virgate in* Shelfeld *which Henry gave in exchange for the piggery and pannage; and grant in free alms of quittance of suit of hundred courts for the abbey and its men of those lands* [1193 × 1221]

B f 109r; C ff 57v–58r

Omnibus sancte matris ecclesie filiis ad quos presens scriptum pervenerit Willelmus comes Sudsex(ie), salutem. Sciatis me concessisse et presenti carta mea confirmasse deo et ecclesie sancte Marie de Rading(ia) et abbati et conventui eiusdem loci,^{a} pro animabus patris^b et matris mee et pro anima Adeleidis regine, matris patris mei, et maxime pro salute mea et uxoris mee et liberorum meorum et omnium antecessorum et successorum meorum, donationes quas Ioc(elinus), frater Adeleidis regine, et Henricus de Percy, filius eius, eis fecerunt. Videlicet, totam terram que fuit Rodberti de Dudelesfald, et totam terram Theod(ri)ci, et totam terram que fuit Edwini Hunte, cum omnibus ad easdem terras pertinentibus, et preter hec essarta que tres prefati homines occupaverant de dominio memorati Iocelini, et unam virgatam terre de Kneppe quam Andreas tenuit, et totam terram de Fernhurst que pertinuit ad Esshiete, cum omnibus in eadem terra^c manentibus vel ad illam pertinentibus, et molendinum de Sutton(a) cum solita sequela et terris et stagnis et omnibus eius pertinentiis quas hactenus habuit, et preterea dimidiam virgatam terre in Shelfeld^d quam Godwinus Ruffus tenuit quam Henricus de Percy eis dedit in escambium porcarie quam habere debebant in boscis^e et parcis^f et defensis suis, sicut carte predictorum Ioc(elini) et Henrici quas inde habent testantur. Preterea, ex propria largitione mea dedi et concessi et hac eadem carta mea confirmavi predictis abbati et conventui de Rading(ia) et omnibus hominibus eorum de predictis terris et tenementis omnem libertatem et quietantiam de omnibus sectis hundredorum in omnibus rebus ad me et^g ad heredes meos pertinentibus in liberam, puram et perpetuam elemosinam pro salute mea et omnium meorum in perpetuum. T(estibus).^{h}

^a *Insert* et *C* ^b *Insert* mei *C* ^c villa *C*
^d Shefeld' *C* ^e bosco *C* ^f parco *C*
^g vel *C* ^h *Om. in C*

This confirmation is by the grandson of Queen Adeliza and William d'Aubigny I, earl of Arundel (or Sussex). He succeeded his father, William d'Aubigny II, in Dec. 1193 and died in Feb. 1221.

557 Confirmation by William [d'Aubigny], 4th earl of Sussex, of the same gifts to Reading Abbey by Jocelin [of Louvain] and Henry de Percy as confirmed in no. 556, and of the grant by his father, Earl William [d'Aubigny III], of quittance of suit of hundred courts. Witnesses^a [omitted] [1221 × 24]

B ff 109v-110r; C f 58v

^a *Om. in C*

The dating limits are those of his earldom. The text of this confirmation is *mutatis mutandis* virtually identical to that of no. 556, the only significant differences in reading of place-names being *Knappa* for *Kneppe*, *Essyete* (*Esscheite* C) for *Esshiete*, and *Selfold'* for *Shelfeld*.

558 Final concord in the king's court at Chichester in the octave of St Martin, 7 Edward I, before John of Reigate (*Reygate*), William of Northborough (*Norhtburg'*), Geoffrey of Lewknor (*Leukenore*), Solomon of Rochester (*Rovecestr'*) and Richard of Boyland (*Boylaund'*),^a justices-in-eyre, and others, between Richard of Diddlesfold (*Dudelesfold'*), seeking, and Abbot Robert [of Burgate] of Reading, holding by Adam Scot his attorney, concerning 140 acres of land in Petworth (*Petteworthe*). Assize of mort d'ancestor. Richard recognized the land to be the right of the abbot and abbey of Reading, in return for which the abbot leased it to him for life for an annual render of 20s at three terms, viz., 6s 8d each at the Purification of St Mary, the Nativity of St John Baptist and Michaelmas, and suit of the abbot's court of Diddlesfold every three weeks, for all service, custom and exaction. The abbot and his successors shall warrant the land to Richard during his life, but afterwards the land shall revert to the abbot and abbey of Reading quit of Richard's heirs, to be held of the chief lords of the fee by the services appurtenant to it in perpetuity 18 Nov. 1279

B f 13r
Pd. (abstract) *An Abstract of Feet of Fines ... Sussex*, ed. L. F. Salzmann, ii (Sussex Rec. Soc., vii, 1908), 112 (from PRO foot: CP 25(1)/235/29/15)

^a *B has* Hoylaund' (*in error*)

559   Record of the action brought by the abbot of Reading against
William Dawtrey (*de Alta Ripa*) for recovery of the customs and right
services which he owes from his free tenement held of the abbot in
Sutton (*Sutton'*) and *Kneppe* in Fernhurst (*Farnhurst*). The abbot
claims that, although William holds a mill and 2 virgates of land in
these vills for an annual service of 34s, which he at one time paid,
he is now refusing to do so at a loss to the abbot to the value of
100s, etc. The case is settled by concord; namely, William recognized
that he and his heirs should, and would, pay the rent, and the abbot
remits damages. William further acknowledged a debt of 119s 4d in
arrears of the rent, of which he will pay half at the Purification of
St Mary, 8 [? Edward I], and half at the feast of St John Baptist in
the following year   [? 1279 × 80]

B f 12v

William is probably to be identified with the William Dawtrey who in 1284-5 held
6 carucates in Full Sutton (Yorks. E. R.) of a Percy under-tenancy of the Honour of
Chester (*EYC*, xi. 255; *Aids*, vi. 47). The regnal year of this action is most probably,
therefore, of Edward I.

BEARLEY

560 Gift and quitclaim by Gerard son of William of Bearley (*Burle*) to Reading Abbey of all the land with appurtenances which the said William of Bearley sometime gave him in Bearley (*Burghel'*). To be held freely by rendering annually to John of Bearley (*Burgl'*)[a] 2d at Michaelmas for all custom, demand and secular service. For this the abbey has given him £10 of silver. Warranty and sealing. Witnesses[b] [omitted]   [c. 1220 x c. 1249]

B ff 129v-130r; C f 74r

[a] Burlegh' C
[b] Om. in C

The donor was a member of the family which held a considerable estate in Bearley (possibly the manor) in the 12th and 13th centuries (*Sir Christopher Hatton's Book of Seals*, 109-10; *VCH Warks.*, iii. 43-4). Its members are difficult to distinguish. It appears, however, that John of Bearley, who confirmed Gerard's gift (no. 562), was his uncle, since in a deed to Bordesley Abbey a John of Bearley, son of William of Bearley, confirmed a gift made by Gerard his nephew, son of his brother William (*Cat. Anc. Deeds*, i, B 782); this deed dates from some time near 1221, since three of its witnesses (Robert de Valle, William of Edstone and Thomas Gery) appear in the Warwickshire eyre of that year, the first of them frequently (see *Warks. Eyre 1221-2*, index *sub nominibus*). In that same eyre John of Bearley was convicted of disseising Hugh of Bearley and Gerard son of William of common of pasture in Bearley belonging to their free tenement there, and the surety for his amercement was his brother, William of Bearley (*ibid.*, 295-6). The present deed to Reading appears to involve the same John, Gerard and William; accordingly, and since John was apparently dead by 1249 (*VCH Warks.*, iii. 43), it is dated c. 1220 × c. 1249.

560a Note of a charter by William of Bearley (*Burleg'*)[a] to Gerard, his son, concerning the same land   [? before 1221]

B f 130r; C f 74r

[a] Burgle C

Before no. 560 and most probably before the action in the eyre of 1221 (see no. 560 n.).

561 Confirmation by William of Bearley (*Burle*) to Reading Abbey of the gift by Gerard, his son, of all the land with rents and all other appurtenances which he sometime held in the vill of Bearley (*Burgle*), as Gerard's charter to the abbey witnesses. For this the abbey has given William 1 mark of silver. Sealing. Witnesses[a] [omitted]

[*c.* 1220 × *c.* 1249]

B f 130r; C f 74r

[a] *Om. in C*

Date as for no. 560.

562 Confirmation by John of Bearley (*Burgle*) to Reading Abbey of the gift by Gerard son of William of Bearley (*Burle*)[a] of all the land which he sometime held with rents and all other appurtenances in the vill of Bearley (*Burle*), as Gerard's charter to the abbey witnesses. Also gift to the abbey of the 2d rent which he was accustomed to receive from that land. For this the abbey has given him 20s sterling. Sealing. Witnesses[b] [omitted]   [*c.* 1220 × *c.* 1249]

B f 130r; C f 74r

[a] Burgle *C*   [b] *Om. in C*

Date as for no. 560.

563 Gift by Richard *Fiselet* to Reading Abbey of all the land with appurtenances which he sometime held of John of Bearley (*Burgle*) in Bearley. To be held freely by rendering annually, on behalf of the donor and his heirs, to John of Bearley[a] and his heirs 3d at Easter for all custom, demand and secular service. Warranty. For this the abbey has given him £15 sterling. Sealing. Witnesses[b] [omitted]

[13th cent.; not later than 1258]

B f 130v; C f 74v

[a] Burle *C*   [b] *Om. in C*

The deed wss entered in the original section of B. It has not been possible to establish which of the two Johns of Bearley who held Bearley before 1258 is named here (see *VCH Warks.*, iii. 43).

564 Gift in free alms by John of Bearley (*Burle*)[a] to Reading Abbey of the 3d annual rent which Richard *Fiselet* used to pay him at Easter for the land which he held of him in Bearley (*Burgle*). Also confirmation of the said Richard's gift of the same land to the abbey, as Richard's charter to the abbey witnesses. Warranty and sealing. Witnesses[b] [omitted]   [13th cent.; not later than 1258]

B f 130r; C f 74r-v

[a] Burgle *C*   [b] *Om. in C*

Date as for no. 563.

565 Gift by Richard son of Nicholas of Warwick (*Warwik*) to Reading Abbey of the whole meadow of *Langeford* [in Bearley]*ᵃ* with appurtenances which Simon Bagot sometime sold to him, viz., that lying between the meadow of W(illiam) of Bearley (*Burle*) and the meadow of Hugh the parson. To be held freely, with free entry and exit, by rendering annually to him and his heirs 1 pair of gloves, price 1d, at Easter for all custom, demand and secular service. Sealing. Witnesses*ᵇ* [omitted]   [13th cent.; not later than 1258]

B f 130v; C f 74v

ᵃ *Supplied from rubrics in B,C*
ᵇ *Om. in C*

This deed was entered in the original section of B. Simon Bagot is possibly identifiable with the last Bagot lord of Preston Bagot, who was dead by 1242-3 (*Fees*, ii. 957; *VCH Warks.*, iii. 143). In view of the reference to Simon Bagot, this meadow may have been in Preston Bagot (cf. no. 577 n.).

BIRMINGHAM

566 Record of the action *ᵃ*[before M(artin) of Littlebury (*Lit(l)ebir'*) and his fellow justices-in-eyre at Warwick, 46 Henry III]*ᵃ* on a complaint by the abbot of Reading that William of Birmingham (*Bermingham*) and his bailiffs of Birmingham (*Burmingham*) are distraining the abbot and his men of Rowington (*Rouwynton'*) for tolls and other customs, etc., in the town (*villa*) of Birmingham contrary to the abbot's liberties. Through his attorney the abbot claims that he and his men are quit of toll and custom throughout England on merchandise put up for sale or on anything bought for their own use, whereas William and his bailiffs of Birmingham (*Bermingham*) take 1d for every horse sold or bought there, ½d for every ox, 1d for 5 sheep and 1d for a cart. After depositions from both parties, the jury decide that the abbot's men of Rowington who hold of him in chief and who do not engage in trade as an occupation (*mercandizas non exercentes*) ought to be quit of all kinds of toll, and that, when such men come into Birmingham and sell or buy for their own use, and are willing to swear that they are the abbot's men, they shall be quit of all tolls and customs. However, merchants of the abbot's homage who engage in trade professionally (*publice mercandizas de foro in forum exercentes*) were always used to paying toll on their merchandise time out of mind, like other outsiders (*extranei*). Therefore, William *sine die*, and the abbot in mercy for false claim   [June × July] 1262

B ff 231v-232r

Rubric (in margin): (I)nrotulacio facta coram M. de Lit(l)ebir' et sociis suis itinerantibus apud Warr' inter abbatem de Rading' et Willelmum de Bermigham, anno regni regis Henrici filii regis Johannis xlvi.

a-a Supplied from rubric

The justices sat at Warwick 5 June—20 July, 1262 (D. Crook, *Records of the General Eyre*, 131). William of Birmingham was lord of Birmingham under the Somery family (*VCH Warks.*, vii. 58) and in the same eyre was in dispute with his lord, Roger de Somery, over the customs and services due (*Warks. Feet of Fines*, i. 181).

CLAVERDON

567 *Grant by Roger, earl of Warwick, to Reading Abbey and all its men, of freedom from tolls, stallage, passage-money and all exactions and customs, within or without a borough, throughout his land; and grant to the abbey and its men of Rowington and* Lamfretuna *of common of pasture in his wood and pasture in Claverdon* [c. 1133 × 53]

A f 91r; A ff 92v-93r; B f 123r; C ff 67v-68r

R(ogerius) comes Warewic(ensis)*ᵃ* omnibus baronibus, senescallis et prepositis et baillivis*ᵇ* suis, salutem. Sciatis me dedisse et concessisse, pro salute anime mee et omnium antecessorum et successorum meorum, omnem quietantiam et libertatem monachis de Rading(ia) et omnibus hominibus eorum in tota terra mea, infra burgum et extra burgum, vendendi ᶜet emendiᶜ sine theloneo et stallagio et omni consuetudine et exactione. Quare volo et firmiter precipio quod predicti monachi et omnes*ᵈ* homines eorum sint quieti de theloneis et stallagiis*ᵉ* et passagiis et omnibus exactionibus et consuetudinibus in tota terra mea. Et nullus eos disturbet super forisfactum meum. Preterea concessi prefatis monachis et omnibus hominibus eorum de Rochintun(a)*ᶠ* et de Lamfretun(a)*ᵍ* communionem pasture omni peculio suo in bosco et pastura mea in Claverdona liberam et quietam ab omni consuetudine. [Testibus.]*ʰ*

ᵃ For expansion see no. 578; Wareuic' *A ff 92v-93r,* Warwik *B,* Warewik' *C*
ᵇ ballivis *C*
ᶜ-ᶜ Interlined in A f 91r
ᵈ Interlined in A ff 92v-93r
ᵉ stalagiis *A ff 92v-93r*
ᶠ Rochinton' *A ff 92v-93r,* Ruchintona *B,C*
ᵍ Lamfreton' *A ff 92v-93r, B,C*
ʰ Om. in A f 91r and C, supplied from other texts

After Adeliza d'Ivry's gift of the manor of Rowington (no. 602) and before the earl's death in 1153.

568 *Confirmation of the same by Waleran, earl of Warwick*

[1184 × 1204]

B f 123r-v; C f 68r

Walerannus comes Warwik[a] omnibus baronibus, senescallis et prepositis et ballivis suis, salutem. Sciatis me concessisse et hac mea carta confirmasse, pro salute anime mee et omnium antecessorum et successorum meorum, omnem quietantiam et libertatem monachis de Rading(ia) et omnibus hominibus eorum quam pater meus R(ogerus) comes eis dedit et concessit et carta sua confirmavit, scilicet ut emant et vendant in tota terra mea, infra burgum et extra burgum, sine theloneo et stallagio et omni consuetudine et exactione. Quare volo et firmiter precipio quod predicti monachi et omnes homines eorum sint quieti de theloneis et stallagiis et passagiis et omnibus exactionibus et consuetudinibus in tota terra mea. Et nullus eos disturbet super forisfactum meum. Preterea concessi prefatis monachis [*f 123v*] et omnibus hominibus eorum de Rokint(ona) et de Lamfert(ona) communionem pasture omnibus animalibus suis in bosco et pastura mea in Claverdon(a) liberam et quietam ab omni consuetudine et exactione. T(estibus).[b]

[a] Warewik *C*
[b] *Om. in C*

The dating limits are those of Waleran's earldom.

569 *Final concord in the king's court at Warwick, in an assize of mort d'ancestor, by which Robert Meverel quitclaimed to Reading Abbey 15 acres of land in Claverdon, and the abbey gave him 5s*   23 Oct. 1194

B f 176v; C f 105r

Hec est finalis concordia facta in curia domini regis apud Warwik die dominica proxima post festum sancti Luce evangeliste [18 Oct.], anno regni regis Ricardi vi., coram Gaufr(edo) filio P(etri), Tedbaldo de Valain(es),[a] Michaele Belet, Henrico de Wichint(ona), magistro Aristot(ele), iustic(iariis) domini regis, et aliis baronibus et fidelibus domini regis ibidem tunc presentibus, inter Robertum Meverel, petentem, et abbatem de Rading(ia), tenentem per Robertum monachum positum loco eiusdem abbatis in curia domini regis ad lucrandum vel perdendum, de .xv. acris terre in Claverdon(a), unde recognitio de morte antecessoris summonita fuit inter eos in curia domini regis. Scilicet quod predictus Robertus quiet'clamavit[b] de se et de[c] heredibus suis predicto abbati et conventui et eorum successoribus totas predictas .xv. acras terre in Claverdone; et pro hac quiet(a)clamatione,[d] fine et concordia predictus

abbas et conventus dederunt predicto Roberto .v. solidos sterlingorum.

^a Walein' C   ^b quietumclamavit C
^c Om. in C   ^d quietcl' C

570 Final concord in the king's court at Warwick in the quindene
of Holy Trinity, 46 Henry III, before Martin of Littlebury (*Litle-
byr'*), Walter of Bersted (*Berstede*), Richard of Middleton (*Middelton'*),
Geoffrey of Lewknor (*Leukenore*) and Richard of Hemington (*Hem-
migtone*), justices-in-eyre, and others, between Richard *le Grom* and
Alice his wife, seeking, and Abbot Richard [II][1] of Reading, holding
by Godfrey *le Messager* his attorney, concerning a messuage and 1
virgate of land with appurtenances in Claverdon (*Claverdone*).
Richard and Alice recognized the messuage and land to be the right
of the abbot and abbey of Reading, and quitclaimed them to the
same for themselves and the heirs of Alice for ever, in return for
which the abbot received them and Alice's heirs into all benefits and
prayers of the abbey for ever   18 June 1262

B f 134r; C f 77r-v
Pd. (cal.) *Warks. Feet of Fines*, i. 176 (no. 816) (from PRO foot: CP 25(1)/244/26/
27)

[1] His election was confirmed by the Crown on 26 Mar. 1262 (*Cal. Pat. R. 1258–66*,
207).

571 Gift in free alms by Thomas *Ang'* of Kington (*Kinton'*) to
Reading Abbey of 18d annual rent which he was accustomed to
receive from W. son of Lettice (*Letya*) for a messuage and croft in
the territory of Kington [in Claverdon], viz., 6d each at Michaelmas, the feast of St Thomas the apostle [21 Dec.] and the feast of
the Holy Cross,[1] with homages, services, reliefs, heriots and all other
escheats from W. and his heirs and from the tenement. Warranty
and sealing. Witnesses^a [omitted]   [13th cent.; not later than 1258]

B f 128v; C f 73r

^a Om. in C

This deed was entered in the original section of B.

[1] Probably the Invention of the Holy Cross, 3 May (cf. the rent-payment dates in
no. 620).

HUNSCOTE (IN CHARLECOTE)

572 Gift by Gilbert of Hunscote (*Hunstanescote*) to Abbot Adam [of Lathbury] and the convent of Reading of all the land which Gervase son of *Seyant* sometime held in Hunscote (*Hunstaneskote*)*a* and all the land which Adam son of *Gladewine*b sometime held in the same vill, except for Adam's messuage, in place of which Gilbert has given the messuage called *Pirichroft*.c All to be held freely by rendering annually to him and his heirs 12d on the feast of St John Baptist for all custom, exaction, demand and secular service. Warranty. For this the abbey has granted to Gilbert and Alice, his wife, corrodies and clothing (*corredia et warniamenta*), as is contained in its charter to them [1226 × 38]

A f 110r-v; B f 125r; C f 69v

*d*Hiis testibus: Jacobo, et cetera.

a Hunstanescot' *B,C*	*b* Gledewine *B*, Geldewine *C*
c Pyricroft *B,C*	*d* *B ends with* T', *C ends*

The dating limits are those of Adam of Lathbury's abbacy. Dugdale, and following him *Warks. Place-Names*, 233, have wrongly located Hunscote in Hampton Lucy (see *VCH Warks.*, v. 34 n.2). The abbey later exchanged these lands with William of Norfolk for land in Tiddington and Alveston (see no. 647).

LANGLEY

573 Gift in free alms by Hugh *de Blez* of Langley (*Longeleya*) to Reading Abbey of all the land which he had towards *Birchurst'* called *la Rudinge* in the territory of Langley, extending from the land of Sir Guy Pipard (*Pipard'*) and *Chelewellesiche* between the king's road leading from the wood of Claverdon (*Claverdon'*) towards Langley and the other road from Langley towards the house of Henry *de Birchurst'*. Warranty and sealing. Witnesses*a* [omitted]

[13th cent.; not later than 1258]

B f 124r; C f 68v

a Om. in C

Entered in the original section of B. The donor is perhaps the Hugh de Blez who held of Peter de Nevill and Alice, his wife, in Langley in 1260 (*Cat. Anc. Deeds*, ii, B 1897; *Warks. Feet of Fines*, i. 167); for the lordship of Peter de Nevill and Alice, see *VCH Warks.*, iii. 72. Sir Guy Pipard is perhaps of the same family which had the overlordship of Lapworth in the 13th century (*ibid.*, v. 110). A field name very similar to *la Rudinge* occurs from the 16th century in Rowington (*Warks. Place-Names*, 370), but this appears to be different. For *Chelewellesiche*, see no. 577 n.

574 Confirmation by Robert son of Matthew of Forewood (*Fore-wode*)[1] to Reading Abbey of the entire gift made by Hugh *de Blez* [details exactly as in no. 573]. To be held in free alms and answering in all things to the abbey alone. Witnesses[a] [omitted]

[13th cent.; not later than 1258]

B f 124r; C f 69r

[a] *Om. in C*

Date as for no. 573. It is unclear from this confirmation whether Hugh de Blez held this land of Robert or not, but if so the latter was not his only lord in Langley (see no. 573 n.).

[1] In Wootton Wawen (*Warks. Place-Names*, 243).

574a Note of a charter by Robert *le Waleys* to Hugh *de Blez* concerning the exchange of 1 acre in Langley (*Longel'*)

[13th cent.; not later than 1258]

B f 124r; B f 125v (deleted)[1]

Entered in the original section of B.

[1] Copied in error as the rubric for no. 594, for which the correct rubric was substituted in the same hand.

LAPWORTH

575 Grant by Luke *Sorel* to Reading Abbey that it may assart and cultivate as much as it pleases of the wood called *Eweruge* and of its other adjacent woods near his land in those parts, in return for a grant by Reading Abbey that all the land which he had assarted before the coming of the justices-in-eyre to Coventry, 5 Henry III, shall remain to him and his heirs quit of all claim from the abbey. Neither he nor his heirs shall assart or break up the ground (*frussare*) of his woods or lands in those parts without the abbey's consent. The abbey and its men shall have common of pasture in the said lands and in his woods of Lapworth (*Lappewrðe*) freely and quit of all hindrance from him or his. Concerning the land called Harborough (*Erdbyr'*),[1] in respect of which the abbey recovered common of pasture in the king's court against Herbert the chaplain,[2] *sit sicut esse debuerit absque aliqua conventione quam cum eis vel cum aliquo alio inde fecerim*. Sealing before the king's justices at Coventry at the aforesaid time. Witnesses[a] [omitted]   [Sept. × Oct.] 1221

B f 125v; C f 70r–v

[a] *Om. in C*

The date is that of the main session of the eyre at Coventry in 5 Henry III (*Warks. Eyre 1221-2*, xii). The wood of *Eweruge*, a name now lost, was presumably in Rowington, which borders Lapworth on the east.

1 Harborough Banks, in Lapworth (*Warks. Place-Names*, 289).

2 In Michaelmas term, 1206, the abbot of Reading successfully sued Herbert, chaplain of Lapworth, for having unjustly disseised him of his common of pasture in Lapworth which belonged to his free tenement in Rowington (*Cur. Reg. R.*, iv. 228).

576 Gift in free alms by Odo *Basard'* of Lapworth (*Lappewrð*)*ᵃ* to Reading Abbey, with the assent of his wife and heirs, and for the souls of Luke *Sorel* and his own father and mother and ancestors, of part of his land in the vill of Lapworth, viz., the croft next to *Morsmethe*[1] lying next to the land of Adam *Calf* as far as the king's road to Birmingham (*Birmigham*), extending in length from this road to another croft called *Middelcroft* and from this croft along the ditch as far as the land of Adam *Calf*, the ditch remaining entirely to the abbey. Warranty and sealing. Witnesses*ᵇ* [omitted]   [? 1221 × 58]

B f 124v; C f 69r-v

ᵃ Rubrics have Lappewrðe; *BL Add. Roll 19617 (above, pp. 8-9) has* Lappewrþe
ᵇ Om. in C

Probably after no. 575, since Luke Sorel appears to have died; entered in the original section of B.

1 Possibly The Moors, in Lapworth (*Warks. Place-Names*, 377).

PRESTON BAGOT

577 *Gift by Hugh Fitz Richard, with the assent of his son William, to John of Kington, of Bearley, Acheals between Bearley and the Kington boundary, other land within stated bounds, and* Codesturna, *to be held in fee and inheritance by rendering annually 1 sore-hawk or 6d. John has given him in recognition 3 marks, to his son William ½ mark and a sword, and to Margaret his wife ½ mark*   [1123 × 53]

A f 44v; (noted) B f 129v; C f 73v

Hugo filius Ricardi omnibus amicis et hominibus suis, clericis et laicis, Francis et Anglicis, salutem. Sciant tam posteri quam presentes me dedisse et concessisse, assensu Willelmi filii mei, Iohanni de Kint(ona) pro suo homagio et suo servitio Burgelai, et Acheals inter Burgelaiam et divisam Kintona(m) et de Cholewelles-

iche usque ad Pavenhalam et de Pavenhal(a) la^a Alrennesiche usque
ad viam que venit de Warewic, et per viam usque ad crucem, et
Codesturnam cum omnibus predictis locis pertinentibus per easdem
metas per quas ego et Willelmus et^b filius meus et Stiant faber et
Siwardus forest(arius) perambulavimus. Hoc ei dedi et concessi in
feodo et hereditate illi et heredibus suis tenendum de me et de meis
heredibus libere et quiete et honorifice, pro omni seculari servitio
annuatim reddendo unum nisum sor^a ad Advincula sancti Petri [1
Aug.], et si nisum ad illum terminum non habuisset, ad festum
sancti Michaelis per .vi. denarios quietus sit. Et ipse in recognicione
dedit mihi tres marcas argenti, et Willelmo filio meo dimidiam marcam et unum gladium, et Margarete uxori mee dimidiam marcam.
Huius donationis testes: Willelmus filius meus, Reginaldus frater
domini, Robertus de Turbervilla, Engenulfus, Oseb(ertus) de Lun-
cecumbe, Achi, Stiant faber.

^{a} Sic
^{b} Sic, but possibly redundant

The dating limits are those of Roger earl of Warwick, who confirmed this gift (no.
578). The exact location of this property is uncertain. To judge from later references,
it lay mostly in Preston Bagot (see nos. 585-9) and certainly *Codesturna* was in that
parish (see no. 590), but the property was on another occasion described as in
Claverdon (see no. 584). *Cholewellesiche*, or *Chelewellesiche*, was a water-course
apparently on or near the boundary between Preston Bagot and Claverdon (see *Cat.
Anc. Deeds*, i, B 1706; ii, B 2953; *Sir Christopher Hatton's Book of Seals*, no. 278; above,
no. 573). The best conclusion appears to be that, although part of the property was
called Bearley, it lay largely in Preston Bagot on the Claverdon side and, if *Acheals*
can be identified with Eccles, in Rowington (*Warks. Place-Names*, 369), extended
northwards to Rowington. Hugh Fitz Richard is not known to have held in this
precise area, although he held of the earl of Warwick in Hatton, Snitterfield and
Wroxall nearby (*VCH Warks.*, iii. 116, 168, 217), while the earl of Warwick was also
overlord of Bearley and lord of Claverdon (*ibid.*, 43, 70).

578   *Confirmation by Roger, earl of Warwick, of Hugh Fitz Richard's gift
to John of Kington, of Bearley. John has given him in recognition a white
brachet*   [1123 × 53]

A ff 44v-45r; (noted) B f 129v; C f 74r

Rogerius comes Warewicensis omnibus baronibus et fidelibus suis
Francis et Angl(is) totius honoris sui tam futuris quam presentibus,
salutem. Sciatis me concessisse Iohanni de Chintona [*f45r*] illud
donum quod Hugo filius Ricardi ei fecit de Burgelai, ad tenendum
de eo et heredibus suis ipse et heredes sui; et si in manum meam
inciderit, similiter tenendum de me et de meis heredibus. Et pro hac
concessione ipse dedit mihi in recognitione quendam album brachet.
Et unoquoque anno quendam nisum debet inde dare pro omni

servitio. Itaque volo firmiterque precipio quod ipse et heredes sui
post eum teneant prescriptam Burgelaiam cum suis omnibus appendiciis, sicut carta Hugonis filii Ricardi dividit, plene, honorifice, in
omnibus locis et rebus, consuetudinibus, libertatibus.*

a *Text apparently corrupt here, since the syntax collapses towards the end of the deed and there
is no mention of witnesses*

The dating limits are those of Roger's earldom.

578a   *Note of [?] writ by King Henry [? I] to the earl and countess of
Warwick, on behalf of John of Kington*   [? 1123 × 35]

B f 129v; C f 74r

H(enrici) regis ad comitem et comitissam Warwic'*a* pro eodem*b*
Johanne de Kinton'.

a Warwik' C   *b* Interlined in B

The suggested dating depends upon the king being Henry I and the earl and countess
of Warwick being Roger and Gundreda. In the cartularies this note follows the notes
of Earl Roger's and Countess Gundreda's charters (nos. 578, 579).

579   *Confirmation [in the form of a gift and restoration] by Gundreda,
countess of Warwick, in her widowhood and with the consent of Earl William,
her son, to John of Kington, of Bearley and its [?] appurtenances, as the
charter by Roger earl of Warwick, her husband, witnesses, and in addition the
land of Siward de Codesturna; all to be held of her and her heirs by the
annual render of 1 sore-hawk*   [1153 × 84]

A f 45r-v; (noted) B f 129v; C f 74r

Gundreda comitissa Warewic(ensis) omnibus hominibus suis et amicis suis tam futuris quam presentibus, salutem. Sciatis me hereditarie
et concessu Willelmi comitis, filii mei, dedisse et reddidisse Iohanni
de Kintona Burgelaiam et sibi adiacentia, sicut carta Rogerii comitis
domini mei testatur, in bosco, in plano, in semitis, in aquis et in
omni libertate, scilicet annuatim pro omni servitio reddendo mihi
unum nisum sor; et in crecentia terram Siwardi de Codesturna sibi
et heredibus suis de me et de heredibus meis tenendum per idem
servitium, scilicet pro uno niso sor. [*f 45v*] Testibus: Willelmo comite
filio meo, Willelmo Giffard, Mathillide comitissa,[1] Margareta sorore
comitis,[2] Hugone de Ardena, et multis aliis.

The dating limits are those of William, earl of Warwick. Gundreda was the widow
of Roger, earl of Warwick. She was still living in 1166 (*Red Bk. Exch.*, i. 326), but,
although the date of her death is unknown (*Complete Peerage*, xii. 362), she may well
have died before 1184. In any case, immediate lordship of this estate passed to her

son in her lifetime, since she witnessed his charter confirming the same lands to be held of him (no. 580).

¹ Matilda, second wife of William earl of Warwick, who married her before 28 Dec. 1175 (*Complete Peerage*, xii. 363).

² Margaret, daughter of Earl Roger and Gundreda, although it is perhaps odd that the latter does not here describe her as her daughter (*ibid.*, 362, n. *d*; *EYC*, viii. 10).

580   *Confirmation [in the form of a gift] by William, earl of Warwick, to John of Kington, of Bearley [etc., as in no. 577], with grant that he may convey the land to whomsoever he wishes, for which concession he has given the earl an iron-grey horse and 5 marks*   [1153 × 84]

A f 45r; B f 129r; (noted) B f 129v; C f 73v

Willelmus*ᵃ* comes Warewic(ensis)*ᵇ* omnibus hominibus suis et amicis Francis et Anglicis tam futuris quam presentibus, salutem. Sciatis me dedisse et concessisse et sigillo meo confirmasse Iohanni de Kintona, pro homagio suo et servitio, Burgelai*ᶜ* et Azceals et*ᵈ* de Chelewellesiche usque in Pavenhale et de Pavenhale usque ad*ᵉ* Alrennesiche*ᶠ* usque ad viam que venit de Warew(ica)*ᵍ* et per viam usque ad crucem, et Codesturnam,*ʰ* reddendo annuatim mihi et heredibus meis pro omni servitio seculari in festo sancti Michaelis .vi. denarios. Et sciatis me hanc donationem fecisse prenominato Iohanni de Kintona et cuicumque predictus Iohannes voluerit dare vel devidere*ⁱ* voluerit,*ᵈ* salvo servitio meo. Pro concessu autem isto *ʲ*et donatione*ʲ* dedit mihi predictus Iohannes unum equum ferrant*ᵏ* et .v. marcas. Testibus: domina Gundreda comitissa, et Walera(nno) fratre meo, Roberto de Munfort,*ˡ* *ᵐ*[Hugone de Arden(a), Nigello de Mundevill(a), Philippo de Estleya, Willelmo de Danullez, Roberto filio Odonis, Waltero Revel, Henrico de Lodbrok', Henrico de Vilers, Waltero filio Gerardi, et Baldewino le Poer, et Iordano clerico].

ᵃ The initial letter in A is U	*ᵇ* Warewyk' *B*
ᶜ Burgelaye *B*	*ᵈ Om. in B*
ᵉ in B	*ᶠ* Allrensiche *B*
ᵍ Warewik' *B*	*ʰ* Codesternam *B*
ⁱ dividere *B*	*ʲ⁻ʲ Om. in B*
ᵏ Sic in A; ferant' *B*	*ˡ* Montford' *B*
ᵐ A ends with et multis aliis, *the remainder being taken from B*	

The dating limits are those of William's earldom. In the original compilation of B this charter was merely noted (f 129v), but in the 14th century the text was copied out in full (f 129r).

581   *Gift by John of Kington to Reading Abbey, with his body, of Bearley [etc., as in no. 577], for an annual render of 6d to the earl of Warwick*   [1184 × 93; ? 1189 × 93]

A f 44v; B f 129v; C f 73v

Sciant presentes et futuri quod ego Iohannes de Kintona,[a] pro salute
anime mee [b]et uxoris mee[b] et pro anima patris et matris mee et pro
animabus omnium antecessorum meorum et successorum, dedi cum
corpore meo et concessi et hac carta mea confirmavi deo et sancte
Marie de Rading(ia) et monachis ibidem deo servientibus Burgelaiam[c] cum omnibus pertinentiis suis, et Echles, et totam terram que
est inter Chelewellesiche usque ad Pavenhale, et totam terram que
est inter Pavenhale usque ad Alrennesiche,[d] et totam terram que est
inter Alrennesiche[d] usque ad viam que ducit ad Warewic,[e] et totam
terram per viam usque ad crucem. Concessi etiam predictis monachis Godesturnam[f] cum omnibus pertinentiis suis; ita libere et
quiete sicut ego liberius tenui et quietius, reddendo annuatim comiti
de Warewic[e] .vi. denarios pro omni terreno et seculari servitio.[g] His
testibus: Waltero clerico, Willelmo camberlano, Ernaldo marescallo,
et multis aliis.

[a] Kyngton' C
[c] Burghelaie B,C
[e] Warwic' B, Warewik' C
[g] B ends with T', C ends

[b-b] Om. in B,C
[d] Alrenesiche B,C
[f] Codesturnam B,C

Before Aug. 1193, when the donor was dead (see no. 583), and not earlier than Nov.
1184, when Waleran earl of Warwick, who confirmed the gift (no. 582) became earl.
However, since the land was not included in Richard I's otherwise very full general
confirmation to Reading, dated Sept. 1189 (no. 34), the gift was possibly made after
that date. This deed was probably made at Reading, since all the witnesses were
local Reading men.

582 *Confirmation of the same by Waleran, earl of Warwick, and grant of
common pasture in Claverdon for 16 oxen, 4 cows and 2 draught-animals and
free pannage in Claverdon wood for 40 pigs* [1184 × 93; ? 1189 × 93]

A f46v; B f129v; C f73v

Waleranus[a] comes War(ewicensis)[b] omnibus hominibus suis et amicis tam futuris quam presentibus, salutem. Sciatis me concessisse et
carta mea[c] presenti confirmasse deo et sancte Marie de Rading(ia)
et monachis ibidem deo servientibus donationem quam Iohannes de
Prestona[d] eis fecit de feodo meo, scilicet Burgele[e] cum omnibus pertinentiis suis, et Echeles, et totam terram que est inter Cheleswelle-
sich(e)[f] usque ad Pavenhale, et totam terram que est inter Pavenhale usque ad Alrenesich(e), et totam terram que est inter
Alrenesich(e) usque ad viam que ducit ad War(ewicam),[b] et totam
terram per viam usque ad crucem, et Codesturne cum omnibus
pertinentiis suis, tenendum de me et heredibus meis, reddendo inde
annuatim michi et heredibus meis sex denarios ad festum sancti
Michaelis. Preterea concessi eisdem monachis communem pasturam

in Claverdon(a) sexdecim bobus et quatuor vaccis et duobus avris,^{g} et panagium in bosco de Claverdona quietum quadraginta porcorum. Quare volo ut predicti monachi habeant et teneant hec omnia predicta ita libere et quiete sicut predictus Iohannes ea liberius et melius tenuit et sicut carta Willelmi comitis fratris mei eidem Iohanni confirmavit.^{h}

^{a} Walerannus B,C ^{b} Warwic' B, Warewyk'/Warewik' C
^{c} Om. in C ^{d} Kinton' B, Kyngton' C (see note)
^{e} Burghel' B,C ^{f} Chelewellesich' B,C
^{g} averis B,C ^{h} Add T' B

Date as for no. 581. The text in A is almost certainly wrong in calling Reading's benefactor John of Preston, for the latter was in fact the brother of John of Kington's wife (see no. 583). The correct name, 'of Kington', is given in the B and C texts. A possible reason for the error in A is that, at about the time this entry was made, the abbey was engaged in an action with John of Preston and his sister (no. 583) and that the scribe inadvertently confused the two names. Though not in the original compilation of A, the confirmation was added in the same hand very soon afterwards with a type of undecorated initial different from that of the main text, and it was added to the contemporary table of contents (f 4v). The entry may well have been made, therefore, in 1193.

583   *Final concord in the king's court at Oxford by which John of Preston and Agnes his sister, late the wife of John of Kington, quitclaimed to Reading Abbey 1 carucate of land in Bearley, a third part of which Agnes would hold of the abbey for life*   13 Aug. 1193

B f 176v; C f 105r

Hec est finalis concordia facta in curia domini regis apud Oxon(efordiam) die veneris proxima post festum sancti Laurentii, anno regni regis Ricardi iiii., coram W(altero) Rothom(agensi) archiepiscopo, Godefr(ido)^a Wint(oniensi) et Ricardo Lond(oniensi) episcopis, Gaufr(edo) filio P(etri) et W(illelmo) Marescallo et Roberto de Wittefeld' et Osb(erto) filio Hervei, iustic(iariis) domini regis, et multis aliis domini regis fidelibus ibidem tunc presentibus, inter Iohannem de Preston(a) et Agnetem sororem eius que fuit uxor Iohannis de Kint(ona), petentes, et abbatem de^b Rading(ia), tenentem per W. capellanum et^b confratrem suum positum loco eiusdem abbatis in curia prefata ad lucrandum vel perdendum, de una carucata terre cum pertinentiis in Burghelee,^{c} unde placitum fuit inter eos in eadem curia. Scilicet quod predicti Iohannes et Agnes quiet'clamaverunt in perpetuum de illis et de heredibus eorum predictam carucatam terre cum pertinentiis predicto abbati et conventui de Rading(ia) per sic quod predicta Agnes tenebit in tota vita sua de predicto abbate et conventu tertiam partem predicte carucate terre cum pertinentiis per regale servitium quod ad predictam tertiam partem pertinet pro omni servitio. Et post eius decessum redibit illa tertia pars illius carucate*d* terre quieta prefato abbati et conventui de Rading(ia) in perpetuum.

_a Godfr' C   _b Om. in C
^c Burghlee C   ^d caruce (sic) C

This fine was made in an action for recovery of dower (see no. 584).

584 *Final concord in the king's court at Westminster, in an assize of mort d'ancestor, by which Abbot Hugh [II] and the convent of Reading conceded to Matilda of Kington and her sisters, Margery and Alice, and Robert de Turville and William of Bearley, husbands of Matilda and Margery, and their heirs 1 carucate of land and a wood in Claverdon, saving an annual rent of 6d from Ingram Bagot, which remained to the abbey, and saving the tenement of Agnes of Preston, which remained to her for life as dower; to be held of the abbey for an annual rent of 20s. After Agnes's death her tenement was to revert to the said Matilda, Margery, Alice, Robert and William or their heirs, who would thenceforth pay the abbey 2 marks of silver annually in perpetuity*   17 Nov. 1194

B f 176r-v; C ff 104v-105r

Hec est finalis concordia facta in curia domini regis apud Westm(onasterium) die iovis proxima post festum sancti Martini, anno regni regis Ricardi vi., coram Gaufr(edo) filio P(etri), Tedbaldo de Valain(es),*a* Michaele Belet, Henrico de Wichint(ona), magistro Aristot(ele), iustic(iariis) domini regis, et aliis baronibus et fidelibus domini regis ibidem tunc presentibus, inter Matill(em) de Kinton(a) et Margeriam sororem suam, petentes per Robertum de Turvill(a) et Willelmum de Burlee viros ipsarum positos loco earundem in curia domini regis ad lucrandum vel perdendum, et Aliciam sororem predictarum M(atillis) et M(argerie), petentem per Henricum filium eiusdem Alicie positum loco ipsius in prefata curia ad lucrandum vel perdendum, et Hugonem abbatem et conventum de Rading(ia), tenentes per Robertum camerarium positum loco eiusdem abbatis in prefata curia ad lucrandum vel perdendum, de una carucata*b* terre et .i. bosco cum pertinentiis in Claverd(ona), unde recognitio de morte antecessoris summonita fuit inter eos in curia domini regis. Scilicet quod predicti Hugo abbas et conventus concesserunt predictis Roberto et Matill(i) et Willelmo et Margerie et Alicie et heredibus ipsorum totam predictam carucatam*b* terre et boscum cum pertinentiis in Claverdon(a), preter redditum sex denariorum per annum de Ingeram Baggot*c* qui remanet in perpetuum quietus de predictis R(oberto) et M(atille), W(illelmo) et M(argeria) et Alicia et de heredibus eorum predictis Hugoni abbati et conventui et eorum successoribus, et preter tenementum Agnetis de Preston(a) quod remanet ipsi Agneti in tota vita eius^d sicut dos sua, tenenda de ipso abbate et conventu et de eorum successoribus reddendo inde per annum .xx. solidos sterlingorum quamdiu prefata Agnes vixerit pro omni servitio ad predictum abbatem vel ad successores suos pertinente. Et post decessum ipsius Agnetis predictum tenementum predicte Agnetis redibit ad predictos R(obertum) et M(atillem), W(illelmum) et M(argeriam) et Aliciam vel ad heredes ipsorum sicut ius et hereditas ipsorum. Et preterea post decessum predicte Agnetis predicti Robertus et Matill(is), W(illelmus) et Margeria et Alicia vel heredes eorum reddent in perpetuum per annum predicto abbati et conventui et eorum successoribus .ii. marcas argenti [f176v] ad tres terminos, scilicet ad festum sancti Michaelis .viii. solidos .x. denarios et obolum, et ad Natale domini .viii. solidos .x. denarios et obolum, et ad Inventionem Sancte Crucis .viii. solidos .xi. denarios, pro omni servitio ad predictum abbatem et conventum vel ad successores suos pertinente, salvo forinseco servitio.

^{a} Walein' C ^{b} caruca/carucam C
^{c} Bagot' C ^{d} sua C

The three sisters were clearly the daughters and co-heirs of John of Kington, who made the gift to Reading in no. 581, since in this fine the dower of Agnes of Preston, John's widow (see no. 583), was excluded from the settlement for the time of her life. The settlement concerned the land which John of Kington gave to Reading in no. 581. The rent of 6d paid by Ingram Bagot was presumably in respect of the land, messuage and meadow conveyed to him by John of Kington (see no. 584a). In 1202 the same three sisters (reading 'Margaret' for 'Margery') and two husbands, the plaintiffs in the present fine, quitclaimed 1 carucate in Preston [Bagot] to Clement of Preston and Agnes his wife in an assize of mort d'ancestor (*Warks. Feet of Fines*, i. 23).

584a Note of a charter by John of Kington (*Kinton'*) to Ingram Bagot concerning certain land with a messuage and a small meadow (*pratellum*)   [before Aug. 1193]

B f126r

Before John's death (see no. 581 n.). Ingram Bagot is presumed to have received Preston Bagot from William, earl of Warwick, possibly *c.* 1170 (*VCH Warks.*, iii. 142).

585 *Gift by Alice of Kington, with the assent of her son and heir Henry, to her son Thomas of all her land of Bearley with appurtenances in Preston [Bagot] which she held of Reading Abbey; for an annual render to herself of white gloves, and to the abbey of 8s 10½d*   [1194 × early 13th cent.]

A f87v; (noted) B f129r; C f73v

Sciant presentes et futuri quod ego Alicia de Kintona, assensu et
voluntate Henrici filii mei et heredis, dedi et hac presenti carta mea
confirmavi Thome filio meo et heredibus suis pro homagio et servitio
suo totam terram meam de Burgheleia cum pertinentiis in Prestona
quam tenui de monachis de Rading(ia), tenendam de me et heredibus meis libere et quiete in bosco et in plano et in omnibus libertatibus, reddendo mihi et heredibus meis quasdam cyrotecas albas
ad Pascha annuatim pro omnibus servitiis et exactionibus michi et
heredibus meis pertinentibus, et predictis monachis de Reding' .ix.
solidos .iii. obolos minus tribus terminis, scilicet .iii. solidos ad Natale
et .iii. solidos ad Inventionem Sancte Crucis et .iii. solidos .iii. obolos
minus ad festum sancti Michaelis. Et hanc donationem ego et
heredes mei Thome et heredibus suis warantizabimus contra omnes.
Hiis testibus.

Not in the original section of A, but among the latest of its entries in the first half of
the 13th century. After no. 584, since the donor was one of the sisters who obtained
their father's land from the abbot by that fine, and before no. 588, which dates
possibly 1225 × 50.

586   *Gift by Henry le Notte* [*senior*]*ᵃ to his brother, Thomas, of all his land
in Preston* [*Bagot*], *viz., a third part of Bearley which his mother, Alice, held
of Reading Abbey; for an annual render to himself of white gloves, and to the
abbey of 8s 10½d*   [1194 × early 13th cent.]

A f 87r; (noted) B f 129r; C f 73v

Sciant presentes et futuri quod ego Henricus le Notte dedi et hac
carta mea confirmavi Thome fratri meo et heredibus suis totam
terram meam in Prestona, scilicet tertiam partem de Burghelea cum
pertinentiis suis, quam mater mea Alicia tenuit de monachis de
Rading(ia) pro homagio et servitio suo, tenendam de me et heredibus meis libere et quiete in bosco et in plano et in omnibus libertatibus, reddendo mihi et heredibus meis annuatim quasdam albas
cirotecas ad Pascha pro omnibus servitiis et exactionibus mihi et
heredibus meis pertinentibus, et predictis monachis de Rading(ia)
.ix. solidos tres obolos minus tribus terminis, scilicet .iii. solidos ad
Nathale, .iii. solidos ad Inventionem Sancte Crucis et .iii. solidos tres
obolos minus ad festum sancti Michaelis. Et hanc donationem ego
et heredes mei predicto Thome et heredibus suis warantizabimus
contra omnes. Hiis testibus.

ᵃ *Not in text, but so described in B,C notes and in BL Add. Roll 19617 (see above, p. 9)*

Date as for no. 585. The donor may be the Henry le Notte who occurs in 1199 and
1201 (*Warks. Feet of Fines*, i, nos. 25, 61, 72).

587 *Gift by Juliana of Kington to her brother, Thomas, of all her land in
Bearley of the fee of the abbot of Reading, for an annual render of* [*?*] *white
gloves. For this Thomas has given her 3 marks* [1194 x early 13th cent.]

A f87v; (noted) B f129r; C f73v

Sciant presentes et futuri quod ego Iuliana de Kinton(a) dedi et
concessi et hac presenti carta mea confirmavi Thome fratri meo, pro
homagio et servitio suo, totam terram meam in Burgheleia cum
omnibus pertinentiis suis absque retenemento, scilicet illam terram
que est de feudo abbatis de Rading(ia), habendam et tenendam de
me et heredibus meis ipse et heredes sui iure perpetuo libere et
quiete ab omni seculari [servitio]*ᵃ* et exigentia ad me sive ad heredes
meos pertinente per .l'.*ᵇ* cyrotecas annuatim ad Pascha persolvendas.
Pro hac autem donatione et confirmatione dedit mihi predictus
Thomas .iii. marcas argenti. Hiis testibus.

ᵃ Supplied   *ᵇ Sic; ? for albas (cf. nos. 585-6)*

Date as for no. 585. The notes in B and C describe the land as 'of Bearley in Preston'.

588 Gift in free alms by Thomas of Kington (*Kington'*) to Reading
Abbey of all the land and tenement which he sometime held of the
fee of Bearley (*Burele*),*ᵃ* to be held freely and quit of all custom,
demand, suit of court and secular service. Warranty and sealing.
Witnesses*ᵇ* [omitted]   [? 1225 × 50]

A f87r; B f128v; C f73r

ᵃ Burle B,C
ᵇ Om. in C

This is entered in A after nos. 810-13, which date *c.* 1238 × 50, and in the same, or a
very similar, hand, which also copied no. 589 and nos. 585-8. For the date, see also
no. 589 n. The rubrics of B and C describe the property as 'in the fee of Bearley in
Preston'.

589 Gift by Henry le Notte [junior]*ᵃ* to Reading Abbey of all the
right which he had in the land and tenement which his uncle,
Thomas of Kington (*Kinton'*),*ᵇ* gave to the abbey in free alms, and
of whatever he could have in rent and other things from the same.
Sealing. Witnesses*ᶜ* [omitted]   [? 1225 × 50]

A f87r; B f129r; C f73r-v

ᵃ Not in text, but so described in B,C rubrics and in BL Add. Roll 19617 (see p. 9)
ᵇ Kyngton' C
ᶜ Om. in C

The donor was presumably the son of Henry le Notte, senior, son of Alice of Kington, who made the gift to Thomas in no. 586. The present Henry is perhaps the Henry le Notte who in 1235 held Kington (in Claverdon) as part of a knight's fee of the earl of Warwick (*Fees*, i. 508; *VCH Warks.*, iii. 71, 143), since this fits with the other dating evidence (see no. 588 n.). The rubrics of B and C describe the property as 'in Preston'. The details in nos. 583–9 yield the following genealogy:

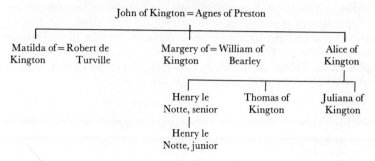

John of Kington = Agnes of Preston

Matilda of = Robert de Margery of = William of Alice of
Kington Turville Kington Bearley Kington

Henry le Thomas of Juliana of
Notte, senior Kington Kington

Henry le
Notte, junior

589a Note of a charter by Matilda of Kington (*Kington'*) to Thomas of Kington concerning a mill and 10 acres of land in Kington [? 1194 × early 13th cent.]

B f 129r; C f 73v

This note follows in B and C those of nos. 585–7, with which it appears to be connected. Kington (in Claverdon) is very near to the other places named in these deeds and it is most probable that Matilda's charter concerned part of the land and tenement given by Thomas to Reading in no. 588. She was one of the daughters and co-heirs of John of Kington (see no. 584) and therefore aunt of Thomas of Kington (see no. 589 n.).

590 *Gift in free alms by William of Bearley to Reading Abbey of the land and tenement which he held of Simon Bagot at* Coddesturn' *in the parish of Preston [Bagot], as is contained in the charters of Simon Bagot and Margery, daughter of Richard son of Pavia of Warwick, but excepting the meadow which Jordan held* [? late 12th × early 13th cent. *or* ? *c.* 1225 × 50]

A f 87v; B ff 127v–128r; C f 72r–v

Sciant presentes et futuri quod ego Willelmus de Burle dedi et concessi et hac presenti carta mea confirmavi deo et ecclesie beate Marie de Rading(ia) et abbati et monachis ibidem deo servientibus, in liberam et*ᵃ* puram et perpetuam elemosinam, totam terram et totum tenementum cum pertinentiis quod aliquando tenui de Symone Bagod*ᵇ* in parochia de Preston(a)*ᶜ* apud Coddesturn' cum mesuagio, curia, pomerio, mora, pratis et cum omnibus aliis pertinentiis et libertatibus in bosco,*ᵈ* in plano, in pasturis, in viis, in aquis, in semitis et in omnibus aliis locis, sicut in cartis Symonis Bagod*ᵇ* et

Margerie filie Ricardi filii Pavie de Warewik'^{e} inde confectis plenius
continetur, excepto tantummodo illo prato quod Iordanus aliquando tenuit. Hec omnia supradicta tenebunt et possidebunt abbas
et monachi^f de Rading(ia) bene et pacifice et quiete sine omni
vexatione et calumpnia de me ^{g}vel de^g heredibus meis de cetero
veniente. Et ego predictus W(illelmus) et heredes mei totam terram
et^h predictum tenementum cum omnibus pertinentiis suis prefatis
abbati et monachis contra omnes homines et feminas in perpetuum
warantizabimus. Et ut hec mea donatio, concessio et confirmatio
perpetuum robur obtineat^i in posterum, hanc presentem cartam
impressione sigilli mei consignavi.^{j} Hiis testibus.

^{a} Om. in B,C ^{b} Bagot B, Bagot' C
^{c} Prestun' B ^{d} Insert et C
^{e} Warwic' B ^{f} Insert ecclesie B,C
$^{g-g}$ vel B, et C ^{h} Insert totum B,C
^{i} optineat B,C ^{j} B,C end

The dating is very insecure. The earlier of the suggested dates is derived from the
quitclaim by Prior Ralph of Wootton Wawen (no. 592), whose dates are very uncertain; the later is based on the fact that this deed was entered among the later
additions in A and on other evidence in the deed itself. Simon Bagot may be he who
was lord of Preston Bagot from some time after 1221 to 1242-3 (see no. 593 n.), while
Margery's father, Richard son of Pavia, occurs as a vintner in Warwick as late as
1221 (*Warks. Eyre 1221-2*, 369).

590a Notes of the following:
  (i) charter by Simon Bagot to William of Bearley (*Burlegh'*) con-
      cerning a messuage at *Coddesturne*;
  (ii) charter by Margery of Warwick (*Warwic'*)^a to W(illiam) of
      Bearley concerning land in Preston [Bagot] (*Prestona*)

B f 128r; C f 72v

^{a} Warewik' C

These are clearly the charters mentioned in no. 590.

591 *Gift by William of Bearley to Reading Abbey of the meadow which
belonged to Jordan of Preston [in Preston Bagot],*[1] *for which the abbey has
given him 10s to free himself from the Jews*

[? early 13th cent. *or* ? *c.* 1225 × 58]

B f 128r; C f 72v

Sciant presentes et futuri quod ego W(illelmus) de Burle. dedi, concessi et hac presenti carta mea confirmavi abbati et conventui de
Rading(ia) pratum meum quod fuit Jordani de Preston(a) cum
omnibus pertinentiis suis et cum omni haytio^a quod est inter pratum

predictum et moram predicti Willelmi, habend(um) et tenend(um) de me et heredibus meis libere et quiete ab omni seculari servitio. Pro hac autem donatione et confirmatione dederunt mihi predictus abbas et conventus .x. solidos ad liberandum me de judaismo. Ut autem concessio mea rata et stabilis sit, appositione sigilli mei confirmavi. T(estibus).[b]

[a] hayicio C   [b] Om. in C

Not entered in A; in the original section of B. It is clearly later than no. 590, since William here gives the meadow excepted from that gift. For discussion of the possible alternative dates, see no. 590 n.

[1] The rubrics of B,C say 'in Preston'.

591a Note of a charter by the same to the prior of Wootton [Wawen] (*Wottone*) concerning the tenement of *Coddesturne*
[? late 12th *or* ? early 13th cent.]

B f 128r

Presumably before nos. 590 and 592, which, respectively, give and quitclaim the tenement to Reading.

592 *Quitclaim by Prior Ralph and the convent of Wootton [Wawen] to Reading Abbey of all their right in the land and tenement which belonged to William of Bearley at and around* Coddeston' *in the parish of Preston [Bagot]. Reading Abbey has given them 16½ marks as purchase price and entry-fine*   [? late 12th × early 13th cent. *or* ? *c.* 1225 × 50]

A f 87v; B f 128r; C f 72v

Sciant presentes et futuri quod ego Rad(ulfus) prior de Wothton'[a] et fratres ibidem deo servientes remisimus et concessimus et hac presenti carta nostra[b] confirmavimus deo et ecclesie beate Marie de Rading(ia) et abbati et monachis ibidem deo servientibus totum ius nostrum et clamium quod aliquando habuimus et habere potuimus in tota terra et in toto tenemento quod fuit Willelmi de Burle in parochia[c] de Preston(a) apud Codeston'[d] et circa Coddeston',[d] predictis abbati et monachis tenend(um) et habend(um) et possidend(um) quiet(um) de nobis et de successoribus nostris in perpetuum. Pro hac vero remissione et ʿquieta clamationeʿ et confirmatione dederunt nobis predicti abbas et monachi sexdecim marcas et dimidiam argenti nomine emptionis et gersume. Et quia volumus quod hec nostra remissio et ʿquieta clamatioʿ et confirmatio rata sit et stabilis in perpetuum perseveret, appositione sigilli nostri presentem paginam corroboravimus.[f] Hiis testibus.

a Wotton' *B,C*   *b Interlined in A*
c parrochia *B*   *d* Coddesturne *B,C*
e-e quiet'cl' *B*, quietcl' *C*   *f B ends with* T', *C ends*

Prior Ralph is said to occur ? late 12th century, before Prior Gerard who is said to occur ? early 13th century (*Heads of Relig. Houses*, 113), but these dates are very uncertain and some of the evidence in no. 590, to which this quitclaim is related, suggests the possibility of a later date (see no. 590 n.). The deed is entered in A in the same hand as no. 590.

593 Gift by Simon Bagot to Reading Abbey of the following [in Preston Bagot]:*a* all the land which Geoffrey *Chimbel* held, and 2 acres of land appurtenant to the mill, with the wood lying between the said land and the said 2 acres, to be held in free alms by rendering annually to Simon and his heirs 6d at Michaelmas; the strip of cultivated land (*cultura*) extending from the said land to the road leading to Beaudesert (*Beaudesert*) with meadows, moors, pastures and all other appurtenances, in length and breadth as far as the bridge of *Esseford*, by rendering annually 6d at Michaelmas; two mills with the entire multure of his house and suit of his men of Preston [Bagot] (*Preston'*) with all fisheries and water-courses appurtenant to the mills and ways leading to the mills, in free alms by rendering annually 6d at Michaelmas for all service; a 4-foot plot of his land (*spatium quatuor pedum terre mee*) along one side of the water-courses to improve the ponds of the said mills as shall be expedient. If the abbey or its tenants should incur danger or loss through the alteration of the water-courses by him or his heirs to the value of 6d, they would pay 20s as a penalty within the octave following; if the damages were more than 6d, they would double the penalty, all damages and impediments to be rectified by the view of two lawful men of Rowington (*Rokint(ona)*). All coming to the mills or ponds shall have free entry and exit over his land. All the above to be held freely and quit of all secular service [etc.] and of all suits of court, by the said annual rent of 18d. Warranty. For this the abbey has given him 40 marks of silver, in his great need, to acquit himself against the Jews. Witnesses*b* [omitted]   [? 1221 × 38]

B ff 126v–127v; C ff 71v–72r

a Not in text, supplied from rubrics
b Om. in C

The donor was lord of Preston Bagot, held of the earl of Warwick (*VCH Warks.*, iii. 142–3). Although a Simon Bagot occurs in 1202 (*Warks. Feet of Fines*, i. 23) and was prominent in the Warwickshire eyre of 1221 (see *Warks. Eyre 1221–2*, index *sub nomine*), he is not thought to have become lord of the manor until after 1221, when a Hugh Bagot was apparently in possession (*ibid.*, 268; *VCH Warks.*, iii. 142). Simon was still living in 1238 (*Cur. Reg. R.*, xvi. 50), but appears to have died by 1242–3 (*Fees*, ii.

957). This deed cannot be later than 1238 at the latest, since Simon subsequently reduced the rent payable by the abbey for these possessions in the time of Abbot Adam of Lathbury, 1226–38 (see no. 595).

593a Note of a charter between Simon Bagot and *Ketell'* concerning two mills in Preston [Bagot] (*Preston'*) [? 1221 × 38]

B f 128r; C f 72v

Possibly after Simon became lord of Preston Bagot (see no. 593 n.) and presumably before no. 593, since the mills are probably those given to Reading in that deed.

594 Gift in free alms by Simon Bagot to Reading Abbey of a parcel (*parcella*) of land, 12 feet wide, extending from *la Stoniforde* to the meadow of John *Cotewill'*, in order to improve Reading's mill pond. Warranty and sealing. Witnesses*a* [omitted] [? 1221 × 38]

B ff 125v–126r; C f 70v

a Om. in C

In view of the purpose of the gift, probably not much later than no. 593, *q.v.*

595 Remission and quitclaim by Simon Bagot to Abbot Adam [of Lathbury] and the convent of Reading of 12d of the 18d which they used to pay him for mills, meadows, lands and a grove in Preston [Bagot] (*Prestona*), so that neither Simon nor his heirs shall claim or be able to claim more than 6d annually. Warranty of the mills [etc.] by the said service of 6d annually. For this the abbey has given him 1 quarter of wheat (*frumentum*), 1 quarter of rye (*siligo*) and 2 quarters of oats (*avena*). Sealing. Witnesses*a* [omitted] [1226 × 38]

B f 127v; C f 72r

a Om. in C

The dating limits are those of Adam of Lathbury's abbacy.

596 Quitclaim by Nichola (*Nicholaa*), widow of Simon Bagot of Preston (*Preston'*), to Reading Abbey of all her right in the land and meadow which she had from the abbey as her dower. For this the abbey has given her 1 mark of silver as entry-fine. She has sworn before good and worthy men that she will never resist this quitclaim. Witnesses*a* [omitted] [1238 × 58]

B f 127v; C f 72r

a Om. in C

Simon Bagot was still living in 1238 (see no. 593, n.), and this quitclaim was entered in the original section of B. The cartulary rubrics describe Nichola's dower as 'in Preston'.

596a   Note of a chirograph relating to the same   [1238 × 58]

B f 127v

Date as for no. 596.

597   Gift in free alms by Thomas Bagot (*Bagod*)[a] to Reading Abbey of a parcel (*particula*) of land, 2 perches long and 22 feet wide, lying between his own land and the water running to the mill of Preston [Bagot] (*Preston'*), and starting at his land and extending as far as the abbey's land, in order to improve the pond of the said mill. For this the abbey has given him 18d sterling. Warranty and sealing. Witnesses[b] [omitted]   [? 1221 × 38]

B f 126v; C f 71r-v

[a] Bagot' C   [b] *Om. in C*

Reference to the mill pond suggests that this acquisition was made by the abbey at about the same time as no. 594.

598   Gift in free alms by John *de Cotevill'* to Reading Abbey of a parcel (*particula*) of land which Thomas Bagot (*Bagod*)[a] gave him for his homage and service in the vill of Preston [Bagot] (*Prestone*), lying between the water running to the mill of Preston [Bagot] and his own meadow on the west. Warranty and sealing. Witnesses[b] [omitted]   [? 1221 × 38]

B f 126v; C f 71r

[a] Bagot C   [b] *Om. in C*

Date as for no. 597. John *de Cotewile* occurs in 1249 (*Cat. Anc. Deeds*, i, B 779).

599   Gift in free alms by Alfred son of Godfrey *de Mundesl(e)*[a] to Reading Abbey of the homage and service of John *de Coteville* which he owed him and his heirs, viz., 1 pair of gloves annually at Easter or ½d. Also grant in free alms of whatever he had or could have in or by the same John within the bounds of Preston [Bagot] (*Preston'*). Warranty and sealing. Witnesses[b] [omitted]   [? 1225 × 50]

A ff 87v–88r; B f 126v; C f 71r

[a] Mundesleye B,C   [b] *Om. in C*

Entered in A in the same hand as nos. 590 and 592; possibly contemporary with nos. 597–8, although how the present donor became involved is not clear.

600 Gift in free alms by Ralph Pauncefoot (*Paunsefot*) to Reading Abbey of 2s annual rent which John *de Cotevill'* was accustomed to pay him for the free tenement which he held of him in the vill of Preston [Bagot] (*Preston'*), with the homage of John and his heirs and all other escheats which might arise from John or his heirs. Warranty and sealing. Witnesses[a] [omitted]   [? c. 1220 × 58]

B f 128r–v; C ff 72v–73r

[a] *Om. in C*

Dating very uncertain, but possibly of the same period as nos. 597–9 and not later than 1258, since the deed was entered in the original section of B.

601 Final concord in the king's court at Warwick in the octave of the Purification, 13 Edward I, before John des Vaux (*de Vallibus*), William *de Saham*, John of Mettingham (*Metingham*) and master Thomas of Siddington (*Sudinton'*), justices-in-eyre, and others, between Abbot Robert [of Burgate] of Reading, plaintiff by Edward *le Someter'* as attorney, and Thomas *de Edinton'*[a] and Isabel, his wife, on a plea by the abbot that the latter should acquit him of the service which William Beauchamp (*de Bello Campo*), earl of Warwick, was demanding from the free tenement which the abbot held of them in Preston Bagot (*Prestone Bagot*), namely, 2 virgates of land, 2 mills and 4 acres of meadow. The abbot complained that, although he held these as free alms by the service of 6d annually, the earl is distraining him for scutage at the rate of 5s 6d for a 40-shilling scutage. In settlement Thomas and Isabel recognized the said tenements to be the right of the abbot and abbey of Reading, to be held of them and the heirs of Isabel for 6d annually at Michaelmas for all service, suit of court, custom and exaction; and they and the heirs of Isabel will warrant the same as free alms and acquit the abbot and his successors and the abbey against the earl and his heirs and all others of the said scutage and all other secular services and aids. For this the abbot remitted to Thomas and Isabel all damages which he said he had incurred by their failure to acquit him of the said scutage hitherto   9 Feb. 1285

B f 177r; C f 105v
Pd. (cal.) *Warks. Feet of Fines*, ii. 2–3 (no. 988) (from PRO foot: CP 25(1)/244/32/9)

[a] *PRO foot has* Etindon'

Clearly Thomas *de Edinton'* and Isabel had succeeded to the lordship which Simon Bagot formerly had over these tenements when he gave them to the abbey (no. 593) and later reduced the rent due to him and his heirs to 6d (no. 595). By the time of Simon Baget's death, between 1238 and 1242/3, his lands in Preston Bagot had been disposed of to sub-tenants (*VCH Warks.*, iii. 143). The overlordship belonged to the earls of Warwick (*ibid.*, 142). Despite this fine, Guy Beauchamp, earl of Warwick, made in 1311 a similar demand for scutage from the abbot, who had to sue Isabel's heir, Roger of Stoke, for acquittance (*Year Books of Edward II 1310-11*, ed. G. J. Turner (Selden Soc., xxvi, 1911), 76).

ROWINGTON

602 *Gift by Adeliza d'Ivry to Reading Abbey of the vill of Rowington* [*c.* 1133]

A f 36r; B f 123v; C f 68r
Pd. Kennett, *Parochial Antiquities*, i. 111

Sciant tam presentes quam futuri sub Christiana religione constituti quod ego Adelitia*ᵃ* de Ivri*ᵇ* concessi ecclesie sancte dei genitricis Marie de Rading(ia) et fratribus ibidem deo servientibus, pro salute anime mee et patris mei atque matris mee et omnium antecessorum meorum, perpetuo iure possidendam villam nomine Rokintonam cum omnibus ad eam pertinentibus. Et ne hoc aliqua rerum labentium varietate deleri valeat, decrevi istud presenti scripto assignare et confirmare subscriptis testibus.*ᶜ* Testibus:*ᵈ* Walterio capellano, Rodulfo Macro, Roberto de Vivario, Roberto de Bosco Herberti, Roberto Dagoberto, Willelmo de Waregrava.

ᵃ Adeliz *B,C*	*ᵇ* Ivery *B*, Iveri *C*
ᶜ C ends	*ᵈ B ends*

The date is probably approximately the same as that of Henry I's confirmation (no. 603). The donor was the daughter of Hugh de Grandmesnil, who had held the manor in 1086 (*VCH Warks.*, iii. 149), and widow of Roger d'Ivry, who died possibly *c.* 1100 (Orderic Vitalis, iv. 230; *The Domesday Monachorum of Christ Church Canterbury*, ed. D. C. Douglas (1944), 56-7—both sources call her Adelina, but the Reading charters seem conclusive that her name was Adeliza, like her mother's). Before her gift to Reading, Adeliza had already granted part of it to Ralph Macer (see no. 611), who witnessed the present deed.

603 Confirmation (*concessi*) in free alms by King Henry I to Reading Abbey of the manor of Rowington in Warwickshire, to be held of him in chief as his own alms, which manor Adeliza d'Ivry (*de Evereio*) gave with his consent; and precept that the abbey shall hold it as freely and with the same liberties as it holds any alms of the king's demesne [28 May × 2 Aug.] 1133

A ff 14v-15r; B f 18r
Pd. *Regesta*, ii. 377 (no. cclxviii); (cal.) *ibid.*, 261 (no. 1757); Kennett, *Parochial Antiquities*, i. 111; Farrer, *Itin.*, 150 (no. 713), reprinted from *EHR*, xxxiv (1919), 574

... in presentia et audientia subscriptorum: *R(ogerii) episcopi Sar(esburiensis), Henrici episcopi Wint(oniensis), Nigelli Eliensis ecclesie electi, Bernardi episcopi Sancti David, Roberti comitis Gloec(estrie), Stephani comitis Morit(onii), Willelmi comitis Warenn(e), Roberti de Ver, Roberti de Curci, B(riani) filii comitis, Hugonis Bigoti, Unfr(edi) de Buhun, Alberici de Ver, Ricardi Bass(et). Apud Wdestoc(am),*ª anno incarnationis domini nostri I(hesu) Christi M.C.xxxiii, peracta feliciter in domino.

ª–ª T' *B*

Nigel was nominated as bishop of Ely on 28 May and consecrated on 1 Oct., 1133; Henry I left England for the last time on 2 Aug. 1133 (*Regesta*, ii, p. xxxi). Cartulary A notes another charter [by the same] concerning the same.

604 Precept by King Henry I to the sheriff, justice, barons and ministers of Warwickshire that the land and men of the abbot of Reading of Rowington are to be quit of plea, plaint, shire and hundred, etc., and that the abbot shall try any case of larceny or murder arising there and have the forfeiture and justice, since the king has determined that the abbey, of which he is the founder, shall be free of these   [July 1133]

A f 15r; B f 18r
Pd. *Regesta*, ii. 379 (no. cclxxiv); (cal.) *ibid.*, 268 (no. 1789)

T(este)ª R(oberto) de Curci. Apud Burn(am).

ª B ends

While the king was at Westbourne (Sussex) shortly before his last crossing to Normandy.

605 Precept by King Stephen to the sheriff and barons of Warwickshire that the land and men of the abbot of Reading of Rowington are to be quit of pleas, plaints, shires and hundreds, etc., and that the abbot shall try any case of larceny or murder arising there and have the forfeiture and justice, as King Henry I conceded and ordered by his writ   [1136 × 54; prob. 1140 × 54]

A f 19v; B f 29r
Pd. *Regesta*, iii. 254 (no. 687)

Testibus:ª R. cancellario, et W(illelmo) Mart(el). Apud Oxen(efordiam).

ª B ends

The narrower dating limits depend upon R. the chancellor being Robert de Gant, who held office 1140–54, for the possibility of which compare the witness-lists and place-dates of nos. 14–15. The text follows closely that of no. 604.

606   Precept by King Stephen to the bishop of Worcester, *^athe earl of Warwick and the justice, sheriff, barons and ministers of Warwickshire^a* that the abbot of Reading shall hold his land and men of Rowington as freely and with all quittance of pleas, plaints, shires, hundreds and causes (*occasiones*) as in the time of King Henry I, since the abbey is in the king's protection   [1135 × 39]

> Original charter: BL Add. Ch. 19580
> B f 29r; (? noted) A f 19v[1]
> Pd. *Arch. Journ.*, xx. 292; *Trans. Royal Soc. Lit.*, 2nd ser., xi. 11; *Regesta*, iii. 254 (no. 688); (cal.) Hurry, *Reading Abbey*, 161

Teste^b R(oberto) de Ver. Apud Westm(onasterium).

Endorsed: Stephani regis de Rokintona [*12th cent.*]
Size: 170 × 88 mm
Seal: Stephen's first seal in white wax on tongue partially re-sewn on to main body of writ; obverse, king seated frontally, legend +STE.....ANGLORVM...; reverse, king mounted, legend + STEPHANV.....

^{a-a} et cetera B   ^b B ends

The dating limits are derived from the circumstance that the original is sealed with Stephen's first seal, which he abandoned after the arrest of the bishops in June, 1139 (*Regesta*, iii, pp. xv–xvi).

[1] A follows its text of no. 605 with *Item carta eiusdem de eodem.*

607   Mandate and precept by King Stephen to R(oger), earl of Warwick, and his ministers that the land and men of Reading Abbey of Rowington are to be quit of danegeld and all other exactions, as in the time of King Henry I and as King Henry's and his charters witness; and they are to have peace   [1139 × 53]

> Original charter: BL Add. Ch. 19582
> B f 29r; (? noted) A f 18v[1]
> Pd. *Arch. Journ.*, xx. 293; *Trans. Royal Soc. Lit.*, 2nd ser., xi. 26; *Regesta*, iii. 254 (no. 689); (cal.) Hurry, *Reading Abbey*, 161

Teste^a R(icardo) de Luci. Apud Rading(iam).

Endorsed: Stephani regis de protectione de Rokint(ona) [*12th cent.*]
Size: 145 × 74 mm
Seal: fragment of Stephen's second seal in white wax on tongue; obverse, king seated frontally; reverse, king mounted

^a B ends

The king adopted his second seal after the arrest of the bishops in June, 1139 (*Regesta*, iii, pp. xv–xvi); Roger, earl of Warwick, died 12 June, 1153.

¹ This is a marginal note, after the text of no. 10, reading: *Item tres alie carte de protectione Rokint(one).*

608 *Precept by King Henry II to the justice, sheriff and others of Warwickshire that the abbot of Reading's men of Rowington are to be quit of pleas [etc.] as in the time of King Henry I, and that the abbot shall try any case of larceny or murder there* [1155 × 58]

A ff 25v–26r; B f 26r

Henricus rex Anglie ᵃet dux Norm(annie) et Aquit(anie) et comes Andeg(avie)ᵃ iustic(iario), vicecomiti, baronibus et ministris suis de Warwicsc(ira), salutem. Precipio quod terra et homines abbatis Rading(ensis) de Rokintona sint quieti de placitis et querelis et schirisᵇ et hundredis et omnibusᶜ rebus. Et si latrocinium [*f 26r*] vel murdrum in ea evenerit, ipse illud placitet et forisfactum inde habeat et iustitiam, sicut solebat habere tempore regis H(enrici) avi mei et sicut ipsius H(enrici) regis carta testatur. Testibus:ᵈ T(homa) cancellario, et comite Reginaldo. Apud Norhantonam.

ᵃ⁻ᵃ et cetera *B* ᵇ syris *B*
ᶜ *A has* aliis *deleted at this point* ᵈ *B ends*

While Thomas Becket was chancellor and the king was in England—he was absent from Aug. 1158 to Jan. 1163, by which time Becket was archbishop. The text follows closely those of nos. 604–5.

609 *Mandate and precept by King Henry II to the bishop of Worcester, Henry brother of the earl of Warwick, Thurstan de Montfort and Walter Bisseche to allow to Reading Abbey and its men of Rowington all common of wood and field which they had in the time of King Henry I* [1155 × 58]

A f 24r; B f 26v

H(enricus) rex Angl(orum) ᵃet dux Norm(annorum) et Aquit(anorum) et comes And(egavorum)ᵃ episcopo Wig(orniensi) ᵇet Henrico fratri comitis de Warewic et Tustino de Munfort et Waltero Bisseche,ᵇ salutem. Mando et firmiter vobisᶜ precipio quatinusᵈ permittatis habere monachis de Rading(ia) et hominibus suis de Rochintonaᵉ omnem communionem de bosco et de plano quam solebant habere tempore H(enrici) regis avi mei. Et nisi feceritis iust(itia) mea de Warewicsireᶠ faciat fieri, ne amplius clamorem audiam pro penuria recti. T(este)ᵍ Thoma cancellario. Apud Norhanton(am).

ᵃ⁻ᵃ et cetera *B* ᵇ⁻ᵇ et cetera *B* ᶜ *Transfer to after* Mando *B*
ᵈ quod *B* ᵉ Rokinton' *B* ᶠ Warwicsir' *B*
ᵍ *B ends*

Date as for no. 608. In 1166 Thurstan de Montfort held 10¼ knights' fees of the earl of Warwick, including the nearby manor of Beaudesert (*Red Bk. Exch.*, i. 325; *VCH Warks.*, iii. 45). Very little is known about Henry, brother of the earl of Warwick (*Complete Peerage*, xii (2), 362 n. *d*). In A the writ was entered at the foot of the folio after the original composition, but in a smaller version of the same hand, and was added to the table of contents (cf. no. 29).

610   *Precept by King Henry II to the earl of Warwick and others of War-wickshire that the lands, goods and men of Reading Abbey, and particularly Rowington, are to be quit of shires, hundreds, pleas, danegeld, tolls, gelds, plaints, murders, etc., as in the time of King Henry I*

[1154 × 75; ? 1154 × 72]

A f 26r; B f 26r

Henricus rex Anglie *a*et dux Norm(annie) et Aquit(anie) et comes Andegavie*a* comiti de Warwicsc(ira)*b* et omnibus baronibus et ius-tic(iario) et vicecomiti et ministris suis de Warwicsc(ira), salutem. Precipio vobis quod in bona pace dimittatis omnes terras et res et homines monachorum de Rading(ia) et nominatim Rokintonam ita quietas*c* de sciris*d* et hundredis et placitis et danegeld(is) et theloneis et omnibus geldis et querelis et murdr(is) et omnibus rebus, sicut quietiores fuerunt tempore regis H(enrici) avi mei et sicut carta ipsius regis H(enrici) testatur. Et prohibeo ne quis super hoc sibi vel rebus suis iniuriam vel contumeliam faciat. Testibus:*e* comite Regin-aldo, et Ricardo de Hum(eto) constabulo. Apud Wareng(efordiam).

a-a et cetera *B*	*b* Warwic' *B*	*c* quietos *B*
d syris *B*	*e* *B ends*	

Reginald, earl of Cornwall, died 1 July, 1175; the king returned to England from Normandy in May, 1175 (Eyton, 190). Richard de Humez was constable of Nor-mandy 1154–80. However, since the king is not styled *dei gratia*, the date may be not later than May, 1172, the king being in France from then until July, 1174 (*ibid.*, 167, 179).

611   *Final peace and concord, by the mediation of King Henry II at Dorch-ester, by which Margaret, daughter of Ralph Macer, and Elias her son recognized an earlier agreement between her parents and Abbot Anscher of Reading, to which she had agreed, concerning a tenement of 3 virgates and an assart which her parents had previously held of Adeliza d'Ivry and which, according to the said agreement, they were to hold of the abbey for life only. Margaret and Elias quitclaimed the tenement to Reading Abbey in return for 100s. Because Margaret did not have a seal of her own, her part of this chirograph was placed for custody in Kenilworth Priory*

15 Jan. [1173 × 84; ? 1180 × 84]

B f 175v; C f 104r–v

Hec est finalis pax et concordia que facta est inter monachos de*a*
Rading(ia) et Margar(etam)*b* filiam Rad(ulf)i*c* Macri de tenemento
quod clamabat in Rokint(ona), mediante domino nostro rege
H(enrico) .ii., xviii. kl' Februarii apud Dorecestr(iam).*d* Videlicet
quod iamdicta Marg(areta)*b* cum filio suo Helya recognovit et concessit donationem quam pater suus et mater sua et ipsamet
M(argareta) cum eis olim fecerant ecclesie Rading(ensi) de .iii. virgatis terre et .i. assarto in Rokinton(a) liberam et quietam ab omni
calumpnia de se et de*a* heredibus suis. Et cyrographum olim factum
inter patrem suum R(adulfum) Macr(um) et ecclesiam Rad-
ing(ensem) 'de predicta donatione' recognovit, cuius talis est tenor.

Sciant presentes et futuri quod ego frater Anscher(us)*f* abbas Rad-
ing(ensis), consilio fratrum nostrorum et assensu totius conventus,
concessi Rad(ulf)o Macro et uxori eius Emme quamdiu vixerint
tenere de nobis terram quam in Rokint(ona) ante nos tenuerunt*g* de
Adelyza de Iverio, scilicet tres virgatas, quarum unam tenet Rannulfus de predicto Rad(ulfo), pro eodem servitio quod ipse Adelyza
inde habebat. Similiter concessi eisdem additamentum de bosco ad
sartandum quod concesserat ipsi Rad(ulfo) ipsa Adelyza dum mor-
eretur. Ipsi vero ambo concesserunt et donationem super altare
sancte Marie de Rading(ia) fecerunt de predicta terra et de addi-
tamento ut, post finem vite illorum, sine calumpnia hereditarii iuris
in dominium nostrum redeant non tantum terra et additamentum
sed etiam omne superfactum quod ibidem facient. Hoc quoque
totum concessit Margar(eta) filia eorum.   [1130 × 35]

Hoc cyrographum recognoverunt et concesserunt predicta
M(argareta)*b* et Helyas filius eius, actor materni negotii, pro se et
pro suis,*h* affirmantes et recognoscentes in curia domini regis nullum
suorum ius aliquod habere in predicto tenemento nisi ecclesiam
Rading(ensem). Et hanc nove recognitionis et concessionis cartam
super altare sancte Marie de Rading(ia) optulerunt, acceptis inde a
monachis Rading(ensibus) .C. solidis sterlingorum per voluntatem
domini regis. Insuper in fide et veritate sua iuraverunt quia, si qui
super hoc monachis adversari voluerint, ipsi pro posse suo in omni
curia illis assistent et predictum tenorem verificabunt et contra
omnes warantizabunt et in quantum poterint nocere volentes dis-
turbabunt. Et quia predicta M(argareta) non habuit proprium sigillum quod huic scripto apponeret, convenit inter nos ut pars huius
cyrographi que predictam M(argaretam) contingebat ad memoriale
mansura*i* in ecclesia de Kenillewrþe*j* canonicis legittime custodienda
committeretur. Hiis testibus, et cetera.

a *Om. in C*   *b* Marger' *C*
c Radulphi *C*   *d* Corcestr' (*sic*) *C*

e-e Interlined in B   *f* Anscheri(us) C
g Interlined in B   *h* B has asserentes *deleted*
i mansur' B, mansurum C   *j* Kenilwrþe C

The date is probably not long before that of Henry II's confirmation (no. 612). The fine was made before the king at Dorchester, but in view of the reference to the altar of Reading Abbey this chirograph may have been made at Reading. The text contains two particularly interesting passages, namely, the primitive form of the warranty clause (cf. *Transcripts of Charters relating to Gilbertine Houses*, ed. F. M. Stenton (Lincoln Rec. Soc. 1922), xxviii–xxix) and the security arrangements made to cover Margaret's lack of a seal of her own.

611a Note of another fine concerning the same in the same words but without the final clause relating to Margaret's seal

[1173 × 84; ? 1180 × 84]

B f 175v.

Whether this was of exactly the same date as no. 611 is unknown.

612 *Confirmation of the same settlement by King Henry II*

[1173 × 84; ? 1180 × 84]

A ff 22v–23r; B ff 26v–27r

Henricus dei gratia rex Angl(orum) *a*et dux Norm(annorum) et Aquitan(orum) et comes And(egavorum) archiepiscopis, episcopis, abbatibus, comitibus, baronibus, iustic(iariis), vicecomitibus et omnibus ministris et fidelibus suis totius Anglie, salutem.*a* Sciatis me concessisse et presenti carta mea confirmasse conventionem que facta fuit coram me inter monachos de Rading(ia) et Margaretam filiam Rad(ulfi) Macri de tenemento quod ipsa clamabat in Rokintona, scilicet tres virgatas terre et unum essartum que ipsa Margareta et Elyas*b* filius eius coram me recognoverunt predictum Rad(ulfum) patrem ipsius Marg(arete) et Emmam matrem eius et ipsam Marg(aretam) donasse Rading(ensi) monasterio. Scilicet quod predicta M(argareta) et Elias*b* filius eius concesserunt monasterio de Rading(ia) totam prenominatam terram liberam et quietam ab omni calumpnia de se et heredibus suis. Et pro hac conventione receperunt a predictis monachis centum solidos esterlingorum,*c* et *d*quietum clamaverunt*d* de se et heredibus suis totum ius quod dicebant se habere in prefata terra. Quare volo et firmiter precipio quod prescripta conventio inter pre[*f 23r*]dictos monachos et predictam Margaretam et Eliam*b* filium eius facta, secundum quod cirographum suum testatur, stabilis et rata permaneat et firmiter et inconcusse teneatur. Testibus:*e* Rannulfo de Glanvilla, Roberto filio Bernardi, Willelmo de Stuttevill(a), Gerardo de Camvill(a), Alano de Fur-

nell(is), Willelmo de Bending(es), Willelmo Ruffo, Willelmo de Ier-
punvilla. Apud Wintoniam.

^{a-a} et cetera *B*   ^b Hel' *B*
^c sterlingorum *B*   ^{d-d} quiet'clamaverunt *B*
^e *B ends*

The inclusion of *dei gratia* in the royal style, on which Cartulary A seems generally
scrupulous, dates this confirmation not earlier than 1173. It is also earlier than
Michaelmas 1184, by which time Robert fitz Bernard was dead (*PR 30 Henry II*,
130). However, since Rannulf de Glanville heads the witness-list, it may be not earlier
than 1180, when he was appointed justiciar (Eyton, 231).

613 *Notification by Hugh fitz Richard that, when he claimed part of the
land and wood of Rowington, the monk Ingulf custos of that vill secured an
arrangement, with the aid of honourable men and a payment of 20s to Hugh,
that both parties with their men should perambulate the boundaries; and accordingly the correct boundaries between Shrewley and Rowington were perambu-
lated. As a result Hugh, with the counsel of his wife Margaret and of his son
William, handed over what he had claimed to Reading Abbey as its
right*   [*c.* 18 June 1150]

A ff 41v-42r; B f 123v; C f 68r-v
Pd. (in part) van Caenegem, *Royal Writs*, 73

Hugo filius Ricardi omnibus ^ahominibus et amicis^a suis clericis et
laicis, Francis et Anglicis, salutem. Sciatis quod ego, consilio aliquo-
rum hominum meorum, clamavi partem unam terre et nemoris de
Rokint(ona) et monachus quidam Ingulfus nomine, qui tunc custos
eiusdem ville fuit, per se et per multos honorabiles^b viros, me requi-
sivit et, ut hoc facerem, mihi .xx. solidos dedit ut supra terram unde
calumpnia fuit ipse cum suis, ego vero cum meis, ad divisas peram-
bulandas convenissemus. Et nos eo anno quo Radulfus comes Cestrie
me venantem cepit, secunda dominica post Pentecosten, scilicet
.xiiii. kl' Iulii, super^c terram venimus et precepimus nostris ut, supra
fidem quam deo et nobis debebant, rectas divisas inter Scraveleiam
et Rokintonam perambularent. His^d auditis, nobis sequentibus pro-
cesserunt, ex parte monachi, Tancwardus^e filius Walderii et Wlfricus
de Halefalga cum multis aliis, de mea parte, Herdingus de Scraveleia
et Helfricus de Nunneleia^f cum pluribus aliis, et preceptum legaliter
ut iuramento affirmabant fecerunt. Ego autem, metuens, si ecclesiam
Radingensem in aliquo diminuerem, periculum anime mee incur-
rere, consilio sponse mee Margarete^g et Willelmi filii mei et heredis
et aliorum amicorum meorum, deo et sancte Marie et conventui
Rading(ensi) pro salute anime mee et meorum ea que clamaveram
de me et de omnibus heredibus meis in perpetuum ut rectum su-
pradicte ecclesie dimisi.^h Huius rei restes sunt: Stephanus [*f 42r*] pres-

biter de Rokint(ona), Robertus presbiter de Hattona, Turstanus de
Monte Forte, et multi alii.

^{a-a} amicis et hominibus *B,C*   ^b venerabiles *C*
^c supra *B,C*   ^d Hiis *B,C*
^e Tanqwardus *B,C*   ^f Nunheleya *B,C*
^g Marg' *B*, Marger' *C*   ^h *B ends with* T', *C ends*

The earl of Chester named in this deed is Rannulf de Gernon, who died in 1153.
Betwen 1100 and 1250 the second Sunday after Whitsun fell on 18 June only in
1150, 1161, 1172 and 1245; hence the year in question can only be 1150 (see van
Caenegem, *Royal Writs*, 73 n 2). This deed has been described as 'a fine example of
a popular recognition' (*ibid.*, 78). Hugh fitz Richard was lord of Hatton, in which
parish Shrewley lay, although there seems to be no other evidence that he held
Shrewley itself (*VCH Warks.*, iii. 116–17). Ingulf was clearly a monk of Reading
placed in charge of Rowington; on the possible Cluniac origin of his status there, see
B. R. Kemp, 'The Monastic Dean of Leominster', *EHR*, lxxxiii (1968), 514 n. 2.

614   *Notification by Hugh fitz Rivhard that he and the monk of Reading,
Ingulf,* custos *of Rowington, caused their free men to recognize on oath what
common of pasture there ought to be between them, the verdict being that the
men of Rowington should have common of pasture in the wood of Shrewley as
the men of Hugh did, while Hugh's men should have common of pasture in the
abbot's wood of Aspley as the abbot's men did*   [*c.* 18 June 1150]

A f90r-v; B ff 123v-124r; C f 68v

Sciant presentes et futuri quod ego Hugo filius Ricardi et quidam
monachus de Rading(ia) nomine Ingulfus, qui tunc custos Ro-
chint(one)^a fuit, anno quo Randulfus^b comes Cestrie me venantem
cepit, congregari fecimus homines francos, scilicet milites, clericos et
franchelanos,^c ut per iuramentum recognosceretur que communio
pasture inter nos esse deberet. Iuraverunt ergo,^d ex parte monachi,
Thangwardus^e filius Walderii et Wlfricus de Halefalga et Edwardus,^f
et,^g ex parte mea, Hardingus^h de Scraveleia et Helfricus de Nuneleia
[*f90v*] cum pluribus aliis, quod homines de Rokint(ona) deberent
habere communionem pasture in bosco de Scraveleia ubique sicut
homines mei, et homines meiⁱ deberent habere communionem [pas-
ture]^j in bosco abbatis ^kde Aspeleia^k sicut homines abbatis. Unde
ego, per hos legales homines abbatis de Rading(ia) et per meos de
rei veritate certificatus, hanc hominibus^l meis et hominibus abbatis
communionem^m hinc inde sigilli mei testificatione et appositione confirmavi et heredibus meis in perpetuum confirmatam et confirman-
dam mandavi.ⁿ Testibus:^o Stephano presbitero de Rokintun(a),
Roberto presbitero de Hatton(a),^p Turstano^q de Munford',
Rad(ulfo) de Cheinei, Enisant, Willelmo Mac(ro), Rad(ulfo) filio
Hugonis, Reinaldo fratre meo, Iohanne de Kinton(a), Ingenulfo,

Rad(ulfo) de Belemare, Roberto Flamanc, le halimot de Kinton(a)
et 'homines mei' de Scraveleia et de Hectona.

a de Rokint' *B,C*	*b* Rad' *C*
c frankel' *B,C*	*d* igitur *B,C*
e Tanqwardus *B,C*	*f* Eylwardus *B,C*
g Om. in *B,C*	*h* Herdingus *B,C*
i Interlined in *A*	*j* Om. in *A, supplied from B,C*
k-k qui voca[tur] Aespeleya *B,C*	*l* Interlined in *A, om. in B,C*
m Insert pasture *B,C*	*n* C ends
o B ends	*p* A has Hamton', *but cf. no. 613*
q A has Turctano	*r-r* Sic in *A; ? rectius* hominibus meis

The names of the jurors and witnesses suggest that this deed passed at the same time
as no. 613.

615 *Quitclaim by Robert of Fullready to Reading Abbey, at the request of
his wife and children, of the land which Jordan, his father-in-law, held of the
abbey in Rowington and which he gave and quitclaimed to the monks when
they received him as a brother* [*c.* 1180 × 93]

A f 42r; B f 124v; C f 69v

Sciant presentes et futuri quod ego Robertus de*a* Fulreda,*b* voluntate
et petitione uxoris mee et liberorum meorum, ex parte ipsorum
concessi et 'quietam clamavi*c* pro salute anime mee et ipsorum deo
et ecclesie de Rading(ia) terram quam Iurdanus*d* socer meus in
Rokint(ona) de prefata ecclesia tenuit, quam et monachis ibidem
deo servientibus dedit et 'quietam clamavit*e* de se et heredibus suis
die quando eum in fratrem susceperunt. Ut autem hec concessio
rata in perpetuum habeatur, sigilli mei appositione ipsam corro-
boro.*f* Testibus:*g* Willelmo camberlano, Raerio, Willelmo dispensatore, Willelmo pincerna, Ricardo de Rokint(ona), Walterio clerico
de Rading(ia), et Waltero Peg, et multis aliis.

a Om. in *C*	*b* Fulred'e *B*, Fulred' *C*
c-c quietcl' *C*	*d* Iordanus *B,C*
e-e [?] quiettcl' *C*	*f* C ends
	g B ends

This deed was entered in the original section of A and is therefore not later than
1193. Apart from Richard of Rowington, all the witnesses are Reading folk who
witness in the years after 1186 (see, e.g., nos. 841–4) and of whom William *dispensator*
also witnesses in 1173 × 86 (no. 830).

616 *Concession by William* de Frainose *and his heirs to Abbot H. and the
convent of Reading of their land of* Smalelie *with appurtenant meadow, which
were of their inheritance and lay in the midst of the abbey's demesne, in*

exchange for a croft which belonged to Daniel Tagge *and which was near their house and more convenient*   [1186 × 1213]

A f95r; B f125v; C f70v

Sciant presentes et futuri quod ego Willelmus de*a* Frainose et heredes mei concessimus dominis nostris H. abbati Rading(ensi) eiusdemque loci conventui terram nostram de Smalelie*b* cum prato eiusdem terre pertinenti, que fuerunt de heretagio nostro, pro excambio unius crofte que fuit Danielis Tagge, que propinqua est domui nostre. Hanc quidem concessionem eis fecimus, quia predicta terra de Smaleleie*b* et predictum pratum iacent in medio dominio eorum et prefata crofta nobis vicina est et commodior.*c* His testibus.

a Om. *in* C   *b* Smaleleia B,C
c B ends with T', C ends

The abbot is either Hugh II (1186–99) or Elias (1200–1213). The rubric of A locates the land in Rowington.

617 *Gift in free alms by Henry de Montfort to Reading Abbey of the whole tenement in* Sterte *which Adam son of Roger held [bounds given]. For this the abbey has given him for his need 8 marks of silver*   [? late 12th cent.]

A f90r; B f124v; C f69r

Sciant presentes et futuri quod ego Henricus de Munfort,*a* pro salute anime mee et uxoris mee et filiorum et filiarum mearum et pro anima patris mei et matris et omnium predecessorum et successorum meorum, dedi et hac mea carta confirmavi in puram et perpetuam elemosinam et ab omni seculari servitio et exactione liberam ecclesie*b* et monachis de Rading(ia) totum tenementum in Sterte quod Adam filius*c* Rogeri tenuit, scilicet per rivulum qui descendit per boscum de Laþurde usque ad alium rivulum qui est inter boscum de Rochinton(a),*d* et sursum per eundem rivulum usque ad tenementum Thome, et a tenemento Thome usque ad predictum rivulum de Laþurde. Volo igitur ut predicti monachi predictum tenementum teneant bene et in pace, plene et honorifice in omnibus. Prefati autem monachi, pro quadam necessitate mea, .viii. marcas argenti mihi dederunt, ut in hoc et aliis magis eis*e* obligatus tenear, et ad elemosinam istam manutenendam obnoxior efficiar.*f* *g* His testibus: Enger(o) Bagot, Willelmo clerico, Simone clerico de Rochint(ona), Roberto de Munf(ort), Henrico filio Roberti, Helia de Bosco, Gautero clerico, Osmundo senescallo, Osmundo de Aclee, Rad(ulfo) hostiario, Archimbaudo, Lamberto coco, Alemanno coco, Ricardo de Rochint(ona), Iohanne Banast(re), Iohanne de Chataine, Waltero Peg, Rogero de camera abbatis.

^a Muntfort' *B,C*　　　　　　　　　^b *A has* eclesie
^c *A repeats* filius　　　　　　　　　^d Rokint' *B*, Rokynton' *C*
^e *Interlined in A*　　　　　　　　　^f *A has* eficiar
^g *B ends with* T', *C ends*

Not entered in the original section of A, but among additions of the late 12th or early 13th century. The donor was lord of a number of places in Warwickshire in the late 12th century, including Beaudesert, near Rowington (*VCH Warks.*, iii. 45); the rubrics of B and C describe *Sterte* as 'at Rowington'. Of the witnesses no fewer than seven (Walter clerk, Osmund *de Aclee*, Archimbaud, Lambert cook, Alemann cook, John *de Chataine* and Roger of the chamber) were Reading folk who witnessed a deed by Abbot H. of Reading, dating 1186 × 1213 (no. 844). Robert de Montfort witnessed a deed by William, earl of Warwck, 1153 × 84 (no. 580).

618　Gift in free alms by Richard of [?] Ockley (*Hacle*) to Reading Abbey, for the health of his soul and of that of Richard *Bulluc* his uncle, of all the lands which the latter sometime held, viz., 9 selions of arable land in *Sachardescroft* which he had by gift of W(illiam) of Bearley (*Burleg'*), 2½ acres in *Lamfert(on')* which he had by gift of Robert Freeman (*Freman*), 1 acre in *Lamfert(on')* which he had by gift of Thomas Freeman, ½ acre of land in *Lamfert(on')* which he had by gift of Robert *de Wodegate*, and a parcel (*particula*) of land at *Wodegat(e)* which he had by gift of Robert *de Wodegate*. Warranty and sealing. Witnesses^a [omitted]　　　　　[? *c*. 1225 × 58]

B f 125r-v; C f 70r

^a *Om. in C*

Dating uncertain. The family of Ockley, *alias* Bulloc, seems to have been a Berkshire family, which may have derived an interest in Warwickshire through Reading Abbey's possessions there. A Richard *de Acle* was a juror for the vill of Bray in 1248 (Clanchy, *Berks. Eyre of 1248*, 297), and by a deed in the Reading Almoner's Cartulary (D f 61r), perhaps dating from the middle years of the 13th century, Richard *Bulluc de Ocley* and his wife, Matilda, made a gift in Reading to Walter Vachell. A presumably earlier Richard *de Accle* or *de Acle* witnessed deeds by Abbot Joseph in Reading, 1173 × 86 (nos. 834-5), and he may be the same as a Richard *Bulloc* who, with other Reading folk, wtnessed a deed by Warin fitz Gerold in Sawbridgeworth in 1204 × 15 (no. 392). It seems likely that this latter is the uncle named in the present deed, and that the former is the present donor. The deed cannot be later than 1258, since it appears in the original section of B. Although the cartulary rubrics do not say so, the lands were presumably in Rowington (see nos. 619, 620).

618a　Note of five charters to Richard *Bulluc* concerning the same lands by William of Bearley (*Burleg'*), Robert Freeman (*Freman*), Thomas Freeman, Robert *de Wodegate* and Roger *de Wodeg(ate)*

B f 125v (in margin)

These charters are listed individually in BL Add. Roll 19617 (see above, p. 8) with brief details largely as in no. 618, but with an extra detail relating to the land which

Richard acquired from Roger *de Wodegate*. The list runs: charter of Thomas *Freman* to Richard *Bulluc* concerning 1 acre of land in *Lanfortune*; charter of Robert *Freman* to the same concerning 2½ [acres] of land in *Lanfortun'*; charter between Robert *de Wodegate* and the same concerning ½ acre of land in *Lanfortun'*; charter between Roger *de Wodeg(ate)* and the same concerning a parcel of land at *Wodegate* of the forinsec wood; charter between William of Bearley (*Burleg'*) and the same concerning 9 selions of land in *Stacardescroft*.

619 Gift by Abbot Richard [de Corjon] and the convent of St Evroul (*de Sancto Ebrulfo*) to Reading Abbey of the whole service of all their tenants of *Launfreford'* and *la Wodegate*, with an annual rent of 10s and with all escheats, reliefs, suits of court and all other services, to be held freely by Reading in perpetuity. For this Reading Abbey has given them 28 marks sterling as entry-fine. Warranty and sealing with the donors' seals. Witnesses[a] [omitted] [1247 × 69]

B f 134v; C f 77v

[a] *Om. in C*

The dating limits are those of Abbot Richard de Corjon of St Evroul (*Gallia Christiana*, xi. 824). The deed is clearly a sale and the tenants concerned were presumably among those on the carucate of land in Rowington which St Evroul held in 1191 × 1204 (Round, *Cal. Docs. France*, 230). The deed was not entered in the original section of B, but very soon afterwards, and may therefore be of *c.* 1260.

619a Note of a charter of final concord between Roger of Pillerton (*Pilardint(ona)*) and Robert, his brother, concerning the wood of *la Wodeyate*   [not later than 1258]

B f 126r

Entered in the original section of B. The identity of these brothers is uncertain, but they were clearly related to the William son of Roger of Pillerton and Robert son of Roger of Pillerton who occur in a fine of 1262 involving *inter alia* 40d rent in *Wodegate* (*Warks. Feet of Fines*, i. 173). Persons called 'of Pilerton' occur in Pillerton in the 13th century (see *VCH Warks.*, v. 133 n. 6), but a family of that name also held Pinley in Rowington in the 12th century (*ibid.*, iii. 150; below no. 624) and it was no doubt in this area that *la Wodeyate* lay.

620 Agreement [in chirograph form][a] between Reading Abbey and Nicholas son of Hugh of Cutshill (*Curteshale*) [in Claverdon] concerning the water of *Lamferton'* which runs over the abbot of Reading's land of Rowington (*Rokint'*). The abbot has conceded that Nicholas and his heirs shall have the course of the water through the land of Rowington as far as the mill of Cutshill for an annual rent of 12d, viz., 4d each at the feast of St Thomas the apostle [21 Dec.], the Invention of the Holy Cross [3 May] and Michaelmas. If ever they withhold the rent, the abbey may withdraw the water-course from them. Nicholas has sworn on the Gos-

pels to be faithful and to pay the rent at the stated terms. Witnesses[b]
[omitted]   [? 13th cent.; not later than 1258]

B f 126r; C f 70v

[a] *Not in text, but so described in B,C rubrics*
[b] *Om. in C*

Entered in the original section of B. The parishes of Claverdon and Rowington are
directly adjacent.

621 *Sale by Roger de St John to Reading Abbey of his wood called* Iveleya
*for 9 marks of silver. He will warrant it as his enclosure so that, if the abbey
wishes to clear it, it shall have the tree-roots and timber, but the land shall
then remain to him*   [*c.* 1176 × 1214 *or* 1242 × 58]

B f 126r; C f 71r

Noverint omnes ad quos presens scriptum pervenerit quod ego
Rog(erus) de Sancto Johanne vendidi monachis de Rading(ia) boscum meum quod apellatur[a] Iveleya pro .ix. marcis argenti totaliter
et integre. Istum boscum eis warantizabo per hanc conventionem
sicut clausum meum, ita quod, si velint assartare, radices extracte[b]
eis cedant et omnes carettas suas ad buscam cotidie et alias si voluerint illuc mittent donec penitus extrahatur. Terra autem quieta
mihi remanebit post asportationem lignorum.[c] T(estibus).

[a] *Sic in B;* appellatur *C*
[b] extecte (*sic*) *C*
[c] *C ends*

The vendor's identity is uncertain. No-one of that name appears to occur in Warwickshire in the 12th and 13th centuries, and, apart from the early Roger de St John
who held in Sussex and Hampshire and was dead in 1130 (Round, *The Genealogist*,
new ser. xvi. 3), the only men of that name I have found are two members of the St
John family of Swallowfield, near Reading (Berks.) and Stanton St John (Oxon.)
(*VCH Berks.*, iii. 268; *VCH Oxon.*, v. 284). If one of these is involved, the sale was
made either by Roger, who succeeded by 1176 and died in or before 1214, or Roger,
who came of age in 1242/3 and was killed at Evesham in 1265 (*VCH Oxon.*, v. 284);
however, since the deed was entered in the original section of B, it cannot be later
than 1258. The location of the wood is equally uncertain. Although it is entered in
the Warwickshire section of the cartularies, the rubrics simply read: *Cyrographum inter
conventum Rading' et Rogerum de Santo Johanne de quodam bosco.*

621a Note of a final concord between Isabel, daughter of Gilbert,
and Richard *le Bonde* and J(oan), his wife, concerning two parts of
1 virgate of land in Rowington (*Rokint'*) and a third part of 1 virgate
of land   [3 Nov. 1240]

B f 176r

The foot of this fine is PRO CP 25(1)/243/19/29, calendared in *Warks. Feet of Fines*, i. 116 (no. 581). It is dated the morrow of All Souls, 25 Henry III. The fine was made in an assize of mort d'ancestor and, with regard to the third part of 1 virgate, Richard and Joan had been vouched to warranty by John Cumin and Eleanor, his wife.

622 Quitclaim by William son of Alexander of Bushwood (*Bissopwde*) to the abbot of Reading and his men of Rowington (*Rokint'*) of all his right in common of pasture in the wood of Rowington called Finwood (*Inwode*),[1] and remission of the claim which he sometime proposed to make before Silvester [Everdon] bishop of Carlisle, Roger of Thirkleby (*Turkeby*) and the other justices-in-eyre at Warwick. For this the abbot has given him 10s sterling. Sealing. Witnesses*a* [omitted]   [*c.* July 1252]

B f 125r; C ff 69v–70r

a Om. in C

The justices sat at Warwick 8–22 July 1252 (Crook, *General Eyre*, 117).

[1] See *Warks. Place-Names*, 218.

623 Final concord in the king's court at Westminster in the octave of St Hilary, 40 Henry III, before Roger of Thirkleby (*Turkeby*) and John of Wyville (*Wyvill'*), justices, and others, between Abbot Richard [I] of Reading, plaintiff, and Reginald *de Morton'* and Joan his wife, defending, concerning 1 messuage and 1 carucate of land in Rowington (*Rokint'*). Plea of convention. Reginald and Joan recognized the messuage and land to be the right of the abbot and abbey of Reading, as the latter have them by their gift, to be held in free alms. Warranty. The abbot has received them and their heirs into all benefits and prayers of Reading Abbey for ever

20 Jan. 1256

B ff 175v–176r; C f 104v
Pd. (cal.) *Warks. Feet of Fines*, i. 161 (no. 758) (from PRO foot: CP 25(1)/244/24/27)

The foot has an endorsement that Robert *le Baud* put in his claim.

624 *Notification by Simon, bishop of Worcester, to Warin, prior of Worcester, and others that on the dedication of the church of Rowington Roger of Pillerton conceded to that church the whole parish and tithe of Pinley, as his father had conceded them; and precept that the church of Rowington shall hold the same in peace*   [1125 × c. 1142; ? c. 1133 × c. 1142]

A f 53v; B f 201r; C f 122v

Simon dei gratia Wigornensis episcopus Warino priori ecclesie Wire-
cestrie et omnibus archidiaconis suis et omnibus fidelibus et filiis
Wigornensis ecclesie, salutem *et paternam benedictionem.* Notificamus dilectioni vestre quod Rog(erius) de Pilherdingtune[b] in dedicatione ecclesie de Rokintuna in presentia mea totam parrochiam et
decimam de Pileneie[c] cum omnibus rebus eidem parrochie pertinentibus predicte ecclesie de Rokintun(a) absque omni calumpnia et
retractione[d] inconcusse inviolabiliterque in perpetuum tenendas concessit, sicut pater suus donationem inde super altare predicte ecclesie
ponendo firmius meliusque concesserat. Volo itaque et episcopali
auctoritate precipio ut supramemorata ecclesia de Rokint(una) parrochiam et decimam de Pileneia[e] cum omnibus rebus eis pertinentibus sine omni diminutione, inquietatione et molestia honorifice[f] et
in pace teneat, sicut supramemoravimus patrem predicti Rogerii de
Pileneia eundemque Rog(erium) dedisse et concessisse. Valete.

a-a Om. in B,C	[b] Pilherdint' B,C	[c] Pilneie C
[d] retractatione B,C	[e] Pileneie C	[f] honorabiliter B,C

After Simon became bishop of Worcester and while Warin was prior of Worcester,
c. 1124–c. 1142 (*Heads of Relig. Houses*, 82; see also *Fasti 1066–1300*, ii. 102). However,
although the act does not refer to Reading Abbey, it seems likely that it was given
after the latter's acquisition of Rowington, in which case it would date after c. 1133
(see no. 602). Roger was no doubt the son of the R. de Pillerton who founded a
Cistercian priory for nuns on his land of Pinley late in Henry I's reign (*VCH Warks.*,
ii. 82; iii. 150; *Mon. Ang.*, iv. 115), at which time he had clearly safeguarded the
parochial and tithe rights of Rowington church, in whose parish Pinley lay. It is
notable that towards the end of this act Roger of Pillerton is also called Roger of
Pinley.

625 *Settlement, with the assent of Reading Abbey, between the church of
Rowington and the nuns of Pinley[1] on a complaint by Robert,[2] rector of
Rowington, that they were withholding lesser tithes. Their corn tithes shall be
paid in full to Rowington church, but the nuns shall give a pension of 2 lbs of
wax annually for their lesser tithes, in return for which Rowington church has
released their own lesser tithes to them in perpetuity* [1195 × 1213]

C f 154v

Hec est compositio facta de assensu domini abbatis et conventus de
Redyng' inter ecclesiam de Rowyngton' et sanctimoniales sancte
Marie de Pinel' super querela eisdem sanctimonialibus pro detentione minutarum decimarum per magistrum Robertum rectorem
ecclesie eiusdem de Rowynton' mota. Videlicet quod eedem sanctimoniales, preter decimas bladi sui dicte ecclesie de Rowyngton' integre persolvend(as), solverent[a] singulis annis in vigilia beati Laurentii eidem ecclesie de Rowyngton' duas libras cere nomine
omnium minutarum decimarum suarum in perpetuum. Dicta vero

ecclesia de Rowyngton' per hanc pensionem relaxavit et in pace
dimisit eisdem sanctimonialibus omnes proprias minutas decimas
libere et integre in perpetuum percipiendas. Hanc autem compositionem fideliter et sine dolo observandam utraque pars tactis sacrosanctis evangeliis iuravit et sigillis partium hinc inde appositis cor-
roboravit. Hiis testibus: domino Symone camerario de Radyng',
domino Walter(o) capellano abbatis, magistro H. persona de Claverdone, et aliis.

a *Ms has* solventes

The date is established by the presence of Simon chamberlain of Reading among the
witnesses. He acquired this office after 28 Oct. 1195, when Robert was chamberlain
(see no. 519), and was elected abbot in 1213. By this agreement Rowington church
retained the greater tithes of the nuns. The text is among the later 14th-century
additions in C.

¹ Pinley Priory (see no. 624 n.).
² Probably Robert of Hailes (see no. 628).

626 *Grant by Henry [de Sully], bishop of Worcester, to Reading Abbey of
an annual pension of 40s from its church of Rowington for the maintenance of
the abbey's hospitality, saving however to the abbey the tithes of its demesne of
Rowington for its own use*   [12 Dec. 1193 × 24/25 Oct. 1195]

A f 72v (crossed through); A f 73v

Universis Christi fidelibus ad quos presens carta pervenerit Henricus
dei gratia Wigornensis episcopus, eternam in domino salutem. Licet
ex officio suscepti regiminis omnium subditorum nostrorum utilitati
studiose teneamur prospicere, specialius tamen eos fovere, diligere et
eorum commoditati attentius studere debemus quos et morum ho-
nestas et artioris religionis sacer ordo reddit conmendabiles. Noverit
igitur universitas vestra nos, considerata honesta*a* conversatione
monachorum de Rading(ia) et eorum circa hospitum susceptionem
pia sollicitudine, divine pietatis intuitu eisdem monachis concessisse
et presenti carta confirmasse annuum canonem quadraginta solidorum de ecclesia eorum de Ruchinton(a)*b* annis singulis percipiendum ad sustentandam*c* domus sue hospitalitatem, salvis etiam memoratis monachis *d*de Rading(ia)*d* decimis*a* de dominio suo de
Ruchinton(a),*b* quas habent in usus proprios. Et ut hec nostra concessio et confirmatio sepedictis monachis de Rading(ia) omni tempore rata et inconvulsa permaneat, eam presenti scripto*e* sigilli nostri
appositione munito roboravimus. Hiis testibus:*f* magistro Willelmo
de Tuneberg', magistro Iordano de Wichewane, magistro Gregorio
de Hallaph', magistro Arnaldo de Bathon(ia).

a *Interlined in A f 72v*   *b* Ruchincton' *A f 73v*   *c* ? sustendam *A f 73v*
d-d *Om. in A f 73v*   *e* *Insert* et (*sic*) *A f 73v*   *f* *A f 73v ends*

The dating limits are those of Henry de Sully's pontificate. The entry crossed through on A f72v was made very soon after the original compilation of that cartulary in a hand extremely close to that of the main text; the entry on f73v was made in an early 13th-century hand. The act was apparently not entered in B and certainly not in C. It would seem that the act may have been obtained initially in connection with the establishment of the hospital outside the abbey gate (see e.g. nos. 158-160, 203, 205, 208, 224), but that its terms were never carried out in full.

627 *Inspeximus and confirmation of the same by Huert [Walter], archbishop of Canterbury, primate and legate* [Apr. 1195 × Feb. 1198]

A f72v; C f121v

H(ubertus)[a] dei gratia Cant(uariensis) archiepiscopus, [b]totius Anglie primas et apostolice sedis legatus, universis sancte matris ecclesie filiis ad quos presens scriptum pervenerit,[b] salutem [c]in eo qui est salus omnium.[c] Ad universitatis vestre volumus devenire notitiam nos venerabilis fratris nostri H(enrici) Wigornensis episcopi literas inspexisse in hec verba.

Universis[d] Christi fidelibus ad quos presens carta pervenerit [etc., quoting in full the act of Bishop Henry de Sully (no. 626) according to the text on A f72v, reading *ad sustendam*[e] for *ad sustentandam*, *Ruchintun(a)*[f] for *Ruchinton(a)* and concluding with [g]*His testibus,*[g] and having the same words *honesta* and *decimis* interlined[h]].

Nos igitur, canonice concessioni venerabilis fratris nostri grato concurrentes assensu, eam presentis scripti testimonio et sigilli nostri appositione duximus corroborandam. Hiis testibus.

[a] Sub' (*sic*) C
[c-c] *Om. in* C
[e] ad sustinendam C
[g-g] Test' et cetera C
[b-b] et cetera C
[d] *A has* Wniversis
[f] Rokynt' C
[h] *C has them not interlined*

While the archbishop exercised legatine authority (see no. 207 n.). For his interest in the hospital outside the abbey gate, see nos. 203, 205, 208.

628 *Grant by Walter [de Gray], bishop of Worcester, to Reading Abbey that it may appropriate the church of Rowington after the death of the parson, master R(obert) of Hailes, saving sufficient provision for a vicar. The bishop has granted this partly for the soul of his father, buried in Reading Abbey* [5 Oct. 1214 × Nov. 1215]

C f121v

Universis sancte matris ecclesie filiis W(alterus)[a] dei gratia Wigorn(iensis) episcopus, salutem. Cum monachos Radyng(ensis) monasterii singulari quadam prerogativa caritatis amplectamur, attendentes fervorem religionis que in eodem monasterio vigere dinoscitur et hospitalitatis communitatem que indistincte patet cuilibet transeunti, tanto nos reputamus ad promotionem eorum procurandam specialius obligatos, quanto ipsos collata sibi beneficia in meliores usus noscimus conversuros. Cupientes igitur bonis eiusdem domus aliquid adicere propter quod tante caritatis opera debeant augmentari, dictis monachis ibidem deo servientibus et in perpetuum servituris ecclesiam de Rokynt(ona) cum omnibus ad eam pertinentibus divine pietatis intuitu et pro anima patris nostri, cuius penes ipsos corpus requiescit, concessimus et auctoritate pontificali confirmavimus, post decessum magistri R(oberti)*b* de Hayles eiusdem ecclesie persone, in usus proprios convertendam, salva competenti sustentatione vicarii eidem ecclesie pro tempore servituri, salvis nobis et successoribus nostris iur(e) pontificali et parrochiali. Ut autem hec nostra confirmatio perpetue firmitatis robur optineat, eam presentis scripti testimonio cum sigilli nostri*c* appositione duximus muniendam.

a Expansion taken from rubric; see also no. 630
b For expansion, see no. 633
c Ms has mei marked for deletion, and nostri interlined

The dating limits are those of Walter de Gray's pontificate of Worcester (see *Fasti 1066-1300*, ii. 101). His father was probably John de Grey of Rotherfield (Oxon.), a few miles north of Reading (*DNB*, xxiii. 208; Nichols, *Hist. Leics.*, iii. 682).

629 *Grant by Walter [de Gray], bishop of Worcester, that Reading Abbey may appropriate the church of Rowington, which is of its gift, after the death of the parson, master R(obert) of Hailes, and may, whenever it becomes vacant, enter possession of the church without mandate or assent of the bishop or his officials*   [5 Oct. 1214 × Nov. 1215]

C ff 121v-122r

Universis Christi fidelibus, et cetera, W(alterus)*a* dei gratia Wigorn(iensis) episcopus, salutem. Noverit universitas vestra nos, divine pietatis intuitu, concessisse abbati et monachis Radyng' ecclesiam de Rokynt(ona), que ad eorum spectat donationem, post decessum magistri R(oberti)*b* de Hayles eiusdem ecclesie persone, in usus proprios convertendam. Et ideo volumus ut, quandocumque predictam ecclesiam vacare [*f 122r*] contigerit, dicti abbas et monachi, non expectato mandato nostro aut requisito assensu nostro vel officialium nostrorum, possessionem prenominate ecclesie valeant ingredi sine omni contradictione. Et in huius concessionis testimonium has litteras nostras patentes eis duximus faciendas. Valete.

a Rubric indicates the same bishop as in no. 628
b For expansion, see no. 633

The dating limits are those of Walter de Gray's pontificate of Worcester.

630 *Confirmation of nos. 628–9 by Silvester [of Evesham], bishop of Worcester* [3 July 1216 × 16 July 1218]

C f 122r

Universis sancte matris ecclesie filiis, et cetera, S(ilvester) dei gratia Wigorn(iensis) episcopus, salutem. Cum ex suscepti pastoralis officii regimine plantare debeamus religionem et fovere plantatam quam, si forte in nobis non habemus, in aliis tamen augere tenemur et conservare, attendentes in locis religiosis illud coram deo et hominibus specialius prefulgere quod ex ipso fonte caritatis frequentius exercetur, ipsa opera cartitatis in eis augere decrevimus et nutrire. Verum quia hospitum susceptio mater est et magistra inter cetera caritatis opera, dicente domino 'hospes fui et col(legistis) me',[1] considerantes eam studiosa copiositate in abbatia Radyng(ensi) continuo vigere, inspecta donatione et confirmatione quam bone memorie W(alterus) de Gray predecessor noster fecit abbati Radyng(ensi) et sacro eiusdem loci conventui super ecclesia de Rokyntun(a) cum eam vacare contigerit in proprios eorum usus convertendam, divine pietatis intuitu et ob favorem et amorem quem erga dictam domum habemus, prenominatam donationem et confirmationem memoratis abbati et conventui Radyng' concedimus et auctoritate pontificali confirmamus, sicut eam dictus predecessor noster eis per cartas suas concessit et confirmavit. Et ut hec nostra donatio et confirmatio perpetue firmitatis robur optineat, eam presentis scripti testimonio cum sigilli nostri appositione duximus muniendam. Hiis testibus.

The dating limits are those of Silvester's pontificate.

[1] Matth. 25: 35. The Vulgate has *eram* in place of *fui*.

631 *Grant by Silvester [of Evesham], bishop of Worcester, that Reading Abbey may appropriate the church of Rowington [etc., in the same terms as no. 629]* [3 July 1216 × 16 July 1218]

C f 122r

Universis Christi fidelibus, et cetera, S(ilvester) dei gratia Wigorn(iensis) episcopus, salutem. Noverit universitas vestra nos, divine pietatis intuitu, concessisse abbati et monachis Radyng' ecclesiam de Rokynt(ona), que ad eorum spectat donationem, post decessum magistri R(oberti)[a] de Hayles, et cetera ut supra in principio huius pagine.[b]

[a] *For expansion, see no. 633*   [b] *Referring to the act of Walter de Gray, no. 629*

The dating limits are those of Silverter's pontificate.

632   Confirmation by W(alter) [de Cantilupe], elect of Worcester, of the grant which W(alter) [de Gray], archbishop of York, made to Reading Abbey when he was bishop of Worcester concerning the church of Rowington (*Rokynt(ona)*), and of the confirmation of the same by Silvester [of Evesham], bishop of Worcester, after inspection of their instruments. Sealing. Given A.D. 1236

30 Aug. 1236 × 24 Mar. 1237

C f 122r

The bishop was elected 30 Aug. 1236 and consecrated 3 May, 1237 (*Fasti 1066–1300*, ii. 101). Assuming the year to begin on 25 March, the year 1236 given in this act would run to 24 March, 1237.

633   Notification by Prior W(illiam) [of Bedford] and the convent of Worcester that W(alter) [de Gray], archbishop of York, when he was bishop of Worcester, granted to Reading Abbey that it might appropriate the church of Rowington (*Rokynt(ona)*) after the death of Robert, then rector of the same, and enter possession of the same on its own authority; and that this was confirmed by Silvester [of Evesham], bishop of Worcester, and by W(alter) [de Cantilupe], elect of Worcester, with their consent. Sealing. *Valete*

[1237; ? 25 Mar. × 3 May 1237]

C f 122v; Worcester, Dean and Chapter Liberary, A.4 (Register I), f 69v
Pd. *Cartl. Worc.*, 255 (from Worcester Register I, minor variants only)

The Annals of Worcester record this act under the year 1237: *Confirmavimus abbati et conventui Radingis ecclesiam de Rugintune* (*Ann. Mon.*, iv. 428). Assuming that the year began on 25 March and that Walter de Cantilupe was still bishop-elect, the act would date between the beginning of the year and the bishop's consecration on 3 May.

634   Confirmation by Walter [de Cantilupe], bishop of Worcester, of the grant which Walter [de Gray], archbishop of York, made to Reading Abbey when he was bishop of Worcester concerning the church of Rowington (*Rokinton(a)*), and of the confirmation of the same by Silvester [of Evesham], bishop of Worcester, after inspection of their instruments; and assignment to the abbey of all tithes of corn, beans and peas growing in the fields of the parish, and all lesser tithes of its court (*curia*), and all tithes of hay and of the parishioners. The perpetual vicar, instituted or to be instituted by the bishop or his successors at the abbey's presentation, shall have all other appurtenances of the church and bear all due and customary archidiaconal, synodal and other burdens. Sealing. Witnesses [omitted]   [1237 × 66; ? 1237 × 60]

A f 110v; C f 122r–v

The outside dating limits are those of the bishop's pontificate, but, since the act is among 13th-century additions in A, it is probably not later than 1260 at the latest. The first part of this act is in effect a re-issue of no. 632.

635 Notification by master Thomas, official of W(alter) [de Cantilupe], bishop of Worcester, that he has received a mandate from the bishop [quoted in full] that, if the abbot of Reading shall provide him with letters patent containing a competent vicarage for the bishop's ordination in the church of Rowington (*Rokynt(ona)*), he shall permit the abbey to have free administration of the church; and that, since he has received from R.[1] of Kempsey (*Kemes(eie)*), chamberlain of the abbey, letters of the abbot and convent to this effect, he has permitted the same. Sealing with the seals of the official and of the local [rural] dean, who was present. *Valete* [1237 × 58]

C f 122v; B f 201r (part only)[2]

During Cantilupe's pontificate and, since it was entered in the original section of B, not later than 1258. Whether it preceded or followed no. 634 is uncertain.

[1] Possibly Roger, who occurs as chamberlain in 1254 and 1262 (see no. 860; *Cal. Pat. R. 1258–66*, 207).

[2] See above, p. 5. The surviving text in B begins in the middle of the address of the quoted bishop's mandate.

636 Licence by King Edward III to Thomas *de la Ryvere* and Richard *Godemon*, for a fine, to alienate in mortmain to Reading Abbey a messuage, 69 acres of land and $8\frac{1}{2}$ acres of meadow in Rowington (*Roughynton'*), co. Warwickshire, to find a monk chaplain to celebrate daily in the abbey church for the good estate of Thomas while he lives and for his soul after death in perpetuity. Licence also to the abbot and convent to receive and hold the same.[a] By a fine of 10 marks[a] 1 Apr. 1344

C f 227r
Pd. *Cal. Pat. R. 1343–5*, 223 (from Patent Roll)

Teste me ipso apud Marleburgh' primo die Aprilis, anno regni nostri Anglie xviii, regni vero nostri Francie quinto.

[a-a] *Added after dating clause*

636a Note of a licence by King Edward III to acquire the land of John *Croupes* in Rowington (*Rowynton'*), in the time of Abbot Henry [1342 × 61; prob. 1 Apr. 1344]

C f 225v

The only abbot of Reading called Henry was Henry of Appleford, 1342–61. However, since this note clearly relates to a mortmain licence and no other is recorded for Rowington in these years, it almost certainly refers to no. 636.

637 Agreement, indented, between the abbot and convent of Reading, Salisbury diocese, appropriators of the parish church of Rowington (*Rowynton'*), Worcester diocese, on the one part, and the prioress and convent of Pinley (*Pynlegh'*) of the Cistercian Order, Worcester diocese, on the other, over the tithes of a windmill of the nuns recently built within the tithe-boundaries of Rowington parish (*de molendino ventriteo sive ad ventum earumdem religiosarum mulierum infra fines limites seu decimaciones parochie ecclesie de Rowynton' supradicte noviter constructo*). The abbot and convent of Reading claimed that the tithes belonged by common right to them and their church of Rowington, but the nuns claimed that they were exempt from paying tithes by a special privilege of the Apostolic See granted to all Cistercians. Settlement by the mediation of common friends, viz., that the nuns shall pay for the tithes annually to the abbot and convent and their church of Rowington 6 measures or strikes of corn according as the multure of the mill allows (*sex modios alias sex stryk(as) bladi prout molendum obvenerit eidem molendino*) in equal portions at Michaelmas and the Annunciation in perpetuity; and the abbot and convent remit to the nuns the tithes and all arrears and the costs of this dispute. Sealing *alternatim*　　　　　　　　　　　　24 Sept. 1348

B f 131r

Dat' quoad priorissam et conventum de Pynlegh' in capitulo loci eiusdem die mercurii proxima post festum sancti Mathei apostoli et evangeliste [21 Sept.], anno domini millesimo CCC.xl.viii.

This document contains one of the few certain references to the nuns of Pinley being of the Cistercian Order (see Knowles and Hadcock, 275). The case is mentioned in *VCH Warks.*, iii. 154.

TIDDINGTON (IN ALVESTON)

638 Gift by Reginald son of John of Kempsey (*Kemes(eye)*) to Reading Abbey of 1 virgate of land in Tiddington (*Tydinton'*) which John, his father, sometime held of Maurice *de Bromhale*[1] and afterwards gave to him. To be held freely, saving to the heirs of the said Maurice an annual rent of 2s which the abbey shall pay to Walter *de Bromhal(e)*, son and heir of Maurice, and his heirs at Tiddington, viz., 12d each at Michaelmas and the Annunciation, for all secular service, exaction, custom, demand, etc. Warranty. For this the abbey has given him 100s sterling. Witnesses[a] [omitted]

　　　　　　　　　　　　　　　　　　　[13th cent., before 29 Oct. 1242]

B f 132r; C f 75v

[a] *Om. in C*

This was confirmed by Worcester cathedral priory in a deed which cannot be later than 29 Oct. 1242 (see no. 640). Walter son of Maurice *de Bromhal'* occurs as a tenant of the priory in Tiddington in 1201 × 4 or 1209 × 12 (*Cartl. Worc.*, 12). For notices of Maurice's charter to John of Kempsey and of the latter's to his son Reginald, see no. 642b, (i) and (iii).

¹ Possibly Broomhall (Cheshire).

639 Confirmation by Walter son of Maurice *de Bromhal(e)* to Reading Abbey of the gift by Reginald son of John of Kempsey (*Kemes(eye)*) of 1 virgate of land in Tiddington (*Tydinton'*) which John of Kempsey sometime held of Maurice *de Bromhal(e)*, his father. To be held freely by rendering annually to him and his heirs 2s, viz., 12d each at Michaelmas and the Annunciation, for all service, exaction and demand. Warranty. For this the abbey has given him in his great need 1 mark of silver and a tunic. Sealing. Witnesses[a] [omitted]   [13th cent., before 29 Oct. 1242]

B f 132r–v; C f 75v

[a] *Om. in C*

Date as for no. 638.

640 Grant, in chirograph form, by Prior William and the convent of Worcester that Reading Abbey shall hold of them in perpetuity the virgate of land in Tiddington (*Tydinton'*) which Walter *de Bromhale* held of them and which Maurice, his father, sold to John of Kempsey (*Kemes(eye)*). The abbey shall pay to the prior and convent at Tiddington 3s sterling annually, viz., 18d each at Michaelmas and the Annunciation, for all service, exaction and custom, saving a payment of 3s sterling, like a relief (*quasi nomine relevii*), each time there is a new abbot of Reading. Distraining clause for this payment. Mutual sealing. Witnesses[a] [omitted]   [1222 × 29 Oct. 1242]

B f 133v; C ff 76v–77r; Worcester, Dean and Chapter Library, A.2 (Registrum Prioratus), p. 85; ibid., A.4 (Register I), f 3v

Pd. *Registrum Prioratus Beatae Mariae Wigorniensis*, ed. W. H. Hale (Camden Soc., 1865), 85b (from Registrum Prioratus); *Cartl. Worc.*, 13 (from Register I)—minor variants, but for *tenuit* in line 11 of the latter, the Reading texts have *tenuerint*

[a] *Om. in C*

The prior of Worcester is either William Norman (1222–24) or William of Bedford (1224–29 Oct. 1242). The requirement that Reading shall pay anything like a relief is wholly exceptional among the abbey's possessions.

641   Final concord in the king's court at Westminster in 1 month from Holy Trinity, 6 Henry III, before Martin of Pattishall (*Pat(es)hull'*), Ralph *Hareng*, Stephen of Seagrave (*Segrave*), Thomas *de Hayden'*, Robert of Lexington (*Lexint'*), justices, and others, between Abbot Simon of Reading, seeking, and Simon of Chelsfield (*Chelefeld'*) and Agnes, his wife, holding, concerning 2 virgates of land in Tiddington (*Tidinton'*). Simon and Agnes recognized the land to be the right of the abbot and abbey of Reading, and quitclaimed the same for themselves and the heirs of Agnes. For this the abbot gave them 10 marks of silver   26 June 1222

B ff 176v-177r; C f 105v
Pd. (cal.) *Warks. Feet of Fines*, i. 61 (no. 313) (from PRO foot: CP 25(1)/243/13/3)

For discussion, see no. 642b n.

642   Gift by Simon of Chelsfield (*Chelefeld'*) and Agnes *de Chamel*, his wife, to Reading Abbey of 2 virgates of land in the territory of Tiddington (*Tydinton'*), viz., the virgate which *Gery* of Tiddington held, with the messuage near to *Fortheie*, and the virgate which Henry son of Osbert held, with the messuage near the house which belonged to Alfric of Tiddington. To be held by perpetual right freely of Alard of Bentley (*Benethleya*)[a] and his heirs by the service of 3s 2d annually, payable at the appointed terms, for all secular service, exaction and demand, as the donors held and ought to hold the land of the said Alard and his heirs. Also concession of all their land, buildings and rents in Stratford[-upon-Avon] (*Stratford'*), to be held freely by the service due to the lords of the fee. Warranty. For this the abbey has given them, in their great need and for the great benefit of them and their heirs, 40 marks of silver. Sealing with the seals of Simon and Agnes. They have handed over to the abbey all charters and writings made either to John of Kempsey (*Kemes(eye)*) or to themselves concerning the same. Witnesses[b] [omitted]   [prob. June 1222]

B f 131v; C ff 74v-75r

[a] Benetheleya C   [b] Om. in C

The date is probably approximately the same as that of the final concord (no. 641). For discussion, see no. 642b n.

642a   Note of another charter concerning the same in almost the same words   [prob. June 1222]

B f 131v

Date as for no. 642.

642b   Notes of the following:

(i) charter by Maurice *de Bromhal(e)* to John of Kempsey (*Kemes(eye)*) concerning 1 virgate of land in Tiddington (*Tydinton'*)   [before 1212]

(ii) three charters by John of Kempsey to Agnes, his wife, concerning 2 virgates of land in Tiddington. *ªThe one with the cross is betterª*   [before 1212]

(iii) charter by John of Kempsey concerning 1 virgate of land in Tiddington which he gave to Reginald his son   [before 1212]

(iv) charter by Alard of Bentley (*Benethleya*) to John of Kempsey (*Kemeseye*), and to whom he wished to assign, concerning 1 virgate of land in Tiddington   [before 1212]

(v) another by the same to the same, and to whom he wished to assign, concerning another virgate of land in Tiddington   [before 1212]

(vi) two charters by the same to Agnes of Tiddington, and to whom she wished to give or assign, concerning 2 virgates of land in Tiddington   [before 1222; ? before 1212]

(vii) charter by Henry son of Osbert concerning 1 virgate of land in Tiddington which he quitclaimed to John of Kempsey   [before 1212]

(viii) chirograph between Walter son of Maurice and Agnes of Tiddington concerning 1 virgate of land in Tiddington   [before 1222; ? before 1212]

B f 132r; C f 75r–v

ª-ª Om. in C

These notices concern title-deeds relating to three distinct properties. Items (i) and (iii) relate to the virgate which is the subject of nos. 638–40; items (ii) and (iv)–(vii) relate to the 2 virgates which are the subject of nos. 641–642a and 643; and item (viii) relates to the first virgate dealt with in no. 644. It is clear that John of Kempsey held of Maurice *de Bromhale* and of Alard of Bentley. After John's death, which had occurred by 1212 at the latest (see no. 644 n.), his widow, Agnes (called either 'of Tiddington' or 'de Camel'), married Simon of Chelsfield; and in 1222 Agnes and Simon quitclaimed to Reading the 2 virgates which Agnes's first husband had received from Alard of Bentley (no. 641). Most of the deeds noted here are clearly those handed over to Reading in no. 642.

643   Confirmation by Richard of Bentley (*Benethleg'*), son of Alard, to Reading Abbey of all the land in Tiddington (*Tydinton'*) which sometime belonged to John of Kempsey (*Kemes(eye)*) and which the abbey afterwards acquired from Simon of Chelsfield (*Chelefeld'*) and Agnes, his wife, as fully as Richard's father conceded it to the said

John and afterwards to the said Agnes in her widowhood,[1] concerning which a chirograph was made in the king's court between the abbey and the said Simon and Agnes. To be held freely by rendering annually to him and his heirs 3s 2d at the appointed terms for all service, exaction and demand. Warranty. Witnesses[a] [omitted]

[1222 × 56]

B f 133r; C f 76r

[a] *Om. in C*

This confirmation clearly relates to the land given in no. 642 and quitclaimed in the final concord of 1222 (no. 641). However, since no. 642 refers to Alard of Bentley as apparently still living, the present confirmation must be later. It cannot be later than 1256, since by then Richard had given the 38d rent to Worcester priory (Worcester Cathedral Ms B 8; charter witnessed by William of Luddington, who had apparently been succeeded by his son, Ralph, by 1256—*VCH Warks.*, iii. 265). The abbot of Reading's tenure of the land under Richard of Bentley is referred to in *Reg. Prioratus ... Wigorniensis* (Camden Soc., 1865), 81a.

[1] Alard of Bentley's charters to John of Kempsey and his widow, Agnes, concerning 2 virgates in Tiddington are no. 642b (iv)-(vi).

643a Note of two charters by W(illiam) of Shottery (*Soter'*) concerning a quitclaim of farm at Tiddington (*Tydinton'*)   [? *c.* 1229]

B f 133r

Dating uncertain, but in 1229 a case concerning service between the abbot of Reading and William of Shottery was left *sine die* on account of the latter's illness (*Cur. Reg. R.*, xiii. 319). William of Shottery occurs in 1221 (*Warks. Eyre 1221-2*, nos. 602, 779).

644 Grant by Simon of Chelsfield (*Chelefeld*) and Agnes *de Kamel*, his wife, to Reading Abbey of all their right in the farm which they sometime had from Walter son of Maurice *de Bromhal(e)* and his heirs of 1 virgate of land in Tiddington (*Tydinton'*) which John of Kempsey (*Kemes(eye)*) held at farm of Maurice, father of the said Walter.[1] This they had for a term appointed between them and Walter with an agreement that the latter would not sell or give the land at farm except to Simon and Agnes or to whom they wished to assign the land and agreement.[2] Also grant of all their right in the custody of 1 virgate of land in Tiddington which *Hathewy* held, whose messuage (*mansum*) is the last in Tiddington towards Stratford[-upon-Avon] (*Stratford'*). All to be held by the abbey in accordance with the concession and agreement made to them, as the deeds made either to them or to John of Kempsey, which they have handed to the abbey, testify. Sealing with the seals of Simon and Agnes, and warranty. Witnesses[a] [omitted]   [? *c.* 1222]

B ff 131v-132r; C f 75r

a Om. in C

Possibly of approximately the same date as nos. 641–2, but not concerned with the same land. The virgate which Simon and Agnes sometime held of Walter son of Maurice *de Bromhale* is identifiable with the second of the virgates confirmed to Reading by Worcester cathedral priory in 1258, namely, the virgate which Walter sold to the priory (see no. 648), since it is clearly the virgate which 'Simon the knight and Agnes his wife' held of Walter and which he sold to the priory for 20s in either 1201 × 4 or 1209 × 12 (*Cartl. Worc.*, 12).

¹ It is possible that no. 642b (i) related to this.
² Possibly the chirograph referred to in no. 642b (viii).

645 Gift by Walter son of Maurice *de Bromhal(e)* to Reading Abbey of 1 virgate of land which *Hathewi*ᵃ sometime held in the vill of Tiddington (*Tydint'*),ᵇ to be held freely by rendering annually to the donor and his heirs 2s, viz., 12d each at Michaelmas and the Annunciation, for all service, exaction and demand. Warranty. For this the abbey has given him 1 mark of silver and a tunic in his great need. Sealing. Witnessesᶜ [omitted]   [? *c.* 1222 × 1258]

B f 132v; C ff 75v-76r

a Hathewy C
b Tydinton' C
c Om. in C

Presumably after no. 644 and, since it was entered in the original section of B, not later than 1258.

646 Demise and gift by Walter *de Bromhal(e)* to Reading Abbey of 1 virgate of land in Tiddington (*Tydint'*)ᵃ which Agnes *de Kamel*, formerly wife of John of Kempsey (*Kemes(eye)*), sometime held of him at farm, and afterwards the abbot of Reading in the same way by his and Agnes's deeds (*per me et per ipsam*). To be held freely by rendering to him and his heirs annually on that land at Tiddington (*Tydinton'*) at Easter 1 pair of gloves for all service, exaction and demand. Warranty. For this the abbey has given him, in his great need and for his great profit, 6 marks of silver beyond the other agreement which it previously had from him concerning the said land. Sealing. Witnessesᵇ [omitted]   [? *c.* 1222 × 1258]

B ff 132v-133r; C f 76r

a Tydinton' C
b Om. in C

Date as for no. 645.

647 Gift by William of Norfolk (*Norfok*)*ª* to Reading Abbey of half a hide of land, with messuage, garden and meadow, which Alfred of Penn Hall (*Penhulle*)¹ sometime gave him in the vill of Tiddington (*Tidint'*);*ᵇ* also of half a virgate of land which Isabel daughter of Mary of Alveston (*Alvest'*) sometime gave him in the vill of Alveston (*Alveston'*);² and also of 3 acres of land in *Blakebreche* which Thomas of Alveston sometime gave him, with a meadow called *Lutlehamme* and a piece (*pecia*) of land called *Blakebuttes* in the vill of Alveston. All to be held freely by rendering annually to him and his heirs 15½d at Michaelmas for all custom, exaction, demand and secular service. Warranty. For this the abbey has given him in exchange all the land with messuage which Gilbert of Hunscote (*Hunstanescote*) gave to it in Hunscote. Sealing. Witnesses*ᶜ* [omitted]   [1226 × 58]

A f 111v; B f 133r-v; C f 76v

ª Norfolk' *C*   *ᵇ* Tydinton' *B,C*   *ᶜ* Om. in *C*

Not earlier than 1226, since the gift by Gilbert of Hunscote was made in the abbacy of Adam of Lathbury, 1226-38 (see no. 572), and before May, 1258, when the present gifts were confirmed by Worcester cathedral priory (see no. 648). William of Norfolk already held 1 carucate of land in Hunscote by 1221 (*Warks. Eyre 1221-2*, 238-9; discussed *ibid.*, xxxi-xxxii). He was apparently dead in 1262 (*Warks. Feet of Fines*, i. 174).

¹ In Pensax (Worcs.).   ² See no. 647b, n.

647a Notes of the following:
   (i) charter by Ralph son of Richard of Exhall (*Eccleshal'*)¹ to William of Norfolk (*Norfok*)*ª* concerning half a hide of land in Tiddington (*Tydinton'*)
   (ii) charter by Alfred of Penn Hall (*Penhull'*) to Ralph son of Richard of Exhall (*Eccles'*) concerning half a hide of land in Tiddington
   (iii) charter by the same to William of Norfolk concerning half a hide of land in Tiddington²
   (iv) charter by Agnes, widow of Alfred of Penn Hall, concerning a third part of 2 virgates of land in Tiddington
   (v) charter by Thomas of Alveston (*Alveston'*) to William of Norfolk concerning 3 acres of land in *Blakebrech(e)*

B f 133v; C f 76v

ª Norfolk' *C*

These clearly included the title-deeds which passed to Reading Abbey with William of Norfolk's gift in no. 647. Item (iv) is to be dated not earlier than 1230, since Alfred of Penn Hall was still living in the period 1230-33 (*Cartl. Worc.*, 149).

¹ Near Alcester (Warks.).

² In either 1201 × 4 or 1209 × 12 Alfred of Penn Hall gave to Worcester priory for 15s two virgates of land which William of Norfolk held of him by inheritance in Tiddington (*Cartl. Worc.*, 224).

647b Note of a charter by Isabel of Alveston (*Alvestone*) to William of Norfolk (*Norfok*) concerning half a virgate of land in Alveston

[before Sept. 1221]

B f 124v

It was presumably by this deed that William of Norfolk acquired the half-virgate in Alveston which was the subject of an action in the Warwickshire eyre of 1221 (*Warks. Eyre 1221-2*, nos. 705, 1202). It was clearly also another of the title-deeds relating to his gift to Reading in no. 647.

648 Agreement, in chirograph form, by which Prior Thomas and the convent of Worcester conceded to Abbot Richard [I] and the convent of Reading in perpetuity the following: 1 virgate in Tiddington (*Tydinton*') of the tenement formerly belonging to Walter son of Maurice *de Bromhal(e)*; 1 virgate of the same tenement which the said Walter sold to Worcester Priory; 2 virgates of the tenement formerly belonging to Richard of Bentley (*Benetlegh*'); and 2½ virgates of the tenement of William of Norfolk (*Northfolk*'). To be held freely by rendering annually to Worcester Priory at Alveston (*Alveston*') 10s, viz., 5s each at the Annunciation and at Michaelmas, for all service and exaction. The abbot shall do suit of the priory's court at Alveston through his attorney by reasonable summons; the abbey shall in no way enter further into any part of the priory's fee without its consent; and each new abbot of Reading shall pay to the priory 10s as a relief (*nomine relevii*) for the said lands, apart from the said annual rent. Sealing *alternatim*. Done on the Wednesday in the week of Pentecost, A.D. 1258

15 May 1258

B f 134r; C f 77r; Worcester, Dean and Chapter Library, A.4 (Register I), f 65r
Pd. *Cartl. Worc.*, 243 (from Register I—minor variants only)

Not entered in the original section of B, but very soon afterwards. This agreement was noted in the Worcester Annals (*Ann. Mon.*, iv. 445). Cf. also *Reg. Prioratus ... Wigorniensis* (Camden Soc., 1865), 81a-81b.

WARWICK

649 *Gift in free alms by Stephen de Morton to Reading Abbey, with the consent of her heir William, of specified lands in the suburb of Warwick which named individuals held of him at the time when he became a monk*

[1184 × 89]

A f 43v; B f 122v; C f 67r

Sciant presentes et futuri quod ego Stephanus de Mortona dedi et concessi deo et sancte Marie de Rading(ia) et monachis ibidem deo servientibus, pro salute anime mee et antecessorum meorum[a] et successorum meorum, in perpetuam elemosinam libere et quiete tenendam terram de[b] Warewic[c] in suburbio quam tempore conversionis mee tenuit filius Pagani pro .xvi. denariis, et terram quam Runild tenuit iuxta domum predicti filii Pagani versus austrum pro .xx. denariis,[d] et terram quam Rog(erus) fornerius tenuit pro .x. denariis proximam iuxta fossatum versus orientem, et terram quam Edit[e] vidua tenuit pro .viii. denariis super vicum apud Avene. Hanc autem donationem feci et carta mea confirmavi presente Willelmo herede meo idem concedente, ita scilicet quod idem Willelmus et heredes eius prefatas terras ab omni exactione et servitio terreno adquietabunt[f] sicut liberam et quietam elemosinam.[g] His testibus: Waltero de Oxoneford, Willelmo Child, Willelmo de Bathe, et multis aliis.

[a] Om. in B,C   [b] in B,C   [c] Warwik' B, Warewik' C
[d] A has dener'   [e] Edith B, Edith' C   [f] acquietabunt B,C
[g] B ends with T', C ends

The gift was confirmed by Waleran, earl of Warwick, who succeeded to the title in Nov. 1184 (no. 650); and was included in Richard I's general confirmation to Reading in Sept. 1189 (no. 34).

650   *Confirmation of the same by Waleran, earl of Warwick*

[1184 × prob. 1189]

A f46v; B f122v; C f67r

Waleranus[a] comes Warewic[b] omnibus hominibus suis et amicis tam futuris quam presentibus, salutem. Notum sit vobis omnibus me concessisse et hac mea presenti carta confirmasse deo et sancte Marie de Radinges et monachis ibidem deo servientibus totas illas terras quas Stephanus de Mortona tempore conversionis sue eis dedit et Willelmus filius suus eis confirmavit, sicut carta ipsius Stephani testatur.[c] His testibus.

[a] Walerannus B,C
[b] Warwik B, Warewik' C
[c] B ends with T', C ends

After Waleran became earl in Nov. 1184 and, since the gift was confirmed by Richard I in 1189 (no. 34), probably not later than 1189, although this confirmation was not entered in the original composition of A but very soon afterwards (see above, p. 3).

651   *Confirmation by William son of Stephen de Morton to Reading Abbey of his father's gift in the suburb of Warwick; and, since William is a brother*

of the abbey, gift in free alms of the land which John the mercer, called
'Little', held of him in the suburb of Warwick

[1184 × c.1193; ? 1184 × 89]

A f46v; B f122v; C f67v

Sciant presentes et futuri quod ego Willelmus filius Stephani de
Moretun(a)*[a]* concessi et hac carta mea confirmavi abbatie*[b]* de Rad-
ing(ia), pro salute patris mei et pro salute anime mee et heredum
meorum, omnem donationem quam pater meus Stephanus dedit
eidem abbatie*[b]* *[c]*in suburbio de Warewic.*[d]* Insuper, quia frater sum
eiusdem domus, ex dono meo dono predicte abbatie*[b]* et hac carta
mea confirmo terram totam quam Iohannes mercerius, cognomento
Parvulus, de me tenuit in suburbio de Warewic*[d]* in perpetuam ele-
mosimam et liberam ab omni seculari servitio et exactione.*[e]* His
testibus: Radulfo senescallo de Rading(ia), Raimundo mercatore, et
multis aliis.

[a] Morton' B,C   *[b]* abbathie C   *[c]* Insert de terra sua B,C
[d] Warwik B, Warewik' C   *[e]* B ends with T', C ends

After no. 649 and, since it was entered very soon after the original composition of A,
probably not later than 1193 and possibly not long after nos. 649–50. The two
witnesses are Reading folk. The reference to William as a 'brother' of the abbey
should probably be understood in the sense of one who has been admitted to confraternity.

652   *Gift and confirmation in free alms by William de Morton to Reading*
Abbey of the land which his father, Stephen, gave in the suburb of Warwick
when he became a monk at Reading; and, in increase of the said alms, gift of
the 3 shillings worth of land which Leysinus *held of him and other specified*
lands, for which the abbey has given him 34s and an iron-grey horse worth
16s   [late 12th × early 13th cent.]

B ff 122v–123r; C f67v.

Sciant presentes et futuri quod ego W(illelmus) de Morton(a) dedi
et presenti carta mea confirmavi, pro salute anime mee et pro anima
Stephani patris mei et matris mee et omnium antecessorum et successorum meorum, deo et monachis de*[a]* Rading(ia) totam terram
quam Stephanus pater meus eis dedit in suburbio de Warwik,*[b]*
quando apud Rading(iam) monachus devenit, in liberam et perpetuam elemosinam. Insuper dedi prefatis monachis, ad incrementum
predicte elemosine, tres solidatas terre quas Leysinus de me tenuit,
scilicet terram illam totam iuxta domum Ivonis pistoris, et terram
proximam fonti Quenild*[c]* ad sinistram versus [f123r] occidentem
quam predictus Leysinus de me tenuit pro .xii. denariis, insuper ex
alia parte aque totam terram quam pontarius tenuit. Hanc autem

elemosinam totam et integram ego et heredes mei predictis monachis warantizabimus per omnia, pro .xxxiiii. solidis et pro quodam equo ferrando .xvi. solidorum quos mihi dederunt. T(estibus).*

a Om. in C   *b Warewik' C*   *c Qenild C*

Although this deed was not entered in A, it presumably dates not long after no. 651.

653   *Gift in free alms by William de Morton to Reading Abbey of 2 shillings worth of land which Leisinus held of him in the suburb of Warwick, for which the abbey has given him 34s*   [late 12th × early 13th cent.]

A f91r; B f123r; C f67v

Sciant presentes et futuri quod ego Willelmus de Mortun(a),* pro anima patris mei et matris mee et omnium antecessorum nostrorum* et successorum meorum, dedi in perpetuam elemosinam et hac carta mea confirmavi deo et monachis de Rading(ia) illas duas solidatas terre in suburbio de Warewic* quas* Leisinus de me tenuit. Quare volo et heredibus et successoribus meis firmiter precipio ut prefati monachi prefatam terram in* bene et in pace, integre et honorifice, in omnibus teneant. Hanc autem terram ego et heredes mei predictis monachis per omnia warantizabimus, propter .xxxiiii. solidos quos predicti monachi mihi dederunt.* Testibus:* Raimundo et Alano mercatoribus, Rad(ulfo) Wille, Willelmo vinitore, Iohanne de Rameiseia, Huberto forestario, Osmundo de Acle, Osmundo emptore, Simone clerico, Reginaldo serviente de Rokint(ona), Willelmo filio Pavie,[1] et multis aliis.

a Morton' B,C   *b Sic in A; om. in B,C*
c Warwik B   *d A has quam, but quas is correct, as in B,C*
e Om. in B,C   *f C ends*   *g B ends*

Not entered in the original section of A, but among additions of the late 12th or early 13th century. The first four witnesses and Osmund *de Acle* are Reading folk.

[1] Cf. Richard son of Pavia of Warwick (no. 590).

MARLBOROUGH

654 Notification by Empress Matilda, daughter of King Henry, to John the Marshal and to the sheriff of Wiltshire and the men of Marlborough, that she has given to Reading Abbey, for the health of her soul and those of King Henry I and all her kinsmen, the land of Herbert son of Fulcher, who has become a monk at Reading, with houses and all appurtenances. The abbey shall hold it as freely as it holds all its other possessions given by her father and as Herbert held it   [Feb. × Apr. 1141]

A f 15v; B f 19v
Pd. *Regesta*, iii. 258 (no. 700)

*His testibus: H(enrico) episcopo Wintonie, et A(lexandro) episcopo Lincoln(ie), et R(oberto) comite Gloec(estrie), et Milone constabulo, et Hunfr(edo) de Buhun dapifero. Apud Radingiam.

a *B ends with* T'

After the battle of Lincoln (2 Feb. 1141) and before the Empress assumed the title *Domina Anglorum* (7/8 Apr. 1141)—see no. 537 n. The rubrics of A and B locate the land in Marlborough, and this is corroborated by nos. 655–6.

655 *Precept by King Henry II to John the Marshal to restore to Reading Abbey the land which Herbert son of Fulcher gave to it when he became a monk*   [1156 × 65]

A f 26r; B f 27v

Henricus rex Anglie *et dux Norm(annie) et Aquit(anie) et comes Andeg(avie)* Iohanni Maresc(allo),*b* salutem. Precipio quod iuste et sine dilatione reddas monachis de Rading(ia) terram de Merleberga quam Herebertus*c* filius Fulcherii eis dedit die qua monachus devenit. Quod nisi feceris, iusticia mea faciat fieri. T(este)*d* domina Imperatrice. Apud Rothomagum.

a–a et cetera *B*
b Marisc' *B*
c Herb' *B*
d *B ends*

Henry did not return to Normandy as king until Jan. 1156 (Eyton, 16); John the Marshal died in 1165 before Michaelmas (*Complete Peerage*, x, App. G, 95). The king was in Normandy *c.* Feb.–May, 1165 (Eyton, 77–9).

656   *Final concord in the court of John, count of Mortain, at Marlborough, by which Adam the Falconer recognized Reading Abbey's right in a messuage in Marlborough which belonged to Herbert son of Fulcher, and the abbey leased the same to him and his heirs for an annual service of 2s, saving the service due to the count; the monks will have right of lodging in the messuage when they come to Marlborough*   22 Apr. 1192

B f 172v; C f 102v

Hec est finalis concordia facta in curia domini Iohannis comitis Morit(onii) apud Merleberg(am) proximo die ante festum sancti Georgii [23 Apr.], anno regni regis Ricardi tertio, coram Stephano Ridell' eiusdem comitis cancellario, Willelmo comite Sar(esburie), Hamone de Valom', Willelmo de Monteacut(o), Ricardo Flandr(ensi), Rad(ulfo) Morin', Thoma filio Willelmi, Alardo filio Willelmi et aliis baronibus et fidelibus domini comitis tunc ibi presentibus, inter Willelmum Hese monachum, positum loco abbatis Rading(ensis) ad lucrandum et perdendum, et Adam Ostritiarium, de uno mesuagio in Merleberg(a) quod fuit Herberti filii Fulcherii, unde placitum fuit inter eos in curia domini*a* comitis. Scilicet quod idem Adam recognovit ipsis monachis Rading(ensibus) ius suum de predicto mesuagio, et monachi concesserunt ipsi Ade predictum mesuagium tenendum ipsi et heredibus suis de monasterio Rading(ensi) per servitium .ii. solidorum per annum ipsi monasterio pro omni servitio reddendorum, salvo debito servitio domini comitis inde. Et monachi Rading(enses) habebunt hostelagium suum in predicto mesuagio cum Merleberg(am)*b* venerint.

a dicti C
b Merleberge C

SALISBURY

657   Gift in free alms by Peter the chaplain, son of Seman of Salisbury (*Saresbiri*), to Reading Abbey of all the land within the walls of Salisbury, with buildings and appurtenances, which he held of Richard of Milford (*Moleford*)*a* for the service of 1 lb of cumin, to be held by the abbey of Richard and his heirs for the same service; and of all the land, with buildings and appurtenances, which he held of Nicholas of Wiltshire (*Wiltesire*) for the service of 12d, to be held by the abbey of Nicholas and his heirs for the same service. Witnesses*b* [omitted]   [13th cent., before *c.* 1230]

A f 107r; B f 118r–v; C f 65r

a Moleford' B,C
b Om. in C

This deed was entered in A with mainly 13th-century documents of before *c.* 1230. Richard of Milford occurs in 1236 (*Fees*, i. 587) and 1249 (*Civil Pleas of the Wiltshire Eyre, 1249*, ed. M. T. Clanchy (Wilts. Rec. Soc., xxvi, 1971), 108, 118). A Nicholas of Wiltshire occurs in 1249 (*ibid.*, 104-5), but this notice reveals that there were two men of that name, father and son, the elder of whom was dead in 1249.

STRATTON ST MARGARET

658 *Gift in free alms by William [d'Aubigny], earl of Chichester, to Reading Abbey of the fee of 6 hides of land which Richard de Marcy holds of Robert Corbucion in Stratton [St Margaret] for 20s, to be held by the abbey freely, saving the service of Robert Corbucion. William's wife, Queen Adeliza, and his son, William, give and concede this with him*

[*c.* 1140 × 51; ? *c.* 1145 × 51]

A f44r-v

Willelmus comes Cicestrie omnibus hominibus suis omnibusque sancte dei ecclesie filiis Francis et Anglicis, clericis [*f44v*] et laicis, salutem. Sciatis me dedisse et concessisse deo et ecclesie sancte Marie de Rading(ia) eiusdemque ecclesie conventui in elemosinam in perpetuum feodum quod Ricardus de Maisi tenet de Roberto Corbuceon in Strettona, videlicet .vi. hidas terre, pro .xx. solidis. Quare volo et firmiter precipio ut illam terram teneant bene et in pace, libere et quiete et honorifice, in bosco et plano, in pratis et pascuis, in viis et semitis, in aquis et extra, cum thol et theam et sacca et socca et infangenetheof et cum omnibus liberis consuetudinibus eidem terre pertinentibus, salvo servitio Roberti Corbuceon, hoc idem mecum dante et concedente Aelide regina uxore mea et Willelmo filio nostro. Testibus: Henrico de Essexia, Radulfo filio Sevari, Adelardo Flemeng, magistro Serlone, Roberto de Alta Ripa, et multis aliis.

After the donor became earl of Chichester (or Arundel) in *c.* 1140 and before the death of Queen Adeliza in 1151, but, since the couple did not marry until 1138, their son William, whose date of birth is unknown, could not have been old enough to approve the gift until *c.* 1145 at the earliest. This deed was not entered in the later cartularies of Reading because the gift did not take permanent effect. In all other references the gift is said to be of 4 hides rather than the 6 stated here. It was included in the general confirmation to Reading by Pope Eugenius III (1145-53) as '4 hides of Stratton in Wiltshire by gift of Richard de Marcy of the fee of William d'Aubigny' (see no. 143), the same being included also in the general confirmations by Popes Adrian IV and Alexander III (nos. 145, 151); it appears also in the diocesan confirmation by Jocelin de Bohun as '4 hides in Stratton by gift of Richard de Marcy' (no. 180); but no royal confirmation mentioned it and no later references to Reading's tenure have been found. Moreover, the text of no original deed by Richard de Marcy concerning this gift appears to exist, so that he may have become a monk at Reading and attempted to bring his land with him. In 1166 William d'Aubigny stated that

Henry I had enfeoffed him with 15 knights of the Corbucion fee (*Red Bk. Exch.*, i. 397), but, although one might suppose from this that the 6 (or 4) hides in Stratton St Margaret had been held by William son of Corbucion in 1086, in fact the vill was at that date held of the king by Nigel the Physician (*VCH Wilts.*, ii. 157). Moreover, Robert Corbucion does not appear to have been among the 12th-century holders of the lands held in chief in 1086 by William son of Corbucion (see *Sir Christopher Hatton's Book of Seals*, no. 153 n.). The subsequent history of the estate is obscure, but in 1226 × 28 Stratton St Margaret was described as an escheat of the Crown which Margery de Ripariis held by gift of King John (*Fees*, i. 380), while in 1242 × 3 there were six separate estates there, in none of which was Reading Abbey recorded as having an interest (*ibid.*, ii. 730, 738).

WORCESTER

659 *Grant by Adam son of Peter and Roger of Oxford, reeves of Worcester, and the whole community of the city of Worcester that Abbot Adam [of Lathbury] and the convent of Reading and their successors, and their men and tenants and their heirs throughout England, shall have free entry and exit at Worcester and freedom to buy and sell without toll and demand [etc.], free of all pleas, plaints [etc.] and amercements, both in and out of fairs, with all the liberties granted to them by Kings Henry I, Henry II, John and Henry III. They have made this grant on account of the unjust demands which they made on the abbot and his men, concerning which the reeves and community were impleaded before the justices-in-eyre at Worcester, 19 Henry III*

[*c.* 12 × 26 July 1235]

A f 102v; E f 95r–v
Pd. *Mon. Ang.*, iv. 57 (no. x)

Sciant presentes et futuri quod nos Adam filius Petri et Rog(erus) de Oxon(efordia), prepositi Wigorn(ie), Robertus Neel, Aluredus le Draper, Johannes Cumin, Petrus Colle, Johannes Franceis,*a* Willelmus Franceis,*a* Ricardus clericus, Robertus de Sancto Godewelle,*b* Rad(ulfus) Cumpainun, Alexander le Draper, Albinus Franceis, Ricardus de Bureford', Johannes Pricht,*c* Ricardus Cumin, Rog(erus) Cumin, Walt(erus) Rup, Nicholaus Andr(eas), Galfridus*d* le Peet, Willelmus Rokulf, Walt(erus) de Wigemor', Walt(erus) Burewald, Johannes Cradan, Walt(erus) le Bufle, Aluredus tinctor, Johannes Bricht,*e* Osbertus Claudus, Johannes Albinus, Walt(erus) Kinterel*f* et tota communa civitatis Wigorn(ie), assensu et voluntate eiusdem commune, concessimus pro nobis et heredibus nostris et hac presenti carta nostra confirmavimus Ade abbati Rading(ensi) et conventui eiusdem loci et eorum successoribus et ecclesie de Rading(ia) et omnibus hominibus et tenentibus eiusdem domus et eorum heredibus de quacumque patria Angl(ie) fuerint in perpetuum quod habeant liberum introitum et exitum in villa nostra Wigorn(ie) et in omni potestate nostra quotienscumque et quandocumque venerint, et libere vendant et emant omnimodas mercandisas*g* et libere venalia sua descendant ubicumque et quandocumque voluerint ad placitum suum infra Bohale¹ et extra quieti de omni genere theolonei*h* et demande et passagiis et*i* stallagiis et pontagiis et de omni genere clausure et de omnibus placitis et*j* querelis, occasionibus et sectis et de omnibus amerciamentis infra nundinas et extra et de omnibus vexationibus, cum omnibus libertatibus quas reges Angl(ie), videlicet rex Henricus fundator ecclesie de Rading(ia) et rex Henricus secundus et rex Johannes filius regis Henrici et rex Henricus filius regis Johannis, eis dederunt. Hanc concessionem fecimus propter iniustam vexationem quam fecimus dicto abbati et hominibus suis contra libertates cartarum suarum, unde inplacitati fuimus coram domino Willelmo de Eboraco, abbate[2] de Teukebir(ia),[k] Willelmo de Insula, Rad(ulfo) de Norwiz, Mauricio le Butiler, justic(iariis) domini regis tunc itinerantibus apud Wigorn(iam), anno regni regis Henrici filii regis Johannis nonodecimo. Et quia volumus quod predicta concessio a nobis et heredibus nostris dicto abbati et hominibus suis et eorum heredibus sine omni vexatione et inpedimento rata et stabilis sicut supradictum est in perpetuum permaneat, commune sigillum civitatis nostre huic scripto apposuimus.[l] Hiis testibus: domino Waltero de Bello Campo, Yvone de Bello Campo.

[a] Fraunceis *E*	[b] Godewello *E*	[c] Prihc *E*
[d] Gauf' *E*	[e] *Sic in A, ? rectius* Pricht; Prihc *and insert* iuvenis *E*	
[f] Kuinterel *E*		

[g] merchandisas *and insert* exceptis coriis et pellibus recentibus et pannis laneis crudis et filo laneo *E*   [h] thelon' *E*   [i] *Insert* de *E*

[j] *Om. in* E   [k] Teok'bir' *E*   [l] *E ends with* Test'

Presumably during the justices' session at Worcester (Crook, *General Eyre*, 92). The clause of exception included in the E text should be noted. Since this grant was not included in Reading's later cartularies, but was entered in the Leominster cartulary, it was presumably of chief interest to the abbey's Herefordshire lands and men. For the reeves of Worcester, see *Cartl. Worc.*, xl–xli.

[1] Presumably the market hall.

[2] The abbot was Robert of Forthampton.